D1702036

Macroeconomic Theory

Macroeconomic Theory

Jean-Pascal Bénassy

OXFORD
UNIVERSITY PRESS

2011

OXFORD
UNIVERSITY PRESS

Oxford University Press, Inc., publishes works that further
Oxford University's objective of excellence
in research, scholarship, and education.

Oxford   New York
Auckland   Cape Town   Dar es Salaam   Hong Kong   Karachi
Kuala Lumpur   Madrid   Melbourne   Mexico City   Nairobi
New Delhi   Shanghai   Taipei   Toronto

With offices in
Argentina   Austria   Brazil   Chile   Czech Republic   France   Greece
Guatemala   Hungary   Italy   Japan   Poland   Portugal   Singapore
South Korea   Switzerland   Thailand   Turkey   Ukraine   Vietnam

Copyright © 2011 by Jean-Pascal Bénassy

Published by Oxford University Press, Inc.
198 Madison Avenue, New York, New York 10016
www.oup.com

Oxford is a registered trademark of Oxford University Press

All rights reserved. No part of this publication may be reproduced,
stored in a retrieval system, or transmitted, in any form or by any means,
electronic, mechanical, photocopying, recording, or otherwise,
without the prior permission of Oxford University Press.

Library of Congress Cataloging-in-Publication Data

Bénassy, Jean-Pascal.
Macroeconomic theory / Jean-Pascal Bénassy.
    p. cm.
Includes bibliographical references and index.
ISBN 978-0-19-538771-1
1. Macroeconomics. I. Title.
HB172.5.B44 2010
339—dc22   2009046111

Contents

Introduction   xii

    The Object of the Book   xii
    Organization of the Book   xiii
    An Overview of the Book   xiii
    Acknowledgments   xviii

1 Growth   3

    1.1 Introduction   3
    1.2 The Solow-Swan Model   4
    1.3 Short-run Equilibrium and Dynamics   6
    1.4 The Golden Rule   9
    1.5 Technical Progress and Growth   11
    1.6 Convergence   12
    1.7 A Model with Two Accumulated Factors   16
    Appendix 1.1: The CES Production Function   18
    Appendix 1.2: Embodied Technical Progress   20
    Problems   22

2 Output, Inflation, and Stabilization   24

    2.1 Introduction   24
    2.2 The Basic Keynesian Models   25
    2.3 The Phillips Curve   29

	2.4 Phillips Curve Dynamics	31
	2.5 Expectations and Policy Effectiveness	34
	Appendix 2.1: The Baumol-Tobin Demand for Money	38
	Appendix 2.2: Indexation	39
	Appendix 2.3: Imperfect Information and the Choice of Economic Instruments	41
	Problems	43
3	**Rational Expectations**	**45**
	3.1 Introduction	45
	3.2 Rational Expectations: A Simple Definition	46
	3.3 The Muth Model	47
	3.4 Rational Expectations and Policy Effectiveness	49
	3.5 Expectations and Stability: The Cagan Model	50
	3.6 Solutions to a Stochastic Dynamic Equation	54
	3.7 Learning and Rational Expectations	57
	Appendix 3.1: Signal Extraction and Adaptive Expectations	60
	Problems	62
4	**Intertemporal Equilibria with Optimizing Agents**	**65**
	4.1 Introduction	65
	4.2 A Ramsey Model with Exogenous Incomes	66
	4.3 An Overlapping Generations Model	70
	4.4 Overlapping Generations and Money	76
	4.5 A Ramsey-OLG Model	78
	Appendix 4.1: A Basic Dynamic Equation	81
	Problems	83
5	**Nonclearing Markets and Imperfect Competition**	**85**
	5.1 Introduction	85
	5.2 Walrasian Theory: The Missing Parts	86
	5.3 Nonclearing Markets and Imperfect Competition	87
	5.4 A Macroeconomic Example	97
	5.5 Shocks and Correlations	108
	Appendix 5.1: Quantity Signals: An Example	111
	Appendix 5.2: Alternative Rigidities	113
	Problems	114
6	**Uncertainty and Financial Assets**	**118**
	6.1 Introduction	118
	6.2 Choice under Uncertainty and Risk Aversion	119

6.3	Equilibrium with Complete Markets	121
6.4	Complete versus Incomplete Markets	125
6.5	Asset Pricing: A Benchmark Case	127
6.6	The Risk-free Rate and the Risk Premium	129
6.7	Risk Aversion and Substitutability	132
	Appendix 6.1: Incomplete Markets and the Risk-free Rate Puzzle	135
	Appendix 6.2: Arrow-Debreu Equilibria with Several Physical Goods	139
	Problems	142

7 The Ramsey Model — 145

7.1	Introduction	145
7.2	The Ramsey Model	146
7.3	Market Equilibrium	147
7.4	Efficiency	151
7.5	Ricardian Equivalence	152
7.6	Government Spending and Dynamics	154
7.7	Exogenous Technical Progress	155
7.8	The Ramsey Model in Discrete Time	155
	Appendix 7.1: Government Spending with Distortionary Taxation	156
	Problems	159

8 Overlapping Generations — 161

8.1	Introduction	161
8.2	The Diamond Model	162
8.3	Market Equilibrium	163
8.4	Optimality	166
8.5	Pensions	169
8.6	Debt Dynamics	174
	Problems	177

9 Endogenous Growth — 180

9.1	Introduction	180
9.2	The AK Model	181
9.3	Technical Progress and Endogenous Growth	183
9.4	The Romer Model	184
9.5	Endogenous Productivity Increases	190
9.6	A Model Without Scale Effects	194
	Appendix 9.1: Capital and Transitional Dynamics	195
	Appendix 9.2: Stochastic Productivity Increases	198
	Problems	201

10 Competitive Business Cycles — 205

10.1 Introduction — 205
10.2 The DSGE Methodology — 207
10.3 A Particular Case — 209
10.4 Depreciation and Propagation — 211
10.5 Intertemporal Substitution and Labor Fluctuations — 213
10.6 Asset Pricing — 215
10.7 Sunspots — 217
10.8 Endogenous Cycles — 220
Appendix 10.1: Employment Lotteries — 224
Appendix 10.2: Output and Capital in the Cycle — 227
Problems — 231

11 Money — 235

11.1 Introduction — 235
11.2 Why Money? — 236
11.3 The Fragility of OLG Money — 240
11.4 Money in the Utility Function — 242
11.5 Cash in Advance — 245
11.6 Puzzles and Paradoxes — 247
11.7 A Non-Ricardian Solution — 251
11.8 A Ramsey-OLG Monetary Model — 255
Appendix 11.1: Money as a Medium of Exchange: An Informational Argument — 259
Appendix 11.2: Proportional Money Transfers — 262
Appendix 11.3: The Weil Model — 263
Problems — 267

12 Money and Cycles — 270

12.1 Introduction — 270
12.2 A Simple Monetary Model — 271
12.3 Imperfect Competition — 275
12.4 Signal Extraction and Nominal Price Stickiness — 277
Appendix 12.1: The Full Information Equilibrium — 284
Appendix 12.2: The Imperfect Information Equilibrium — 285
Problems — 287

13 Nominal Rigidities and Fluctuations — 291

13.1 Introduction — 291
13.2 Early Models — 292

13.3 Nominal Rigidities and Correlations ... 298
13.4 Three Models of Nominal Rigidities ... 301
13.5 A DSGE Model with Sticky Prices ... 308
13.6 The DSGE Model: Properties and Extensions ... 312
Appendix 13.1: Menu Costs ... 316
Appendix 13.2: Real and Nominal Rigidities ... 318
Appendix 13.3: Impulse Response Functions and Propagation ... 320
Appendix 13.4: Disinflation ... 322
Appendix 13.5: Price Dynamics ... 329
Problems ... 333

14 Consumption, Investment, Inventories, and Credit — 337

14.1 Introduction ... 337
14.2 Consumption ... 338
14.3 Investment ... 343
14.4 Inventories ... 349
14.5 Credit ... 354
Appendix 14.1: An Imperfect Competition Accelerator ... 359
Appendix 14.2: Inventories ... 361
Problems ... 365

15 Unemployment: Basic Models — 369

15.1 Introduction ... 369
15.2 A Simple Framework ... 370
15.3 Three Classic Trade Union Models ... 372
15.4 Insiders and Outsiders ... 377
15.5 Efficiency Wages ... 380
15.6 Implicit Contracts ... 385
Appendix 15.1: Centralization and Unemployment ... 389
Problems ... 394

16 A Dynamic View of Unemployment — 397

16.1 Introduction ... 397
16.2 A Simple Dynamic Framework ... 398
16.3 A Few Dynamic Relations ... 399
16.4 The Shirking Model ... 401
16.5 Matching in the Labor Market ... 404
Problems ... 410

17 Policy: The Public Finance Approach — 413

17.1 Introduction ... 413

17.2 Issues in Policy Design	414
17.3 The Friedman Rule	415
17.4 Tax Smoothing	418
17.5 Optimal Ramsey Taxation	421
17.6 Optimal Seigniorage	423
Appendix 17.1: The Cost of Distortionary Taxation	425
Appendix 17.2: Optimal Seigniorage in an OLG Model	429
Problems	431

18 Stabilization Policies   434

18.1 Introduction	434
18.2 Optimal Monetary and Fiscal Financing	436
18.3 Government Information and the Policy Effectiveness Debate	439
18.4 Interest Rate Rules and Determinacy	445
Appendix 18.1: Model Uncertainty and Stabilization	450
Appendix 18.2: Instrument Instability	451
Appendix 18.3: The Ineffectiveness Argument: A Simple Model	454
Appendix 18.4: Fiscal Policy and Determinacy	456
Appendix 18.5: The Pigou Effect and Global Determinacy	459
Problems	463

19 Dynamic Consistency and Credibility   466

19.1 Introduction	466
19.2 The Dynamic Consistency Intuition	467
19.3 Capital Taxation and Dynamic Consistency	468
19.4 Monetary Policy and Credibility	470
19.5 Solutions to the Credibility Problem	474
Appendix 19.1: Reputation and Credibility	478
Problems	481

20 Political Economy   483

20.1 Introduction	483
20.2 Arrow's Impossibility Theorem	484
20.3 The Median Voter	486
20.4 Voting and Redistribution	489
20.5 The Political Economy of Budget Deficits	491
20.6 Platform Heterogeneity	493
Appendix 20.1: The Political Economy of Deficits	496
Problems	500

A Mathematical Appendix · 502

- A.1 Matrices · 502
- A.2 Functions · 506
- A.3 Static Optimization · 510
- A.4 Dynamic Optimization · 513
- A.5 Dynamic Programming · 516
- A.6 Noncooperative Games · 518
- A.7 Stochastic Variables · 524
- A.8 Time Series and Stochastic Processes · 529
- A.9 Solutions to a Rational Expectations Dynamic Equation · 533
- A.10 Dynamic Systems · 536
- A.11 Determinacy · 540
- A.12 Some Useful Calculations · 544
- A.13 References · 547

Bibliography · 548

Index · 578

Introduction

The Object of the Book

This book is meant to a primer in macroeconomics for graduate students. To make it reader-friendly to first-year students, the first two chapters provide a summary of the concepts that should already be mastered. The next eighteen chapters progressively develop the central concepts of modern macroeconomics, with the aim of being as comprehensive as possible,[1] while offering, for each topic, the models that will deliver the results in the most simple manner.

While writing this book, I have sought to achieve two main goals. The first one has been to present, whenever possible, models with explicit and rigorous microeconomic foundations, however simple they may be. Indeed, the evolution of macroeconomics in the last decades has been characterized by an inexorable move away from ad hoc models and toward models with such foundations. This has been a highly valuable development. So I have endeavoured to show in the most simple and pedagogical way the enormous progress that has been achieved in this regard.[2]

---

1. One domain, though, is not represented in this book, international macroeconomics. But this is a whole field in itself, which deserves a textbook of its own.

2. Although my personal preference is clearly toward microfounded models, I believe one should not be dogmatic about this issue. There are some ad-hoc models that are just too elegant and insightful to be ignored, so that I have resolutely included a number of them in this book.

My second goal has been to give for each topic the simplest possible formalization. Over the years, the field of economics has become increasingly technical. This is a positive development, which has allowed us to push forward the frontiers of the domain. This has sometimes led to a tendency to write overcomplicated models. I have tried to show, by way of many examples, that one can tackle conceptually difficult issues with simple models. Moreover these models come with explicit solutions, which is the most effective way to convey the basic economic intuitions.

Organization of the Book

Each chapter covers a specific topic, using a homogeneous set of models. It contains a "main body," which represents the central elements to be taught, as well as a few appendixes.

Basically, it is not necessary, in a first reading, to go through the appendixes to have a full understanding of the main text. Some appendixes are more technical than the main body of the chapter, whereas some others, although nontechnical, have a slightly different emphasis. These appendixes should be seen as optional additional teaching material that each professor may (or may not) teach, depending on personal preferences.

As evidenced in its title, this book is centered on macroeconomic theory, and its primary purpose is to teach the concepts and instruments of macroeconomic analysis. Some chapters have a few numbers designed to give some sense of magnitude. These are not intended to represent any significant empirical contribution and should obviously be supplemented by proper empirical references in reading lists.

At the end of each chapter are a few problems that hopefully represent some interesting developments of the material in the chapter. Solutions are posted on the Web site www.oup.com/us/MacroeconomicTheorySolutions.

Finally, to make the book fully self-contained, there is a mathematical appendix that gives the necessary mathematical results. This should be seen more as a set of cooking recipes than a rigorous mathematical treatise.

An Overview of the Book

The first two chapters give a quick panorama of the main models used in undergraduate teaching and of the state of macroeconomics at the outset of the 1970s.

Chapter 1 studies growth theory using the famous Solow-Swan model. It shows how growth results from two sources: capital accumulation (part of which may be human capital accumulation) and technical progress. At this stage technical progress is exogenous, and the equations giving capital accumulation are also given exogenously.

Chapter 2 studies the traditional models of output, employment, and inflation determination in the Keynesian tradition. We describe successively the IS-LM model, the AD-AS model and the Phillips curve. We also describe the famous debate on stabilization in the Keynesian mode, which prompted the relative decline of Keynesian ideas and the move toward more microfounded macroeconomic models.

The next four chapters describe four fundamental building blocks of the modern approach to macroeconomics.

Chapter 3 describes the concept of rational expectations (RE), somehow an extension to stochastic environments of the idea of perfect foresight. This has become the natural benchmark for expectations, because before RE many results were simply due to expectational errors. As it turns out, rational expectations introduce a number of hitherto unknown questions, and we study successively issues of stability, solution multiplicity, learning, and signal extraction.

Chapter 4 studies various deterministic models with infinite horizons where all decisions are taken by maximizing agents. Such models with stochastic shocks, and under the name of "dynamic stochastic general equilibrium models", have become the workhorse of modern macroeconomics. Since these models are intrinsically complex, we start here with simple deterministic versions. These differ essentially by the "demographics" of consumers. We begin with a model with a single infinitely lived consumer. We then move to "overlapping generations" where new households, each with a finite life, are born every period, and these generations overlap during part of their lives. We finally study a synthetic model where agents are infinitely lived, but new ones are born each period.

Chapter 5 studies rigorous models of nonclearing markets and imperfect competition, a necessary step towards giving microfoundations to models of Keynesian inspiration. We first give a simple description of the concepts describing price and quantity decisions in a nonclearing markets framework. We then give a simple macroeconomic example of price and quantity determination under various assumptions of price and wage rigidity. We finally show that the response to stochastic shocks and the associated correlations between various variables depend very much on the rigidities assumed.

Chapter 6 is concerned with the introduction of uncertainty at the individual and general equilibrium level. It starts with the problem of individual choice in uncertain environments, describes expected utility theory and presents a few measures of risk aversion. It then presents a few models of general equilibrium. We review the so-called complete markets and incomplete markets models and show how the concepts developed apply, in particular, to the pricing of financial assets. We finally introduce the concept of "nonexpected utility," which allows us to disentangle the notions of risk and substitutability.

The next three chapters study various models of growth with explicit microfoundations.

Chapter 7 studies the famous Ramsey model. Ramsey (1928), decades ahead of his time, described a rigorous model of growth where an infinitely lived maximizing consumer arbitrages at every instant of time between consuming and investing capital. The Ramsey model is in many respects a benchmark, which displays properties like intertemporal efficiency, or Ricardian equivalence.

Chapter 8 studies models of growth where the demographic structure is that of overlapping generations (OLG). We begin with an extensive study of the simplest model, due to Diamond (1965), where the agents live two periods. This allows us to show that a number of properties of the benchmark Ramsey model do not survive the change in the demographic assumptions. Market equilibria can be inefficient, fiscal policy matters. We also investigate the important issue of pensions.

Chapter 9 studies endogenous growth. Until this chapter the main explanation of growth, technical progress, was taken as exogenous. Endogenous growth theory makes technical progress the result of conscious profit-maximizing activities by individuals or firms. We start with a first model where productivity growth results from returns to diversity in production and the desire of agents to secure rents through creating new diversified products. We then move to a model where research and development increases directly productivity. We also investigate the issue of the so-called scale effects.

Chapter 10 presents the first models of fluctuations using the methodology of "dynamic stochastic general equilibrium" (DSGE) models, that is, models of general intertemporal equilibrium where the economy is subject to various shocks, such as technology shocks. To introduce difficulties progressively, this chapter considers "real" (i.e., nonmonetary) economies, where moreover all markets are assumed to clear in the Walrasian mode. These were the first models introduced in this line of research and for that reason were called "real business cycles." We investigate notably the allocation of consumption and investment in the cycle, asset pricing, and the role of intertemporal substitution in labor supply. This chapter also studies two alternative representations of competitive business cycles: sunspots, where shocks extraneous to the system nevertheless influence economic activity, and endogenous business cycles, where the economy is intrinsically unstable and deterministic cyclical trajectories arise.

Chapter 11 introduces money. Until this chapter we considered "real" economies where exchange is carried through some kind of unspecified barter. Although this simplification is acceptable to study topics such as long-run growth trends, it is clearly inadequate for short-run fluctuations. Introducing money is not such an easy task. Monetary exchange is a restriction on possible trades, and money is an asset that is strictly dominated in rates of return. So we indicate a number of formalizations that allow us to sustain the existence of monetary exchange. We then show that many traditional formalizations of money actually lead to puzzles and paradoxes, and we show some ways to overcome them. We finally describe a model that somehow synthesizes Ramsey, OLG, and money.

Chapter 12 introduces money into the model of fluctuations described in chapter 10. We first show that introduction of money per se is not a cause for extra fluctuations, as nominal variables can adjust fully to nominal money shocks. The same result is obtained for imperfect competition. We finally introduce imperfect information in the tradition of Lucas's (1972) seminal article and show that misperception of various shocks can give a role to monetary shocks in fluctuations.

Chapter 13 studies dynamic stochastic general equilibrium models with nonclearing markets and imperfect competition. Although dynamic models with market clearing (whether with perfect or imperfect competition) can potentially produce fluctuations in response to demand shocks, these seem to be of insufficient magnitude and persistence when one comes to numerical evaluations. So a successful answer to these problems has been to introduce various forms of nominal price or wage rigidities into the system. In this chapter we introduce several formalizations of such rigidities, and it turns out that several of them allow to obtain substantial and persistent responses to nominal shocks. As in the previous chapters our inquiry is conducted via explicitly solved models, which allow to have a clearer grasp of the mechanisms at work.

Chapter 14 studies in a more "partial equilibrium" framework a number of important topics that would have led to a less elegant exposition in the full general equilibrium framework of chapters 7 to 13. We start with consumption, and study successively consumption smoothing, the case of certainty equivalence, precautionary savings. We then move to investment, and describe the rationale and working out of the most standard investment model involving installation costs. We also show how to obtain an "accelerator" in an imperfectly competitive framework. We then consider an often ignored topic, that of inventories. We first show how storability of a good will induce firms not to ration customers, the usual assumption in macroeconomics. We also show that, although production smoothing is one of the functions of inventories, volatility of production may nevertheless be higher than that of sales. We finally relate inventories and production to price making in an imperfect competition framework. Last in this chapter we study credit, which had been left implicit in the previous developments, and we show how credit rationing may arise from imperfect information reasons (adverse selection or moral hazard).

We then have two chapters devoted to the issue of unemployment. Chapter 15 describes, in a unified one-period model, a number of basic models of unemployment. We first describe the three traditional models of interaction between firms and trade unions (monopoly union, efficient bargaining, right to manage), and then the theories of insiders–outsiders, efficiency wages and various forms of implicit contracts.

Chapter 16 puts the unemployment problem in a more dynamic and intertemporal framework, emphasizing flows in and out of unemployment. After describing the general framework, we give a dynamic version of the efficiency wage model seen in the previous chapter. We then describe a workhorse of recent dynamic analysis of unemployment, the matching function.

Chapters 17 to 19 study a number of central issues and debates concerning monetary and fiscal policy. Chapter 17 presents the "public finance" approach to policy, whose central purpose is to minimize distortions associated with the financing of public spending. We start with two classic examples, the Friedman rule and tax smoothing. We then move to one of the pillars of this approach, Ramsey taxation. We then apply these principles to the issue of optimally combining money creation and regular taxes to finance government spending.

Chapter 18 studies stabilization policies, that is, the optimal government reactions to shocks on the economy. We give two important examples of optimal policy in microfounded models. We begin with a model of optimal seigniorage under uncertainty, which links the issues of stabilization and public finance in a Walrasian framework. We then move to a non-Walrasian setting and study the famous "policy effectiveness" debate initiated by Sargent and Wallace in 1975. We find that adequate policies circumvent the ineffectiveness argument. We then study another type of potential economic instability, which can be created by government policy itself. In the same 1975 article, Sargent and Wallace showed that nominal interest rate pegging would create indeterminacy in prices. A similar problem occurs with the more recent "Taylor rules." We reexamine the issue in a microfounded model and find that a revival of the old Pigou effect allows us to find simple rules guaranteeing global determinacy.

Chapter 19 studies the problem of time consistency, which arises in many aspects, fiscal and monetary, of policy making. In a nutshell, that problem arises whenever a policy decided, say, at time 0 for a time t posterior to 0, is not optimal anymore when time t has come. We first give a very simple characterization of that problem and then move to examples pertaining to both fiscal policy and monetary policy. We finally give a number of solutions to solve that credibility problem.

Chapter 20 relates macroeconomics to political economy, that is, the study of decision making when decisions are taken not by a single individual but by politicians representing highly heterogeneous interests. We first describe Arrow's "impossibility theorem." We then show that adequate restrictions to preferences can lead to a solution, describe the famous median voter theorem, and apply it to the problem of redistribution. That theorem predicts that all politicians will have similar platforms, which is not realistic, so we describe a model of "probabilistic voting," which predicts different platforms for different politicians. We also show how the possibility of alternating between politicians with different goals may lead to government deficits in circumstances where political stability would lead to balanced budgets.

Finally, a mathematical appendix gives in a simple and self-contained manner a number of results and recipes that are useful for a number of developments in the main text.

Acknowledgments

While writing this book I have incurred an enormous debt toward Jean-Olivier Hairault, Jean-Pierre Laffargue, François Langot, and Alexander Meyer-Gohde. Their insightful comments on earlier versions of this book brought many improvements to the manuscript. I nevertheless retain all responsibility for any remaining deficiencies.

Macroeconomic Theory

Monopoly Theory

1

Growth

1.1 Introduction

Explaining the relative levels of development of various countries, as well as their rates of growth, is certainly one of the most striking and mysterious challenges in macroeconomics.

A first mystery is this: how did we arrive at the huge degree of inequality we observe today? Until the end of the eighteenth century, disparities between countries were relatively moderate, as many of them were still little above subsistence levels for most of the population. Things changed dramatically in the past two centuries. Then occurred what some authors have called "the great divergence," that is, an unprecedented and steady rise in inequality among countries (this is described, for example, in Bourguignon and Morrisson, 2002).

To have an idea of the magnitudes, a good source is the Penn World Table (Heston, Summers, and Aten, 2009).[1] As an (extreme) example, in 2007 (the latest year available) the Democratic Republic of Congo, a large country with rich mining resources, had a level of gross domestic product (GDP) per capita 110 times smaller that that of the United States. This is simply stupefying.

Now, observing such a degree of inequality, one would expect that there should be a natural movement of people, factors of production, and ideas,

---

1. The Penn World Table presents a set of homogeneous data for a large number of countries, starting around 1950. We use version 6.3. An earlier published version is Summers and Heston (1991). The reader can find longer series for a selected set of countries in Maddison (1982, 1989, 1991, 1995, 2001).

which would bring these countries closer to each other. So the natural intuition would be that some form of convergence should take place, with poorer countries catching up with the rich ones. The actual record is much more complex. For example Barro and Sala-i-Martin (1995) plot for two samples of countries the growth rate of per capita GDP over the period 1960–85 against per capita GDP (in logs) at the beginning of the period (1960). If convergence is taking place, the slope should be negative. For a first sample of Organisation for Economic Cooperation and Development countries, the slope is clearly negative, apparently validating the intuition. When the sample is extended to a large set of 118 countries, the picture changes completely, as the relation is, if anything, slightly positive. The same picture emerges if the period is extended to the longer period 1960–2000 (Barro and Sala-i-Martin, 2004).

The picture one gets is that there are somehow "convergence clubs," made of similar countries, but there is no general tendency for the disparition of inequalities.

Faced with such a diversity of facts, we describe in chapters 1, 7, 8, and 9 a variety of models. For example the "exogenous growth" model of this chapter leads to results of (conditional) convergence, whereas the endogenous growth models of chapter 9 naturally generate different rates of growth.

We begin in this chapter with the so-called exogenous growth models, and section 1.2 presents the most classic model of the domain, the Solow-Swan model. Section 1.3 describes the short-run equilibrium and the dynamics of that model. Section 1.4 studies efficiency and notably the famous "golden rule." Section 1.5 introduces exogenous technical progress. Section 1.6 studies the problem of convergence across different economies. Section 1.7 presents a model with two accumulated factors, physical and human capital.

1.2 The Solow-Swan Model

The Solow-Swan model[2] explains principally increases in national production by factor accumulation. We expose in this chapter the continuous time version of the model.

1.2.1 The Production Function

At time t output Y_t is produced with two factors of production: capital K_t and labor L_t, according to the production function:

$$Y_t = F(K_t, L_t) \qquad (1)$$

---

2. The central reference is Solow (1956). Swan (1956) contemporaneously proposed a similar model.

The function F is assumed to be homogeneous of degree 1:

$$F(\lambda K_t, \lambda L_t) = \lambda F(K_t, L_t) \tag{2}$$

An example that we shall use again and again is the so-called Cobb-Douglas production function:

$$Y_t = A K_t^\alpha L_t^{1-\alpha} \tag{3}$$

Since the function F is homogeneous of degree 1, one can represent productive possibilities in a simpler manner by deflating all variables by the size of the labor force. We thus define variables per head:

$$y_t = \frac{Y_t}{L_t} \qquad k_t = \frac{K_t}{L_t} \tag{4}$$

and therefore:

$$y_t = \frac{Y_t}{L_t} = \frac{F(K_t, L_t)}{L_t} = F\left(\frac{K_t}{L_t}, 1\right) = f(k_t) \tag{5}$$

with:

$$f(k) = F(k, 1) \qquad f'(k) > 0 \qquad f''(k) < 0 \tag{6}$$

It is generally assumed that the function f has the shape indicated in figure 1.1 and that it satisfies the Inada conditions (Inada, 1964):

$$f'(0) = \infty \qquad f'(\infty) = 0 \tag{7}$$

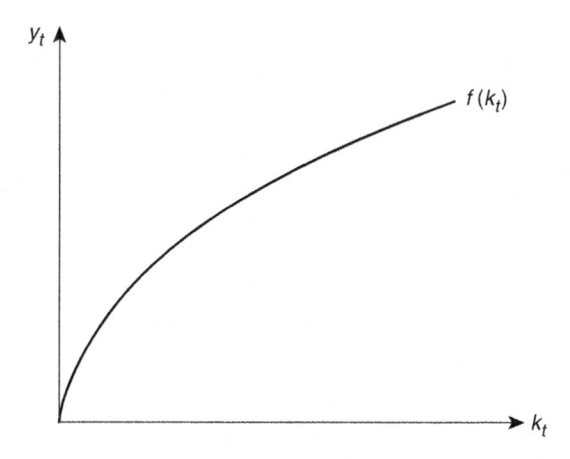

Figure 1.1 The production function

Note that the Inada conditions are clearly satisfied by the Cobb-Douglas production function (formula 3):

$$f(k) = Ak^\alpha \tag{8}$$

There are others that do not satisfy it. For example we describe in appendix 1.1 a class of functions called CES (for constant elasticity of substitution), some of which do not satisfy the Inada conditions.

1.2.2 Factor Accumulation

We first assume that the working population grows at a constant rate n:

$$\frac{\dot{L}_t}{L_t} = n \tag{9}$$

Capital accumulation results from two antagonistic effects. First, a fraction δ of the capital stock depreciates per unit of time. On the other hand, firms invest in time t a flow of output I_t. The law governing the evolution of capital is thus:

$$\dot{K}_t = I_t - \delta K_t \tag{10}$$

To fully describe this law of evolution, we must still indicate which fraction of output will be invested and which will be consumed. It is assumed that agents save and invest a fixed fraction s of period t production Y_t:

$$I_t = sY_t = sF(K_t, L_t) \tag{11}$$

where s, the savings rate, is assumed to be constant (we shall derive the optimal savings behavior of the consumer in chapters 7 to 9). The final equation giving capital dynamics is thus:

$$\dot{K}_t = sF(K_t, L_t) - \delta K_t \tag{12}$$

1.3 Short-run Equilibrium and Dynamics

1.3.1 The Short-run Equilibrium

A central assumption of the model is that in the short run the relative prices of factors adjust so that capital and labor are always fully employed. Let us call ω_t the real wage and κ_t the marginal product of capital. We have:

$$\omega_t = \frac{\partial F(K_t, L_t)}{\partial L_t} \qquad \kappa_t = \frac{\partial F(K_t, L_t)}{\partial K_t} \qquad (13)$$

Of course, since the function F is homogeneous of degree 1, we have the classic identity:

$$L_t \frac{\partial F(K_t, L_t)}{\partial L_t} + K_t \frac{\partial F(K_t, L_t)}{\partial K_t} = F(K_t, L_t) \qquad (14)$$

which, in view of (13), can be rewritten:

$$\omega_t L_t + \kappa_t K_t = Y_t \qquad (15)$$

Under constant returns to scale, the incomes of the various factors completely exhaust the value of output.

The two equalities (13) can be rewritten, using the function f:

$$\omega_t = f(k_t) - k_t f'(k_t) \qquad \kappa_t = f'(k_t) \qquad (16)$$

1.3.2 The Dynamics of the Solow-Swan Model

We thus have a dynamic system in the two variables labor and capital (equations 9 and 12). Homogeneity of the function F will enable us to reduce this to a dynamic system in one single variable, the amount of capital per head k_t. Indeed we deduce from equations (9) and (12) that:

$$\dot{k}_t = \frac{\dot{K}_t}{L_t} - \frac{K_t}{L_t}\frac{\dot{L}_t}{L_t} = \frac{sF(K_t, L_t) - \delta K_t}{L_t} - n\frac{K_t}{L_t} \qquad (17)$$

which simplifies as:

$$\frac{\dot{k}_t}{k_t} = \frac{sf(k_t)}{k_t} - (\delta + n) \qquad (18)$$

This dynamic equation has been represented in figure 1.2. Capital per head will converge toward the long-run equilibrium value k^* obtained by equating to 0 the right-hand side of (18), which yields:

$$(\delta + n) k^* = sf(k^*) \qquad (19)$$

We see, which is intuitive, that the equilibrium value of capital per head k^* is an increasing function of the savings rate s, a decreasing function of the population's rate of growth n, and of the capital's depreciation rate δ.

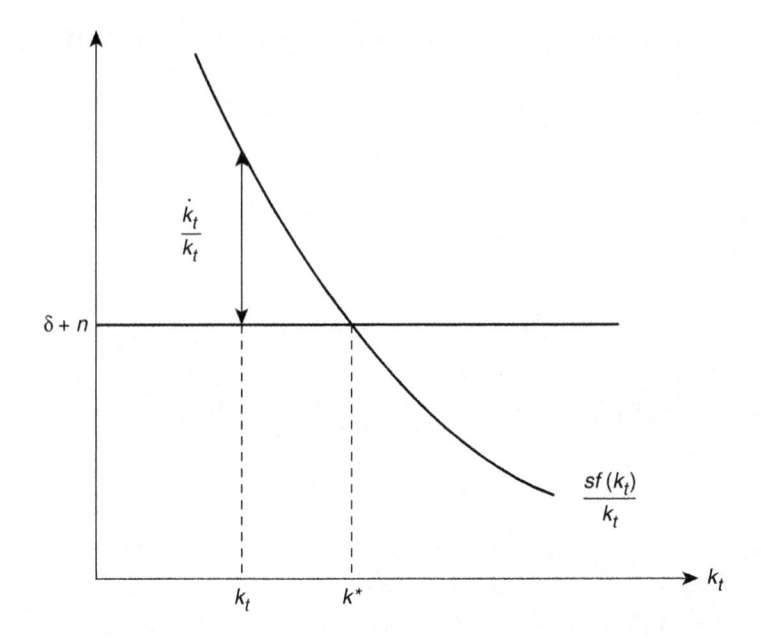

Figure 1.2 Capital dynamics

1.3.3 The Speed of Convergence: A Cobb-Douglas Example

We now give an example where the dynamics can be computed explicitly. Assume that the production function is of the Cobb-Douglas type:

$$f(k) = Ak^\alpha \tag{20}$$

We can first compute, via formula (19), the stationary level of capital per head:

$$k^* = \left(\frac{sA}{\delta + n}\right)^{1/(1-\alpha)} \tag{21}$$

Now we also compute the whole dynamic path. Let us rewrite equation (18):

$$\dot{k}_t = sAk_t^\alpha - (\delta + n)k_t \tag{22}$$

Multiply both sides by $k_t^{-\alpha}$:

$$k_t^{-\alpha}\dot{k}_t = sA - (\delta + n)k_t^{1-\alpha} \tag{23}$$

which is rewritten as:

$$\frac{1}{1-\alpha}\frac{dk_t^{1-\alpha}}{dt} = sA - (\delta+n)k_t^{1-\alpha} \qquad (24)$$

This differential equation has the solution:

$$k_t^{1-\alpha} = \frac{sA}{\delta+n} + \left(k_0^{1-\alpha} - \frac{sA}{\delta+n}\right)e^{-(1-\alpha)(\delta+n)t} \qquad (25)$$

We see that the higher the parameter $(1-\alpha)(\delta+n)$ will be, the faster convergence will be. Note in particular that the closer α is to 1, the slower the convergence to the steady state.

1.4 The Golden Rule

Until now we took the savings rate s as exogenous. One may ask what would be the best savings rate from the point of view of society, and we shall define here the best savings rate as the one that maximizes consumption per head in the stationary state. Intuitively one sees that the savings rate must neither be too high nor too low: $s=0$ or $s=1$ would both yield zero consumption in the long run. The optimal savings rate will thus be solution of the following program:

$$\text{Maximize } (1-s)f(k^*) \quad \text{s.t.}$$

$$(\delta+n)k^* = sf(k^*)$$

where k^* is the equilibrium value of capital per head. Taking k^* as our working variable, this is equivalent to:

$$\text{Maximize } f(k^*) - (\delta+n)k^*$$

which immediately yields the optimal value of the capital per head, $\hat{k}$, given by:

$$f'(\hat{k}) = \delta + n \qquad (26)$$

Equation (26), which gives the optimal level of capital per head, is called the golden rule, and $\hat{k}$ the golden rule capital (Phelps, 1961, 1966).

The optimal savings rate is deduced from it by:

$$\hat{s} = \frac{(\delta + n)\hat{k}}{f(\hat{k})} = \frac{\hat{k}f'(\hat{k})}{f(\hat{k})} \qquad (27)$$

As an example, consider the Cobb-Douglas function $f(k) = Ak^\alpha$. In that case:

$$\hat{s} = \alpha \qquad (28)$$

The optimal savings rate is exactly equal to the share of profits in production.

Note that if the amount of capital is higher than that given by the golden rule, the dynamic equilibrium is particularly inefficient because, by reducing the level of capital, one could increase consumption at all times.

This is demonstrated in figure 1.3, which shows the dynamic effects of a reduction in the savings rate s. The savings rate is initially equal to s_0, and decreases to $s < s_0$ at time t_0. We see that the effects are quite different, depending on the position of s_0 with respect to $\hat{s}$. If $s_0 < \hat{s}$, there is first an increase and then a fall in consumption per head. But if $s_0 > \hat{s}$ we see that the trajectory of consumption is perpetually above the initial one. The equilibrium with a too high savings rate is not even Pareto optimal, and thus particularly inefficient.

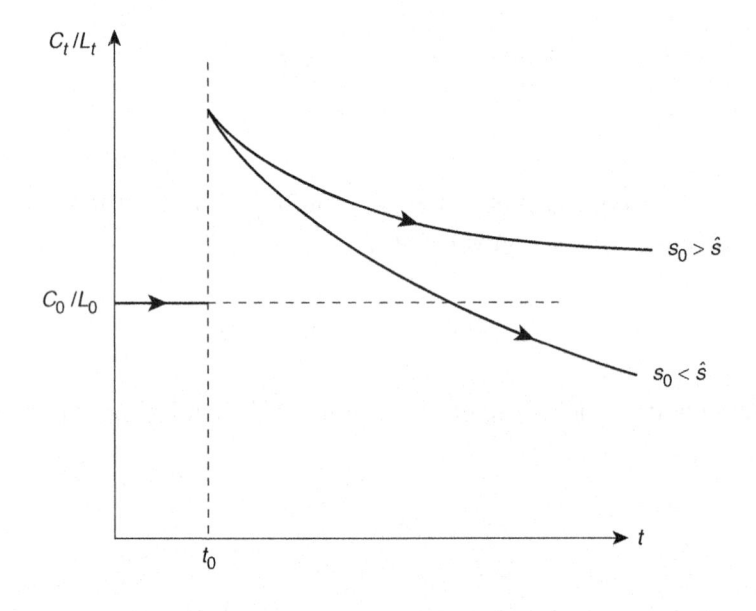

Figure 1.3 The effects of a reduction in the savings rate

1.5 Technical Progress and Growth

1.5.1 The Solow Residual

Although the foregoing model is most useful in explaining output growth by the accumulation of productive factors, some of its predictions are clearly contradicted by the facts. First, the model predicts a constant production per head in the long run. What is observed in most countries is, on the contrary, an uninterrupted (although fluctuating) growth of production per head.

Second, according to the model, output growth is 100 percent explained by the accumulation of capital. For example, assuming a Cobb-Douglas function and log-differentiating equation (8) one obtains:

$$\dot{y}_t/y_t = \alpha \dot{k}_t/k_t \qquad (29)$$

so that a regression of $\dot{y}_t$ on $\dot{k}_t$ should have a R^2 equal to 1. What one obtains instead is something of the form:

$$\dot{y}_t/y_t = \alpha \dot{k}_t/k_t + \dot{z}_t/z_t \qquad (30)$$

where the variable z_t, often called the Solow residual (Solow, 1957), fluctuates around a positive average.

1.5.2 Technical Progress

So everything happens as if the production function $F(K_t, L_t)$ was not stable in time but there was an extra factor, called "technical progress," which enables more production with the same quantity of factors. One can, for example, generalize the production function (1) to:

$$Y_t = F(K_t, L_t, t) \qquad \frac{\partial F(K_t, L_t, t)}{\partial t} \geq 0 \qquad (31)$$

This is still quite general, and there are multiple, more specific ways of formalizing this technical progress. One popular representation is that of "factor augmenting" technical progress, which is formalized as follows:

$$Y_t = F(B_t K_t, A_t L_t) \qquad \dot{A}_t \geq 0 \qquad \dot{B}_t \geq 0 \qquad (32)$$

The factor A_t is called labor augmenting technical progress, B_t capital augmenting technical progress. The interpretation is that production is function of "effective labor" and "effective capital." For a given amount of factor, technical progress augments the value of the "effective factor."

1.5.3 Balanced Growth

As it turns out, this model has a steady state if technical progress is of the "labor augmenting" type,[3] that is, technical progress of the form:

$$Y_t = F(K_t, A_t L_t) \qquad \frac{\dot{A}_t}{A_t} = \gamma_A \qquad (33)$$

One might fear having to redo the whole analysis in that case. Actually, the analysis will be identical to that without technical progress, simply by replacing everywhere L_t by "effective labor" $\Lambda_t = A_t L_t$, and n by $n + \gamma_A$. The variable k_t becomes:

$$k_t = \frac{K_t}{\Lambda_t} = \frac{K_t}{A_t L_t} \qquad (34)$$

In the steady state, variables per head grow at the rate γ_A, instead of being constant.

1.6 Convergence

We saw at the beginning of this chapter that an important puzzle in growth economics was the issue of convergence.[4] So a natural question to ask is: does the Solow-Swan model predict convergence among economies?

To answer that question we consider a set of countries indexed by i. Then from formula (18), the growth of capital in country i is equal to:

$$\frac{\dot{k}_{it}}{k_{it}} = \frac{s_i f(k_{it})}{k_{it}} - (\delta_i + n_i) \qquad (35)$$

To make the discussion more transparent, we assume that all countries have a Cobb-Douglas production function with the same exponent α:

$$f(k_{it}) = A_i k_i^\alpha \qquad (36)$$

---

3. For a proof, see for example Barro and Sala-i-Martin (1995) or problem 1.2.
4. A (very) partial list of works on growth empirics and convergence is Barro (1991); Barro and Sala-i-Martin (1991, 1992); Baumol (1986); Baumol and Wolff (1988); De Long (1988); Dowrick and Nguyen (1989); Durlauf, Johnson, and Temple (2005); Durlauf and Quah (1999); Jones (1997a, 1997b); Mankiw, Romer, and Weil (1992); Pritchett (1997); Quah (1996a, 1996b); and Temple (1999). Expositions are found in Barro and Sala-i-Martin (1995, 2004), De la Fuente (1997), Helpman (2004), Sala-i-Martin (1996).

so that the rates of growth are:

$$\frac{\dot{k}_{it}}{k_{it}} = s_i A_i k_{it}^{\alpha-1} - (\delta_i + n_i) \qquad (37)$$

The dynamics of each country is thus characterized by a vector of parameters:

$$z_i = (s_i, A_i, \delta_i, n_i) \qquad (38)$$

We may consider several cases.

1.6.1 Absolute Convergence

If all countries considered have the same fundamental parameters, that is, if $z_i = z$, then there is *absolute convergence*, which means that the countries with lower levels of capital per head also have higher rates of growth of capital per head (formula 37). This is represented in figure 1.4, which pictures the case of two countries who have different levels of capital per head k_1 and k_2 but the same parameters (s, A, δ, n). The levels of capital per head will get closer and become equal asymptotically.

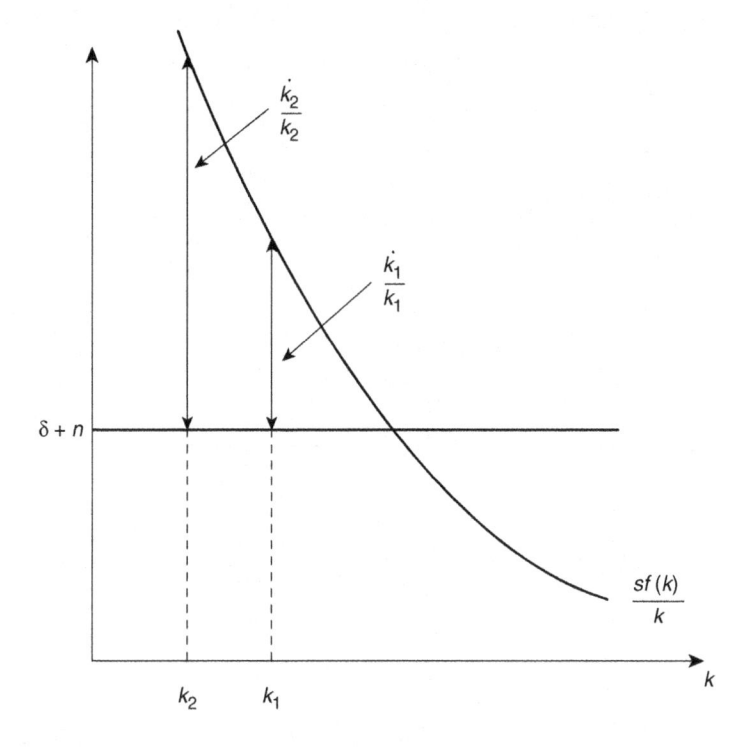

Figure 1.4 Absolute convergence

1.6.2 Conditional Convergence

If the two countries have different parameters, there may be an apparent divergence. This is shown in figure 1.5, which pictures two countries that have the same A, δ, and n, but different savings rates, s_1 and s_2. We see that although country 1 has a capital per head greater than that of country 2, it nevertheless grows faster. We have somehow absolute divergence.

This is not the end of the story as, although we do not have absolute convergence, we have, however, in this case *conditional convergence*, which means that, controlling for the different values of the fundamental parameters, a lower capital leads to a higher rate of growth.

To express the notion of conditional convergence in a more precise way, let us continue to use Cobb-Douglas production functions (formula 36) and consider the particular case where only the savings rate s_i are different. Then formula (35) is rewritten:

$$\frac{\dot{k}_{it}}{k_{it}} = (\delta + n)\left[\left(\frac{k_i^*}{k_{it}}\right)^{1-\alpha} - 1\right] \qquad (39)$$

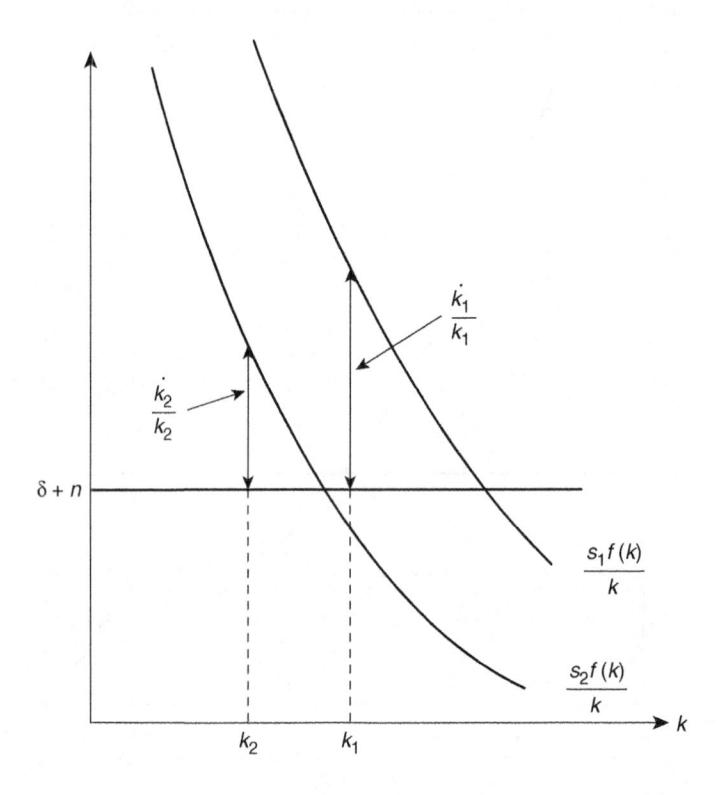

Figure 1.5 Absolute divergence and conditional convergence

where k_i^*, the long run capital level of country i, is (formula 21):

$$k_i^* = \left(\frac{s_i A}{\delta + n}\right)^{1/(1-\alpha)} \quad (40)$$

We see that what matters in this example is not the absolute level of capital but the ratio of that level to the long-run value of capital. Of course, if the δ_i's and n_i's were different, there would still be a different form of conditional convergence, although its expression would be a little more complicated.

1.6.3 Conditional and Unconditional Convergence: An Example

We want to show here in a simple example that, even though conditional convergence is at work, one may find a *positive* relation between capital and growth, and therefore "absolute divergence."

We consider a set of countries that have the same A, δ, and n, but differ only by their savings rate, s_i. We have for each country i (equation 37):

$$\frac{\dot{k}_{it}}{k_{it}} = s_i A k_{it}^{\alpha-1} - (\delta + n) \quad (41)$$

Equation (41) shows that, controlling for s_i, we have a negative relation between capital and capital growth, and thus conditional convergence.

We now investigate absolute convergence, and for that we will be a little more specific about trajectories. Assume that at some early point in history all countries had the same level of capital k_0. Then the dynamic path of capital for country i is given by equation (25):

$$k_{it}^{1-\alpha} = \frac{s_i A}{\delta + n} + \left(k_0^{1-\alpha} - \frac{s_i A}{\delta + n}\right) e^{-\theta t} \quad (42)$$

with:

$$\theta = (1-\alpha)(\delta + n) \quad (43)$$

Imagine that the values of the s_i's are not directly observable. But from equation (42) there is a relation between k_{it} and s_i. In fact we have:

$$s_i = \frac{(\delta + n)\left(k_{it}^{1-\alpha} - e^{-\theta t} k_0^{1-\alpha}\right)}{A\left(1 - e^{-\theta t}\right)} \quad (44)$$

Inserting this into (41) we find:

$$\frac{\dot{k}_{it}}{k_{it}} = \frac{(\delta + n) e^{-\theta t}}{1 - e^{-\theta t}} \left[1 - \left(\frac{k_0}{k_{it}} \right)^{1-\alpha} \right] \tag{45}$$

We see that now the relation between $\dot{k}_{it}/k_{it}$ and k_{it} is positive. There is thus somehow "absolute divergence."

1.7 A Model with Two Accumulated Factors

So far we have assumed that there is a single accumulated factor, physical capital. As we will see, some studies have had difficulties matching some empirical results with this simple model. In the spirit of Uzawa (1965), we extend this model to two accumulated factors, physical and human capital, and see that this allows us to solve some of the puzzles.

1.7.1 The Model

We decompose productive labor into "raw labor" L_t, whose evolution is taken exogenous as before, and human capital H_t which can be accumulated. Accordingly the production function is:

$$Y_t = K_t^\alpha H_t^\beta (A_t L_t)^{1-\alpha-\beta} \tag{46}$$

with:

$$\frac{\dot{A}_t}{A_t} = \gamma_A \tag{47}$$

The accumulation equation for capital is the same as in the Solow-Swan model:

$$\dot{K}_t = s_K Y_t - \delta K_t \tag{48}$$

and the equation for human capital is similar:

$$\dot{H}_t = s_H Y_t - \delta H_t \tag{49}$$

Define the quantities per unit of effective raw labor:

$$y_t = \frac{Y_t}{A_t L_t} \qquad k_t = \frac{K_t}{A_t L_t} \qquad h_t = \frac{H_t}{A_t L_t} \tag{50}$$

Equations (48) and (49) are rewritten:

$$\dot{k}_t = s_K y_t - (n + \gamma_A + \delta) k_t \tag{51}$$

$$\dot{h}_t = s_H y_t - (n + \gamma_A + \delta) h_t \tag{52}$$

1.7.2 Steady States

From (46), (51), and (52) we easily compute the steady-state values:

$$k^* = \left(\frac{s_K^{1-\beta} s_H^{\beta}}{n + \gamma_A + \delta} \right)^{1/(1-\alpha-\beta)} \tag{53}$$

$$h^* = \left(\frac{s_K^{\alpha} s_H^{1-\alpha}}{n + \gamma_A + \delta} \right)^{1/(1-\alpha-\beta)} \tag{54}$$

Inserting these into the production function we find the following value of income per capita in steady state:

$$\log\left(\frac{Y_t}{L_t}\right) = \log A_0 + \gamma_A t + \frac{\alpha}{1-\alpha-\beta} [\log s_K - \log(n + \gamma_A + \delta)]$$

$$+ \frac{\beta}{1-\alpha-\beta} [\log s_H - \log(n + \gamma_A + \delta)] \tag{55}$$

1.7.3 An Empirical Application

Recall that the equation corresponding to (55) for the one factor case is (it is enough to take $\beta = 0$):

$$\log\left(\frac{Y_t}{L_t}\right) = \log A_0 + \gamma_A t + \frac{\alpha}{1-\alpha} [\log s_K - \log(n + \gamma_A + \delta)] \tag{56}$$

Mankiw, Romer, and Weil (1992) first estimate equation (56) for a panel of 75 countries. They find:

$$\frac{\alpha}{1-\alpha} = 1.43 \tag{57}$$

This corresponds to $\alpha = 0.59$. There is clearly a problem because the share of capital in income is about one third.

They then proceed to estimate the two factors equation (55) and find:

$$\frac{\alpha}{1-\alpha-\beta} = 0.71 \qquad \frac{\beta}{1-\alpha-\beta} = 0.74 \qquad (58)$$

These correspond to $\alpha = 0.29$ and $\beta = 0.30$. These numbers are now consistent with the observed distribution of income, because workers' income includes the remuneration of both raw labor and human capital.

Appendix 1.1: The CES Production Function

We saw in this chapter a first example of a production function, the Cobb-Douglas function:

$$Y = AK^\alpha L^{1-\alpha} \qquad (59)$$

This function has an elasticity of substitution between capital and labor equal to 1. Another popular example is the Leontief production function, where no substitution is possible between factors, which are used in fixed proportions:

$$Y_t = A \min\left(\frac{K}{a}, \frac{L}{b}\right) \qquad (60)$$

We now describe a particularly useful production function (Arrow, Chenery, Minhas, and Solow, 1961) known as CES (for "constant elasticity of substitution"), which synthesizes the two preceding cases and several others.

$$Y_t = A\left[\alpha\left(\frac{K}{a}\right)^\eta + (1-\alpha)\left(\frac{L}{b}\right)^\eta\right]^{1/\eta} \qquad \eta \leq 1 \qquad (61)$$

It is easy to see that in the limit case $\eta = 0$, one obtains a Cobb-Douglas function:

$$Y = A\left(\frac{K}{a}\right)^\alpha \left(\frac{L}{b}\right)^{1-\alpha} \qquad (62)$$

For $\eta = -\infty$, one obtains a Leontief function:

$$Y = A \min\left(\frac{K}{a}, \frac{L}{b}\right) \qquad (63)$$

and finally, for $\eta = 1$, a function with perfectly substitutable factors:

$$Y = A\left[\frac{\alpha K}{a} + \frac{(1-\alpha)L}{b}\right] \tag{64}$$

We should note that the Inada conditions are not always satisfied, for example, for $0 < \eta \leq 1$.

A CES Function with Many Inputs

The CES function just described has two inputs. In this book, we repeatedly use CES functions with many inputs. Let us thus assume that there are N inputs indexed by $i = 1, \ldots, N$. Denote as X_i the amount of input i. We shall assume a symmetrical production function, and the CES function is expressed as:

$$Y = N\left(\frac{1}{N}\sum_{i=1}^{N} X_i^\eta\right)^{1/\eta} \qquad \eta \leq 1 \tag{65}$$

This function has been parameterized so that, if $X_i = X$, then $Y = NX$. Denote as P the price of output, and P_i the price of input i. The demand for input i is obtained by maximizing profit:

$$PY - \sum_{i=1}^{N} P_i X_i \tag{66}$$

subject to the production function (65). This yields:

$$\frac{NX_i}{Y} = \left(\frac{P_i}{P}\right)^{-1/(1-\eta)} \tag{67}$$

We note that the closer η is to 1, that is, the more substitutable the inputs, the more elastic the input demand, and therefore the more competitive the corresponding market.

A Continuous Version

We can go to the limit and assume that there is an infinity of inputs. In that case, it is convenient to represent inputs as indexed by $i \in [0, 1]$. The CES function is accordingly written:

$$Y = \left(\int_0^1 X_i^\eta\right)^{1/\eta} \tag{68}$$

and the demand for input i:

$$\frac{X_i}{Y} = \left(\frac{P_i}{P}\right)^{-1/(1-\eta)} \tag{69}$$

Appendix 1.2: Embodied Technical Progress

In the main body of the chapter, technical progress accrues no matter when the capital equipment is produced or installed. This is called "disembodied" technical progress. Anybody who works, say, with computers, knows that to benefit from the latest technology, one has to buy the latest computer. Technical progress is embodied in capital. We shall now see, following Solow (1960), how to model this.

First, we have to use two time scales. As before, time t will denote "current time," when production takes place. The index v will denote vintages of capital. For example K_{vt} will denote the amount of capital installed at time v (i.e., of vintage v) and still in use at time t. Similarly L_{vt} will denote the amount of work used on vintage v capital. So there will be a production function for vintage v:

$$Y_{vt} = F(K_{vt}, L_{vt}, v) \qquad \partial F(K_{vt}, L_{vt}, v)/\partial v \geq 0 \tag{70}$$

where Y_{vt} is output produced with capital of vintage v. Note that the third argument of the function, which captures technical progress, is v, which means that the technical progress affecting each vintage is function of the time where the machine was constructed and not of the time t when it is used.

Aggregation

Aggregate output and labor are simply obtained by summing the amounts corresponding to all vintages:

$$Y_t = \int_{-\infty}^{t} Y_{vt} dv \tag{71}$$

$$L_t = \int_{-\infty}^{t} L_{vt} dv \tag{72}$$

In general, the relation between the two will depend on the whole stream of investments I_v, $v \leq t$. There are cases, however, where one can write:

$$Y_t = F(J_t, L_t) \tag{73}$$

where J_t is some measure of aggregate capital. To show this, let us first assume that capital depreciates exponentially:

$$K_{vt} = e^{-\delta(t-v)} I_v \qquad (74)$$

where I_v is capital investment at time v. Let us also assume that technical progress is of the capital augmenting type:

$$F(K_{vt}, L_{vt}, v) = F(B_v K_{vt}, L_{vt}) \qquad (75)$$

Now, because the markets are competitive, the marginal productivity of labor is equal to the real wage for all vintages:

$$\frac{\partial F(B_v K_{vt}, L_{vt})}{\partial L_{vt}} = \omega_t \qquad \forall v \qquad (76)$$

Because F is homogeneous of degree 1, the partial derivative is homogeneous of degree 0. It is thus a function of $B_v K_{vt}/L_{vt}$, and this quantity has the same value, say, ψ_t, for all vintages, so that:

$$B_v K_{vt} = \psi_t L_{vt} \qquad \forall v \qquad (77)$$

Let us aggregate (77) across all vintages:

$$\int_{-\infty}^{t} B_v K_{vt} dv = \psi_t \int_{-\infty}^{t} L_{vt} dv = \psi_t L_t \qquad (78)$$

and denote:

$$J_t = \int_{-\infty}^{t} B_v K_{vt} dv = \int_{-\infty}^{t} B_v e^{-\delta(t-v)} I_v dv \qquad (79)$$

We can now compute the value of aggregate output:

$$Y_t = \int_{-\infty}^{t} F(B_v K_{vt}, L_{vt}) dv = \int_{-\infty}^{t} F\left(\frac{B_v K_{vt}}{L_{vt}}, 1\right) L_{vt} dv \qquad (80)$$

Inserting (77) into (80) we find:

$$Y_t = F(\psi_t, 1) \int_{-\infty}^{t} L_{vt} dv = F(\psi_t, 1) L_t = F(\psi_t L_t, L_t) = F(J_t, L_t) \qquad (81)$$

where J_t is given by (79).

So under assumptions (74) and (75), heterogeneous vintages can be aggregated in the global production function (73).

Problems

Problem 1.1: Transition in a Dual Economy

The economy comprises two sectors, 1 and 2. They produce the same good, which can be both consumed or invested. The "modern" sector, 1, uses capitalistic techniques described by the production function:

$$Q_{1t} = F(K_t, L_{1t}) = A K_t^\alpha L_{1t}^{1-\alpha}$$

where Q_{1t} is the quantity produced by sector 1, K_t the stock of capital in the modern sector, and L_{1t} employment in sector 1. Firms maximize profits and pay to their workers a real wage ω_t, which is determined competitively.

The "traditional" sector, 2, produces the same good with a technique using only labor. Its production is equal to:

$$Q_{2t} = B L_{2t} \qquad B > 0$$

where L_{2t} is employment in sector 2.

The aggregate labor force $L_t = L_{1t} + L_{2t}$ grows at the rate $n > 0$. It is also assumed that taken together, entrepreneurs and workers in the modern sector save and invest a constant proportion s of their total income.

1. Determine, depending on the value of K_t/L_t, the characteristics of the short-run equilibrium, and notably the employment in each sector.
2. Call $k_t = K_t/L_t$ the ratio of capital to total population. Give the expression of dk_t/dt as a function of k_t.
3. Describe the various possible dynamic evolutions. Show that, depending notably on the values of s and n, the modern sector may take over the whole economy, or in the contrary regress to 0.

Problem 1.2: Steady Growth and Labor Augmenting Technical Progress

We want to show that, to have steady-state growth, technical progress must be of the labor augmenting type (see, notably, Barro and Sala-i-Martin, 1995). So we assume a CES production function:

$$Y_t = [\alpha (B_t K_t)^\eta + (1-\alpha)(A_t L_t)^\eta]^{1/\eta}$$

with:

$$A_t = e^{at} \qquad B_t = e^{bt} \qquad L_t = e^{nt}$$

and the usual capital accumulation equation:

$$\dot{K}_t = sY_t - \delta K_t$$

1. Show that to obtain steady growth one must have either a Cobb-Douglas production function ($\eta = 0$) or labor augmenting technical progress ($b = 0$).

2

Output, Inflation, and Stabilization

2.1 Introduction

In the previous chapter we studied the long-run evolution of output. To make these long-run issues particularly transparent, we made the simplifying assumption that all markets clear at every instant in time, and all factors of production (capital and labor) are fully employed.

This is, of course, an unrealistic assumption and another fundamental branch of macroeconomic theory, starting with the pathbreaking contributions of Keynes (1936) and Hicks (1937), studied imbalances between supply and demand in the short run, as well as policies designed to suppress or alleviate these imbalances. In this chapter we concentrate on three central issues: (1) how to model economies out of competitive Walrasian equilibrium, (2) how to represent the inflationary process in a world of sticky prices and wages, and (3) can and should the government actively intervene so as to stabilize output, employment, or inflation?

In section 2.2 we present a number of historical models, notably the most traditional Keynesian models, the "Keynesian cross," the IS-LM and the AD-AS models, which are still the workhorses of undergraduate macroeconomics.

These models are essentially static and based on temporary price and wage rigidities. To introduce dynamics, in section 2.3 we study the Phillips curve, which depicts the evolution of wages in response to unemployment. Section 2.4 introduces expectations and shows how the interaction of the Phillips curve and the evolution of expectations determines the joint dynamics of inflation and unemployment.

Finally, in section 2.6 we turn to a particularly important issue, that of government policy effectiveness. It is shown notably that hypotheses on information and expectations formation are absolutely central in assessing whether government can actually control the evolution of employment and output.

2.2 The Basic Keynesian Models

In models of Keynesian inspiration that we will now study, the level of income is the central variable of adjustment.[1] Implicit is the assumption that prices and wages do not fully adjust, and as a consequence quantities must bear at least part of the adjustment. Microfoundations for this type of situations are studied in chapter 5. Meanwhile, we describe a number of models in this tradition.

We study three particularly well-known Keynesian models: the Keynesian cross, the IS-LM model, and the AD-AS model.

2.2.1 The Keynesian Cross

Keynesian models start from the equality between total output Y_t and the sum of consumption C_t, investment I_t and governement spending G_t:

$$Y_t = C_t + I_t + G_t \tag{1}$$

In the simplest Keynesian cross model, investment and government spending are exogenous, whereas consumption is given by a consumption function:

$$C_t = C(Y_t - T_t) \qquad 0 < C_Y = \frac{\partial C}{\partial (Y_t - T_t)} < 1 \tag{2}$$

where T_t is real taxes. Output is thus given by the following equation:

$$Y_t = C(Y_t - T_t) + I_t + G_t \tag{3}$$

This equation is pictured in figure 2.1, commonly known as the Keynesian cross.

---

1. That this is a central feature of Keynesian economics appears quite clearly in the following quotation by Keynes (1937, p. 250): "As I have said above, the initial novelty lies in my maintaining that it is not the rate of interest, but the level of incomes that ensures equality between savings and investment."

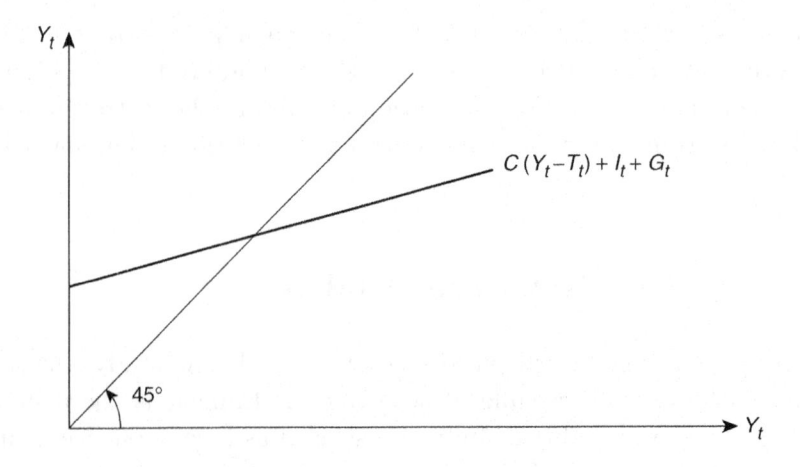

Figure 2.1 The Keynesian cross

From equation (3) one derives the famous multiplier:

$$\frac{\partial Y_t}{\partial G_t} = \frac{1}{1 - C_Y} > 1 \qquad (4)$$

Because the multiplier is greater than 1, we have the remarkable result that an increase in government spending increases consumption, in contradiction to the traditional "crowding-out" effect.

If the increases in taxes and government spending are equal, we obtain Haavelmo's (1945) balanced budget multiplier:

$$\frac{\partial Y_t}{\partial G_t} = 1 \qquad \text{if } dT_t = dG_t \qquad (5)$$

2.2.2 The IS-LM Model

As compared to the previous model, the IS-LM model (Keynes, 1936; Hicks, 1937), does not take investment as exogenous but makes it dependent on at least the interest rate:

$$Y_t = C(Y_t - T_t) + I(i_t) + G_t \qquad IS \qquad (6)$$

where i_t is the nominal interest rate. Actually the rate of interest appearing in the IS curve should be a real rather than a nominal interest rate, and the investment function should be written $I(i_t - \pi_t^e)$, where π_t^e is the expected rate of inflation. For the time being we shall treat π_t^e as given in the

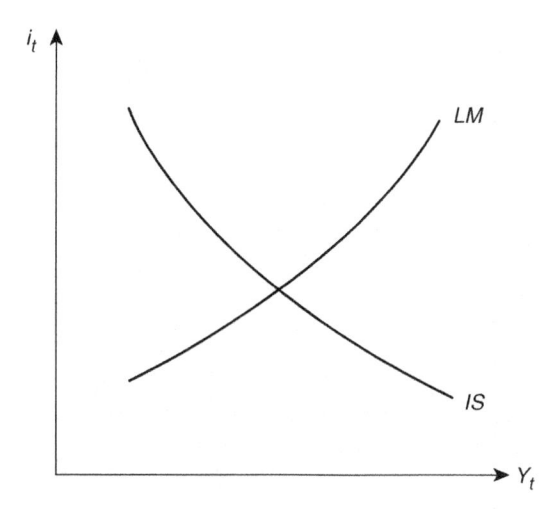

Figure 2.2 The IS-LM model

short run, and omit it from the investment function to simplify notation. Sections 2.4 and 2.5 will explore specifically various roles of inflationary expectations.

Of course this leaves the interest rate to be determined. This is done through the equation of demand for money, the so-called LM curve:

$$\frac{M_t}{P_t} = \mathcal{M}(Y_t, i_t) \qquad LM \qquad (7)$$

where M_t is the quantity of money and P_t the nominal price level. A simple justification for such a demand for money is given in appendix 2.1. The IS and LM curves are represented in figure 2.2.

If prices and wages are assumed fixed, one can directly analyze the effects of economic policies in period t, either graphically (figure 2.2), or by differentiating equations (6) and (7).

The hypothesis of price rigidity, however, is not realistic, and this model is more often used in its version with fixed wages and flexible prices.

2.2.3 The AD-AS Model

We thus assume a rigid wage and flexible price. The price level is determined by the intersection of supply and demand for goods. To obtain the demand equation (named AD, like "aggregate demand"), we eliminate the interest

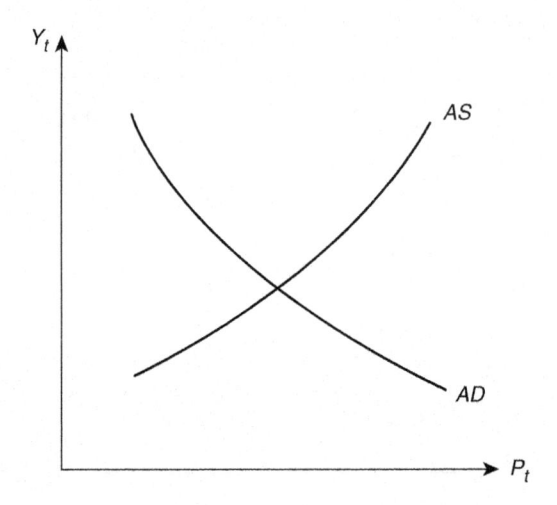

Figure 2.3 The AD-AS model

rate i_t between the two IS and LM equations, which yields:

$$Y_t = D\left(\frac{M_t}{P_t}, G_t, T_t\right) \qquad AD \qquad (8)$$

To obtain the supply-side equation (named AS, like "aggregate supply"), we compute the supply of output by firms. Assume they have a production function $Y_t = F(L_t)$. Their supply is obtained as the quantity of output that maximizes firms' profits, that is, the solution in Y_t of:

$$\text{Maximize } P_t Y_t - W_t L_t \quad \text{s.t.}$$
$$Y_t = F(L_t)$$

which yields the output supply function:

$$Y_t = F\left[F'^{-1}\left(\frac{W_t}{P_t}\right)\right] = S\left(\frac{W_t}{P_t}\right) \qquad AS \qquad (9)$$

Again we can find the effects of economic policies either graphically (figure 2.3), or by differentiating equations (8) and (9).

2.2.4 Policy in Traditional Keynesian Models

We now study (very briefly) the issue of policy in the foregoing models. Let us consider, for example, the AD-AS model. Assume there is a constant supply of labor L_0, so that full employment output is equal to $Y_0 = F(L_0)$.

Output, Inflation, and Stabilization

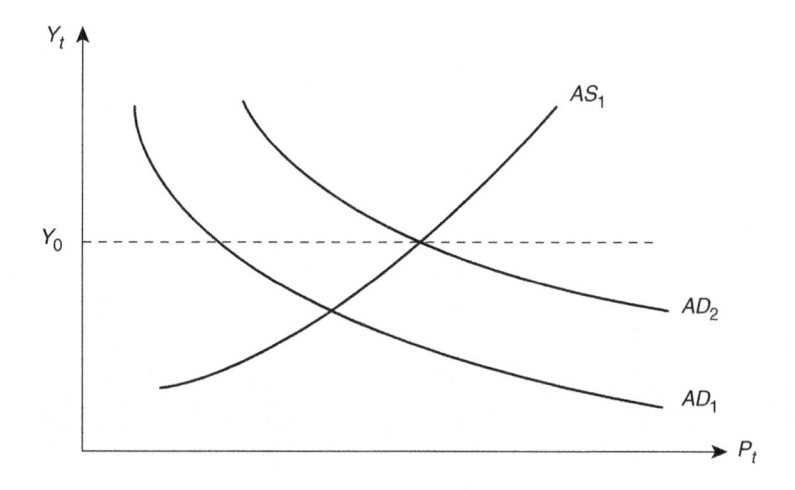

Figure 2.4 An expansionary demand policy

The "initial situation" corresponds to the two curves AD_1 and AS_1 in figure 2.4. These two curves intersect at a value Y_1 inferior to Y_0, thus producing unemployment. Now, to obtain full employment, all that is needed is to move the AD curve upward to a position like AD_2, so that it intersects AS_1 at $Y = Y_0$. This upward move can be obtained by traditional demand expansion policies, like increasing M_t or G_t or reducing T_t. We may note that these expansionary demand policies also lead to higher prices.

2.3 The Phillips Curve

We clearly see that if one wants, starting from an AD-AS model, to study the effects over time of an economic policy, it is necessary to know the evolution of wages. Numerous debates actually took place around this law of evolution of wages. In a famous article, Phillips (1958) showed that over a period of almost a century (1861–1957) there existed a surprisingly stable relation between wage increases and the level of unemployment. Empirically, one obtains a relation of the type:

$$\dot{w}_t = \Phi(u_t) \qquad \Phi(u^*) = 0 \qquad \Phi' < 0 \qquad (10)$$

where $w_t = LogW_t$ and u_t is the rate of unemployment. The unemployment rate u^* is called, depending on authors, natural rate of unemployment or noninflationary rate of unemployment. This relation (figure 2.5) is nowadays generally known as the Phillips curve. We may note that stable wages occur for a positive u^*, and not for $u = 0$. Implicit in this is that there are

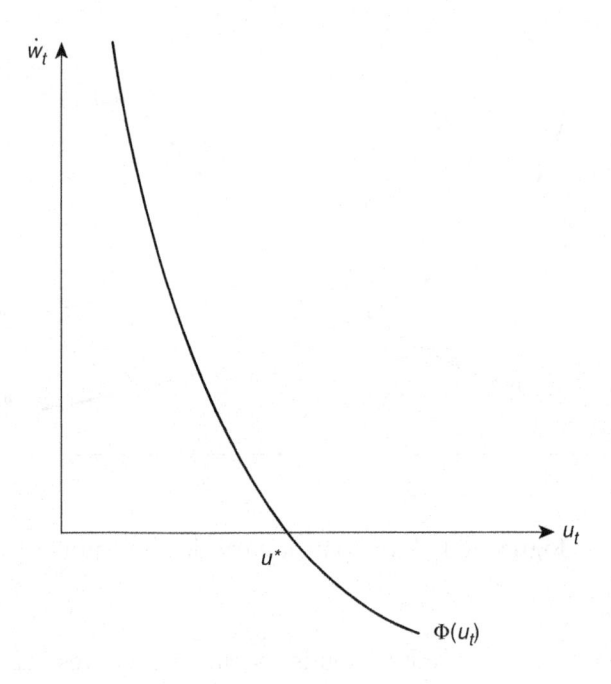

Figure 2.5 The Phillips curve

frictions in the labor market. We encounter such a frictional labor market in chapter 16.

A number of authors, starting with Samuelson and Solow (1960), investigated whether this Phillips curve could be used for policy purposes. If the government considers the rate u^* as satisfying, it will naturally choose the combination of stable wages and the unemployment rate u^*. However, this rate u^* has a priori no particular optimality property, and may actually be "too high."[2] The government may then want to "buy" a decrease in unemployment in exchange for a little inflation, so that it will choose a point like point A in figure 2.6.

The problem is that, as soon as such policies were implemented in a systematic manner,[3] the Phillips curve, which had remained stable for a century, became totally unstable, drifting toward the northeast in the $(u_t, \dot{w}_t)$ graph.

The explanation was given by Friedman (1968) and Phelps (1967, 1968): wage earners are not concerned with nominal wages but by the *real* value of

---

2. We shall see, for example, in chapter 5, that market power on the goods and labor markets may result in inefficiently low employment and output.

3. This occurred in the 1960s and early 1970s, when expansionary fiscal or monetary policies were implemented in many industrialized countries.

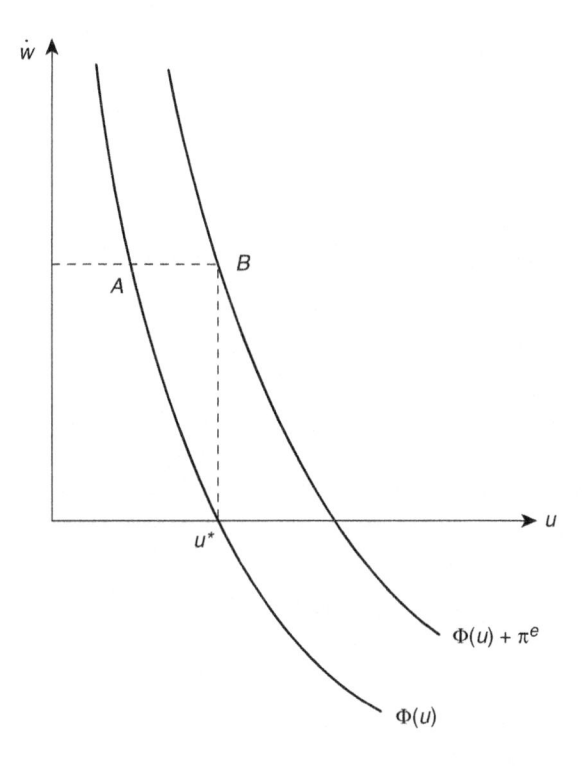

Figure 2.6 The Phillips curve and inflationary expectations

these wages. Consequently in an inflationary period, expected price increases will be integrated in the negotiations, so that the "augmented" Phillips curve will be written:

$$\dot{w}_t = \pi_t^e + \Phi(u_t) \qquad \Phi(u^*) = 0 \qquad (11)$$

where π_t^e is expected inflation. This is represented in figure 2.6. The Phillips curve will thus naturally move in time. The stability during the period covered by Phillips's article is simply due to the fact that this was a long period during which there was no sustained inflation.

2.4 Phillips Curve Dynamics

We now show how to combine the "static" AD-AS model with a dynamic evolution of wages given by an expectations-augmented Phillips curve.

The short-run equilibrium is described by two equations of AD-AS type, which we rewrite under a simplified linearized logarithmic form, taking only monetary policy into account:

$$y_t = m_t - p_t \qquad AD \qquad (12)$$

$$y_t = \xi\left(p_t - w_t\right) \qquad AS \qquad (13)$$

Wages evolve according to a Phillips curve, modified to take into account inflationary expectations:

$$\dot{w}_t = \pi_t^e + \phi\left(y_t - y^*\right) \qquad (14)$$

where π_t^e is expected inflation for the period and y^* the natural level of activity. We assume that government policy consists in choosing a money growth rate:

$$\dot{m}_t = \mu \qquad (15)$$

To close the model, there remains to indicate how inflationary expectations π_t^e are formed, and we assume that they evolve according to a scheme of "adaptive expectations" (Cagan, 1956):

$$\dot{\pi}_t^e = \vartheta\left(\dot{p}_t - \pi_t^e\right) \qquad (16)$$

These are called adaptive expectations because the expectations are modified so as to partly reduce the discrepancy between expected inflation and the actually observed inflation.

2.4.1 Stationary State

The stationary state of this economy is characterized by:

$$y_t = y^* \qquad \pi_t^e = \dot{p}_t = \dot{w}_t = \mu = \pi^* \qquad (17)$$

Let us define the intermediate variable:

$$\varkappa_t = m_t - w_t \qquad (18)$$

From (12) and (13) we can compute the stationary state value $\varkappa^*$:

$$\varkappa^* = \frac{(1+\xi)\, y^*}{\xi} \qquad (19)$$

2.4.2 Dynamics

To characterize dynamics around the stationary state, let us first solve the two AD-AS equations (12) and (13):

$$p_t = \frac{m_t + \xi w_t}{1+\xi} = m_t - \frac{\xi \varkappa_t}{1+\xi} \qquad (20)$$

$$y_t = \frac{\xi(m_t - w_t)}{1+\xi} = \frac{\xi \varkappa_t}{1+\xi} \qquad (21)$$

We transform the system of equations into a two-dimensional system in $(\varkappa_t, \pi_t^e)$.

$$\dot{\varkappa}_t = \dot{m}_t - \dot{w}_t = -(\pi_t^e - \pi^*) - \frac{\phi\xi}{1+\xi}(\varkappa_t - \varkappa^*) \qquad (22)$$

$$\dot{\pi}_t^e = \vartheta(\dot{p}_t - \pi_t^e) = -\frac{\vartheta}{1+\xi}(\pi_t^e - \pi^*) + \frac{\vartheta\phi\xi^2}{(1+\xi)^2}(\varkappa_t - \varkappa^*) \qquad (23)$$

or in matrix form:

$$\begin{bmatrix} \dot{\pi}_t^e \\ \dot{\varkappa}_t \end{bmatrix} = \begin{bmatrix} -\vartheta/(1+\xi) & \vartheta\phi\xi^2/(1+\xi)^2 \\ -1 & -\xi\phi/(1+\xi) \end{bmatrix} \begin{bmatrix} \pi_t^e - \pi^* \\ \varkappa_t - \varkappa^* \end{bmatrix} \qquad (24)$$

The characteristic polynomial giving the roots is thus:

$$\psi(\lambda) = \lambda^2 + \frac{\vartheta + \xi\phi}{1+\xi}\lambda + \frac{\vartheta\phi\xi}{1+\xi} = 0 \qquad (25)$$

We see that the real part of the roots is always negative. The system will thus converge toward the equilibrium. The type of convergence (cyclical or not) is determined by whether the roots are real or complex.

We can, for example, see what happens if the government wants to engineer a disinflation. Assume that the initial situation is a growth rate of money, and a rate of inflation, equal to μ_0. Assume that the government wants to reduce permanently inflation by reducing the growth rate of money from μ_0 to $\mu_1 < \mu_0$. The dynamic path of unemployment and inflation is pictured in figure 2.7. As we see, this disinflation ends up being successful, but it is paid by a long period with higher than usual unemployment. In the world of this Phillips curve, disinflations are costly. We return to this problem, notably in chapter 13.

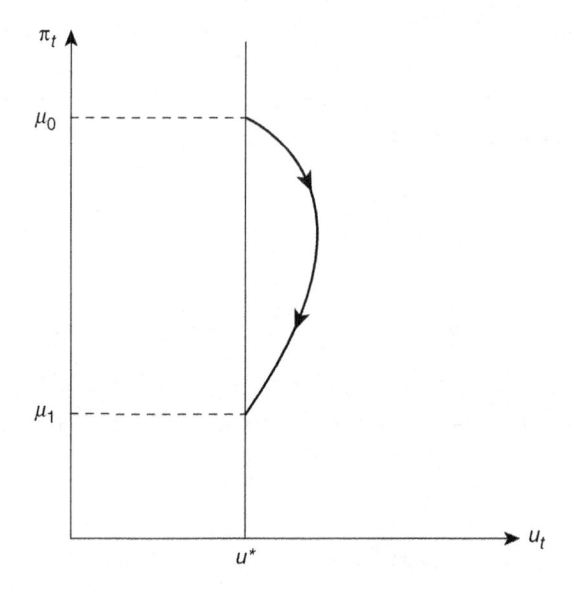

Figure 2.7 A disinflation

2.5 Expectations and Policy Effectiveness

We saw in section 2.2 that, in the world of AD-AS or IS-LM models, policy is particularly simple. Notably demand policies seem particularly powerful to fight unemployment. In the early 1970s, a number of articles challenged this view, and questioned notably the capacities of activist demand policies to stabilize employment and output (Lucas, 1972, 1976; Sargent and Wallace, 1975, 1976).

The models around which the debate centered pictured the economy as subject to stochastic shocks, which could potentially throw the economy off balance. We study the issue of policy effectiveness in simplified AD-AS models where stochastic shocks have been added. Because such shocks are easier to handle in discrete time, we correlatively move from continuous to discrete time.

2.5.1 The Model

We consider the following log-linear model:

$$y_t = \xi \left(p_t - w_t \right) \tag{26}$$

$$y_t = m_t - p_t + \varepsilon_t \tag{27}$$

$$w_t = p_t^e + \omega \tag{28}$$

Equation (26) represents the supply of firms (it can be derived rigorously from a Cobb-Douglas production function). Equation (27) is a log-linearized version of the aggregate demand curve AD, which is subject to a random shock ε_t. Equation (28) represents wage formation: wages are fixed at the beginning of period t on the basis of price expectations p_t^e. The parameter ω is somehow a "target real wage."

The value of the random variable ε_t is revealed *after* w_t and m_t have been decided. A central variable will turn out to be the price expectation p_t^e. We assume that it is formed on the basis of information from periods *anterior* to period t.

2.5.2 The Natural Rate of Activity and Government Policy

Combining equations (26) and (28), we can rewrite the value of y_t under the form:

$$y_t = y^* + \xi \left(p_t - p_t^e \right) \tag{29}$$

with:

$$y^* = -\omega \xi \tag{30}$$

The output level y^* is the "natural rate of activity," that is, that which will occur if agents do not make expectational mistakes. Note that this natural rate may be too low from a social point of view, for example, if workers have too much bargaining power, and as a consequence the target real wage ω is "too high." The government may thus be tempted to have an activist economic policy aimed at raising the activity level above the natural rate y^*.

In what follows we assume that the government tries to stabilize the activity level around a value $\bar{y} > y^*$. The government tries to minimize:

$$E \left(y_t - \bar{y} \right)^2 \tag{31}$$

It will use as a policy tool the quantity of money m_t.

2.5.3 Output and Price Dynamics

Let us eliminate the price and wage level between equations (26), (27), and (28). We obtain:

$$(1 + \xi) y_t = y^* + \xi \left(m_t - p_t^e \right) + \xi \varepsilon_t \tag{32}$$

Because the objective is to stabilize y_t around $\bar{y}$, we would like the deterministic part of this expression to be equal to $\bar{y}$. This yields:

$$(1+\xi)\bar{y} = y^* + \xi\left(m_t - p_t^e\right) \tag{33}$$

One deduces the monetary policy:

$$m_t = p_t^e + \bar{y} + \frac{\bar{y} - y^*}{\xi} \tag{34}$$

Combining (27), (29), and (34), we find the values of output and price:

$$y_t = \bar{y} + \frac{\xi \varepsilon_t}{1+\xi} \tag{35}$$

$$p_t - p_t^e = \frac{\bar{y} - y^*}{\xi} + \frac{\varepsilon_t}{1+\xi} \tag{36}$$

We first see that, except for a white noise, y_t is stabilized around $\bar{y}$. As for price dynamics, equation (36) tells us that it will depend on the particular expectations scheme. We now study these dynamics under various expectations formulas.

2.5.4 Static Price Expectations

Assume to start with that expectations are static, that is, that agents expect the same price to prevail as in the previous period:

$$p_t^e = p_{t-1} \tag{37}$$

Then equation (36) becomes:

$$\pi_t = p_t - p_{t-1} = \frac{\bar{y} - y^*}{\xi} + \frac{\varepsilon_t}{1+\xi} \tag{38}$$

We see that the reduction in unemployment is paid by positive average inflation, which is higher, the higher the target level of activity $\bar{y}$ is. There is thus an inflation-unemployment trade-off, which is more favorable when ξ is high.

Of course it is hard to believe that faced with a positive average inflation (equation 38) agents will continue to anticipate stable prices; we now assume that agents adapt their expectations schemes to this inflationary situation.

Output, Inflation, and Stabilization

2.5.5 Static Inflation Expectations

We now assume that the agents anticipate that inflation, not absolute prices, will remain the same, that is:

$$\pi_t^e = \pi_{t-1} \tag{39}$$

or:

$$p_t^e = p_{t-1} + \pi_{t-1} \tag{40}$$

where $\pi_{t-1} = p_{t-1} - p_{t-2}$ is the inflation rate precedingly observed. Equation (36) then becomes:

$$p_t = p_{t-1} + \pi_{t-1} + \frac{\bar{y} - y^*}{\xi} + \frac{\varepsilon_t}{1+\xi} \tag{41}$$

or in terms of inflation:

$$\pi_t = \pi_{t-1} + \frac{\bar{y} - y^*}{\xi} + \frac{\varepsilon_t}{1+\xi} \tag{42}$$

We now see that to reach the activity level $\bar{y}$, one needs not a permanent inflation anymore but a permanent *increase* in the inflation rate!

2.5.6 Perfect Foresight

In both preceding cases, agents make systematic expectational mistakes. Of course one may wonder what would happen if agents did not make such mistakes. This is called "rational expectations," and the next chapter is devoted to that issue. To get an advance flavor of it, we study a simplified version of our model with no uncertainty, that is, $\varepsilon_t = 0$. In that case, the hypothesis of no expectational mistake boils down to perfect foresight:

$$p_t^e = p_t \tag{43}$$

To solve the problem, let us rewrite the two equations (27) and (29) with $\varepsilon_t = 0$:

$$y_t = m_t - p_t \tag{44}$$

$$y_t = y^* + \xi(p_t - p_t^e) \tag{45}$$

If $p_t^e = p_t$, one immediately deduces from (44) and (45):

$$y_t = y^* \tag{46}$$

$$p_t = m_t - y^* \tag{47}$$

So we see that (1) one will never be able to do better on average than the natural level of activity y^*; (2) monetary policies only influence prices, not output.

This is strikingly at variance with the results of sections 2.5.4 and 2.5.5. The next chapter further investigates this issue in a model with stochastic shocks.

Appendix 2.1: The Baumol-Tobin Demand for Money

We present here a very simple formalization, due to Baumol (1952) and Tobin (1956), which yields a demand for money of the form (7).

We assume that an agent has an income Y, which he wants to spend during a period of length T. He can keep his wealth either as money or as interest-bearing asset in the bank (which we call "bonds" for short). This asset yields a nominal interest rate i over the period T. Money is the only medium of exchange, so he cannot purchase directly goods with bonds, and therefore every once in a while he has to transform bonds into money to make his purchases.

The agent will organize as follows. Initially he has all his wealth Y in the bank. To have cash when needed for his transactions, he makes n trips to the bank. Each trip costs an amount c. Each time he withdraws Y/n units of money, which he spends regularly during the time interval T/n, that is, until his next trip to the bank. As a result, his money and bond holdings look as in figure 2.8, which is drawn for $n = 4$.

The agent chooses the number of trips n so as to minimize total costs. These total costs consist of the cost of the n trips to the bank, that is, nc, and the cost of interest forgone because he holds money. If M is the average holding of money, this cost is equal to iM. So the agent minimizes total cost:

$$iM + nc \tag{48}$$

Now it is easy to see (figure 2.8) that the average quantity of money is:

$$M = \frac{Y}{2n} \tag{49}$$

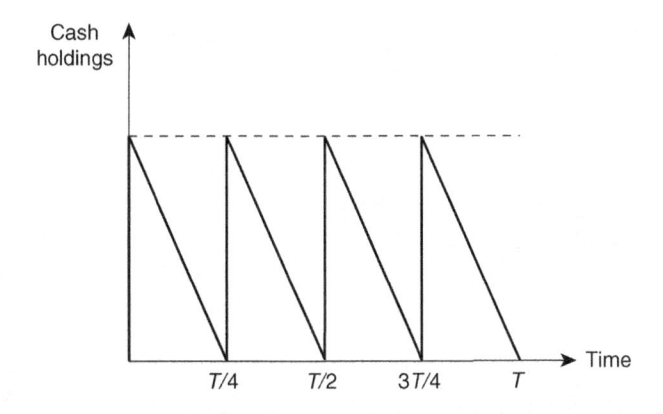

Figure 2.8 Trips to the bank and cash holdings

so that the agent chooses n so as to minimize:

$$\frac{iY}{2n} + nc \tag{50}$$

Optimizing with respect to n, and omitting the fact that n should be an integer, we find the optimal number of trips:

$$n^* = \sqrt{\frac{iY}{2c}} \tag{51}$$

Inserting this into formula (49) we find the optimum quantity of money:

$$M = \frac{1}{2}\sqrt{\frac{cY}{2i}} \tag{52}$$

Appendix 2.2: Indexation

We consider an economy subject to both technology and demand shocks, and we want to study to what extent wage indexation can help stabilizing the economy (Fischer 1977b; Gray, 1976, 1978).

The Model

We assume that the production function is isoelastic:

$$Y_t = A_t L_t^{1-\alpha} \tag{53}$$

where A_t is a technology shock. Going to logarithms:

$$y_t = a_t + (1 - \alpha) \ell_t \tag{54}$$

The goods market clears, so the real wage is equal to the marginal productivity of labor:

$$w_t - p_t = a_t - \alpha \ell_t + Log(1 - \alpha) \tag{55}$$

We also have a demand function:

$$y_t = m_t - p_t + \varepsilon_t \tag{56}$$

where ε_t is a demand shock. Finally we have an equation that shows how wages are indexed:

$$w_t - w_0 = \gamma (p_t - p_0) \qquad 0 \leq \gamma \leq 1 \tag{57}$$

where γ is the coefficient of indexation, and w_0 and p_0 are "benchmark" wage and price levels. We can solve for the level of employment, omitting irrelevant constants:

$$\ell_t = \frac{\gamma a_t + (1 - \gamma) \varepsilon_t}{1 - \gamma + \alpha \gamma} \tag{58}$$

Optimal Indexation

We want to minimize the variance of ℓ_t, which we compute from (58) as:

$$\text{Var}(\ell_t) = \frac{\gamma^2 \sigma_a^2 + (1 - \gamma)^2 \sigma_\varepsilon^2}{(1 - \gamma + \alpha \gamma)^2} \tag{59}$$

This is minimal for:

$$\gamma = \gamma^* = \frac{\alpha \sigma_\varepsilon^2}{\sigma_a^2 + \alpha \sigma_\varepsilon^2} \tag{60}$$

We see that the larger the variance of the monetary shock as compared to that of the real shock, the higher the coefficient of indexation.

Appendix 2.3: Imperfect Information and the Choice of Economic Instruments

In this chapter, we followed the IS-LM and AD-AS traditions, taking the quantity of money as the instrument of monetary policy. But interest rates can be chosen as well as the basic instrument of monetary policy. As it turns out, whether the government uses one or the other is not really important if the government has full information about shocks when making policy decisions, as we shall see shortly. In a very insightful article Poole (1970) showed that if information is imperfect, it actually makes a difference to set monetary policy in terms of m_t or i_t, and he indicated the conditions that should lead the government to choose one or the other. We describe his results in a simple static IS-LM model.

A Log-linearized Version

The basic model is a log-linearized version of the IS-LM model.[4] It consists of two equations:

$$y_t = -bi_t + \varepsilon_t \qquad IS \qquad (61)$$

$$m_t - p_t - y_t = -ci_t - v_t \qquad LM \qquad (62)$$

where ε_t and v_t are, respectively, a real demand shock and a money velocity shock. Because we concentrate on monetary policy, we have omitted government spending and taxes from these equations.

Policy Under Full Information

We first study as a benchmark the case where the government has full information about the two shocks ε_t and v_t. It aims at minimizing the variance of y_t. Now monetary policy can be implemented in at least two ways: setting the quantity of money m_t as a function of all shocks, or setting the nominal interest rate i_t as a function of all shocks. As it turns out, the two following equivalent policies allow to fully stabilize y_t at 0 at all times.

$$i_t = \frac{\varepsilon_t}{b} \qquad (63)$$

$$m_t - p_t = -\frac{c}{b}\varepsilon_t - v_t \qquad (64)$$

---

4. A version with flexible prices in an AD-AS framework is in problem 2.1. A full dynamic general equilibrium version is in Collard and Dellas (2005).

Optimal Policy Under Imperfect Information

Of course if the government knew all the shocks immediately, policy would be an easy task. In reality, government does not observe the underlying shocks, only some of the resulting variables, and not all of them. To make things concrete, we assume that the government can observe neither the shocks nor output nor prices. It can, however, observe immediately the two monetary policy variables m_t and i_t.[5]

In fact, there are more general monetary policies, as it is easy to see that the two policies of setting money or the interest rate are both particular cases of policies of the form:

$$m_t = \chi i_t, \tag{65}$$

A policy of setting the quantity of money corresponds to $\chi = 0$, a policy of setting the interest rate to $\chi = \infty$.

The short-run equilibrium is solution of the system of equations (61), (62), and (65). Solving for the level of output we find:

$$y_t = \frac{(\chi + c)\varepsilon_t + bv_t}{\chi + c + b} \tag{66}$$

We can immediately compute the variance of y_t as a function of the parameter χ:

$$\operatorname{Var}(y_t) = \frac{b^2 \sigma_v^2 + (\chi + c)^2 \sigma_\varepsilon^2}{(\chi + c + b)^2} \tag{67}$$

With the help of this formula, we can first compare the two policies of interest and money setting. Let us start with money setting. Making $\chi = 0$ in formula (67) we find the corresponding variance:

$$\mathcal{V}_m = \frac{b^2 \sigma_v^2 + c^2 \sigma_\varepsilon^2}{(c + b)^2} \tag{68}$$

Symmetrically for interest rate setting, let us make $\chi = \infty$ in formula (67). We obtain the corresponding variance:

$$\mathcal{V}_i = \sigma_\varepsilon^2 \tag{69}$$

---

5. Note that although there are two monetary variables, there is only one "degree of freedom," since these two variables are linked by the equilibrium condition on the bonds market.

Now setting the quantity of money will be better than setting the interest rate if $\mathcal{V}_m < \mathcal{V}_i$, that is, if:

$$b\sigma_v^2 < (2c+b)\sigma_\varepsilon^2 \qquad (70)$$

We see that which of the two policies is best will depend fundamentally on the relative size of the two shocks.

Now of course, in general, neither the policy of interest setting nor the policy of setting the quantity of money will be the best policy among all policies defined by (65). To find this best policy, we minimize the variance in (67) with respect to χ. This yields the optimal value χ^*:

$$\chi^* = \frac{b\sigma_v^2}{\sigma_\varepsilon^2} - c \qquad (71)$$

As should be expected, this optimal value also depends on the ratio between the variances of shocks.

Problems

Problem 2.1: Price Flexibility, Indexation, and the Money Multiplier

Consider the following AD-AS model in logarithms (fiscal variables are omitted for simplicity):

$$y_t = m_t - p_t$$

$$y_t = \xi(p_t - w_t)$$

1. Compute and compare the multipliers $\partial y_t / \partial m_t$ for fixed and flexible prices.
2. Assume now that wages are indexed on prices according to the formula:

$$w_t - w_0 = \gamma(p_t - p_0) \qquad 0 \le \gamma \le 1$$

where w_0 and p_0 are benchmark wage and price. Compute the multiplier $\partial y_t / \partial m_t$ and compare to the two previous ones.

Problem 2.2: International Trade and the Multiplier

We want to show how trade with foreign economies modifies the multipliers.

1. We first consider as a benchmark a closed economy with rigid wages and flexible prices. The equilibrium is a simplified version of the model of section 2.2.3 and is represented by the following AD-AS equations:

$$Y = C(Y, P) + G \qquad 0 < C_Y < 1 \qquad C_P < 0$$
$$Y = S(P) \qquad\qquad S_P > 0$$

   Compute the multiplier $\partial Y / \partial G$.

2. We now assume there are two countries indexed 1 and 2 (this model is based on Branson and Rotemberg, 1980). They produce and consume the same good, with a common price P. The consumption functions are $C_1(Y_1, P)$ and $C_2(Y_2, P)$, the supply functions $S_1(P)$ and $S_2(P)$. Give the equations describing the international equilibrium, and compute the multiplier $\partial Y_1 / \partial G_1$. Compare with the closed economy multiplier.

Problem 2.3: The Poole Model with Endogenous Prices

We extend the model that we saw in appendix 2.3 by endogenizing prices. So we have the same IS-LM equations:

$$y_t = -b i_t + \varepsilon_t \qquad\qquad IS$$
$$m_t - p_t - y_t = -c i_t - v_t \qquad LM$$

We add an AS curve:

$$y_t = \xi (p_t - w_t) \qquad\qquad AS$$

As in appendix 2.3, we assume that the government aims to stabilize output, that is, to minimize the variance of y_t.

1. Compute the optimal monetary policy under full information.
2. Compute the optimal monetary policy under the form $m_t = \chi i_t$ assuming that government knows neither the shocks nor output nor prices.

3

Rational Expectations

3.1 Introduction

We saw in the previous chapter that in dynamic models many important results strongly depend on the agents' expectations schemes. A problem with the expectations schemes that we studied in chapter 2 is that they are exogenous, and thus can be completely at variance with the actual functioning of the model studied. We saw a case where expectation of stable prices gave rise to steady inflation, and another case where expectation of stable inflation created accelerating inflation.

To solve this discrepancy between expectations schemes and the actual dynamics of the economy, John Muth (1961) proposed in a seminal article the notion of *rational expectations*. This was followed by many important contributions, notably Lucas (1972, 1973, 1976) and Sargent and Wallace (1973, 1975).[1]

The basic idea is that rational expectations are consistent with the actual dynamics of the model. If the model is deterministic, rational expectations will coincide with perfect foresight. If the model is stochastic, the generalization gives rise to many novel cases. Notably, as we shall see, as compared with exogenous expectations schemes, this hypothesis changes many results concerning both the dynamics of the economy and the impact of economic policies.

---

1. Collections of important articles on the subject can be found in Lucas and Sargent (1981) and Miller (1994).

We begin in section 3.2 by giving definitions of rational expectations. Section 3.3 then describes the original Muth (1961) model, which, although more microeconomic than macroeconomic, shows how a number of results on the propagation of shocks and stability are turned upside down. Section 3.4 pursues the discussion of chapter 2 on the effectiveness of government policy and shows that the striking result obtained under the assumption of perfect foresight (chapter 2, section 2.5.6) carries through in a stochastic environment. Section 3.5 studies a very famous model of inflation, the Cagan (1956) model. The original model has adaptive expectations. We study that version first, and then a rational expectations version due to Sargent and Wallace (1973). The stability conditions turn out to be strikingly different.

Section 3.6 studies the set of solutions to a simple dynamic equation with rational expectations. Although the basic equation is extremely simple, we find a very rich set of different solutions. In section 3.7 we study the question of whether learning converges toward rational expectations, a legitimate problem because, after all, economic agents are not born with rational expectations, and they must somehow learn them at some point.

3.2 Rational Expectations: A Simple Definition

In its most demanding definition, we say that an agent has rational expectations if he knows the probability distribution of every variable in the future, conditional of course on his current information. For example, if he throws a die, he knows that each of the six numbers will come out with probability 1/6.

In many applications the models are linear, and what matters is the expectation of the variable, not its entire probability distribution. The traditional definition in that case is that expectations are rational if the expectation X_t^e of a variable X_t is equal to the expectation of that variable, based on the "true" model, and conditional on the information held by the agent at the time he makes his prevision. For example, if the prevision is made in period $t-1$ for period t:

$$X_t^e = E_{t-1}(X_t) = E(X_t \mid \mathcal{I}_{t-1}) \qquad (1)$$

where E is the expectation operator and $\mathcal{I}_{t-1}$ is the information available to the forecaster up to period $t-1$.

3.3 The Muth Model

We now present the original model of Muth (1961). Although not a macroeconomic one, it will already show us a number of striking properties.

3.3.1 The Model

Let us consider a market with random demand:

$$D_t = a - bp_t + \varepsilon_t \tag{2}$$

Production takes time, and thus supply depends on the price expected by producers at the time when they launch their production decisions, denoted as p_t^e:

$$S_t = cp_t^e \tag{3}$$

Market equilibrium thus yields:

$$cp_t^e = a - bp_t + \varepsilon_t \tag{4}$$

The dynamics will depend, as we saw in the previous chapter, on the way expectations are formed. We assume in all cases that, because they form their expectations before the market is held, suppliers do not yet know ε_t, so p_t^e must be based on information up to period $t-1$. We study two expectations schemes satisfying this condition.

3.3.2 Naive Expectations and Dynamics

Let us first consider a naive expectations scheme: when they take their production decisions, producers expect for period t the price they observed in $t-1$:

$$p_t^e = p_{t-1} \tag{5}$$

Combining (4) and (5), we obtain the equilibrium price in period t:

$$p_t = \frac{a - cp_{t-1} + \varepsilon_t}{b} \tag{6}$$

We see that this creates a "cobweb" dynamics, which may even be explosive if $c > b$ (figure 3.1).

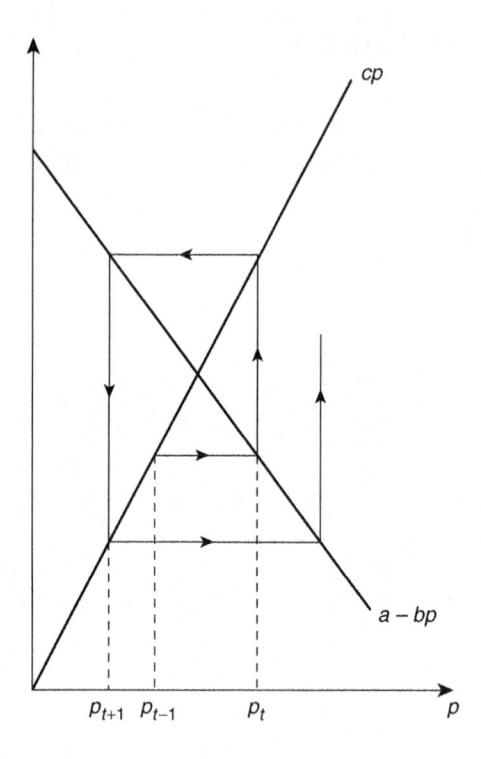

Figure 3.1 Unstable cobweb dynamics

Even if dynamics is not explosive $(c < b)$, we see, iterating formula (6), that the price in period t will depend on all past shocks:

$$p_t = \frac{a}{b+c} + \frac{1}{b}\sum_{i=0}^{\infty}\left(-\frac{c}{b}\right)^i \varepsilon_{t-i} \qquad (7)$$

3.3.3 Rational Expectations

We now assume that the expected price p_t^e is equal to the rational expectation of p_t, conditional on period t information:

$$p_t^e = E_{t-1}(p_t) \qquad (8)$$

To find the value of the rational price expectation $p_t^e = E_{t-1}(p_t)$, we start from the equality between demand and supply (equation 4):

$$cp_t^e = a - bp_t + \varepsilon_t \qquad (9)$$

We take the mathematical expectation of both sides conditional on the information available at time $t-1$:

$$cp_t^e = a - bp_t^e \tag{10}$$

from which we deduce:

$$p_t^e = \frac{a}{b+c} \tag{11}$$

and thus, combining (9) and (11):

$$p_t = \frac{a}{b+c} + \frac{\varepsilon_t}{b} \tag{12}$$

Compared with the dynamics under naive expectations, we can see at least two striking differences: (1) the dynamics is never explosive, even if $c > b$, and (2) the price today depends only on the shock today, instead of the whole sequence of past shocks, as in equation (7).

3.4 Rational Expectations and Policy Effectiveness

We saw in the preceding chapter that in a deterministic version of a simple policy model, the assumption of perfect foresight made monetary policy totally ineffective, whereas it was effective with exogenous expectations schemes. We shall reintroduce stochastic shocks and study the model under the hypothesis of rational expectations. We will see that similar striking results obtain.[2]

Let us recall the two basic equations (equations 27 and 29 in chapter 2):

$$y_t = m_t - p_t + \varepsilon_t \tag{13}$$

$$y_t = y^* + \xi \left(p_t - p_t^e \right) \tag{14}$$

We continue to assume that the government, using m_t as its policy variable, tries to stabilize the activity level around a value $\bar{y} > y^*$, that is, the government tries to minimize:

$$E \left(y_t - \bar{y} \right)^2 \tag{15}$$

---

2. Central references for this debate are Lucas (1972, 1976), Sargent and Wallace (1975, 1976).

We now assume that agents form their expectations "rationally" on the basis of period $t-1$ information, that is:

$$p_t^e = E_{t-1}(p_t) \tag{16}$$

To solve the problem, we first need to compute the value of p_t^e. For that, let us take the expectation of (13) and (14) as of period $t-1$:[3]

$$E_{t-1}(y_t) = E_{t-1}(m_t) - E_{t-1}(p_t) \tag{17}$$

$$E_{t-1}(y_t) = y^* + \xi\left[E_{t-1}(p_t) - E_{t-1}(p_t^e)\right] = y^* \tag{18}$$

Combining (17) and (18) we find the rational expectation of prices:

$$E_{t-1}(p_t) = E_{t-1}(m_t) - y^* \tag{19}$$

Combining this with (13) and (14), we finally obtain the value of production:

$$y_t = y^* + \frac{\xi}{1+\xi}\left[m_t - E_{t-1}(m_t)\right] + \frac{\xi\varepsilon_t}{1+\xi} \tag{20}$$

We thus see that (1) as in the deterministic model, one will never be able to do better on average than the natural level of activity y^*. (2) The best monetary policies, which minimize the variance of y_t, are "predictable" policies, that is, policies of the form:

$$m_t = E_{t-1}(m_t) \tag{21}$$

3.5 Expectations and Stability: The Cagan Model

We move to a famous macroeconomic model, the Cagan (1956) model, which was initially designed to see whether price dynamics could degenerate into hyperinflation.

We actually compare the dynamics of that model under two different expectations schemes, adaptive expectations (as in the original Cagan model) and rational expectations (the corresponding version was developed

---

3. Note that in equation (18) we use $E_{t-1}\left[E_{t-1}(p_t^e)\right] = E_{t-1}(p_t^e)$, which is a particular case of the "law of iterated expectations" (mathematical appendix A.8.3)

by Sargent and Wallace, 1973). As we shall see, the differences are even more startling than for the Muth model.

3.5.1 The Original Cagan Model

The Cagan model comprises first an equation of demand for money,[4] which is in logarithmic form:

$$m_t^d - p_t = -\alpha \pi_t^e \qquad (22)$$

where π_t^e is expected inflation. All markets are assumed to clear so that in particular money demand is equal to the quantity of money:[5]

$$m_t^d = m_t \qquad (23)$$

where π_t^e is expected inflation. Combine (22) and (23). We obtain:

$$m_t - p_t = -\alpha \pi_t^e \qquad (24)$$

To study the dynamics of the model, we have to specify how inflationary expectations and money evolve over time. As for expectations, Cagan uses the hypothesis of *adaptative expectations*:

$$\dot{\pi}_t^e = \frac{d\pi_t^e}{dt} = \vartheta \left(\pi_t - \pi_t^e \right) \qquad (25)$$

The idea is that if actual inflation is different from expectations, these expectations will be revised in the direction of actual inflation, hence the name adaptive expectations. The parameter ϑ represents the speed of expectations adaptation and plays a crucial role in the dynamics.

We also have to specify how money supply m_t changes in time. We make the simple assumption that money grows at a constant rate μ:

$$\dot{m}_t = \mu \qquad (26)$$

Differentiate (24):

$$\alpha \dot{\pi}_t^e = \pi_t - \mu \qquad (27)$$

---

4. A justification for such a money demand is in appendix 4.1.
5. Goldman (1972) extends the Cagan model and stability conditions to the case where, due to price sluggishness, the demand for money is not always equal to the supply, and equation (23) is not always satisfied.

Combining with (25) we find:

$$\pi_t = \frac{\mu - \alpha\vartheta\pi_t^e}{1 - \alpha\vartheta} \tag{28}$$

Inserting (28) into (27) we find the dynamics of expectations:

$$\dot{\pi}_t^e = \frac{\vartheta}{1 - \alpha\vartheta}(\mu - \pi_t^e) \tag{29}$$

Finally, combining (28) and (29), we obtain the dynamics of inflation:

$$\dot{\pi}_t = \frac{\vartheta}{1 - \alpha\vartheta}(\mu - \pi_t) \tag{30}$$

The steady-state value of π_t and π_t^e is μ. Inflation will converge toward μ if $\alpha\vartheta < 1$. If $\alpha\vartheta > 1$, inflation will diverge, and hyperinflation will set in. There is a self-reinforcing mechanism through which high inflationary expectations lead to low money demand and high demand for goods. These increase inflationary pressures, which themselves lead to higher inflationary expectations, and so on.

3.5.2 Rational Expectations

We move to the study of the rational expectations version of the Cagan model, which was pioneered by Sargent and Wallace (1973). We first study the deterministic case, which boils down to perfect foresight. We may note that the case of perfect foresight ($\pi_t^e = \pi_t$) corresponds to $\vartheta = \infty$ (equation 25), and thus to the "unstable case." We can actually see that directly, as equations (24) and (25) are now replaced by a single equation:

$$m_t - p_t = -\alpha\pi_t = -\alpha\frac{dp_t}{d_t} \tag{31}$$

Equation (31) can actually be rewritten:

$$\frac{d\left(e^{-t/\alpha}p_t\right)}{dt} = -\frac{1}{\alpha}e^{-t/\alpha}m_t \tag{32}$$

This can be integrated as:

$$e^{-t/\alpha}p_t - p_0 = -\frac{1}{\alpha}\int_0^t e^{-s/\alpha}m_s ds \tag{33}$$

which is rewritten as:

$$p_t = e^{t/\alpha}\left[p_0 - \frac{1}{\alpha}\int_0^t e^{-s/\alpha} m_s ds\right] \tag{34}$$

This formula shows that the price will explode at an exponential rate, unless the initial price p_0 is chosen so that the limit, when t goes to infinity, of the term into brackets in (34) is 0, that is, if:

$$p_0 = \frac{1}{\alpha}\int_0^\infty e^{-s/\alpha} m_s ds \tag{35}$$

We see in equation (35) that the price is fully determined by the future values of money supply. We may note that this is in total contradiction with the traditional Cagan model under adaptive expectations, where the current price is history-determined. Actually, in this model there is no reason the initial price should be history-determined. Sargent and Wallace (1973) turned the problem upside down and decided that the criterion of selection of the initial price would be precisely that the price does not explode at infinity. More precisely, we want:

$$\lim_{t\to\infty} e^{-t/\alpha} p_t = 0 \tag{36}$$

which yields (35). Now inserting (35) into (34) we obtain the value of the price for any time t:

$$p_t = \frac{1}{\alpha}\int_t^\infty e^{-(s-t)/\alpha} m_s ds \tag{37}$$

As an example, we apply this formula to a simple experiment: assume that the quantity of money has been stable at M_0 (and expected to be so) until time t_0. At time t_0 it is announced that at time $t_0 + \theta$ money will jump from M_0 to δM_0 with $\delta > 1$. It is easy to compute with formula (37) that:

$$p_t = \begin{cases} m_0 & t < t_0 \\ m_0 + e^{-(t_0+\theta-t)} Log\delta & t_0 < t < t_0 + \theta \\ m_0 + Log\delta & t_0 + \theta < t \end{cases} \tag{38}$$

This is pictured in figure 3.2, which shows that the price makes a discrete jump at the time of the announcement and then increases continuously toward its long-run value.

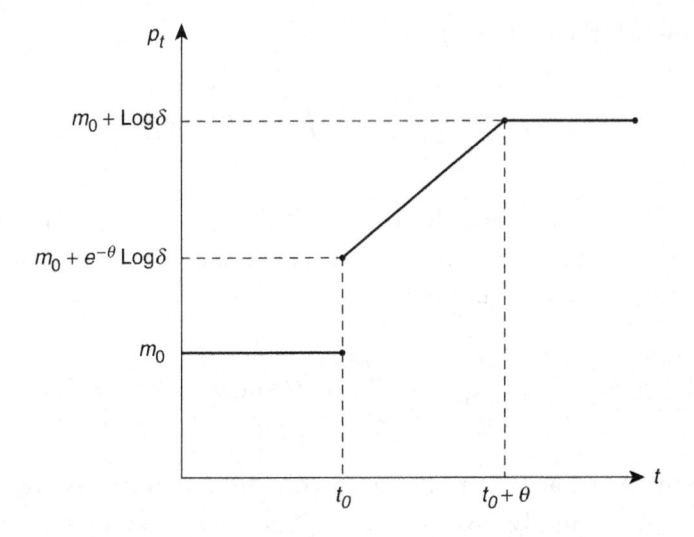

Figure 3.2 Discontinuous price dynamics

3.6 Solutions to a Stochastic Dynamic Equation

We now consider a discrete time, stochastic version of the Cagan model and study the set of its solutions. We shall see that although extremely simple, this model has a very rich set of potential dynamics.

3.6.1 The Model

The model consists essentially of a demand for money function, which is the discrete time translation of the money demand in equation (24):

$$m_t - p_t = -\alpha \pi_t^e = -\alpha \left(E_t p_{t+1} - p_t \right) \tag{39}$$

The expectation sign is due to the fact that we will now consider a stochastic money process m_t, and therefore future prices will in general be also stochastic. This equation can be rewritten:

$$p_t = a E_t p_{t+1} + (1-a) m_t \tag{40}$$

with:

$$a = \frac{\alpha}{1+\alpha} \tag{41}$$

Rational Expectations

3.6.2 The Fundamental Solution

One solution to this equation when $a < 1$ is particularly easy to obtain by successive forward iterations of equation (40). For example rewrite (40) for $t+1$, and insert the value into (40). We obtain:

$$p_t = (1-a)\, m_t + a\,(1-a)\, E_t m_{t+1} + a^2 E_t p_{t+2} \qquad (42)$$

If we repeat similar substitutions until period T we obtain:

$$p_t = (1-a) \sum_{j=0}^{T-1} a^j E_t m_{t+j} + a^T E_t p_{t+T} \qquad (43)$$

At this stage, we make the hypothesis that the last term goes to 0 as T goes to infinity:

$$\text{Lim}_{T \to \infty}\, a^T E_t p_{t+T} = 0 \qquad (44)$$

In that case, we see that the unique solution satisfying (44) is:

$$p_t^f = (1-a) \sum_{j=0}^{\infty} a^j E_t m_{t+j} \qquad (45)$$

This is called the *fundamental solution*, hence the superscript f. We note that this formula looks very much like the one we found in the deterministic continuous time case (formula 37).

3.6.3 Bubble Solutions

We now look for more general solutions to equation (40) when $a < 1$, which do not necessarily satisfy restriction (44). For that let us denote b_t the difference between the price and its fundamental value:

$$b_t = p_t - p_t^f \qquad (46)$$

The variable b_t is often called a *bubble* (hence the notation b_t) because, as we will see, it often has a tendency to grow (and sometimes explode). Combining (40), (45), and (46), we find that the dynamic equation governing b_t is:

$$b_t = a E_t b_{t+1} \qquad (47)$$

This equation has an infinity of solutions. First, it has a set of deterministic solutions:

$$b_t = \frac{b_0}{a^t} \qquad (48)$$

where the initial value b_0 is arbitrary. But it has also many stochastic solutions. For example if $\mathcal{M}_t$ is a martingale, that is, a stochastic process such that $E_t \mathcal{M}_{t+1} = \mathcal{M}_t$ (see mathematical appendix A.8.8), then:

$$b_t = \frac{\mathcal{M}_t}{a^t} \qquad (49)$$

is also a solution. These multiple solutions have a common feature: they are "explosive," in the sense that they grow like $1/a^t$ in expected value. Of course, if one does not accept such explosive solutions, then the only remaining solution is the fundamental solution. On the other hand, it is not always possible to find economic reasons to rule them out.[6]

3.6.4 Indeterminacies and Sunspots

We move to the case $a > 1$, and see that the problem of the multiplicity of solutions becomes even more acute. To find the solutions in a simple manner, let us proceed in two steps. In the first step we look for a particular solution where prices would be perfectly predictable from one period to the next, that is:

$$p_{t+1} = E_t p_{t+1} \qquad (50)$$

In such a case, equation (40) becomes:

$$p_{t+1} = \frac{p_t}{a} - (1-a)\frac{m_t}{a} \qquad (51)$$

Operating repeated backward substitutions we obtain:

$$p_t = \frac{p_{t-T}}{a^T} - (1-a)\sum_{j=1}^{T} \frac{m_{t-j}}{a^j} \qquad (52)$$

---

6. The literature on bubbles has become quite large, notably as several different types of bubbles have been identified and studied. The interested reader can start with the useful surveys by Brunnermeier (2008), Camerer (1989), and Iraola and Santos (2008).

We assume that:

$$\text{Lim}_{T\to\infty} \frac{p_{t-T}}{a^T} = 0 \tag{53}$$

Letting T go to infinity in formula (52), we obtain the "backward solution" p_t^b (Blanchard, 1979):

$$p_t^b = -(1-a)\sum_{j=1}^{\infty} \frac{m_{t-j}}{a^j} \tag{54}$$

Note that if m_t is stationary, this will always converge because $|a| > 1$. In a second step, let us call δ_t the discrepancy between the price and the backward solution:

$$\delta_t = p_t - p_t^b \tag{55}$$

Combining (40), (54), and (55) we obtain:

$$\delta_t = aE_t\delta_{t+1} \tag{56}$$

As in the previous section, this equation has an infinity of solutions, deterministic or stochastic, which grow like $1/a^t$ in expected value. But because $a > 1$, these solutions remain bounded, and there is no economic ground to eliminate them. We thus have a genuine problem of multiplicity.

The multiple solutions of the type that we just described are often associated with the idea of "sunspots." A sunspot is a stochastic variable extraneous to the system, but which nevertheless has real effects on the economy because agents coordinate their actions on them.

The foregoing model is based on an "ad hoc" dynamic equation, and a number of authors have investigated whether sunspot equilibria could arise in rigorously specified models. The answer is yes, and we return to this issue in chapter 10.

3.7 Learning and Rational Expectations

Of course, economic agents are not born with rational expectations, and one may wonder whether simple learning processes may actually lead to rational expectations. We describe a simple model due to Evans (1985).[7]

---

7. The issue of learning and rational expectations is surveyed in Evans and Honkapohja (1999, 2001, 2008).

3.7.1 The Model and Rational Expectations Solution

Let us consider the following simple model:

$$x_t = aE_{t-1}x_{t+1} + \varepsilon_t \qquad 0 < a < 1 \tag{57}$$

where ε_t is a white noise. We consider a family of solutions of the form:

$$x_t = \lambda x_{t-1} + \gamma \varepsilon_{t-1} + \delta \varepsilon_t \tag{58}$$

Before introducing learning, we first derive the rational expectations solutions of the form (58). Let us forward equation (58) one period:

$$x_{t+1} = \lambda x_t + \gamma \varepsilon_t + \delta \varepsilon_{t+1} \tag{59}$$

and take the expectation as of $t-1$:

$$E_{t-1}x_{t+1} = \lambda E_{t-1}x_t = \lambda \left(\lambda x_{t-1} + \gamma \varepsilon_{t-1} \right) \tag{60}$$

Let us insert this into (57):

$$x_t = a\lambda \left(\lambda x_{t-1} + \gamma \varepsilon_{t-1} \right) + \varepsilon_t \tag{61}$$

Now let us replace on the left-hand side x_t by its expression (58):

$$\lambda x_{t-1} + \gamma \varepsilon_{t-1} + \delta \varepsilon_t = a\lambda \left(\lambda x_{t-1} + \gamma \varepsilon_{t-1} \right) + \varepsilon_t \tag{62}$$

Identifying to 0 the terms in x_{t-1}, ε_{t-1}, and ε_t, we obtain, respectively:

$$\lambda = a\lambda^2 \tag{63}$$

$$\gamma = a\lambda\gamma \tag{64}$$

$$\delta = 1 \tag{65}$$

We see that there are two sets of solutions. The first is the "fundamental" solution:

$$\lambda = 0 \qquad \gamma = 0 \qquad \delta = 1 \tag{66}$$

There is another set of "nonfundamental" solutions given by:

$$\lambda = \frac{1}{a} \qquad \gamma \text{ free} \qquad \delta = 1 \tag{67}$$

Since $0 < a < 1$ these look similar to the bubble solutions seen in section 3.6.3 above

We will now have to answer two questions on learning: (1) does learning converge? (2) If it does, toward which type of solutions?

3.7.2 Learning and Expectational Stability

Assume now that the agents do not know the model but try to learn about it. The learning process occurs in successive steps indexed by n. At each step the agent has a model of the economy, with a forecasting rule of the same type as (58), but with coefficients indexed by n:

$$x_t = \lambda_n x_{t-1} + \gamma_n \varepsilon_{t-1} + \delta_n \varepsilon_t \tag{68}$$

Let us now find the dynamics that will be associated to (68). First, forward (68) one period:

$$x_{t+1} = \lambda_n x_t + \gamma_n \varepsilon_t + \delta_n \varepsilon_{t+1} \tag{69}$$

and take the expectation at time $t-1$:

$$E_{t-1} x_{t+1} = \lambda_n E_{t-1} x_t = \lambda_n \left(\lambda_n x_{t-1} + \gamma_n \varepsilon_{t-1} \right) \tag{70}$$

Insert (70) into (57):

$$x_t = a\lambda_n \left(\lambda_n x_{t-1} + \gamma_n \varepsilon_{t-1} \right) + \varepsilon_t \tag{71}$$

If agents have the model (68) in mind at stage n, the actual dynamics will be (71). It is now assumed that agents update their forecasting rule so that their updated rule for stage $n+1$:

$$x_t = \lambda_{n+1} x_{t-1} + \gamma_{n+1} \varepsilon_{t-1} + \delta_{n+1} \varepsilon_t \tag{72}$$

is the same as (71). Identifying the terms in (71) and (72) one by one we find:

$$\lambda_{n+1} = a\lambda_n^2 \tag{73}$$

$$\gamma_{n+1} = a\lambda_n \gamma_n \tag{74}$$

$$\delta_{n+1} = 1 \tag{75}$$

We first note that the solutions of the system of equations (63) to (65) are fixed points of the dynamic process (73) to (75), so the learning process is consistent with the "true" solutions.

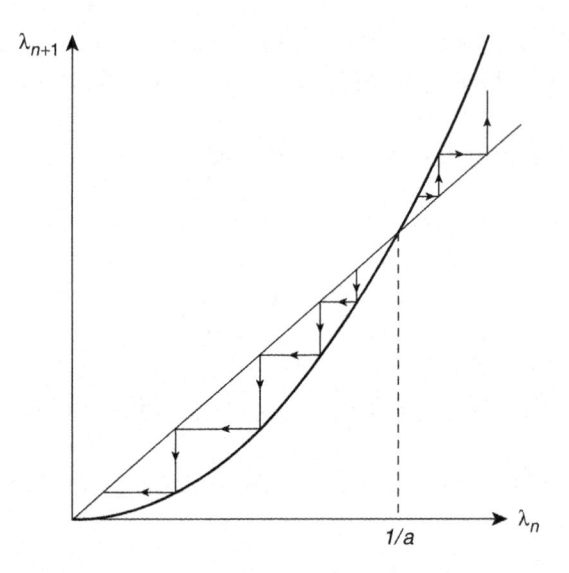

Figure 3.3 Learning dynamics

If we consider the dynamics of the system (73), (74), and (75), we see that the nonfundamental solutions with $\lambda = 1/a$ are always unstable. The "fundamental" solution with $\lambda = 0$ is stable, provided one starts with a value $\lambda_0 < 1/a$ (figure 3.3). Note that the lower a, the more chances are that one will converge toward the fundamental solution.

Appendix 3.1: Signal Extraction and Adaptive Expectations

Up to now, it might appear that rational expectations and, say, adaptive expectations, are alternative and antagonistic expectations schemes. In an insightful article Muth (1960) showed that adaptive expectations can actually be rational. When the observed variable is the sum of permanent and temporary shocks that the agents cannot disentangle, rational expectations lead to a forecasting formula that is exactly the traditional adaptive expectations formula.

Let us thus assume that the observed variable x_t is the sum of two stochastic processes with different autoregressive roots:

$$x_t = \frac{u_t}{1 - \rho \mathcal{L}} + \frac{\varepsilon_t}{1 - \mu \mathcal{L}} \tag{76}$$

where $\mathcal{L}$ is the lag operator (see mathematical appendix, section A.8.4), u_t and ε_t are independent white noises and $\mu > \rho$. We want to put this process under the form:

$$(1 - \rho\mathcal{L})(1 - \mu\mathcal{L}) x_t = (1 - \mu\mathcal{L}) u_t + (1 - \rho\mathcal{L}) \varepsilon_t = (1 - \lambda\mathcal{L}) z_t \qquad (77)$$

where z_t is the innovation of x_t:

$$z_t = x_t - E_{t-1} x_t \qquad (78)$$

Computation of the Autoregressive Root

Let us start from the equality:

$$(1 - \mu\mathcal{L}) u_t + (1 - \rho\mathcal{L}) \varepsilon_t = (1 - \lambda\mathcal{L}) z_t \qquad (79)$$

We can compute the variances of both sides and equal them:

$$(1 + \lambda^2) \sigma_z^2 = (1 + \mu^2) \sigma_u^2 + (1 + \rho^2) \sigma_\varepsilon^2 \qquad (80)$$

and similarly for the the covariances at lag one:

$$\lambda \sigma_z^2 = \rho \sigma_\varepsilon^2 + \mu \sigma_u^2 \qquad (81)$$

Combining (80) and (81), we find that λ is solution of:

$$\Psi(\lambda) = \lambda^2 - \lambda \chi + 1 = 0 \qquad (82)$$

with:

$$\chi = \frac{(1 + \mu^2) \sigma_u^2 + (1 + \rho^2) \sigma_\varepsilon^2}{\mu \sigma_u^2 + \rho \sigma_\varepsilon^2} \qquad (83)$$

We can compute:

$$\Psi(0) = 1 > 0 \qquad (84)$$

$$\Psi(1) = -\frac{(1 - \rho)^2 \sigma_\varepsilon^2 + (1 - \mu)^2 \sigma_u^2}{\rho \sigma_\varepsilon^2 + \mu \sigma_u^2} < 0 \qquad (85)$$

$$\Psi(\rho) = \frac{(\mu - \rho)(1 - \mu\rho) \sigma_u^2}{\rho \sigma_\varepsilon^2 + \mu \sigma_u^2} > 0 \qquad (86)$$

$$\Psi(\mu) = \frac{(\rho - \mu)(1 - \mu\rho) \sigma_\varepsilon^2}{\rho \sigma_\varepsilon^2 + \mu \sigma_u^2} < 0 \qquad (87)$$

We see that λ is between ρ and μ:

$$\rho < \lambda < \mu \qquad (88)$$

Adaptive Expectations

Let us start with the expectation at lag one:

$$E_t x_{t+1} = x_{t+1} - z_{t+1} = \left[1 - \frac{(1 - \rho \mathcal{L})(1 - \mu \mathcal{L})}{(1 - \lambda \mathcal{L})}\right] x_{t+1}$$

$$= \frac{(\rho + \mu - \lambda - \mu \rho \mathcal{L}) x_t}{1 - \lambda \mathcal{L}} \tag{89}$$

Let us take the particular case where $\mu = 1$ and $\rho = 0$, that is, one shock is permanent and the other is purely transitory. Then formula (89) becomes:

$$E_t x_{t+1} = \frac{(1 - \lambda) x_t}{1 - \lambda \mathcal{L}} \tag{90}$$

which can be transformed into:

$$E_t x_{t+1} - E_{t-1} x_t = (1 - \lambda)(x_t - E_{t-1} x_t) \tag{91}$$

in which we recognize a traditional adaptive expectations formula.

Problems

Problem 3.1: Policy Ineffectiveness

We consider an extension of the AD-AS system that we saw in section 3.4:

$$y_t = m_t - p_t + b E_{t-1}(p_{t+1} - p_t) + \varepsilon_t \quad AD$$

$$y_t = y^* + \xi (p_t - p_t^e) \quad AS$$

with:

$$p_t^e = E_{t-1} p_t$$

The AD curve comes from an IS-LM system where demand is a negative function of the expected real interest rate, and thus a positive function of expected inflation.

1. Compute the value of output y_t.
2. We assume that monetary policy m_t is a function of past events only. Show that monetary policy has no influence on output (policy ineffectiveness).

Problem 3.2: Learning and Sunspots

We investigate whether a modification of the model that we studied in section 3.7 can give rise to sunspots, and whether learning can lead to such sunspots. We replace equation (57) giving the dynamics of x_t by:

$$x_t = aE_{t-1}x_{t+1} + bE_{t-1}x_t + \varepsilon_t \qquad 0 < a < 1$$

where ε_t is a white noise. As compared to the model of section 3.7, we have added the term $bE_{t-1}x_t$.

1. We consider a family of solutions of the form:

$$x_t = \lambda x_{t-1} + \gamma \varepsilon_{t-1} + \delta \varepsilon_t$$

   Characterize the rational expectations solutions. Are there sunspot type solutions?

2. We assume that agents learn by updating functions of the type:

$$x_t = \lambda_n x_{t-1} + \gamma_n \varepsilon_{t-1} + \delta_n \varepsilon_t$$

   The updating procedure is exactly the same as in section 3.7. Characterize the dynamics of the parameters λ_n, γ_n, and δ_n, and indicate whether the system can converge toward sunspot solutions.

Problem 3.3: Permanent and Temporary Shocks: Expectations Several Steps Ahead

We studied in appendix 3.1 how to predict the next realization of a stochastic process x_t, which is the sum of two nonobservable stochastic processes with different autoregressive roots:

$$x_t = \frac{u_t}{1 - \rho \mathcal{L}} + \frac{\varepsilon_t}{1 - \mu \mathcal{L}}$$

with:

$$0 \leq \rho < \mu \leq 1$$

We showed that x_t could be expressed under the form:

$$x_t = \frac{(1 - \lambda \mathcal{L}) z_t}{(1 - \rho \mathcal{L})(1 - \mu \mathcal{L})}$$

where z_t is the innovation in x_t:

$$z_t = x_t - E_{t-1}x_t$$

and λ is solution of:

$$\lambda^2 - \lambda\chi + 1 = 0$$

$$\chi = \frac{(1+\mu^2)\sigma_u^2 + (1+\rho^2)\sigma_\varepsilon^2}{\mu\sigma_u^2 + \rho\sigma_\varepsilon^2}$$

1. Compute the expectation of x_t at various higher lags, that is, $E_t x_{t+j}$ for $j > 1$.

4

Intertemporal Equilibria with Optimizing Agents

4.1 Introduction

In the previous chapter, we introduced rational expectations in traditional and otherwise ad hoc models. An important aspect of recent progress in macroeconomics has been the replacement of such ad hoc models by fully microfounded ones, for example, models where all agents take their consumption and investment decisions through explicit intertemporal maximization.

Such models will be described and applied notably to the issues of growth (chapters 7, 8, and 9) and fluctuations (chapters 10, 12, and 13). Before moving to these more specialized topics, we want to describe in a simple framework the models that are most used in the field.

In particular we study two famous and alternative models: the Ramsey model (Ramsey, 1928; Cass, 1965; Koopmans, 1965), and the overlapping generations (OLG) model (Allais, 1947; Samuelson, 1958; Diamond, 1965), as well as a third model, somehow intermediate between the two.

The central difference between the Ramsey and OLG models is in the demographics. In the Ramsey model, households are represented as a single infinitely lived consumer, which may actually represent a dynasty of identical representative consumers, but with a single utility function and a single budget constraint.

On the contrary, in the OLG model, households are pictured as a sequence of overlapping families, each with its own utility function and budget constraint. In the simplest version, each family lives two periods and overlaps only with the previous family (when young) and the next one (when old). We will see in this and later chapters that this demographic difference creates a number of important differences in the properties of the two models.

Although our ultimate purpose is to study growth and fluctuations models with explicit capital acccumulation, we will find out that a number of salient features of these models are purely due to their respective demographic structures. So, to make the exposition more pedagogic, before going to the Ramsey and OLG models with explicit capital accumulation, we present in this chapter simplified versions of these models without capital, where income is taken as exogenous. This will allow us to better understand the different structures of these models, notably as far as long-run equilibria and transitory dynamics are involved.

We first present, in section 4.2, a Ramsey model with exogenous incomes. This is very much a benchmark model, which has a single dynamic equilibrium and good efficiency properties.

We then move in section 4.3 to the model of overlapping generations. In the simple model, we present here, each agent lives two periods. Although this might seem a minor modification, it turns out to have fairly striking consequences; notably, there is more than one long-run equilibrium, and equilibria can be Pareto inefficient.

The two models we study in sections 4.2 and 4.3 are real. In section 4.4, we present a different OLG model, due to Samuelson (1958), where money serves as a store of value.

Finally, it is clear that the Ramsey and OLG models represent somehow two polar cases, and a model bridging the gap between them will clearly be a welcome addition. So we present in section 4.4 a third model, a Ramsey-OLG model, developed by Blanchard (1985), Weil (1989a), and Buiter (1988), which combines the long-lived households of the Ramsey model and the OLG structure, and is thus somehow a synthesis of the two previous models.

4.2 A Ramsey Model With Exogenous Incomes

The economy is populated with a single dynasty of identical representative households. There is neither birth nor death. The representative household lives forever, has an exogenous perishable income Y_t in period t, and maximizes the utility function

$$\sum_t \beta^t U(C_t) \qquad \beta < 1 \tag{1}$$

where β is the discount rate. The agents pay taxes T_t in real terms. There is no capital, but agents can nevertheless transfer purchasing power between periods through a real asset (this can be thought of as government debt). Let us denote as r_t the real interest rate on assets accumulated in $t-1$, and R_t the gross real interest rate:

$$R_t = 1 + r_t \qquad (2)$$

Denoting as D_t the amount of government debt held by the household at the beginning of period t, the budget constraint of the household is:

$$D_{t+1} = R_{t+1}\left(D_t + Y_t - T_t - C_t\right) \qquad (3)$$

The household maximizes utility (1) subject to the sequence of budget constraints (3).

4.2.1 The Intertemporal Budget Constraint

We can aggregate all budget constraints (3) into an intertemporal budget constraint. For that let us define the discount factors:

$$\Delta_t = \frac{1}{(1+r_1)\ldots(1+r_t)} \qquad \Delta_0 = 1 \qquad (4)$$

Multiply the period t budget constraint (3) by the discount factor Δ_{t+1}:

$$\Delta_{t+1} D_{t+1} = \Delta_t \left(D_t + Y_t - T_t - C_t\right) \qquad (5)$$

Summing all these equalities from time 0 to infinity, and assuming that $\Delta_t D_t$ goes to 0 as t goes to infinity,[1] we obtain the household's intertemporal budget constraint:

$$\sum_{t=0}^{\infty} \Delta_t C_t = D_0 + \sum_{t=0}^{\infty} \Delta_t Y_t - \sum_{t=0}^{\infty} \Delta_t T_t \qquad (6)$$

---

1. This is the so-called transversality condition. See mathematical appendix, section A.4.3

4.2.2 The Euler Equation

The household maximizes utility (1) subject to the intertemporal budget constraint (6), so it solves the following program:

$$\text{Maximize} \sum_t \beta^t U(C_t) \quad \text{s.t.}$$

$$\sum_{t=0}^{\infty} \Delta_t C_t = D_0 + \sum_{t=0}^{\infty} \Delta_t Y_t - \sum_{t=0}^{\infty} \Delta_t T_t$$

The Lagrangian is:

$$\sum_{t=0}^{\infty} \beta^t U(C_t) + \lambda \left[D_0 + \sum_{t=0}^{\infty} \Delta_t Y_t - \sum_{t=0}^{\infty} \Delta_t T_t - \sum_{t=0}^{\infty} \Delta_t C_t \right] \tag{7}$$

The first-order condition for consumption C_t is:

$$\beta^t U'(C_t) = \lambda \Delta_t \tag{8}$$

Let us forward this one period:

$$\beta^{t+1} U'(C_{t+1}) = \lambda \Delta_{t+1} = \frac{\lambda \Delta_t}{R_{t+1}} \tag{9}$$

Eliminating λ between equations (8) and (9) we obtain the so-called *Euler equation:*

$$U'(C_t) = \beta R_{t+1} U'(C_{t+1}) \tag{10}$$

This essentially says that you do not get any extra utility increase by moving consumption from one period to the next.

4.2.3 Market Equilibrium

The equilibrium condition on the goods market is for each period t:

$$Y_t = C_t + G_t \tag{11}$$

where G_t is government spending in real terms. Inserting (11) into the Euler equation (10), we obtain the value of the gross real interest rate:

$$R_t = \frac{\Delta_{t-1}}{\Delta_t} = \frac{U'(Y_{t-1} - G_{t-1})}{\beta U'(Y_t - G_t)} \qquad (12)$$

For example if $U(C_t) = Log C_t$ and:

$$\frac{Y_t - G_t}{Y_{t-1} - G_{t-1}} = \zeta \qquad (13)$$

Then:

$$R_t = \frac{\zeta}{\beta} \qquad (14)$$

We may note that what matters is the growth rate of society's income net of government spending.

4.2.4 Ricardian Equivalence

We now study an important property, that of Ricardian equivalence. Ricardian equivalence says that, as long as the government plans to respect its long-run budget constraint in all circumstances, fiscal policy (i.e., the specific values of taxes and debt in each period) becomes irrelevant.[2]

To examine this issue rigorously, let us start with the government's budget constraint:

$$D_{t+1} = R_{t+1}(D_t + G_t - T_t) \qquad (15)$$

Using the same method as for the household, these constraints can be aggregated into the government's intertemporal budget constraint:

$$\sum_{t=0}^{\infty} \Delta_t T_t = D_0 + \sum_{t=0}^{\infty} \Delta_t G_t \qquad (16)$$

---

2. The issue of Ricardian equivalence emerged notably with the article by Barro (1974). The connection with Ricardo came up in the ensuing discussion with Buchanan (1976) and O'Driscoll (1977). Surveys on Ricardian equivalence can be found in Abel (2008), Barro (1989), and Bernheim (1987).

Inserting this into the household's budget constraint (6), we obtain the final form of the household's intertemporal budget constraint:

$$\sum_{t=0}^{\infty} \Delta_t C_t = \sum_{t=0}^{\infty} \Delta_t Y_t - \sum_{t=0}^{\infty} \Delta_t G_t \qquad (17)$$

We note a striking property: both taxes and the initial government debt have disappeared from this budget constraint, so this model indeed has the Ricardian equivalence property. As we will see below, the problem of Ricardian equivalence turns out to be important for a number of policy issues.

4.3 An Overlapping Generations Model

4.3.1 The Model

The demography of the OLG model[3] is quite different from that of the Ramsey model. In the simplest version, which we use here, households live two periods. Households born in period t receive perishable incomes y_1 in period t and y_2 in period $t+1$. Their utility function is:

$$U(c_{1t}) + \beta U(c_{2t+1}) \qquad (18)$$

where β is again the discount rate, and c_{1t} and c_{2t+1} are consumptions in t and $t+1$, respectively. Consumers can transfer wealth from period t to period $t+1$ through a real asset, which we can again think of as public debt. The household saves an amount s_t in period t, and receives in $t+1$ a gross real return R_{t+1} on it, so that its budget constraints are:

$$c_{1t} + s_t = y_1 \qquad (19)$$

$$c_{2t+1} = R_{t+1} s_t + y_2 \qquad (20)$$

Eliminating s_t we can aggregate these two constraints into a single intertemporal budget constraint:

$$c_{1t} + \frac{c_{2t+1}}{R_{t+1}} = y_1 + \frac{y_2}{R_{t+1}} \qquad (21)$$

---

3. The overlapping generations model has been notably developed by Allais (1947), Samuelson (1958), Diamond (1965), and Gale (1973).

We assume that there are N_t households born in t. In period t coexist N_t households born in t and N_{t-1} households born in $t-1$. To lighten the exposition we ignore government spending from now on, so that the equilibrium condition on the goods market is:

$$N_t c_{1t} + N_{t-1} c_{2t} = N_t y_1 + N_{t-1} y_2 \qquad (22)$$

or if $N_t = (1+n) N_{t-1}$:

$$c_{1t} + \frac{c_{2t}}{1+n} = y_1 + \frac{y_2}{1+n} \qquad (23)$$

4.3.2 Optimal Consumptions

The young consumer maximizes his utility (18) subject to the budget constraint (21), that is, he solves the following optimization program:

$$\text{Maximize } U(c_{1t}) + \beta U(c_{2t+1}) \quad \text{s.t.}$$

$$c_{1t} + \frac{c_{2t+1}}{R_{t+1}} = y_1 + \frac{y_2}{R_{t+1}}$$

which yields the following first-order condition:

$$U'(c_{1t}) = \beta R_{t+1} U'(c_{2t+1}) \qquad (24)$$

We may note the formal similarity of this condition with the Euler equation in the Ramsey model.

4.3.3 Steady States

We first study market equilibrium steady states, where consumptions per head are constant in time:

$$c_{1t} = c_1 \qquad c_{2t} = c_2 \qquad \forall t \qquad (25)$$

These consumptions and the gross real interest rate R are solutions of the system of three equations, coming from (21), (23), and (24):

$$c_1 + \frac{c_2}{1+n} = y_1 + \frac{y_2}{1+n} \qquad (26)$$

$$c_1 + \frac{c_2}{R} = y_1 + \frac{y_2}{R} \qquad (27)$$

$$U'(c_1) = \beta R U'(c_2) \qquad (28)$$

Looking at equations (26) and (27), we see that there are two possible steady states. The first, and obvious one, is that where all households simply consume their endowment in each period:

$$c_1 = y_1 \qquad c_2 = y_2 \qquad (29)$$

The associated real interest rate is, from equation (28):

$$R = \frac{U'(c_1)}{\beta U'(c_2)} = \frac{U'(y_1)}{\beta U'(y_2)} \qquad (30)$$

We call this the *autarkic* interest rate because in this equilibrium each generation consumes exactly its endowment, and thus somehow lives in full autarky. Note that this equilibrium looks somewhat similar to the simplified Ramsey model in section 4.2.

There is now a novelty with respect to the Ramsey model. There exists another type of steady state, which was uncovered by Samuelson (1958), and where:

$$R = 1 + n \qquad (31)$$

Samuelson (1958) called it the "biological rate of interest." Following chapter 1 and anticipating chapter 8, we call it the *golden rule* rate of interest. It corresponds indeed to the stationary equilibrium that yields the highest utility level. To characterize this equilibrium, let us maximize utility $U(c_1) + \beta U(c_2)$ subject to the stationary feasibility constraint (26). This yields the first-order condition:

$$U'(c_1) = \beta(1+n)U'(c_2) \qquad (32)$$

We already saw (equation 28) that the first-order condition for a household faced with an interest rate R is:

$$U'(c_1) = \beta R U'(c_2) \qquad (33)$$

Comparing (32) and (33), we see that the steady state with the highest utility corresponds indeed to a gross real interest rate $R = 1 + n$.

4.3.4 Dynamics

To simplify the description of the dynamics, we take a logarithmic utility function, that is, $U(c_t) = Log c_t$. Then, combining the first-order condition (24) with the budget constraint (21), we obtain the consumption function of the young household:

$$c_{1t} = \frac{1}{1+\beta}\left(y_1 + \frac{y_2}{R_{t+1}}\right) \quad (34)$$

The old household has saved s_{t-1} in the previous period, and therefore enters period t with holdings of government debt d_t equal to:

$$d_t = R_t s_{t-1} \quad (35)$$

Since it will die at the end of the period, this old household consumes these assets d_t totally plus its second-period endowment y_2:

$$c_{2t} = y_2 + d_t \quad (36)$$

Finally we have the equation of equilibrium in the goods market:

$$c_{1t} + \frac{c_{2t}}{1+n} = y_1 + \frac{y_2}{1+n} \quad (37)$$

Eliminating c_{1t} and c_{2t} between equations (34), (36), and (37), we obtain the gross interest rate as a function of debt holdings:

$$R_{t+1} = \frac{(1+n)y_2}{\beta(1+n)y_1 - (1+\beta)d_t} \quad (38)$$

We note that for an equilibrium to exist, the amount of debt must be inferior to the following level:

$$d_t < \frac{\beta(1+n)y_1}{1+\beta} \quad (39)$$

Combining equations (19), (34), (35), and (38), we obtain a dynamic equation showing the evolution in time of asset holdings per head d_t:

$$d_{t+1} = \frac{y_2 d_t}{\beta(1+n)y_1 - (1+\beta)d_t} \quad (40)$$

4.3.5 Steady-state Equilibria

We see that there are two steady states, one with $d_t = 0$, corresponding to the autarkic interest rate $R = y_2/\beta y_1$, the other one with:

$$d_t = \frac{\beta(1+n)y_1 - y_2}{1+\beta} = d^* \qquad (41)$$

corresponding to the golden rule interest rate $R = 1 + n$. To further study the dynamics, let us (following Gale, 1973), classify economies into (a) "Samuelson" economies where, in steady state, young agents are lenders at the golden rule interest rate; and (b) "classical" economies where, in steady state, young agents are borrowers at the golden rule interest rate.

The dynamics of the Samuelson and classical cases are represented in figures 4.1 and 4.2, respectively.

We see notably that the golden rule equilibrium is unstable in the Samuelson case and stable in the classical case. Conversely, the autarkic equilibrium is stable in the Samuelson case and unstable in the classical case.

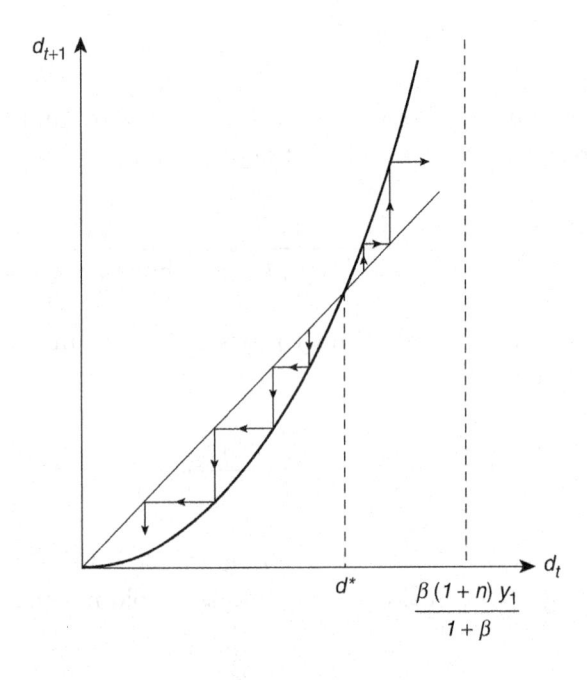

Figure 4.1 The OLG model: Samuelson case

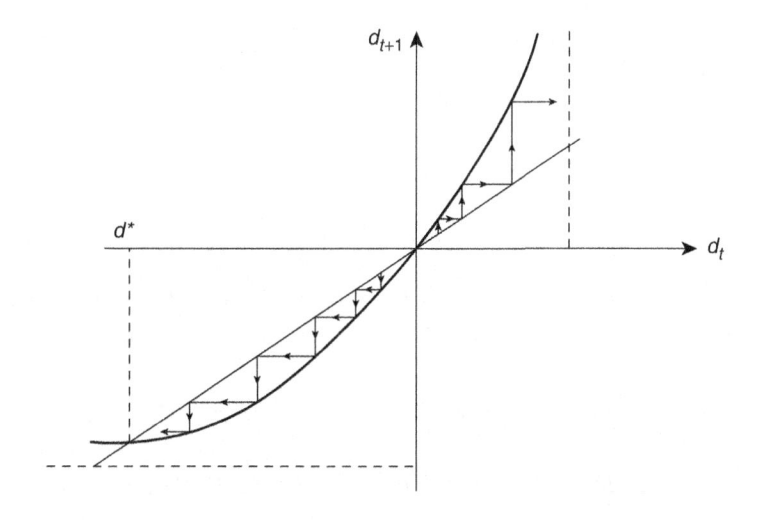

Figure 4.2 The OLG model: classical case

4.3.6 Taxes and Ricardian Equivalence

We shall now see that as we might have expected, Ricardian equivalence does not hold in the OLG model. To show this in the simplest manner possible, we consider a simple fiscal policy where the government levies in each period real taxes per head τ_1 on the young household and τ_2 on the old household. The budget constraints (19) and (20) become:

$$c_{1t} + s_t = y_1 - \tau_1 \tag{42}$$

$$c_{2t+1} = R_{t+1}s_t + y_2 - \tau_2 \tag{43}$$

and consequently the consumption function of the young household:

$$c_{1t} = \frac{1}{1+\beta}\left(y_1 - \tau_1 + \frac{y_2 - \tau_2}{R_{t+1}}\right) \tag{44}$$

The evolution of aggregate public debt D_t is:

$$D_{t+1} = R_{t+1}\left(D_t - N_t\tau_1 - N_{t-1}\tau_2\right) \tag{45}$$

Let us now assume that these taxes balance in the aggregate, so that:

$$N_t\tau_1 + N_{t-1}\tau_2 = 0 \tag{46}$$

and that initial debt is 0. Then (45) and (46) imply that debt will be 0 in all periods. The autarkic steady state is then particularly easy to compute and will be characterized by:

$$c_{1t} = y_1 - \tau_1 \qquad c_{2t} = y_2 - \tau_2 \qquad (47)$$

$$R = \frac{y_2 - \tau_2}{\beta(y_1 - \tau_1)} \qquad (48)$$

We see that contrary to the Ramsey model, consumptions and the interest rate clearly depend on fiscal policy, and Ricardian equivalence therefore does not hold.

4.4 Overlapping Generations and Money

We now study a different version of the OLG model, the one pioneered by Samuelson (1958). In this model, money, that is, intrinsically useless pieces of paper, serves as a store of value between one period and the next.

4.4.1 An OLG Model

We consider a highly streamlined version of Samuelson (1958). As in the model of section 4.3, the economy is populated with households that live two periods. They receive an exogenous real income y_1 and y_2 the first and second period, respectively. They consume c_{1t} and c_{2t+1} in t and $t+1$ and have a utility function:

$$Log\, c_{1t} + \beta Log\, c_{2t+1} \qquad (49)$$

The difference with the previous model is that households now save under the form of money, of which there is a fixed quantity M in the economy.

4.4.2 The Dynamic Equilibrium

Each household has two budget constraints, one for each period of its life:

$$p_t c_{1t} + M_t = p_t y_1 \qquad (50)$$

$$p_{t+1} c_{2t+1} = M_t + p_{t+1} y_2 \qquad (51)$$

where M_t is the amount of money saved from t to $t+1$. The young household maximizes utility (49) subject to these budget constraints, so its program is:

$$\text{Maximize } Log c_{1t} + \beta Log c_{2t+1} \quad \text{s.t.}$$

$$p_t c_{1t} + M_t = p_t y_1$$

$$p_{t+1} c_{2t+1} = M_t + p_{t+1} y_2$$

This yields the consumption function of the young:

$$p_t c_{1t} = \frac{1}{1+\beta} \left(p_t y_1 + p_{t+1} y_2 \right) \tag{52}$$

The old household arrives in the second period of its life with a quantity of money M. Furthermore, it has real income y_2. So its consumption c_{2t} is given by:

$$p_t c_{2t} = M + p_t y_2 \tag{53}$$

The condition for equilibrium in the goods market is:

$$c_{1t} + c_{2t} = y_1 + y_2 \tag{54}$$

Combining (52), (53), and (54), we obtain:

$$(1+\beta) M = \beta y_1 p_t - y_2 p_{t+1} \tag{55}$$

The first result we get is that if there is a stationary equilibrium price p^*, it will be given by:

$$\frac{M}{p^*} = \frac{\beta y_1 - y_2}{1+\beta} \tag{56}$$

We see that for the long-run price to be positive, we must have:

$$\frac{\beta y_1}{y_2} > 1 \tag{57}$$

We now move to the study of dynamics. Using (56), equation (55) can be rewritten as:

$$p_{t+1} - p^* = \frac{\beta y_1}{y_2} (p_t - p^*) \tag{58}$$

where we see that the equilibrium p^* is locally determinate (see mathematical appendix, section A.11) if $\beta y_1 > y_2$. This corresponds to condition (57) for $p^* > 0$.

Before we study this model further in chapter 11, we use it, because of its simplicity, in chapters 5 and 10. In both cases we make assumptions equivalent to (57), so that a monetary equilibrium actually exists.

4.5 A Ramsey-OLG Model

As we indicated above, it would be useful to have a model that is intermediate between the Ramsey and OLG models. We describe in this section a model first proposed by Blanchard (1985), and further developed by Weil (1989a) and Buiter (1988). This model is somehow a synthesis between the Ramsey model and the OLG model of section 4.3. As in the Ramsey model, the households are infinitely lived, but as in the OLG model, new generations appear over time.

The original model (Blanchard, 1985) had both births and deaths.[4] But it appeared later that the important difference was birth, not death (Weil, 1989; Buiter, 1988) so we shall describe, to simplify, a model with only births, and infinite lives. To facilitate the exposition, we also describe, as in the previous sections, a simple version of the model without production and with exogenous incomes.

4.5.1 The Model

New generations of households are born in each period. Denote by N_t the number of households alive at time t. $N_t - N_{t-1}$ households are born in period t, and we assume $N_t \geq N_{t-1}$. We often work with a constant rate of growth of the population $n \geq 0$, so that $N_t = (1+n)^t$.

Consider a household born in period j. We denote by c_{jt} and y_{jt} its consumption and endowment at time $t \geq j$. This household maximizes the following utility function:

$$U_{jt} = \sum_{s=t}^{\infty} \beta^{s-t} Log\, c_{js} \qquad (59)$$

Household j begins period t with a wealth that consists of an amount of public debt d_{jt} (which includes interest payments). The goods market opens, and the household sells its endowment y_{jt}, pays taxes τ_{jt} in real terms, and consumes c_{jt}. Consequently, the budget constraint for this

---

[4]. In the model with death, each agent has a constant probability of death. This is made tractable by using an ingenious life insurance scheme due to Yaari (1965).

household is:

$$d_{jt+1} = R_{t+1}\left(d_{jt} + y_{jt} - \tau_{jt} - c_{jt}\right) \qquad (60)$$

4.5.2 Aggregation

Aggregate quantities are obtained by summing the various individual variables. Because there are $N_j - N_{j-1}$ agents in cohort j, these aggregates are equal to:

$$Y_t = \sum_{j\leq t}\left(N_j - N_{j-1}\right) y_{jt} \qquad T_t = \sum_{j\leq t}\left(N_j - N_{j-1}\right) \tau_{jt} \qquad (61)$$

$$C_t = \sum_{j\leq t}\left(N_j - N_{j-1}\right) c_{jt} \qquad D_t = \sum_{j\leq t}\left(N_j - N_{j-1}\right) d_{jt} \qquad (62)$$

4.5.3 Incomes and Taxes

We now describe how incomes and taxes are distributed among households. We assume that all households have the same income and taxes, so equation (61) simplifies to:

$$y_{jt} = y_t = \frac{Y_t}{N_t} \qquad \tau_{jt} = \tau_t = \frac{T_t}{N_t} \qquad (63)$$

Real income per head grows at the rate ζ, so that:

$$\frac{y_{t+1}}{y_t} = \zeta \qquad \frac{Y_{t+1}}{Y_t} = (1+n)\zeta \qquad (64)$$

4.5.4 Government

Another important part of the model is the government. Government owes a total amount of real debt D_t. The evolution of government debt is described by the government's budget constraint:

$$D_{t+1} = R_{t+1}\left(D_t - T_t + G_t\right) \qquad (65)$$

4.5.5 Dynamics

As an example of the dynamics of this model, we study the dynamics of interest rates and assets in the case where $G_t = T_t = 0$. Then equation (65) becomes:

$$D_{t+1} = R_{t+1} D_t \qquad (66)$$

It is shown in appendix 4.1 that the dynamics of debt and interest rates are given by the following equation:

$$Y_{t+1} = \beta(1+n) R_{t+1} Y_t - (1-\beta) n D_{t+1} \qquad (67)$$

which becomes, in view of (66):

$$Y_{t+1} = \beta(1+n) R_{t+1} Y_t - (1-\beta) n R_{t+1} D_t \qquad (68)$$

We can solve for the real interest rate:

$$R_{t+1} = \frac{Y_{t+1}}{\beta(1+n) Y_t - (1-\beta) n D_t} \qquad (69)$$

Note again that as in the OLG model, debt D_t must not be too high for an equilibrium to exist. Combining (66) and (69), we obtain the equation of evolution of D_t:

$$D_{t+1} = R_{t+1} D_t = \frac{Y_{t+1} D_t}{\beta(1+n) Y_t - (1-\beta) n D_t} \qquad (70)$$

and the debt-to-income ratio D_t/Y_t:

$$\frac{D_{t+1}}{Y_{t+1}} = \frac{D_t/Y_t}{\beta(1+n) - (1-\beta) n D_t/Y_t} \qquad (71)$$

As in the OLG model, this dynamic equation admits two long-run equilibria, the autarkic and golden rule, with, respectively:

$$\frac{D_t}{Y_t} = 0 \qquad R_t = \frac{\zeta}{\beta} \qquad (72)$$

$$\frac{D_t}{Y_t} = \frac{\beta(1+n) - 1}{(1-\beta) n} \qquad R_t = \zeta(1+n) \qquad (73)$$

As in section 4.3.4, we can classify economies into Samuelson economies, corresponding to $\beta(1+n) > 1$, and classical economies, corresponding to $\beta(1+n) < 1$. The Samuelson case is represented in figure 4.3.

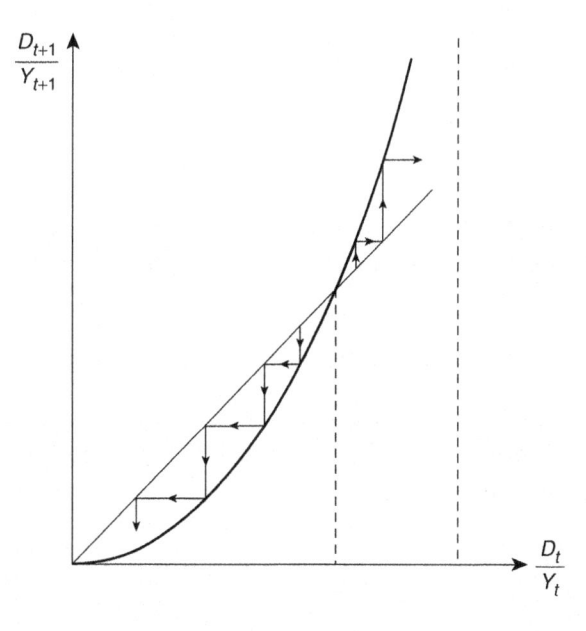

Intertemporal Equilibria with Optimizing Agents

Figure 4.3 The Ramsey-OLG model: Samuelson case

We note that the dynamic and stability properties of this Ramsey-OLG model are very similar to those of the OLG model of section 4.3 (compare figures 4.1 and 4.3). The same is true in the classical case, and thus we omit the corresponding figure that would look like figure 4.2.

Appendix 4.1: A Basic Dynamic Equation

In this appendix we derive the dynamic equation (67). Let us again use the real discount factors seen in section 4.2.1:

$$\Delta_t = \frac{1}{(1+r_1)\ldots(1+r_t)} \qquad \Delta_0 = 1 \qquad (74)$$

and apply them to the budget constraint (60). This yields:

$$\Delta_{s+1} d_{js+1} = \Delta_s \left(d_{js} + y_{js} - \tau_{js} - c_{js} \right) \qquad (75)$$

If we aggregate all budget constraints (75) from time t to infinity, and assume that $\Delta_s d_{js}$ goes to 0 as s goes to infinity (this is again the transversality condition), we obtain household j's intertemporal budget constraint:

$$\sum_{s=t}^{\infty} \Delta_s c_{js} = \Delta_t d_{jt} + \sum_{s=t}^{\infty} \Delta_s (y_s - \tau_s) \qquad (76)$$

Maximizing the utility function (59) subject to the intertemporal budget constraint (76) yields household j's consumption function:

$$\Delta_t c_{jt} = (1 - \beta) \left[\Delta_t d_{jt} + \sum_{s=t}^{\infty} \Delta_s (y_s - \tau_s) \right] \qquad (77)$$

Summing this across the N_t agents alive in period t, we obtain the aggregate consumption C_t:

$$\Delta_t C_t = (1 - \beta) \left[\Delta_t D_t + N_t \sum_{s=t}^{\infty} \Delta_s (y_s - \tau_s) \right] \qquad (78)$$

In equilibrium we have $C_t = Y_t$ (we assume $G_t = 0$ to simplify formulas), so the equilibrium equation is:

$$\Delta_t Y_t = (1 - \beta) \left[\Delta_t D_t + N_t \sum_{s=t}^{\infty} \Delta_s (y_s - \tau_s) \right] \qquad (79)$$

Let us divide both sides by N_t:

$$\Delta_t y_t = (1 - \beta) \left[\frac{\Delta_t D_t}{N_t} + \sum_{s=t}^{\infty} \Delta_s (y_s - \tau_s) \right] \qquad (80)$$

We rewrite this equation for $t+1$ and subtract it from (80). We obtain:

$$\Delta_t y_t - \Delta_{t+1} y_{t+1} = (1 - \beta) \left[\frac{\Delta_t D_t}{N_t} - \frac{\Delta_{t+1} D_{t+1}}{N_{t+1}} + \Delta_t (y_t - \tau_t) \right] \qquad (81)$$

Multiply the government's budget equation (65) by Δ_{t+1}/N_t:

$$\frac{\Delta_{t+1} D_{t+1}}{N_t} = \frac{\Delta_t}{N_t} (D_t - T_t) = \frac{\Delta_t D_t}{N_t} - \Delta_t \tau_t \qquad (82)$$

and insert it into equation (81):

$$\Delta_{t+1} y_{t+1} = \beta \Delta_t y_t - (1 - \beta) \left(\frac{1}{N_t} - \frac{1}{N_{t+1}} \right) \Delta_{t+1} D_{t+1} \qquad (83)$$

Now multiply equation (83) by N_{t+1}/Δ_{t+1}:

$$Y_{t+1} = \beta \frac{N_{t+1}}{N_t} R_{t+1} Y_t - (1-\beta)\left(\frac{N_{t+1}}{N_t} - 1\right) D_{t+1} \qquad (84)$$

Assume, finally, $N_{t+1}/N_t = 1 + n$. We obtain:

$$Y_{t+1} = \beta(1+n) R_{t+1} Y_t - (1-\beta) n D_{t+1} \qquad (85)$$

which is equation (67).

Problems

Problem 4.1: The Demand for Money

Consider an overlapping generations structure where households have the following utility function:

$$U_t = \frac{C_{t+1}^{1-\theta}}{1-\theta} - \frac{L_t^{1+\nu}}{1+\nu} \qquad \nu > 0 \qquad \theta \geq 0$$

The household maximizes utility subject to the budget constraints:

$$W_t L_t = M_t$$

$$P_{t+1}^e C_{t+1} = M_t$$

1. Compute the demand for money as a function of W_t and P_{t+1}^e.
2. Assume that the production function is:

$$Y_t = L_t$$

and that all markets clear. Show that the following relation holds:

$$\frac{M_t}{P_t} = \left(\frac{P_{t+1}^e}{P_t}\right)^{-\alpha}$$

What is the value of α?

Problem 4.2: The OLG Model: An Intertemporal Optimum

We consider an overlapping generations endowment economy. Each agent has an exogenous income y_1 when young and y_2 when old. The household of generation t consumes c_{1t} when young and c_{2t+1} when old. It has the following utility function:

$$U_t = Log c_{1t} + \beta Log c_{2t+1}$$

The population grows at rate n. We want to compute an intertemporal optimum according to the criterion developed by Samuelson (1967, 1968) for OLG economies:

$$V = \sum_t \phi^t U_t$$

where ϕ represents the relative weight of generations.

1. Compute the values of consumptions c_{1t} and c_{2t} in such an intertemporal optimum. How do they depend on ϕ?

Problem 4.3: Pareto Optimality of Autarkic Equilibria in the Ramsey-OLG Model

We derive conditions under which the autarkic equilibrium is a Pareto optimum in the Ramsey-OLG model. We assume that agents born in period j have a utility function:

$$U_j = \sum_{t=j}^{\infty} \beta^{t-j} U(c_{jt})$$

Each agent receives in period t an income y_t independent of the date he was born. We consider autarkic equilibria where each agent consumes exactly his endowment:

$$c_{jt} = y_t \qquad \forall t \quad \forall j \leq t$$

1. Show that if $\beta(1+n) > 1$, the autarkic equilibrium is Pareto dominated.
2. Show that if $\beta(1+n) < 1$ the autarkic equilibrium is Pareto efficient.

5

Nonclearing Markets and Imperfect Competition

5.1 Introduction

Looking at the first four chapters, we see that there is a serious conceptual gap between chapters 1, 3, and 4 on one hand, and chapter 2 on the other. In chapters 1, 3, and 4, it is always assumed, implicitly or explicitly, that all markets perpetually clear, and supply equals demand in all circumstances.

In chapter 2, on the contrary, most models display unemployment, that is, an excess supply on the labor market, and sometimes excess supply on the goods market as well. This is handled formally by adding output as an argument of various functions, but this is clearly an ad hoc formalization so far.

Our purpose in this chapter is to show how to formalize such situations of market imbalances in a way that is as rigorous as the Walrasian one and to give a few simple macroeconomic applications. The theories we shall develop synthesize the Walrasian, Keynesian, and imperfect competition theories, and they will provide a coherent formalization of both price and quantity formation outside Walrasian equilibrium.

Section 5.2 briefly recalls the central features of Walrasian theory to identify the points where it has to be generalized. Section 5.3 gives a simple description of the microfoundations of the more general theories already outlined. Section 5.4 gives a simple macroeconomic application of the foregoing theories. The same model is successively studied under the assumptions of Walrasian equilibrium, rigid prices and wages, and imperfect competition on the goods and labor markets.

An important feature of modern macroeconomics is studying the correlations between economic variables generated by various models. Section 5.5 introduces stochastic shocks into the model of section 5.4, showing that both the response to shocks and the resulting correlations depend in a fundamental manner on the assumptions on price and wage rigidities.

5.2 Walrasian Theory: The Missing Parts

Here we briefly describe the characteristics of the Walrasian model[1] and then outline how it has to be generalized to deal with nonclearing markets and imperfect competition.

5.2.1 The Walrasian Paradigm

Consider an economy where goods indexed by $h = 1, \cdots, \ell$ are exchanged among agents indexed by $i = 1, \cdots, n$. Call p_h the price of good h, and p the price vector:

$$p = (p_1, \cdots, p_h, \cdots, p_\ell) \qquad (1)$$

Denote by d_{ih} and s_{ih} the demand and supply of good h by agent i. The Walrasian mechanism can be summarized as an atemporal "dialogue" between the agents in the economy and the famous Walrasian auctioneer.

All agents receive from the auctioneer the same price signal p, and assume that they will be able to exchange whatever they want at this price system. In turn, each agent i sends to the auctioneer his Walrasian demands and supplies, obtained through maximization of his own objective function. Of course, demands and supplies depend on the price system. We denote them as:

$$d_{ih} = d_{ih}(p) \qquad s_{ih} = s_{ih}(p) \qquad (2)$$

The auctioneer changes the price system through the famous tâtonnement process until a Walrasian equilibrium price vector p^* is reached.

---

1. The founding reference is Walras (1874). Modern representations and extensions are found in Arrow and Debreu (1954), Debreu (1959), and Arrow and Hahn (1971).

This equilibrium price p^* is characterized by the equality of aggregate demand and aggregate supply in all markets:

$$\sum_{i=1}^{n} d_{ih}(p^*) = \sum_{i=1}^{n} s_{ih}(p^*) \qquad \text{for all } h = 1, \cdots, \ell \qquad (3)$$

Transactions are equal to the demands and supplies at this price system. No quantity constraint is experienced by any agent, because demands and supplies match on all markets.

5.2.2 The Missing Elements

The Walrasian story is a good description of reality for the few real-world markets, such as the stock market (which inspired Walras), where the equality between demand and supply is ensured institutionally by an actual auctioneer. For all other markets, where there is no auctioneer and which function in a decentralized manner, the Walrasian story is clearly incomplete. Two important problems in the Walrasian model deserve to be stressed here:

- The first concerns prices: as was pointed out by Arrow (1959) himself, "there is no place for a rational decision with respect to prices as there is with respect to quantities." The price formation mechanism is assumed; it is not the consequence of rational behavior.
- In the absence of an auctioneer, transactions occur at nonequilibrium prices. The theory says nothing about how this is done, and how potential imbalances in turn react on quantities and prices.

We will now fill these gaps and describe a consistent theory of the functioning of decentralized market economies when no auctioneer is present. We will find that a complete formalization of such decentralized markets must include quantity signals as well as price signals. These quantity signals are central not only for quantity decisions but also in the process of price making by agents internal to the system.[2]

5.3 Nonclearing Markets and Imperfect Competition

We now present a simplified theory of nonclearing markets and imperfect competition. We describe successively how transactions are realized in a

---

2. These theories have been developed in full-fledged general equilibrium frameworks, notably in Drèze (1975, 1991) and Bénassy (1975, 1976, 1977, 1988). The concepts are compared in Silvestre (1982, 1983). See Bénassy (1990, 2002b) for synthetic presentations.

market where demand and supply do not match, how quantity signals are formed in the process, how demands and supplies respond to these quantity signals, and finally how prices are set in a framework with quantity signals and imperfect competition.

5.3.1 Transactions in Nonclearing Markets

In nonmarket-clearing models we must make an important distinction that by nature is not made in market-clearing models: that between demands and supplies, on the one hand, and the resulting transactions, on the other. We distinguish them by different notations.

Consider a particular market where n agents, indexed by $i = 1, \ldots, n$ exchange a particular good against money. Because we shall be considering a single market, we omit its index h.

Transactions, that is, purchases and sales of goods, are denoted d_i and s_i. They are the actual exchanges carried on markets. Therefore, aggregate purchases must be equal to aggregate sales. With n agents in the economy, this is written

$$D = \sum_{i=1}^{n} d_i = \sum_{i=1}^{n} s_i = S \qquad (4)$$

Demands and supplies, denoted $\widetilde{d}_i$ and $\widetilde{s}_i$, are signals that represent the exchanges agents wish to carry. Since the price is not necessarily market-clearing, they do not automatically match on the market, and we may have:

$$\widetilde{D} = \sum_{i=1}^{n} \widetilde{d}_i \neq \sum_{i=1}^{n} \widetilde{s}_i = \widetilde{S} \qquad (5)$$

From any such set of possibly inconsistent demands and supplies, the exchange process must generate consistent transactions satisfying equation (4). Evidently, as soon as $\widetilde{D} \neq \widetilde{S}$, some demands and supplies cannot be satisfied in the exchange process and some agents must be "rationed", in the sense that they cannot achieve their desired demand or supply.[3] In real life this "rationing" is done through a variety of procedures, such as, among others, queueing, proportional rationing, or priority systems, depending on

---

3. We should note that, although some agents do not reach their preferred transaction, there need not be rationing in the popular sense of the word. For example, if producers carry inventories, consumers will usually not be rationed, even when production is smaller than demand. This relation between inventories and rationing is studied in chapter 14.

the particular organization of each market. We call transactions scheme, or *rationing scheme*, the mathematical representation of the exchange process in the market being considered. It gives the transactions of each agent as a function of the demands and supplies of all agents present in that market. Before studying the properties of these schemes, we give the simplest possible example, where only two agents are present in the market considered (a slightly more elaborate example appears in appendix 5.1). Agent 1 demands $\tilde{d}_1$, and agent 2 supplies $\tilde{s}_2$. In such a simple market, the transaction is naturally the minimum of demand and supply:

$$d_1 = s_2 = \min(\tilde{d}_1, \tilde{s}_2) \tag{6}$$

We successively study a number of properties of rationing schemes.

Voluntary Exchange

The first property we consider is a very natural one in a free market economy, namely, that of *voluntary exchange*, according to which no agent can be forced to purchase more than he demands or sell more than he supplies. This is expressed by:

$$d_i \leq \tilde{d}_i \tag{7}$$

$$s_i \leq \tilde{s}_i \tag{8}$$

Such a condition is quite natural and actually verified in most markets. It is clearly satisfied by (6). Under voluntary exchange agents fall into two categories: "rationed" agents, for which $d_i < \tilde{d}_i$ or $s_i < \tilde{s}_i$, and "nonrationed" ones, for which $d_i = \tilde{d}_i$ or $s_i = \tilde{s}_i$.

Frictionless Markets

A rationing scheme in a market is *frictionless* if there are not both rationed demanders and rationed suppliers in that market. The intuitive idea behind this is that in a market without frictions, a rationed buyer and a rationed seller should be able to meet and exchange until one of the two is not rationed anymore.

Together with the voluntary exchange assumption (equations 7 and 8), this assumption implies the "short-side" rule, according to which agents on the short side of the market can realize their desired transactions:

$$\tilde{D} \geq \tilde{S} \Rightarrow s_i^* = \tilde{s}_i \qquad \text{for all } i \qquad (9)$$

$$\tilde{S} \geq \tilde{D} \Rightarrow d_i^* = \tilde{d}_i \qquad \text{for all } i \qquad (10)$$

It also yields the "rule of the minimum," which says that the aggregate level of transactions is equal to the minimum of aggregate demand and supply:

$$D = S = \min(\tilde{D}, \tilde{S}) \qquad (11)$$

Although the assumption of frictionless markets is implicit in many macroeconomic models, we should note that the concepts that follow do not actually depend on this assumption. In fact, there are some fields in macroeconomics where frictions in the transaction process play a central role, as we see in chapter 16 (the matching function). Such frictions may arise, for example, if one market is the aggregation of several submarkets. Then the aggregate market may not satisfy the rule of the minimum even though each of the submarkets is itself frictionless (figure 5.1).

5.3.2 Quantity Signals

It is quite clear that because they cannot trade what they want, at least the rationed agents must perceive some quantity signals in addition to the price signals. Let us first look at an example of how this occurs.

An Example

To see how quantity signals are formed in the transaction process, we begin with the example already seen (equation 6):

$$d_1 = s_2 = \min(\tilde{d}_1, \tilde{s}_2) \qquad (12)$$

Now, as transactions take place, quantity signals are clearly sent across the market: faced with a supply $\tilde{s}_2$, and under voluntary exchange, demander 1 knows that she will not be able to purchase more than $\tilde{s}_2$. Symmetrically supplier 2 knows that she cannot sell more than $\tilde{d}_1$. Each agent thus receives from the other a "quantity signal," respectively denoted $\bar{d}_1$ and $\bar{s}_2$, that tells

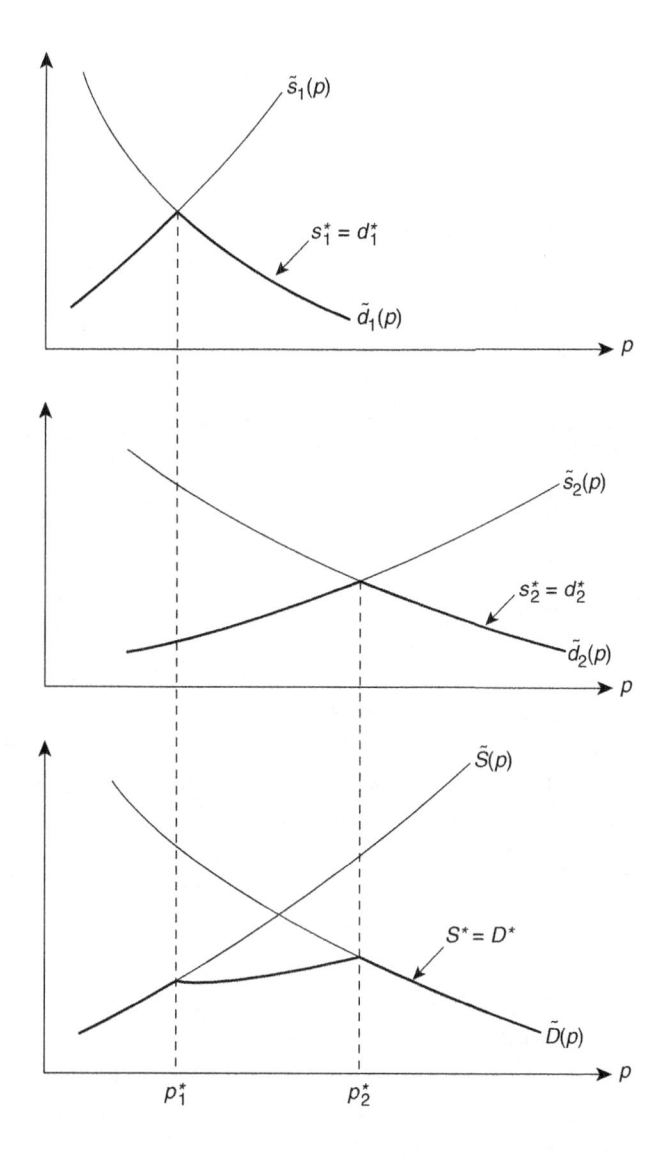

Figure 5.1 Aggregation and market frictions

her the maximum quantity she can respectively buy and sell. So the rationing scheme (12) can be alternatively be expressed as:

$$d_1 = \min(\widetilde{d}_1, \overline{d}_1) \tag{13}$$

$$s_2 = \min(\widetilde{s}_2, \overline{s}_2) \tag{14}$$

with:

$$\overline{d}_1 = \widetilde{s}_2 \qquad \overline{s}_2 = \widetilde{d}_1 \tag{15}$$

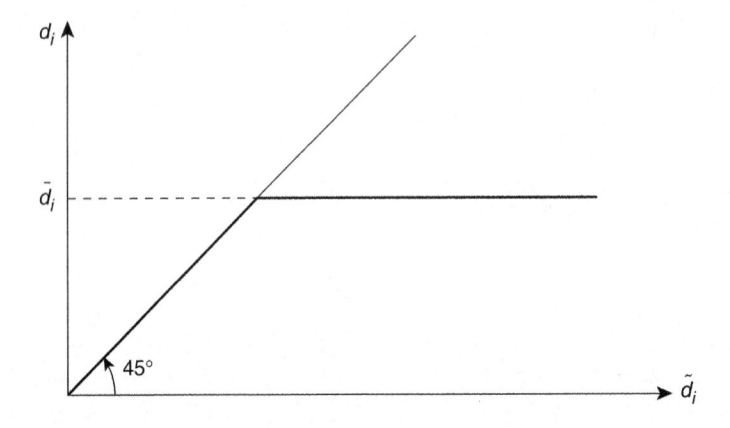

Figure 5.2 Demand and purchase

Quantity Signals

It turns out that many rationing schemes, and actually those we study in what follows, share the simple representation given by equations (13) and (14). Every agent i receives in the market a quantity signal, respectively $\bar{d}_i$ or $\bar{s}_i$ on the demand or supply side, which tells her the maximum quantity she can buy or sell. So the rationing scheme is simply rewritten:

$$d_i = \min(\tilde{d}_i, \bar{d}_i) \qquad (16)$$

$$s_i = \min(\tilde{s}_i, \bar{s}_i) \qquad (17)$$

where the quantity signals are functions of the demands and supplies of the *other* agents in the market (appendix 5.1 gives another example). The relation between the demand $\tilde{d}_i$ and purchase d_i looks as in figure 5.2 (and similarly for the relation between sale s_i and supply $\tilde{s}_i$).

Further, it is clear that the quantity signals perceived by the agents should have an effect on demand, supply, and price formation. This is the relationship we explore next.

5.3.3 Effective Demands and Supplies

We now examine how demands and supplies are formed when markets do not clear, and for that purpose we develop a theory of *effective demands and supplies*, which are functions of both price and quantity signals.[4]

---

4. The theory of effective demand was developed by Patinkin (1956), Clower (1965), Leijonhufvud (1968), Barro and Grossman (1971), and Bénassy (1975).

A Definition

When formulating effective demands and supplies, agent i knows that her transactions will be related to them by equalities like (13) and (14).

Maximizing the expected utility of the resulting transactions may lead to complex calculations (especially if constraints are stochastic). In the case of deterministic constraints, which is what we consider here, there exists a simple and workable definition that generalizes Clower's (1965) seminal insight: effective demand (or supply) of a particular good is the trade that maximizes the agent's criterion subject to the usual constraints *and* to the quantity constraints on the *other* markets. We turn to a well-known example.

The Employment Function

A good illustrative example of this definition of effective demand and supply is the employment function due to Patinkin (1956) and Barro and Grossman (1971). Consider a firm with a diminishing returns to scale production function $Y = F(L)$, and faced with a price P and a nominal wage W. The Walrasian labor demand is equal to $F'^{-1}(W/P)$. Assume now that the firm faces a constraint $\overline{Y}$ on its sales of output (in a complete macroeconomic model, such as will be developed in section 5.4, $\overline{Y}$ is equal to total demand from the other agents). By the foregoing definition, the effective demand for labor $\tilde{L}^d$ is the solution in L of the program:

$$\text{Maximize } PY - WL \quad \text{s.t.}$$
$$Y = F(L)$$
$$Y \leq \overline{Y}$$

This yields

$$\tilde{L}^d = \min\left[F'^{-1}\left(\frac{W}{P}\right), F^{-1}(\overline{Y})\right] \tag{18}$$

So the effective demand for labor has two forms: the Walrasian one $F'^{-1}(W/P)$ if the sales constraint is not binding, or, if this constraint is binding, a more Keynesian form equal to the quantity of labor just necessary to produce the output demand $F^{-1}(\overline{Y})$. We immediately see in this example that effective demand can have various functional forms, which intuitively explains why non-Walrasian models can have multiple regimes (as we will discover in section 5.4).

5.3.4 Price Making and Imperfect Competition

We are now ready to address the problem of price making by agents internal to the system. The general idea relating the concepts of this section to those of the preceding ones is that price setters change their prices so as to manipulate the quantity constraints they face, that is, to increase or decrease their possible sales or purchases. Various price-setting scenarios integrating the foregoing ideas can actually be envisioned. We focus on a particular (and realistic for many markets) pricing process in which a single seller quotes the price and faces demanders that act as price takers.[5]

Consider, thus, a seller i who sets the price P_i in a particular market, also indexed by i. As we saw, once the price setter has posted his price, demands are expressed, and this seller faces a constraint $\bar{s}_i$ that is equal to the sum of all other agents' demands:

$$\bar{s}_i = \sum_{j \neq i} \tilde{d}_j = \tilde{D}_i \qquad (19)$$

If we consider the market *before* seller i sets his price P_i, we see that he does not, contrarily to a price taker, consider his quantity constraint $\bar{s}_i$ as parametric. Rather, we have, in view of (19):

$$\bar{s}_i = \bar{s}_i(P_i) = \tilde{D}_i(P_i) \qquad (20)$$

How do we compute the demand $\tilde{D}_i(P_i)$? It turns out that a rigorous derivation of an "objective demand curve" in a multimarket setting requires a sophisticated general equilibrium argument.[6] We do not go into the complexities of a full general equilibrium definition of objective demand, but rather give a simple example, based on Dixit and Stiglitz (1977), which has become a workhorse for many macroeconomic models and we will be using repeatedly in this book. As we shall see, it leads to simple isoelastic demand curves, and this allows us to shortcut many computations.

Let us assume that final output Y is produced via a continuum of intermediate goods Y_i indexed by $i \in [0, 1]$. The production function is CES (see appendix 1.1):

$$Y = \left(\int_0^1 Y_i^\eta \right)^{1/\eta} \qquad 0 < \eta < 1 \qquad (21)$$

---

5. Alternatives are, for example, prices determined by the demanders (monopsony), or prices bargained between the two sides of the market.

6. Such general equilibrium constructions have been proposed, following the seminal article by Negishi (1961), by Gabszewicz and Vial (1972) for Cournotian quantity games, and Bénassy (1988, 1990) for price games. See Bénassy (2002b) for explicit macroeconomic applications.

Let P be the price of output and P_i the price of intermediate good i. The firms producing Y maximize their profit:

$$PY - \int_0^1 P_i Y_i \tag{22}$$

subject to the production function (21). The result of this maximization is:

$$\tilde{D}_i(P_i) = Y_i = Y\left(\frac{P_i}{P}\right)^{-1/(1-\eta)} \tag{23}$$

We may note here that although each firm i appears as a "monopolist" on its market, this does not mean necessarily that it has much market power. Indeed, the elasticity of this demand curve is $-1/(1-\eta)$, so if η is close to 1 the demand curve will be extremely elastic and the outcome close to the competitive one.

Price Making

Once the demand curve is known, price setting proceeds along lines that are traditional in imperfect competition theories: the price setter maximizes his profits subject to the constraint that his sales can be no greater than the amount given by the demand curve on the markets he controls.

For example, consider a firm i with a cost function $\mathcal{C}_i(Y_i)$, and assume that it faces a demand curve $\tilde{D}_i(P_i)$. The program giving the optimal price and production of the firm is thus simply written:

$$\text{Maximize } P_i Y_i - \mathcal{C}_i(Y_i) \quad \text{s.t.}$$

$$Y_i \leq \tilde{D}_i(P_i)$$

To solve this, we first note that the price setter will always choose a combination of P_i and Y_i such that he is "on" the demand curve, that is, such that $Y_i = \tilde{D}_i(P_i)$. If he were not, he could increase the price P_i without modifying Y_i, thus increasing his profits. So the solution is first characterized by:

$$Y_i = \tilde{D}_i(P_i) \tag{24}$$

Inserting (24) into the expression of profits and maximizing, we obtain the first-order condition

$$\mathcal{C}'_i(Y_i) = \frac{\epsilon(P_i) - 1}{\epsilon(P_i)} P_i \tag{25}$$

where:

$$\epsilon(P_i) = -\frac{\partial Log \tilde{D}_i(P_i)}{\partial Log P_i} > 0 \qquad (26)$$

If the demand curve has the form (23), then $\epsilon(P_i) = 1/(1-\eta)$, and equation (25) further simplifies as:

$$C'_i(Y_i) = \eta P_i \qquad (27)$$

Both equations (25) and (27) are the well-known "marginal cost equals marginal revenue" condition, in which we see that the firm will choose a price high enough that it will not only want to serve the actual demand but even be willing to serve more demand at the price it has chosen. In fact, the firm would be happy to meet demand up to the level $C'^{-1}_i(P_i)$, which, in view of (25) or (27), is bigger than actual production Y_i. Thus, there is in our sense an "excess supply" of the good, although this excess supply is fully voluntary on the part of the price setter.

The imperfectly competitive price and production are determined by equations (24) and (25). They are drawn together in figure 5.3, where $\tilde{S}_i(P_i) = C'^{-1}_i(P_i)$ is the "competitive" supply of the firm. The resulting equilibrium corresponds to point M (like "monopolistic competition").

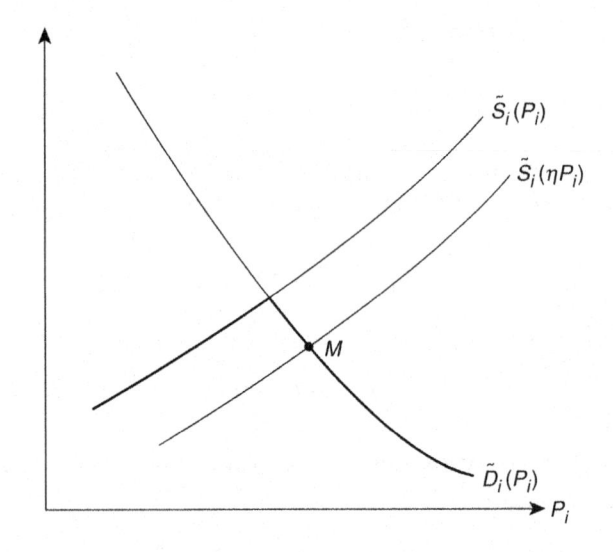

Figure 5.3 The imperfect competition equilibrium

Figure 5.3 also shows the "fixprice allocations" given by the minimum of supply and demand, that is,

$$Y_i = \min\left[\widetilde{D}_i(P_i), \widetilde{S}_i(P_i)\right] \tag{28}$$

This is represented by the heavy line in figure 5.3. In this figure we see that the imperfectly competitive solution corresponds to one of the "fixprice" points, and one that is in the excess supply zone.

5.4 A Macroeconomic Example

We now show in this section how the concepts just described can be used to construct a wide variety of macroeconomic models. We consider a simple economy and study successively equilibria of this economy under the following assumptions on price and wage formation: (1) Walrasian equilibrium, (2) rigid prices and wages, and (3) imperfect competition in the goods and labor markets.

We will learn that both employment and output determination, as well as the effects of economic policies, can be very different, depending not only on the pricing scheme but even, for a given pricing scheme, on which endogenously determined regime the economy will be in. All these models are studied in the framework of the same economy, which we now describe.

5.4.1 The Economy

We consider a very simple dynamic monetary economy of the type that was pioneered by Samuelson (1958), and that we described in chapter 4 (section 4.4). The households in this economy live two periods each, so that in each period coexist young and old households.

There are three goods—output, labor, and money—and in each period two markets where output and labor are exchanged against money at the price P_t and wage W_t, respectively. We assume that these markets are frictionless so that transactions in each market are equal to the minimum of supply and demand. We denote by Y_t and L_t, respectively, the output and labor transactions.

There are firms, households, and the government. The aggregate firm has a strictly concave production function:

$$Y_t = F(L_t) \qquad F'(L_t) > 0 \qquad F''(L_t) < 0 \tag{29}$$

The firm maximizes profits $\Pi_t = P_t Y_t - W_t L_t$. These profits are redistributed to the young households.

Households work L_t and consume C_{1t} in the first period of their life. They save a quantity of money M_t, which they spend in the second period to consume C_{2t+1}. Accordingly, their budget constraints for the two periods are:

$$P_t C_{1t} + M_t = W_t L_t + \Pi_t - P_t T_t \tag{30}$$

$$P_{t+1} C_{2t+1} = M_t \tag{31}$$

where T_t is the real value of taxes levied by the government. Households have the simple utility function:

$$Log C_{1t} + \beta Log C_{2t+1} - \Gamma(L_t) \tag{32}$$

where $\Gamma(L_t)$ is the disutility of labor, with

$$\Gamma'(L_t) > 0 \qquad \Gamma''(L_t) > 0 \tag{33}$$

Using equation (31), we will actually use utility function (32) under the following form, where the variables of choice pertain to period t:

$$Log C_{1t} + \beta Log(M_t/P_{t+1}) - \Gamma(L_t) \tag{34}$$

Finally, the government has a demand for output G_t and, as already seen, taxes an amount T_t in real terms from the household. As a consequence its budget constraint is

$$M_t - M_{t-1} = P_t(G_t - T_t) \tag{35}$$

We can describe government policy by any two of the three variables G_t, T_t, and M_t, the third one being deduced through the government budget constraint (35).

5.4.2 Walrasian Equilibrium

We derive as a benchmark the Walrasian equilibrium of this economy. We begin by computing the Walrasian demands and supplies in the output and labor markets. Maximization of the firm's profits under the production function $F(L)$ yields labor demand and output supply:

$$L_t^d = F'^{-1}\left(\frac{W_t}{P_t}\right) \tag{36}$$

$$Y_t^s = F\left[F'^{-1}\left(\frac{W_t}{P_t}\right)\right] \tag{37}$$

The old household simply spends the quantity of money M_{t-1} carried from the previous period:

$$C_{2t} = \frac{M_{t-1}}{P_t} \tag{38}$$

Maximization of the young household's utility function (34), subject to the budget constraint (30), yields the first-order conditions for consumption and labor, respectively:

$$M_t = \beta P_t C_{1t} \tag{39}$$

$$\Gamma'(L_t) = \frac{\beta W_t}{M_t} \tag{40}$$

We also have the equilibrium condition on the goods market:

$$Y_t = C_t + G_t = C_{1t} + C_{2t} + G_t \tag{41}$$

Combining equations (36) to (41), we find that the values of L_t, Y_t, P_t, and W_t in Walrasian equilibrium (when it exists) are given by:

$$(1+\beta)F'(L_t) = [F(L_t) - T_t]\Gamma'(L_t) \tag{42}$$

$$Y_t = F(L_t) \tag{43}$$

$$\frac{W_t}{P_t} = F'(L_t) \tag{44}$$

$$P_t = \frac{(1+\beta)M_{t-1}}{\beta(Y_t - G_t) + T_t - G_t} \tag{45}$$

From (45) we see that a necessary condition for the existence of a Walrasian equilibrium is:

$$G_t < \frac{\beta Y_t + T_t}{1+\beta} \tag{46}$$

where $Y_t = F(L_t)$ and L_t is the solution of (42). This condition says that the real spending of the government must not be too high. From (41), (42), and (43) we deduce:

$$\frac{\partial Y_t}{\partial G_t} = 0 \qquad \frac{\partial C_t}{\partial G_t} = -1 \qquad (47)$$

So there is a 100 percent crowding out of private consumption by government expenditures. Now from (42) and (43) we can also compute:

$$\frac{\partial L_t}{\partial T_t} > 0 \qquad \frac{\partial Y_t}{\partial T_t} > 0 \qquad (48)$$

The intuition for this result is that an increase in taxes makes the household poorer. Consequently, it consumes less leisure, and thus, other things equal, works more. As a result, labor and output increase.

5.4.3 Fixprice-fixwage Equilibria

We now turn to the model under the assumption, polar to that of the Walrasian model, that the price P_t and wage W_t are completely rigid in the period considered.[7] A remarkable feature of such models is that they endogenously produce multiple regimes. As is well known, this model has three possible regimes, most often called:[8]

- Keynesian unemployment, with excess supply of both output and labor.
- Classical unemployment, with excess supply of labor and excess demand for goods.
- Suppressed inflation, with excess demand for both labor and output.

We consider these three regimes in turn.

Keynesian Unemployment

The Keynesian regime exhibits excess supply in both markets. In particular, the young household faces a binding constraint $\bar{L}_t$ in the labor market,

---

7. This fixprice model was first proposed by Barro and Grossman (1971, 1976). An early precursor is Solow and Stiglitz (1968). The adaptation in this section borrows from Bénassy (1977, 1990, 2002b).
8. The classical-Keynesian distinction is due to Hunt and Sherman (1972).

so that its effective consumption demand $\tilde{C}_{1t}$ is the solution in C_{1t} of the following program:

$$\text{Maximize } LogC_{1t} + \beta Log(M_t/P_{t+1}) - \Gamma(L_t) \quad \text{s.t.}$$

$$P_t C_t + M_t = W_t L_t + \Pi_t - P_t T_t$$

$$L_t \leq \overline{L}_t$$

Because the second constraint is binding in this Keynesian regime, this yields:

$$\tilde{C}_{1t} = \frac{1}{1+\beta}\left(\frac{W_t \overline{L}_t + \Pi_t - P_t T_t}{P_t}\right) \tag{49}$$

Equation (49) can be rewritten, since $\overline{L}_t$ is equal to the actual sale of labor L_t, and $\Pi_t = P_t Y_t - W_t L_t$:

$$\tilde{C}_{1t} = \frac{Y_t - T_t}{1+\beta} \tag{50}$$

This is a standard Keynesian consumption function, with a propensity to consume equal to $1/(1+\beta)$. Because there is excess supply on the goods market, output Y_t is equal to total output demand:

$$Y_t = C_{1t} + C_{2t} + G_t = \frac{Y_t - T_t}{1+\beta} + \frac{M_{t-1}}{P_t} + G_t \tag{51}$$

This equation yields a "Keynesian" level of output:

$$Y_t = \frac{1+\beta}{\beta}\left(\frac{M_{t-1}}{P_t} + G_t - \frac{T_t}{1+\beta}\right) = Y_{kt} \tag{52}$$

We recognize in (52) a traditional Keynesian multiplier formula where $(1+\beta)/\beta$ is the multiplier and the term in parentheses is the so-called autonomous demand. This multiplier results from the interaction of two effects. First, in view of the employment function (equation 18), more demand for goods creates a higher demand for labor. Second, in view of the consumption function (49), more demand for labor results in a higher demand for goods. The compounding of these two mutually reinforcing effects will multiply autonomous demand variations.

Labor transactions are equal to the firm's labor demand, itself equal to the quantity of labor necessary to produce Y_{kt}:

$$L_t = F^{-1}(Y_{kt}) = L_{kt} \tag{53}$$

We can also compute total private consumption $C_t = C_{1t} + C_{2t} = Y_t - G_t$:

$$C_t = \frac{1+\beta}{\beta}\left(\frac{M_{t-1}}{P_t} + \frac{G_t - T_t}{1+\beta}\right) \tag{54}$$

We note that production, employment, and private consumption are increased by decreases in taxes or increases in government spending. The traditional results of Keynesian multiplier analysis are thus fully valid in this regime.

Perhaps the most striking property of the Keynesian equilibrium is that an increase in government spending *increases* private consumption (formula 54). Unlike in the Walrasian equilibrium, there is thus no crowding out; quite on the contrary: although the government collects real output from the private sector, more of it is available for private consumption. This is a remarkable by-product of the inefficiency of the Keynesian multiplier state.

Classical Unemployment

In this case there is an excess supply of labor and an excess demand for goods. The firm is thus on the short side in both markets, so it is able to carry out its Walrasian plan, so that:

$$L_t = F'^{-1}(W_t/P_t) = L_{ct} \tag{55}$$

$$Y_t = F[F'^{-1}(W_t/P_t)] = Y_{ct} \tag{56}$$

We immediately see that Keynesian policies have no impact on employment and production. In fact, it is easy to check that the main effect of a Keynesian policy would be to aggravate excess demand on the goods market. The only thing that affects employment and production is the level of real wages. This validates the classical view that there is unemployment because "real wages are too high."

Suppressed Inflation

In this regime, there is excess demand in both markets.[9] In particular, since there is excess demand for labor, the consumer's first-order condition on the labor market (40) is satisfied, that is:

$$\Gamma'(L_t) = \frac{\beta W_t}{M_t} \tag{57}$$

Since $M_t = M_{t-1} + P_t G_t - P_t T_t$, the corresponding quantity of labor, which we denote as L_{it}, is given by:

$$\Gamma'(L_{it}) = \frac{\beta W_t}{M_{t-1} + P_t G_t - P_t T_t} \tag{58}$$

The corresponding output, denoted Y_{it}, is what can be produced with available labor supply, namely:

$$Y_{it} = F(L_{it}) \tag{59}$$

We may note that in this regime the economic policy variables have effects completely opposite to those in the Keynesian regime. In particular, increases in government spending *diminish* employment and production, whereas higher taxes increase production!

The Complete Picture

As we have seen, the three regimes of our model display strikingly different properties concerning the determination of employment and production and the economy's response to policy variables. It is therefore important to know for which values of the exogenous parameters M_{t-1}, P_t, W_t, G_t, and T_t the three regimes obtain. We can easily check that the nature of the regime and the resulting level of output and employment are determined by finding the lowest of the three possible output levels computed above (equations 52, 56, and 59), that is,

$$Y_t = \min(Y_{kt}, Y_{ct}, Y_{it}) \tag{60}$$

The separation of these three regimes involves five parameters, M_{t-1}, P_t, W_t, G_t, and T_t. It turns out that if we take $T_t = 0$, we can represent

---

9. Clearly this regime is not very realistic for free market economies. But it was useful to explain the functioning of some centrally planned economies (Portes, 1981).

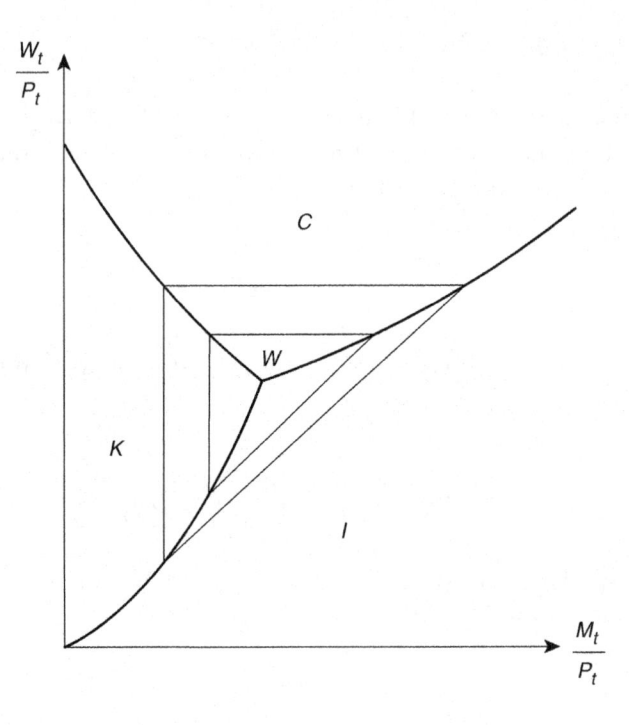

Figure 5.4 The three regimes

everything as a function of only two synthetic parameters, M_t/P_t and W_t/P_t. This is done in figure 5.4. The triangles are iso-employment or iso-output lines. The highest level of employment and production occurs at W, the Walrasian equilibrium point. Region K corresponds to Keynesian unemployment, region C to classical unemployment, and region I to suppressed inflation.

In figure 5.4 we see that even if the real wage is "right" (that is, equal to its Walrasian equilibrium level, which corresponds to the horizontal line going through W), we may have inefficiently low values of employment and output due to insufficient or excessive demand in the output market.

Inefficiency Properties

We now highlight in this particular macroeconomic example a remarkable inefficiency property of multiplier equilibria, namely, that there can be Pareto improving trades at the *given* price system.[10] We will now verify this fact in the regime of Keynesian unemployment.

---

10. See notably Bénassy (1975, 1990) for general statements.

So assume that we are in the interior of the Keynesian regime. Since $L_{kt} < L_{ct}$, we have:

$$F'(L_t) < \frac{W_t}{P_t} \tag{61}$$

so the firm could increase its real profit by directly buying labor for output. Consider the household. Because it is unconstrained in the goods market and constrained on the labor market, we have

$$\frac{1}{P_t}\frac{\partial U}{\partial C_{1t}} = \frac{\partial U}{\partial M_t} > -\frac{1}{W_t}\frac{\partial U}{\partial L_t} \tag{62}$$

so that the household would also gain in directly selling labor for output.

So both the firm and household would strictly gain in exchanging directly output for labor. Nevertheless, this simple Pareto-improving trade remains unattained in equilibrium. This striking inefficiency explains the surprising effects of Keynesian policies that we already saw.

5.4.4 An Imperfectly Competitive Model

We will now endogenize prices and wages in a framework of imperfect competition. We assume that firms set prices and that households set wages.[11]

The Equilibrium

To characterize the equilibrium, we successively consider the optimal actions of the firm and household. Consider first the firm, and assume that it faces demand curves of the form:

$$\xi_t P_t^{-1/(1-\eta)} \qquad 0 < \eta < 1 \tag{63}$$

where ξ_t is a variable "position" parameter (note that we derived a demand curve of this type in section 5.3.4). The optimal actions of the firm are given

---

11. This model is adapted from Bénassy (1977, 1987, 1990, 2002b). Models of the same type can be found in Negishi (1977, 1979), Hart (1982), Snower (1983), Weitzman (1985), Blanchard and Kiyotaki (1987), Dixon (1987), Sneessens (1987), Jacobsen and Schultz (1990), and several others. The field is surveyed in Silvestre (1993, 1995), Dixon and Rankin (1994).

by the program:

$$\text{Maximize } P_t Y_t - W_t L_t \quad \text{s.t.}$$

$$Y_t = F(L_t)$$

$$Y_t \leq \xi_t P_t^{-1/(1-\eta)}$$

The first-order conditions for this program yield:

$$\frac{W_t}{P_t} = \eta F'(L_t) \tag{64}$$

We may note that due to the isoelastic demand curve, ξ_t disappears from this first-order condition. Suppose that the household similarly faces demand curves for labor of the form:

$$\zeta_t W_t^{-1/(1-\chi)} \qquad 0 < \chi < 1 \tag{65}$$

where ζ_t is a position parameter. The program yielding the household's optimal decisions is

$$\text{Maximize } Log C_{1t} + \beta Log(M_t/P_{t+1}) - \Gamma(L_t) \quad \text{s.t.}$$

$$P_t C_{1t} + M_t = W_t L_t + \Pi_t - P_t T_t$$

$$L_t \leq \zeta_t W_t^{-1/(1-\chi)}$$

The first-order conditions for consumption and labor are respectively:

$$M_t = \beta P_t C_{1t} \tag{66}$$

$$\Gamma'(L_t) = \frac{\beta \chi W_t}{M_t} \tag{67}$$

To complete the model, we add to the first-order conditions (64), (66), and (67) four equations that hold in all versions of the model. These are the production function:

$$Y_t = F(L_t) \tag{68}$$

the budget constraint of the young household:

$$P_t C_{1t} + M_t = W_t L_t + \Pi_t - P_t T_t \tag{69}$$

the consumption of the old:

$$C_{2t} = \frac{M_{t-1}}{P_t} \tag{70}$$

and the equality between production and total demand:

$$Y_t = C_{1t} + C_{2t} + G_t \tag{71}$$

Solving the system of equations (64) and (66) to (71), we find that the values of Y_t, L_t, P_t, and W_t in equilibrium (when it exists) are given by:

$$[F(L_t) - T_t]\Gamma'(L_t) = \chi\eta(1+\beta)F'(L_t) \tag{72}$$

$$Y_t = F(L_t) \tag{73}$$

$$\frac{W_t}{P_t} = \eta F'(L_t) \tag{74}$$

$$P_t = \frac{(1+\beta)M_{t-1}}{\beta(Y_t - G_t) + T_t - G_t} \tag{75}$$

We may first note that the Walrasian equilibrium is a particular limit case of this equilibrium when both η and χ go to 1 (compare equations 42–45 and equations 72–75), that is when the demand curves (63) and (65) become infinitely elastic, as one would naturally expect.

Properties of the Equilibrium

We can first remark that the allocation in our imperfectly competitive equilibrium has, at first sight, properties similar to those of a Keynesian allocation, as described in section 5.3.3, and notably that we are somehow in a general excess supply regime. Indeed, equation (64) shows that the firm would be willing, at the equilibrium price and wage, to produce and sell more goods if the demand was forthcoming. Similarly equation (67) shows that the household would like to sell more labor at the going price and wage if there was more demand for it. In figure 5.4 the equilibrium values of W_t and P_t would correspond to a point *within* region K. We will now see that this similarity does not extend to the effects of government policy.

Government Policy

We ask whether the Keynesian-style government policies that are successful in the regime of Keynesian unemployment are still as successful in this imperfectly competitive framework. We find that they are not.

Let us consider the effects of an increase in government spending G_t. From formulas (72) and (73) we see that it does not have any impact on Y_t and L_t, and therefore decreases consumption by 100 percent. There is full crowding out, and this is definitely not Keynesian.

If we consider an increase in taxes T_t, we see that it increases employment and production (formulas 72 and 73). This is the contrary of what happens in the Keynesian regime. The mechanism is actually the same as in Walrasian equilibrium: the household gets poorer, and therefore supplies more labor.

One may wonder why some authors thought they had found in such models a foundation for the Keynesian multiplier. The reason is simple: they usually studied a model with balanced budget $T_t = G_t$. In such a case, output appears to be an increasing function of G_t (but in fact is an increasing function of T_t), hence the mistake.

All in all, we see that this model yields an allocation that has Keynesian inefficiency properties but reacts to government policy in a way somewhat similar to that of a Walrasian model.

Although highly simplified, the model of this section has shown us the potential richness of the approach outlined in section 4.3, because we can obtain within the *same* model results belonging to the Walrasian, Keynesian, and imperfect competition paradigms, and still a few others, as we shall see in the next section and appendix 5.2.

5.5 Shocks and Correlations

To describe the concepts in the simplest manner, we concentrated in the previous section on a purely deterministic version of our simple macroeconomic model. On the other hand, an important aspect of modern macroeconomics is to describe how various variables in the economy react to exogenous shocks and evaluate the correlations between endogenous variables arising from such shocks.

To study this issue, we consider a simplified version of the model of the previous section, to which we add some stochastic shocks. This will allow us to compute both the economy's response to these shocks and some resulting correlations. We will see that these may be dramatically different depending not only on the price-wage formation scheme, but even, under the same scheme, on the regime the economy is in.

Of course, we will not try to study all possible situations exhaustively, but rather concentrate on a few examples where the differences are particularly striking. We successively consider the fixprice version of the model, as well as two versions not yet studied: one with rigid wages and flexible prices, the other with rigid prices and flexible wages.

5.5.1 The Model

We first take particular specifications for the utility and production functions:

$$U_t = LogC_{1t} + \beta LogC_{2t+1} - \frac{L_t^{1+\nu}}{1+\nu} \qquad \nu > 0 \tag{76}$$

$$Y_t = A_t L_t^{1-\alpha} \tag{77}$$

where A_t is a stochastic technology shock. Second, we assume that $T_t = 0$, so that the evolution of the quantity of money is given by:

$$M_t = M_{t-1} + P_t G_t \tag{78}$$

and M_t is also a stochastic shock.

We study how the economy reacts to the shocks A_t and M_t in various situations, as well as some of the correlations this generates.

5.5.2 Fixprice-fixwage Equilibria

We begin our inquiry with the fixprice-fixwage version studied in section 5.4.3. We shall then move to alternative combinations of rigidities.

Equilibrium Output and Employment

Using formulas in section 5.4.3, we can compute output and employment in the Keynesian unemployment regime (formulas 52 and 53):

$$Y_{kt} = \frac{1+\beta}{\beta} \frac{M_t}{P_t} \qquad L_{kt} = \left(\frac{1+\beta}{\beta} \frac{M_t}{A_t P_t}\right)^{1/(1-\alpha)} \tag{79}$$

in the classical unemployment regime (formulas 55 and 56):

$$Y_{ct} = A_t^{1/\alpha} \left[\frac{(1-\alpha) P_t}{W_t}\right]^{(1-\alpha)/\alpha} \qquad L_{ct} = \left[\frac{(1-\alpha) A_t P_t}{W_t}\right]^{1/\alpha} \tag{80}$$

and finally in the repressed inflation regime (formulas 58 and 59):

$$Y_{it} = \left(\frac{\beta W_t}{\xi M_t}\right)^{1/\nu} \qquad L_{it} = A_t \left(\frac{\beta W_t}{\xi M_t}\right)^{(1-\alpha)/\nu} \qquad (81)$$

The Effects of Technology and Monetary Shocks

We now point out a few cases where the same shock has opposite effects depending on the regime.

We start with technology shocks. As we shall see, notably in chapter 10, an important issue of recent macroeconomics has been evaluate the impact of technology shocks on the economy.

If we look at formulas (79) and (80), we note a particularly striking result, since positive technology shocks have a negative impact on employment in the Keynesian regime but a positive impact on employment in the classical unemployment regime.

Moving to monetary shocks, we observe in formulas (79) and (81) that monetary shocks have a positive impact on employment and output in the Keynesian unemployment regime and a negative impact in the repressed inflation regime.

Many modern dynamic macroeconomic models are constructed as if there was a unique given price-wage scheme and, within this scheme, a unique "regime." What we just saw demonstrates that this can be quite misleading in some situations.

5.5.3 Alternative Rigidities

We now study two combinations of rigidity and flexibility that have been popular in recent research. The first is fixed wages combined with flexible prices; the second, fixed prices combined with flexible wages.

Fixed Wages, Flexible Prices

Assume that the wage W_t is fixed at the beginning of period t, before values of the shocks are revealed, and that the price P_t clears the goods market. We show in appendix 5.2 that employment, output, and the real wage are given by (we suppress all irrelevant constants):

$$L_t = \frac{M_t}{W_t} \tag{82}$$

$$Y_t = A_t \left(\frac{M_t}{W_t}\right)^{1-\alpha} \tag{83}$$

$$\frac{W_t}{P_t} = A_t \left(\frac{M_t}{W_t}\right)^{-\alpha} \tag{84}$$

Fixed Prices, Flexible Wages

Symmetrically assume that the price P_t is fixed at the beginning of period t before values of the shocks are revealed, and the wage W_t clears the labor market. Appendix 5.2 derives the values of output, employment and the real wage, again suppressing all irrelevant constants:

$$Y_t = \frac{M_t}{P_t} \tag{85}$$

$$L_t = \left(\frac{M_t}{A_t P_t}\right)^{1/(1-\alpha)} \tag{86}$$

$$\frac{W_t}{P_t} = A_t^{-\nu/(1-\alpha)} \left(\frac{M_t}{P_t}\right)^{(1-\alpha+\nu)/(1-\alpha)} \tag{87}$$

A Comparison

Here again we see that the effect of shocks can be totally different depending on the price-wage scheme. For example, a positive shock on money M_t has a negative effect on the real wage in the fixed-wage case, a positive one in the fixed-price case.

The same type of results can be found for some covariances and correlations. For example, the covariance between labor and the real wage is negative in the fixed-wage case, positive in the fixed-price case.

Appendix 5.1: Quantity Signals: An Example

We considered in the main text a particularly simple rationing scheme with only two agents. Here we present something a little more elaborate, a queue, and show how transactions and quantity signals are formed in that transaction process (for a more general theory, see, for example, Bénassy, 1990).

In a queueing system, the demanders (or the suppliers) are ranked in a predetermined order and served according to that order. Let there be n demanders ranked in the order $i = 1, \cdots, n$, each having a demand $\tilde{d}_i$, and a supplier, indexed by 0, who supplies $\tilde{s}_0$. When the turn of demander i comes, the maximum quantity he can obtain is what demanders before him (that is, agents $j < i$) have not taken, namely:

$$\tilde{s}_0 - \sum_{j<i} d_j = \max\left(0, \tilde{s}_0 - \sum_{j<i} \tilde{d}_j\right) \qquad (88)$$

The level of his purchase is simply the minimum of this quantity and his demand:

$$d_i = \min\left[\tilde{d}_i, \max\left(0, \tilde{s}_n - \sum_{j<i} \tilde{d}_j\right)\right] \qquad (89)$$

As for the supplier, he sells the minimum of his supply and of total demand:

$$s_0 = \min\left(\tilde{s}_0, \sum_{i=1}^{n} \tilde{d}_i\right) \qquad (90)$$

It is easy to verify that whatever the demands and supplies, aggregate purchases and sales always match.

Now it is clear that the rationing scheme represented by (89) and (90) can be represented as a function of quantity signals $\bar{d}_i$ and $\bar{s}_0$:

$$d_i = \min\left(\tilde{d}_i, \bar{d}_i\right) \qquad s_0 = \min\left(\tilde{s}_0, \bar{s}_0\right) \qquad (91)$$

with:

$$\bar{d}_i = \max\left(0, \tilde{s}_0 - \sum_{j<i} \tilde{d}_j\right) \qquad i = 1, \cdots, n \qquad (92)$$

$$\bar{s}_0 = \sum_{j=1}^{n} \tilde{d}_j \qquad (93)$$

As we indicated in section 3.2, each quantity signal is a function of the demands and supplies of the *other* agents.

Appendix 5.2: Alternative Rigidities

In the main body of this chapter we studied a few polar cases of price and wage rigidities. We consider here two additional intermediate schemes: rigid wages with flexible prices, and rigid prices with flexible wages.

The Model

We study the model of section 5.5. Let us recall the utility and production functions:

$$U_t = LogC_{1t} + \beta LogC_{2t+1} - \frac{L_t^{1+\nu}}{1+\nu} \qquad \nu > 0 \tag{94}$$

$$Y_t = A_t L_t^{1-\alpha} \tag{95}$$

where A_t is a stochastic technology shock. The other shock is the quantity of money M_t. We study this economy under two regimes: (1) fixed wages with flexible prices, and (2) fixed prices with flexible wages. We begin with a few equilibrium conditions.

Equilibrium Conditions

An equation will be valid in all situations, the production function:

$$Y_t = A_t L_t^{1-\alpha} \tag{96}$$

If the goods market clears, the real wage is equal to marginal productivity:

$$\frac{W_t}{P_t} = (1-\alpha) A_t L_t^{-\alpha} \tag{97}$$

Now the household solves the program:

$$\text{Maximize } LogC_{1t} + \beta Log(M_t/P_{t+1}) - \frac{L_t^{1+\nu}}{1+\nu} \qquad \text{s.t.}$$

$$P_t C_{1t} + M_t = W_t L_t + \Pi_t$$

The first-order conditions yield the two following relations:

$$\beta P_t Y_t = (1+\beta) M_t \tag{98}$$

$$\beta \frac{W_t}{M_t} = L_t^\nu \tag{99}$$

Fixed Wages, Flexible Prices

Assume that the wage W_t is fixed at the beginning of period t before values of the shocks are revealed, and that the price P_t clears the goods market. We further assume that labor demand is satisfied at the fixed wage. Condition (99) is not valid, but equations (96), (97), and (98) are valid. Solving the corresponding system, we find the equilibrium values of employment, output and the real wage:

$$L_t = \frac{(1-\alpha)(1+\beta)}{\beta} \frac{M_t}{W_t} \tag{100}$$

$$Y_t = A_t \left[\frac{(1-\alpha)(1+\beta)}{\beta} \frac{M_t}{W_t} \right]^{1-\alpha} \tag{101}$$

$$\frac{W_t}{P_t} = A_t (1-\alpha)^{1-\alpha} \left(\frac{1+\beta}{\beta} \frac{M_t}{W_t} \right)^{-\alpha} \tag{102}$$

Fixed Prices, Flexible Wages

Symmetrically assume that the price P_t is fixed at the beginning of period t before values of the shocks are revealed, and that the wage W_t clears the labor market. We assume that goods demand is satisfied at the fixed price. Condition (97) is thus not valid, but equations (96), (98), and (99) are still valid. Solving the corresponding system we find the values of output, employment, and the real wage:

$$Y_t = \frac{1+\beta}{\beta} \frac{M_t}{P_t} \tag{103}$$

$$L_t = \left(\frac{1+\beta}{\beta} \frac{M_t}{A_t P_t} \right)^{1/(1-\alpha)} \tag{104}$$

$$\frac{W_t}{P_t} = \frac{\xi}{\beta} \left(\frac{1+\beta}{\beta} \right)^{\nu/(1-\alpha)} A_t^{-\nu/(1-\alpha)} \left(\frac{M_t}{P_t} \right)^{(1-\alpha+\nu)/(1-\alpha)} \tag{105}$$

Problems

Problem 5.1: Aggregation and Market Frictions

We consider a good that is sold at the same price p in a multiplicity of spatially separated micromarkets (one may think for example of the market for newspapers). The average demand and supply in each micromarket are:

$$D(p) = A - Bp$$

$$S(p) = Cp$$

In the absence of any perturbation, the Walrasian price and transaction would be in each of the micromarkets:

$$p^* = \frac{A}{B+C} \qquad Y^* = \frac{AC}{B+C}$$

We assume that the demand on each micromarket is subject to a stochastic demand shock ω, where ω is uniformly distributed on the interval $[-\sigma, \sigma]$. Each micromarket is frictionless, so the transaction $\tau(p, \omega)$ on the market hit by the shock ω is equal to the minimum of supply and demand on the micromarket:

$$\tau(p, \omega) = \min(A - Bp + \omega, Cp)$$

Aggregate transactions are the sum of all transactions on the micromarkets:

$$T(p) = \frac{1}{2\sigma} \int_{-\sigma}^{\sigma} \tau(p, \omega) \, d\omega$$

1. Show that there is a minimum and maximum prices, p_m and p_M such that:

$$p \leq p_m \implies T(p) = Cp$$
$$p \geq p_M \implies T(p) = A - Bp$$

2. Compute the aggregate transactions $T(p)$ for $p_m < p < p_M$ and show that in that case:

$$T(p) < \min(A - Bp, Cp)$$

Problem 5.2: Multiple Regimes and Asymmetric Price Flexibility

Although this may have been a realistic feature for some planned economies, a somewhat unappealing aspect of the fixprice model of section 5.4.3 is that in some regimes consumers are rationed on the goods market. We can obtain a similar model with multiple regimes while totally eliminating consumer rationing. To obtain this, instead of assuming full price and wage rigidity, we assume that the price and the real wage are rigid downwards, but flexible upward:

$$P_t \geq \bar{P}_t \qquad \frac{W_t}{P_t} \geq \omega_t$$

The rest of the assumptions are the same. Firms have a production function:

$$Y_t = F(L_t) \qquad F'(L_t) > 0 \qquad F''(L_t) < 0$$

and households a utility function:

$$LogC_{1t} + \beta LogC_{2t+1} - \Gamma(L_t)$$

The government has a demand for output G_t and taxes an amount T_t in real terms.

As a consequence of our assumption on asymmetric price flexibility we now have three regimes: (a) excess supply on the two markets; (b) excess supply on the labor market, and the goods market cleared; (c) both markets cleared.

1. Compute the level of output and employment in each of the three regimes.
2. What are the effects of government policies in each of the regimes?

Problem 5.3: Market Power and Welfare

One would usually think that if a group has market power, an increase in this market power will increase the welfare of the group. We now construct a model similar to that of section 5.4.4 and find a surprising relation between workers' market power in the labor market and their welfare.

We use the model of section 5.4.4, taking $G_t = T_t = 0$, because government is not involved in the results. Workers-consumers work L_t, consume C_{1t} and C_{2t+1}, and their utility function is (formula 32):

$$U_t = LogC_{1t} + \beta LogC_{2t+1} - \Gamma(L_t)$$

Their first-period budget constraint is:

$$P_t C_{1t} + M_t = W_t L_t + \Pi_t$$

where M_t is monetary savings.

Recall that the demand function for labor $\xi_t P_t^{-1/(1-\chi)}$ has elasticity $-1/(1-\chi)$, so that $1/\chi$ can be taken as an index of the market power of workers on the labor market.

1. Compute the value of employment in the imperfectly competitive equilibrium.
2. Compute the utility of workers.
3. Show that workers' welfare is inversely related to their market power, i.e.

$$\frac{\partial U}{\partial \chi} > 0$$

6

Uncertainty and Financial Assets

6.1 Introduction

Most economic decisions are taken in uncertain environments. In this chapter we study how to model individual choices when agents are faced with uncertain events, now or in the future. We then examine a number of concepts that extend the traditional Walrasian equilibrium concepts to situations of uncertainty. We finally indicate the role of financial assets and show how they are priced in various institutional contexts.

Section 6.2 exposes the traditional expected utility maximization theory and presents a few concepts of risk aversion. Section 6.3 moves to a situation of general equilibrium with many agents and presents the most classic model of general equilibrium under uncertainty, the Arrow-Debreu model. This is also called a model with "complete markets" because it allows agents to exchange economic goods conditionally on any possible event, in a sense that will be made clear.

The Arrow-Debreu model implies an unrealistically high number of markets. Section 6.4 moves to models of "incomplete markets." We give a general definition of financial securities. We then describe the difference between complete and incomplete markets.

Section 6.5 gives a first example of theories of asset pricing. It considers a benchmark model in which the complete and incomplete markets equilibria yield the same allocations and shows how to price a financial asset in both cases.

Section 6.6 uses the pricing formulas to compare safe and risky assets. It derives the riskless rate, as well as the "risk premium" on risky securities. Up to section 6.6 we use the traditional expected utility model. It turns out that in such models a confusion often arises between risk aversion measures and parameters depicting intertemporal substitution. In section 6.7 we expose the problem, and show a possible answer, the so-called nonexpected utility. As an example and application, we generalize an asset pricing formula to such a nonexpected utility framework.

6.2 Choice Under Uncertainty and Risk Aversion

In this section we study the behavior of an agent who has to take decisions under uncertainty. Uncertainty is represented by "states of nature"[1] indexed by $s \in S$. The set S can be discrete or continuous. For example, there may be two states of nature, respectively, "it rains" and "it does not rain." The same "physical" good will be a different economic good depending on the state of nature under which it is consumed. For example, an umbrella will obviously yield different utility depending on whether it rains or not.

The probability of state of nature s is π_s, with:

$$\sum_{s \in S} \pi_s = 1 \qquad (1)$$

The agent has to rank uncertain outcomes represented by a random variable x. The value of this variable x when the state of nature is s is denoted x_s.

6.2.1 Expected Utility

The expected utility hypothesis says that there exists a utility function $U(x)$ such that the agent's choices over various stochastic outcomes corresponds to maximizing the expected utility of these outcomes (Von Neumann and Morgenstern, 1944), that is, to maximizing the quantity:

$$\sum_{s \in S} \pi_s U(x_s) \qquad (2)$$

One says that the agent is *risk neutral* if the expected utility of the agent depends only on the mean $E(x_s)$ and not at all on the distribution of

---

1. These are also sometimes called "states of the world" or "events" in the literature.

the x_s:

$$E\left[U\left(x_s\right)\right] = U\left[E\left(x_s\right)\right] \tag{3}$$

This will occur if the function U is linear in x. Now a contrario, we say that the agent displays *risk aversion* if:

$$E\left[U\left(x_s\right)\right] < U\left[E\left(x_s\right)\right] \tag{4}$$

This notably occurs if the function U is concave.

6.2.2 Measures of Risk Aversion

Economists have sought to measure the degree of risk aversion by quantifying, for example, the trade-off between the mean and the variance. We describe a few concepts and measures, notably associated to the names of Pratt (1964) and Arrow (1971).

Imagine the following experiment: starting from a deterministic value x, one adds a random variable ε of mean 0 and variance σ^2:

$$E\left(\varepsilon\right) = 0 \qquad E\left(\varepsilon^2\right) = \sigma^2 \tag{5}$$

The individual has the choice between the stochastic outcome $x + \varepsilon$ or a sure outcome $x - z$. The *absolute* risk premium z_a is defined by:

$$E\left[U\left(x+\varepsilon\right)\right] = U\left(x - z_a\right) \tag{6}$$

This premium z_a is thus the income the agent is willing to pay to get rid of the uncertainty. The more risk averse the agent is, the higher this risk premium.

We can relate the degree of risk aversion to characteristics of the utility function. Doing a second-degree development of the left-hand side of (6) for infinitesimal values of the variable ε, we find that:

$$z_a = -\frac{U''(x)}{U'(x)}\frac{\sigma^2}{2} \tag{7}$$

We can define the index of absolute risk aversion $\mathcal{R}_a$ (Pratt, 1964):

$$\mathcal{R}_a = -\frac{U''(x)}{U'(x)} \tag{8}$$

so that the index of absolute risk aversion and the risk premium are related by:

$$z_a = \mathcal{R}_a \frac{\sigma^2}{2} \qquad (9)$$

The following family of utility functions has constant absolute risk aversion (CARA):

$$U(x) = Ae^{-\lambda x} + B \qquad \mathcal{R}_a = \lambda \qquad (10)$$

Similarly, we can define a *relative* risk premium z_r by:

$$E\{U[x(1+\varepsilon)]\} = U[x(1-z_r)] \qquad (11)$$

and we find:

$$z_r = -\frac{xU''(x)}{U'(x)} \frac{\sigma^2}{2} \qquad (12)$$

The quantity:

$$\mathcal{R}_r = -\frac{xU''(x)}{U'(x)} \qquad (13)$$

is called the degree of relative risk aversion, and we have:

$$z_r = \mathcal{R}_r \frac{\sigma^2}{2} \qquad (14)$$

The following family of functions has constant relative risk aversion (CRRA):

$$U(x) = Ax^{1-\theta} + B \qquad \mathcal{R}_r = \theta \qquad (15)$$

$$U(x) = A Log x + B \qquad \mathcal{R}_r = 1 \qquad (16)$$

6.3 Equilibrium with Complete Markets

We now describe a very influential representation of general equilibrium under uncertainty, due to Arrow (1953, 1963) and Debreu (1959). This model traditionally serves as the central benchmark to which other concepts are compared.

6.3.1 The Model

We consider here a simple economy with only one "physical" good.[2] Agents are indexed by $i \in I$. As indicated, uncertainty is represented by states of nature $s \in S$. The probability of state s is π_s with:[3]

$$\sum_s \pi_s = 1 \quad \forall i \tag{17}$$

We denote by c_{is} the consumption of the good by agent i in state s. Agent i has a utility function $U_i(c_{is})$. He ranks various consumption bundles according to their expected utility:

$$\sum_s \pi_s U_i(c_{is}) \tag{18}$$

Finally agent i has an endowment y_{is} in state of nature s.

6.3.2 Complete Markets and the Arrow-Debreu Equilibrium

We start with a system of complete markets. By this we mean that each agent can buy the good *conditionally* on any state of nature that will occur. Accordingly there will be a price vector:

$$p = \{p_s \mid s \in S\} \tag{19}$$

The price p_s is the price paid for receiving one unit of the good if the state of nature s occurs, nothing in the other states of nature. The budget constraint of agent i is:

$$\sum_{s \in S} p_s c_{is} = \sum_{s \in S} p_s y_{is} \tag{20}$$

Agent i's program is to maximize utility (18) subject to the budget constraint (20), that is:

$$\text{Maximize} \sum_s \pi_s U_i(c_{is}) \quad \text{s.t.}$$

$$\sum_{s \in S} p_s c_{is} = \sum_{s \in S} p_s y_{is}$$

---

2. The more general case, where there are $H > 1$ physical goods, is treated in appendix 6.2.
3. We assume here that all agents have the same "objective" probability for state s. The Arrow-Debreu theory is actually more general and allows each agent i to have her own subjective probability π_{is} for state s. To make the change, it is enough to replace π_s with π_{is} in the expected utility of agent i (equation 18). For simplicity, we keep he notation π_s throughout.

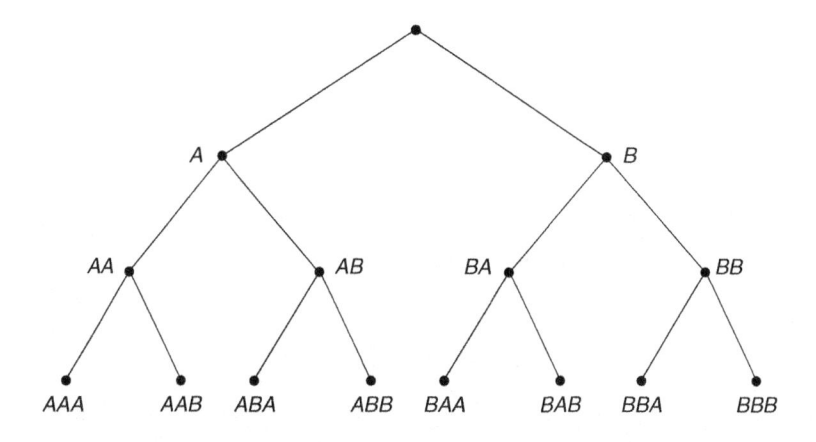

Figure 6.1 An event tree and the states of nature

This yields demand functions $c_{is}(p)$. An Arrow-Debreu equilibrium is characterized by a vector of prices p^* such that:

$$\sum_i c_{is}(p^*) = \sum_i y_{is} \qquad \forall s \qquad (21)$$

One may picture the equilibrium process as consisting of two stages. In the first stage, "at the beginning of times," all contingent markets are open and contracts for all contingent commodities are traded on these markets. In the second stage, the state of nature s is revealed, contracts are executed, and consumption takes place.

Of course, in reality there is no unique period in which all activity takes place and uncertainty is revealed. The theory generalizes naturally to a sequence of periods $1, \ldots T$. As time progresses from 1 to T, the full state of nature is progressively revealed, and transactions take place. Although notation becomes more complicated, the corresponding concept is essentially the same (Debreu, 1959).

The unfolding of dates and events looks somehow as in the event tree of figure 6.1. This figure shows a situation where in each of three successive periods an event A or B will occur randomly (one may think of flipping of a coin). At the end we have eight possible states of nature.

6.3.3 Insurance through Complete Markets

We now show on a particular example that the existence of complete markets may allow individual agents to be completely insured against their individual risks. In particular we show that if total resources are constant across states of nature, that is, if:

$$\sum_i y_{is} = Y_s = Y \quad \forall s \tag{22}$$

then each agent is fully insured against the variability of her income. Recall agent i's budget constraint is (equation 20):

$$\sum_s p_s c_{is} = \sum_s p_s y_{is} \tag{23}$$

and her utility:

$$\sum_s \pi_s U_i(c_{is}) \tag{24}$$

Agent i maximizes utility (24) subject to the budget constraint (23). Call λ_i the Lagrange multiplier of the budget constraint. The first-order conditions are:

$$\pi_s \frac{dU_i}{dc_{is}} = \lambda_i p_s \quad \forall i \quad \forall s \tag{25}$$

which can be rewritten:

$$c_{is} = C_i\left(\frac{\lambda_i p_s}{\pi_s}\right) \quad C_i = U_i'^{-1} \tag{26}$$

Summing these across agents we find:

$$\sum_i c_{is} = \sum_i C_i\left(\frac{\lambda_i p_s}{\pi_s}\right) = \sum_i y_{is} = Y_s \tag{27}$$

If Y_s is the same for all s, then p_s/π_s is the same for all states. Because prices are defined up to a multiplicative constant we can take:

$$p_s = \pi_s \tag{28}$$

This means from (26) that c_{is} is independent of the state of nature:

$$c_{is} = c_i \quad \forall s \tag{29}$$

Agent i is fully insured. We can compute agent i's (constant) consumption by combining (23) and (29):

$$c_{is} = c_i = \sum_s \pi_s y_{is} \qquad (30)$$

With constant aggregate income, each agent is fully insured. If aggregate income Y_s is not constant across states, full insurance will not occur, but the agents' consumptions will usually be less volatile than their incomes.

6.4 Complete versus Incomplete Markets

Of course, a complete set of financial markets, as we assumed in the previous section, is rather unrealistic, and reality is characterized by a situation of *incomplete markets*. In such a situation the agents have access to various securities, whose number is typically inferior to the number S of states of nature.

6.4.1 Securities

A security j is defined as a financial asset that gives a specified amount of money Z_s^j for every state of nature s, that is, it is defined by an array:

$$\left(Z_1^j, \ldots, Z_s^j, \ldots, Z_S^j \right) \qquad (31)$$

Assume that there are J securities indexed by $j \in \{1, \ldots, J\}$. The characteristics of these securities are summarized in the *payoff matrix* (table 6.1):

$$\begin{bmatrix} Z_1^1 & .. & Z_s^1 & .. & Z_S^1 \\ Z_1^j & .. & Z_s^j & .. & Z_S^j \\ Z_1^J & .. & Z_s^J & .. & Z_S^J \end{bmatrix}$$

Table 6.1: A payoff matrix

As an example, in the Arrow-Debreu world of the previous section, there are $J = S$ "Arrow securities", which yield one unit of money in state s

and nothing in the others, so that the payoff matrix is particularly simple (table 6.2).

$$\begin{bmatrix} 1 & 0 & 0 & 0 \\ 0 & 1 & 0 & 0 \\ 0 & 0 & 1 & 0 \\ 0 & 0 & 0 & 1 \end{bmatrix}$$

Table 6.2: The payoff matrix: Arrow securities

Let us denote Q^j as the price of security j. That security can be alternatively described by its rates of return in every state, that is, by an array:

$$\left(R_1^j, \ldots, R_s^j, \ldots, R_S^j\right) \quad (32)$$

with:

$$R_s^j = \frac{Z_s^j}{Q^j} \quad (33)$$

Let us give another example that we will use shortly, that of a safe bond, which gives the *same* payment (which we normalize to 1) in every state of nature. The array of payments for such a bond is:

$$(1, \ldots, 1, \ldots, 1) \quad (34)$$

If the price of this bond is Q, the gross rate of return is $R = 1/Q$.

6.4.2 Complete and Incomplete Markets

We say that markets are *complete* if one can, by adequate combination of all available assets, reproduce the full set of Arrow securities. For example, if there are two states of nature and two securities with returns:

$$(a, b) \quad \text{and} \quad (c, d) \quad (35)$$

The markets are complete if:

$$ad - bc \neq 0 \quad (36)$$

because indeed, we have the following linear combinations:

$$(1, 0) = \frac{d}{ad - bc}(a, b) - \frac{b}{ad - bc}(c, d) \quad (37)$$

$$(0,1) = -\frac{c}{ad-bc}(a,b) + \frac{a}{ad-bc}(c,d) \qquad (38)$$

Otherwise the markets are called *incomplete*. We may note that $ad - bc$ is the determinant of the payoff matrix. In general if $J = S$, the condition for complete markets is that the determinant of the payoff matrix be different from zero.

An example of incomplete markets, which we study shortly, is that where the only available asset is either the safe bond of formula (34), or a more general financial security, such as (31).

6.5 Asset Pricing: A Benchmark Case

We now turn to the problem of the pricing of financial assets in both complete or incomplete markets settings. To make the exposition particularly simple, we start with a special benchmark case where the two equilibria yield the same allocation.[4]

The model has two periods. In the first period, all agents have a sure income Y_0. In the second period, a state of nature $s \in S$ occurs with probability π_s, and all agents have the same income Y_s in state s. They also have the same utility:

$$U(C_0) + \beta \sum_s \pi_s U(C_s) \qquad (39)$$

We want to find the price Q in the first period of a security that will deliver in the second period an array of payments:

$$(Z_1, \ldots, Z_s, \ldots, Z_S) \qquad (40)$$

6.5.1 The Complete Markets Case

To find the value of the security (40), we first determine the value of Arrow securities and then find the price of (40) as a weighted sum of these Arrow securities.

We normalize the price system so that the price in the first period is equal to one. We denote by p_s the price of a unit of account delivered in the second period in state s. The budget constraint of the representative consumer is:

$$C_0 + \sum_s p_s C_s = Y_0 + \sum_s p_s Y_s \qquad (41)$$

---

4. Appendix 6.1 develops a model in which the complete markets and incomplete markets equilibria are different, which notably allows us to give at least a partial answer to the so-called risk-free rate puzzle.

The consumer maximizes utility (39) subject to the budget constraint (41). The Lagrangian is:

$$U(C_0) + \beta \sum_s \pi_s U(C_s) - \lambda \left(C_0 + \sum_s p_s C_s \right) \tag{42}$$

and the first-order conditions:

$$U'(C_0) = \lambda \tag{43}$$

$$\beta \pi_s U'(C_s) = \lambda p_s \tag{44}$$

Because of the symmetry of the model, all agents end up consuming their endowments:

$$C_0 = Y_0 \tag{45}$$

$$C_s = Y_s \tag{46}$$

Combining (43) to (46), we find the price of an elementary Arrow security, which yields one unit of income in state s:

$$p_s = \frac{\beta \pi_s U'(C_s)}{U'(C_0)} = \frac{\beta \pi_s U'(Y_s)}{U'(Y_0)} \tag{47}$$

Now to reproduce security (40), we only need to take a quantity Z_s of each Arrow security s. The price of the security will thus be:

$$Q = \sum_{s \in S} p_s Z_s = \sum_{s \in S} \frac{\beta \pi_s Z_s U'(Y_s)}{U'(Y_0)} \tag{48}$$

For example, if the asset is the safe bond (34), the price of that safe bond is:

$$Q = \sum_s p_s = \sum_s \frac{\beta \pi_s U'(Y_s)}{U'(Y_0)} \tag{49}$$

which corresponds to a gross real interest rate R given by:

$$\frac{1}{R} = \beta \sum_s \pi_s \frac{U'(Y_s)}{U'(Y_0)} \tag{50}$$

Uncertainty and Financial Assets

6.5.2 Incomplete Markets

We now move to a situation of incomplete markets and assume that instead of the S Arrow securities, the only asset available is security (40). If households purchase $\mathcal{A}$ units of this asset in the first period, the budget constraints for the two periods are:

$$C_0 = Y_0 - Q\mathcal{A} \tag{51}$$

$$C_s = Y_s + \mathcal{A}Z_s \tag{52}$$

and the program of the household is:

$$\text{Maximize } U(Y_0 - Q\mathcal{A}) + \beta \sum_s \pi_s U(Y_s + \mathcal{A}Z_s) \tag{53}$$

The first-order condition with respect to $\mathcal{A}$ is:

$$QU'(Y_0 - Q\mathcal{A}) = \beta R \sum_s \pi_s Z_s U'(Y_s + \mathcal{A}Z_s) \tag{54}$$

Again, because of the symmetry, at equilibrium $\mathcal{A} = 0$, so this equation becomes:

$$Q = \beta \sum_s \pi_s \frac{Z_s U'(Y_s)}{U'(Y_0)} \tag{55}$$

Note that equations (48) and (55) are identical. The price of the security is the same whether or not markets are complete. This is due to the fact that, because the model is symmetrical, financial markets are inactive, and therefore whether markets are complete or incomplete does not matter.

We will see in appendix 6.1 a case in which whether markets are complete or not does matter.

6.6 The Risk-free Rate and the Risk Premium

To illustrate the foregoing results, we use formulas (48) and (55) to compare the prices of two assets; a safe bond (indexed B) and a risky security (indexed R).

We assume that the utility function is isoelastic:

$$U(C_t) = \frac{C_t^{1-\theta}}{1-\theta} \qquad \theta > 0 \qquad (56)$$

The parameter θ is the coefficient of relative risk aversion. The higher θ, the more risk averse the agents are.

6.6.1 The Pricing Formula

Using the pricing formulas (49) or (55) with the utility function (56) we find that the price of the asset is:

$$Q = \beta E\left[Z_s \left(\frac{Y_s}{Y_0}\right)^{-\theta}\right] \qquad (57)$$

To evaluate (57), we assume that $y_s = Log\,(Y_s/Y_0)$ is a normal variable with mean μ_Y and variance σ_Y^2. Accordingly, we repeatedly use the following formula for log-normal variables (mathematical appendix, formula A.166): if $Log\,Z$ is a normal variable with mean μ and variance σ^2, then:

$$E\left(Z^k\right) = \exp\left(k\mu + \frac{k^2\sigma^2}{2}\right) \qquad (58)$$

6.6.2 A Safe Bond

Consider first a safe asset, some "real bond," indexed B, with constant payments $Z_{Bs} = 1$. The price Q_B of that asset is thus, from (57):

$$Q_B = \beta E\left(\frac{Y_s}{Y_0}\right)^{-\theta} \qquad (59)$$

and using formula (58):

$$Q_B = \beta \exp\left(-\theta\mu_Y + \frac{\theta^2\sigma_Y^2}{2}\right) \qquad (60)$$

6.6.3 A Risky Security

Now consider a risky security, indexed R, whose return is proportional to output growth, that is, Z_{Rs} is proportional to Y_s/Y_0. We also want, to compare it meaningfully with the safe bond above that it has the same average return, that is, 1. So, for this asset:

$$Z_{Rs} = \frac{Y_s/Y_0}{E\left(Y_s/Y_0\right)} \qquad (61)$$

and, using formula (57), the price Q_R of this risky asset is given by:

$$Q_R = \frac{\beta}{E\left(Y_s/Y_0\right)} E\left[(Y_s/Y_0)^{1-\theta}\right] \qquad (62)$$

which, using again formula (58), yields:

$$Q_R = \beta \exp\left[-\theta \mu_Y + \left(\theta^2 - 2\theta\right) \frac{\sigma_Y^2}{2}\right] \qquad (63)$$

6.6.4 The Risk Premium

We can compare the prices of the bond and the risky asset:

$$\frac{Q_B}{Q_R} = \exp\left(\theta \sigma_Y^2\right) > 1 \qquad (64)$$

Although both assets have the same expected payments, the safe bond always commands a premium over the risky asset. In accordance with basic intuition, this premium is higher (a) the more risk averse the consumers are, and (b) the more volatile income is.

Although formula (64) is very intuitive, we must mention that it has given rise to one of the most famous empirical puzzles in economics, the equity premium puzzle (Mehra and Prescott, 1985). In a nutshell, if one takes "historical" values of Q_B/Q_R and σ_Y^2, one finds that an unrealistically high value of risk aversion θ would be needed for formula (64) to match the data.[5]

---

5. There is actually a large body of literature on the subject. For overviews, see Campbell (1999), Kocherlakota (1996), Siegel and Thaler (1997).

6.7 Risk Aversion and Substitutability

As it turns out, in the traditional expected utility formalization of attitudes toward risk we just described, there naturally arises a confusion between risk aversion and indices of intertemporal substitutability between goods. We expose this confusion in a very simple example and then show how a more general formalization allows us to disentangle the two concepts. We finally use this formalization to give a new pricing formula for a risk-free asset.

6.7.1 The Confusion

Let us consider the following two-period utility function:

$$C_0^{1-\theta} + \beta C_1^{1-\theta} \qquad (65)$$

We just defined the parameter θ as the index of relative risk aversion. Let us now put ourselves in a purely deterministic setting and consider the optimal consumption choice of a consumer who has incomes Y_0 and Y_1 in periods 0 and 1 and who is faced with a gross real interest rate R. The program of this consumer is:

$$\text{Maximize} \quad C_0^{1-\theta} + \beta C_1^{1-\theta} \quad \text{s.t.}$$

$$C_0 + \frac{C_1}{R} = Y_0 + \frac{Y_1}{R}$$

The first-order conditions yield:

$$\frac{C_1}{C_0} = (\beta R)^{1/\theta} \qquad (66)$$

We see that in formula (66) the parameter θ also appears as the inverse of the elasticity of substitution between first- and second-period consumption.

6.7.2 Nonexpected Utility

We now give a brief description of a generalization of the Von Neumann–Morgenstern expected utility, which allows us to separate the coefficient of risk aversion and the intertemporal elasticity of substitution.

The most standard version of expected utility has the following intertemporal utility function:

$$V_t = E_t \left[\sum_{s=t}^{\infty} \beta^s U(C_s) \right] \qquad (67)$$

We may note that this can be obtained recursively as:

$$V_t = U(C_t) + \beta E_t V_{t+1} \qquad (68)$$

As we saw, this representation of preferences somehow mixes two a priori distinct concepts—risk aversion and the intertemporal elasticity of substitution. This is particularly conspicuous if one takes the particular case of an isoelastic U:

$$V_t = E_t \left(\sum_{s=t}^{\infty} \beta^s C_s^{1-\theta} \right) \qquad (69)$$

As in (65), the parameter θ turns out to represent both the coefficient of relative risk aversion and the inverse of the (constant) elasticity of intertemporal substitution.

To escape this problem, following Kreps and Porteus (1978), a number of authors (Epstein and Zin, 1989; Farmer, 1990; Weil, 1990) use a different representation of preferences that disentangles the two parameters. These preferences, which are often called *nonexpected utility*, can be represented recursively as:

$$V_t = \mathcal{U}(C_t, E_t V_{t+1}) \qquad (70)$$

Rather than going into the general theory, we give an example where both the coefficient of relative risk aversion and the intertemporal elasticity of substitution are constant but independent. Assume that there is a terminal date T. The preferences in this example are defined recursively by:

$$V_T(C_T) = C_T^{1-\gamma} \qquad (71)$$

$$V_t = \left[C_t^{1-\theta} + \beta (E_t V_{t+1})^{(1-\theta)/(1-\gamma)} \right]^{(1-\gamma)/(1-\theta)} \qquad (72)$$

where, as we shall see, θ is the inverse of the elasticity of substitution and γ the coefficient of relative risk aversion. We make a few remarks.

First if $\gamma = \theta$, formula (72) yields:

$$V_t = C_t^{1-\theta} + \beta E_t V_{t+1} \qquad (73)$$

Integrating forward, we find the traditional formula (69).

Now if there is no uncertainty, formula (72) can be solved forward and we obtain:

$$V_t = \left(\sum_{s=t}^{T} \beta^s C_s^{1-\theta} \right)^{(1-\gamma)/(1-\theta)} \qquad (74)$$

and it is easy to compute that the intertemporal elasticity of substitution is indeed $1/\theta$.

As an example, the next subsection shows how this generalization of the utility functions modifies the price of the safe bond we derived in section 6.6.

6.7.3 The Risk-free Rate

We use the same basic model as in sections 6.5 and 6.6. Today's income is equal to Y_0, tomorrow's income is a stochastic variable Y_s. The difference is that the utility function is now, using the formulation in (72):

$$C_0^{1-\theta} + \beta \left[E\left(C_s^{1-\gamma}\right) \right]^{(1-\theta)/(1-\gamma)} \qquad (75)$$

We consider a riskless bond, indexed B, and derive its price Q_B. If agents save an amount B of this riskless bond, their budget constraints are:

$$C_0 = Y_0 - Q_B B \qquad (76)$$

$$C_s = Y_s + B \qquad (77)$$

Inserting (76) and (77) into (75), we find that households will maximize:

$$(Y_0 - Q_B B)^{1-\theta} + \beta \left[E\left(Y_s + B\right)^{1-\gamma} \right]^{(1-\theta)/(1-\gamma)} \qquad (78)$$

The first-order conditions with respect to B yield:

$$Q_B (Y_0 - Q_B B)^{-\theta} = \beta \left[E\left(Y_s + B\right)^{1-\gamma} \right]^{(\gamma-\theta)/(1-\gamma)} E\left(Y_s + B\right)^{-\gamma} \qquad (79)$$

Because the problem is symmetrical, at equilibrium $B = 0$ and this equation simplifies to:

$$Q_B = \beta \left[E \left(\frac{Y_s}{Y_0} \right)^{1-\gamma} \right]^{(\gamma-\theta)/(1-\gamma)} E \left(\frac{Y_s}{Y_0} \right)^{-\gamma} \tag{80}$$

As in section 6.6, we assume that Y_s/Y_0 is normally distributed with mean μ_Y and variance σ_Y^2. Then using formula (58), (80) becomes:

$$Q_B = \beta \exp \left[-\theta \mu + \frac{(\gamma\theta - \theta + \gamma)\sigma_Y^2}{2} \right] \tag{81}$$

Note that the safe rate of interest is an increasing function of risk aversion γ, an intuitive result. Also note that this property did not appear in the expression of Q_B that we found earlier (equation 60), when we had not yet disentangled risk aversion and intertemporal substitutability.

Appendix 6.1: Incomplete Markets and the Risk-free Rate Puzzle

Sections 6.5 to 6.7 studied a benchmark case where the economy had the same equilibrium allocations under complete or incomplete markets.

We introduce some heterogeneity among consumers. As a consequence, we see that the complete markets and incomplete markets equilibria are not the same anymore. In particular, we find that the interest rate is lower under incomplete markets than under complete markets (Weil, 1992). So the realistic assumption of incomplete markets can help solving the "risk-free rate puzzle."[6]

The Model

The models of sections 6.5 to 6.7 had only aggregate uncertainty, represented by the state of nature s, and the corresponding stochastic aggregate income Y_s. To create some heterogeneity, we add to this aggregate uncertainty idiosyncratic uncertainty as follows: each agent i is hit by an idiosyncratic shock denoted X_i. His income is $X_i Y_s$, that is, the product of the aggregate shock Y_s and his own idiosyncratic shock X_i. We assume

---

6. The risk-free rate puzzle (Weil, 1989b) refers to the difficulty of reproducing, in dynamic stochastic general equilibrium models with reasonable parameterizations, the low risk-free interest rate observed in reality.

that all variables X_i have exactly the same distibution, more precisely the variables $x_i = LogX_i$ are i.i.d. normal variables with the same mean μ_X and variance σ_X^2. We want that expected aggregate income not be changed by these idiosyncratic shocks, which means:

$$E(X_i) = 1 \qquad (82)$$

or, in view of the log-normal distribution of X:

$$\mu_X + \frac{\sigma_X^2}{2} = 0 \qquad (83)$$

We also assume an isoelastic utility function, the same for all agents:

$$U(C_i) = \frac{C_i^{1-\theta}}{1-\theta} \qquad (84)$$

Complete Markets

We give here (without proof) the basic characteristics of the complete markets equilibrium. It turns out that consumptions are the same as in section 6.5. Intuitively this is due to the fact that all agents are fully insured against their idiosyncratic uncertainty, so if the aggregate state is s the consumptions are:

$$C_0 = Y_0 \qquad C_s = Y_s \qquad (85)$$

The price p_s for one contingent unit of account depends only on the aggregate state s:

$$p_s = \frac{\beta \pi_s U'(Y_s)}{U'(Y_0)} \qquad (86)$$

As a consequence the price of a bond Q_C (the subindex C is for "complete" markets) is given by:

$$Q_C = \beta \sum_s \pi_s \frac{U'(Y_s)}{U'(Y_0)} = \beta E\left[\frac{U'(Y_s)}{U'(Y_0)}\right] \qquad (87)$$

Note that (86) and (87) are exactly the same as (47) and (49). Now let us take the particular utility function (84). Then (87) becomes:

$$Q_C = \beta E\left(\frac{Y_s}{Y_0}\right)^{-\theta} \qquad (88)$$

As in section 6.6, we assume that $Log\,(Y_s/Y_0)$ is a normal variable with mean μ_Y and variance σ_Y^2, so that using the traditional formula for log-normal variables (formula 58) we finally obtain:

$$Q_C = \beta \exp\left(-\theta\mu_Y + \frac{\theta^2\sigma_Y^2}{2}\right) \qquad (89)$$

Incomplete Markets

We now assume incomplete markets. The only available financial asset is a safe bond. The budget constraints of an agent are (we omit the index i because all agents are identical ex ante):

$$C_0 = Y_0 - Q_I B \qquad (90)$$

$$C_s = XY_s + B \qquad (91)$$

where B is the number of bonds purchased and Q_I is the price of the bond (the subindex I is for "incomplete" markets). The household maximizes $U(C_0) + \beta EU(C_s)$ subject to the constraints (90) and (91), that is, its program is:

$$\text{Maximize } U(Y_0 - Q_I B) + \beta E\left[U(XY_s + B)\right]$$

The first-order condition in B is:

$$U'(Y_0 - Q_I B) = \beta R E\left[U'(XY_s + B)\right] \qquad (92)$$

When the bonds market opens, uncertainty has not yet been resolved. Because all agents are identical ex ante, in equilibrium $B = 0$, so that Q_I is given by (92) with $B = 0$:

$$Q_I = \frac{\beta E\left[U'(XY_s)\right]}{U'(Y_0)} \qquad (93)$$

which yields with the utility function in equation (84):

$$Q_I = \beta E\left(\frac{XY_s}{Y_0}\right)^{-\theta} \qquad (94)$$

We again use the formula for log-normal distributions:

$$E\left(Z^k\right) = \exp\left(k\mu + \frac{k^2\sigma^2}{2}\right) \qquad (95)$$

Applying it to (94) we find:

$$Q_I = \beta \exp\left(-\theta\mu_Y + \frac{\theta^2\sigma_Y^2}{2} - \theta\mu_X + \frac{\theta^2\sigma_X^2}{2}\right) \qquad (96)$$

Now we assumed $E(X) = 1$, so that (equation 83):

$$\mu_X = -\frac{\sigma_X^2}{2} \qquad (97)$$

and (96) becomes:

$$Q_I = \beta \exp\left[-\theta\mu_Y + \frac{\theta^2\sigma_Y^2}{2} + \frac{\theta(1+\theta)\sigma_X^2}{2}\right] \qquad (98)$$

A Comparison

We compare bond prices under complete and incomplete markets. Combining (89) and (98), we find:

$$Q_I = Q_C \exp\left[\frac{\theta(1+\theta)\sigma_X^2}{2}\right] \qquad (99)$$

or, in terms of the gross real interest rates $R_C = 1/Q_C$ and $R_I = 1/Q_I$:

$$R_C = R_I \exp\left[\exp\frac{\theta(1+\theta)\sigma_X^2}{2}\right] \qquad (100)$$

We see that the interest rate is smaller under incomplete markets. The reason is that each agent is "more insured" in the complete markets economy than in the incomplete markets economy.

More precisely, in the incomplete markets economy, because the bonds market is inactive, each agent is left in the end with his initial income $X_i Y_s$. In the complete markets economy, agents are insured against their idiosyncratic risk, and each receives the aggregate income Y_s. The individual consumptions are "more random" under incomplete markets than under complete markets, and as a result agents accept a lower interest rate in the incomplete markets economy to "insure" themselves.

Appendix 6.2: Arrow-Debreu Equilibria with Several Physical Goods

We consider the model presented in section 6.3, but this time we assume that there are many "physical goods" indexed by $h \in H$. As in section 6.3, agents are indexed by $i \in I$, and states of nature by $s \in S$, with probabilities π_s:

$$\sum_s \pi_s = 1 \qquad (101)$$

We denote by c_{ihs} the consumption of good h by agent i in state s, and c_{is} the vector of consumptions in state s:

$$c_{is} = \{c_{ihs} \mid h \in H\} \qquad (102)$$

Agent i has a utility function $U_i(c_{is})$, where c_{is} is now a vector. She ranks various consumption bundles according to their expected utility:

$$\sum_s \pi_s U_i(c_{is}) \qquad (103)$$

Finally agent i has an endowment y_{ihs} of good h in state of nature s.

Complete Markets and the Arrow-Debreu Equilibrium

We again assume a system of complete markets. There is a market for each "economic good" indexed by both h and s, with a price p_{hs}. So there are HS markets.

The price p_{hs} is the price paid for receiving one unit of good h if the state of nature s occurs, nothing in the other states of nature. We denote by p the full price vector:

$$p = \{p_{hs} \mid h \in H, s \in S\} \qquad (104)$$

The budget constraint of agent i is:

$$\sum_{s \in S} \sum_{h \in H} p_{hs} c_{ihs} = \sum_{s \in S} \sum_{h \in H} p_{hs} y_{ihs} \qquad (105)$$

So agent i's program is to maximize utility (103) subject to the budget constraint (105), that is:

$$\text{Maximize} \sum_s \pi_s U_i(c_{is}) \quad \text{s.t.}$$

$$\sum_{s \in S} \sum_{h \in H} p_{hs} c_{ihs} = \sum_{s \in S} \sum_{h \in H} p_{hs} y_{ihs}$$

This yields demand functions $c_{ihs}(p)$. An Arrow-Debreu equilibrium is characterized by a vector of prices p^* such that:

$$\sum_i c_{ihs}(p^*) = \sum_i y_{ihs} \quad \forall h \quad \forall s \qquad (106)$$

The first theorem of welfare says that under very mild conditions an equilibrium is a Pareto optimum. Conversely, the second theorem of welfare says that under slightly more demanding conditions, a Pareto optimum can be obtained as an equilibrium under suitable transfers.

Implementation through Financial Securities and Spot Markets

Although it is a most useful benchmark, the equilibrium with complete markets is not very realistic, as it would require HS markets to be operated, and this can be a huge number.

We shall now see (Arrow, 1953, 1963) that one can implement the same allocations with a much smaller number of markets. The basic idea is that in a first stage, and before uncertainty is resolved, S financial markets will be used to transfer ex ante purchasing power across states of nature. Then one waits for uncertainty to be resolved, and when a particular state of nature has occurred, H spot markets are opened where goods and the financial assets are traded. That means that we need only $S + H$ markets instead of SH, a much smaller number.

The Spot Markets

Let us place ourselves in the second stage. We denote by $\bar{p}_{hs}$ the "spot price" of good h in state of nature s, and Υ_{is} the number of units of income (which can be negative) that agent i has transferred in state of nature s. Then the budget constraint of agent i in state of nature s is:

$$\sum_{h \in H} \bar{p}_{hs} c_{ihs} = \sum_{h \in H} \bar{p}_{hs} y_{ihs} + \Upsilon_{is} \qquad (107)$$

and thus, if a particular state s occurs, agent i solves the following program:

$$\text{Maximize } U_i(c_{is}) \quad \text{s.t.}$$

$$\sum_{h \in H} \bar{p}_{hs} c_{ihs} = \sum_{h \in H} \bar{p}_{hs} y_{ihs} + \Upsilon_{is}$$

The Markets for Financial Securities

Now we consider the situation in period 0, when agent i must determine the amounts Υ_{is}. Denote as q_s the price of a contingent claim for state s, that is, more precisely the price for obtaining one unit of income if state s occurs. The budget constraint in period 0 is:

$$\sum_s q_s \Upsilon_{is} = 0 \tag{108}$$

which simply expresses that agent i transfers purchasing power from some states to the others, at relative prices given by the prices q_s of the Arrow securities. To determine the Υ_{is} agent i will solve the program:

$$\text{Maximize } \sum_s \pi_s U_i(c_{is}) \quad \text{s.t.}$$

$$\sum_s q_s \Upsilon_{is} = 0$$

$$\sum_{h \in H} \bar{p}_{hs} c_{ihs} = \sum_{h \in H} \bar{p}_{hs} y_{ihs} + \Upsilon_{is} \quad \forall s$$

The first constraint is the budget constraint in the first stage (equation 108). The second set of constraints simply brings together the budget constraints for all states s in the second stage (equation 107 for all s).

To complete our description of this equilibrium, we add the condition that financial markets are in equilibrium for all states of nature:

$$\sum_{i \in I} \Upsilon_{is} = 0 \quad \forall s \tag{109}$$

The Equivalence

Recall the program giving demands in an Arrow-Debreu equilibrium:

$$\text{Maximize} \sum_s \pi_s U_i(c_{is}) \quad \text{s.t.}$$

$$\sum_{s \in S} \sum_{h \in H} p_{hs} c_{ihs} = \sum_{s \in S} \sum_{h \in H} p_{hs} y_{ihs}$$

We see (Arrow, 1953, 1963) that if utility functions are strictly concave, the last two programs will lead to the same allocation if:

$$p_{hs} = q_s \bar{p}_{hs} \tag{110}$$

Under condition (110), the budget constraints are the same, and so are the consumption decisions of the agents.

Problems

Problem 6.1: The Curse of Early Information Revelation

Many people would naturally believe that early information about "states of nature" is a good thing, because it somehow reduces uncertainty. We describe an insightful model due to Hirshleifer (1971), where early revelation of information is actually detrimental because it destroys the potential mutual insurance possibilities that exist when the information about states of nature is not yet revealed.

The economy has only one "physical" good and two states of nature, indexed 1 and 2. To make the exposition more compact, we call "good 1" and "good 2" the "contingent goods" delivered, respectively, in states 1 and 2.

There are two agents, X and Y, who consume x_1 and x_2, and y_1 and y_2 in the two states of nature. The utilities of X and Y are, respectively:

$$\pi Log x_1 + (1 - \pi) Log x_2$$

$$\pi Log y_1 + (1 - \pi) Log y_2$$

where π is the probability of state 1, and $1 - \pi$ the probability of state 2. Finally the initial endowments of the two agents are:

$$\bar{x}_1 = a \qquad \bar{x}_2 = 1 - a \qquad a < 1$$

$$\bar{y}_1 = 1 - a \qquad \bar{y}_2 = a$$

Uncertainty and Financial Assets

1. Assume that the state of nature is not known in the first period. There is a contingent goods market where the agents can exchange good 1 against good 2. Call p the market price of good 2 in terms of good 1. (a) Compute the equilibrium value of p, and (b) compute the expected utilities of the two agents.
2. Assume now that agents learn in the first period which state of nature will occur in the second period. What will be the transactions on the contingent market? Compute the expected utilities of the two agents.
3. Compare the expected utilities in the two cases. Interpret.

Problem 6.2: Actuarial Fairness and Insurance

An agent has an income Y and faces the risk of an accident, which has a probability π. In the case where the accident occurs, she makes a loss $L < Y$. Now she can subscribe to an insurance scheme through which she can get a payment I in case of accident, by paying an insurance premium equal to pI. As a consequence her final consumption is equal to:

$$C = Y - pI$$

if no accident occurs, and:

$$C = Y - L + I - pI$$

if the accident occurs. The agent evaluates her expected utility using a Von Neumann–Morgenstern utility function $U(C)$ strictly concave in its argument.

1. Compute the demand of insurance I as a function of p.
2. One says that the insurance is actuarially fair if $p = \pi$. What is the demand for insurance in that case?

Problem 6.3: Self-protection and Insurance

We consider the same framework as in problem 6.2, but now we assume that the representative agent can influence the probability of an accident by paying a "self-protection cost" x. In that case his income is $Y - x$ and the probability of accident $\pi(x)$ with $\pi'(x) < 0$ and $\pi''(x) > 0$.

1. Characterize the values of x and I at the social optimum. Show that if $-\pi'(0) > 1/L$ it is optimal to have a positive value of x.

2. Show that this optimum can be attained if x is observable and the insurance company can make the individual insurance premium conditional on the value of self-protection x.
3. We assume that the insurance company cannot observe x, and therefore the premium is independent of x. What is the equilibrium value of x? Is the equilibrium efficient? Why?

Problem 6.4: Pricing of a Risky Asset Under Nonexpected Utility

In section 6.6 we showed how to price a risky asset with the traditional expected utility. We now extend the result to a framework of nonexpected utility where notably the coefficients of risk aversion and intertemporal substitutability are clearly disentangled.

We assume that agents consume C_0 in the first period and C_s in the second, where s denotes states of nature. They maximize the following utility:

$$C_0^{1-\theta} + \beta \left[E \left(C_s^{1-\gamma} \right) \right]^{(1-\theta)/(1-\gamma)}$$

The agent receives an exogenous income Y_0 in the first period and in the second period a random income that takes the value Y_s in state of nature s.

As in section 6.6.3, the risky security we consider gives a payment Z_s in the state of nature s, with:

$$Z_s = \frac{Y_s/Y_0}{E\left(Y_s/Y_0\right)}$$

So the payment is proportional to the random income, but has an expected value of 1.

1. Denote as Q_R the price of this risky asset, and $\mathcal{A}$ the quantity of assets bought by the agents in the first period. Write the first- and second-period budget constraints and the program of utility maximization.
2. Write the first-order conditions. Because of the symmetry of the problem, at equilibrium $\mathcal{A} = 0$. Deduce the price Q_R of the asset.
3. We now assume that $Log\left(Y_s/Y_0\right)$ is a normal variable with mean μ_Y and variance σ_Y^2. Using formula (58) in the chapter, compute the price of the risky asset.
4. Comparing with the price of a safe asset in section 6.7.3, compute the risk premium.

7

The Ramsey Model

7.1 Introduction

This chapter presents a most famous model of growth, the Ramsey model (Ramsey, 1928; Cass, 1965; Koopmans, 1965). As in the Solow-Swan model presented in chapter 1, the rate of growth in this model is essentially determined by the evolution of the technology, assumed exogenous, so it belongs to the category of exogenous growth models. On the other hand, now all agents will make their consumption and investment decisions through explicit intertemporal maximization.

Among all models with intertemporal dynamic optimization, the characteristic of the Ramsey model is that households are represented as a single dynasty of infinitely lived households. This dynasty may actually include an increasing number of households-workers, but the important thing is that all these households have a single utility function and a single budget constraint.

Section 7.2 presents the basic Ramsey model in continuous time, as in the original Ramsey contribution. To economize on notation, we start with a model without technical progress, as many properties of the model are actually independent of this technical progress. Section 7.3 describes the intertemporal market equilibrium. Section 7.4 investigates the efficiency properties of the market equilibrium. Section 7.5 studies an important property of the Ramsey model, which we already encountered in chapter 4: Ricardian equivalence. Section 7.6 shows how the introduction of government spending modifies the dynamics of the model. Section 7.7 introduces explicit exogenous technical progress and shows how the basic model is adapted to incorporate such technical progress.

Finally, section 7.8 presents the Ramsey model in discrete time. This is useful for several reasons. First it will show us on a precise example how to go from continuous to discrete time. Second, the main alternative to the Ramsey model, the overlapping generations model (chapters 4 and 8), is set by construction in discrete time, and this will facilitate the comparison. Third, an important development in modern macroeconomics has been to add stochastic elements to Ramsey-type models. Such models, which will be studied in chapters 10, 12, and 13, are almost exclusively set in discrete time settings. So our discrete time version will facilitate later comparisons.

7.2 The Ramsey Model

7.2.1 Production

The representation of production is the same as in the Solow-Swan model. Producers have a constant returns technology:

$$Y_t = F(K_t, A_t L_t) \tag{1}$$

where A_t is an index of labor augmenting technical progress. Actually until section 7.6, we assume that $A_t = 1$, so that the production function is:

$$Y_t = F(K_t, L_t) \tag{2}$$

Capital depreciates at the rate δ, so the dynamic equation governing the accumulation of capital is:

$$\dot{K}_t = I_t - \delta K_t = Y_t - C_t - \delta K_t \tag{3}$$

We assume that the workforce grows at the rate n:

$$L_t = L_0 e^{nt} \tag{4}$$

As in chapter 1, we define per capita variables:

$$y_t = \frac{Y_t}{L_t} \qquad k_t = \frac{K_t}{L_t} \qquad c_t = \frac{C_t}{L_t} \tag{5}$$

The Ramsey Model

and the associated production function:

$$y_t = f(k_t) = F(k_t, 1) \tag{6}$$

Finally (3) is rewritten in per capita terms:

$$\dot{k}_t = y_t - c_t - (\delta + n) k_t \tag{7}$$

7.2.2 Households

Households maximize discounted utility:[1]

$$V = \int_0^\infty e^{-\rho t} U(c_t) \, dt \tag{8}$$

The budget constraint of the household is:

$$C_t + \dot{K}_t = \omega_t L_t + r_t K_t \tag{9}$$

where r_t is the rate of return on capital. Note that at this stage we assume that households only save under the form of capital. In section 7.5 we introduce government debt, and a household's assets will then be the sum of capital and debt.

In per capita terms the budget constraint (9) becomes:

$$c_t + \frac{dk_t}{dt} + nk_t = \omega_t + r_t k_t \tag{10}$$

7.3 Market Equilibrium

7.3.1 First-order Conditions

Equilibrium of the firms implies:

$$r_t = f'(k_t) - \delta \tag{11}$$

$$\omega_t = f(k_t) - k_t f'(k_t) \tag{12}$$

---

1. Some authors assume that per capita utilities are weighted by the size of the population, that is, they assume that the maximand in the integral is $e^{-\rho t} L_t U(c_t)$ instead of $e^{-\rho t} U(c_t)$.

Now the problem of the household is to maximize utility (8) subject to the budget constraint (10), that is:

$$\text{Maximize} \int_0^\infty e^{-\rho t} U(c_t)\, dt \quad \text{s.t.}$$

$$c_t + \frac{dk_t}{dt} + nk_t = w_t + r_t k_t$$

Let us write the current value Hamiltonian (see mathematical appendix, section A.4.2):

$$\mathcal{H}_t = U(c_t) + \lambda_t (w_t + r_t k_t - c_t - nk_t) \qquad (13)$$

The first-order conditions are:

$$\lambda_t = U'(c_t) \qquad (14)$$

$$\dot{\lambda}_t = \rho \lambda_t - \frac{\partial \mathcal{H}_t}{\partial k_t} = \lambda_t (\rho + n - r_t) \qquad (15)$$

Combining the two first-order conditions (14) and (15), we obtain the so-called Euler equation:

$$\frac{U''(c_t)}{U'(c_t)} \frac{dc_t}{dt} = \rho + n - r_t \qquad (16)$$

7.3.2 The Transversality Condition

Condition (16) is a necessary condition for optimality. But to be fully optimal, the household's program must satisfy another optimality condition, the so-called transversality condition (mathematical appendix, section A.4.3), which is expressed here as:

$$\lim_{t \to \infty} e^{-\rho t} k_t U'(c_t) = 0 \qquad (17)$$

The interpretation of this condition is straightforward: imagine a contrario that the limit of the quantity in (17) is strictly positive. This means that by selling all or some of the capital accumulated, the household could increase

7.3.3 The Dynamic Equations

From (6) and (7) we have the equation of evolution of capital per head:

$$\dot{k}_t = f(k_t) - (\delta + n) k_t - c_t \tag{18}$$

We saw the dynamic optimality equation:

$$\frac{U''(c_t)}{U'(c_t)} \frac{dc_t}{dt} = \rho + n - r_t \tag{19}$$

Let us define $\theta(c_t)$ as:

$$\theta(c_t) = -\frac{c_t U''(c_t)}{U'(c_t)} \tag{20}$$

We recognize the inverse of the intertemporal elasticity of substitution. Now using (11) and (20), equation (19) is rewritten:

$$\frac{1}{c_t} \frac{dc_t}{dt} = \frac{f'(k_t) - \rho - \delta - n}{\theta(c_t)} \tag{21}$$

7.3.4 Steady States

We have two dynamic equations, (18) and (21), in c_t and k_t. These two equations and the dynamics are represented in figure 7.1.

The vertical line is the $\dot{c}_t = 0$ locus, whose equation is (from 21):

$$f'(k_t) = \rho + \delta + n \tag{22}$$

The bell-shaped curve is the $\dot{k}_t = 0$ locus, whose equation is (from 18):

$$c_t = f(k_t) - (\delta + n) k_t \tag{23}$$

Let us denote as c^* and k^* the steady-state values. They are simply the solutions in c_t and k_t of the system of the two equations (22) and (23).

7.3.5 Dynamics and the Saddle Path

Figure 7.1 depicts the dynamics of the system. The arrows show the direction of variation of each variable. Figure 7.1 shows that the economy displays saddle path dynamics.

We now show that the saddle path, that is, the trajectory labeled (1) in figure 7.2, is the only admissible trajectory.

Imagine first that the economy follows a trajectory above the saddle path such as the trajectory labeled (2) in figure 7.2. We see that the economy will reach in finite time a point on the $\dot{k}_t = 0$ line with positive consumption. Because $\dot{k}_t = -c_t$ on that line, the capital would have to become negative, which is impossible.

Now imagine that the economy follows a trajectory below the saddle path, such as the trajectory labeled (3) in figure 7.2. We want to show that the economy will save too much capital and not satisfy the transversality condition (17). For that, let us evaluate the derivative of the logarithm of the expression in (17):

$$dLog\left[e^{-\rho t} k_t U'(c_t)\right] = -\rho + \frac{\dot{k}_t}{k_t} + \frac{U''(c_t)}{U'(c_t)} \frac{\dot{c}_t}{c_t} \tag{24}$$

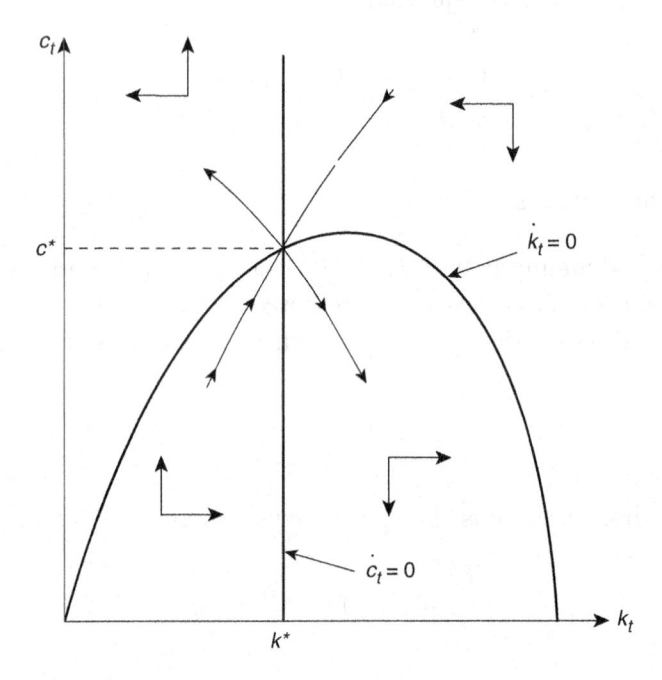

Figure 7.1 The dynamics of consumption and capital

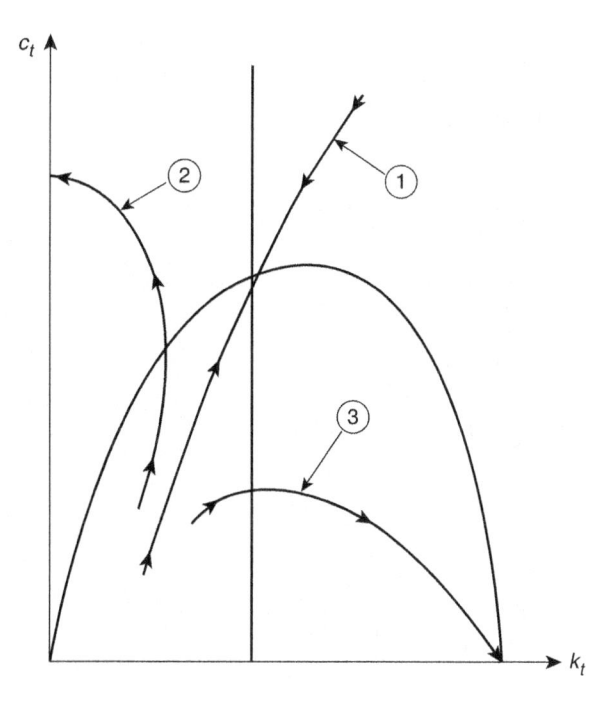

Figure 7.2 Saddle path dynamics

Combining with (18) and (19), we obtain:

$$dLog\left[e^{-\rho t}k_t U'(c_t)\right] = \frac{f(k_t) - c_t}{k_t} - r_t \quad (25)$$

Because c_t goes to 0 along trajectories such as that labeled (3), and because $f(k_t) > r_t k_t$, at some point this derivative becomes positive, and the quantity in (17) will not go to 0, violating the transversality condition.

7.4 Efficiency

The first theorem of welfare says that a market equilibrium, when it exists, is a Pareto optimum. There are, however, qualifications to this theorem, and we see in the next chapter a model where the market equilibrium may not be a Pareto optimum. Here we investigate the efficiency issue directly for the Ramsey model.

The physical constraint to which the economy is subject is the equation of accumulation of capital, which we recall here in its per capita version:

$$\dot{k}_t = f(k_t) - (\delta + n)k_t - c_t \quad (26)$$

Because there is only one aggregate agent, the optimum will simply be obtained by maximizing the intertemporal utility (8) subject to constraint (26), that is, the optimum will be solution of the following program:

$$\text{Maximize} \int_0^\infty e^{-\rho t} U(c_t) \, dt \quad \text{s.t.}$$

$$\dot{k}_t = f(k_t) - (\delta + n)k_t - c_t$$

The current-value Hamiltonian for this problem is:

$$\mathcal{H}_t = U(c_t) + \lambda_t [f(k_t) - (\delta + n)k_t - c_t] \tag{27}$$

and the first-order conditions, with respect to c_t and k_t, respectively:

$$U'(c_t) = \lambda_t \tag{28}$$

$$\dot{\lambda}_t = \rho \lambda_t - \frac{\partial \mathcal{H}_t}{\partial k_t} = \lambda_t [\delta + n + \rho - f'(k_t)] \tag{29}$$

We have also the transversality condition:

$$\lim_{t \to \infty} e^{-\rho t} k_t U'(c_t) = 0 \tag{30}$$

Combining equations (28) and (29), we obtain:

$$\frac{U''(c_t)}{U'(c_t)} \frac{dc_t}{dt} = \delta + n + \rho - f'(k_t) \tag{31}$$

This equation also characterizes the market equilibrium, as can be checked by combining equations (11) and (19). The transversality conditions are also the same, and the market equilibrium is an optimum.

7.5 Ricardian Equivalence

We shall now introduce government into the picture. The government spends G_t, taxes T_t in real terms, and has a debt D_t, also in real terms. Government debt evolves according to the government's budget constraint:

$$\dot{D}_t = r_t D_t + G_t - T_t \tag{32}$$

The consumer can now save and accumulate both capital K_t and debt D_t. Consequently, the consumer's budget constraint in period t is now:

$$C_t + \dot{K}_t + \dot{D}_t = \omega_t L_t + r_t K_t + r_t D_t - T_t \tag{33}$$

Note that we have taken the same rate of return r_t on capital and debt. If this was not the case, the asset with the lowest return would simply not be held at all.

We write the household's and government's intertemporal budget constraints, and for that it will be convenient to use the real discount factors:

$$\Delta_t = \exp\left(-\int_0^t r_s ds\right) \tag{34}$$

Using these to integrate equation (32) we find the government's intertemporal budget constraint:

$$\int_0^\infty \Delta_t T_t dt = D_0 + \int_0^\infty \Delta_t G_t dt \tag{35}$$

Of course, for this to be valid, it must be that the government has a "well-behaved" fiscal policy, in the sense that $\Delta_t D_t$ must go to 0 as time goes to infinity.

Symmetrically the intertemporal budget constraint of the household is now written:

$$\int_0^\infty \Delta_t C_t dt = D_0 + K_0 + \int_0^\infty \Delta_t \omega_t L_t dt - \int_0^\infty \Delta_t T_t dt \tag{36}$$

Subtracting (35) from (36), we obtain:

$$\int_0^\infty \Delta_t C_t dt = K_0 + \int_0^\infty \Delta_t \omega_t L_t dt - \int_0^\infty \Delta_t G_t dt \tag{37}$$

Both government debt and taxes have completely disappeared from the household's intertemporal budget constraint! All that matters is the sequence of government spendings G_t. How it is financed is irrelevant, provided (of course) that the government plans to balance its budget in the long-run. So the property of *Ricardian equivalence*, which we already saw in chapter 4, also holds in the presence of capital.

The intuitive reason for Ricardian equivalence is that in the consumer's budget constraint, the value of governmental debt is exactly compensated by the discounted value of taxes that the government will have to levy to repay the debt. We saw in chapter 4 that this Ricardian equivalence property disappears if we abandon the single infinitely lived agent formalization of this chapter.

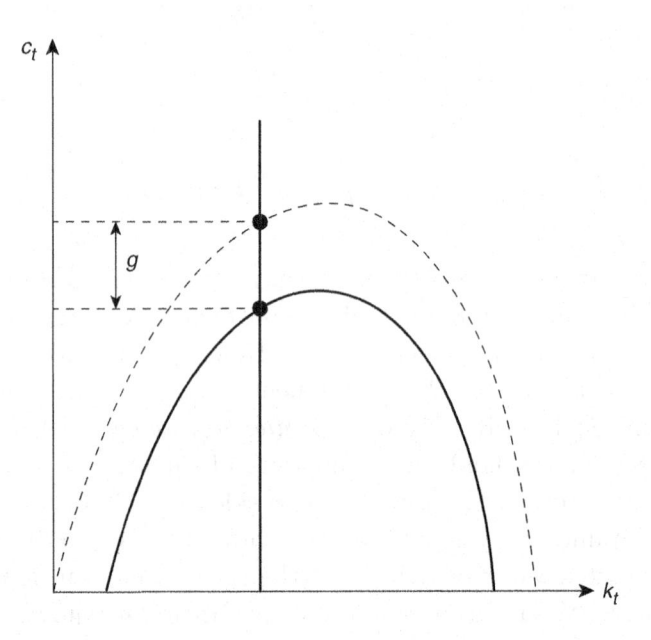

7.6 Government Spending and Dynamics

We will now study how the dynamics of the economy is modified by government spending. In this section we assume nondistortionary lump-sum taxation. The case of government spending financed by distortionary proportional taxation is treated in appendix 7.1.

Let us assume that the government spends G_t in real terms, which it finances by lump-sum taxation. Equation (3) becomes:

$$\dot{K}_t = I_t - \delta K_t = Y_t - C_t - G_t - \delta K_t \tag{38}$$

or in per capita terms, since $y_t = f(k_t)$:

$$\dot{k}_t = f(k_t) - (\delta + n) k_t - c_t - g_t \tag{39}$$

with:

$$g_t = \frac{G_t}{L_t} \tag{40}$$

Imagine that we start from a stationary state with $g = 0$, and that government spending jumps to $g > 0$. In the initial situation the locus $\dot{k}_t = 0$ is the dashed line (figure 7.3). When government spending changes to g, the

Figure 7.3 Government spending and dynamics

The Ramsey Model

locus $\dot{k}_t = 0$ goes down by g (solid line), whereas the locus $\dot{c}_t = 0$ stays unchanged. Consequently, because the predetermined variable k_t does not have to move, the economy will jump directly to the new stationary state.

7.7 Exogenous Technical Progress

We will now assume that there is exogenous technical progress, that is, that A_t in formula (1) is an increasing function of time:

$$\frac{\dot{A}_t}{A_t} = \gamma_A \tag{41}$$

A few things have to be changed in the analysis. First, we take as a working variable, instead of L_t, the variable "effective labor":

$$\Lambda_t = A_t L_t \tag{42}$$

We also replace the rate of growth of population n by $n + \gamma_A$. Finally, because the argument of U is now C_t/Λ_t instead of C_t/L_t, the discount rate ρ has be reinterpreted accordingly.

7.8 The Ramsey Model in Discrete Time

We give a discrete time version of the Ramsey model. Population increases at the rate n:

$$L_t = L_0 (1+n)^t \tag{43}$$

Capital depreciates at the rate δ, so that the dynamic equation governing the accumulation of capital is:

$$K_{t+1} = (1-\delta) K_t + I_t \tag{44}$$

Households maximize the following discounted utility:

$$\sum_0^\infty \beta^t U(C_t) \tag{45}$$

and the households' budget constraints are:

$$C_t + K_{t+1} = \omega_t L_t + R_t K_t - T_t \tag{46}$$

Households maximize utility (45) subject to the budget constraints (46). The corresponding Lagrangian is:

$$\sum_0^\infty \beta^t \left[U(C_t) + \lambda_t \left(\omega_t L_t + R_t K_t - T_t - C_t - K_{t+1} \right) \right] \quad (47)$$

and the first order conditions for consumption and capital:

$$\lambda_t = U'(C_t) \quad (48)$$

$$\lambda_t = \beta R_{t+1} \lambda_{t+1} \quad (49)$$

Combining (48) and (49) we obtain:

$$U'(C_t) = \beta R_{t+1} U'(C_{t+1}) \quad (50)$$

This is somehow the discrete time version of the Euler equation. The interpretation of this formula is straightforward: imagine that the consumer decides to consume less at time t, by an infinitesimal quantity ε. The immediate loss in utility is $U'(C_t)\varepsilon$. The quantity ε is invested, yielding next period an extra income $R_{t+1}\varepsilon$, and thus a utility gain of $\beta R_{t+1} U'(C_{t+1})\varepsilon$. In equilibrium the gain and loss in utility exactly compensate, so that:

$$\beta R_{t+1} U'(C_{t+1}) \varepsilon = U'(C_t) \varepsilon \quad (51)$$

which is equation (50).

Appendix 7.1: Government Spending with Distortionary Taxation

We now assume that government spending G_t is financed by a proportional, distortionary tax on income, so it is given by:

$$G_t = \tau \left(\omega_t L_t + r_t K_t \right) \quad (52)$$

where τ is the given tax rate. The budget constraint of the household is now:

$$C_t + \dot{K}_t = (1 - \tau)\left(\omega_t L_t + r_t K_t \right) \quad (53)$$

In per capita terms, the budget constraint (53) becomes:

$$c_t + \frac{dk_t}{dt} + nk_t = (1 - \tau)(\omega_t + r_t k_t) \quad (54)$$

and that of the government:

$$g_t = \tau\left(\omega_t + r_t k_t\right) \tag{55}$$

First-order Conditions

Equilibrium of the firms implies as above:

$$r_t = f'\left(k_t\right) - \delta \tag{56}$$
$$\omega_t = f\left(k_t\right) - k_t f'\left(k_t\right) \tag{57}$$

Now the problem of the household is to maximize utility subject to the budget constraint (54), that is:

$$\text{Maximize} \int_0^\infty e^{-\rho t} U\left(c_t\right) dt \quad \text{s.t.}$$

$$c_t + \frac{dk_t}{dt} + nk_t = (1-\tau)\left(\omega_t + r_t k_t\right)$$

Let us write the current-value Hamiltonian:

$$\mathcal{H}_t = U\left(c_t\right) + \lambda_t \left[(1-\tau)\left(\omega_t + r_t k_t\right) - c_t - nk_t\right] \tag{58}$$

The first-order conditions are:

$$\lambda_t = U'\left(c_t\right) \tag{59}$$

$$\dot{\lambda}_t = \rho\lambda_t - \frac{\partial \mathcal{H}_t}{\partial k_t} = \lambda_t \left[\rho + n - (1-\tau) r_t\right] \tag{60}$$

Combining these two first-order conditions, we obtain a new Euler equation, which now depends on the tax rate:

$$\frac{U''\left(c_t\right)}{U'\left(c_t\right)} \frac{dc_t}{dt} = \rho + n - (1-\tau) r_t \tag{61}$$

The Dynamic Equations

So the dynamics is given by the equation of evolution of capital:

$$\dot{k}_t = f(k_t) - (\delta + n) k_t - c_t - g_t \quad (62)$$

and the Euler equation (61). Define $\theta(c_t)$ as before as:

$$\theta(c_t) = -\frac{c_t U''(c_t)}{U'(c_t)} \quad (63)$$

Using (56) and (63), equation (61) is rewritten:

$$\frac{1}{c_t}\frac{dc_t}{dt} = \frac{(1-\tau)[f'(k_t) - \delta] - \rho - n}{\theta(c_t)} \quad (64)$$

Now:

$$g_t = \tau(\omega_t + r_t k_t) = \tau[f(k_t) - \delta k_t] \quad (65)$$

and so equation (62) is rewritten:

$$\dot{k}_t = (1-\tau)[f(k_t) - \delta k_t] - nk_t - c_t \quad (66)$$

The Effects of a Tax Increase

We have two dynamic equations in c_t and k_t, equations (64) and (66). We first note that these two equations are quite similar to (21) and (18) (which correspond to $\tau = 0$), and the dynamics will look similar to that depicted in figure 7.1.

We want to find the effects of, say, an increase in τ. From (64), the $\dot{c}_t = 0$ locus has for equation:

$$(1-\tau)[f'(k_t) - \delta] = \rho + n \quad (67)$$

while, from (66), the $\dot{k}_t = 0$ locus has for equation:

$$c_t = (1-\tau)[f(k_t) - \delta k_t] - nk_t \quad (68)$$

These equations are represented in figure 7.4, which shows how these two curves move when the tax rate increases from 0 to $\tau > 0$. The dashed lines correspond to a zero tax rate, the solid lines to a positive tax rate.

We see that here, contrary to the lump-sum case, additional distortionary taxes to finance government spending reduce not only consumption but also the stationary level of capital.

The Ramsey Model

Problems

Problem 7.1: Explicit Dynamics: Government Spending

Households have an intertemporal logarithmic utility function:

$$U = \sum_t \beta^t Log C_t$$

Firms have a Cobb-Douglas production function:

$$Y_t = A K_t^\alpha L_t^{1-\alpha}$$

Capital depreciates fully in one period, so that:

$$K_{t+1} = I_t$$

We further assume that the government wants to carry public spending G_t in the amount:

$$G_t = \zeta Y_t$$

These government expenses are financed by a lump-sum tax $T_t = G_t$.

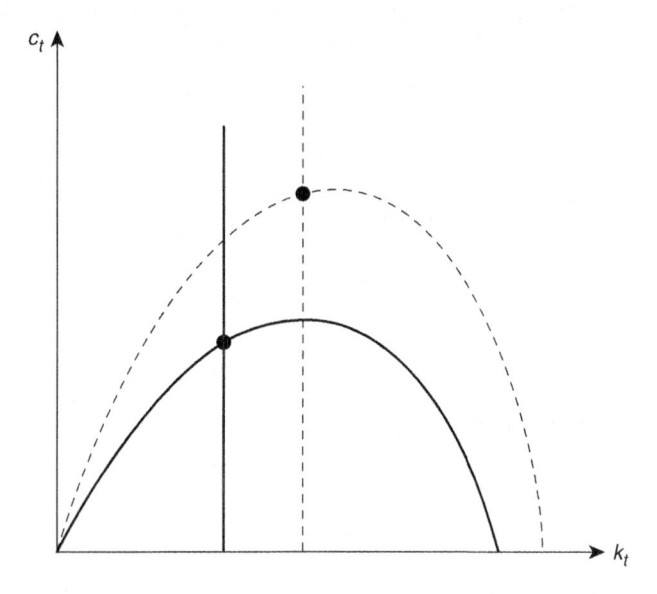

Figure 7.4 An increase in the tax rate

1. Write the first-order conditions of the household.
2. Compute consumption and investment.

Problem 7.2: Explicit Dynamics: Distortionary Taxation

We take the same model as in problem 7.1, but we assume that G_t is financed by a proportional tax on all components of income Y_t:

$$G_t = \tau Y_t$$

The budget is balanced, so that $\tau = \zeta$.

1. Compute the dynamics of the economy.
2. What is the effect of distortionary taxation on investment?

Problem 7.3: Labor versus Capital Taxation

Distortionary taxes are levied proportionally on labor and capital income. We assume that these tax rates are constant in time, and denote them τ_ℓ and τ_k, respectively. Government spending is a given fraction of national income:

$$G_t = \zeta Y_t$$

We compute the optimal τ_ℓ and τ_k associated to ζ. We assume a Cobb-Douglas production function and 100 percent depreciation:

$$Y_t = A K_t^\alpha L_t^{1-\alpha}$$

$$K_{t+1} = I_t$$

The utility function is logarithmic:

$$U = \sum \beta^t Log C_t$$

We finally assume that the government budget is balanced in each period.

1. Derive the first-order conditions.
2. Compute consumption and investment as a function of income and the tax rates.
3. Find the optimal tax rates τ_ℓ and τ_k.

8

Overlapping Generations

8.1 Introduction

In this chapter we study a discrete time model, the overlapping generations (OLG) model, due notably to Allais (1947), Samuelson (1958), and Diamond (1965).[1] The particularity of the OLG model is that households are not pictured as a single dynasty, as in the Ramsey model, but as a sequence of overlapping families, each with its own utility function and budget constraint. In the simplest version, which we study in this chapter, each family lives two periods and overlaps only with the previous family (when young) and the next one (when old). We see that this demographic difference creates a number of important changes, notably the possibility of Pareto dominated equilibria and the failure of Ricardian equivalence, so that government's debt and fiscal policy will matter. The dynamics of the economy are also seriously modified, as notably the economy usually has more than one steady state.

Section 8.2 presents the most classic OLG model, in which the agents have two-period lives (Diamond, 1965). Section 8.3 describes the market equilibrium of this economy. Section 8.4 studies efficiency and shows that some equilibria can be Pareto dominated. Section 8.5 studies the issue of pensions, for which the OLG model is particularly adequate in view of its explicit life cycle structure. Section 8.6 studies the dynamics of the economy when agents can accumulate both debt and capital.

---

1. For a synthesis on the overlapping generations model, see De la Croix and Michel (2002).

8.2 The Diamond Model

8.2.1 Households

Each household lives two periods. There are N_t young households born in period t. Each young household inelastically supplies one unit of labor, so that the total supply of labor L_t is equal to N_t, which we assume grows at the rate n:

$$\frac{L_{t+1}}{L_t} = \frac{N_{t+1}}{N_t} = 1 + n \qquad (1)$$

Consider the household born in t. When young (in period t) it consumes c_{1t} and saves s_t. When old (in period $t+1$) it does not work and consumes c_{2t+1}. Its budget constraints for the two periods are thus:

$$c_{1t} + s_t = \omega_t \qquad (2)$$

$$c_{2t+1} = R_{t+1} s_t \qquad (3)$$

where ω_t is the real wage and R_{t+1} the gross rate of return in period $t+1$ on period t savings. Households maximize their utility, given by:

$$U(c_{1t}) + \beta U(c_{2t+1}) \qquad (4)$$

where β is the discount rate.

8.2.2 Firms

We assume that firms have a production function homogeneous of degree 1:

$$Y_t = F(K_t, L_t) \qquad (5)$$

We could actually take the more general form:

$$Y_t = F(K_t, A_t L_t) \qquad (6)$$

where A_t is exogenous technical progress. As we pointed out in chapter 7, the analysis with the simpler form (5) carries through with (6), replacing L_t by $A_t L_t$. To save on notation, from now on we use the simpler form (5).

Capital depreciates at the rate δ so that:

$$K_{t+1} = (1-\delta) K_t + I_t \tag{7}$$

We define the per worker[2] production function f:

$$y_t = f(k_t) \qquad y_t = \frac{Y_t}{L_t} \qquad k_t = \frac{K_t}{L_t} \tag{8}$$

The derivatives of the original and per worker functions F and f are related by:

$$\frac{\partial F(K_t, L_t)}{\partial K_t} = f'(k_t) \tag{9}$$

$$\frac{\partial F(K_t, L_t)}{\partial L_t} = f(k_t) - k_t f'(k_t) \tag{10}$$

8.3 Market Equilibrium

8.3.1 Households

The savings s_t of young households in period t are solution of the following program:

$$\text{Maximize } U(c_{1t}) + \beta U(c_{2t+1}) \quad \text{s.t.}$$

$$c_{1t} + s_t = \omega_t$$

$$c_{2t+1} = R_{t+1} s_t$$

The first-order conditions for this program yield:

$$U'(c_{1t}) = \beta R_{t+1} U'(c_{2t+1}) \tag{11}$$

Combining this first-order condition with the budget constraints, we obtain a savings function of the form:

$$s_t = S(\omega_t, R_{t+1}) \tag{12}$$

---

2. Here we have to differentiate between per worker and per capita variables because in period t there are N_t workers but $N_t + N_{t-1}$ households alive.

As an example, if we take a isoelastic utility function:

$$U(c) = \frac{c^{1-\theta}}{1-\theta} \qquad (13)$$

then savings are equal to:

$$S(\omega_t, R_{t+1}) = \frac{\omega_t}{1 + \left(\beta R_{t+1}^{1-\theta}\right)^{-1/\theta}} \qquad (14)$$

In the particular logarithmic case, corresponding to $\theta = 1$, savings is a constant fraction of real wage income:

$$S(\omega_t, R_{t+1}) = \frac{\beta \omega_t}{1+\beta} \qquad (15)$$

8.3.2 Firms

If a quantity of capital K_t is used in period t, then total output available consists of production and undepreciated capital, that is, it is equal to:

$$(1-\delta) K_t + F(K_t, L_t) \qquad (16)$$

Consequently R_t, the marginal rate of return on K_t, is equal to:

$$R_t = \frac{\partial}{\partial K_t}\left[(1-\delta) K_t + F(K_t, L_t)\right] = 1 - \delta + f'(k_t) \qquad (17)$$

8.3.3 Capital Dynamics

Capital in period $t+1$ is equal to savings of period t. Because only the N_t young households save, we have:

$$K_{t+1} = N_t s_t \qquad (18)$$

Using variables per worker, this becomes:

$$k_{t+1} = \frac{s_t}{1+n} \qquad (19)$$

Combining equations (12) and (19), we obtain the equation of evolution of capital per worker:

$$k_{t+1} = \frac{S(\omega_t, R_{t+1})}{1+n} \qquad (20)$$

with:

$$\omega_t = f(k_t) - k_t f'(k_t) \tag{21}$$

and R_t is given by (17). Combining (17), (20), and (21), we obtain the equation giving the dynamic evolution of capital:

$$k_{t+1} = \frac{1}{1+n} S\left[f(k_t) - k_t f'(k_t), 1 - \delta + f'(k_{t+1})\right] \tag{22}$$

The equilibrium value of capital per worker, k^*, is obtained by replacing k_{t+1} and k_t in equation (22) with k^*, which yields:

$$k^* = \frac{1}{1+n} S\left[f(k^*) - k^* f'(k^*), 1 - \delta + f'(k^*)\right] \tag{23}$$

Whether there exists a unique value for k^* and whether the dynamic system (22) leads toward it does not have a simple answer in general.[3] Let us first take the traditional example of a logarithmic utility function:

$$U(c_{1t}) + \beta U(c_{2t+1}) = Log c_{1t} + \beta Log c_{2t+1} \tag{24}$$

Then formula (22) becomes:

$$k_{t+1} = \frac{\beta}{(1+n)(1+\beta)} \left[f(k_t) - k_t f'(k_t)\right] \tag{25}$$

If we further assume a Cobb-Douglas production function:

$$F(K_t, L_t) = A K_t^\alpha L_t^{1-\alpha} \tag{26}$$

then:

$$f(k) = Ak^\alpha \qquad f'(k) = \alpha A k^{\alpha-1} \tag{27}$$

and the dynamic equation (25) becomes:

$$k_{t+1} = \frac{\beta(1-\alpha)A}{(1+n)(1+\beta)} k_t^\alpha \tag{28}$$

which is represented in figure 8.1.

---

3. Because the shape of the function in the right-hand side can be complex. See Galor and Ryder (1989) for a thorough study of that issue.

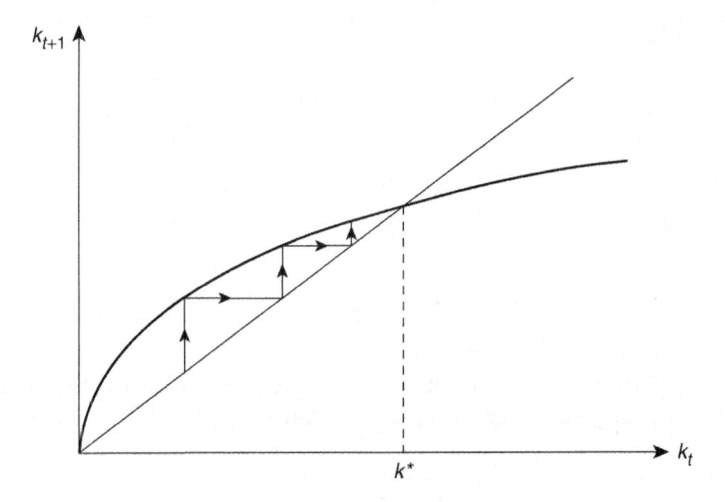

Figure 8.1 Capital dynamics

In this case k_t will converge monotonically toward the unique equilibrium value k^* given by:

$$k^* = \left[\frac{\beta(1-\alpha)A}{(1+n)(1+\beta)}\right]^{1/(1-\alpha)} \quad (29)$$

We also see that in this case, steady-state capital per worker is an increasing function of the savings rate of workers $\beta/(1+\beta)$, and a decreasing function of the population's growth rate n, just as in the Solow-Swan model.

8.4 Optimality

We now investigate the optimality properties of this model. Compared with the Ramsey model in the previous chapter, we encounter a number of novelties. First, we shall see that the market equilibrium may not be a Pareto optimum. Second, the optimality criterion to be used is not as clear as in the Ramsey model, where there is a single dynasty. Here, due to the coexistence of an infinity of generations, several criteria can be envisioned. We begin with Pareto optimality.

8.4.1 Pareto Optima

In period t the condition depicting balance on the goods market is written:

$$N_t c_{1t} + N_{t-1} c_{2t} + K_{t+1} = F(K_t, L_t) + (1-\delta)K_t \quad (30)$$

We will use this equation in terms of variables per worker:

$$c_{1t} + \frac{c_{2t}}{1+n} + (1+n)k_{t+1} = f(k_t) + (1-\delta)k_t \qquad (31)$$

We can find necessary conditions characterizing Pareto optima by maximizing a weighted sum, with arbitrary weights ζ_t, of the utilities of all generations, subject to all dynamic resource equations:

$$\text{Maximize} \sum_t \zeta_t \left[U(c_{1t}) + \beta U(c_{2t+1}) \right] \qquad \text{s.t.}$$

$$c_{1t} + \frac{c_{2t}}{1+n} + (1+n)k_{t+1} = f(k_t) + (1-\delta)k_t \qquad \forall t$$

The Lagrangian for this program is:

$$\sum_t \zeta_t \left[U(c_{1t}) + \beta U(c_{2t+1}) \right]$$
$$+ \sum_t \lambda_t \left[f(k_t) + (1-\delta)k_t - c_{1t} - \frac{c_{2t}}{1+n} - (1+n)k_{t+1} \right] \qquad (32)$$

We obtain the following first-order conditions:

$$\zeta_t U'(c_{1t}) = \lambda_t \qquad (33)$$

$$\beta \zeta_t U'(c_{2t+1}) = \frac{\lambda_{t+1}}{1+n} \qquad (34)$$

$$\lambda_{t+1} \left[1 - \delta + f'(k_{t+1}) \right] = (1+n)\lambda_t \qquad (35)$$

Eliminating the ζ_t and λ_t, we obtain the necessary condition:

$$U'(c_{1t}) = \beta \left[1 - \delta + f'(k_{t+1}) \right] U'(c_{2t+1}) = \beta R_{t+1} U'(c_{2t+1}) \qquad (36)$$

We may note that this condition has a strong resemblance with the discrete time Euler equation that we saw in chapter 7 (section 7.8).

8.4.2 The Golden Rule

There is usually an infinity of Pareto optima satisfying condition (36), so we now use a more discriminating criterion and compute the optimal level of capital in a steady state. We define this optimal capital level, which we will call "golden rule" and denote as $\hat{k}$, as the one that maximizes the utility of the representative household.

In steady state the resource constraint is equation (31), where time indices have been suppressed, that is:

$$c_1 + \frac{c_2}{1+n} = f(k) - (\delta + n)k \qquad (37)$$

The capital level $\hat{k}$ will result from maximizing the utility of the representative household $U(c_1) + \beta U(c_2)$ subject to constraint (37), that is:

$$\text{Maximize} \quad U(c_1) + \beta U(c_2) \quad \text{s.t.}$$

$$c_1 + \frac{c_2}{1+n} = f(k) - (\delta + n)k$$

We see that the resolution of this program can be somehow broken into two steps. In the first step, one maximizes $f(k) - (\delta + n)k$, which yields the golden rule capital $\hat{k}$ (Phelps, 1961):

$$f'(\hat{k}) = \delta + n \qquad (38)$$

In the second step, one finds the first- and second-period consumptions by solving the program:

$$\text{Maximize } U(c_1) + \beta U(c_2) \quad \text{s.t.}$$

$$c_1 + \frac{c_2}{1+n} = f(\hat{k}) - (\delta + n)\hat{k}$$

Note that because $R_t = 1 - \delta + f'(k_t)$ (formula 17), formula (38) can be rewritten:

$$\hat{R} = 1 + n \qquad (39)$$

The golden rule is thus characterized by a real interest rate equal to the growth rate of the population. We recognize Samuelson's (1958) "biological" rate of interest, which we encountered in chapter 4.

8.4.3 Overaccumulation and Inefficiency

We now explore a possibility that did not occur in the Ramsey model, that of inefficient equilibria.

Let us consider a steady state. We say that there is overaccumulation of capital if the amount of capital per worker is superior to the value given by the golden rule, that is, if:

$$f'(k) < \delta + n = f'(\hat{k}) \qquad (40)$$

We show that in this case it is possible to improve the situation of *all* generations, which means that the initial situation is not even Pareto optimal. Let us recall the equation of goods market equilibrium expressed in variables per worker (equation 31):

$$c_{1t} + \frac{c_{2t}}{1+n} + (1+n)k_{t+1} = f(k_t) + (1-\delta)k_t \qquad (41)$$

Assume that until period 0, the economy has been in a steady state with capital per worker $k_0 > \hat{k}$. Imagine that starting with period 1, k_t decreases to the level k_1, with $\hat{k} \leq k_1 < k_0$. Using equation (41), one finds that, compared with the reference trajectory corresponding to k_0, feasible consumption variations (which will be denoted with Δ) are given by:

$$\Delta\left(c_{1t} + \frac{c_{2t}}{1+n}\right) = \Delta\left[f(k_t) + (1-\delta)k_t - (1+n)k_{t+1}\right] \qquad (42)$$

We separate the cases $t=0$ and $t \geq 1$. For $t=0$, (42) yields:

$$\Delta\left(c_{10} + \frac{c_{20}}{1+n}\right) = (1+n)(k_0 - k_1) > 0 \qquad (43)$$

and for $t \geq 1$:

$$\Delta\left(c_{1t} + \frac{c_{2t}}{1+n}\right) = [f(k_1) - (\delta+n)k_1] - [f(k_0) - (\delta+n)k_0] > 0 \qquad (44)$$

We see that all generations benefit from this change. The initial equilibrium was thus not a Pareto optimum.

8.5 Pensions

We now see that the foregoing model and developments are particularly relevant to study the debate between advocates of a "fully funded" pension system and those of a "pay-as-you-go" pension system.[4]

---

4. Early contributions on the pensions issue are Feldstein (1974, 1976) and Samuelson (1975). For a survey, see Feldstein and Liebman (2002).

In a pension system, the government collects a premium x_t from young households and gives a pension z_{t+1} to old households. As a result, the budget constraints for young and old are:

$$c_{1t} + s_t = \omega_t - x_t \qquad (45)$$

$$c_{2t+1} = R_{t+1}s_t + z_{t+1} \qquad (46)$$

We study two classic pension systems, the fully funded system and the pay-as-you-go system, which differ essentially in the way x_t and z_{t+1} are related.

To make the exposition more transparent, we again use the simple logarithmic utility function:

$$Log c_{1t} + \beta Log c_{2t+1} \qquad (47)$$

8.5.1 The Fully Funded System

In the fully funded system the government collects a premium x_t, and invests this sum on financial markets where it is used, just as private savings, to finance capital accumulation. It has the same rate of return as private capital, so that:

$$z_{t+1} = R_{t+1}x_t \qquad (48)$$

The household's budget constraints are thus:

$$c_{1t} + s_t = \omega_t - x_t \qquad (49)$$

$$c_{2t+1} = R_{t+1}s_t + R_{t+1}x_t \qquad (50)$$

We see that, compared with the case without pensions, the households' intertemporal budget constraint is exactly the same, that is:

$$c_{1t} + \frac{c_{2t+1}}{R_{t+1}} = \omega_t \qquad (51)$$

The chosen level of savings is:

$$s_t = \frac{\beta \omega_t}{1+\beta} - x_t \qquad (52)$$

We see that agents reduce their savings by the exact amount of pension payments. Finally, capital accumulation is given by:

$$K_{t+1} = N_t (s_t + x_t) = \frac{\beta N_t \omega_t}{1+\beta} \qquad (53)$$

Compared with a system without pensions, the introduction of a fully funded pension system is thus totally neutral.

8.5.2 The Pay-as-you-go System

In a pay-as-you-go system, the government collects premia from the young generation and distributes them immediately to the old generation. Calling z_t the payments to the old in period t, we thus have:

$$N_t x_t = N_{t-1} z_t \qquad (54)$$

or, because $N_t = (1+n) N_{t-1}$:

$$z_t = (1+n) x_t \qquad (55)$$

and the budget constraints become:

$$c_{1t} + s_t = \omega_t - x_t \qquad (56)$$

$$c_{2t+1} = R_{t+1} s_t + (1+n) x_{t+1} \qquad (57)$$

To make the effect of the pension premium x_t more transparent, we shall assume from now on that $x_{t+1} = x_t$. Accordingly each household chooses savings s_t by maximizing its utility with given x_t:

$$\text{Maximize } Log(\omega_t - x_t - s_t) + \beta Log\left[R_{t+1} s_t + (1+n) x_t\right] \qquad (58)$$

This yields the savings of each individual household:

$$s_t = \frac{\beta}{1+\beta}(\omega_t - x_t) - \frac{1+n}{(1+\beta) R_{t+1}} x_t \qquad (59)$$

Now we use the following relations:

$$k_{t+1} = \frac{s_t}{1+n} \qquad (60)$$

$$\omega_t = f(k_t) - k_t f'(k_t) \qquad (61)$$

$$R_{t+1} = 1 - \delta + f'(k_{t+1}) \qquad (62)$$

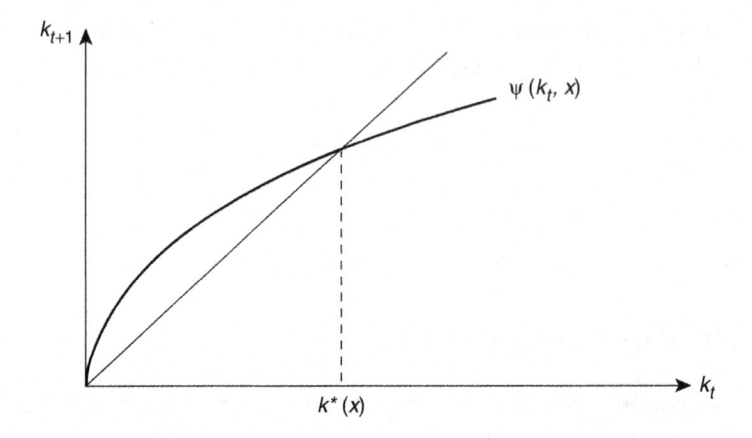

[Figure: Pensions and capital dynamics — curve ψ(kₜ, x) intersecting 45° line at k*(x)]

Figure 8.2 Pensions and capital dynamics

which, combined with (59), give us the dynamic equation of capital accumulation:

$$k_{t+1} = \frac{\beta\left[f(k_t) - k_t f'(k_t) - x_t\right]}{(1+\beta)(1+n)} - \frac{x_t}{(1+\beta)\left[1 - \delta + f'(k_{t+1})\right]} \qquad (63)$$

To have a more compact notation, we rewrite equation (63) as:

$$k_{t+1} = \Psi(k_t, x_t) \qquad (64)$$

with the following partial derivatives:

$$\Psi_k > 0 \qquad \Psi_x < 0 \qquad (65)$$

This is represented in figure 8.2 for a constant x_t. In this figure we have implicitly assumed that the steady-state capital $k^*(x)$ is dynamically stable, as in the Cobb-Douglas case of figure 8.1. This means in particular that, at least at the steady-state k^*:

$$\Psi_k < 1 \qquad (66)$$

8.5.3 Pay-as-you-go and Welfare

We saw that the introduction of a fully funded system was neutral with respect to a system without pensions. We want to investigate the effect of the introduction of a pay-as-you-go system. We limit ourselves to the study of steady states and assume that contributions x_t are constant in time and equal to x.

In a first step, we want to know the effect of increased pay-as-you-go contributions on capital accumulation. More specifically, we want to find the effect of an increase in x on the stationary value of capital k^*. From equation (64), this stationary value is simply given by:

$$k^*(x) = \Psi\left[k^*(x), x\right] \qquad (67)$$

Differentiating we find that:

$$\frac{dk^*(x)}{dx} = \frac{\Psi_x}{1 - \Psi_k} \qquad (68)$$

In view of (65), and if we assume (66), the level of capital in steady state will be a decreasing function of x. This is pictured in figure 8.3, which compares the cases $x_t = 0$ and $x_t = x > 0$.

Now we ask about the effect of an increase in x on welfare, and we see that the question has no unequivocal answer, since it clearly depends on the starting point.

If the initial situation is characterized by an insufficient level of capital, then the introduction of a pay-as-you-go system will worsen things, because the new equilibrium level of capital will be even further from the golden rule optimum.

If, on the contrary, the initial state is characterized by overaccumulation, the introduction of a pay-as-you-go retirement system will go in the right direction because it will reduce the level of capital, which was too high in the first place. This result is in the same spirit as that of section 8.4.3,

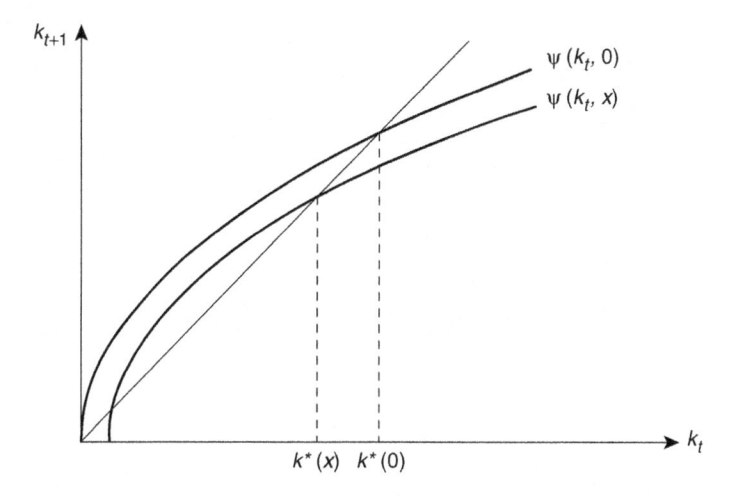

Figure 8.3 Pay-as-you-go and steady state capital

where we saw that an exogenous decrease in capital would lead to a Pareto improvement if one starts from a situation of overaccumulation.

8.6 Debt Dynamics

We assumed so far that households could only save under the form of physical capital. But we saw in chapter 4 that the possibility of saving under the form of government debt dramatically changed the dynamics of the economy. We now assume that households can save both capital and government debt, and we shall see that, contrarily to what happens in the Ramsey model, debt matters.

To make the exposition simple, we continue to use the logarithmic utility function:

$$Log c_{1t} + \beta Log c_{2t+1} \tag{69}$$

8.6.1 Dynamic Equations

As in chapter 4, let us denote as D_t the total amount of real government debt held by consumers at the beginning of period t (including interest payments), and $d_t = D_t/N_t$ debt per worker. Total savings is now shared between capital accumulation and debt:[5]

$$N_t s_t = K_{t+1} + \frac{D_{t+1}}{R_{t+1}} \tag{70}$$

Dividing by N_t this yields, in terms of variables per worker:

$$s_t = (1+n) k_{t+1} + \frac{(1+n) d_{t+1}}{R_{t+1}} \tag{71}$$

On the other hand, with the utility function (69) savings per worker are given by:

$$s_t = \frac{\beta \omega_t}{1 + \beta} \tag{72}$$

---

5. The coefficient $1/R_{t+1}$ for next period's government debt D_{t+1} is due to the fact that D_{t+1} includes interest payments, and is thus worth D_{t+1}/R_{t+1} in period t.

Combining (71) and (72) we obtain a first dynamic equation:

$$(1+n)\,k_{t+1} + \frac{(1+n)\,d_{t+1}}{R_{t+1}} = \frac{\beta w_t}{1+\beta} = \frac{\beta\left[f(k_t) - k_t f'(k_t)\right]}{1+\beta} \qquad (73)$$

The other dynamic equation represents the evolution of debt. To have a simpler exposition we assume that there is no taxation,[6] so the debt evolves according to:

$$D_{t+1} = R_{t+1} D_t \qquad (74)$$

or in terms of variables per worker:

$$d_{t+1} = \frac{R_{t+1}}{1+n} d_t = \frac{1 - \delta + f'(k_{t+1})}{1+n} d_t \qquad (75)$$

8.6.2 Steady States

We see that, as in the simplified model of chapter 4, the dynamic system admits two types of steady states. In the first, debt is zero, and capital and the rate of return are the same as in the market equilibrium of section 8.3:

$$d^* = 0 \qquad R^* = 1 - \delta + f'(k^*) \qquad (76)$$

where, from equation (73), k^* is the solution of:

$$(1+n)\,k^* = \frac{\beta}{1+\beta}\left[f(k^*) - k^* f'(k^*)\right] \qquad (77)$$

There is also a second long-run equilibrium, the golden rule, with nonzero debt and a rate of return equal to the rate of growth of the population:

$$\hat{R} = 1 + n \qquad f'(\hat{k}) = \delta + n \qquad (78)$$

where, from equation (73), $\hat{d}$ is given by:

$$\hat{d} = \frac{\beta}{1+\beta}\left[f(\hat{k}) - \hat{k} f'(\hat{k})\right] - (1+n)\,\hat{k} \qquad (79)$$

---

6. There are, of course, many other possible cases. See some alternative assumptions in De la Croix and Michel (2002).

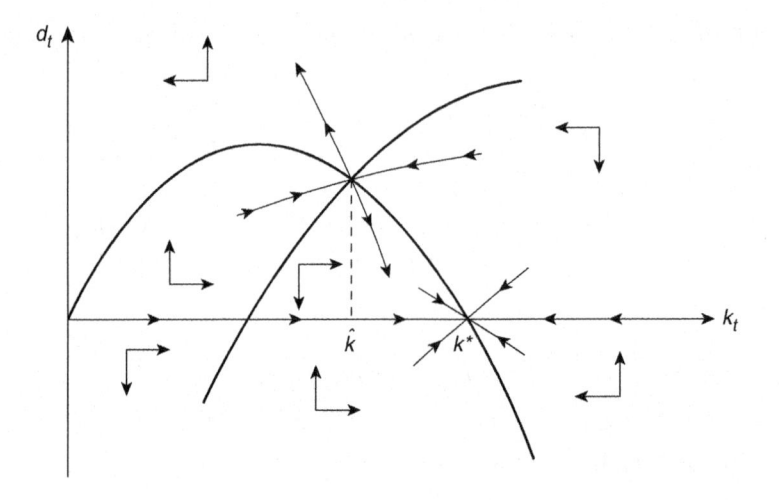

Figure 8.4 Capital and debt dynamics

8.6.3 The Dynamics of Capital and Debt

Figure 8.4 describes capital and debt dynamics in the (k_t, d_t) plane. It is drawn for the case where long-term debt at the golden rule is positive.

From equations (73) and (75), the $k_{t+1} = k_t$ locus has for equation:

$$d_t = \frac{\beta \omega_t}{(1+\beta)(1+n)} - k_t = \frac{\beta [f(k_t) - k_t f'(k_t)]}{(1+\beta)(1+n)} - k_t \qquad (80)$$

This is the bell-shaped curve that starts at the origin. From equation (75), the $d_{t+1} = d_t$ locus has actually two branches. The first branch is simply the horizontal axis:

$$d_t = 0 \qquad (81)$$

The second branch has as equation:

$$1 + n = R_{t+1} = 1 - \delta + f'(k_{t+1}) \qquad (82)$$

This is actually equivalent to $k_{t+1} = \hat{k}$, or, using (73):

$$d_t = \frac{\beta [f(k_t) - k_t f'(k_t)]}{1+\beta} - (1+n)\hat{k} \qquad (83)$$

This is the upward-sloping curve in figure 8.4. We see that the dynamics around the golden rule is a saddle path. On the other hand, the equilibrium with zero debt is stable.[7]

Problems

Problem 8.1: Generalized Golden Rules

We investigate a generalization of the golden rule, based on a criterion due to Samuelson (1967, 1968), which consists in weighting the utilities of the various generations by some "social rate of discount," ϕ. The utility criterion, as viewed from period s, will be:

$$\sum_{t=s-1}^{\infty} \phi^t \left[U(c_{1t}) + \beta U(c_{2t+1}) \right] \qquad \phi < 1$$

The sum starts with period $s - 1$ because the old member of that generation is still alive in period s. We may note that maximizing the utility of the representative household, as we did for finding the golden rule, somehow boils down to taking the particular case $\phi = 1$.

The per worker production function is still:

$$y_t = f(k_t)$$

and the equation of goods market balance:

$$c_{1t} + \frac{c_{2t}}{1+n} + (1+n) k_{t+1} = f(k_t) + (1-\delta) k_t$$

1. Derive the first-order conditions that characterize the dynamic equilibrium of this economy.
2. Compute the steady-state value of the gross real interest rate. Compare with the value that we found in section 8.4.

---

7. Tirole (1985) studies a similar model, with a slightly different interpretation of the results. The reason is that, whereas we define D_t as traditional real debt (as in the original Diamond model), in Tirole (1985) that second asset is considered as a bubble, hence the difference.

Problem 8.2: Taxation and Capital Accumulation

We show that the way taxes are collected affects capital accumulation in an OLG economy. Assume that households have the following utility function:

$$LogC_1 + \beta LogC_2$$

They receive an exogenous real income Y when young. They can invest an amount of capital K, which will give them an income AK in the second period. The government spends G, which is entirely financed by lump-sum taxes.

1. Assume that government taxes young households in a lump sum by an amount $T_1 = G$. What is the level of capital accumulation?
2. Assume that government taxes old households in a lump sum by an amount $T_2 = G$. What is the level of capital accumulation?
3. Compare the answers in (1) and (2).

Problem 8.3: Labor versus Capital Taxation

As in problem 7.3, we study proportional distortionary taxation to see which of capital or labor income should preferably be taxed. Again we assume a Cobb-Douglas production function and 100 percent depreciation:

$$Y_t = AK_t^\alpha L_t^{1-\alpha}$$

$$K_{t+1} = I_t$$

but instead of Ramsey consumers we have an OLG structure with constant population where generation t has the utility function:

$$U_t = LogC_{1t} + \beta LogC_{2t+1}$$

The government maximizes the discounted sum of utilities:

$$\sum \phi^t U_t = \sum \phi^t \left(LogC_{1t} + \beta LogC_{2t+1} \right)$$

Government spending is a given fraction of national income:

$$G_t = \zeta Y_t$$

Government taxes labor and capital income at the constant rates τ_ℓ and τ_k, so that total taxes are equal to:

$$T_t = \tau_\ell \omega_t L_t + \tau_k R_t K_t$$

We finally assume that the government budget is balanced period by period:

$$T_t = G_t$$

1. Compute the dynamics of this economy.
2. Find the optimal tax rates τ_ℓ and τ_k.
3. The results are different from those of problem 7.3. Compute the optimal and market rates of savings and interpret this difference.

9

Endogenous Growth

9.1 Introduction

In the models of the two previous chapters, as in the Solow-Swan model, the rate of growth is exogenous and does not depend on any decision by firms or the production sector. In particular, it does not depend on the rate of factor accumulation, but is determined by the rates of growth of population and (exogenous) technical progress.

In this chapter we study models of *endogenous growth*, where in particular (1) the rate of growth is sensitive to the rate of factor accumulation, and (2) technical progress is an economic activity that results from rational decisions by households and firms.

Besides its obvious theoretical interest, from an empirical point of view endogenous growth is a most welcome addition to our toolbox if we want to explain such phenomena as the "great divergence" that we mentioned in chapter 1 without putting all the weight of the explanation on exogenous, and thus unexplained factors.

Although it has become a major subject of study only recently, the history of endogenous growth goes farther back than is usually thought. For example, the two famous models of Harrod (1939) and Domar (1946) had elements of endogenous growth. The problem is that they actually had *two* potentially inconsistent different rates of growth: one, exogenous, was based on the rate of growth of the population, the other, endogenous, was based on savings and the capital-output ratio. This discrepancy posed a serious problem in the profession until the two aspects were reconciled with a variable capital-output ratio in the Solow-Swan model. But the endogenous growth aspect had disappeared. In an early article, Frankel (1962) built a Solow-Swan-type model with growth made endogenous.

Rigorous endogenous growth really starts with the seminal work of Romer (1986, 1987, 1990), who embeds a number of features conducive to endogenous growth (increasing returns, research) into full-fledged dynamic maximizing models. Lucas (1988) explores models with two accumulated factors and global constant returns. After that, the development of the field has been exponential.[1]

Section 9.2 studies the simplest model of endogenous growth, the so-called AK model. Section 9.3 presents a number of reflections on the particular nature of technical progress as an input to growth.

Sections 9.4, 9.5, and 9.6 present in a simple unified framework a few alternative models that emphasize the role of research in endogenous growth. Section 9.4 presents the seminal model by Romer (1987, 1990) where technical progress occurs through returns to diversification among horizontally differentiated products. Growth results from the increase in the number of varieties, which is done through (costly) research. Section 9.5 presents a different model, in which the central mechanism is that the productivity of each production process can be increased through research.

Both models of sections 9.4 and 9.5 display scale effects, through which, for example, the size of the economy has a positive influence on the growth rate. In section 9.6 it is shown that a simple modification of the model can suppress this surprising property.

9.2 The AK Model

We begin by studying the simplest possible model of endogenous growth with maximizing consumers, called the AK model (Rebelo, 1991) because the production function is linear in capital, which is the only factor of production:[2]

$$Y_t = AK_t \tag{1}$$

Note already that this production function is homogeneous of degree 1 in the accumulated factor, capital, a feature that appears in some form

---

[1]. Overviews of the field can be found in Aghion and Howitt (1998), Grossman and Helpman (1991b), Howitt (2008), and Romer (1994).

[2]. A model of similar inspiration, but with two accumulated factors, physical and human capital, is the subject of problem 9.2.

or the other in models of endogenous growth. We note also that because the parameter A is constant, the growth we obtain will not come, as in the two previous chapters, from exogenous increases in the "technological parameter" A.

We expose a discrete time version of the AK model. Problem 9.1 gives a continuous time version.

Capital depreciates at the rate δ, so it evolves as:

$$K_{t+1} = (1-\delta) K_t + I_t \tag{2}$$

In period t the household's income consists of the value of production plus undepreciated capital, so that its budget constraint is:

$$K_{t+1} + C_t = (1-\delta) K_t + Y_t = (1-\delta) K_t + AK_t \tag{3}$$

Households have the following intertemporal utility:

$$\sum_t \beta^t Log C_t \tag{4}$$

They maximize utility (4) subject to the budget constraints (3). The Lagrangian for this maximization program is thus:

$$\sum_t \beta^t \left\{ Log C_t + \lambda_t \left[(1-\delta+A) K_t - C_t - K_{t+1} \right] \right\} \tag{5}$$

The first-order conditions for C_t and K_t are, respectively:

$$\lambda_t = \frac{1}{C_t} \tag{6}$$

$$\lambda_t = \beta (1-\delta+A) \lambda_{t+1} \tag{7}$$

Combining (6) and (7) we find the rate of growth of consumption (assuming an interior solution):

$$\frac{C_{t+1}}{C_t} = \beta (1-\delta+A) \tag{8}$$

We see that the rate of growth of consumption, which is also the rate of growth of the economy, depends on both technology (via δ and A) and on the households' rate of intertemporal preferences via β. Recall that in the Solow-Swan model parameters like δ and A did not influence the growth rate, only the level of production.

To characterize fully our intertemporal equilibrium, we have to determine how the production in period t, $Y_t = AK_t$, is allocated between consumption and investment. Because the ratio of the two is not predetermined, the economy settles on a balanced path from the start, so that, combining equations (2) and (8):

$$\frac{K_{t+1}}{K_t} = 1 - \delta + \frac{I_t}{K_t} = \frac{C_{t+1}}{C_t} = \beta(1 - \delta + A) \qquad (9)$$

which yields, combining with (1), the ratio of investment to output:

$$\frac{I_t}{Y_t} = \frac{\beta A - (1 - \beta)(1 - \delta)}{A} \qquad (10)$$

9.3 Technical Progress and Endogenous Growth

We just saw with the AK model that endogenous growth can arise if technology in a Ramsey-type model has constant returns to scale in the accumulated factors. But we saw in chapter 1 (section 1.7) that total returns to traditional accumulated factors (physical and human capital) seem to be less than one in reality.

Consequently recent research on endogenous growth has put more emphasis on the role of technical progress and has sought to endogenize the evolution of the variable representing the state of technology, that is, the parameter A_t in the Solow-Swan, Ramsey, or AK models. Before giving examples of models achieving such a goal, we underscore a few aspects that differentiate such theories from traditional growth theories (the discussion that follows is essentially taken from Romer, 1990).

9.3.1 Rivalry and Excludability

We first describe two potential characteristics of economic goods that will allow us to highlight the specific features of research activities. These are rivalry and excludability.

A purely *rival* good has the property that its use by one economic agent precludes its use by another agent. A contrario the use of a purely *nonrival* good limits in no way its use by another agent.

A good is *excludable* if its owner can prevent other agents from using it.

Private economic goods in traditional theory are both rival and excludable. At the other end of the spectrum, public goods are nonrival and nonexcludable. The goods we are most interested in here are nonrival but excludable. The typical example is a design for a production process.

Once the design exists, it can potentially be used by an unlimited number of people, so it is nonrival. But agents can be excluded from its use, for example, by a patent system, and it is thus excludable.

9.3.2 Returns to Scale and Market Structure

The presence of nonrival inputs creates a number of substantial changes in the assumptions traditionally used in growth theory. To make things precise, let us denote Z_t as the quantity of "traditional" rival inputs and A_t the amount of nonrival inputs (this can be thought of, for example, as the level of technical knowledge). The production function is $F(A_t, Z_t)$. The traditional "homogeneity" argument applies only to the rival outputs so that:

$$F(A_t, \lambda Z_t) = \lambda F(A_t, Z_t) \qquad (11)$$

A first consequence is that the production function is not concave anymore because for $\lambda \leq 1$:

$$F(\lambda A_t, \lambda Z_t) \leq F(A_t, \lambda Z_t) = \lambda F(A_t, Z_t) \qquad (12)$$

Moreover, differentiating (11) with respect to λ, we find:

$$F(A_t, Z_t) = Z_t F_Z(A_t, Z_t) \qquad (13)$$

and thus, if the nonrival input A_t is productive (i.e., $F_A > 0$):

$$F(A_t, Z_t) < A_t F_A(A_t, Z_t) + Z_t F_Z(A_t, Z_t) \qquad (14)$$

If all factors were paid at their marginal productivity, firms would make losses and shut down. This explains why a number of authors, starting with Romer, developed models in which imperfect competition is the natural market structure. We study such models in the next three sections.

9.4 The Romer Model

Here we describe the seminal model by Romer (1990). We use a simplified version without capital, because capital does not play a central role here. A version with capital is given in appendix 9.1.

9.4.1 The Model

Time is discrete. There are three sectors of production. Output is produced with the help of intermediate goods indexed by i. Each intermediate good i is produced by a monopolistically competitive firm i with production function:

$$y_{it} = \ell_{it} \qquad (15)$$

The range of intermediate goods existing at time t is $[0, N_t]$. These intermediate goods $i \in [0, N_t]$ are combined by competitive firms to produce output Y_t according to the production function:

$$Y_t = N_t^{1+\nu} \left(\frac{1}{N_t} \int_0^{N_t} y_{it}^\eta di \right)^{1/\eta} \qquad 0 \leq \eta < 1 \qquad \nu \geq 0 \qquad (16)$$

The parameter η is an index of substitutability between the various intermediate goods. The elasticity of the demand curves for intermediates will turn out to be $-1/(1-\eta)$. The more substitutable the goods are (i.e., the closer η is to 1), the more elastic the demand curves will be, and thus the more competitive the market. Therefore, the parameter η will also be interpreted as an index of competitiveness between the intermediate goods producers.

A second important parameter in the production function (16) is the parameter ν, which represents the extent of "returns to diversification" (Dixit and Stiglitz, 1977; Ethier, 1982) in the sense that for a given total labor input, output will be larger the larger N_t. To show this, let us call L_t the total amount of labor employed in the production of intermediate goods:

$$L_t = \int_0^{N_t} \ell_{it} di \qquad (17)$$

and consider a symmetrical situation where:

$$\ell_{it} = \ell_t = \frac{L_t}{N_t} \qquad y_{it} = y_t = \frac{L_t}{N_t} \qquad (18)$$

Then, combining (16) and (18), we find:

$$Y_t = N_t^\nu L_t \qquad (19)$$

so the parameter ν measures indeed the extent of the "returns to diversification."

Finally the number of intermediate goods can be increased by undertaking research. The reason agents want new goods is that to each good i is associated a "patent," which gives its owner the exclusive right to produce and sell that good.

The research sector produces new intermediate goods, and thus new patents. The production function in the research sector shows how much the number N_t of intermediate goods expands as a function of the quantity of labor H_t devoted to research:

$$\frac{N_{t+1} - N_t}{N_t} = aH_t \qquad (20)$$

Households are infinitely lived and endowed with a total aggregate flow of labor Λ in each period. They consume C_t in period t and maximize discounted utility:

$$U = \sum_t \beta^t Log C_t \qquad (21)$$

The budget constraint of households is:

$$C_t + v_t \left(N_{t+1} - N_t\right) = \omega_t \Lambda + \pi_t N_t \qquad (22)$$

where v_t is the price of a patent, ω_t the real wage, and π_t the flow of real profits that an existing patent yields.

9.4.2 The Market Equilibrium

Let us take final output as the numéraire, and denote as p_{it} the relative price of intermediate good i. The firms producing final output maximize profits:

$$Y_t - \int_0^{N_t} p_{it} y_{it} di = N_t^{1+\nu} \left(\frac{1}{N_t} \int_0^{N_t} y_{it}^\eta di\right)^{1/\eta} - \int_0^{N_t} p_{it} y_{it} di \qquad (23)$$

which yields the following demand for y_{it}:

$$y_{it} = \frac{Y_t}{N_t^{1+\nu}} \left(\frac{p_{it}}{N_t^\nu}\right)^{-1/(1-\eta)} \qquad (24)$$

Firm i maximizes profit $p_{it} y_{it} - \omega_t \ell_{it}$ subject to the production function $y_{it} = \ell_{it}$ and the demand curve (24). In view of the linear production function (15), the marginal cost of producing each intermediate good is constant and equal to the real wage ω_t. With constant marginal cost and

Endogenous Growth

the isoelastic demand curve (24), the price is simply obtained by applying the corresponding monopolistic markup $1/\eta$ to the marginal cost, that is:

$$p_{it} = p_t = \frac{\omega_t}{\eta} \tag{25}$$

Actually, the market solution will be symmetric in the various intermediates i, so we shall give from now on most equilibrium relations without mentioning the corresponding index i.

Because the final goods sector is competitive, the price p_{it} of an intermediate good i is simply equal to its marginal productivity $\partial Y_t / \partial x_{it}$, which yields in a symmetrical situation:

$$p_{it} = p_t = N_t^\nu \tag{26}$$

Because the research sector is also competitive, from (20) the real wage ω_t and the value v_t of a patent for an additional good i are related by:

$$v_t = \frac{\omega_t}{aN_t} \quad \text{if} \quad N_{t+1} > N_t \tag{27}$$

Call $\ell_t = L_t/N_t$ the employment in one of the intermediate industries. The flow of profits π_t accruing to the holder of a patent is:

$$\pi_t = p_t y_t - \omega_t \ell_t = \frac{(1-\eta)p_t L_t}{N_t} \tag{28}$$

Now we have to derive the optimal intertemporal choices of the households, who can choose between consuming now or accumulating new patents via increases in N_t. Their optimization program consists in maximizing utility (21) subject to the budget constraints (22):

$$\text{Maximize} \sum_t \beta^t Log C_t \quad \text{s.t.}$$

$$C_t + v_t (N_{t+1} - N_t) = \omega_t \Lambda + \pi_t N_t$$

The Lagrangian is:

$$\sum_t \beta^t \left\{ Log C_t + \lambda_t \left[\omega_t \Lambda + \pi_t N_t - C_t - v_t (N_{t+1} - N_t) \right] \right\} \tag{29}$$

and the first-order conditions in C_t and N_t:

$$\lambda_t = \frac{1}{C_t} \tag{30}$$

$$\lambda_t v_t = \beta \lambda_{t+1} \left(v_{t+1} + \pi_{t+1} \right) \tag{31}$$

To complete the solution, we have additional conditions of equilibrium on goods and labor markets. The first is that consumption be equal to final goods output, which, assuming that a total quantity of labor L_t is used in the production of intermediates, is written:

$$C_t = Y_t = N_t^\nu L_t \tag{32}$$

Second, the quantities of labor H_t used in research, and L_t used in producing intermediate goods, must sum up to Λ:

$$L_t + H_t = \Lambda \tag{33}$$

These equations fully define the dynamics of the economy. Combining (20), (25), (26), (27), (28), (32), and (33), we obtain the dynamic equation giving the evolution of L_t:

$$\frac{1}{L_t} = \frac{\beta}{1 + a\Lambda} \frac{1}{L_{t+1}} + \frac{\beta a (1 - \eta) + \eta a}{\eta (1 + a\Lambda)} \tag{34}$$

Because the coefficient of $1/L_{t+1}$ is smaller than 1, we have a determinate steady state with constant L_t, where the economy settles immediately (mathematical appendix, section A.11). From (34), this steady-state value of L_t, which we denote as L, is given by (if we have an interior maximum):

$$L_t = L = \frac{\eta \left[(1 - \beta) + a\Lambda \right]}{\beta a (1 - \eta) + \eta a} \tag{35}$$

This results in a constant rate of growth γ_N of the number N_t of goods and patents:

$$\gamma_N = \frac{N_{t+1} - N_t}{N_t} = a (\Lambda - L) = \frac{\beta a (1 - \eta) \Lambda - \eta (1 - \beta)}{\beta (1 - \eta) + \eta} \tag{36}$$

Note that the rate of growth of patents is an increasing function of the monopolistic markup $1/\eta$. The intuition is the following: a low value of η leads to a higher markup, and therefore a higher rate of return for intermediates. Consequently agents will invest more in patents, thus creating more growth.

We may note also that the rate of growth depends positively on the size of the working population Λ. This is called, the "scale effect." Clearly it is a little strange, as there is no compelling reason why a larger economy should grow faster than a smaller one. We return to this issue in section 9.6.

9.4.3 The Social Optimum

Computation of the social optimum will actually be easier than that of the market solution, as we can immediately consider a symmetric situation. All that has to be done is to choose which quantity of labor L_t will be devoted to the production of intermediate goods, the rest, $\Lambda - L_t$, being devoted to research. Because $C_t = N_t^\nu L_t$, the program giving the optimal path is:

$$\text{Maximize} \sum_t \beta^t Log\left(N_t^\nu L_t\right) \quad \text{s.t.}$$

$$Log N_{t+1} - Log N_t = Log\left[1 + a\left(\Lambda - L_t\right)\right]$$

The Lagrangian for this program is:

$$\sum_t \beta^t \left\{\nu Log N_t + Log L_t + \lambda_t \left[Log\left(1 + a\Lambda - aL_t\right) + Log N_t - Log N_{t+1}\right]\right\} \tag{37}$$

This Lagrangian is concave in L_t and $Log\ N_t$. The first-order conditions are:

$$\frac{1}{L_t} = \frac{a\lambda_t}{1 + a\Lambda - aL_t} \tag{38}$$

$$\lambda_{t-1} = \beta\left(\lambda_t + \nu\right) \tag{39}$$

Because the coefficient of λ_t in (39) is smaller than 1, λ_t immediately settles to its steady-state value, which from (39) is:

$$\lambda_t = \frac{\beta\nu}{1-\beta} \tag{40}$$

Inserting this into (38), we find:

$$L_t = L = \frac{(1-\beta)(1 + a\Lambda)}{a(1 - \beta + \beta\nu)} \tag{41}$$

from which we can compute the optimal rate of growth of patents γ_N^*:

$$\gamma_N^* = \frac{\beta a \nu \Lambda - (1-\beta)}{1 - \beta + \beta \nu} \qquad (42)$$

9.4.4 Comparing Market Outcome and Social Optimum

Looking first at formulas (36) and (42), we see that there is no a priori ranking between the market equilibrium rate of growth γ_N and the optimal one γ_N^*, so the amount of research, and accordingly the growth rate, can be too high or too low.

But formulas (36) and (42) also give us the key to a result found in the early literature, i.e. that the amount of research was always found to be too low. These early models, instead of production function (16), used the original Dixit-Stiglitz (1977) aggregator function:

$$Y_t = \left(\int_0^{N_t} y_{it}^{\eta} di \right)^{1/\eta} \qquad 0 \leq \eta < 1 \qquad (43)$$

We see that this is equivalent to taking for the parameter ν measuring the "returns to diversity" in formula (16) the particular value $\nu = 1/\eta - 1$. Inserting this value of ν into formulas (36) and (42) we obtain:

$$\gamma_N = \frac{\beta a (1-\eta) \Lambda - \eta (1-\beta)}{\beta (1-\eta) + \eta} \qquad (44)$$

$$\gamma_N^* = \frac{\beta a (1-\eta) \Lambda - \eta (1-\beta)}{\beta (1-\eta) + \eta (1-\beta)} \qquad (45)$$

Under this particular specification, the market rate of growth of patents γ_N is systematically lower than the socially optimal one γ_N^*. This result was thus only due to the choice of a particular value for the returns to specialization (Bénassy, 1998).

9.5 Endogenous Productivity Increases

In the model we now describe,[3] technical progress does not come from a larger range of intermediate goods but from increases in the productivity q_{it} of industries producing each of these goods.

---

3. The initial contributions in this area are Aghion and Howitt (1992); Grossman and Helpman (1991a); and Segerstrom, Anant, and Dinopoulos (1990). The model in this and the next section derives from Smulders and Van de Klundert (1995), Van de Klundert and Smulders (1996), and Young (1998). Appendix 9.2 describes a model with a stochastic technical progress function.

9.5.1 The Model

As in the previous model, households supply in each period a total quantity of labor Λ and have an intertemporal utility function:

$$U = \sum_t \beta^t Log C_t \qquad (46)$$

Consumption goods are produced by competitive firms with a production function:

$$Y_t = N \left(\frac{1}{N} \int_0^N y_{it}^\eta di \right)^{1/\eta} \qquad (47)$$

Note that since the issue of returns to diversity will not play any role here, we have, as compared to production function (16), suppressed returns to diversity ($\nu = 0$) and taken a fixed number of varieties ($N_t = N$).

The intermediate inputs y_{it} are produced by monopolistically competitive firms with the technology:

$$y_{it} = q_{it} \ell_{it} \qquad (48)$$

where q_{it} is the productivity in sector i. Productivities may differ across firms during a period, but at the end of each period all firms have costlessly access to the best technology, which we denote $\bar{q}_t$:

$$\bar{q}_t = \max_i q_{it} \qquad (49)$$

At the beginning of period t all firms have freely access to the technology $\bar{q}_{t-1}$. Starting from this common level of productivity, each firm i can raise its productivity from $\bar{q}_{t-1}$ to q_{it} at a labor cost h_{it}:[4]

$$h_{it} = \Psi \left(\frac{q_{it}}{\bar{q}_{t-1}} \right) \qquad \Psi' > 0 \qquad \Psi'' > 0 \qquad (50)$$

This may include a fixed cost, in which case $\Psi(1) > 0$.

---

4. The reader may note that "technical progress" occurs in the period where labor is spent. A usual assumption in the literature is that there is a one-period lag; this is explored in problem 9.4. The results do not differ much, but the derivation is a little longer.

9.5.2 The Short-run Equilibrium

The firms producing the final good maximize profits in real terms:

$$Y_t - \int_0^N p_{it} y_{it} \, di = N \left(\frac{1}{N} \int_0^N y_{it}^\eta \, di \right)^{1/\eta} - \int_0^N p_{it} y_{it} \, di \qquad (51)$$

where p_{it} is the relative price (with respect to output) of intermediate good i. Maximization in y_{it} yields the demand for intermediate i:

$$y_{it} = \frac{Y_t}{N} p_{it}^{-1/(1-\eta)} \qquad (52)$$

Now the firms producing the intermediate goods maximize period t profits, that is:

$$p_{it} y_{it} - \omega_t \ell_{it} - \omega_t h_{it} \qquad (53)$$

subject to (48), (50), and (52). Maximization in p_{it} yields the traditional "markup" equation:

$$p_{it} = \frac{\omega_t}{\eta q_{it}} \qquad (54)$$

Inserting (48), (50), (52), and (54) into (53), firm i's profit (53) becomes:

$$(1-\eta) \frac{Y_t}{N} \left(\frac{\eta q_{it}}{\omega_t} \right)^{\eta/(1-\eta)} - \omega_t \Psi \left(\frac{q_{it}}{\bar{q}_{t-1}} \right) \qquad (55)$$

The first-order condition on q_{it} is:

$$\eta \frac{Y_t}{N} \left(\frac{\omega_t}{\eta} \right)^{-\eta/(1-\eta)} q_{it}^{\eta/(1-\eta)-1} = \frac{\omega_t}{\bar{q}_{t-1}} \Psi' \left(\frac{q_{it}}{\bar{q}_{t-1}} \right) \qquad (56)$$

We see that all sectors will choose the same level of productivity, so that:

$$q_{it} = q_t = \bar{q}_t \qquad (57)$$

Now in equilibrium, the real wage is equal to productivity q_t divided by the markup $1/\eta$:

$$\omega_t = \eta q_t \qquad (58)$$

Using (57) and (58), equation (56) simplifies as:

$$\frac{Y_t}{q_t N_t} = \frac{q_t}{q_{t-1}} \Psi'\left(\frac{q_t}{q_{t-1}}\right) \qquad (59)$$

Let us denote the gross rate of growth of productivity as $\mathcal{G}_t$:

$$\mathcal{G}_t = \frac{q_t}{q_{t-1}} \qquad (60)$$

Equation (59) is rewritten:

$$\frac{Y_t}{q_t N} = \mathcal{G}_t \Psi'(\mathcal{G}_t) \qquad (61)$$

Now the condition of equilibrium on the labor market is that labor used in research and labor used in production in each sector sum up to Λ/N, that is:

$$\Psi(\mathcal{G}_t) + \frac{Y_t}{q_t N} = \frac{\Lambda}{N} \qquad (62)$$

Combining (61) and (62) we obtain the equation giving the rate of growth:

$$\Psi(\mathcal{G}_t) + \mathcal{G}_t \Psi'(\mathcal{G}_t) = \frac{\Lambda}{N} \qquad (63)$$

We may note that, as in the model of section 9.4, we again have 'scale effects', because by differentiating equation (63) we obtain:

$$[2\Psi'(\mathcal{G}_t) + \mathcal{G}_t \Psi''(\mathcal{G}_t)] d\mathcal{G}_t = d\left(\frac{\Lambda}{N}\right) \qquad (64)$$

so that:

$$\frac{\partial \mathcal{G}_t}{\partial (\Lambda/N)} > 0 \qquad (65)$$

9.6 A Model Without Scale Effects

In the two models of sections 9.4 and 9.5 studied so far, the rate of growth is an increasing function of the size of the population Λ. We now show that these surprising scale effects are not a necessary feature of this type of models.[5]

To achieve this, we consider the model of section 9.5, but instead of having a fixed number of sectors N, we assume that there is free entry, and thus the number of sectors N_t is endogenously determined so as to drive profits to zero, as in standard monopolistic competition.

Using the expression of profits (55) with endogenous N_t, the zero-profits condition is:

$$(1-\eta) \frac{Y_t}{N_t} \left(\frac{\eta q_{it}}{\omega_t} \right)^{\eta/(1-\eta)} = \omega_t \Psi \left(\frac{q_{it}}{\bar{q}_{t-1}} \right) \tag{66}$$

Since $\omega_t = \eta q_t$, this free entry condition simplifies as:

$$\frac{1-\eta}{\eta} \frac{Y_t}{q_t N_t} = \Psi \left(\frac{q_t}{q_{t-1}} \right) \tag{67}$$

Combining (61) and (67), we find that the equilibrium rate of growth is given by:

$$(1-\eta) \mathcal{G}_t \Psi'(\mathcal{G}_t) = \eta \Psi(\mathcal{G}_t) \tag{68}$$

We note immediately that the rate of growth no longer depends on the size of the economy. It depends, however, on the shape of the technical progress function Ψ, and on the parameter η representing the degree of competitiveness.

9.6.1 The Effect of Competition

To see how the rate of growth depends on competitiveness in this model, let us differentiate equation (68) giving $\mathcal{G}_t$:

$$[(1-2\eta) \Psi'(\mathcal{G}_t) + (1-\eta) \mathcal{G}_t \Psi''(\mathcal{G}_t)] d\mathcal{G}_t = [\Psi(\mathcal{G}_t) + \mathcal{G}_t \Psi'(\mathcal{G}_t)] d\eta \tag{69}$$

We see that we have $d\mathcal{G}_t/d\eta > 0$ if the expression in brackets in front of $d\mathcal{G}_t$ is positive. But one can check that the second-order condition for the

---

5. See, notably, Dinopoulos and Thompson (1998), Eicher and Turnovsky (1999), Howitt (1999), Jones (1995, 1999), Segerstrom (1998), and Young (1998).

maximization of the maximand in (55) is precisely:

$$(1 - 2\eta)\Psi'(\mathcal{G}_t) + (1-\eta)\mathcal{G}_t\Psi''(\mathcal{G}_t) > 0 \qquad (70)$$

so that the rate of growth depends positively on competitiveness in this model, contrary to the horizontal differentiation model.

The reason growth depends positively on competitiveness is the following: individual firms engage in research to be able to have a lower price and to "steal" customers from their competitors. For a given increase in productivity, they will steal more customers the more elastic the demand curve (52) is, that is, the higher η is, hence the positive effect of η on growth.

Of course, this effect might have been counterbalanced by the "profitability" effect we saw in section 9.4, but free entry precisely eliminates that effect by spreading the monopolistic rents among a larger number of intermediate industries.

Appendix 9.1: Capital and Transitional Dynamics

We develop an extension of the model of section 9.4 by including fixed capital. This notably enables us to describe transitional dynamics with a closed-form solution. It will mix both the "catching up" of capital found in the Solow-Swan and Ramsey models and the features of endogenous growth.

The Model

The production function is now:

$$Y_t = N_t^{1+\nu-\alpha} K_t^\alpha \left[\left(\frac{1}{N_t}\int_0^{N_t} y_{it}^\eta di\right)^{1/\eta}\right]^{1-\alpha} \qquad (71)$$

with:

$$0 < \eta < 1 \qquad 0 < \alpha < 1 \qquad (72)$$

This parameterization has been chosen so that (a) for $\alpha = 0$ we obtain the production function in section 9.4 (formula 16); (b) for $\nu = 0$ we obtain the traditional Cobb-Douglas function $Y_t = K_t^\alpha L_t^{1-\alpha}$. To obtain a simple closed-form solution, we assume that capital depreciates fully in one period, so that:

$$K_{t+1} = I_t \qquad (73)$$

The budget constraint of households now includes capital:

$$C_t + K_{t+1} + v_t \left(N_{t+1} - N_t \right) = \omega_t \Lambda + \pi_t N_t + R_t K_t \qquad (74)$$

The other equations are the same as in section 9.4.

Market Equilibrium

A few equations are the same (equations 25, 27, and 28), where we suppress the index i because equilibrium will be symmetrical:

$$p_t = \frac{\omega_t}{\eta} \qquad (75)$$

$$v_t = \frac{\omega_t}{a N_t} \qquad (76)$$

$$\pi_t = \frac{(1-\eta) p_t L_t}{N_t} \qquad (77)$$

The price p_t of intermediates in terms of the final good is equal to their marginal productivity, that is, in a symmetrical situation:

$$p_t = (1-\alpha) N_t^\nu K_t^\alpha L_t^{-\alpha} \qquad (78)$$

and similarly the value of output is:

$$Y_t = N_t^\nu K_t^\alpha L_t^{1-\alpha} \qquad (79)$$

Households solve the following program:

$$\text{Maximize} \sum_t \beta^t Log C_t \quad \text{s.t.}$$

$$C_t + K_{t+1} + v_t \left(N_{t+1} - N_t \right) = \omega_t \Lambda + \pi_t N_t + R_t K_t$$

The Lagrangian is:

$$\sum_{t=0}^{\infty} \beta^t \left\{ Log C_t + \lambda_t \left[\pi_t N_t + R_t K_t - C_t - K_{t+1} - v_t \left(N_{t+1} - N_t \right) \right] \right\} \qquad (80)$$

and the first-order conditions:

$$\lambda_t = \frac{1}{C_t} \tag{81}$$

$$\lambda_t = \beta \lambda_{t+1} R_{t+1} \tag{82}$$

$$\lambda_t v_t = \beta \lambda_{t+1} \left(v_{t+1} + \pi_{t+1} \right) \tag{83}$$

Together with $R_t = \alpha Y_t / K_t$, equations (81) and (82) yield:

$$K_{t+1} = I_t = \alpha \beta Y_t \tag{84}$$

$$C_t = (1 - \alpha \beta) Y_t \tag{85}$$

Combining it with (76), (77), and (81), equation (83) is rewritten:

$$\frac{\omega_t}{aC_t} \frac{N_{t+1}}{N_t} = \frac{\beta \omega_{t+1}}{aC_{t+1}} + \frac{\beta (1-\eta) p_{t+1} L_{t+1}}{C_{t+1}} \tag{86}$$

We further have from (78) and (79):

$$p_t L_t = (1 - \alpha) Y_t \tag{87}$$

Combining (75), (85), (86), and (87), we obtain the dynamic equation in L_t:

$$\frac{1}{L_t} = \frac{\beta}{1+a\Lambda} \frac{1}{L_{t+1}} + \frac{a \left[\beta (1-\eta) + \eta \right]}{\eta (1+a\Lambda)} \tag{88}$$

Because the coefficient of $1/L_{t+1}$ is smaller than 1, the solution is a constant $L_t = L$ given by:

$$L = \frac{\eta \left[(1-\beta) + a\Lambda \right]}{\beta a (1-\eta) + \eta a} \tag{89}$$

so that the rate of growth γ_N in the number of intermediates is:

$$\gamma_N = \frac{N_{t+1}}{N_t} = 1 + a(\Lambda - L) = \frac{\beta a (1-\eta) \Lambda + \beta}{\beta (1-\eta) + \eta} \tag{90}$$

Transitional Dynamics

Let us recall equation (79) giving output with constant labor:

$$Y_t = N_t^\nu K_t^\alpha L^{1-\alpha} \qquad (91)$$

Combining with (84) we find:

$$\frac{K_{t+1}}{K_t} = \frac{Y_t}{Y_{t-1}} = \left(\frac{N_t}{N_{t-1}}\right)^\nu \left(\frac{K_t}{K_{t-1}}\right)^\alpha \qquad (92)$$

or going to logarithms, and using (90):

$$k_{t+1} - k_t = \alpha\left(k_t - k_{t-1}\right) + \nu Log\left[\frac{\beta a\left(1-\eta\right)\Lambda + \beta}{\beta\left(1-\eta\right)+\eta}\right] \qquad (93)$$

Equation (93) combines elements in the Solow-Swan-Ramsey tradition with features of endogenous growth. The first term in the right-hand side represents the catching up of capital when it is not in steady state, as we saw in chapters 1 and 7. The second term shows how this steady state is influenced by all parameters that intervene in endogenous growth, as we saw in section 9.4.

Appendix 9.2: Stochastic Productivity Increases

In section 9.5 we described a model of endogenous productivity increases where productivity improvements in each industry are a deterministic function of labor invested into research and development. We now describe a model where the productivity increases are stochastic.[6] The model has a number of common points with the model of section 9.5, but to diversify the exposition we shall give a continuous time version of the model.

The Model

Households supply in each period a total quantity of labor Λ and have an intertemporal utility function:

$$U = \int_0^\infty e^{-\rho t} Log C_t dt \qquad (94)$$

---

6. The initial contributions in this area are Aghion and Howitt (1992); Grossman and Helpman (1991a); Segerstrom, Anant, and Dinopoulos (1990). Our exposition follows Grossman and Helpman (1991b). A comprehensive exposition is in Aghion and Howitt (1998).

Consumption goods are produced by competitive firms with a production function:

$$LogY_t = \int_0^1 Log y_{it} di \qquad (95)$$

Intermediate input y_{it} is produced by firms in sector i. Each sector i is organized as a duopoly. There is a "leader" and a "follower." The leader, who is the only one to produce, has the production function:

$$y_{it} = q_{it} \ell_{it} \qquad (96)$$

where q_{it} is the productivity of the leading firm in sector i, and ℓ_{it} the quantity of labor used for the production of the intermediate.

Now productivities and the leader-follower status evolve over time. If any of the two firms invests a quantity of labor h_{it} during the infinitesimal time interval $[t, t+dt]$, its productivity will rise to λq_{it} ($\lambda > 1$) with probability $\kappa_{it} dt$, and will stay unchanged with probability $1 - \kappa_{it} dt$, with:

$$\kappa_{it} = a h_{it} \qquad (97)$$

where h_{it} is the amount of labor devoted to research in sector i. When a productivity rise occurs in one firm, the other firm has free access to the "previous" technology, that is, the productivity of the follower is always $1/\lambda$ times the "frontier" productivity.

We should note that only the follower undertakes research in this framework. Indeed, because the productivity of the follower is always $1/\lambda$ times that of the leader, the leader would waste resources doing research while gaining no competitive advantage.[7]

Equilibrium Relations

Let r_t denote the real interest rate. From (94) we have the traditional Euler relation:

$$\frac{\dot{C}_t}{C_t} = r_t - \rho \qquad (98)$$

Let us denote v_{it} as the value of a share of the leading firm in sector i, and π_{it} the profits in that sector. With probability $\kappa_{it} dt$, the leader loses

---

7. For models where there is no automatic catching up, and where all firms may be interested in doing research, see, for example, Aghion, Harris, Howitt, and Vickers (2001).

everything, and with probability $1 - \kappa_{it}dt$, the leader has the usual rate of return $(\pi_{it} + \dot{v}_{it})/v_{it}$. The expected return must be equal to the safe rate of return r_t, so that we obtain the arbitrage relation:

$$\frac{\pi_{it}}{v_{it}} + \frac{\dot{v}_{it}}{v_{it}} - \kappa_{it} = r_t \qquad (99)$$

Now we consider a follower in sector i. If he spends an amount of labor $h_{it}dt$, this will cost $\omega_t h_{it}dt$. On the other hand, it will bring him the value v_{it} with probability $\kappa_{it}dt = ah_{it}dt$, and thus an expected value $ah_{it}v_{it}dt$. Equating the two we find the value of the firm:

$$v_{it} = \frac{\omega_t}{a} \qquad (100)$$

where ω_t is the real wage. We have also the steady-state relation:

$$\frac{\dot{\omega}_t}{\omega_t} = \frac{\dot{C}_t}{C_t} \qquad (101)$$

The price is:

$$p_{it} = \lambda \omega_t \qquad (102)$$

and thus the profits in real terms:

$$\pi_{it} = (\lambda - 1)\omega_t \ell_{it} \qquad (103)$$

where ℓ_{it} is the amount of work used for production in sector i. Production labor and research labor must sum to Λ in every sector i:

$$\ell_{it} + h_{it} = \Lambda \qquad (104)$$

Combining (97) to (104), we obtain:

$$\kappa_{it} = \kappa = \frac{(\lambda - 1)a\Lambda - \rho}{\lambda} \qquad (105)$$

We can compute from (95) and (96):

$$Log Y_{t+dt} - Log Y_t = \int_0^1 \left(Log q_{it+dt} - Log q_{it}\right) di \qquad (106)$$

But $Log q_{it+dt} - Log q_{it}$ is equal to $Log\lambda$ with probability κdt and equal to zero with probability $1 - \kappa dt$. The integral in (106) is equal to:

$$Log Y_{t+dt} - Log Y_t = \kappa Log\lambda dt \qquad (107)$$

so that the rate of growth of output is:

$$\gamma_Y = \frac{1}{Y_t}\frac{dY_t}{dt} = \kappa Log\lambda \qquad (108)$$

which, using (105), becomes:

$$\gamma_Y = \frac{(\lambda - 1)a\Lambda - \rho}{\lambda} Log\lambda \qquad (109)$$

We see that, quite intuitively, the rate of growth depends positively on λ, a, and Λ and negatively on ρ.

Problems

Problem 9.1: The AK Model in Continuous Time

We study here the AK model (section 9.2) in continuous time. The production function is the same:

$$Y_t = AK_t$$

Capital depreciates at the rate δ, so capital evolves as:

$$\dot{K}_t = I_t - \delta K_t$$

The households maximize the following intertemporal utility, where ρ is the continuous discount rate and $1/\theta$ is the intertemporal elasticity of substitution (the logarithmic utility in section 9.2 corresponds to $\theta = 1$):

$$\int_0^\infty e^{-\rho t}\frac{C_t^{1-\theta} - 1}{1 - \theta} dt$$

under the budget constraint:

$$C_t + I_t = AK_t$$

1. Derive the first-order conditions of the household's intertemporal maximization program.
2. Compute the rate of growth of the economy.

Problem 9.2: Endogenous Growth with Physical and Human Capital

We consider here an endogenous growth model with two accumulated factors, physical and human capital (Uzawa, 1965; Lucas, 1988). We denote with K_t and H_t the amounts of physical and human capital available at the beginning of period t.

The production functions for output Y_t and "human capital goods" X_t are, respectively:

$$Y_t = A_Y K_{Yt}^\alpha H_{Yt}^{1-\alpha}$$

$$X_t = A_X K_{Xt}^\alpha H_{Xt}^{1-\alpha}$$

where K_{Yt} is the amount of physical capital devoted to the production of output, and so on. Of course, we have:

$$K_{Yt} + K_{Xt} = K_t \qquad H_{Yt} + H_{Xt} = H_t$$

Output Y_t is divided between consumption C_t and investment I_t. The production of human capital goods X_t can only be used to increase the stock of human capital. To simplify the computations, we assume that physical and human capital fully depreciate in each period, so that:

$$K_{t+1} = I_t \qquad H_{t+1} = X_t$$

Households maximize the expected value of their discounted intertemporal utility:

$$\sum_t \beta^t Log C_t$$

subject to the budget constraints:

$$C_t + I_t + Q_t H_{t+1} = R_t K_t + \omega_t H_t$$

where K_t and H_t are accumulated physical and human capital, Q_t is the real price of human capital, and R_t is the real return on physical capital. To keep the model simple, we assume that the labor market is competitive.

1. Show that the dynamic equilibrium of the economy is characterized by:

$$\frac{K_{Yt}}{K_t} = \frac{H_{Yt}}{H_t} = 1 - \beta + \beta\alpha$$

$$\frac{K_{Xt}}{K_t} = \frac{H_{Xt}}{H_t} = \beta(1-\alpha)$$

$$C_t = \frac{1-\beta}{1-\beta+\beta\alpha} Y_t$$

$$K_{t+1} = \frac{\beta\alpha}{1-\beta+\beta\alpha} Y_t$$

2. Going to logarithms (denoted by lowercase letters), show that the growth rates of physical and human capital are given by:

$$k_{t+1} - k_t = Log A_Y - (1-\alpha)(k_t - h_t) + Log(\beta\alpha)$$

$$h_{t+1} - h_t = Log A_X + \alpha(k_t - h_t) + Log[\beta(1-\alpha)]$$

3. Compute the steady-state rate of growth.

Problem 9.3: The Romer Model: Continuous Time

We present a simple version of the Romer (1990) model in continuous time. Households are infinitely lived and endowed with a constant aggregate flow of labor Λ. They consume C_t and maximize discounted utility:

$$\int_0^\infty e^{-\rho t} Log C_t \, dt$$

The production function in the research sector becomes in continuous time:

$$\frac{\dot{N}_t}{N_t} = a H_t$$

and the budget constraint of households is:

$$C_t + v_t \dot{N}_t = \omega_t \Lambda + \pi_t N_t$$

The rest of the model is the same as in section 9.4.

1. Compute the intertemporal market equilibrium.
2. Compute the intertemporal optimum and compare it with the market equilibrium

Problem 9.4: Productivity Increases with a Delay

We consider the model of section 9.5, but instead of assuming that productivity increases occur in the period where research labor is spent (formula 50 in chapter 9):

$$h_{it} = \Psi\left(\frac{q_{it}}{\bar{q}_{t-1}}\right)$$

we assume that productivity increases take place in the next period:

$$h_{it} = \Psi\left(\frac{q_{it+1}}{\bar{q}_t}\right)$$

All other assumptions are the same.

1. Derive the first-order conditions of the firm and household.
2. Derive the equation giving the growth rate of productivity for a given number N of intermediates. How does it compare to that in section 9.5 (equation 63)?

10

Competitive Business Cycles

10.1 Introduction

After studying in the three preceding chapters various representations of the growth process, here we will study another very important topic: fluctuations. In view of the large number of issues involved, we approach this area progressively and introduce various hypotheses successively here and in chapters 12 and 13.

This chapter presents some basic models of fluctuations, assuming competitive markets in "real" models. Chapter 12 introduces money and nominal shocks, as well as imperfect competition and imperfect information. Chapter 13 introduces in the monetary model nominal rigidities and nonclearing markets, with or without imperfect competition.

The contributions on competitive business cycles in this chapter can be, broadly speaking, classified into three main lines of research. The first one, which will occupy most of this chapter as well as chapters 12 and 13, is that of dynamic stochastic general equilibrium (DSGE) models, in line with the seminal contribution of Kydland and Prescott (1982). In this line of work, the economic system is usually viewed as stable but permanently subject to various stochastic shocks. Fluctuations result from the optimal responses of agents to these shocks. The typical model in this area is an optimal growth model, for example of the Ramsey or overlapping generations type, with stochastic shocks added. The first shocks to be considered were productivity shocks, some sort of stochastic Solow residuals (Kydland and Prescott, 1982). Because these were real shocks, and they occurred in a real model, the corresponding models were initially called real business cycles (RBC) models (Long and Plosser, 1983). Later on, money, market imperfections, and other types of shocks were introduced and, as we indicated, the corresponding models took the more general name of dynamic stochastic general equilibrium (DSGE) models.

This line of research has met with great success among macroeconomists. A first obvious reason is that the models in that line have rigorous microfoundations. A second reason is that they integrate the theories of growth and fluctuations in a unified framework. A third reason is that they allow a natural confrontation with reality. Indeed, the functioning of DSGE models generates stochastic trajectories for all variables of the model. Correlations, impulse response functions, and other statistics can be computed and compared to those observed in reality.

Section 10.2 describes the basic RBC methodology, introducing technology shocks into a Ramsey growth model. These models are usually solved numerically in the literature. We adopt a complementary line of exposition in this and the next chapters. We successively consider various simplified versions of the model, each emphasizing a particular and important aspect of the cycle. All these models are solved analytically, which will give us a better comprehension of the mechanisms at work.

Section 10.3 gives a well-known particular example where a simple exact solution to a stochastic model and its dynamics can be explicitly computed. Section 10.4 investigates the role of depreciation in the propagation mechanism, that is, on the dynamic effects of shocks on endogenous variables, such as output. Section 10.5 concentrates on labor fluctuations and the mechanisms of intertemporal labor substitution. Section 10.6 shows how the prices of various assets can be computed using the simple first-order conditions of the model.

A second line of research, which we outline in section 10.7, is associated with the idea of sunspots, the basic idea of which we already saw in chapter 3. The typical sunspot model usually has an infinity of rational expectations equilibria "indexed" on stochastic variables, sunspots, which are extraneous to the economic system under study. Section 10.7 shows by way of a microfounded example that shocks that are intrinsically irrelevant can nevertheless have an influence on the economy.

Finally, a third line of research, sketched in section 10.8, is that of endogenous cycles. Contributors to that line of thought usually view the economy as inherently unstable, at least locally around the steady state. Initial contributions were in the Keynesian tradition and combined a destabilizing accelerator à la Samuelson (1939), and other features, such as floors and ceilings, or a Phillips curve, which exerted a stabilizing influence. The combination of these resulted in cycles. These models, however, had no rigorous microfoundations, and there are more recent vintages that do have such foundations. A typical model and references are presented in section 10.8.

10.2 The DSGE Methodology

As indicated, the basic idea behind DSGE models is to view the economy as subject to sequences of shocks. These can be technology shocks, monetary or government spending shocks, or taste shocks. For example, if the shock is a technology shock, which we denote as a stochastic variable A_t, the production function can be written:

$$Y_t = A_t F(K_t, L_t) \qquad (1)$$

All agents maximize their expected intertemporal utility, or their discounted profits, subject to (a) the realized shocks that have actually already hit the economy, and (b) the expectations of future shocks.

As already mentioned, contrary to the earlier situation where the treatments of growth and fluctuations were completely separated (as is exemplified, for example, by the lack of connections between chapters 1 and 2), here they are integrated within the same model, as notably technology shocks will produce both growth and fluctuations.

10.2.1 A Standard RBC Model

We expose here a standard RBC model.[1] To lighten the exposition we concentrate on one type of shocks, technology shocks, which was the first introduced historically. The methodology clearly applies to other shocks (see, for example, problems 10.1 and 10.2, as well as chapters 12 and 13). Let us consider a real economy with an aggregate production function as above:

$$Y_t = A_t F(K_t, L_t) \qquad (2)$$

where A_t is a stochastic productivity shock. Capital depreciates at the rate δ, so the equation of evolution of capital is:

$$K_{t+1} = (1-\delta) K_t + I_t \qquad (3)$$

---

1. A collection of main articles on the subject is Kydland (1995). Overviews of the field can be found in Lucas (1987); King, Plosser, and Rebelo (1988a, 1988b); Plosser (1989); Cooley (1995); King and Rebelo (1999); and Rebelo (2005).

The representative consumer is infinitely lived and maximizes discounted expected utility:[2]

$$E \sum_t \beta^t \left[U(C_t) - \Gamma(L_t) \right] \qquad \Gamma'(L_t) > 0 \qquad \Gamma''(L_t) > 0 \qquad (4)$$

where $\Gamma(L_t)$ is the disutility of labor. In each period the consumer is subject to the budget constraint:

$$C_t + K_{t+1} = \omega_t L_t + R_t K_t \qquad (5)$$

where R_t is the gross real rate of return on capital and ω_t the real wage. Equilibrium on the goods market requires:

$$C_t + I_t = Y_t \qquad (6)$$

10.2.2 First-order Conditions

The first-order conditions of the firm yield:

$$\omega_t = \frac{\partial Y_t}{\partial L_t} = A_t \frac{\partial F(K_t, L_t)}{\partial L_t} \qquad (7)$$

$$R_t = 1 - \delta + \frac{\partial Y_t}{\partial K_t} = 1 - \delta + A_t \frac{\partial F(K_t, L_t)}{\partial K_t} \qquad (8)$$

The household maximizes the utility function (4) subject to all budget constraints (5). The Lagrangian of this program is:

$$E \left\{ \sum_t \beta^t \left[U(C_t) - \Gamma(L_t) \right] + \sum_t \beta^t \lambda_t \left(\omega_t L_t + R_t K_t - C_t - K_{t+1} \right) \right\} \qquad (9)$$

and the first-order conditions with respect to C_t, L_t, and K_t are, respectively:

$$\lambda_t = U'(C_t) \qquad (10)$$

$$\Gamma'(L_t) = \lambda_t \omega_t \qquad (11)$$

$$\lambda_t = \beta E_t \left(\lambda_{t+1} R_{t+1} \right) \qquad (12)$$

Solving the model in its most general version would turn out to be quite clumsy, and one generally has to use numerical simulations. As we indicated,

---

2. Note that this methodology is not restricted to the (most commonly used) Ramsey model. Problem 10.4 develops a real business cycle in a simple OLG type structure.

to better understand the underlying mechanisms, in the next sections we successively study a number of simplified versions with explicit solutions, each emphasizing a particular important aspect of the model.

10.3 A Particular Case

To develop our intuition, we first examine a well-known particular case, found in Long and Plosser (1983) and McCallum (1989a), and for which a simple exact closed-form solution exists.

10.3.1 The Model

The economy has a Cobb-Douglas aggregate production function:

$$Y_t = A_t K_t^\alpha L_t^{1-\alpha} \qquad (13)$$

We make two further simplifying assumptions, which will allow us to solve the model easily. First, capital depreciates fully in one period (i.e., we take $\delta = 1$ in equation 3), so that capital tomorrow is equal to investment today:

$$K_{t+1} = I_t \qquad (14)$$

Second, the utility of consumers is logarithmic in consumption, so that the intertemporal utility function is:

$$\sum_t \beta^t \left[Log C_t - \Gamma(L_t) \right] \qquad (15)$$

10.3.2 Resolution

The first-order conditions of the firm (equations 7 and 8) simplify to:

$$\omega_t = \frac{(1-\alpha) Y_t}{L_t} \qquad (16)$$

$$R_t = \frac{\alpha Y_t}{K_t} \qquad (17)$$

The first-order conditions (11) and (12) for the consumer are the same, and (10) becomes:

$$\lambda_t = \frac{1}{C_t} \qquad (18)$$

Using (14), (17), and (18), equation (12) becomes:

$$\frac{I_t}{C_t} = \alpha\beta E_t\left(\frac{C_{t+1} + I_{t+1}}{C_{t+1}}\right) = \alpha\beta + \alpha\beta E_t\left(\frac{I_{t+1}}{C_{t+1}}\right) \qquad (19)$$

which solves as:

$$\frac{I_t}{C_t} = \frac{\alpha\beta}{1 - \alpha\beta} \qquad (20)$$

Combining (6) and (20) we obtain:

$$I_t = \alpha\beta Y_t \qquad (21)$$

$$C_t = (1 - \alpha\beta) Y_t \qquad (22)$$

Now we combine (11), (16), (18), and (22). We find that employment is constant and equal to the value L given by:

$$L\Gamma'(L) = \frac{1 - \alpha}{1 - \alpha\beta} \qquad (23)$$

10.3.3 Correlations

Whether a DSGE model is solved analytically or numerically, at some point one may want to compare correlations, impulse response functions, and other statistical indicators to their real-life counterparts.

As we will briefly see, the simplicity of this model is paid by an extremely low approximation of its basic statistics to reality.

Let us first start with consumption C_t and investment I_t, both of which are here proportional to income Y_t. This means that consumption and investment have the same volatility (in logs). This is quite far from reality, where the variance of investment is much higher than that of consumption. Problem 10.4 actually shows a model that has a simple analytic solution and captures the difference of reaction of consumption and investment in a simple manner.

Another well-known problem is the real wage. Combining equation (16) with $L_t = L$ we obtain:

$$\omega_t = \frac{(1 - \alpha) Y_t}{L} \qquad (24)$$

We see that the correlation coefficient between ω_t and Y_t is equal to 1, much higher than the correlation in reality.[3] We see in chapter 13 that the introduction of nominal rigidities is one way of improving that aspect.

10.4 Depreciation and Propagation

We now go one step in the direction of more realism and generalize the model of section 10.3 by replacing the assumption of full capital depreciation ($\delta = 1$) by a value of δ between 0 and 1 (a commonly found value is 0.025 per quarter, thus very far from the value of 1 above).

Introducing a realistic rate of depreciation allows us to understand a "puzzle" described by Cogley and Nason (1993, 1995). What they found is that in standard RBC models the dynamics of output almost exactly mimics that of the productivity shock. In other words, there is practically no "propagation" mechanism in the standard RBC model. This is what we find analytically next.

10.4.1 A Simple Formalization

The traditional equation depicting the evolution of capital is:

$$K_{t+1} = (1-\delta) K_t + I_t \qquad 0 < \delta \leq 1 \qquad (25)$$

To have a simple explicit solution, we replace it by the following log-linear approximation (Hercowitz and Sampson, 1991):[4]

$$K_{t+1} = \Lambda K_t^{1-\delta} I_t^{\delta}, \qquad 0 < \delta \leq 1 \qquad (26)$$

where the parameter Λ is calibrated so that (25) and (26) are consistent in stationary state.[5] The full depreciation case studied in section 10.3 corresponds to $\delta = 1$ and $\Lambda = 1$. The rest of the model is the same as in section 10.3.

---

3. For example, King and Rebelo (1999) report a correlation of 0.98 for the standard RBC model (thus quite close to our value of 1), versus 0.12 for U.S. data.

4. A model based on the actual depreciation formula (25) is found in appendix 10.2.

5. For example, if capital is constant in stationary state, then K_{t+1} must be equal to K_t for $I_t = \delta K_t$, which yields $\Lambda = \delta^{-\delta}$.

10.4.2 Dynamics and Propagation

One can prove (Hercowitz and Sampson, 1991; or problem 10.3) that the dynamics of the model is characterized by a constant quantity of labor $L_t = L$ and the following consumption and investment functions:

$$C_t = \frac{1 - \beta(1 - \delta + \alpha\delta)}{1 - \beta + \beta\delta} Y_t \qquad (27)$$

$$I_t = \frac{\alpha\beta\delta}{1 - \beta + \beta\delta} Y_t \qquad (28)$$

which generalize equations (21) and (22) to the case $\delta < 1$. Combining equations (13) and (28), and taking logarithms, we find:

$$k_{t+1} = (1 - \delta) k_t + \delta y_t \qquad (29)$$

On the other hand, taking the logarithm of the production function:

$$y_t = \alpha k_t + (1 - \alpha) \ell + a_t \qquad (30)$$

Combining the two (we omit irrelevant constants), we find the dynamic equation in k_t:

$$k_{t+1} = (1 - \delta + \alpha\delta) k_t + \delta a_t \qquad (31)$$

or using the lag operator $\mathcal{L}$ (mathematical appendix A.8.4):

$$k_{t+1} = \frac{\delta a_t}{1 - (1 - \delta + \alpha\delta) \mathcal{L}} \qquad (32)$$

From this we deduce output:

$$y_t = a_t + \frac{\alpha \delta a_{t-1}}{1 - (1 - \delta + \alpha\delta) \mathcal{L}} \qquad (33)$$

We can see first that capital is more persistent than in the preceding section, because the autoregressive root $1 - \delta + \alpha\delta$ in formula (31) is quite bigger than α, which was the value we found in section 10.3.

Now the propagation effects on output are, on the contrary, quite smaller. Indeed, we see in equation (33) that the second-period effect of a technology shock is only equal to $\alpha\delta$ times the first period effect. This is much smaller that the value α we previously obtained. The effects of technology shocks on output die very quickly, and thus there is little propagation, which explains the Cogley and Nason (1993, 1995) puzzle.

10.5 Intertemporal Substitution and Labor Fluctuations

We now turn to another important topic; explaining labor fluctuations in the cycle. A number of authors, notably Lucas and Rapping (1969), emphasized that intertemporal substitution between labor at different dates could explain labor fluctuations even with market clearing. The intuition is that if there is a high elasticity of substitution between, say, labor in period t and labor in period $t+1$, then a relatively small variation in relative wages between the two periods can be accompanied by large movements in the quantity of labor.

We investigate this issue in a simplified model without capital accumulation. In view of the results of the preceding section, this suppression of capital should not quantitatively affect the results too much.

10.5.1 The Model

We assume a simple production function:

$$Y_t = A_t L_t^{1-\alpha} \qquad (34)$$

The households have the following intertemporal utility:

$$U = \sum_t \beta^t \left(\frac{C_t^{1-\theta}}{1-\theta} - \frac{L_t^{1+\nu}}{1+\nu} \right) \qquad (35)$$

where ν and θ will turn out to be the inverse of the intertemporal elasticities of substitution for labor and consumption, respectively.

Because we have suppressed capital accumulation, there must be another asset that enables households to transfer purchasing power from one period to the other. This will be a real asset, government debt, denoted D_t. Consequently households are subject to a sequence of budget constraints:

$$D_{t+1} = R_{t+1} \left(D_t + \omega_t L_t + \Upsilon_t - C_t \right) \qquad (36)$$

where Υ_t is *real* period t profits.

10.5.2 First-order Conditions

Households maximize their utility (35) subject to the budget constraints (36). The Lagrangian is:

$$\sum_t \beta^t \left\{ \frac{C_t^{1-\theta}}{1-\theta} - \frac{L_t^{1+\nu}}{1+\nu} + \lambda_t \left[R_{t+1} D_t + R_{t+1} \omega_t L_t - R_{t+1} C_t - D_{t+1} \right] \right\} \quad (37)$$

The first-order conditions with respect to C_t, L_t, and D_t are, respectively:

$$C_t^{-\theta} = \lambda_t R_{t+1} \quad (38)$$

$$L_t^{\nu} = \lambda_t R_{t+1} \omega_t \quad (39)$$

$$\lambda_{t-1} = \beta \lambda_t R_{t+1} \quad (40)$$

10.5.3 Intertemporal Substitution and Labor Supply

Combining (39) at times t and $t-1$, and (40), we find:

$$\frac{L_t}{L_{t-1}} = \left(\frac{\omega_t}{\beta R_t \omega_{t-1}} \right)^{1/\nu} \quad (41)$$

We see that, other things equal, a high degree of intertemporal substitution for labor (low ν) will create large labor fluctuations in response to variations in the real wages.

However this is not the end of the story because relation (41) is a partial equilibrium one, and the real wages ω_t and ω_{t-1} in (41) are themselves endogenous variables. To obtain the full response of labor to shocks, we complete the solution of the model with the supply side.

10.5.4 Labor Fluctuations

From the production function (34), we compute the real wage ω_t:

$$\omega_t = (1-\alpha) A_t L_t^{-\alpha} \quad (42)$$

Combining (34), (38), (39), (42), and $C_t = Y_t$, we find, in logarithms and omitting irrelevant constants:

$$\ell_t = \frac{(1-\theta) a_t}{\alpha + \nu + \theta - \alpha\theta} \quad (43)$$

In accordance with the intuition indicated above, we find that a low value of ν, that is, a high degree of intertemporal labor substitutability, will lead (other things equal) to a larger response of labor to shocks. A problem is that labor substitution seems to be limited in reality (see, for example, Killingsworth and Heckman, 1986; and Pencavel, 1986). Appendix 10.1 presents an ingenious device, due to Hansen (1995) and Rogerson (1998), which allows to obtain an apparently high elasticity of labor supply even if the parameter ν is high.

Now we also see that whether shocks will result in labor fluctuations depends not only on the intertemporal substitutability of labor but also on that of consumption. For example in the particular case of logarithmic utility for consumption ($\theta = 1$), there will be no response of labor to shocks, even if labor is highly substitutable (low ν). The shocks are fully absorbed by movements in real wages.

10.6 Asset Pricing

DSGE models have also been widely used to derive the prices of various financial or real assets. This potential use has not been apparent in the models we presented so far, as the only assets we considered explicitly were capital or debt.

Following chapter 6, we now introduce other assets, and see that the first-order conditions naturally give us the prices of these assets.[6]

10.6.1 The Consumption Capital Asset Pricing Model

To simplify the exposition, we ignore both capital accumulation and labor supply and assume that income is given by an exogenous stochastic process. Accordingly, the problem of the representative household is:

$$\text{Maximize } E \sum_t \beta^t U(C_t) \quad \text{s.t.} \tag{44}$$

$$C_t + Q_t \mathcal{A}_t = Y_t + Z_t \mathcal{A}_{t-1} \tag{45}$$

where Y_t is an exogenous stochastic income, $\mathcal{A}_t$ is the real quantity of the asset, Z_t is the real payment in period t on the asset invested in $t-1$, and Q_t is the real price of the asset. The Lagrangian for this program is:

$$\sum_t \beta^t \left[U(C_t) + \lambda_t \left(Y_t + Z_t \mathcal{A}_{t-1} - C_t - Q_t \mathcal{A}_t \right) \right] \tag{46}$$

---

6. See, notably, Breeden (1979), Lucas (1978). These issues are surveyed, for example, in Guvenen and Lustig (2008a, 2008b) and Singleton (1990).

The first-order conditions for C_t and $\mathcal{A}_t$ are:

$$\lambda_t = U'(C_t) \tag{47}$$

$$\lambda_t Q_t = \beta E_t \left(\lambda_{t+1} Z_{t+1}\right) \tag{48}$$

Combining (47) and (48), we obtain the fundamental asset pricing equation:

$$Q_t = \beta E_t \left[\frac{U'(C_{t+1})}{U'(C_t)} Z_{t+1} \right] \tag{49}$$

This model is usually called the consumption CAPM (capital asset pricing model) because it shows that the important thing is how the asset's returns correlate with the household's consumption pattern in time.

We can rewrite the asset pricing formula (49) directly as a function of returns R_t:

$$U'(C_t) = \beta E_t \left[R_{t+1} U'(C_{t+1}) \right] \tag{50}$$

where R_{t+1}, the gross return on the asset, is equal to Z_{t+1}/Q_t. As an application, we use this relation to compare the price of some safe and risky assets.

10.6.2 Risk and Returns

We start with a safe asset, with constant real return R, and rewrite equation (50):

$$U'(C_t) = \beta E_t \left[R U'(C_{t+1}) \right] \tag{51}$$

For variable returns, equation (50) can be rewritten, using the definition of covariance (mathematical appendix, section A.7.4):

$$U'(C_t) = \beta \operatorname{Cov}\left[R_{t+1}, U'(C_{t+1})\right] + \beta E_t\left(R_{t+1}\right) E_t\left[U'(C_{t+1})\right] \tag{52}$$

Combining (51) and (52), we obtain:

$$R - E_t\left(R_{t+1}\right) = \frac{\operatorname{Cov}\left[R_{t+1}, U'(C_{t+1})\right]}{E_t\left[U'(C_{t+1})\right]} \tag{53}$$

To illustrate this, consider for example the case where returns are negatively correlated with consumption (i.e. positively with the marginal utility of consumption). Formula (53) tells us that investors will then accept an average return smaller than that of the safe asset. The intuitive reason is that the corresponding asset acts as "insurance", and investors are ready to pay for such insurance, as we already saw in chapter 6.

10.7 Sunspots

A sunspot is somehow a state of nature (chapter 6) that has no intrinsic effect on the economy. The idea that such sunspots can nevertheless influence the economy in some circumstances because the agents coordinate their actions on them was first implemented in rigorous microfounded models by Shell (1977), Azariadis (1981a), and Cass and Shell (1983). The reader will find a number of good overviews in Benhabib and Farmer (1999), Chiappori and Guesnerie (1991), Farmer (1993), Guesnerie and Woodford (1992), and Shell (2008).

We shall not try to give the most general statements on the subject, but we work by way of an example and describe a simple and rigorous model, taken from Azariadis and Guesnerie (1986), which displays such sunspot equilibria.

10.7.1 The Model

We consider an overlapping generations (OLG) model[7] with money of the same type as that described in chapter 4, section 4.4. Households live two periods. An agent of generation t works L_t when young and consumes C_{t+1} when old. Her utility function is:

$$U_t = C_{t+1} - \frac{L_t^2}{2} \tag{54}$$

The production function is:

$$Y_t = L_t \tag{55}$$

The produced good is perishable, so to transfer purchasing power from the first period to the second, the agents use a nonperishable good (we call it "money" for short), of which there is a fixed quantity, equal to 1, in the economy. We denote P_t as the price of the perishable good in terms of money.

---

7. Although we present an OLG version of sunspots, sunspots can arise as well in Ramsey type models. See, for example, Farmer and Guo (1994), Benhabib and Farmer (1994, 1996), and Benhabib and Wen (2004), some of which also perform calibration exercises similar to those of the traditional RBC models.

10.7.2 Deterministic Trajectories and Indeterminacy

Old agents hold all the money, and spend it in their old age, so the demand for the good is equal to:

$$C_t = \frac{1}{P_t} \tag{56}$$

On the other hand, in view of the production function (55), the supply of goods is equal to the supply of labor by the young, itself the solution of the maximization program:

$$\text{Maximize } \frac{P_t L_t}{P_{t+1}} - \frac{L_t^2}{2}$$

whose solution is:

$$L_t = \frac{P_t}{P_{t+1}} \tag{57}$$

and because:

$$L_t = Y_t = C_t = \frac{1}{P_t} \tag{58}$$

equation (57) can be rewritten:

$$\frac{1}{P_{t+1}} = \left(\frac{1}{P_t}\right)^2 \tag{59}$$

Figure 10.1 depicts this dynamic system in the plane $(1/P_t, 1/P_{t+1})$. We see that there are two long-run equilibria, corresponding, respectively, to:

$$P_t = 1 \quad L_t = 1 \tag{60}$$

and:

$$P_t = \infty \quad L_t = 0 \tag{61}$$

The first is the golden rule equilibrium, the second the autarkic equilibrium where there is no communication between generations because the real value of money is 0.

What we see immediately in figure 10.1 is that although the golden rule equilibrium is locally determinate, the system as a whole is globally indeterminate. In particular, there is an infinity of admissible perfect

Competitive Business Cycles

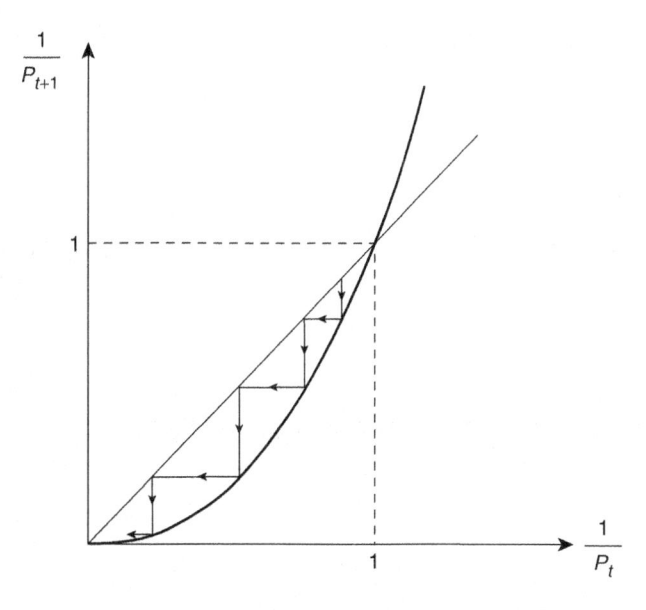

Figure 10.1 Price dynamics and indeterminacy

foresight trajectories that start anywhere between the autarky and golden rule, and which all converge toward autarky.

Sunspots are often associated to such indeterminacies in the literature, and we will see that this indeterminate model produces sunspot-type dynamics.

10.7.3 Sunspots

We consider stochastic dynamic equilibria and see that sunspot equilibria can arise in this economy. Formula (58) still holds. On the other hand, because future prices are stochastic, the program giving the labor supply of the young is now:

$$\text{Maximize } E_t \left(\frac{P_t L_t}{P_{t+1}} - \frac{L_t^2}{2} \right)$$

which yields the labor supply:

$$L_t = E_t \left(\frac{P_t}{P_{t+1}} \right) \qquad (62)$$

so that the dynamic equilibrium equation (59) is replaced by:

$$\left(\frac{1}{P_t}\right)^2 = E_t\left(\frac{1}{P_{t+1}}\right) \tag{63}$$

To show that sunspot equilibria can arise, we construct two sequences $\{q_t \mid t = 1\ldots\infty\}$ and $\{\pi_t \mid t = 1\ldots\infty\}$ defined recursively by:

$$q_{t+1} = \frac{q_t^2}{\theta} \qquad \pi_{t+1} = \frac{1-\theta}{q_t^2 - \theta} \tag{64}$$

where the two arbitrary numbers θ and q_0 are such that:

$$0 < \theta < 1 \qquad q_0 > 1 \tag{65}$$

Since $q_{t+1} > q_t$ and $q_0 > 1$, we have:

$$q_t > 1 \quad \text{and} \quad 0 < \pi_t < 1 \quad \forall t \tag{66}$$

We define the sequence of random prices by:

$$\text{If } P_{t-1} = 1 \qquad P_t = P_{t-1} \tag{67}$$

$$\text{If } P_{t-1} \neq 1 \qquad P_t = \begin{cases} q_t & \text{with probability } 1 - \pi_t \\ 1 & \text{with probability } \pi_t \end{cases} \tag{68}$$

This stochastic sequence satisfies the dynamic equilibrium equation (63) and thus constitutes a dynamic sunspot equilibrium.

Of course, to have a full description of the dynamics, one should indicate how a particular path will be chosen among the infinity of possible paths. For example, the dynamics of learning in such a context are investigated in Woodford (1990a).

10.8 Endogenous Cycles

As indicated in the introduction, early models of endogenous cycles were Keynesian in inspiration, and most of them based on an investment function of the "accelerator" type.[8] These models, however, had no rigorous foundations.

---

8. Traditional models of the cycle with an investment accelerator date back to Samuelson (1939), Kaldor (1940), and Hicks (1950). Various formalizations can be found in Goodwin (1951, 1982), Rose (1967), Chang and Smyth (1971), Schinasi (1982), Bénassy (1984), and Dana and Malgrange (1984). For a synthetic presentation, see Gabisch and Lorenz (1987).

The seminal model of a Walrasian endogenous cycle in a microfounded OLG setting is due to Benhabib and Day (1982), and we shall now present it briefly.[9]

10.8.1 The Model

We consider a simple OLG model. Agents born in period t have incomes y_1 in period t and y_2 in period $t+1$. They consume c_{1t} in t and c_{2t+1} in period $t+1$. Their utility function is $V(c_{1t}, c_{2t+1})$. The household's intertemporal budget constraint is:

$$c_{1t} + \frac{c_{2t+1}}{R_{t+1}} = y_1 + \frac{y_2}{R_{t+1}} \qquad (69)$$

where R_{t+1} is the real rate of return from period t to period $t+1$.

10.8.2 Dynamics

The young household maximizes utility $V(c_{1t}, c_{2t+1})$ subject to the budget constraint (69), which yields:

$$c_{1t} = c_{1t}(R_{t+1}) \qquad (70)$$

We further have the equilibrium condition on the goods market:

$$c_{1t} + c_{2t} = y_1 + y_2 \qquad (71)$$

Combining equations (69), (70), and (71) and assuming that (70) is invertible (this will be the case in the example below), we obtain an equation that relates c_{1t+1} to c_{1t}:

$$c_{1t+1} = f(c_{1t}) \qquad (72)$$

---

9. A model of similar type with Ramsey consumers appears in the early contribution by Benhabib and Nishimura (1979). An example of a two period cycle in an OLG model appears in Gale (1973). A collection of the main articles can be found in Benhabib (1992), and the field is surveyed in Benhabib (2008) and Boldrin and Woodford (1990). Some learning dynamics are studied in Grandmont (1985).

10.8.3 Cycles

We now give general conditions for the existence of cycles and present a simple example. First, we define a cycle in this discrete time framework. Consider a continuous dynamic one-dimensional system:

$$x_{t+1} = f(x_t) \tag{73}$$

A cycle of period n consists of n values $x_1, \ldots, x_n$ such that:

$$x_2 = f(x_1) \quad x_3 = f(x_2) \ldots x_n = f(x_{n-1}) \quad x_1 = f(x_n) \tag{74}$$

The existence of cycles clearly depends on the shape of the function f. Figure 10.2 shows a unimodal function f (that is a function with a single "hump"), which naturally generates cyclical trajectories. Indeed, figure 10.2 shows a cycle of period 3 where first-period consumption c_{1t} oscillates between the three values c, c', and c''.

One may wonder whether something further can be said about the periodicity of potential cycles. For that we use Sarkovskii's theorem (Sarkovskii, 1964). Consider a continuous dynamic one-dimensional system:

$$x_{t+1} = f(x_t) \tag{75}$$

and the following ordering $\succ$ of the integers:

$$3 \succ 5 \succ 7 \succ \ldots \succ 2.3 \succ 2.5 \succ 2.7$$
$$\ldots \succ 2^k.3 \succ 2^k.5 \succ 2^k.7 \succ \ldots \succ 2^m \succ \ldots \succ 8 \succ 4 \succ 2 \succ 1 \tag{76}$$

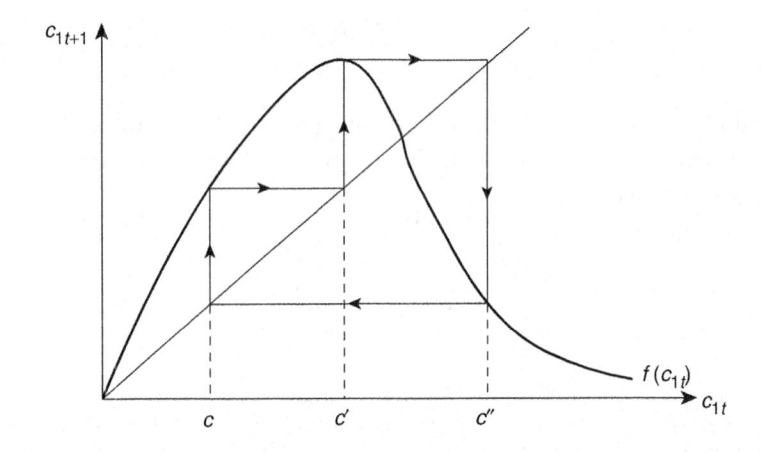

Figure 10.2 A period 3 cycle

That is, this ordering starts with the odd integers (except 1) in ascending order. Then these same odd integers, still in ascending order, but multiplied by successive powers of two, $2, 2^2, 2^k \ldots$, and finally all powers of 2 in descending order.

Sarkovskii's theorem says that if f is continuous and has a cycle of period n, then it has cycles of period n', where $n' \prec n$.

An immediate application of this theorem is, for example, to show that, because it has a cycle of period 3, the dynamic system of figure 10.2 has cycles of any integer period!

Of course, not all of these cycles are stable. To assess how many cycles will be stable, we use another theorem, from Singer (1978). Consider a one-dimensional, three times continuously differentiable and unimodal dynamic system:

$$x_{t+1} = f(x_t) \tag{77}$$

and define the Schwarzian derivative as:

$$\frac{f'''(x)}{f'(x)} - \frac{3}{2}\left[\frac{f''(x)}{f'(x)}\right]^2 \tag{78}$$

Then, if this Schwarzian derivative is negative, f has at most one (locally) stable cycle.

10.8.4 An Example

Let us consider the foregoing model with $y_1 = 0$ and the particular utility function (Benhabib and Day, 1982):

$$V(c_{1t}, c_{2t+1}) = ac_{1t} - \frac{b}{2}c_{1t}^2 + c_{2t+1} \tag{79}$$

Then one can compute that:

$$f(c_{1t}) = c_{1t}(a - bc_{1t}) \tag{80}$$

The function f has the shape indicated in figure 10.2. Because $f''' = 0$, the Schwarzian derivative (formula 78) is negative and, from Singer's theorem, there is thus only one locally stable cycle. For this cycle to be nondegenerate, it must not be reduced to the steady state, and therefore the steady state should be locally unstable. The corresponding condition is that the slope of f at the steady state must be greater than 1 in absolute value.

From (80) this slope is easily computed as equal to $2 - a$, so this yields the condition:

$$a > 3 \tag{81}$$

Under condition (81), there exist stable cycles of periodicity equal or superior to 2.

Appendix 10.1: Employment Lotteries

As we saw in section 10.6, even though a strong intertemporal labor substitution mechanism may be present, stochastic shocks do not necessarily lead to employment variations of the magnitude observed in reality. We present a different formalization of the labor market, developed by Hansen (1985) and Rogerson (1988), which creates a larger variability of employment in response to shocks.

The characteristics of this formalization are the following: (1) labor is indivisible, (2) workers choose lotteries over employment, and (3) workers are completely insured on their labor income.

The Model

We denote consumption by C_t, labor by L_t. Households maximize the intertemporal utility function:

$$\sum \beta^t \left[U(C_t) - \Gamma(L_t) \right] \tag{82}$$

with:

$$U' > 0 \quad U'' < 0 \quad \Gamma' > 0 \quad \Gamma'' > 0 \tag{83}$$

Labor is indivisible. Each household can either work ($L_t = L_0$), or not work at all ($L_t = 0$). Work is allotted among workers according to a system of employment lotteries, whereby each worker chooses a probability of working π_t, and then works:

$$L_t = L_0 \qquad \text{with probability } \pi_t \tag{84}$$

$$L_t = 0 \qquad \text{with probability } 1 - \pi_t \tag{85}$$

Inspite of this heterogeneity in work, each worker is fully insured on her labor income and receives the same income $\pi_t \omega_t$ whether or not she actually works.

Lotteries and the Elasticity of Labor Supply

If a household chooses a lottery with probability π_t, its expected amount of work L_t will be:

$$L_t = \pi_t L_0 \tag{86}$$

Now it will consume the same amount in both states, so its expected utility is:

$$\pi_t \left[U(C_t) - \Gamma(L_0) \right] + (1 - \pi_t) \left[U(C_t) - \Gamma(0) \right] \tag{87}$$

Using (86) and eliminating irrelevant constants, the expected utility (87) becomes:

$$U(C_t) - \frac{L_t}{L_0} \left[\Gamma(L_0) - \Gamma(0) \right] \tag{88}$$

We see that even though the "intrinsic" disutility of labor $\Gamma(L_t)$ may be very inelastic, things happen as if the disutility of labor was linear in L_t (and thus labor supply highly elastic and intertemporally substitutable). We now show that this results in a stronger reaction of employment to shocks in an explicitly dynamic model.

Dynamics

As in section 10.5, we assume that households have the following intertemporal utility:

$$U = \sum_t \beta^t \left(\frac{C_t^{1-\theta}}{1-\theta} - \frac{L_t^{1+\nu}}{1+\nu} \right) \tag{89}$$

and we have a simple production function:

$$Y_t = A_t L_t^{1-\alpha} \tag{90}$$

The only asset that can be transferred from period to period is government debt, D_t. The household's budget constraint is:

$$D_{t+1} = R_{t+1} \left(D_t + \omega_t \pi_t L_0 + \Upsilon_t - C_t \right) \tag{91}$$

where Υ_t is *real* profits.

First-order Conditions

The total level of employment is:

$$L_t = \pi_t L_0 \qquad (92)$$

and the real wage:

$$\omega_t = (1-\alpha) A_t L_t^{-\alpha} \qquad (93)$$

Because households work L_0 with probability π_t, and 0 with probability $1 - \pi_t$, their period t utility is:

$$\frac{C_t^{1-\theta}}{1-\theta} - \pi_t \frac{L_0^{1+\nu}}{1+\nu} \qquad (94)$$

Households maximize the expected value of utility (94) subject to the budget constraints (91). The Lagrangian is:

$$\sum_t \beta^t \left\{ \frac{C_t^{1-\theta}}{1-\theta} - \pi_t \frac{L_0^{1+\nu}}{1+\nu} + \lambda_t \left[R_{t+1} D_t + R_{t+1} \omega_t \pi_t L_0 - R_{t+1} C_t - D_{t+1} \right] \right\} \qquad (95)$$

and the first-order conditions with respect to C_t, π_t and D_t are, respectively:

$$C_t^{-\theta} = \lambda_t R_{t+1} \qquad (96)$$

$$\frac{L_0^\nu}{1+\nu} = \lambda_t R_{t+1} \omega_t \qquad (97)$$

$$\lambda_{t-1} = \beta \lambda_t R_{t+1} \qquad (98)$$

Combining (90), (93), (96), (97), and $C_t = Y_t$, we find, in logarithms and omitting irrelevant constants:

$$\ell_t = \frac{(1-\theta) a_t}{\alpha + \theta - \alpha\theta} \qquad (99)$$

To evaluate the effect of employment lotteries, we recall the value of employment in the "traditional" case (equation 43):

$$\ell_t = \frac{(1-\theta) a_t}{\alpha + \nu + \theta - \alpha\theta} \qquad (100)$$

We see that, as compared to equation (100), the value of employment under employment lotteries (equation 99) would correspond to the case where $\nu = 0$, that is, the case where labor supply is extremely elastic. This will result, other things equal, in a greater volatility of labor.

Appendix 10.2: Output and Capital in the Cycle

One of the initial important themes of the RBC literature was that capital accumulation, being the central dynamic mechanism linking successive periods, would also play a central role in the dynamic propagation of shocks to all macroeconomic variables and (notably) output. We now investigate this problem in an RBC model more general than that of section 10.3, for which we give an analytical solution.[10] To make the exposition clearer, we concentrate here on the dynamics of output and capital accumulation and on the propagation issue, taking a constant labor supply.

The Model

As compared to the models of section 10.3 and 10.4, we keep the same Cobb-Douglas production function:

$$Y_t = A_t K_t^\alpha L_t^{1-\alpha} \tag{101}$$

but we use the "original" equation for capital dynamics with a depreciation rate δ:

$$K_{t+1} = (1 - \delta) K_t + I_t \tag{102}$$

As we indicated, we ignore fluctuations in labor and assume that labor supply is exogenous and constant in each period:

$$L_t = L_0 \tag{103}$$

Instead of a logarithmic utility, we take a more general isoelastic utility function:

$$E \sum_t \beta^t \frac{C_t^{1-\theta}}{1-\theta} \qquad \theta > 0 \tag{104}$$

Finally, to concentrate on the endogenous persistence and propagation effects, we assume that productivity shocks $a_t = Log A_t$ are i.i.d. white noises (the case of autocorrelated productivity shocks is treated in problem 10.5).

---

10. Analytical studies of the standard RBC model are found in Campbell (1994) and Lau (2002).

The Dynamics of Capital and Output

It is proved in the next subsection that the dynamics of capital k_t and output y_t are given by:

$$k_{t+1} = \lambda k_t + \phi a_t \tag{105}$$

$$y_t = \alpha k_t + a_t \tag{106}$$

where λ is solution of the characteristic polynomial:

$$\Psi(\lambda) = \beta \lambda^2 - (1 + \beta + \zeta)\lambda + 1 = 0 \tag{107}$$

and ϕ is given by:

$$\phi = \lambda \beta \xi \tag{108}$$

with:

$$\xi = \frac{1 - \beta + \beta \delta}{\alpha \beta} \qquad \zeta = \frac{\alpha \beta^2 \xi (\xi - \delta)(1 - \alpha)}{\theta} > 0 \tag{109}$$

Derivation of the Dynamic Equations

We derive the foregoing dynamics (equation 105) in a number of steps.

First-order Conditions

With the Cobb-Douglas production function (101), the first-order conditions of the firm yield:

$$\omega_t = \frac{\partial Y_t}{\partial L_t} = \frac{(1-\alpha)Y_t}{L_t} \tag{110}$$

$$R_t = 1 - \delta + \frac{\partial Y_t}{\partial K_t} = 1 - \delta + \frac{\alpha Y_t}{K_t} \tag{111}$$

Households maximize the utility function (104) subject to the budget constraints:

$$C_t + I_t = \omega_t L_t + R_t K_t \tag{112}$$

The Lagrangian of this program is:

$$\sum_t \beta^t \left[\frac{C_t^{1-\theta}}{1-\theta} + \lambda_t (\omega_t L_t + R_t K_t - C_t - I_t) \right] \tag{113}$$

and the first-order conditions on C_t and K_t:

$$\lambda_t = C_t^{-\theta} \tag{114}$$

$$\lambda_t = \beta E_t \left(\lambda_{t+1} R_{t+1}\right) \tag{115}$$

Combining equations (114) and (115) yields:

$$C_t^{-\theta} = \beta E_t \left(R_{t+1} C_{t+1}^{-\theta}\right) \tag{116}$$

Steady States

We denote with A_0, R_0, Y_0, C_0, I_0, and K_0 the steady-state values of the various variables. In view of equations (102), (111), and (116):

$$\frac{I_0}{K_0} = \delta \qquad R_0 = \frac{1}{\beta} \tag{117}$$

$$\frac{Y_0}{K_0} = \frac{1 - \beta + \beta\delta}{\alpha\beta} = \xi \tag{118}$$

Dynamic Equations

We log-linearize equations (111) and (116) around the steady state, denoting $c_t = Log\left(C_t/C_0\right)$, and similarly for the other variables. Omitting irrelevant constants, the intertemporal consumption function (equation 116) becomes:

$$\theta E_t c_{t+1} = \theta c_t - \alpha\beta\xi\left(1 - \alpha\right) E_t k_{t+1} \tag{119}$$

Now we consider the capital accumulation equation (102). Log-linearizing it around the stationary state, we obtain:

$$k_{t+1} = \frac{1}{\beta} k_t + (\delta - \xi) c_t + \xi a_t \tag{120}$$

We combine the two dynamic equations (119) and (120) to obtain a single equation in capital. This yields (note that because k_{t+1} is known in t, there is no need to put an expectation operator in front of it):

$$(1 + \beta + \zeta) k_{t+1} - \beta E_t k_{t+2} - k_t = \beta\xi a_t \tag{121}$$

with:

$$\zeta = \frac{\alpha\beta^2\xi\left(\xi - \delta\right)\left(1 - \alpha\right)}{\theta} > 0 \tag{122}$$

Resolution

We conjecture a solution of the form:

$$k_{t+1} = \lambda k_t + \phi a_t \qquad (123)$$

Iterating (123) and taking the expectation as of period t, we obtain:

$$E_t k_{t+2} = \lambda^2 k_t + \lambda \phi a_t \qquad (124)$$

Insert (123) and (124) into (121), we obtain:

$$[\lambda(1+\beta+\zeta) - \beta\lambda^2 - 1]k_t + [\phi(1+\beta+\zeta) - \beta\lambda\phi - \beta\xi]a_t = 0 \qquad (125)$$

Equating to 0 the term in k_t, we find:

$$\Psi(\lambda) = \beta\lambda^2 - (1+\beta+\zeta)\lambda + 1 = 0 \qquad (126)$$

which is equation (107). Equating to 0 the term in a_t yields:

$$(1+\beta+\zeta - \beta\lambda)\phi = \beta\xi \qquad (127)$$

which, using (126), can be rewritten $\phi = \lambda\beta\xi$, which is equation (108).

We finally check that the autoregressive root λ is between 0 and 1, so we compute:

$$\Psi(0) = 1 > 0 \qquad (128)$$

$$\Psi(1) = -\zeta < 0 \qquad (129)$$

and λ is indeed between 0 and 1. The other root is $1/\beta\lambda$.

An Example

In the case where $\theta = 1$ and $\delta = 1$, which corresponds to the case treated in section 10.3, then:

$$\xi = \frac{1}{\alpha\beta} \qquad \zeta = \frac{(1-\alpha)(1-\alpha\beta)}{\alpha} \qquad (130)$$

and therefore:

$$\lambda = \alpha \qquad \phi = 1 \qquad (131)$$

as we found in section 10.3.

Depreciation, Persistence, and Propagation

We can compute, differentiating (107):

$$\frac{\partial \lambda}{\partial \zeta} < 0 \qquad (132)$$

so that persistence is a decreasing function of the composite parameter ζ. Because $\partial \zeta / \partial \delta > 0$ we find that, as intuition would suggest, low depreciation will make capital more persistent.

This does not imply, however, a strong propagation mechanism on output. Indeed, in view of equations (105) and (106), the first-period impact of a productivity shock on output is a_t, and the second-period effect is:

$$\alpha \phi a_t = \lambda \left(1 - \beta + \beta \delta\right) a_t \qquad (133)$$

Let us take some usual values for a quarterly model: $\beta = 0.99$, $\delta = 0.025$. Because $\lambda < 1$, we find that the second period effect is less than 0.035 times that of the first period. Although in that case the persistence of capital is quite high, the propagation of shocks to output is very low, and we again illustrate the Cogley and Nason (1993, 1995) puzzle on low propagation.

Problems

Problem 10.1: Alternative Shocks: Government

We introduce a different shock—a government spending shock—into the simple model of section 10.3. The utility function is the same:

$$\sum_t \beta^t \left[LogC_t - \Gamma\left(L_t\right)\right]$$

and so is the production function:

$$Y_t = A_t K_t^\alpha L_t^{1-\alpha}$$

We introduce government, which levies taxes T_t in real terms, and purchases a stochastic amount of goods G_t. As a result, the budget constraint of the household is now:

$$C_t + I_t = \omega_t L_t + R_t K_t - T_t$$

We assume:

$$G_t = \zeta_t C_t \tag{134}$$

where $\zeta_t \geq 0$ is a stochastic variable. Finally equilibrium on the goods market is now written:

$$C_t + I_t + G_t = Y_t \tag{135}$$

The rest of the model is the same as in section 10.3.

1. Compute consumption and investment as a function of output and the government shock ζ_t.
2. Compute the employment level as a function of the government shock.

Problem 10.2: Alternative Shocks: The Households

We reconsider the model of section 10.3, but we introduce shocks on the propensity to consume and on the disutility of work. The utility function becomes:

$$\sum \beta^t \left[\phi_t \text{Log} C_t - \xi_t \Gamma(L_t)\right] \tag{136}$$

where ϕ_t is a demand shock and ξ_t is a labor supply shock. The rest of the model is the same as in section 10.3.

1. Derive the market equilibrium and compute the optimal consumption and investment as a function of the shocks ϕ_t and ξ_t.
2. Characterize the equilibrium quantity of labor. How does it react to shocks?

Problem 10.3: Incomplete Capital Depreciation

We solve the model of section 10.4, due to Hercowitz and Sampson (1991). Compared with the standard RBC model, the essential change is that we replace the traditional equation depicting the evolution of capital:

$$K_{t+1} = (1-\delta) K_t + I_t \qquad 0 < \delta \leq 1$$

by the following log-linear approximation:

$$K_{t+1} = \Lambda K_t^{1-\delta} I_t^\delta, \qquad 0 < \delta \leq 1$$

The production function is still:

$$Y_t = A_t K_t^\alpha L_t^{1-\alpha}$$

and the household's budget constraint:

$$C_t + I_t = \omega_t L_t + \kappa_t K_t$$

where κ_t denotes the marginal productivity of capital $\partial Y_t/\partial K_t$. The household maximizes the expectation of its utility:

$$E_0 \sum_t \beta^t [Log C_t - \Gamma(L_t)]$$

1. Give the first-order conditions.
2. Compute the ratios of consumption and investment to output.
3. Compute the level of employment.

Problem 10.4: An RBC Model with Generations

We study and solve analytically a simple model with generations where, as in reality, investment and consumption can react differently to productivity shocks. The model is adapted from Huffman (1993), who studies the more general case where agents have a positive probability of death.

The population grows at the rate n, and the supply of labor also grows at the rate n. Each generation of households lives forever, works only in the first period of its life, and consumes in all periods by saving under the form of capital. The household of generation τ has a utility function:

$$\sum_{t=\tau}^{\infty} \beta^t Log C_t$$

which it maximizes subject to the budget constraints:

$$C_t + K_{t+1} = \omega_t L_t \quad t = \tau$$
$$C_t + K_{t+1} = R_t K_t \quad t > \tau$$

Finally the production function is Cobb-Douglas:

$$Y_t = A_t K_t^\alpha L_t^{1-\alpha}$$

1. Compute the values of consumption and investment as functions of capital and output.
2. Show how consumption and investment respond to technology shocks.

Problem 10.5: An RBC model with Autocorrelated Shocks

We study here the model of appendix 10.2, but instead of assuming that technology shocks are i.i.d. white noises, we assume that they are autocorrelated:

$$a_t = \frac{\varepsilon_t}{1 - \rho \mathcal{L}}$$

Except for that change, the rest of the model is the same.

1. Following the same method as in appendix 10.2, derive a dynamic equation linking successive values of capital.
2. Conjecture a solution for capital dynamics of the form:

$$k_{t+1} = \lambda k_t + \phi a_t$$

Compute the new values of λ and ϕ, and compare them to the values found in appendix 10.2.

11

Money

11.1 Introduction

Money is a very special good that performs the three functions of unit of account (or numéraire), medium of exchange, and store of value. Its study is thus generally separated from that of other goods.[1] Introducing money in rigorous dynamic models actually poses a number of difficult conceptual problems.

1. As we shall see, using one particular good as money actually corresponds to a restriction on possible exchanges as compared, for example, with a barter system. We will have to explain why it is profitable to society to restrict trades in such a way.

2. Money is used as a store of value even though it has no intrinsic value itself. Moreover, it is strictly dominated in terms of rates of return by other financial assets. We will construct models where money can survive while being so dominated.

In section 11.2 we show that there are good economic reasons, in terms of both information and transactions costs, for the adoption of monetary exchange. In section 11.3 we continue the study of the Samuelson (1958) monetary model, which we already saw in chapter 4 (section 4.4), and where

---

[1]. For overviews of three different vintages on the topic, the reader should consult Niehans (1978), McCallum (1989b), and Walsh (1998).

money is a pure store of value. We will see that money in this model is extremely fragile.

In the following two sections we describe two classic models where the existence of a monetary equilibrium is more robust and where money can coexist in equilibrium with other assets that dominate it in terms of rates of return. In section 11.4 we study money in the utility function (MIUF) models and in section 11.5 cash in advance (CIA) models.[2]

Following the majority of the literature, MIUF and CIA formalizations are embedded in dynamic general equilibrium models. To have a simple and homogeneous exposition, sections 11.4 and 11.5 use the Ramsey-type model with an infinitely lived agent, which we studied in chapters 4 and 7. But in section 11.6 we see that a number of disturbing paradoxes arise in such "Ricardian"[3] monetary models. One may thus naturally want to explore alternative frameworks.

Going in this direction, we show in section 11.7 how the paradoxes disappear in non-Ricardian models, which are essentially monetary extensions of overlapping generations (OLG) models. Finally, in section 11.8 we present a "monetary Ramsey-OLG model," which is a synthesis of the preceding models. We show that this model displays the famous "Pigou effect", and, as a simple application, solves the famous interest rate pegging puzzle.

11.2 Why Money?

To precisely characterize monetary exchange as compared to, say, barter exchange, we use the concept of an "exchange relation" (Clower, 1967), that is, the list of pairs of goods that can be exchanged directly against each other. Each pair corresponds to a market. Figure 11.1 represents, in an economy with four goods, the exchange relation for a barter and a monetary economy.

The existence of a market for the exchange of two goods is indicated by a cross in the corresponding box. In a barter economy, the exchange relation is "maximal," that is, there is a market for every pair of goods. So with ℓ goods there are $\ell(\ell-1)/2$ markets, or trading posts. In a monetary economy instead, all exchanges must go through a single good, money (good 1 in figure 11.1), so that the number of markets is $\ell - 1$.

We see that monetary exchange corresponds to a clear limitation of possible exchanges. A first reason appears immediately for wanting such a limitation: $\ell - 1$ trading posts are less costly for society to operate than

---

2. There is also a third approach, where money provides utility because it allows to economize on shopping costs. See, for example, McCallum and Goodfriend (1987), McCallum (1989b).
3. By "Ricardian" we mean models where, as in the Ramsey model, Ricardian equivalence holds.

Goods	1	2	3	4
1	▨	X	X	X
2	X	▨	X	X
3	X	X	▨	X
4	X	X	X	▨

Barter

Goods	1	2	3	4
1	▨	X	X	X
2	X	▨		
3	X		▨	
4	X			▨

Money

Figure 11.1 The exchange relation

$\ell(\ell-1)/2$. We will see that there are some further reasons, in terms of both information and other transactions costs, in favor of monetary exchange.

11.2.1 A Basic Example

To make these points, we use a simple four-goods economy (Niehans, 1969). We assume that the auctioneer has done his job, in the sense that excess demands sum to 0 for every single good. We take the simple matrix of excess demands Δ depicted in table 11.1, with agents in columns, goods in rows.

$$\Delta = \begin{bmatrix} -1 & +1 & 0 & 0 \\ 0 & -1 & +1 & 0 \\ 0 & 0 & -1 & +1 \\ +1 & 0 & 0 & -1 \end{bmatrix}$$

Table 11.1 The excess demand matrix

This matrix of excess demands has the famous "absence of double coincidence of wants" property. This means that exchanges cannot be carried by direct trades between pairs of agents but must involve indirect trades. The matrix Δ in table 11.1 is a typical case of this lack of double coincidence of wants. The ultimate flows corresponding to this matrix are shown in figure 11.2.

The problem is that implementing these ultimate trades may not be feasible in the absence of some coordinating device. In a decentralized economy, every transfer of goods must have a counterpart of equal value. As a result, to one set of ultimate trades can be associated several alternative payment arrangements (figures 11.3 and 11.4).

Figure 11.3 depicts monetary exchange with good 1 as money, whereas figure 11.4 depicts a hybrid payments arrangement where both goods 1 and 3 are used partially as means of exchange. We now review two classic

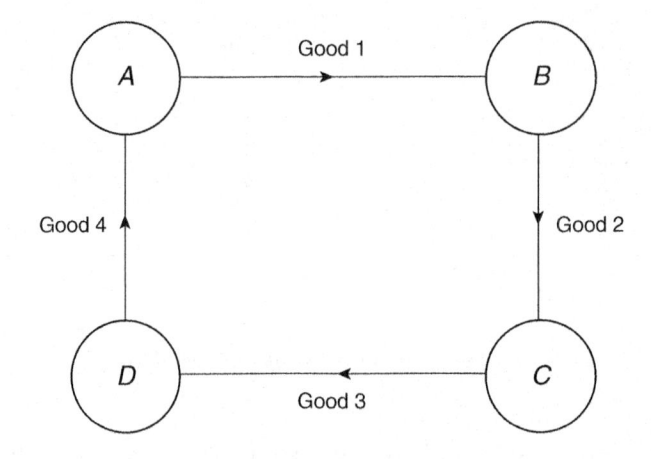

Figure 11.2 The ultimate trade flows

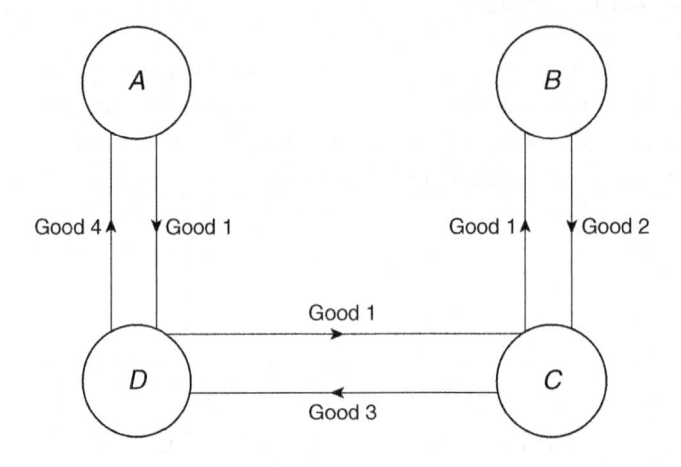

Figure 11.3 Monetary exchange

arguments, based on information and transactions costs, showing why it is efficient to use monetary exchange.

11.2.2 An Informational Argument

The first argument says that it is socially beneficial to have a single means of exchange for informational reasons.[4] A simple example will make

---

4. These informational arguments have been notably developed in Veendorp (1970), Ostroy (1973), Ostroy and Starr (1974), Jones (1976).

Money

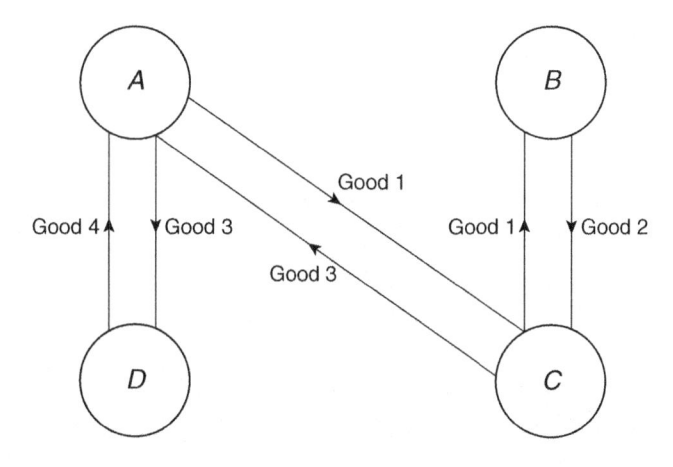

[Figure: diagram with nodes A (top-left), B (top-right), C (bottom-right), D (bottom-left). Arrows labeled: A↔D with "Good 4" (up) and "Good 3" (down); B↔C with "Good 1" (up) and "Good 2" (down); A→C "Good 1"; C→A "Good 3".]

Figure 11.4 An alternative payment arrangement

the point. Imagine you are in a "fruit economy" and you want to exchange your strawberries for bananas. Because there is no double coincidence of wants, there is nobody in the economy who wants to directly buy your bananas against strawberries, and you will have to use another fruit as an intermediate for exchange. The problem is that, if all trades are allowed, you have no idea which fruit (apples, pears, cherries, etc.) to use as a medium of exchange, and you are likely to make mistakes, that is, choose a medium of exchange that no banana owner will want. Appendix 11.1 gives an example where, although all agents choose their medium of exchange on the basis of the market demands they have observed, everybody ends up choosing the wrong medium of exchange and no trade takes place.

Of course, this informational problem is completely solved in a monetary economy since all trades are made against money. The trader above will simply sell her strawberries for money, and then acquire bananas against the money she has obtained.

11.2.3 A Transactions Costs Argument

The foregoing argument tells us that a single medium of exchange is better than many, but somehow does not give us a clue as to which good will finally be chosen as the medium of exchange. Transactions costs give a natural answer to that question (see notably Niehans, 1969).

Let us go back to figures 11.3 and 11.4 and assume there is a cost for transporting one good from one agent to the other, which we suppose, to simplify the argument, is independent of the agents concerned. Let us denote κ_1, κ_2, κ_3, and κ_4 these costs for goods 1, 2, 3, and 4, respectively.

Assume that good 1 has the lowest cost:

$$\kappa_1 < \kappa_2 \quad \kappa_1 < \kappa_3 \quad \kappa_1 < \kappa_4 \tag{1}$$

The cost of operating monetary exchange with good 1 as money, as in figure 11.3, is:

$$3\kappa_1 + \kappa_2 + \kappa_3 + \kappa_4 \tag{2}$$

whereas the cost of operating the hybrid system with goods 1 and 3 as partial monies, as in figure 11.4, is:

$$2\kappa_1 + \kappa_2 + 2\kappa_3 + \kappa_4 \tag{3}$$

Because $\kappa_1 < \kappa_3$, the monetary system is less expensive to operate than the hybrid system. Clearly the same argument can be made, not only with the hybrid system of figure 11.4 but with other payments arrangements as well, so that the monetary system with good 1 as money is the least costly to operate.

11.3 The Fragility of OLG Money

We have just seen why it would be useful to society to have a monetary exchange system for informational and transactions costs reasons. An important issue remains: agents must be willing to hold money as a store of value. We have already seen in chapter 4 a first model of that type, Samuelson's (1958) OLG model with money. We show in this section that money is extremely fragile in that model. We will then move to models where monetary equilibrium is more robust.

11.3.1 An OLG Model

First recall briefly the central features of the model. Households live two periods. They consume c_{1t} and c_{2t+1} in the first and second period of their lives, and have a utility function:

$$Log c_{1t} + \beta Log c_{2t+1} \tag{4}$$

They receive exogenous real incomes y_1 and y_2 in the first and second period. They can save from one period to the next under the form of money, of which there is a fixed quantity M in the economy.

11.3.2 The Dynamic Equilibrium and Indeterminacy

We saw in chapter 4, section 4.4 that the dynamics of equilibrium prices is given by:

$$y_2 p_{t+1} + (1+\beta) M = \beta y_1 p_t \tag{5}$$

We already noted that the condition for both the existence of a positive long-term equilibrium price and local determinacy around it was:

$$\frac{\beta y_1}{y_2} > 1 \tag{6}$$

If $\beta y_1 < y_2$, there will not even be local determinacy. But the situation is actually worse if we study global determinacy. For that purpose, it will be more enlightening to study the dynamic evolution of real money balances M/p_t. Equation (5) can be rewritten as:

$$\frac{M}{p_{t+1}} = \frac{(M/p_t) y_2}{\beta y_1 - (1+\beta)(M/p_t)} \tag{7}$$

If we place ourselves in the case where local determinacy holds, that is, if $\beta y_1 > y_2$, there will be two long-run equilibrium values for money balances:

$$\frac{M}{p} = 0 \quad \text{and} \quad \frac{M}{p} = \frac{M}{p^*} = \frac{\beta y_1 - y_2}{1+\beta} \tag{8}$$

The equilibrium p^* is locally determinate, but the system as a whole is globally indeterminate because there is an infinity of trajectories starting with prices above p^* and converging to the autarkic state $M/p = 0$ (figure 11.5).

We see that money as a store of value is quite fragile in this model, for at least three reasons:

1. Even when money is the sole asset, the system will be locally determinate only when condition (6) is satisfied.
2. Even in that "favorable" case, the system as a whole is not globally determinate, as we just saw.
3. Finally, we have placed ourselves in a model where there is no alternative asset. If agents could save, say, under the form of bonds with a positive return, money would be driven out of the system.

We will now study two models in which the services of money as facilitating exchange are more formally acknowledged, and where the presence of money is less fragile.

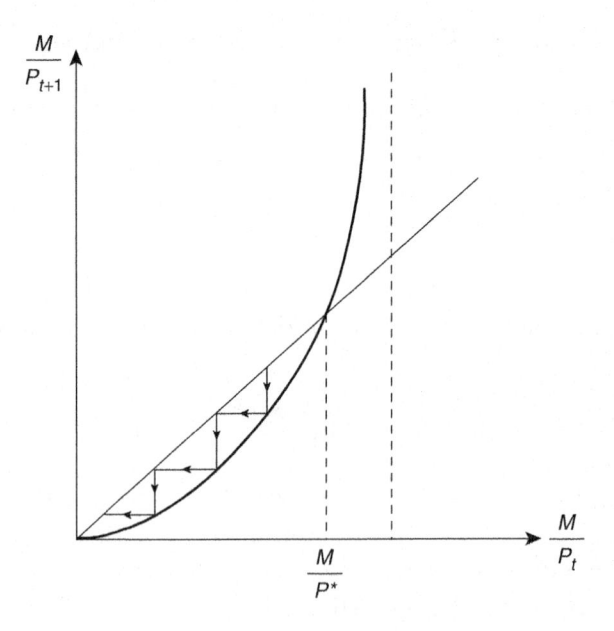

Figure 11.5 Global indeterminacy

11.4 Money in the Utility Function

We investigate a first model, called "money in the utility function" MIUF, coming from Patinkin (1956), Sidrauski (1967), and Brock (1974, 1975), which allows money and bonds to coexist in a dynamic general equilibrium. The basic idea is that money yields directly some "liquidity services," so that real money balances M_t/P_t will appear, together with consumption, in the utility function.

11.4.1 The Basic Model

We assume that the intertemporal utility of the households has the following form:

$$\sum_t \beta^t V\left(C_t, \frac{M_t}{P_t}\right) \qquad (9)$$

where M_t is the quantity of money held by the agent at the end of period t and the function V is concave and homogeneous in its two arguments. The budget constraint in each period is:

$$C_t + \frac{M_t}{P_t} + \frac{B_t}{P_t} = Y_t - T_t + \frac{M_{t-1}}{P_t} + \frac{(1+i_{t-1})B_{t-1}}{P_t} \qquad (10)$$

where Y_t is real income and T_t a lump-sum tax expressed in real terms. We assume that real income Y_t is exogenous. The household maximizes the utility function (9) subject to the budget constraints (10). The corresponding Lagrangian is:

$$\sum_t \beta^t V\left(C_t, \frac{M_t}{P_t}\right)$$

$$+ \sum_t \beta^t \lambda_t \left[\frac{M_{t-1}}{P_t} + \frac{(1+i_{t-1})B_{t-1}}{P_t} + Y_t - T_t - C_t - \frac{M_t}{P_t} - \frac{B_t}{P_t}\right] \quad (11)$$

Let us denote:

$$V_{ct} = \frac{\partial V(C_t, M_t/P_t)}{\partial C_t} \qquad V_{mt} = \frac{\partial V(C_t, M_t/P_t)}{\partial (M_t/P_t)} \quad (12)$$

The first-order conditions with respect to C_t, B_t, and M_t are, respectively:

$$\lambda_t = V_{ct} \quad (13)$$

$$\frac{\lambda_t}{P_t} = \beta(1+i_t) E_t\left(\frac{\lambda_{t+1}}{P_{t+1}}\right) \quad (14)$$

$$\frac{\lambda_t}{P_t} = \frac{V_{mt}}{P_t} + \beta E_t\left(\frac{\lambda_{t+1}}{P_{t+1}}\right) \quad (15)$$

11.4.2 The Demand for Money

Combining equations (13), (14), and (15), we obtain:

$$\frac{V_{mt}}{V_{ct}} = \frac{i_t}{1+i_t} \quad (16)$$

Equation (16) defines a demand for money of the form:

$$\frac{M_t}{P_t C_t} = \mathcal{M}\left(\frac{i_t}{1+i_t}\right) \quad (17)$$

Let us consider as an example a constant elasticity of substitution (CES) utility:

$$V\left(C_t, \frac{M_t}{P_t}\right) = \frac{1}{1-\theta}\left[C_t^{1-\theta} + \varpi\left(\frac{M_t}{P_t}\right)^{1-\theta}\right] \qquad \theta \geq 0 \quad (18)$$

where θ is somehow the inverse of the elasticity of substitution between consumption and real money balances. Then:

$$\frac{V_{mt}}{V_{ct}} = \varpi \left(\frac{M_t}{P_t C_t}\right)^{-\theta} \tag{19}$$

and this yields a demand for money:

$$\frac{M_t}{P_t C_t} = \varpi^{1/\theta} \left(\frac{i_t}{1+i_t}\right)^{-1/\theta} \tag{20}$$

11.4.3 Solving the Model: An Example

We show an example of how one can explicitly solve for the equilibrium prices and interest rates. Assume that the households have the following utility function:

$$V\left(C_t, \frac{M_t}{P_t}\right) = Log C_t + \varpi Log\left(\frac{M_t}{P_t}\right) \tag{21}$$

The first-order conditions (13), (14), and (15) are now written:

$$\lambda_t = \frac{1}{C_t} \tag{22}$$

$$\frac{\lambda_t}{P_t} = \beta (1+i_t) E_t \left(\frac{\lambda_{t+1}}{P_{t+1}}\right) \tag{23}$$

$$\frac{\lambda_t}{P_t} = \frac{\varpi}{M_t} + \beta E_t \left(\frac{\lambda_{t+1}}{P_{t+1}}\right) \tag{24}$$

Combining first (22) and (23), we obtain:

$$\frac{1}{P_t C_t} = \beta (1+i_t) E_t \left(\frac{1}{P_{t+1} C_{t+1}}\right) \tag{25}$$

This equation replaces, in this monetary economy, the Euler equation in real economies. We now combine (22) and (24) and obtain:

$$\frac{1}{P_t C_t} = \frac{\varpi}{M_t} + \beta E_t \left(\frac{1}{P_{t+1} C_{t+1}}\right) \tag{26}$$

which solves as:

$$\frac{1}{P_t C_t} = \varpi \sum_{s=t}^{\infty} \beta^{s-t} E_t \left(\frac{1}{M_s} \right) \tag{27}$$

and because C_t is equal to Y_t, which is exogenous, this gives us the equilibrium price level. Now combining (16) and (27) we find the interest rate:

$$\frac{1+i_t}{i_t} = \frac{V_{ct}}{V_{mt}} = \frac{M_t}{\varpi P_t C_t} = \sum_{s=t}^{\infty} \beta^{s-t} E_t \left(\frac{M_t}{M_s} \right) \tag{28}$$

We may note that if the quantity of money grows at the rate β, the nominal interest rate will be equal to 0. The basic intuition comes from Friedman (1969): in this simple model, the gross real interest rate is equal to $1/\beta$. If money decreases at the rate β, prices also decrease at the rate β. The nominal interest rate, which is the sum of the real interest rate and the rate of inflation, will be driven to 0. This result is of interest because, as we shall see in chapter 17, a zero nominal interest rate has appealing optimality properties.

11.5 Cash in Advance

The basic idea of cash in advance (CIA) models, initially proposed by Clower (1967), is that transactions must be paid in cash, moreover in cash already held *before* the transaction. This reflects the indispensable role of money in the transactions process.

This CIA constraint imposes a cost of holding money because otherwise the corresponding sum could be held under the form of interest-bearing assets.

The CIA constraint can take several forms, depending on the timing of transactions. A simple traditional way to express this constraint is the following:

$$P_t C_t \leq M_{t-1} \tag{29}$$

where M_{t-1} is the quantity of money accumulated at the end of the period $t-1$. A problem with this formulation is that if an agent is at the beginning of her life, then she cannot consume at all—a bad start.

So we will consider a formulation of the CIA constraint that will allow more flexibility, and in particular allow agents to consume even in the first period of their lives. To achieve this, each period is broken into two subperiods (Helpman, 1981; Lucas, 1982). In the first subperiod, the agent visits financial markets, where she can in particular acquire money against debt, thus solving the above problem. In the second subperiod, she visits the other markets, notably the goods markets, where she will be subject to the cash in advance constraint.[5]

Let us be more formal and denote by Ω_t the amount of financial assets, transmitted from period $t-1$, the household has at the beginning of period t. Things occur in two steps. First, the household goes to the financial market where it shares its wealth Ω_t between money and bonds:

$$M_t + B_t = \Omega_t \tag{30}$$

In a second step, the household consumes C_t, satisfying the CIA constraint:

$$P_t C_t \leq M_t \tag{31}$$

In this second step, households also receive exogenous real income Y_t and pay lump-sum real taxes T_t, so their wealth at the beginning of the next period is:

$$\Omega_{t+1} = M_t + (1+i_t) B_t + P_t Y_t - P_t T_t - P_t C_t \tag{32}$$

Combining (30) and (32), we obtain the following budget constraint:

$$\Omega_{t+1} = (1+i_t) \Omega_t - i_t M_t - P_t C_t + P_t Y_t - P_t T_t \tag{33}$$

Households maximize their discounted utility:

$$\sum_t \beta^t U(C_t) \tag{34}$$

subject to the CIA constraint (31) and the budget constraint (33). The Lagrangian is:

$$\sum_t \beta^t \left[U(C_t) + \nu_t \left(\frac{M_t}{P_t} - C_t \right) \right]$$

$$+ \sum_t \beta^t \lambda_t \left[(1+i_t) \frac{\Omega_t}{P_t} + Y_t - T_t - C_t - i_t \frac{M_t}{P_t} - \frac{\Omega_{t+1}}{P_t} \right] \tag{35}$$

---

[5]. There is an alternative version of the CIA model (Svensson, 1985) where agents visit first the goods market and then the assets markets.

and the first-order conditions, with respect to C_t, Ω_t, and M_t:

$$U'(C_t) = \lambda_t + \nu_t \qquad (36)$$

$$\frac{\lambda_t}{P_t} = \beta E_t \left[(1 + i_{t+1}) \frac{\lambda_{t+1}}{P_{t+1}} \right] \qquad (37)$$

$$\nu_t = \lambda_t i_t \qquad (38)$$

Combining (36), (37), and (38), we get the following relation:

$$\frac{U'(C_t)}{P_t} = \beta (1 + i_t) E_t \left[\frac{U'(C_{t+1})}{P_{t+1}} \right] \qquad (39)$$

which is also a monetary version of the Euler equation for this CIA economy.

11.5.1 A Logarithmic Example

We assume:

$$U(C_t) = Log C_t \qquad (40)$$

In that case, equation (39) becomes:

$$\frac{1}{P_t C_t} = \beta (1 + i_t) E_t \left(\frac{1}{P_{t+1} C_{t+1}} \right) \qquad (41)$$

which, using the CIA constraint $P_t C_t = M_t$, yields the nominal interest rate:

$$\frac{1}{1 + i_t} = \beta E_t \left(\frac{M_t}{M_{t+1}} \right) \qquad (42)$$

Again, we see that if the money supply grows at the rate β the nominal interest rate will be driven to 0.

11.6 Puzzles and Paradoxes

We have just seen how money can be introduced in an operational way into the traditional model with an infinitely lived household. We saw two different ways, MIUF and CIA. However, these models deliver a number of paradoxical answers to some central questions in monetary economics, so they should be modified to take these problems into account (Bénassy,

2007). We investigate the paradoxes in this section and then indicate (in the next section) a possible direction to fix them.

To make the exposition simple, we adopt in this section the CIA model with logarithmic utility function that was described in section 11.5. Households maximize the following intertemporal utility:

$$\sum_t \beta^t Log C_t \qquad (43)$$

and they are subject in each period to a CIA constraint:

$$P_t C_t \leq M_t \qquad (44)$$

11.6.1 The Liquidity Puzzle

We saw in chapter 2 that in the traditional IS-LM model the response to an increase in the quantity of money is a decrease in the nominal interest rate, the so-called liquidity effect. This liquidity effect, which dates back at least to Keynes (1936) and Hicks (1937), appears to be found in the data (see, for example, Christiano, Eichenbaum, and Evans, 1999).

The problem is that this liquidity effect seems difficult to obtain in the monetary models just described. In fact, in these models the nominal interest rate actually tends to increase in response to a monetary injection. Formally, the mechanism will appear most clearly if we recall equation (42):

$$\frac{1}{1+i_t} = \beta E_t \left(\frac{M_t}{M_{t+1}} \right) \qquad (45)$$

To find the effect of a monetary shock we need to know the response of $E_t \left(M_t / M_{t+1} \right)$ to a shock on M_t. Many authors describe the dynamics of money under the form of an autoregressive process:

$$\log \left(\frac{M_t}{M_{t-1}} \right) = \frac{\varepsilon_t}{1 - \rho \mathcal{L}} \qquad 0 \leq \rho < 1 \qquad (46)$$

In this formula ε_t is an i.i.d. stochastic variable and $\mathcal{L}$ is the lag operator. Most empirical evaluations find a value of ρ around 0.5. In such a case $E_t \left(M_t / M_{t+1} \right)$ is decreasing in M_t and therefore the nominal interest rate will *increase* in response to a positive monetary shock. So the nominal interest rate goes in the direction opposite to that predicted by the traditional liquidity effect.

11.6.2 Interest Rate Pegging and Nominal Price Indeterminacy

We now consider a different monetary experiment, where the government pegs the nominal interest rate, letting the quantity of money adapt endogenously. As we will see, this may lead prices to be totally indeterminate (Sargent and Wallace, 1975).

There is nominal indeterminacy if, whenever a price sequence is an equilibrium, then any price sequence multiple of the first one is also an equilibrium.[6] It was first pointed out by Sargent and Wallace (1975) that pegging nominal interest rates could lead to such nominal indeterminacy. At the time, they did not use a model with explicit intertemporal maximization, so it is useful to restate the problem in the framework of the maximizing model just described. To make things simplest, assume there is no uncertainty and that the nominal interest rate is pegged at the value i_t in period t. The first-order condition (41) is then rewritten:

$$P_{t+1} C_{t+1} = \beta \left(1 + i_t\right) P_t C_t \qquad (47)$$

Let us define nominal discount rates:

$$\Lambda_t = \frac{1}{(1 + i_0) \ldots (1 + i_{t-1})} \qquad \Lambda_0 = 1 \qquad (48)$$

Simple manipulations of the intertemporal household and government budget constraints with the logarithmic utility function (43) yield the household's consumption function:

$$\Lambda_t P_t C_t = (1 - \beta) \sum_{s=t}^{\infty} \Lambda_s P_s Y_s \qquad (49)$$

Because markets clear, $C_t = Y_t$ for all t, and inserting this into (49) we obtain the equilibrium equations:

$$\Lambda_t P_t Y_t = (1 - \beta) \sum_{s=t}^{\infty} \Lambda_s P_s Y_s \qquad \forall t \qquad (50)$$

Equations (50) are homogeneous of degree 1 in prices, so that if a sequence P_t is a solution of all these equations, then any sequence multiple of that one will also be a solution. There is thus nominal indeterminacy, and the disturbing Sargent and Wallace (1975) result is valid in this maximizing framework.

---

6. For a useful discussion of the differences between nominal and real indeterminacy, see McCallum (1986).

11.6.3 The Fiscal Theory of the Price Level

In recent years, a challenging theory of price determinacy in monetary economies has developed: the fiscal theory of the price level (FTPL).[7] What the FTPL says is that even in circumstances where monetary policy is not sufficient to bring determinacy, for example, in the case of a pure interest rate peg, as the one we just saw, adequate fiscal policies can still restore determinacy. The fiscal policies that achieve determinacy are such that the government's intertemporal budget constraint is not balanced in all circumstances. In fact, the intuition behind the theory is that unless one starts from a particular price level, the government's real liabilities would explode in time.

More precisely, there is an equilibrium path, corresponding to a particular initial price, where the government balances its intertemporal budget constraint. In off-equilibrium paths, where the economy starts from a different price level, the government's real liabilities will be explosive.

To show the mechanics of the FTPL, we consider a simple policy of interest rate pegging, which is the typical situation where the FTPL holds. To simplify the exposition we assume that the pegged interest rate is constant in time, so that:

$$i_t = i_0 \qquad \forall t \tag{51}$$

Let us recall the government budget equation:

$$\Omega_{t+1} = (1 + i_t)\Omega_t - i_t M_t - P_t T_t \tag{52}$$

We have to specify fiscal policy, and we assume that the government has fiscal policies of the form:

$$P_t T_t = i_t B_t + (1 - \gamma)\Omega_t + \delta P_t Y_t \qquad \gamma \geq 0 \qquad \delta \geq 0 \tag{53}$$

This formula has three terms. (a) The term $i_t B_t$ is interest paid on bonds. If there was only this term, government budget would be balanced at all times. (b) The term $\delta P_t Y_t$ says that the governement taxes a fraction δ of national income. (c) The term $(1 - \gamma)\Omega_t$ says that the government may want to withdraw a fraction $1 - \gamma$ of its outstanding financial liabilities. If γ is greater than 1, this actually corresponds to an expansion of government liabilities. The FTPL, as we will see, corresponds notably to a large value of γ.

---

7. This is notably due to Leeper (1991), Sims (1994), and Woodford (1994, 1995).

Combining (52) and (53) with $\Omega_t = M_t + B_t$, we find:

$$\Omega_{t+1} = \gamma \Omega_t - \delta P_t Y_t \tag{54}$$

Turning now to nominal income $P_t Y_t$, the first-order condition (47) and $C_t = Y_t$ yield, under the interest peg $i_t = i_0$:

$$P_{t+1} Y_{t+1} = \beta (1 + i_0) P_t Y_t \tag{55}$$

Dividing (54) by (55) we obtain:

$$\frac{\Omega_{t+1}}{P_{t+1} Y_{t+1}} = \frac{\gamma}{\beta (1 + i_0)} \frac{\Omega_t}{P_t Y_t} - \frac{\delta}{\beta (1 + i_0)} \tag{56}$$

Since $\Omega_t/P_t Y_t$ is a nonpredetermined variable, the condition for determinacy is that the coefficient of $\Omega_t/P_t Y_t$ be greater than 1 (mathematical appendix, section A.11), that is:

$$\gamma > \beta (1 + i_0) \tag{57}$$

Combining (56) and (57) we see that to achieve determinacy, the parameter γ must be high enough that the ratio of government liabilities to income is explosive on off-equilibrium paths. A number of peole would view that as an adventurous policy in real-life situations.

11.7 A Non-Ricardian Solution

We now show that a solution to the three puzzles of the preceding section can be found by moving to a non-Ricardian framework where new agents are born in time and Ricardian equivalence does not hold. To make the demonstration simple we shall use a monetary OLG model in the tradition of Samuelson (1958) together with a cash in advance constraint.[8] We will see that it delivers answers strikingly different from those obtained in the Ricardian model.

---

8. The point can be made in more sophisticated models, such as the Ramsey-OLG monetary model described in section 11.8. See Bénassy (2007).

11.7.1 The Model

The household side is represented by overlapping generations of consumers. Households born in period t live for two periods, t and $t+1$, and receive real income Y_t when young. They consume C_{1t} in period t, C_{2t+1} in period $t+1$, and their utility is:

$$Log\, C_{1t} + \beta Log\, C_{2t+1} \tag{58}$$

In each period of its life, a household born in period t is submitted to a CIA constraint:

$$P_t C_{1t} \leq M_{1t} \qquad P_{t+1} C_{2t+1} \leq M_{2t+1} \tag{59}$$

Total consumption and money are:

$$C_t = C_{1t} + C_{2t} \qquad M_t = M_{1t} + M_{2t} \tag{60}$$

As in the model of section 11.6, call Ω_t the total amount of financial assets that the agents have at the beginning of period t. Because young households are born without any assets, Ω_t is entirely in the hands of old households. To simplify the exposition, we assume that taxes T_t are levied only on young households.

11.7.2 Equilibrium

Let us start with the old households who arrive in period t with financial assets Ω_t. In view of the 100 percent CIA constraint (formula 59), old households transform all their financial assets Ω_t into money and spend it, so their consumption is equal to:

$$C_{2t} = \frac{\Omega_t}{P_t} \tag{61}$$

We now study the problem of the young household. If it consumes C_{1t} in the first period, it must acquire a quantity of money $P_t C_{1t}$ to satisfy the CIA constraint, and therefore borrows $P_t C_{1t}$ from the central bank, so that it holds a quantity of money and bonds (a negative amount of bonds corresponds to borrowing at the interest rate i_t):

$$M_{1t} = P_t C_{1t} \qquad B_{1t} = -P_t C_{1t} \tag{62}$$

As a consequence, it will hold at the end of period t a quantity of financial assets equal to:

$$\Omega_{t+1} = M_{1t} + (1+i_t) B_{1t} + P_t Y_t - P_t T_t - P_t C_{1t}$$
$$= P_t Y_t - P_t T_t - (1+i_t) P_t C_{1t} \qquad (63)$$

Combining (61) and (63), we find that second-period consumption is equal to:

$$C_{2t+1} = \frac{\Omega_{t+1}}{P_{t+1}} = \frac{P_t Y_t - P_t T_t - (1+i_t) P_t C_{1t}}{P_{t+1}} \qquad (64)$$

Inserting this into the utility function (58), we find that the young household will choose its first period consumption C_{1t} so as to maximize:

$$Log C_{1t} + \beta Log\left[P_t Y_t - P_t T_t - (1+i_t) P_t C_{1t}\right] \qquad (65)$$

which yields the first-period consumption function:

$$C_{1t} = \frac{1}{1+\beta} \frac{Y_t - T_t}{1 + i_t} \qquad (66)$$

Combining with (61) we obtain total consumption:

$$C_t = C_{1t} + C_{2t} = \frac{1}{1+\beta} \frac{Y_t - T_t}{1+i_t} + \frac{\Omega_t}{P_t} \qquad (67)$$

Now the equation of equilibrium on the goods market is $C_t = Y_t$, which yields:

$$Y_t = \frac{1}{1+\beta} \frac{Y_t - T_t}{1+i_t} + \frac{\Omega_t}{P_t} \qquad (68)$$

We have also a second equilibrium equation saying that in view of the CIA constraint (59), the total quantity of money M_t is equal to $P_t C_t = P_t Y_t$, that is:

$$M_t = P_t Y_t \qquad (69)$$

So the equilibrium is characterized by the two equations (68) and (69). We shall see that it has none of the paradoxical properties we saw in section 11.6.

11.7.3 The Liquidity Effect

Let us first assume, to study the liquidity issue, that the quantity of money is exogenous. We combine equations (68) and (69) and solve for the interest rate. We find:[9]

$$1 + i_t = \frac{1}{1+\beta} \frac{Y_t - T_t}{Y_t} \frac{M_t}{M_t - \Omega_t} \qquad (70)$$

There is clearly a liquidity effect because:[10]

$$\frac{\partial i_t}{\partial M_t} = -\frac{1}{1+\beta} \frac{Y_t - T_t}{Y_t} \frac{\Omega_t}{(M_t - \Omega_t)^2} < 0 \qquad (71)$$

11.7.4 Interest Pegging and Price Determinacy

Let us again consider the issue of price determinacy under interest rate pegging, and assume that the nominal interest rate is exogenously given at the level i_t in period t. We can solve equation (68) for the price level:

$$P_t = \frac{(1+\beta)(1+i_t)\Omega_t}{(\beta + i_t + \beta i_t) Y_t + T_t} \qquad (72)$$

We see that whatever the level of i_t, the price level is fully determinate, and the indeterminacy result of Sargent and Wallace (1975) disappears. We further see that:

$$\frac{\partial P_t}{\partial i_t} = \frac{-(1+\beta)\Omega_t(Y_t - T_t)}{[(\beta + i_t + \beta i_t)Y_t + \alpha T_t]^2} < 0 \qquad (73)$$

so that the price depends negatively on the interest rate, as is usually expected.

We now give a brief intuition about this result. In the Ricardian model, the basic dynamic equation, the Euler equation, relates P_t to P_{t+1}. Because both P_t and P_{t+1} are nonpredetermined variables, there is nothing that makes them determinate.

On the contrary, we see here in equation (68) that P_t is related to Ω_t. Because Ω_t is inherited from the past, this gives a "nominal anchor" that helps making the price determinate. This relation between P_t and Ω_t is itself

---

9. Note that $M_t - \Omega_t$ in the denominator of the last fraction is always positive because it is equal to $P_t C_{1t}$.
10. Note that this is, of course, not the only way to solve the liquidity puzzle. See notably Lucas (1990), Christiano and Eichenbaum (1992), and Fuerst (1992).

due to the fact that consumption depends on the real value of financial assets Ω_t/P_t (equation 67). This is called the "Pigou effect" (Pigou, 1943), or "real balance effect" (Patinkin, 1956). We study it in more depth in section 11.8.

11.7.5 Fiscal Policy and Determinacy

We finally reexamine the fiscal theory of the price level. We consider the same fiscal policy examined in section 11.6.3:

$$P_t T_t = i_t B_t + (1 - \gamma)\Omega_t + \delta P_t Y_t \qquad \gamma \geq 0 \qquad \delta \geq 0 \qquad (74)$$

Let us combine it with the identity $\Omega_t = M_t + B_t$ and the two equilibrium equations (68) and (69). We obtain:

$$P_t Y_t = \frac{\beta(1 + i_0) + \gamma}{\beta(1 + i_0) + \delta} \qquad (75)$$

We see that, unlike with the FTPL, there is no need to have a high γ to obtain price determinacy. Price determinacy can occur under fully reasonable fiscal policies.

11.7.6 A Summary

We have just seen that the Ricardian model (section 11.6) and the OLG model of this section display strikingly different properties. (a) A positive shock on money leads to a nominal interest rate increase in the Ricardian model, but to a decrease in the OLG model. (b) In the case of a nominal interest rate peg, the Ricardian model displays nominal indeterminacy, whereas in the OLG model the price level is fully determinate. (c) In the Ricardian model, the FTPL associates price determinacy with fiscal policies that make government liabilities explosive, whereas no such policies are required for price determinacy in the OLG model.

Of course, these two models are very different, and we now present a monetary model intermediate between the two, which allows us to study these issues in a more synthetic framework.

11.8 A Ramsey-OLG Monetary Model

We saw in sections 11.6 and 11.7 the enormous differences between the monetary versions of the Ramsey and OLG models. It also appeared that the Pigou effect played a central role in these differences.

Now these two models are polar models, and we would like to have a model that is somehow intermediate between them. As it turns out, such a model has been developed by Weil (1987, 1991). In that model, new generations are born in every period, as in the OLG model, but households are infinitely lived, as in the Ramsey model. As we shall see, this model displays a Pigou effect.

11.8.1 The Economy

The economy is essentially a monetary extension of the Ramsey-OLG model described in chapter 4 (section 4.5). As in that model, we find that for our purposes the important feature is births, not deaths, and so we assume that new generations of households are born each period, but nobody dies.

Denote as N_t the number of households alive at time t. So $N_t - N_{t-1} \geq 0$ households are born in period t. Except for that demographic structure, the model is very similar to that of section 11.6.

Consider a household born in period j. Denote by c_{jt}, y_{jt}, and m_{jt}, its consumption, endowment, and money holdings at time $t \geq j$. This household maximizes the following utility function:

$$U_{jt} = \sum_{s=t}^{\infty} \beta^{s-t} Log\, c_{js} \tag{76}$$

and is submitted in period t to a CIA constraint:

$$P_t c_{jt} \leq m_{jt} \tag{77}$$

Household j begins period t with a financial wealth ω_{jt}. First the bond market opens, and the household lends an amount b_{jt} at the nominal interest rate i_t. The rest is kept under the form of money m_{jt}, so that:

$$\omega_{jt} = m_{jt} + b_{jt} \tag{78}$$

Then the goods market opens, and household j sells its endowment y_{jt}, pays taxes τ_{jt} in real terms, and consumes c_{jt}, subject to the CIA constraint (77). Both income y_{jt} and taxes τ_{jt} are exogenous. The budget constraint for household j is:

$$\omega_{jt+1} = (1 + i_t)\omega_{jt} - i_t m_{jt} + P_t y_{jt} - P_t \tau_{jt} - P_t c_{jt} \tag{79}$$

11.8.2 Aggregation

Aggregate quantities are obtained by summing the various individual variables. There are $N_j - N_{j-1}$ agents in generation j, so, for example, aggregate assets Ω_t and taxes T_t are equal to:

$$\Omega_t = \sum_{j \leq t} (N_j - N_{j-1}) \omega_{jt} \qquad T_t = \sum_{j \leq t} (N_j - N_{j-1}) \tau_{jt} \qquad (80)$$

Similar formulas apply to output Y_t, consumption C_t, money M_t, and bonds B_t. We now describe how endowments and taxes are distributed among households. We assume that all households have the same income and taxes, so that:

$$y_{jt} = y_t = \frac{Y_t}{N_t} \qquad \tau_{jt} = \tau_t = \frac{T_t}{N_t} \qquad (81)$$

Going to aggregate variables, as before, financial wealth Ω_t is the sum of money and bonds:

$$\Omega_t = M_t + B_t \qquad (82)$$

and it evolves according to the government's budget constraint:

$$\Omega_{t+1} = (1 + i_t) \Omega_t - i_t M_t - P_t T_t = \Omega_t + i_t B_t - P_t T_t \qquad (83)$$

We do not give a detailed analytical resolution of the model, which is done in appendix 11.3, but we show through simple examples how the Pigou effect comes into the picture and how it can lead to totally different answers on some central issues.

11.8.3 A Dynamic Equation with a Pigou Effect

A central building block of all dynamic models is the dynamic equation linking successive values of equilibrium prices. For the sake of later comparison, we take the example of an intertemporal logarithmic utility. Then this equation is:

$$P_{t+1} Y_{t+1} = \beta (1 + i_t) P_t Y_t \qquad (84)$$

It results simply from the Euler equation:

$$P_{t+1} C_{t+1} = \beta (1 + i_t) P_t C_t \qquad (85)$$

and from the equilibrium condition $C_t = Y_t$. Note that no financial asset appears in this equation.

Now it is shown in appendix 11.3 that with the same logarithmic utility, and assuming an increasing population N_t, the corresponding dynamic equation becomes:

$$P_{t+1}Y_{t+1} = \beta(1+i_t)\frac{N_{t+1}}{N_t}P_tY_t - (1-\beta)\Omega_{t+1}\left(\frac{N_{t+1}}{N_t}-1\right) \qquad (86)$$

We see that, as soon as $N_{t+1} > N_t$, a term containing financial wealth enters the dynamic equation. Formula (86) shows most clearly how this term totally disappears when, as in the monetary versions of the Ramsey model, the population is constant through time.

As it turns out, introducing the Pigou effect into the picture brings radical changes for some central issues of monetary theory (Bénassy, 2007). As a first example, we return to the famous "nominal indeterminacy" result of Sargent and Wallace (1975), and see that the outcome is dramatically modified.

11.8.4 An Example: Interest Pegging and Determinacy

We assume $N_{t+1} = (1+n)N_t$, so that the dynamic equation (86) simplifies to:

$$P_{t+1}Y_{t+1} = \beta(1+n)(1+i_t)P_tY_t - (1-\beta)n\Omega_{t+1} \qquad (87)$$

which generalizes the traditional equation (84). The interest rate is pegged at i_0. We assume, moreover, that the government has a balanced budget fiscal policy $P_tT_t = i_tB_t$, so that:

$$\Omega_{t+1} = \Omega_t = \Omega \qquad (88)$$

Equation (87) becomes:

$$P_{t+1}Y_{t+1} = \beta(1+n)(1+i_0)P_tY_t - (1-\beta)n\Omega \qquad (89)$$

Applying the Blanchard-Kahn condition (mathematical appendix, section A.11.6) to the nonpredetermined variable P_tY_t, we find that the condition for local determinacy is that the coefficient of P_tY_t be greater than 1, that is:

$$\beta(1+n)(1+i_0) > 1 \qquad (90)$$

Introducing a Pigou effect has a striking effect on the determinacy properties of the model, because under the (mild) condition (90), the system

Money 259

is determinate, whereas it never was in the traditional framework. One may note also that (90) is only a local determinacy result. Global results can be obtained as well in this framework (Bénassy, 2007, 2009).

Appendix 11.1: Money as a Medium of Exchange: An Informational Argument

We now show that if the medium of exchange is not institutionally determined, agents acting in a decentralized manner may end up repeatedly choosing the wrong medium of exchange, therefore increasing the time necessary to the completion of their desired trades. The following example is due to Veendorp (1970).

Let us consider an economy with four agents (A, B, C, D) and four goods $(1, 2, 3, 4)$. To concentrate on the coordination issue, we assume that prices are Walrasian, so that excess demands balance in the aggregate. Initial endowments and excess demands are indicated in the following matrices (table 11.2), where horizontal lines correspond to agents (A, B, C, D) and vertical lines to goods $(1, 2, 3, 4)$.

$$\Xi = \begin{bmatrix} 1 & 0 & 0 & 0 \\ 0 & 1 & 0 & 0 \\ 0 & 0 & 1 & 0 \\ 0 & 0 & 0 & 1 \end{bmatrix} \qquad \Delta = \begin{bmatrix} -1 & +1 & 0 & 0 \\ 0 & -1 & +1 & 0 \\ 0 & 0 & -1 & +1 \\ +1 & 0 & 0 & -1 \end{bmatrix}$$

Table 11.2: Endowments and excess demands

Note that we have a typical case of an absence of double coincidence of wants, where indirect exchange is therefore necessary. We study the functioning of this economy, first under barter exchange, then under monetary exchange.

Barter Exchange

In a barter system, there is a market for each pair of goods, that is, six markets, $(1, 2), (1, 3), (1, 4), (2, 3), (2, 4)$, and $(3, 4)$. Let us assume that in the first round of trading agents try to achieve direct exchanges. For example, agent A goes to market $(1, 2)$ and demands good 2 against good 1. Nothing happens because of the lack of double coincidence of wants, and nobody wants to exchange 2 for 1.

In the second round, agents abandon the idea of direct exchanges and attempt to carry indirect exchanges of length one, and therefore try to pick the best medium of exchange. For example, A has noted that on market $(2,3)$ there was a supply of good 2 (which he wants ultimately) against good 3. He therefore goes to the market $(1,3)$ to acquire good 3 against good 1, with the purpose of reselling it later against good 2 in market $(2,3)$.

If we symmetrically carry the same reasoning for the four agents we find that:

- A will demand 3 against 1.
- C will demand 1 against 3.
- B will demand 4 against 2.
- D will demand 2 against 4.

This time there will be exchanges on markets $(1,3)$ and $(2,4)$. The resulting endowments and excess demands matrices are shown in table 11.3.

$$\Xi = \begin{bmatrix} 0 & 0 & 1 & 0 \\ 0 & 0 & 0 & 1 \\ 1 & 0 & 0 & 0 \\ 0 & 1 & 0 & 0 \end{bmatrix} \qquad \Delta = \begin{bmatrix} 0 & +1 & -1 & 0 \\ 0 & 0 & +1 & -1 \\ -1 & 0 & 0 & +1 \\ +1 & -1 & 0 & 0 \end{bmatrix}$$

Table 11.3: New endowments and excess demands

Again, we are in a situation where no exchange can take place. The problem is that, based on the market signals of the first round, each trader has chosen a different medium of exchange. As a result of these uncoordinated choices, after one round of exchange they end up in essentially the same situation as before they traded.

Monetary Exchange

We now assume that exchanges are monetary. One of the four goods, say, 1, has been chosen as the medium of exchange (money). Accordingly there are only three markets, $(1,2), (1,3)$, and $(1,4)$ and all agents plan trades that go through money. For example, B, who wants ultimately to sell good 2 and purchase good 3, will first demand 1 (money) against 2, with the intention of exchanging it against 3 in the next round.

So in the first round:

- A demands 2 against 1 (money).
- B demands 1 against 2 with the intention of exchanging it against 3 in the next round.
- C demands 1 against 3, with the intention of exchanging it against 4 in the next round.
- D demands 1 against 4.

We see that A and B exchange 1 against 2. As a result the new matrices are as shown in table 11.4.

$$\Xi = \begin{bmatrix} 0 & 1 & 0 & 0 \\ 1 & 0 & 0 & 0 \\ 0 & 0 & 1 & 0 \\ 0 & 0 & 0 & 1 \end{bmatrix} \qquad \Delta = \begin{bmatrix} 0 & 0 & 0 & 0 \\ -1 & 0 & +1 & 0 \\ 0 & 0 & -1 & +1 \\ +1 & 0 & 0 & -1 \end{bmatrix}$$

Table 11.4: Endowments and excess demands after round 1

Because A has obtained his desired exchange, he will not participate in the next rounds. As for the three others, a reasoning similar to the preceding one shows that in the second round:

- B demands 3 against 1.
- C demands 1 against 3, with the intention of exchanging it against 4 in the next round.
- D demands 1 against 4.

We see that B and C exchange 1 against 3. As a result, the new matrices are in table 11.5.

$$\Xi = \begin{bmatrix} 0 & 1 & 0 & 0 \\ 0 & 0 & 1 & 0 \\ 1 & 0 & 0 & 0 \\ 0 & 0 & 0 & 1 \end{bmatrix} \qquad \Delta = \begin{bmatrix} 0 & 0 & 0 & 0 \\ 0 & 0 & 0 & 0 \\ -1 & 0 & 0 & +1 \\ +1 & 0 & 0 & -1 \end{bmatrix}$$

Table 11.5: Endowments and excess demands after round 2

Finally, in the third round:

- C demands 4 against 1.
- D demands 1 against 4.

As a result, C and D exchange 1 against 4 and the new matrices are in table 11.6.

$$\Xi = \begin{bmatrix} 0 & 1 & 0 & 0 \\ 0 & 0 & 1 & 0 \\ 0 & 0 & 0 & 1 \\ 1 & 0 & 0 & 0 \end{bmatrix} \qquad \Delta = \begin{bmatrix} 0 & 0 & 0 & 0 \\ 0 & 0 & 0 & 0 \\ 0 & 0 & 0 & 0 \\ 0 & 0 & 0 & 0 \end{bmatrix}$$

Table 11.6: Endowments and excess demands after round 3

We see that because they have coordinated on the same medium of exchange, the agents do not suffer from the coordination problem present in the barter economy and succeed in achieving their desired trades.

Appendix 11.2: Proportional Money Transfers

So far, according to tradition, we have assumed that money is distributed in a lump sum. A classic alternative assumption (Lucas, 1972) is that existing money holdings are multiplied overnight by the same coefficient for all agents. The budget constraint in each period is:

$$C_t + \frac{M_t}{P_t} + \frac{B_t}{P_t} = Y_t - T_t + \frac{X_t M_{t-1}}{P_t} + \frac{(1+i_{t-1}) B_{t-1}}{P_t} \tag{91}$$

where X_t is the proportional money expansion coefficient. We assume the following MIUF utility function:

$$\sum_t \beta^t V\left(C_t, \frac{M_t}{P_t}\right) \tag{92}$$

Maximizing (92) subject to (91) yields the following first-order conditions with respect to C_t, B_t, and M_t:

$$\lambda_t = V_{ct} \tag{93}$$

$$\frac{\lambda_t}{P_t} = \beta(1+i_t) E_t \left(\frac{\lambda_{t+1}}{P_{t+1}}\right) \tag{94}$$

$$\frac{\lambda_t}{P_t} = \frac{V_{mt}}{P_t} + \beta E_t \left(\frac{\lambda_{t+1} X_{t+1}}{P_{t+1}}\right) \tag{95}$$

Let us again take the example:

$$V\left(C_t, \frac{M_t}{P_t}\right) = Log C_t + \varpi Log\left(\frac{M_t}{P_t}\right) \tag{96}$$

Then the first-order conditions (93), (94), and (95) yield:

$$\frac{1}{P_t C_t} = \beta(1+i_t) E_t \left(\frac{1}{P_{t+1} C_{t+1}}\right) \tag{97}$$

$$\frac{M_t}{P_t C_t} = \varpi + \beta E_t \left(\frac{M_{t+1}}{P_{t+1} C_{t+1}}\right) \tag{98}$$

Equation (98) solves as:

$$\frac{M_t}{P_t C_t} = \frac{\varpi}{1-\beta} \qquad (99)$$

Inserting (99) into (97), we obtain the nominal interest rate:

$$\frac{1}{1+i_t} = \beta E_t \left(\frac{M_t}{M_{t+1}}\right) \qquad (100)$$

Appendix 11.3: The Weil Model

We now describe in a little more detail the Weil (1987, 1991) model that we outlined in section 11.8. We first show how the Pigou effect appears in consumption functions, then derive a dynamic equation, and finally show how the Pigou effect is related to the intergenerational distribution of taxes.

The Household's Consumption Function

Recall the utility function of households born in j:

$$U_{jt} = \sum_{s=t}^{\infty} \beta^{s-t} Log\, c_{js} \qquad (101)$$

and their budget constraint:

$$\omega_{jt+1} = (1+i_t)\omega_{jt} - i_t m_{jt} + P_t y_{jt} - P_t \tau_{jt} - P_t c_{jt} \qquad (102)$$

We assume that i_t is strictly positive. The household will thus satisfy the CIA equation exactly, so that $m_{jt} = P_t c_{jt}$ and the budget constraint (102) is written:

$$\omega_{jt+1} = (1+i_t)\omega_{jt} + P_t y_t - P_t \tau_t - (1+i_t) P_t c_{jt} \qquad (103)$$

We use the following nominal discount factors:

$$\Lambda_t = \frac{1}{(1+i_0)\ldots(1+i_{t-1})} \qquad \Lambda_0 = 1 \qquad (104)$$

Apply the discount factor Λ_{t+1} to the budget constraint (103). We obtain:

$$\Lambda_{t+1}\omega_{jt+1} = \Lambda_t \omega_{jt} + \Lambda_{t+1} P_t (y_t - \tau_t) - \Lambda_t P_t c_{jt} \qquad (105)$$

Summing all these budget constraints from time t to infinity, and assuming that $\Lambda_t \omega_{jt}$ goes to 0 as t goes to infinity (the transversality condition), we find the intertemporal budget constraint of household j:

$$\sum_{s=t}^{\infty} \Lambda_s P_s c_{js} = \Lambda_t \omega_{jt} + \sum_{s=t}^{\infty} \Lambda_{s+1} P_s (y_s - \tau_s) \qquad (106)$$

Maximizing the utility function (101) subject to this intertemporal budget constraint yields household j's consumption function:

$$\Lambda_t P_t c_{jt} = (1 - \beta) \left[\Lambda_t \omega_{jt} + \sum_{s=t}^{\infty} \Lambda_{s+1} P_s (y_s - \tau_s) \right] \qquad (107)$$

Summing this across the N_t agents alive in period t, we get the aggregate consumption function:

$$\Lambda_t P_t C_t = (1 - \beta) \left[\Lambda_t \Omega_t + N_t \sum_{s=t}^{\infty} \Lambda_{s+1} P_s (y_s - \tau_s) \right] \qquad (108)$$

Using the definition of the discount factor Λ_t (equation 104), we find:

$$\Lambda_{s+1} P_s (y_s - \tau_s) = \Lambda_s P_s y_s - \frac{\Lambda_{s+1} (P_s T_s + i_s M_s)}{N_s} \qquad (109)$$

To have a more compact notation, let us define total (nominal) taxes Θ_t as:

$$\Theta_t = P_s T_s + i_s M_s \qquad (110)$$

Then, combining (108), (109), and (110), the consumption function is rewritten as:

$$\Lambda_t P_t C_t = (1 - \beta) \left[\Lambda_t \Omega_t + N_t \sum_{s=t}^{\infty} \Lambda_s P_s y_s - N_t \sum_{s=t}^{\infty} \frac{\Lambda_{s+1} \Theta_s}{N_s} \right] \qquad (111)$$

The three terms in brackets are quite intuitive. On the positive side, the first represents financial assets, the second discounted incomes, while the third negative term is taxes that will be paid by currently alive households.

The Intertemporal Government Budget Constraint

Recall the government budget constraint:

$$\Omega_{t+1} = (1 + i_t)\Omega_t - i_t M_t - P_t T_t \qquad (112)$$

Multiply this budget constraint by Λ_{t+1} and use (110). We obtain:

$$\Lambda_{t+1}\Omega_{t+1} = \Lambda_t \Omega_t - \Lambda_{t+1}\Theta_t \qquad (113)$$

Summing from 0 to infinity we obtain:

$$\Lambda_t \Omega_t = \sum_{s=t}^{\infty} \Lambda_{s+1}\Theta_s \qquad (114)$$

What this means is that the value of financial assets is matched 100 percent by the value of current and future taxes. These taxes include both proper taxes and the money tax.

The Pigou Effect

Now we can use equation (111) in two different ways. In the first we use equation (113) and replace $\Lambda_{s+1}\Theta_s$ with $\Lambda_s \Omega_s - \Lambda_{s+1}\Omega_{s+1}$. This yields:

$$\Lambda_t P_t C_t = (1-\beta)\left[N_t \sum_{s=t}^{\infty} \Lambda_s P_s y_s + \Lambda_t \Omega_t + N_t \sum_{s=t}^{\infty} \frac{\Lambda_{s+1}\Omega_{s+1} - \Lambda_s \Omega_s}{N_s}\right] \qquad (115)$$

Rearranging the terms in Ω_s, we find:

$$\Lambda_t P_t C_t = (1-\beta)\left[N_t \sum_{s=t}^{\infty} \Lambda_s P_s y_s + N_t \sum_{s=t}^{\infty} \Lambda_{s+1}\Omega_{s+1}\left(\frac{1}{N_s} - \frac{1}{N_{s+1}}\right)\right] \qquad (116)$$

We see that as soon as $N_{t+1} > N_t$, terms containing financial wealth enter the dynamic equation. Formula (116) shows most clearly why these terms totally disappear when, as in the monetary versions of the Ramsey model, the population is constant through time.

The Dynamic Equation

Let us now insert the equilibrium condition $C_t = Y_t$ into equation (116) and divide by N_t. We obtain:

$$\Lambda_t P_t y_t = (1-\beta) \left[\sum_{s=t}^{\infty} \Lambda_s P_s y_s + \sum_{s=t}^{\infty} \Lambda_{s+1} \Omega_{s+1} \left(\frac{1}{N_s} - \frac{1}{N_{s+1}} \right) \right] \quad (117)$$

Rewrite equation (117) for $t+1$ and subtract the corresponding equation from (117). We find:

$$\Lambda_t P_t y_t - \Lambda_{t+1} P_{t+1} y_{t+1} = (1-\beta) \left[\Lambda_t P_t y_t + \Lambda_{t+1} \Omega_{t+1} \left(\frac{1}{N_t} - \frac{1}{N_{t+1}} \right) \right] \quad (118)$$

or, after simplification and multiplying by N_{t+1}/Λ_{t+1}:

$$P_{t+1} Y_{t+1} = \beta (1 + i_t) \frac{N_{t+1}}{N_t} P_t Y_t - (1-\beta) \left(\frac{N_{t+1}}{N_t} - 1 \right) \Omega_{t+1} \quad (119)$$

which is equation (86).

The Pigou Effect and Taxes

We have so far shown the existence of the Pigou effect. We now explain its cause and why it arises only when new agents are born in the economy.

We again use equation (111), but this time replace $\Lambda_t \Omega_t$ with $\sum_{s=t}^{\infty} \Lambda_{s+1} \Omega_s$ (equation 114):

$$\Lambda_t P_t C_t = (1-\beta) \left[N_t \sum_{s=t}^{\infty} \Lambda_s P_s y_s + N_t \sum_{s=t}^{\infty} \Lambda_{s+1} \Theta_s \left(\frac{N_s - N_t}{N_s} \right) \right] \quad (120)$$

The expression in brackets consists of two parts. The first is again the traditional term representing discounted incomes. Now the second term represents the discounted value of all taxes that will be paid by agents *who will be born later*. Therein lies the central difference between Ricardian and non-Ricardian models. Recall that in *both* cases financial assets are matched by an equivalent amount of current and future taxes (equation 114), so this is not where the difference lies.

In the Ricardian case, currently alive agents will pay 100 percent of these taxes. Taxes exactly cancel out the value of financial assets, and therefore these financial assets totally disappear from consumption functions and dynamic equations.

In the contrary, in the non-Ricardian case some future (yet unborn) agents will pay part of the taxes, and this represents actual wealth to the currently alive agents, hence the Pigou effect.

Problems

Problem 11.1: OLG Money, Inflation, and Determinacy

In section 11.3 we derived condition (6) for local determinacy in the OLG monetary model. We treated the case of a constant quantity of money M, and now we want to see how the conditions for equilibrium existence and determinacy are modified when government engineers money growth. More precisely, we assume that the government engineers a rate of growth X of money:

$$\frac{M_t}{M_{t-1}} = X$$

This is achieved by giving in period t a lump-sum amount of money $(X-1)M_{t-1}$ to the young household. Consequently, its intertemporal budget constraint is:

$$p_t c_{1t} + p_{t+1} c_{2t+1} = p_t y_1 + p_{t+1} y_2 + (X-1) M_{t-1}$$

1. Derive the consumption functions for the young and old households, as well as the dynamic equation relating successive prices.
2. Find the new condition for local determinacy. How do it relate to the coefficient of monetary expansion?

Problem 11.2: Naive Versus Rational Expectations in the Monetary OLG Model

We want to compare the dynamics of a monetary OLG economy under two alternative expectations schemes: rational expectations and naive expectations. For that we consider the same model as in problem 4.1.

This is an OLG monetary model where households have the following utility function:

$$U_t = \frac{C_{t+1}^{1-\theta}}{1-\theta} - \frac{L_t^{1+\nu}}{1+\nu} \qquad \nu > 0 \qquad \theta > 0$$

As we saw (problem 4.1), the current price P_t and expected future price P_{t+1}^e are related by:

$$\frac{M}{P_t} = \left(\frac{M}{P_{t+1}^e}\right)^{(1-\theta)/(1+\nu)}$$

1. We first assume rational expectations:

$$P_{t+1}^e = P_{t+1}$$

Are the dynamics locally determinate? Globally determinate?

2. We now assume naive expectations:

$$P_{t+1}^e = P_{t-1}$$

Are the dynamics stable? How do they compare to rational expectations?

Problem 11.3: The Money Process and the Nominal Interest Rate

Assume that output Y_t is exogenous and households have the following utility function, which generalizes the one in section 11.4.3.

$$V\left(C_t, \frac{M_t}{P_t}\right) = U(C_t) + \varpi Log\left(\frac{M_t}{P_t}\right)$$

1. Give the dynamic equilibrium equations
2. Compute the current price P_t as a function of current and future money supplies
3. Compute the equilibrium nominal interest rate as a function of current and future money supplies

Problem 11.4: A Synthesis between MIUF and CIA

If we compare the CIA and MIUF formalizations of money, each one has advantages and shortcomings.

The MIUF allows more general formulations, and in particular enables us to have a demand for money that is responsive to the interest rate.

The CIA formulation, on the other hand, represents better the idea that money is necessary to facilitate transactions, because money must be held before the transactions actually take place.

We study a model (Carlstrom and Fuerst, 2001), which is as general as the MIUF model but where the transaction facilitating aspect of money appears better because, as in the CIA model, the money that yields utility must be held before transactions take place.

As in the MIUF model, the agents maximize a utility function, including the services of money:

$$\sum_t \beta^t V\left(C_t, \frac{M_t}{P_t}\right)$$

The rest of the theory looks more like the CIA story. Denote Ω_t as the amount of financial assets at the beginning of period t. In a first stage, the consumer visits the bonds market where she shares her wealth Ω_t between money and bonds:

$$M_t + B_t = \Omega_t$$

The quantity of money M_t is the one that is taken into account in the utility function. In a second stage, the household consumes and receives various incomes, so that its wealth at the beginning of period $t+1$ is:

$$\Omega_{t+1} = (1 + i_t)\Omega_t - i_t M_t - P_t C_t + P_t Y_t - P_t T_t$$

1. Derive the intertemporal first-order conditions of the household.
2. Write the equation corresponding to equation (16) in this chapter.
3. Derive the demand for money for:

$$V\left(C_t, \frac{M_t}{P_t}\right) = \frac{1}{1-\theta}\left[C_t^{1-\theta} + \varpi\left(\frac{M_t}{P_t}\right)^{1-\theta}\right] \qquad \theta \geq 0$$

12

Money and Cycles

12.1 Introduction

In chapter 10 we studied business cycles in "real" economies, under the assumption of perpetual market clearing. In this and the next chapter we want to extend the study to more realistic economies with monetary exchange and also study the impact of imperfect competition and nominal rigidities. As it turns out, introducing nominal rigidities makes a huge difference, and to do things progressively we leave their study to the next chapter. So in this chapter, we continue to assume fully flexible prices, as in chapter 10. But we introduce successively three new and important features: (a) money and monetary shocks, (b) imperfect competition, and (c) imperfect information.

In section 12.2 we add money and monetary shocks to the simple real model that was studied in chapter 10, section 10.3 while maintaining the hypothesis of Walrasian equilibrium in all markets. As we shall see, the introduction of money per se does not necessarily change much of the dynamics of the real sphere.

A number of authors have believed that introducing imperfect competition would create Keynesian features in the corresponding models. We saw in chapter 5 that this was not really the case. But the model of chapter 5 was somewhat static, and we want to continue the argument in a truly dynamic setting. In section 12.3, while keeping the monetary structure, we replace Walrasian equilibrium by monopolistic competition on the goods markets, and we will see that imperfect competition per se does not really create any Keynesian features.

At this stage one might think that money can have only no or little effects in market clearing models, whether under perfect or imperfect competition. To show that this is actually not the case, we describe in section 12.4 an adaptation of the famous Lucas (1972) model, where money has real effects. The reason is an imperfect information problem, because of which the agents cannot disentangle real from monetary shocks. Because of this confusion, monetary shocks, which should be neutral, end up having real effects.

12.2 A Simple Monetary Model

In this section we extend the model of chapter 10 (section 10.3) to include money and monetary shocks.[1] We saw that capital did not create much dynamics in that model, so to both lighten the exposition and concentrate on the specifics of money, we ignore capital in this and the next sections.[2]

12.2.1 The Model

The economy studied is a monetary economy with two markets in each period t: goods for money at the price P_t and labor for money at the (nominal) wage W_t. There are two types of representative agents: firms and households. Firms have a technology:

$$Y_t = A_t L_t^{1-\alpha} \tag{1}$$

where L_t is labor input and A_t a stochastic technological shock.

In period t the representative household works L_t, consumes C_t, and ends the period with a quantity of money M_t. It maximizes the expected value of discounted future utilities with the following utility, of the money in the utility function type (see chapter 11), which now includes real money balances M_t/P_t:

$$U = \sum_{t=0}^{\infty} \beta^t \left[Log C_t + \varpi \, Log \frac{M_t}{P_t} - \Gamma(L_t) \right] \tag{2}$$

---

1. Money was introduced in calibrated "real business cycles" by King and Plosser (1984) and Cooley and Hansen (1989).
2. Similar models with capital can be found in Bénassy (1995, 2002b).

where Γ is an increasing convex function representing the disutility of labor. At the beginning of period t, there is a stochastic multiplicative monetary shock denoted as X_t: money holdings M_{t-1} carried from the previous period are multiplied by X_t, so the household starts period t with a quantity of money $X_t M_{t-1}$. Its budget constraint for period t is thus:

$$P_t C_t + M_t = W_t L_t + \Pi_t + X_t M_{t-1} \qquad (3)$$

where Π_t is distributed profits.

12.2.2 Walrasian Equilibrium

In each period, firms demand labor competitively. The real wage is equal to the marginal productivity of labor:

$$\frac{W_t}{P_t} = \frac{\partial Y_t}{\partial L_t} = (1-\alpha)\frac{Y_t}{L_t} \qquad (4)$$

The representative households maximize the expected value of their discounted utility (2), subject to the sequence of budget constraints (3). The Lagrangian for this program is the expected value of:

$$\sum_{t=0}^{\infty} \beta^t \left[Log C_t + \varpi\, Log \frac{M_t}{P_t} - \Gamma(L_t) + \lambda_t \left(\frac{W_t}{P_t} L_t + \frac{X_t M_{t-1}}{P_t} - C_t - \frac{M_t}{P_t} \right) \right] \qquad (5)$$

The first-order conditions for the consumer's program yield:

$$\frac{1}{C_t} = \lambda_t \qquad (6)$$

$$\Gamma'(L_t) = \lambda_t \frac{W_t}{P_t} \qquad (7)$$

$$\lambda_t = \frac{\varpi P_t}{M_t} + \beta E_t \left(\lambda_{t+1} \frac{X_{t+1} P_t}{P_{t+1}} \right) \qquad (8)$$

The equilibrium condition for money is that the quantity of money M_t demanded by the household be equal to the initial money holdings $X_t M_{t-1}$:

$$M_t = X_t M_{t-1} \qquad (9)$$

Now using (6) and (9), condition (8) is rewritten as:

$$\frac{M_t}{P_t C_t} = \varpi + \beta E_t \left(\frac{M_{t+1}}{P_{t+1} C_{t+1}} \right) \qquad (10)$$

This solves (by repeated forward substitution) as:

$$\frac{M_t}{P_t C_t} = \frac{\varpi}{1 - \beta} \qquad (11)$$

Because in equilibrium $C_t = Y_t$, we obtain the level of real money balances:

$$\frac{M_t}{P_t} = \frac{\varpi}{1 - \beta} Y_t \qquad (12)$$

Finally, combining conditions (6), (7), and the expression of the real wage (4), we find that L_t is constant and equal to L, where L is given by

$$L\Gamma'(L) = 1 - \alpha \qquad (13)$$

12.2.3 Walrasian Dynamics

We briefly describe the dynamic evolution of this Walrasian economy (non-Walrasian dynamics are studied in chapter 13). The equilibrium values of the main variables are given by:

$$L_t = L \qquad (14)$$

$$Y_t = A_t L_t^{1-\alpha} \qquad (15)$$

$$\frac{W_t}{P_t} = (1 - \alpha) \frac{Y_t}{L_t} \qquad (16)$$

$$\frac{M_t}{P_t} = \frac{\varpi}{1 - \beta} Y_t \qquad (17)$$

Looking at the first three equations, we note that, although the economy is perpetually subjected to monetary shocks, fluctuations in real variables are driven by real shocks *only*. In fact, the dynamics of the real variables are the same as in the model without money. We see that the introduction of money per se does not give necessarily a role for monetary shocks.[3]

---

3. Note that the total lack of effect of monetary shocks is due to our specific money creation process and utility for money, and is thus not a robust feature. More general dynamic models with money usually yield small effects for these shocks under market clearing.

Combining equations (14) to (17), we obtain, in logarithms,[4] the expressions for output y_t, Walrasian price p_t^*, Walrasian wage w_t^*, and inflation π_t (we have omitted all irrelevant constants):

$$y_t = a_t \tag{18}$$

$$w_t = w_t^* = m_t \tag{19}$$

$$p_t = p_t^* = m_t - a_t \tag{20}$$

$$\pi_t = m_t - m_{t-1} - (a_t - a_{t-1}) \tag{21}$$

At this point, although we will not embark in any actual calibrations, we may note a few correlations that have puzzled researchers working in this area.

The first problem is that real wages are too procyclical in this model. Combining (19) and (20), we find the real wage:

$$w_t - p_t = a_t \tag{22}$$

Comparing with (18) we find that the coefficient of correlation between the real wage and output is equal to 1:

$$\text{Corr } (w_t - p_t, y_t) = 1 \tag{23}$$

Although this correlation is a little weaker in more general calibrated models where L_t varies, it is usually much higher than what is observed in reality.

The second problem concerns prices. A comparison of equations (18) and (20) shows that prices in this model are countercyclical, whatever the relative size of technological and monetary shocks (we assume that they are independent). For example if a_t and m_t are i.i.d. white noise with variances σ_a^2 and σ_m^2, respectively:

$$\text{Corr } (p_t, y_t) = -\frac{\sigma_a}{(\sigma_a^2 + \sigma_m^2)^{1/2}} < 0 \tag{24}$$

On the other hand, it is usually admitted that there are periods when prices have been countercyclical but also some periods when they have been procyclical.[5] Clearly, this Walrasian model cannot reproduce this variety of experiences in the cyclical behavior of prices.

---

4. Lowercase letters denote the logarithm of the corresponding uppercase variables.
5. See, for example, Cooley and Ohanian (1991) and Smith (1992).

The third problem concerns the correlation between inflation and output (an issue related to the Phillips curve literature). Whereas this correlation is most generally viewed as positive, the Walrasian model above delivers a negative correlation for most sensible specifications of the productivity shocks (equations 18 and 21). Again with i.i.d. a_t and m_t:

$$\text{Corr } (\pi_t, y_t) = -\frac{\sigma_a}{(2\sigma_a^2 + 2\sigma_m^2)^{1/2}} < 0 \qquad (25)$$

We will see in chapter 13 that some nominal rigidities can help alleviate these problems. Before that, we investigate whether imperfect competition by itself can give more impact to money and monetary shocks.

12.3 Imperfect Competition

We combine the monetary model of the previous section with the imperfect competition framework presented in chapter 5 (section 5.4.4), by introducing imperfect competition on goods markets.[6] We will see that it does not change the dynamics very much.

12.3.1 The Model

To introduce imperfect competition in the simplest manner we use a Dixit and Stiglitz (1977), Ethier (1982) type framework. Output Y_t is produced from a continuum of differentiated goods indexed by $j \in [0,1]$:

$$Y_t = \left(\int_0^1 Y_{jt}^\eta dj \right)^{1/\eta} \qquad (26)$$

Each firm j has the same technology as in (1):

$$Y_{jt} = A_t L_{jt}^{1-\alpha} \qquad (27)$$

where A_t is a common technological shock. We denote with L_t the total quantity of labor used in the economy:

$$L_t = \int_0^1 L_{jt} dj \qquad (28)$$

---

6. This model is adapted from Bénassy (1996). Dynamic models with various forms of imperfect competition, calibrated or otherwise, are found in Danthine and Donaldson (1990, 1991, 1992); Rotemberg and Woodford (1992); Devereux, Head, and Lapham (1993); and Hornstein (1993). For surveys, see Rotemberg and Woodford (1995) and Silvestre (1995).

12.3.2 The Demand for Goods

We denote P_{jt} the price of intermediate good j. Output-producing firms choose the amounts Y_{jt} to minimize the cost of producing a given amount of final output Y_t, that is, they solve the following program:

$$\text{Minimize} \int_0^1 P_{jt} Y_{jt} dj \quad \text{s.t.}$$

$$\left(\int_0^1 Y_{jt}^\eta dj \right)^{1/\eta} = Y_t$$

The solution is:

$$Y_{jt} = Y_t \left(\frac{P_{jt}}{P_t} \right)^{-1/(1-\eta)} \tag{29}$$

where P_t is the associated constant elasticity of substitution price index:

$$P_t = \left(\int_0^1 P_{jt}^{-\eta/(1-\eta)} dj \right)^{-(1-\eta)/\eta} \tag{30}$$

12.3.3 First-order Conditions

Now that we have the demand function for goods j, we can derive the first-order conditions for firms and households.

Firms

Intermediate firm j chooses its price P_{jt} to maximize profits subject to its production function and its demand curve, that is, it will solve the program:

$$\text{Maximize} \quad P_{jt} Y_{jt} - W_t L_{jt} \quad \text{s.t.}$$

$$Y_{jt} = A_t L_{jt}^{1-\alpha}$$

$$Y_{jt} = Y_t \left(\frac{P_{jt}}{P_t} \right)^{-1/(1-\eta)}$$

The first-order conditions yield:

$$W_t L_{jt} = (1-\alpha) \eta P_{jt} Y_{jt} \tag{31}$$

or, suppressing the index j, because the equilibrium will be symmetrical:

$$W_t L_t = (1-\alpha) \eta P_t Y_t \tag{32}$$

Households

Households maximize utility subject to budget constraints, that is, they solve the program:

$$\text{Maximize} \quad E\sum_{t=0}^{\infty}\beta^t\left[Log C_t + \varpi\, Log\frac{M_t}{P_t} - \Gamma(L_t)\right] \quad \text{s.t.}$$

$$P_t C_t + M_t = W_t L_t + \Pi_t + X_t M_{t-1}$$

Note that this is the same program as in section 12.2. The first-order conditions are the same, and they yield, notably (equations 6, 7, and 11):

$$\Gamma'(L_t) = \frac{W_t}{P_t C_t} \tag{33}$$

$$\frac{M_t}{P_t C_t} = \frac{\varpi}{1-\beta} \tag{34}$$

Now combining (32) and (33), we find that L_t is constant and equal to L, where:

$$L\Gamma'(L) = (1-\alpha)\eta \tag{35}$$

We see that, as compared to the competitive case (equation 13), the introduction of imperfect competition leads to a lower level of employment (equation 35).

Except for that lower employment, comparing the other equilibrium equations shows that the dynamic properties of this imperfectly competitive model are very similar to those of the corresponding Walrasian model, and notably money has little influence on the real sphere. We find the same conclusion if there is imperfect competition on both goods and labor markets (problem 12.1).

12.4 Signal Extraction and Nominal Price Stickiness

We have seen in sections 12.2 and 12.3 that money shocks may not create specific dynamics in the real sphere, both in Walrasian and imperfect competition settings.

In a famous article, Lucas (1972) showed how, even in a fully competitive environment, imperfect information can lead to price sluggishness and to output and price movements whose relation looks like a Phillips curve. The central idea is that agents live in informationally separated islands. There are both local real shocks and global monetary shocks. If information was perfect, agents should react only to the real local shocks, which have "real" consequences, but not to the purely nominal money shocks, as we will see.

The informational setup is such that agents cannot fully distinguish the real from the monetary shocks, and they have a "signal extraction" problem. As a result, we will see that nominal monetary shocks will have real effects that they would not have under full information.

We now present a simple adaptation of the Lucas (1972) model, with a fully explicit solution, which will make the mechanisms at work clearer.[7]

12.4.1 The Model

Markets and Agents

The economy consists of a continuum of sectors, or islands, indexed by j. Firms in island j are competitive and produce a specific intermediate good (indexed by j) with the following technology:

$$Y_{jt} = L_{jt} \tag{36}$$

where Y_{jt} and L_{jt} are production and employment in island j. We denote by P_{jt} and W_{jt} the price and wage in sector j.

Households consume an aggregate consumption good produced by competitive firms endowed with the following technology of the Cobb-Douglas type:

$$Log\, Y_t = E\left(\Theta_{jt} Log\, Y_{jt}\right) \tag{37}$$

where Θ_{jt} is a local real shock concerning island j, and the expectation E in (37) is taken across all islands j. We assume:

$$E\left(\Theta_{jt}\right) = 1 \tag{38}$$

Equation (38) means that there is no aggregate real shock. We denote by P_t the aggregate price.

---

7. The adaptation in this section is a simplified version of Bénassy (2001b), which considers aggregate technology shocks as well. Other adaptations of the Lucas (1972) model can be found in Azariadis (1981b), McCallum (1984), Hahm (1987), Wallace (1992), and Bénassy (1999). The signal extraction problem has been studied in imperfectly competitive settings by Andersen (1985a, 1985b) and Nishimura (1986, 1992).

Each island j has a population of atomistic households of size 1. The demography of these households is characterized by an overlapping generations structure. All households are identical across islands, so we sometimes omit the index j in describing them. The typical household of generation t works L_t when young and consumes C_{t+1} when old. The utility function of the generation t household is:

$$U_t = C_{t+1} - \frac{L_t^{1+\nu}}{1+\nu} \qquad \nu > 0 \tag{39}$$

Policy

Because households consume one period after they have worked, they must transfer wealth from one period to the next, which is done by accumulating money, the only store of value. Call M_t the quantity of money in t (which is entirely in the hands of old households). Government policy consists in engineering changes in this quantity of money. To be specific, all individual money holdings are multiplied between periods $t-1$ and t by a coefficient X_t, so that aggregate money M_t evolves according to:

$$M_t = X_t M_{t-1} \tag{40}$$

As a result, the intertemporal budget constraint for the old households in island j is:

$$P_{t+1} C_{jt+1} = X_{t+1} M_t = X_{t+1} W_{jt} L_{jt} \tag{41}$$

Stochastic Shocks and Information

Let us call:

$$x_t = Log\, X_t \qquad \theta_{jt} = Log\, \Theta_{jt} \tag{42}$$

We assume that x_t is normal and i.i.d. with mean 0 and variance σ_x^2. The variables θ_{jt} are also normal and i.i.d. with mean μ_θ and variance σ_θ^2, the same for all j. Because Θ_{jt} is log-normal, we use formula (A.164) in the mathematical appendix to compute:

$$E\left(\Theta_{jt}\right) = \exp\left(\mu_\theta + \frac{\sigma_\theta^2}{2}\right) \tag{43}$$

and so, in view of (38), μ_θ and σ_θ^2 are related by:

$$\mu_\theta + \frac{\sigma_\theta^2}{2} = 0 \tag{44}$$

It is further assumed that in period t households and firms in sector j know M_{t-1} and the local variables P_{jt}, Y_{jt}, W_{jt}, and L_{jt}. They do not know the contemporaneous aggregate variables P_t, X_t, or Y_t, which they learn about only in the following period.

12.4.2 Market Equilibrium

We will study both full information and imperfect information equilibria. In this subsection we give a few equilibrium relations that will hold in both cases. First, because the firms producing intermediate goods are competitive, we have:

$$W_{jt} = P_{jt} \tag{45}$$

Second, because the firms producing the aggregate consumption good are competitive, the relative product price of intermediate j will be equal to its marginal productivity, so that:

$$\frac{P_{jt}}{P_t} = \frac{\Theta_{jt} Y_t}{Y_{jt}} \tag{46}$$

Third, the demand for the aggregate consumption good comes from old agents only. They entirely spend their money M_t on it, so the condition of equilibrium on the goods market is simply:

$$Y_t = \frac{M_t}{P_t} \tag{47}$$

Combining (36), (40), (45), (46), and (47) we obtain:

$$W_{jt} L_{jt} = P_{jt} Y_{jt} = \Theta_{jt} M_t = \Theta_{jt} X_t M_{t-1} \tag{48}$$

To compute the equilibrium, we have to find the amount of labor supplied by households. The household in island j maximizes its expected utility:

$$\text{Maximize } E_{jt}\left(\frac{X_{t+1} W_{jt} L_{jt}}{P_{t+1}}\right) - \frac{L_{jt}^{1+\nu}}{1+\nu} \tag{49}$$

where E_{jt} denotes an expectation based on information available in island j only. The first-order condition is:

$$L_{jt}^{\nu} = W_{jt} E_{jt} \left(\frac{X_{t+1}}{P_{t+1}} \right) \qquad (50)$$

12.4.3 Full Information

We first study as a benchmark the case in which agents have full information. In particular, agents in island j know both the local shock Θ_{jt} and the aggregate shock X_t.

To evaluate the expectation $E_{jt}(X_{t+1}/P_{t+1})$ in (50), the households will hold a price theory. More precisely, they conjecture a "quantity theory" relation of the form:

$$P_t = \frac{M_t}{\Lambda} = \frac{M_{t-1} X_t}{\Lambda} \qquad (51)$$

where the parameter Λ will be determined below. Inserting this into (50), we find:

$$L_{jt}^{\nu} = \frac{\Lambda W_{jt}}{M_t} \qquad (52)$$

and, multiplying both sides by L_{jt}, and using (48):

$$L_{jt} = (\Lambda \Theta_{jt})^{1/(1+\nu)} \qquad (53)$$

We see that under full information the quantity of labor employed in sector j depends only on the local real shock. Monetary shocks have no effect.

From equation (38) there is no aggregate technology shock, so we may expect that these local labor movements will cancel in the aggregate. Combining indeed (40), (47), and (51), we obtain aggregate output:

$$Y_t = \Lambda \qquad (54)$$

To have a complete solution, we need only to find the value of Λ, which is done in appendix 12.1 (equation 74), and yields:

$$\Lambda = \exp\left(\frac{\sigma_\theta^2}{2\nu} \right) \qquad (55)$$

We see that money is neutral, as neither aggregate output nor the local quantities of labor depend on the monetary shock. We shall now see that this changes drastically when we introduce imperfect information.

12.4.4 Signal Extraction and Nominal Sluggishness

We now come to our main subject of interest and assume that there is imperfect information. More precisely, young agents in island j know M_{t-1} and the local variables in their island, but they do not know the values of the shocks Θ_{jt} and X_t. Let us recall equation (48):

$$W_{jt}L_{jt} = P_{jt}Y_{jt} = \Theta_{jt}M_t = \Theta_{jt}X_tM_{t-1} \tag{56}$$

We see that, although they do not know Θ_{jt} and X_t individually, households know their product $\Theta_{jt}X_t$. The signal extraction problem consists of trying to evaluate, when the product $\Theta_{jt}X_t$ changes, how much of that change will be attributed to moves in Θ_{jt} and X_t, respectively. As it turns out, the answer depends on relative variances. Let us define:

$$\rho = \frac{\sigma_x^2}{\sigma_x^2 + \sigma_\theta^2} \tag{57}$$

There are classic signal extraction formulas (mathematical appendix, section A.7) for such problems. They notably tell us that the condititional expectation of x_t is:

$$E\left(x_t \mid x_t + \theta_{jt}\right) = \rho\left(x_t + \theta_{jt} - \mu_\theta\right) \tag{58}$$

The parameter ρ thus intuitively represents how much of a shock in $\Theta_{jt}X_t$ is attributable to a shock in X_t. This plays a central role in the solution that follows. Now, as in the preceding section, agents conjecture a price theory:

$$P_t = \frac{M_{t-1}X_t^{1-\gamma}}{\Lambda} \tag{59}$$

The main difference with the full information case is that, whereas γ was equal to 0 under full information, it will turn out to be strictly between 0 and 1 under imperfect information. This means that a money expansion X_t will lead to a less than proportional price increase and will therefore have real effects.

Computing the full solution of the model turns out to be a bit cumbersome, and this is done in appendix 12.2, where it is shown that the equilibrium is characterized by:

$$L_{jt} = (\xi\Lambda)^{1/(1+\nu)}\left(\Theta_{jt}X_t\right)^\gamma \tag{60}$$

$$Y_t = \Lambda X_t^\gamma \tag{61}$$

with:

$$\gamma = \frac{1-\rho}{1+\nu} \tag{62}$$

$$\Lambda = \exp\left[\frac{\gamma^2 \sigma_x^2}{2\nu} + \frac{(1-\rho)\sigma_\theta^2}{2\nu}\right] \qquad \xi = \exp\left(\frac{\gamma^2 \sigma_x^2}{2}\right) \tag{63}$$

We see that money is not neutral anymore: a positive money shock will now have a positive effect on both the levels of local employment and global output.

12.4.5 Positive Results

Because we have obtained closed-form solutions for employment and output, we can derive a number of correlations between macroeconomic aggregates. We will see that, from a positive point of view, our model behaves very much like Lucas's also famous (1973) model.

We start by going to logarithms, which will be denoted by lowercase letters (we ignore irrelevant constants):[8]

$$y_t = \gamma x_t \tag{64}$$

Now prices are deduced from output through $p_t = m_t - y_t$, so that:

$$p_t = m_t - \gamma x_t \tag{65}$$

and denoting as $\pi_t = p_t - p_{t-1}$ the inflation rate:

$$\pi_t = (1-\gamma)x_t + \gamma x_{t-1} \tag{66}$$

Using equations (64), (65), and (66), we can describe a number of positive properties of our model.

---

8. These constants do not matter for the correlations we discuss next, but they would be of utmost importance to do normative policy analysis. For such exercises, see Bénassy (1999, 2001b).

The Phillips Curve

We begin with the inflation–output correlation, associated with the Phillips curve tradition. Using formulas (64) and (66), the covariance is equal to (to simplify computations, we assume that the x_t's are i.i.d.):

$$\text{Cov}(y_t, \pi_t) = \gamma(1-\gamma)\sigma_x^2 \qquad (67)$$

There is a positive correlation between output and inflation, which corresponds to the Phillips curve tradition. It should be noted, however, that, if in a more general version of the model one introduces some *aggregate* productivity shocks, this correlation can actually become negative (Wallace, 1992).

Output Regressions

We now investigate how much output reacts to money expansions by regressing output y_t on money increases x_t. From equation (64), this regression coefficient is:

$$\gamma = \frac{1-\rho}{1+\nu} = \frac{\sigma_\theta^2}{(1+\nu)(\sigma_x^2 + \sigma_\theta^2)} \qquad (68)$$

We see that, as was observed by Lucas (1973), the coefficient of regression of output on money increases is a decreasing function of the variance σ_x^2 of these money increases.

Appendix 12.1: The Full Information Equilibrium

Let us recall the production function:

$$Log\, Y_t = E\left(\Theta_{jt} Log\, Y_{jt}\right) \qquad (69)$$

and the quantity of labor and output on island j (equation 53):

$$Y_{jt} = L_{jt} = (\Lambda\Theta_{jt})^{1/(1+\nu)} \qquad (70)$$

Inserting the values of Y_{jt} (70) into the production function (69), we find:

$$Log Y_t = \frac{E\left(\Theta_{jt} Log\Theta_{jt}\right) + E\left(\Theta_{jt}\right) Log\Lambda}{1+\nu} \qquad (71)$$

From (38) we have $E(\Theta_{jt}) = 1$, and from (54) $Y_t = \Lambda$, so that (71) becomes:

$$Log\Lambda = \frac{E(\Theta_{jt}Log\Theta_{jt})}{\nu} \qquad (72)$$

Formula (A.254) in the mathematical appendix tells us that:

$$E(\Theta_{jt}Log\Theta_{jt}) = \frac{\sigma_\theta^2}{2} \qquad (73)$$

so that, combining (72) and (73), we find the value of Λ for the perfect information case:

$$Log\Lambda = \frac{\sigma_\theta^2}{2\nu} \qquad (74)$$

Appendix 12.2: The Imperfect Information Equilibrium

To evaluate the expectation $E_{jt}(X_{t+1}/P_{t+1})$ in (50), we assume that the household conjectures a price theory, more precisely a relation of the form:

$$P_t = \frac{M_{t-1}X_t^{1-\gamma}}{\Lambda} \qquad (75)$$

where the parameters γ and Λ will be determined next. In view of (75), the expectation in (50) is rewritten:

$$E_{jt}\left(\frac{X_{t+1}}{P_{t+1}}\right) = \frac{\Lambda}{M_{t-1}} E_{jt}\left(\frac{1}{X_t}\right) E_{jt}(X_{t+1}^\gamma) \qquad (76)$$

Because X_{t+1} is log-normal with mean 0 and variance σ_x^2, we have:

$$E_{jt}(X_{t+1}^\gamma) = \exp\left(\frac{\gamma^2\sigma_x^2}{2}\right) = \xi \qquad (77)$$

Signal extraction comes in the evaluation of $E_{jt}(1/X_t)$, because the household in sector j observes the product $\Theta_{jt}X_t$, but not Θ_{jt} or X_t individually. Call $\rho = \sigma_x^2/(\sigma_x^2 + \sigma_\theta^2)$. Going to logarithms and using the traditional signal extraction formulas (mathematical appendix, section A.7), we find that, conditional on the observation of $x_t + \theta_{jt}$, x_t is a normal variable with mean and variance:

$$E\left(x_t \mid x_t + \theta_{jt}\right) = \rho\left(x_t + \theta_{jt} - \mu_\theta\right) \tag{78}$$

$$Var\left(x_t \mid x_t + \theta_{jt}\right) = \rho\sigma_\theta^2 \tag{79}$$

so that, using the formula (A.166) in the mathematical appendix for lognormal distributions:

$$E_{jt}\left(\frac{1}{X_t}\right) = \left(\frac{1}{\Theta_{jt}X_t}\right)^\rho \exp\left(\rho\mu_\theta + \frac{\rho\sigma_\theta^2}{2}\right) \tag{80}$$

and in view of equation (44):

$$E_{jt}\left(\frac{1}{X_t}\right) = \left(\frac{1}{\Theta_{jt}X_t}\right)^\rho \tag{81}$$

Combining (76), (77), and (81), we obtain:

$$E_{jt}\left(\frac{X_{t+1}}{P_{t+1}}\right) = \frac{\Lambda\xi}{M_{t-1}}\left(\Theta_{jt}X_t\right)^{-\rho} \tag{82}$$

Now combine (50) with (48) and (82). This yields:

$$L_{jt} = \left[\Lambda\xi\left(\Theta_{jt}X_t\right)^{1-\rho}\right]^{1/(1+\nu)} \tag{83}$$

Because $Y_{jt} = L_{jt}$, inserting this value into the production function (37), we obtain the level of output:

$$Log Y_t = \frac{Log\left(\Lambda\xi\right) + (1-\rho)Log X_t + (1-\rho) E\left(\Theta_{jt} Log\Theta_{jt}\right)}{1+\nu} \tag{84}$$

Combining the equality $P_t Y_t = M_t = X_t M_{t-1}$ and the price theory (75), we obtain:

$$Y_t = \Lambda X_t^\gamma \tag{85}$$

If the price theory is right, the two expressions giving Y_t in (84) and (85) must be the same. Identifying first the term in X_t, we find the value of γ:

$$\gamma = \frac{1-\rho}{1+\nu} \qquad (86)$$

Identifying the constant terms in (84) and (85), we obtain:

$$\nu Log\Lambda = Log\xi + (1-\rho) E\left(\Theta_{jt} Log\Theta_{jt}\right) \qquad (87)$$

and combining (73), (77), and (87), we obtain the value of Λ for the imperfect information case:

$$Log\Lambda = \frac{1}{\nu}\left[\frac{\gamma^2\sigma_x^2}{2} + \frac{(1-\rho)\sigma_\theta^2}{2}\right] \qquad (88)$$

Problems

Problem 12.1: Money and Imperfect Competition on Goods and Labor Markets

In section 12.3, we studied a dynamic monetary model with imperfect competition on the goods market. We will now see whether and how the results are modified if we introduce imperfect competition on both goods and labor markets.

As in section 12.3, we model imperfect competition on the goods market via a Dixit-Stiglitz (1977) type framework. Output Y_t is produced from a continuum of differentiated goods indexed by $j \in [0,1]$:

$$Y_t = \left(\int_0^1 Y_{jt}^\eta dj\right)^{1/\eta}$$

Each firm j has the same Cobb-Douglas technology as in this chapter (formula 1):

$$Y_{jt} = A_t L_{jt}^{1-\alpha}$$

where A_t is a common technological shock. We denote by L_t the total quantity of labor used in the economy:

$$L_t = \int_0^1 L_{jt} dj$$

We introduce imperfect competition on the labor market as well. Symmetrically to what happens in the goods market, L_t is itself an aggregate of a continuum of differentiated labor types (Snower, 1983), indexed by $i \in [0,1]$:

$$L_t = \left(\int_0^1 L_{it}^\chi di \right)^{1/\chi} \qquad 0 < \chi < 1$$

Households of type i set their wage W_{it}.

1. Derive the first-order conditions for firms and households.
2. Characterize the dynamic general equilibrium, and notably the employment level. What are the differences with the competitive case? And with the case where there is imperfect competition in the goods market only?

Problem 12.2: Lucas's Signal Extraction Model

We give here a simple computable version of Lucas's famous 1972 model.[9] The signal extraction problem concerns aggregate monetary shocks and "local" population shocks.

The economy consists of many isolated subeconomies, islands, indexed by $j \in [0,1]$. Each island j is a "Samuelsonian" (1958) overlapping generations economy. Generation t has N_{jt} members, where N_{jt} is an i.i.d. stochastic variable. Households of generation t work L_{jt} when young and consume C_{jt+1} when old. The utility function of generation t households is:

$$U_{jt} = C_{jt+1} - \frac{L_{jt}^{1+\nu}}{1+\nu} \qquad \nu > 0$$

The technology is linear:

$$Y_{jt} = N_{jt} L_{jt}$$

Households transfer wealth from one period to the next by holding money. We assume that money holdings in island j, M_{jt}, are the same in all islands and equal to M_t. Monetary shocks are the following: all individual money holdings are multiplied between periods $t-1$ and t by a coefficient X_t common to all islands, so that M_t evolves according to:

$$M_t = X_t M_{t-1}$$

---

9. This adaptation comes from Bénassy (1999). Earlier contributions with similar purposes include Azariadis (1981b), McCallum (1984), Hahm (1987), and Wallace (1992).

We now describe the informational problem. As in Lucas (1972), it is assumed that young agents j will not know the values of N_{jt} and X_t until period $t+1$. In period t they know M_{t-1}, P_{jt} and L_{jt}.

To have simple explicit solutions, we make particular assumptions about the distributions of the stochastic variables N_{jt} and X_t. Call n_{jt} and x_t their logarithms. We assume that these are independent normal variables. Money increases x_t have mean 0 and variance σ_x^2. Population n_{jt} has variance σ_n^2 and mean $\mu_n = -\sigma_n^2/2$, so that total population is constant:

$$E(N_{jt}) = \exp\left(\mu_n + \frac{\sigma_n^2}{2}\right) = 1$$

1. Write the utility maximization program of agent j and derive his labor supply.
2. Assume that agent j has a price theory:

$$P_{jt} = \frac{M_{t-1} Z_{jt}^{1-\gamma}}{\Lambda}$$

   where $Z_{jt} = X_t/N_{jt}$ is observable by household j. Compute the equilibrium on island j.
3. Compute the global equilibrium, and notably aggregate output and price as a function of X_t.
4. Show that there is a positive relation between output and inflation.
5. Show that the reaction of output to money is decreasing in the variance of money shocks.

Problem 12.3: Signal Extraction: Lump Sum Money Transfers

In section 12.4 and in problem 12.2 we assumed, as in Lucas (1972), that money injections are proportional to individual money holdings. We now use the traditional assumption of lump-sum money transfers, and see that the positive conclusions of the model turn out to be quite similar.

All the main assumptions of the model are the same as in section 12.4.1, and we do not repeat them here. The difference is in the operation of monetary policy. As in the model of section 12.4, aggregate money supply is multiplied between periods $t-1$ and t by a coefficient X_t:

$$M_t = X_t M_{t-1}$$

Now this money increase is carried out by making lump-sum money transfers $\mathcal{T}_t$ to the old households (or taxing them if there is a decrease in the aggregate quantity of money):

$$T_t = (X_t - 1)M_{t-1}$$

As a result, the budget constraint for the old households in island j is:

$$P_{t+1}C_{jt+1} = W_{jt}L_{jt} + T_{t+1}$$

We assume that young households j know only M_{t-1} and some of the local variables $(W_{jt}, L_{jt}, P_{jt}, Y_{jt})$ but not X_t, P_t, or Θ_{jt}.

1. Write the utility maximization program of agent j and derive her labor supply.
2. Assume that agent j has a price theory:

$$P_t = \frac{M_{t-1}X_t^{1-\gamma}}{\Lambda}$$

   Compute the equilibrium on island j.
3. Derive the full equilibrium, and notably aggregate output as a function of X_t.
4. Show that there is a positive relation between output and inflation, and that the reaction of output to money is decreasing in the variance of money shocks.

13

Nominal Rigidities and Fluctuations

13.1 Introduction

We studied in chapters 10 and 12 a number of dynamic stochastic general equilibrium (DSGE) models, which showed how to model an economy populated with rational maximizing agents and submitted to a number of demand and supply shocks. We studied these models both under the hypothesis of Walrasian market clearing, as in the initial real business cycle (RBC) models, and in a framework of imperfect competition. We want to extend this methodology and consider non-Walrasian economies with nominal rigidities.

A first obvious reason for such an extension is that a number of authors have documented such wage and price rigidities in actual market economies.[1]

There are other reasons why we want to move to such a non-Walrasian framework with nominal rigidities. In chapters 10 and 12 we identified a number of problems with the standard market clearing models. These were not solved by the introduction of imperfect competition by itself. We will see in this chapter that the addition of nominal rigidities allows us to alleviate these problems.

The first problem is that a number of correlations are quite far from their real-world counterparts. For example we saw that real wages are too procyclical or prices too countercyclical.

---

1. See, for example, Carlton (1986), Cecchetti (1986), Kashyap (1995), Taylor (1999), and Bils and Klenow (2004). For an overview on price rigidity from a more theoretical side, see Andersen (1994).

Another important issue is that of the propagation mechanism. Several empirical studies have shown that shocks, and notably demand shocks, have long-lasting effects on employment and output.[2] But the standard RBC model delivers very little propagation and persistence, as we explained in chapter 10.

As it turns out, a number of authors have convincingly demonstrated that the consideration of price and wage rigidities allowed them to substantially improve the capacity of these DSGE models to match the stylized facts.[3] These contributions are usually made in calibrated models. As in previous chapters, we follow a complementary line and consider models with explicit solutions that make more transparent the economic mechanisms at work.

Section 13.2 presents a few early models of wage rigidity, notably associated with the names of Gray (1976), Fischer (1977a), and Taylor (1979, 1980). Section 13.3 shows that even the simplest model of nominal rigidities, like preset wages à la Gray (1976), allows us to substantially improve some important correlations.

We move in section 13.4 to more recent models of price and wage rigidities and present in a simple common framework three schemes of nominal rigidities that have the properties of being highly tractable and allowing us to handle price and wage setting schemes going from full flexibility to full rigidity. We compare the impulse response functions for these schemes and show how their dynamics relate to the Phillips curve literature.

In section 13.5, we demonstrate how to include such rigidities into a rigorous DSGE model. We use the dynamic general equilibrium model of chapter 12 and study its dynamics under a simple scheme of price rigidity. The model displays persistence in output and prices, and we relate the degree of persistence to the fundamentals of the economy. Finally, section 13.6 studies some properties and extensions of the sticky price DSGE model of section 13.5.

13.2 Early Models

We shall describe three early models, due to Gray (1976), Fischer (1977a), and Taylor (1979, 1980). We expose these models within a very simple common framework.

---

2. See notably the recent studies of Christiano, Eichenbaum, and Evans (1999, 2005), Smets and Wouters (2003), and the references therein.

3. The pioneering dynamic model with imperfect competition and preset prices is Svensson (1986). Early works on calibrated models with nominal rigidities are Cho (1993); Hairault and Portier (1993); Cho and Cooley (1995); and Cho, Cooley, and Phaneuf (1997). Recent contributions are Christiano, Eichenbaum, and Evans (2005) and Smets and Wouters (2003).

13.2.1 A Common Walrasian Benchmark

The Walrasian version of the model is based on a system of four equations. The variables y_t, ℓ_t, w_t, p_t, and m_t are the logarithms of output, employment, wages, prices, and money:

$$y_t = a_t + (1-\alpha)\ell_t \tag{1}$$

$$w_t + \ell_t = p_t + y_t \tag{2}$$

$$m_t = p_t + y_t \tag{3}$$

$$\ell_t = \ell \tag{4}$$

Equations (1) and (2) correspond to a isoelastic production function $Y_t = A_t L_t^{1-\alpha}$, where A_t is a technology shock. Equation (3) is a simplified quantity of money equation. Equation (4) says that the labor supply is constant.

Combining (1) to (4), we find that the Walrasian wage w_t^* is proportional to the quantity of money, that is, in logarithms and omitting irrelevant constants:

$$w_t^* = m_t \tag{5}$$

13.2.2 The Gray Model

In the Gray (1976) model, the wage is preset at the expected value of the Walrasian wage:[4]

$$w_t = E_{t-1} w_t^* = E_{t-1} m_t \tag{6}$$

This equation replaces equation (4). Combining (2) and (3), employment is equal to:

$$\ell_t = m_t - w_t \tag{7}$$

which, in view of (6), yields:

$$\ell_t = m_t - E_{t-1} m_t \tag{8}$$

---

4. The article of Gray (1976) is actually more general because it studies not only presetting but also the optimal indexation of wages on prices (appendix 2.2).

Let us assume the following random walk process for money:

$$m_t - m_{t-1} = \varepsilon_t \tag{9}$$

where ε_t, a white noise, is the innovation in the monetary process. Then we find:

$$\ell_t = \ell + \varepsilon_t \tag{10}$$

$$y_t = (1-\alpha)\ell + a_t + (1-\alpha)\varepsilon_t \tag{11}$$

We see two things. (a) because of the nominal wage rigidity, money shocks now have an effect on employment and output. (b) But this effect is very short-lived. Even though the quantity of money given by (9) is persistent, the effect on employment and output lasts only one period and is only related to the innovation on money ε_t.

13.2.3 The Fischer Model

The model by Fischer (1977a)[5] attempts to create more persistence by introducing labor contracts of longer duration. It was customary at that time for trade unions and firms to sign contracts for several years ahead. To mimic this, the labor force is divided in two cohorts.[6] One cohort signs labor contracts in even periods, the other in odd periods. The cohort signing in period t signs contracts for periods t and $t+1$. We denote by $x_{t,t}$ and $x_{t,t+1}$ the contracts signed in period t for periods t and $t+1$, respectively. Similarly to the Gray contract, it is assumed that these are based on information of period $t-1$, and that the contracts take the Walrasian wage w_t^* as a reference, so that:

$$x_{t,t} = E_{t-1} w_t^* = E_{t-1} m_t \qquad x_{t,t+1} = E_{t-1} w_{t+1}^* = E_{t-1} m_{t+1} \tag{12}$$

The aggregate wage w_t in period t is the average of the two contracts signed in $t-1$ and t:

$$w_t = \frac{1}{2}\left(x_{t,t} + x_{t-1,t}\right) = \frac{1}{2}\left(E_{t-1} m_t + E_{t-2} m_t\right) \tag{13}$$

---

5. See also Phelps and Taylor (1977).
6. Actually any number of cohorts can be handled, but we keep it to two to simplify the exposition.

Combining (2), (3), and (13), we find that employment is equal to:

$$\ell_t = m_t - w_t = \frac{(m_t - E_{t-1}m_t) + (m_t - E_{t-2}m_t)}{2} \tag{14}$$

If we take again the monetary process (9), formula (14) yields:

$$\ell_t = \varepsilon_t + \frac{\varepsilon_{t-1}}{2} \tag{15}$$

We see that a shock has an impact for two periods, which is the length of the contract, but no more. We now study a contract, due to Taylor, that allows shocks to have an impact beyond the average duration of each contract.

13.2.4 The Taylor Model

In the Taylor model (Taylor, 1979, 1980), as in the Fischer model, workers sign contracts for two periods. But there are two differences. First the nominal wage contract is the same for periods t and $t+1$, and we denote by x_t the value of the new contract signed in t for periods t and $t+1$. So with the notation of section 13.2.3:

$$x_{t,t} = x_{t,t+1} = x_t \tag{16}$$

Consequently the current aggregate wage is equal to the average of today's and yesterday's new wage contract:

$$w_t = \frac{1}{2}(x_t + x_{t-1}) \tag{17}$$

Second the reference wage for the determination of x_t is not the Walrasian wage w_t^*, but the average wage w_t corrected by a measure of demand on the labor market.[7] So the reference wage for period t will be:

$$w_t + \psi \ell_t \qquad \psi > 0 \tag{18}$$

Because the new contract wage x_t will be in effect in periods t and $t+1$, it is a weighted average of the reference wages in both periods:

$$x_t = b(w_t + \psi \ell_t) + dE_t(w_{t+1} + \psi \ell_{t+1}) \tag{19}$$

---

7. Note that many articles in the literature actually take output y_t as the index of demand. Because we are studying the labor market, it seems more natural to take employment ℓ_t rather than output y_t as the relevant index of market demand.

with:

$$b + d = 1 \qquad (20)$$

Combining (2), (3), (17), and (19), we obtain the following dynamic equation:

$$cx_t = bx_{t-1} + dE_t x_{t+1} + \frac{2\psi b}{1-\psi} m_t + \frac{2\psi d}{1-\psi} E_t m_{t+1} \qquad (21)$$

with:

$$c = \frac{1+\psi}{1-\psi} > 1 \qquad (22)$$

Again we solve for the dynamics in the simple case where m_t is a random walk:

$$m_t - m_{t-1} = \varepsilon_t \qquad (23)$$

We use the method of undetermined coefficients and conjecture a solution of the form:

$$x_t = \lambda x_{t-1} + \mu m_t \qquad (24)$$

Moving (24) forward one period and taking the expectation as of time t we find:

$$E_t x_{t+1} = \lambda x_t + \mu E_t m_{t+1} = \lambda^2 x_{t-1} + \lambda \mu m_t + \mu E_t m_{t+1} \qquad (25)$$

Inserting (23), (24), and (25) into (21) we find:

$$c\lambda x_{t-1} + c\mu m_t = bx_{t-1} + d\left(\lambda^2 x_{t-1} + \lambda \mu m_t + \mu m_t\right) + \frac{2\psi}{1-\psi} m_t \qquad (26)$$

Equating the term in x_{t-1} to 0 we find that the autoregressive root λ is a root of the characteristic polynomial:

$$\Psi(\lambda) = d\lambda^2 - c\lambda + b = 0 \qquad (27)$$

Equating the term in m_t to 0, and using (27) we find that:

$$\mu = 1 - \lambda \qquad (28)$$

Now we can compute:

$$\Psi(0) = b > 0 \tag{29}$$

$$\Psi(1) = b + d - c = 1 - c < 0 \tag{30}$$

so we know that the root λ is between 0 and 1.

Wage and Employment Dynamics

Combining (24) and (28) we obtain:

$$x_t = \lambda x_{t-1} + (1 - \lambda) m_t \tag{31}$$

Recall that the aggregate wage is:

$$w_t = \frac{1}{2}(x_t + x_{t-1}) \tag{32}$$

Combining this with (31) we obtain wage dynamics:

$$w_t = \lambda w_{t-1} + (1 - \lambda) \frac{m_t + m_{t-1}}{2} \tag{33}$$

We now move to the dynamics of employment. Combining (33) and the equality $w_t + \ell_t = m_t$ we obtain:

$$\ell_t = \lambda \ell_{t-1} + \left(\frac{1+\lambda}{2}\right)(m_t - m_{t-1}) = \lambda \ell_{t-1} + \left(\frac{1+\lambda}{2}\right)\varepsilon_t \tag{34}$$

Solving this equation forward, we finally obtain:

$$\ell_t = \frac{1+\lambda}{2} \sum_{j=0}^{\infty} \lambda^j \varepsilon_{t-j} \tag{35}$$

We see that although each contract lasts only two periods, the effects of a money shock on ℓ_t are much more long-lived.

13.3 Nominal Rigidities and Correlations

We now show that the introduction of nominal rigidities changes some important correlations. For that purpose, we compare the correlations in two versions of the same model: Walrasian market clearing versus preset wages à la Gray (1976).[8] The particular model we consider is the model of section 13.2.1. In this section, to have simple calculations, we assume that the monetary and technology shocks m_t and a_t are both i.i.d. white noises with variances:

$$\sigma_m^2 = Var(m_t) \qquad \sigma_a^2 = Var(a_t) \qquad (36)$$

13.3.1 The Walrasian Benchmark

As a benchmark, recall the Walrasian equilibrium values seen above (we omit irrelevant constants):

$$y_t = a_t \qquad w_t = w_t^* = m_t \qquad p_t = p_t^* = m_t - a_t \qquad (37)$$

where a_t and m_t are technology and monetary shocks. In chapter 12 we noted some correlations that puzzled researchers working in the real business cycles area:

$$\text{Corr}(w_t - p_t, y_t) = 1 \qquad (38)$$

$$\text{Corr}(p_t, y_t) = -\frac{\sigma_a}{(\sigma_a^2 + \sigma_m^2)^{1/2}} < 0 \qquad (39)$$

$$\text{Corr}(\pi_t, y_t) = -\frac{\sigma_a}{(2\sigma_a^2 + 2\sigma_m^2)^{1/2}} < 0 \qquad (40)$$

Real wages are "too procyclical," whereas prices and inflation are "too countercyclical." We now consider wage contracts and show that this can help alleviate these problems.

13.3.2 Gray Contracts

As in section 13.2.2, we assume that the labor market does not clear anymore, but that the wage w_t is preset at the beginning of period t as the expected value of the Walrasian wage:

$$w_t = E_{t-1} w_t^* \qquad (41)$$

---

8. Similar results in a full DSGE model were derived in Bénassy (1995).

We already computed the values of employment and output. If m_t is a white noise, equation (8) simplifies to (suppressing irrelevant constants):

$$\ell_t = m_t \tag{42}$$

and, combining (1) and (42), output is:

$$y_t = a_t + (1 - \alpha) m_t \tag{43}$$

The real wage and price are deduced from y_t through the simple formulas:

$$w_t - p_t = y_t - \ell_t \qquad p_t = m_t - y_t \tag{44}$$

We use these relations to throw some light on the cyclical properties of a few variables in response to technological and monetary shocks.

13.3.3 Real Wages

We begin with real wages. To make correlations clearer, let us rewrite output and real wages:

$$y_t = a_t + (1 - \alpha) m_t \tag{45}$$

$$w_t - p_t = a_t - \alpha m_t \tag{46}$$

Technology shocks induce a positive correlation between real wage and output, but money shocks induce inversely a negative correlation between real wage and output. Our model thus combines this last feature, which is characteristic of traditional Keynesian models, with the more standard results of RBC models. The real wage output correlation is:

$$\text{corr}(w_t - p_t, y_t) = \frac{\sigma_a^2 - \alpha(1-\alpha)\sigma_m^2}{(\sigma_a^2 + \alpha^2 \sigma_m^2)^{1/2} \left[\sigma_a^2 + (1-\alpha)^2 \sigma_m^2\right]^{1/2}} \tag{47}$$

The correlation between real wages and output is still 1 if there are *only* technology shocks. But this correlation diminishes as soon as monetary shocks are present and can even become negative.

13.3.4 Prices

Let us now move to the expression of the price level, which, in view of the fact that $E_{t-1}m_t = 0$, can be rewritten as:

$$p_t = \alpha m_t - a_t \qquad (48)$$

Comparing this expression with that of output (45), we see that supply shocks induce a negative correlation between output and prices, but money shocks induce inversely a positive correlation. Again, we have a synthesis of traditional Keynesian features with those of standard RBC models. The price-output correlation is:

$$\operatorname{corr}(p_t, y_t) = \frac{\alpha(1-\alpha)\sigma_m^2 - \sigma_a^2}{(\sigma_a^2 + \alpha^2\sigma_m^2)^{1/2}[\sigma_a^2 + (1-\alpha)^2\sigma_m^2]^{1/2}} \qquad (49)$$

We obtain procyclical prices if monetary shocks are prevalent, and countercyclical prices if technology shocks are prevalent. The different behavior of prices over different historical subperiods may thus simply be due to the relative size of shocks faced by the economies during these periods.

13.3.5 The Inflation-output Correlation

We finally study a third well-known relation in macroeconomics, that between inflation and output, which are usually thought to be positively correlated, at least in the Keynesian tradition. From (48) we deduce inflation:

$$\pi_t = p_t - p_{t-1} = \alpha m_t - \alpha m_{t-1} - a_t + a_{t-1} \qquad (50)$$

Consequently:

$$\operatorname{corr}(\pi_t, y_t) = \frac{\alpha(1-\alpha)\sigma_m^2 - \sigma_a^2}{(2\sigma_a^2 + 2\alpha^2\sigma_m^2)^{1/2}[\sigma_a^2 + (1-\alpha)^2\sigma_m^2]^{1/2}} \qquad (51)$$

This formula shows that the positive inflation-output correlation is associated to the presence of monetary shocks, but that the sign of this correlation can actually be reversed if there are sufficiently strong technological shocks.

13.4 Three Models of Nominal Rigidities

We now describe three more recent and popular models of nominal rigidities. They have at least three advantages. (1) They are quite flexible, ranging from perfect flexibility to total rigidity. (2) Their solutions can be worked out easily. (3) They allow us to build models where shocks, and notably monetary shocks, can have a strong propagation mechanism under realistic parameters.

These models have been used to describe both price and wage rigidities. We model price rigidities here. A symmetrical exposition could be made for wage rigidities.

To better appreciate the similarities and differences between these three schemes, we describe them within a simple common framework (a model with more microeconomic foundations is in section 13.5).

13.4.1 The Common Framework

We take the same basic model as in section 13.2. Consequently the optimal price, absent costs of changing prices, is the Walrasian price, that is, up to a constant:

$$p_t^* = m_t \tag{52}$$

It is assumed that deviating in period t from this optimal price creates a cost equal to:

$$(p_t - p_t^*)^2 = (p_t - m_t)^2 \tag{53}$$

Price setters minimize the discounted intertemporal value of these costs:

$$E \sum_t \beta^t (p_t - p_t^*)^2 = E \sum_t \beta^t (p_t - m_t)^2 \tag{54}$$

13.4.2 The Rotemberg Model

In the first model, which was developed by Rotemberg (1982a, 1982b), it is assumed that in addition to the above costs, the price setters bear a quadratic cost of changing prices, equal to $\delta \left(p_t - p_{t-1}\right)^2$. As a result, price setters minimize the total intertemporal cost which, in addition to the right-hand side of (54), now includes this quadratic price adjustment cost. So they minimize:

$$E \sum_t \beta^t \left[(p_t - m_t)^2 + \delta \left(p_t - p_{t-1}\right)^2\right] \tag{55}$$

We consider only the terms containing p_t. We want to minimize:

$$(p_t - m_t)^2 + \delta (p_t - p_{t-1})^2 + \beta\delta E_t (p_t - p_{t+1})^2 \qquad (56)$$

Differentiating with respect to p_t we find the first-order condition:

$$(1 + \delta + \beta\delta) p_t - \delta p_{t-1} - \beta\delta E_t p_{t+1} = m_t \qquad (57)$$

To solve the dynamic equation (57) we can use formula (A.212) in the mathematical appendix (section A.9) with:

$$\mathcal{A} = 1 + \delta + \beta\delta \qquad \mathcal{B} = \delta \qquad \mathcal{C} = \beta\delta \qquad \mathcal{D} = 1 \qquad (58)$$

so that the solution is:

$$p_t - \lambda p_{t-1} = \frac{\lambda}{\delta} \sum_{j=0}^{\infty} \beta^j \lambda^j E_t m_{t+j} \qquad (59)$$

and the autoregressive root λ is a root of the following characteristic polynomial (equation A.207):

$$\Psi(\lambda) = \beta\delta\lambda^2 - (1 + \delta + \beta\delta)\lambda + \delta = 0 \qquad (60)$$

We want to verify that there is one root between 0 and 1, so we compute:

$$\Psi(0) = \delta > 0 \qquad (61)$$

$$\Psi(1) = -1 < 0 \qquad (62)$$

so the root λ is indeed between 0 and 1. Moreover, differentiating equation (60) we obtain:

$$\frac{\partial \lambda}{\partial \delta} = \frac{\lambda^2}{\delta^2 (1 - \beta\lambda^2)} > 0 \qquad (63)$$

As intuition would suggest, the coefficient of price stickiness λ is an increasing function of the cost of changing prices δ.

13.4.3 The Calvo Model

In the Taylor model that was exposed in section 13.2.4, a contract "dies" with certainty after two periods. In the Calvo model (Calvo, 1983), it is assumed that price contracts die with a constant probability $1 - \gamma$, or continue with probability γ. When a contract disappears, it is renegotiated using all information available at time t. As in the Taylor model we denote x_t as the "new contract" that is renegotiated in period t. An advantage of this formulation is that the average duration of price contracts is a free parameter, which can thus potentially be matched with the average duration of contracts in real life.

We compute this average duration. The probability that a contract lasts j periods is equal to $(1 - \gamma) \gamma^j$. So the expected duration is (formula A.255 in the mathematical appendix):

$$\sum_{j=0}^{\infty} j (1-\gamma) \gamma^j = \frac{\gamma}{1-\gamma} \tag{64}$$

When γ goes from 0 to 1, the average duration of contracts goes from 0 to infinity, so this formulation is particularly flexible.

In period t we have a multiplicity of contracts x_s, $s \leq t$ which have been signed in the past, and we would like to compute the aggregate price p_t as a function of these contracts. For that, we note that because contracts survive with probability γ each period, at time t there remains only a fraction γ^{t-s} of the contracts that have been negotiated in s. Now a fraction $1 - \gamma$ of contracts is renegotiated in each period. Combining the two, we find that contracts x_s are a fraction $(1-\gamma) \gamma^{t-s}$ of total contracts existing at time t. Therefore, the equation giving the aggregate price p_t as a function of past price contracts is:

$$p_t = (1-\gamma) \sum_{s \leq t} \gamma^{t-s} x_s \tag{65}$$

which can be rewritten:

$$p_t - \gamma p_{t-1} = (1-\gamma) x_t \tag{66}$$

Now we have to determine how the "new" contracts x_t are determined. When setting x_t, the agent will minimize:

$$E \sum_t \beta^t \gamma^t (x_t - m_t)^2 \tag{67}$$

Differentiating with respect to x_t we find the first-order condition:

$$x_t = (1 - \beta\gamma) \sum_{j=0}^{\infty} \beta^j \gamma^j E_t m_{t+j} \qquad (68)$$

Combining (66) and (68) we obtain:

$$p_t - \gamma p_{t-1} = (1 - \gamma)(1 - \beta\gamma) \sum_{j=0}^{\infty} \beta^j \gamma^j E_t m_{t+j} \qquad (69)$$

We see that there is an autoregressive root in price dynamics. This root is actually equal to the probability γ that price contracts stay the same from one period to the other, an intuitive result.

If we compare equations (59) and (69), we see that in this simple model the Rotemberg and Calvo models have very similar dynamics (Rotemberg, 1987). In fact these dynamics will be the same if the parameters (β, γ) in the Calvo model and δ in the Rotemberg model are related by:

$$\delta = \frac{\gamma}{(1-\gamma)(1-\beta\gamma)} \qquad (70)$$

13.4.4 The New Keynesian Phillips Curve

As it turns out, the price dynamics in the Calvo and Rotemberg model can be given a very simple expression in terms of inflation. Recall, for example, the dynamic price equation of the Rotemberg model (equation 57):

$$(1 + \delta + \beta\delta) p_t - \delta p_{t-1} - \beta\delta E_t p_{t+1} = m_t \qquad (71)$$

Define the inflation rate $\pi_t = p_t - p_{t-1}$. Then equation (71) can be rewritten:

$$\pi_t = \beta E_t \pi_{t+1} + \frac{m_t - p_t}{\delta} \qquad (72)$$

or, because $m_t - p_t = y_t$:

$$\pi_t = \beta E_t \pi_{t+1} + \frac{y_t}{\delta} \qquad (73)$$

The same exercise can be carried with the Calvo model, and we obtain:

$$\pi_t = \beta E_t \pi_{t+1} + \frac{(1-\gamma)(1-\beta\gamma)}{\gamma} y_t \qquad (74)$$

We see that equations (73) and (74) are both of the form:

$$\pi_t = \beta E_t \pi_{t+1} + \kappa y_t \qquad (75)$$

with $\kappa = (1-\gamma)(1-\beta\gamma)/\gamma$ for the Calvo model and $\kappa = 1/\delta$ for the Rotemberg model.

Equations like (75) have been popular in recent years under the name of "new Keynesian Phillips curve" (Roberts, 1995). It is a Keynesian Phillips curve in the sense that inflation is positively related to a measure of demand. The "new" part comes from the fact that inflation is not backward looking, as the traditional Phillips curve, but has a forward-looking component $\beta E_t \pi_{t+1}$. In section 13.6, we go a little deeper into the properties of that curve.

13.4.5 A Calvo-Fischer Contract

The third contract we study here somehow combines features of the Calvo (1983) and Fischer (1977a) models.[9] The central idea is the same as in the Calvo contract. Notably, each contract terminates randomly with probability $1 - \gamma$, and continues unchanged with probability γ. As a consequence, the average duration of a contract is $\gamma/(1-\gamma)$. The difference with the Calvo contract is that, as in the Fischer model, we do not constrain all contracts decided at a given time to be the same for all future periods.

At time s one will decide contracts for all dates $t \geq s$, and these contracts can be different for all t. Our notation must reflect that, and we shall denote x_{st} as the contract decided at time s to be in effect at time $t \geq s$.

The current aggregate price is a weighted average of all the prices contracted in the past. A fraction γ^{t-s} of contracts signed at time $s \leq t$ is still alive at time t. Now contracts signed in s were themselves a fraction $1 - \gamma$ of total contracts. So the formula giving the aggregate price at time t is:

$$p_t = (1-\gamma) \sum_{s \leq t} \gamma^{t-s} x_{st} \qquad (76)$$

Note that this formula is very similar to that of the Calvo case (equation 65), with x_s replaced by x_{st}. Now the values of the x_{st}'s themselves are given

---

9. The contract described in this section was developed in DSGE models in Bénassy (2002b, 2002c, 2003a, 2003b). Mankiw and Reis (2002) have a similar contract with a different "sticky information" interpretation. Devereux and Yetman (2003) develop a similar contract and compare it to the original Calvo contract.

by the following maximization program:

$$\text{Maximize } E_s \sum_t \beta^{t-s} \gamma^{t-s} (x_{st} - m_t)^2 \qquad (77)$$

This maximization is particularly easy because x_{st} appears in only one term, so we get:

$$x_{st} = E_s m_t \qquad (78)$$

Combining (76) and (78), we obtain the current aggregate price:

$$p_t = (1-\gamma) \sum_{s \le t}^t \gamma^{t-s} x_{st} = (1-\gamma) \sum_{s \le t}^t \gamma^{t-s} E_s m_t \qquad (79)$$

13.4.6 Impulse Response Functions

We now give the output impulse response functions for the Calvo, Rotemberg, and Calvo-Fischer contracts when money increases are given by the following autoregressive process:

$$m_t - m_{t-1} = \frac{\varepsilon_t}{1 - \rho \mathcal{L}} \qquad (80)$$

where $\mathcal{L}$ is the lag operator.

The Calvo and Rotemberg Contracts

Let us start with the Calvo contract, assuming that the probability of survival of each contract is γ. It is proved in appendix 13.3 that the impulse response function of output is:

$$y_t = \frac{\gamma \varepsilon_t}{(1 - \gamma \mathcal{L})(1 - \rho \mathcal{L})} \qquad (81)$$

We see that an increase in γ increases both the effect on impact and the persistence of these effects. Note that there will be a hump in the impulse response function if:

$$\gamma + \rho > 1 \qquad (82)$$

Figure 13.1 shows the impulse response function (IRF) for:

$$\gamma = 4/5 \quad \text{and} \quad \rho = 0.5 \qquad (83)$$

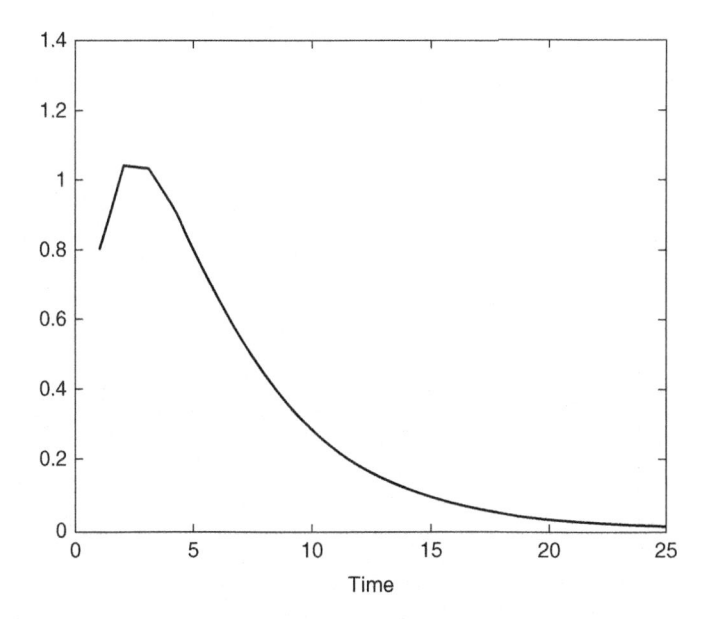

Figure 13.1 IRF for the Calvo and Rotemberg models

The value $\rho = 0.5$ is that found most often in empirical studies. The value $\gamma = 4/5$ corresponds to an average duration of contracts of one year.[10] So we see that reasonable assumptions on nominal rigidities can produce a persistent response of output to monetary shocks.

The IRF for the Rotemberg model is similar, the parameter δ in the Rotemberg model being related to γ by formula (70).

The Calvo-Fischer Contract

Let us assume the same monetary process as in equation (80) and a probability of survival of contracts γ. Then one can compute (appendix 13.3) that the output IRF is:

$$y_t = \frac{\gamma \varepsilon_t}{(1 - \gamma \mathcal{L})(1 - \gamma \rho \mathcal{L})} \qquad (84)$$

There will be a hump in the IRF if:

$$\gamma(1 + \rho) > 1 \qquad (85)$$

---

10. An average duration of one year is considered fairly realistic for wages (see, for example Taylor, 1999). For prices, average durations are less consensual.

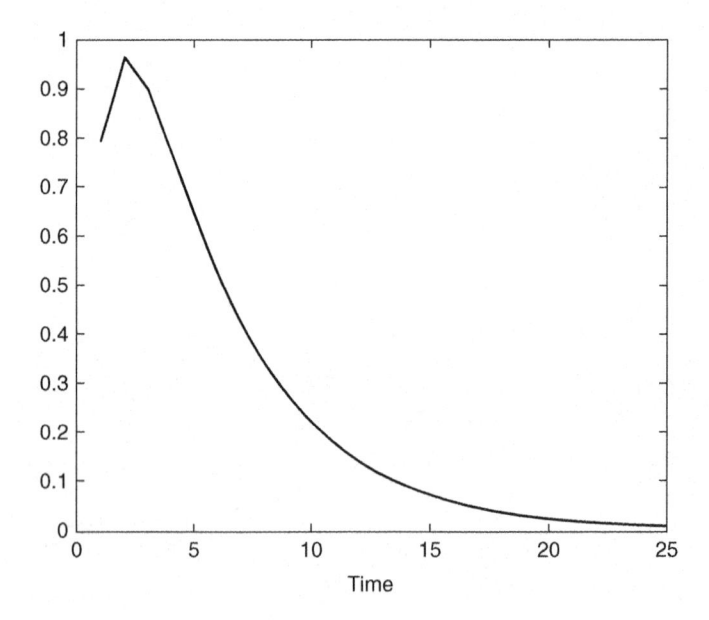

Figure 13.2 IRF for the Calvo-Fischer model

Figure 13.2 shows the IRF to a monetary shock for the same parameter values as in (83).

The similarity of the IRFs for the two contracts described in sections 13.4.3 and 13.4.5 might lead us to believe that such will be the case for any monetary experiment. This is actually not the case, and the time responses can be quite different, as is demonstrated in appendix 13.4, which shows the comparative effects of a disinflationary experiment under both types of contracts.

13.5 A DSGE Model with Sticky Prices

To better highlight the similarities and differences between various schemes of price stickiness, we conducted their study in the framework of a simplified model. We now conduct the same study in a rigorous DSGE model with nominal rigidities, taking as a basis the monetary model with imperfect competition developed in chapter 12. We notably study the issue of propagation with a model embedding quadratic costs of changing prices (Rotemberg, 1982a, 1982b).[11] To simplify the exposition, we put

---

11. Similar models with microeconomic foundations can be found in Jeanne (1998) and Woodford (2003) for Calvo contracts, Ascari (2000) for Taylor contracts, and Bénassy (2002b, 2003a, 2003b) for Calvo-Fischer contracts.

13.5.1 The Model

The model follows closely that of chapter 12 (section 12.3). Households have an intertemporal utility function:

$$U = \sum \beta^t \left[Log C_t + \varpi Log\left(\frac{M_t}{P_t}\right) - \frac{L_t^{1+\nu}}{1+\nu} \right] \qquad \nu > 0 \qquad (86)$$

and are submitted in each period to a budget constraint:

$$P_t C_t + M_t = W_t L_t + \Pi_t + X_t M_{t-1} \qquad (87)$$

where X_t is a multiplicative money shock à la Lucas (1972), and Π_t is distributed profits.

Competitive firms produce final output with intermediate goods indexed by $j \in [0,1]$. They all have the same constant returns to scale production function:

$$Y_t = \left(\int_0^1 Y_{jt}^\eta dj \right)^{1/\eta} \qquad 0 < \eta \le 1 \qquad (88)$$

where Y_t is the level of output and Y_{jt} the amount of intermediate good j used in production. Intermediate goods themselves are produced by monopolistically competitive firms indexed by $j \in [0,1]$. Firm j has a production function:

$$Y_{jt} = A_t L_{jt} \qquad (89)$$

where A_t is a common productivity shock.

The difference with the model of chapter 12 is that we introduce a nominal rigidity. As in Rotemberg (1982a, 1982b), a firm producing intermediate product j incurs (in addition to production costs) a cost of changing prices, which in real terms is equal to:

$$\frac{\zeta}{2} Y_t \left(\frac{P_{jt}}{P_{jt-1}} - 1 \right)^2 \qquad (90)$$

13.5.2 Price Dynamics

We can characterize the dynamics of prices p_t (in logarithms) through the following dynamic equation, derived in appendix 13.5 (equation 206):

$$(1 + \beta + \kappa) p_t - p_{t-1} - \beta E_t p_{t+1} = \kappa (m_t - a_t) \qquad (91)$$

with:

$$\kappa = \frac{\eta (1 + \nu)}{\zeta (1 - \eta)} \qquad (92)$$

We note that (91) is an equation of the form:

$$\mathcal{A} p_t - \mathcal{B} p_{t-1} - \mathcal{C} E_t p_{t+1} = \mathcal{D} z_t \qquad (93)$$

Comparing (91) and (93), we see that we have:

$$\mathcal{A} = 1 + \beta + \kappa \qquad \mathcal{B} = 1 \qquad \mathcal{C} = \beta \qquad \mathcal{D} = \kappa \qquad (94)$$

$$z_t = m_t - a_t \qquad (95)$$

Equation (93) is solved in mathematical appendix A.9 (equation A.212). Taking into account (94) and (95), this solution is:

$$p_t = \lambda p_{t-1} + \lambda \kappa \sum_{j=0}^{\infty} (\beta \lambda)^j E_t z_{t+j} \qquad (96)$$

where the autoregressive root λ is solution of the characteristic equation:

$$\Psi(\lambda) = \beta \lambda^2 - (1 + \beta + \kappa) \lambda + 1 = 0 \qquad (97)$$

We can compute:

$$\Psi(0) = 1 > 0 \qquad (98)$$

$$\Psi(1) = -\kappa < 0 \qquad (99)$$

so that there is indeed one root λ such that $0 < \lambda < 1$. This root λ somehow represents the degree of persistence created by the costs of changing prices.

13.5.3 Price Stickiness and Propagation: An Example

To show in a simple manner how the value of the parameter λ connects to the propagation of shocks, we assume the following simple process for the composite shock z_t:

$$z_t - z_{t-1} = \varepsilon_t \tag{100}$$

where ε_t is an i.i.d. white noise. Let us first take as a benchmark the case where the cost of changing prices is 0, that is, where $\zeta = 0$. In that case κ is infinite and (91) immediately yields:

$$p_t = z_t = m_t - a_t \tag{101}$$

Let us now consider the case where $\zeta > 0$. Using assumption (100), equation (96) becomes:

$$p_t = \lambda p_{t-1} + \frac{\lambda \kappa}{1 - \beta \lambda} z_t \tag{102}$$

Combining (97), (100), and (102), we find that the solution takes the simple form:

$$p_t = z_t - \frac{\lambda \varepsilon_t}{1 - \lambda \mathcal{L}} \tag{103}$$

We see that following a shock, the discrepancy between the price and its benchmark market clearing value z_t is both higher on impact and returns more slowly to 0 when λ is high. The parameter λ appears indeed as a natural parameter to characterize price stickiness.

We can also compute the expression of output. Using $y_t = m_t - p_t$, equation (103) yields:

$$y_t = a_t + \frac{\lambda \varepsilon_t}{1 - \lambda \mathcal{L}} \tag{104}$$

Here also, a higher λ will increase both the effect on impact and its persistence.

13.5.4 Price Stickiness and the Fundamentals

Finally, we want to see how the index of price stickiness and persistence λ relates to the various fundamental parameters of the model. For that purpose, we differentiate equation (97). We find:

$$\frac{\partial \lambda}{\partial \kappa} = -\frac{\lambda^2}{1 - \beta \lambda^2} < 0 \qquad (105)$$

and using the definition of κ (equation 92):

$$\frac{\partial \lambda}{\partial \eta} < 0 \qquad \frac{\partial \lambda}{\partial \zeta} > 0 \qquad (106)$$

As intuition would suggest, the stickiness of prices is an increasing function of the cost of changing prices ζ and a negative function of the competitiveness index η.

13.6 The DSGE Model: Properties and Extensions

We examine in this section a few additional properties of the DSGE model.

13.6.1 The New Keynesian Phillips Curve

We first see that we can obtain through the above DSGE model a more rigorous and general version of the new Keynesian Phillips curve seen in section 13.4.4. Recall the dynamic equation for prices (equation 91):

$$(1 + \beta + \chi) p_t - p_{t-1} - \beta E_t p_{t+1} = \kappa (m_t - a_t) \qquad (107)$$

Denoting inflation as $\pi_t = p_t - p_{t-1}$ and using $m_t - p_t = y_t$, (107) can be rewritten as:

$$\pi_t = \beta E_t \pi_{t+1} + \kappa (y_t - a_t) \qquad (108)$$

where we recognize the new Keynesian Phillips curve of section 13.4.4. Using $y_t - a_t = \ell_t$, equation (108) can be rewritten as:

$$\pi_t = \beta E_t \pi_{t+1} + \kappa \ell_t \qquad (109)$$

The important difference with earlier expressions of this Phillips curve is that the parameter κ in equations (108) and (109) is now related, via formula (92), to the fundamental parameters of the economy.

13.6.2 Real Rigidities and Persistence

So far we have emphasized the role of nominal rigidities in creating disequilibria and persistence in the effects of shocks. A recurrent theme in recent literature[12] is that "real rigidities" enhance the price stickiness created by nominal rigidities. This idea is developed in appendix 13.2, and we illustrate it briefly with the help of the DSGE model of the previous section.

First what are these real rigidities? A popular definition is that there is a real rigidity when a large move in some quantities (like employment or output) is accompanied by a small move in the ratio between two nominal variables (for example, a real wage).

There are of course, even in a single DSGE model, many potential real rigidities. To make the point in a simple manner, we consider a particular real rigidity on the household side. The first-order conditions of the household notably yield the following traditional condition (equation 190 in appendix 13.5):

$$\frac{W_t}{P_t C_t} = L_t^\nu \tag{110}$$

If ν is low, real wage changes will be smaller for a given variation of L_t. So a low value of ν corresponds to a real rigidity in the sense given above.

Now we relate this to the persistence that we found in section 13.5. Recall that the autoregressive root λ is solution of:

$$\beta \lambda^2 - (1 + \beta + \kappa) \lambda + 1 = 0 \tag{111}$$

with:

$$\kappa = \frac{\eta(1+\nu)}{\zeta(1-\eta)} \tag{112}$$

We already saw (equation 105):

$$\frac{\partial \lambda}{\partial \kappa} = -\frac{\lambda^2}{1 - \beta \lambda^2} < 0 \tag{113}$$

so that:

$$\frac{\partial \lambda}{\partial \nu} = \frac{\partial \lambda}{\partial \kappa} \frac{\partial \kappa}{\partial \nu} < 0 \tag{114}$$

---

12. See for example Ball and Romer (1990) and Jeanne (1998).

We see that, other things equal, more real rigidity (a lower ν) leads to a greater price stickiness.

13.6.3 The Natural Rate Property

Many years ago, Phelps (1967, 1968) and Friedman (1968) showed that by proper inclusion of expectations one could obtain a Phillips curve that satisfied the natural rate property, which means that the locus of long-run equilibrium employment-inflation pairs is a vertical at the natural rate of employment.

It was pointed out (McCallum, 1994; McCallum and Nelson, 1999) that, although it is derived under rational expectations, the new Keynesian Phillips curve does not satisfy the natural rate property. Indeed, let us recall equation (109):

$$\pi_t = \beta E_t \pi_{t+1} + \kappa \ell_t \tag{115}$$

Denoting by ℓ^* and π^* the long-run values of ℓ_t and π_t, we find that they are related by:

$$\ell^* = \frac{(1-\beta)\pi^*}{\kappa} \tag{116}$$

As in the "very old" Phillips curve, there is a positive relation between employment and inflation in the long-run. We will see that it is possible to obtain a Phillips curve with the natural rate property in our DSGE model.

Indeed, to eliminate this long-run trade-off, we can simply assume that the benchmark price in equation (90) is not last period's price P_{jt-1}, but last period's price augmented by some inflationary expectation Π_t^e. That is, we take the real cost of changing prices to be:

$$\frac{\varsigma}{2} Y_t \left(\frac{P_{jt}}{\Pi_t^e P_{jt-1}} - 1 \right)^2 \tag{117}$$

The computations of appendix 13.5 are easily reworked with this modification, and as a result the Phillips curve (109) is changed into:

$$\pi_t - \pi_t^e = \beta E_t \left(\pi_{t+1} - \pi_{t+1}^e \right) + \kappa \ell_t \tag{118}$$

Now there are several possible expectations schemes π_t^e that will work. For example, Yun (1996) takes $\pi_t^e = \pi^*$, where π^* is the long-run rate of inflation. Christiano, Eichenbaum, and Evans (2005) take $\pi_t^e = \pi_{t-1}$, where

π_{t-1} is the previouly observed rate of inflation. Of course there are many more possibilities. Let us take, for example, $\pi_t^e = \pi_{t-1}$. Then (118) becomes:

$$\pi_t - \pi_{t-1} = \beta E_t \left(\pi_{t+1} - \pi_t\right) + \kappa \ell_t \tag{119}$$

In a long-run equilibrium:

$$\pi_{t-1} = \pi_t = \pi_{t+1} = \pi^* \tag{120}$$

and we see that the Phillips curve now has the natural rate property.

13.6.4 A Phillips Curve with Wages

Up to now we have considered Phillips curves that apply to prices, unlike the traditional Phillips curve, which relates wage increases to employment. Clearly the same type of reasoning will apply to wages if there is a cost of changing wages.

We now assume that prices are competitive, and there is instead a cost of changing wages, which has the same form as the cost of changing prices (90). It is equal in real terms to:

$$\frac{\zeta}{2} Y_t \left(\frac{W_{it}}{W_{it-1}} - 1\right)^2 \tag{121}$$

We have imperfect competition on the labor market. This is based on the following aggregator structure (Dixit and Stiglitz, 1977; Snower, 1983), which replaces (88):

$$L_t = \left(\int_0^1 L_{jt}^\chi dj\right)^{1/\chi} \qquad 0 < \chi \le 1 \tag{122}$$

The calculations are extremely similar to those of section 13.5 and appendix 13.5, so we do not go through them again.[13] We find that wage dynamics is characterized by the following equation:

$$(1 + \beta + \kappa) w_t - w_{t-1} - \beta E_t w_{t+1} = \kappa m_t \tag{123}$$

with:

$$\kappa = \frac{\chi (1 + \nu)}{\zeta (1 - \chi)} \tag{124}$$

---

13. But see problem 13.5 where the dynamic equation (123) is derived.

Denote wage inflation as:

$$\pi_t^w = w_t - w_{t-1} \qquad (125)$$

Then equation (123) is rewritten, using $m_t = w_t + \ell_t$:

$$\pi_t^w = \beta E_t \pi_{t+1}^w + \kappa \ell_t \qquad (126)$$

Note that this Phillips curve, like the original Phillips curve, relates wage increases to the level of employment. Of course, the traditional Phillips curve was backward looking, and this one is forward looking.

Appendix 13.1: Menu Costs

Menu costs is the popular name for fixed costs of changing prices. Early versions are found in Barro (1972) and Sheshinski and Weiss (1977).

The argument is simplest if we assume that the firm setting the price has a one-period horizon. Assume that at time t, absent any cost of changing prices, the optimal price from the point of view of the firm is p_t^*. If the firm sets a different price p_t, then it incurs a cost $\mathcal{C}(p_t - p_t^*)$, which we represent in figure 13.3.

There is also a fixed cost f of changing the price from the previous price p_{t-1}. This is called the menu cost.

The price setter has two options: (1) leaving the price at the former level and incurring the cost $\mathcal{C}(p_{t-1} - p_t^*)$, or (2) changing the price to p_t^* and

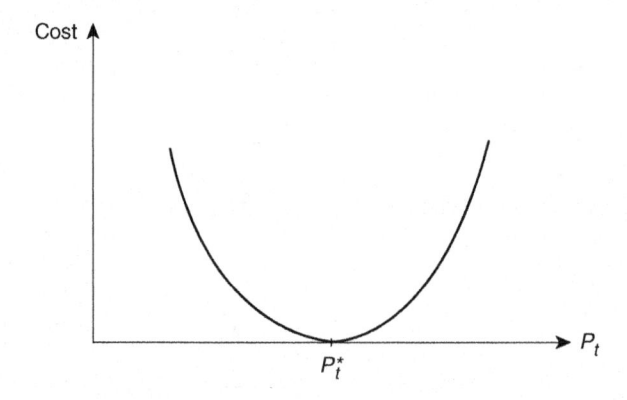

Figure 13.3 The cost of price deviations

incurring the menu cost f. So the strategy is straightforward:

$$\text{If } \mathcal{C}\left(p_{t-1} - p_t^*\right) < f \qquad p_t = p_{t-1} \tag{127}$$

$$\text{If } \mathcal{C}\left(p_{t-1} - p_t^*\right) > f \qquad p_t = p_t^* \tag{128}$$

This simple theory became popular in the mid-1980's because of the "second-order argument" (Akerlof and Yellen, 1985a, 1985b; Mankiw, 1985; Parkin, 1986). As pictured in figure 13.3, near p_t^* the cost of deviating from the optimal price is approximately quadratic. As a consequence, it was claimed, a small menu cost (of the second order) could lead to "large rigidities" (of the first order).

This argument was actually abandoned later because it is valid only if *all* firms at the period considered are at their optimum price, which is normally not the case. In fact, one can find examples where, although menu costs are present and prices are sticky at the individual firm level, the aggregate price is totally flexible. We now outline such an example (Rotemberg, 1983; Caplin and Spulber, 1987).

Assume we are in a situation of steady inflation, for example, because money supply grows at a constant rate μ:

$$m_t = \mu t \tag{129}$$

Each price setter has a so-called $s - S$ policy with $s < S$. The agent somehow watches a relative price index, her price compared to the aggregate price. Because of aggregate inflation, this index diminishes regularly. When the index falls to s, the agent raises her price discontinuously so that this relative index becomes equal to S, and then she does not move her price until the index goes down to s again.

The situation is illustrated in figure 13.4, which considers the case of three price setters with prices p_1, p_2, and p_3.[14] We see that for each price there are periods where it stays fixed and others where it jumps discontinuously. But the aggregate price, that is, the average of the three prices, is equal to:

$$\frac{s+S}{2} + \mu t = \frac{s+S}{2} + m_t \tag{130}$$

and moves in line with the quantity of money. Although there are rigidities and discontinuities at the individual level, the aggregate price looks as if it was perfectly flexible.

---

14. The picture is drawn in discrete time to make the argument easier to read. But the argument carries to continuous time (Rotemberg, 1983; Caplin and Spulber, 1987).

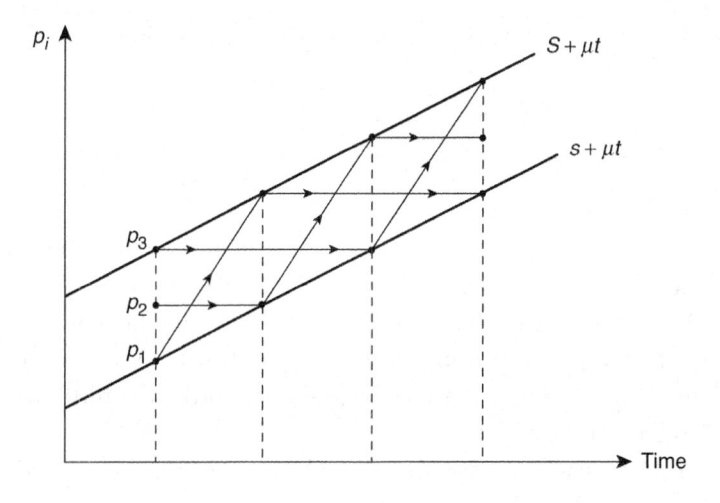

Figure 13.4 Individual price dynamics

Appendix 13.2: Real and Nominal Rigidities

As indicated in section 13.6.2, a recurring theme in the literature on nominal rigidities is that "real" and "nominal" rigidities reinforce each other to produce price stickiness.[15] Nominal rigidities can be any of the mechanisms that we studied in this chapter, such as nominal price or wage contracts, or various costs of changing prices.

We first give a more precise meaning to the notion of real rigidity in a model without nominal rigidity. We then introduce a simple nominal rigidity and show that in this example real rigidity reinforces nominal rigidity.

Real Rigidity

Generally speaking, there is a real rigidity if agents change some relative prices by a small amount in response to shocks in aggregate quantities. To make this a little more precise, we consider a price maker i who has to decide her price p_i. We assume that her utility is:

$$V(m - p, p_i - p) \qquad (131)$$

where all variables are in logarithms. So she is concerned with both the real value of the quantity of money, and the discrepancy between her price and

---

15. See notably Ball and Romer (1990), from which this appendix is adapted, and Jeanne (1998), who analyzes this issue in a DSGE model.

the aggregate price. The unconstrained maximization in p_i yields:

$$V_2(m-p, p_i - p) = 0 \tag{132}$$

where V_2 is the derivative of V with respect to its second argument. We are interested in how much the "relative price" $p_i - p$ changes in response to a shock in $m - p$. So we differentiate (132) totally and find:

$$V_{21} d(m-p) + V_{22} d(p_i - p) = 0 \tag{133}$$

or:

$$\frac{d(p_i - p)}{d(m - p)} = -\frac{V_{21}}{V_{22}} \tag{134}$$

where V_{21} and V_{22} are second derivatives of V. We see that $p_i - p$ will change little in response to $m - p$, that is, there will be greater "real rigidity" if (a) V_{21} is small, or (b) V_{22} is large in absolute value.

Nominal Rigidity

We now add a nominal rigidity under the form of a cost of changing the price:

$$\frac{\zeta (p_i - p)^2}{2} \tag{135}$$

The parameter ζ is somehow an index of nominal rigidity. To simplify computations we have taken the "base price" equal to the aggregate price level p. The price maker i now maximizes:

$$V(m - p, p_i - p) - \frac{\zeta (p_i - p)^2}{2} \tag{136}$$

The first-order condition in p_i is:

$$V_2(m - p, p_i - p) = \zeta (p_i - p) \tag{137}$$

and differentiating it totally we find:

$$\frac{d(p_i - p)}{d(m - p)} = -\frac{V_{21}}{V_{22} - \zeta} \tag{138}$$

We see that for the same index of nominal rigidity ζ, price stickiness is increased by (a) a decrease in V_{21}, or (b) an increase in the absolute value of V_{22}, both of which are associated, by formula (134), to a greater real rigidity. In this example, real rigidities do reinforce the nominal rigidities.

Appendix 13.3: Impulse Response Functions and Propagation

We compute the IRFs for the Calvo and Calvo-Fischer contracts under the same money process:

$$m_t - m_{t-1} = \frac{\varepsilon_t}{1 - \rho\mathcal{L}} \tag{139}$$

Calvo Contracts

Recall the two dynamic equations (66) and (68) linking x_t and p_t:

$$p_t - \gamma p_{t-1} = (1 - \gamma) x_t \tag{140}$$

$$x_t = (1 - \beta\gamma) \sum_{j=0}^{\infty} \beta^j \gamma^j E_t m_{t+j} \tag{141}$$

Using the lag operator, these two formulas are rewritten:

$$p_t = \frac{1 - \gamma}{1 - \gamma\mathcal{L}} x_t \tag{142}$$

$$x_t = \frac{1 - \beta\gamma}{1 - \beta\gamma\mathcal{L}^{-1}} m_t \tag{143}$$

Putting together (142) and (143), we find the expression of the aggregate price level:

$$p_t = \frac{(1-\gamma)(1-\beta\gamma)}{(1-\gamma\mathcal{L})(1-\beta\gamma\mathcal{L}^{-1})} m_t \tag{144}$$

Now:

$$y_t = m_t - p_t \tag{145}$$

So:

$$y_t = \frac{\gamma(1-\beta\mathcal{L}^{-1})(1-\mathcal{L})m_t}{(1-\gamma\mathcal{L})(1-\beta\gamma\mathcal{L}^{-1})} = \frac{\gamma(1-\beta\mathcal{L}^{-1})\varepsilon_t}{(1-\gamma\mathcal{L})(1-\rho\mathcal{L})(1-\beta\gamma\mathcal{L}^{-1})} \tag{146}$$

and because $\mathcal{L}^{-1}\varepsilon_t = 0$,

$$y_t = \frac{\gamma\varepsilon_t}{(1-\gamma\mathcal{L})(1-\rho\mathcal{L})} \tag{147}$$

which is equation (81).

Calvo-Fischer Contracts

Recall equation (79) giving the value of aggregate price:

$$p_t = (1-\gamma) \sum_{s \leq t}^{t} \gamma^{t-s} E_s m_t \qquad (148)$$

This can be rewritten:

$$p_t = (1-\gamma) \sum_{j=0}^{\infty} \gamma^j E_{t-j} m_t \qquad (149)$$

Now:

$$m_t = m_{t-j} + \frac{\varepsilon_{t-j-1}}{1-\rho\mathcal{L}} + \ldots + \frac{\varepsilon_t}{1-\rho\mathcal{L}} \qquad (150)$$

$$E_{t-j} m_t = m_{t-j} + \frac{\rho \varepsilon_{t-j}}{1-\rho\mathcal{L}} + \ldots + \frac{\rho^j \varepsilon_{t-j}}{1-\rho\mathcal{L}}$$

$$= m_{t-j} + \frac{\rho(1-\rho^j)\varepsilon_{t-j}}{(1-\rho)(1-\rho\mathcal{L})} \qquad (151)$$

Combine formulas (149) and (151):

$$p_t = (1-\gamma) \sum_{j=0}^{\infty} \gamma^j \left[m_{t-j} + \frac{\rho(1-\rho^j)\varepsilon_{t-j}}{(1-\rho)(1-\rho\mathcal{L})} \right]$$

$$= (1-\gamma) \sum_{j=0}^{\infty} \gamma^j \left[m_{t-j} + \frac{\rho \varepsilon_{t-j}}{(1-\rho)(1-\rho\mathcal{L})} - \frac{\rho^{j+1} \varepsilon_{t-j}}{(1-\rho)(1-\rho\mathcal{L})} \right] \qquad (152)$$

Now we rewrite (152) using the lag operator $\mathcal{L}$:

$$p_t = (1-\gamma) \sum_{j=0}^{\infty} \left[\gamma^j \mathcal{L}^j m_t + \frac{\rho \gamma^j \mathcal{L}^j \varepsilon_t}{(1-\rho)(1-\rho\mathcal{L})} - \frac{\rho^{j+1} \gamma^j \mathcal{L}^j \varepsilon_t}{(1-\rho)(1-\rho\mathcal{L})} \right]$$

$$= \frac{(1-\gamma) m_t}{1-\gamma\mathcal{L}} + \frac{(1-\gamma)\rho \varepsilon_t}{(1-\rho)(1-\rho\mathcal{L})(1-\gamma\mathcal{L})} - \frac{(1-\gamma)\rho \varepsilon_t}{(1-\rho)(1-\rho\mathcal{L})(1-\gamma\rho\mathcal{L})} \qquad (153)$$

and since $y_t = m_t - p_t$, we find, after simple manipulations:

$$y_t = \frac{\gamma \varepsilon_t}{(1 - \rho \mathcal{L})(1 - \gamma \rho \mathcal{L})} \tag{154}$$

which is equation (85).

Appendix 13.4: Disinflation

We now present a direct application of the price schemes of section 13.4 by studying a very popular experiment and question, namely, are disinflations costly? This question was already present at the time of the old Phillips curve, and the answer appears quite clearly, for example, from figure 2.8 in chapter 2: a disinflation is costly, as it is accompanied by a prolonged period of less that normal employment and output. We will see that under more modern versions of the price mechanism the answer is more contrasted.[16]

The Disinflationary Experiment

We consider a particularly simple disinflationary experiment, which is represented in figure 13.5.

It is assumed that until time $t = 0$ money has been growing at a constant positive rate $\mu > 0$.

$$m_t = \mu t \qquad t \leq 0 \tag{155}$$

and this was initially assumed to last forever. Starting at time $t = 1$ the level of money is stabilized:

$$m_t = 0 \qquad t \geq 1 \tag{156}$$

This new policy is announced at a time $T \leq 1$, and it is fully believed by all agents.

We first study this disinflationary experiment under Calvo contracts, which are the most used in this literature. We will find the remarkable property that this disinflation entails no cost in terms of output. We will then qualify this result by showing that the results can change noticeably if one changes the announcement time or the nature of the contract.

---

16. The results here are notably inspired from Phelps (1978), Taylor (1983), Buiter and Miller (1985), Ball (1994a), Ascari and Rankin (2002), and Mankiw and Reis (2002).

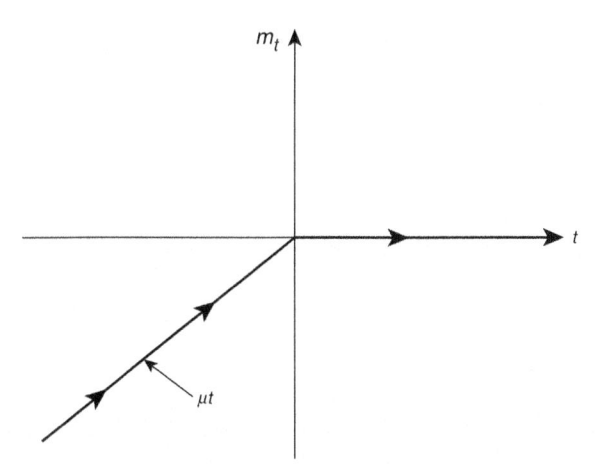

Figure 13.5 A disinflationary money path

To make the following results more striking and transparent, we assume throughout this section that the discount rate is equal to 1:

$$\beta = 1 \tag{157}$$

Problem 13.3 shows how some results are modified if one considers the more general case $\beta < 1$.

Calvo Contracts: A Costless Disinflation

Many years ago Phelps (1978), Taylor (1983), and Buiter and Miller (1985) pointed out that with adequate contracts a disinflation could be engineered without incurring output and employment costs. We study the issue with Calvo-type contracts (those most often associated with the new Keynesian Phillips curve) and show that this surprising result indeed holds. Recall that under Calvo contracts the aggregate price is an aggregate of past values of x_t:

$$p_t = (1-\gamma) \sum_{j=0}^{\infty} \gamma^j x_{t-j} \tag{158}$$

The x_t's themselves are given by (formula 68 with $\beta = 1$):

$$x_t = (1-\gamma) \sum_{j=0}^{\infty} \gamma^j E_t m_{t+j} \tag{159}$$

We assume in this subsection that the new policy is announced at the time when the change occurs, $T = 1$. We study successively what happens before and after the announcement.

Before the Announcement

In periods $t < 1$, before the announcement, money is expected to grow forever at rate μ, so we have:

$$E_t m_{t+j} = \mu(t+j) \qquad \forall t < 1 \qquad \forall j \geq 0 \tag{160}$$

Inserting this into formula (159) we obtain:

$$x_t = (1-\gamma) \sum_{j=0}^{\infty} \gamma^j \mu(t+j) \qquad t < 1 \tag{161}$$

Using formula (A.255) in the mathematical appendix we find that:

$$\sum_{j=0}^{\infty} j\gamma^j = \frac{\gamma}{(1-\gamma)^2} \tag{162}$$

Inserting this into (161) we obtain:

$$x_t = \mu t + \frac{\mu\gamma}{1-\gamma} \qquad t < 1 \tag{163}$$

We note that, if $\mu > 0$, the newly set prices x_t are "ahead" of money μt. Intuitively this is because x_t is an average of current and expected quantities of money. Because money is growing, this average is greater than the current value of money μt. We can compute the aggregate price and output:

$$p_t = (1-\gamma) \sum_{j=0}^{\infty} \gamma^j x_{t-j} = (1-\gamma) \sum_{j=0}^{\infty} \gamma^j \left[\mu(t-j) + \frac{\mu\gamma}{1-\gamma}\right] \tag{164}$$

Using again formula (162) we obtain:

$$p_t = \mu t \tag{165}$$

and thus output:

$$y_t = m_t - p_t = \mu t - p_t = 0 \tag{166}$$

Before the disinflationary announcement, prices follow the quantity of money, and output is perpetually at 0, its "natural" value.

After the Announcement

Because the disinflation is announced at time $T = 1$, the new contracts x_t set at times $t \geq 1$ have a value of 0, since money is expected to be 0 from then on:

$$x_t = 0 \qquad t \geq 1 \qquad (167)$$

Of course, the contracts x_t (which were set at times $t < 1$) have the same value as in formula (163):

$$x_t = \mu t + \frac{\mu \gamma}{1 - \gamma} \qquad t < 1 \qquad (168)$$

Inserting (167) and (168) into (158), we find the expression of the aggregate price:

$$p_t = (1 - \gamma) \sum_{j=t}^{\infty} \gamma^j \left[\mu(t - j) + \frac{\mu \gamma}{1 - \gamma} \right] \qquad (169)$$

From formula (A.256) in the mathematical appendix we know that:

$$\sum_{j=t}^{\infty} j \gamma^j = \frac{t \gamma^t}{1 - \gamma} + \frac{\gamma^{t+1}}{(1 - \gamma)^2} \qquad (170)$$

Inserting this into (169) we find:

$$p_t = 0 \qquad (171)$$

and consequently:

$$y_t = 0 \qquad (172)$$

We see that the disinflation has no cost in terms of output!

Disinflation and the Timing of Announcements

We now want to study how the timing of the announcement of the disinflation influences the dynamics of prices and output. We continue to assume that prices in the economy are determined by contracts of the Calvo type, but we now assume that the disinflation is announced at time $T = 0$ instead of $T = 1$.

Because the disinflationary policy is now announced at time $T = 0$, equations (167) and (168) are replaced by:

$$x_t = 0 \qquad t \geq 0 \qquad (173)$$

$$x_t = \mu t + \frac{\mu \gamma}{1 - \gamma} \qquad t < 0 \qquad (174)$$

and the expression of the aggregate price changes:

$$p_t = (1 - \gamma) \sum_{j=t+1}^{\infty} \gamma^j \left[\mu(t - j) + \frac{\mu \gamma}{1 - \gamma} \right] \qquad (175)$$

which, using again formula (170) yields:

$$p_t = -\mu \gamma^{t+1} \qquad (176)$$

$$y_t = \mu \gamma^{t+1} \qquad (177)$$

We see that, as was found by Ball (1994a), a disinflation can even create a boom! The paths of output for $T = 0$ and $T = 1$ are shown in figure 13.6.

To have an intuition of the underlying mechanism, we compare the path of x_t's in the case where $T = 0$ to the "reference path" corresponding to $T = 1$. The only difference is actually the contract x_0, which is equal to 0 if $T = 0$ and to $\mu \gamma / (1 - \gamma)$ if $T = 1$ (equations 163 and 173). Because x_0 is smaller for $T = 0$, all subsequent aggregate prices p_t are also smaller for $T = 0$ and the output y_t larger. Output was 0 in the reference path $T = 1$, so a larger output actually means a boom for $T = 0$.

We must say that neither this result of a boom nor the result of a painless disinflation in the previous section looks very realistic. Ball (1994b) studies a number of disinflations and finds that they are generally costly.

We will see that a simple modification of the price contract will allow us to obtain a costly disinflation.

Nominal Rigidities and Fluctuations

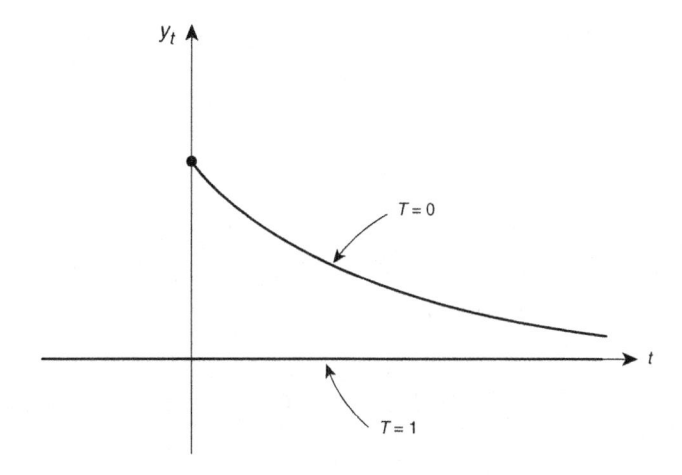

[Figure showing y_t axis with curves labeled $T=0$ and $T=1$]

Figure 13.6 A disinflationary boom

Disinflation with Calvo-Fischer Contracts

We now show that although their IRFs look very similar, the Calvo-Fischer contracts yield a response to disinflation that is strikingly different from that of Calvo contracts. To have a simple benchmark, we assume that the disinflation is announced at $T = 1$ (this is the case of a painless disinflation).

Recall that under Calvo-Fischer contracts, the formula for prices is (formula 79):

$$p_t = (1-\gamma)\sum_{s \leq t} \gamma^{t-s} E_s m_t \qquad (178)$$

We use this formula to compute the path of prices and output, both before and after the announcement of the disinflation.

Before the Announcement

We first compute p_t for $t < 1$. Because the money stabilization is announced at $T = 1$, for any date $s < 1$ before the announcement, money is expected to grow at the rate μ forever, so that:

$$E_s m_t = \mu t \qquad \forall s < 1 \qquad \forall t \geq s \qquad (179)$$

Inserting (179) into (178) we find:

$$p_t = (1-\gamma)\sum_{s \leq t} \gamma^{t-s} E_s m_t = (1-\gamma)\sum_{s<t} \gamma^{t-s}\mu t = \mu t \qquad (180)$$

Prices follow exactly the level of money, and thus:

$$y_t = 0 \quad \forall t < 1 \tag{181}$$

After the Announcement

After the announcement date $T = 1$, all agents know that money will be equal to 0 in the future, so that:

$$E_s m_t = 0 \quad s \geq 1 \quad t \geq s \tag{182}$$

Inserting (179) and (182) into (178) we obtain:

$$p_t = (1 - \gamma) \sum_{s \leq t} \gamma^{t-s} E_s(m_t) = (1 - \gamma) \sum_{s < 1} \gamma^{t-s} \mu t \tag{183}$$

which simplifies to:

$$p_t = \mu t \gamma^t \tag{184}$$

$$y_t = m_t - p_t = -\mu t \gamma^t \tag{185}$$

Now there is an output cost of disinflation, which is represented in figure 13.7 (drawn for $\gamma = 4/5$). The maximum output cost is attained for $t = -1/Log\gamma$. We see that a higher γ will result in a deeper and more protracted recession.

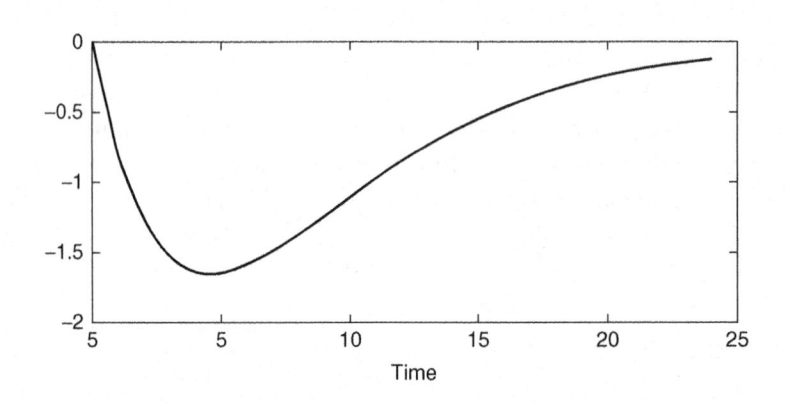

Figure 13.7 A disinflationary slump

Costly Disinflations

We have just seen that it is possible to obtain a costly disinflation by changing the nature of the contracts. Of course this is not the only possibility, and we give a few examples of modifications of the standard framework that allow one to obtain costly disinflations.

A first possibility is another modification of price-wage contracts. Buiter and Jewitt (1981) and Fuhrer and Moore (1995) construct a Taylor-type model where agents care about relative real wages rather than relative nominal wages.

A second possibility is imperfect credibility. It was implicity assumed that the government's announcements about future monetary policy are fully credible. Ball (1995) and Erceg and Levin (2003) show that if the government has imperfect credibility, this will result in costly disinflation.

A third possibility is the adjunction of indexation schemes. Christiano, Eichenbaum, and Evans (2005) use a Calvo-type contract scheme where the contracts that are not renegotiated are automatically indexed on the basis of a past inflation rate, as we saw in section 13.6.3. As a result, inflation has a stronger backward looking component, which makes the results more similar to those of the old Phillips curve.

Appendix 13.5: Price Dynamics

In this appendix we derive the dynamic price equation (91). This will be done in a few steps.

First-order Conditions

Households

Households maximize the discounted utility (86) subject to the budget constraints (87). The Lagrangian is:

$$\sum_t \beta^t \left[Log C_t + \varpi Log\left(\frac{M_t}{P_t}\right) - \frac{L_t^{1+\nu}}{1+\nu} + \lambda_t \left(\frac{W_t L_t + X_t M_{t-1} - P_t C_t - M_t}{P_t}\right) \right]$$
(186)

and the first-order conditions in C_t, L_t, and M_t:

$$\lambda_t = \frac{1}{C_t} \tag{187}$$

$$\frac{\lambda_t W_t}{P_t} = L_t^\nu \tag{188}$$

$$\frac{\lambda_t}{P_t} = \frac{\varpi}{M_t} + \beta E_t\left(\frac{\lambda_{t+1}}{P_{t+1}} X_{t+1}\right) \tag{189}$$

Combining (187) and (188) we find:

$$\frac{W_t}{P_t C_t} = L_t^\nu \tag{190}$$

Combining (187) and (189) and using $X_{t+1} = M_{t+1}/M_t$, we obtain:

$$\frac{M_t}{P_t C_t} = \varpi + \beta E_t\left(\frac{M_{t+1}}{P_{t+1} C_{t+1}}\right) \tag{191}$$

which solves as:

$$\frac{M_t}{P_t C_t} = \frac{\varpi}{1-\beta} \tag{192}$$

Output Firms

Output-producing firms competitively maximize profits:

$$P_t \left(\int_0^1 Y_{jt}^\eta dj\right)^{1/\eta} - \int_0^1 P_{jt} Y_{jt} \tag{193}$$

This yields the demand for intermediate good j:

$$Y_{jt} = Y_t \left(\frac{P_{jt}}{P_t}\right)^{-1/(1-\eta)} \tag{194}$$

The elasticity of these demand curves goes from 1 to infinity (in absolute value) when η goes from 0 to 1, so η appears as a natural index of competitiveness.

Dynamics

Optimal Price Setting

Including the cost of changing prices (90), the real profit of intermediate firm j in period t is:

$$\frac{\Pi_{jt}}{P_t} = \frac{P_{jt}Y_{jt} - W_t L_{jt}}{P_t} - \frac{\zeta}{2} Y_t \left(\frac{P_{jt}}{P_{jt-1}} - 1 \right)^2 \quad (195)$$

Firm j maximizes discounted real profits, multiplied by the marginal utility of consumption, equal to $1/C_t = 1/Y_t$, so that firm j maximizes the expected value of the following criterion:

$$\sum_t \beta^t \frac{\Pi_{jt}}{P_t Y_t} = \sum_t \beta^t \left[\frac{P_{jt}Y_{jt} - W_t L_{jt}}{P_t Y_t} - \frac{\zeta}{2} \left(\frac{P_{jt}}{P_{jt-1}} - 1 \right)^2 \right] \quad (196)$$

Insert into the discounted profits (equation 196) the expression of Y_{jt} (equation 194) and $Y_{jt} = A_t L_{jt}$. We obtain:

$$\sum_t \beta^t \left[\left(\frac{P_{jt}}{P_t} \right)^{-\eta/(1-\eta)} - \frac{W_t}{P_t A_t} \left(\frac{P_{jt}}{P_t} \right)^{-1/(1-\eta)} - \frac{\zeta}{2} \left(\frac{P_{jt}}{P_{jt-1}} - 1 \right)^2 \right] \quad (197)$$

Now insert (190) and $Y_t = C_t$ into (197). Keeping only the terms where P_{jt} appears, we obtain the maximand:

$$\left(\frac{P_{jt}}{P_t} \right)^{-\eta/(1-\eta)} - \left(\frac{Y_t}{A_t} \right)^{1+\nu} \left(\frac{P_{jt}}{P_t} \right)^{-1/(1-\eta)}$$

$$- \frac{\zeta}{2} \left(\frac{P_{jt}}{P_{jt-1}} - 1 \right)^2 - \frac{\beta \zeta}{2} E_t \left(\frac{P_{jt+1}}{P_{jt}} - 1 \right)^2 \quad (198)$$

Let us differentiate with respect to P_{jt}. We obtain the first-order condition:

$$-\frac{\eta}{1-\eta} \left(\frac{P_{jt}}{P_t} \right)^{-1/(1-\eta)} + \frac{1}{1-\eta} \left(\frac{Y_t}{A_t} \right)^{1+\nu} \left(\frac{P_{jt}}{P_t} \right)^{-1/(1-\eta)-1}$$

$$- \zeta \frac{P_t}{P_{jt-1}} \left(\frac{P_{jt}}{P_{jt-1}} - 1 \right) + \beta \zeta E_t \frac{P_t P_{jt+1}}{P_{jt}^2} \left(\frac{P_{jt+1}}{P_{jt}} - 1 \right) = 0 \quad (199)$$

Price Dynamics

All firms j are actually in a symmetric situation, so that in equilibrium $P_{jt} = P_t$. Inserting this into (199) we obtain the dynamic equation for prices:

$$-\frac{\eta}{1-\eta} + \frac{1}{1-\eta}\left(\frac{Y_t}{A_t}\right)^{1+\nu}$$

$$-\zeta\frac{P_t}{P_{t-1}}\left(\frac{P_t}{P_{t-1}} - 1\right) + \beta\zeta E_t \frac{P_{t+1}}{P_t}\left(\frac{P_{t+1}}{P_t} - 1\right) = 0 \qquad (200)$$

We first characterize the long-run equilibrium, where all prices are equal over time. Then (200) yields:

$$\left(\frac{Y_t}{A_t}\right)^{1+\nu} = \eta \qquad (201)$$

or:

$$L_t = \eta^{1/1+\nu} = L_0 \qquad (202)$$

Now we go back to the dynamics. Log-linearizing (200) we find:

$$\frac{\eta(1+\nu)}{1-\eta}(y_t - a_t) - \zeta(p_t - p_{t-1}) + \beta\zeta(E_t p_{t+1} - p_t) = 0 \qquad (203)$$

and since, from (192), $y_t = c_t = m_t - p_t$, this becomes:

$$\eta(1+\nu)(p_t - m_t + a_t) + \zeta(1-\eta)(p_t - p_{t-1})$$

$$+\beta\zeta(1-\eta)(p_t - E_t p_{t+1}) = 0 \qquad (204)$$

We define:

$$\kappa = \frac{\eta(1+\nu)}{\zeta(1-\eta)} \qquad (205)$$

Then formula (204) becomes:

$$(1+\beta+\kappa)p_t - p_{t-1} - \beta E_t p_{t+1} = \kappa(m_t - a_t) \qquad (206)$$

which is equation (91).

Problems

Problem 13.1: The Taylor Model

We consider the Taylor model described in section 13.2, but instead of assuming that the new wage x_t is based on period t information, we assume (actually as in some initial Taylor models) that it is based on period $t-1$ information, so that formula (19) is replaced by:

$$x_t = bE_{t-1}\left(w_t + \psi\ell_t\right) + dE_{t-1}\left(w_{t+1} + \psi\ell_{t+1}\right)$$

Recall that the average wage w_t is related to the x_t's by:

$$w_t = \frac{x_t + x_{t-1}}{2}$$

and that:

$$\ell_t = m_t - w_t$$

Finally, we assume that money follows a random walk:

$$m_t - m_{t-1} = \varepsilon_t$$

1. Derive the dynamic equation governing the new wages x_t.
2. Show that the autoregressive root is the same as when wages are based on period t information.
3. Compute the dynamics of the aggregate wage w_t.
4. Compute the dynamics of employment.

Problem 13.2: Inflation Persistence

Consider the following new Keynesian Phillips curve:

$$\pi_t = \beta E_t \pi_{t+1} + \kappa y_t \qquad 0 < \beta < 1 \qquad \kappa > 0$$

where $\pi_t = p_t - p_{t-1}$ is inflation. The logarithms of price, output, and money are p_t, y_t, and m_t. We assume these are related by:

$$m_t = p_t + y_t$$

1. Compute the dynamics of inflation for:

$$m_t - m_{t-1} = \varepsilon_t$$

where ε_t is a white noise.

2. Show that the response of inflation to monetary shocks is autocorrelated and derive the autoregressive root λ.

Problem 13.3: Disinflation and the Discount Rate

In appendix 13.4 we studied the effects of a disinflation, assuming to simplify that the discount rate $\beta = 1$. We now study the same disinflation assuming $\beta < 1$. To compare it to the benchmark case of a costless disinflation of appendix 13.4, we assume that the disinflation is implemented and announced at time $T = 1$.

Recall that with $\beta < 1$ the new prices x_t are given by:

$$x_t = (1 - \beta\gamma) \sum_{j=0}^{\infty} (\beta\gamma)^j E_t m_{t+j}$$

and the aggregate price by:

$$p_t = (1 - \gamma) \sum_{j=0}^{\infty} \gamma^j x_{t-j}$$

1. Compute the value of new contracts x_t.
2. Compute the value of the aggregate price p_t and output y_t.
3. Compare with the benchmark case $\beta = 1$.

Problem 13.4: Calvo and Calvo-Fischer: Comparative Dynamics

We give an example, inspired from Ball (1994a), where the responses to the same money shock under Calvo and Calvo-Fischer contracts are quite different. The experiment is a one-step money increase announced in advance as follows: we assume that money has been 0, and expected to be so in the future, until date 0. At date 0 it is announced that money will jump from 0 to 1 at date $T > 0$, and stay there forever.

1. Compute the path of prices and output under Calvo contracts (as described in section 13.4.3). Show that there is a slump until time T, and then a boom.

2. Compute the path of prices and output under Calvo-Fischer contracts (as described in section 13.4.5). Show that output remains at 0 until time T, and there is a boom after.

Problem 13.5: A DSGE Model with Sticky Wages

We study a DSGE model with nominal wage stickiness, similar to the model with price stickiness in section 13.5. The basic elements are the same as in section 13.5, and we recall briefly some essentials. Firms have a linear technology:

$$Y_t = A_t L_t$$

The labor index L_t is an aggregate of a continuum of differentiated labor types (Snower, 1983), indexed by $i \in [0,1]$:

$$L_t = \left(\int_0^1 L_{it}^\chi di\right)^{1/\chi}$$

Note that this is similar to the Dixit and Stiglitz (1977) formalization, but applied to labor.

The representative household of type i maximizes the following expected value of discounted future utilities:

$$U = E_0 \sum_{t=0}^\infty \beta^t \left[LogC_{it} + \varpi Log\frac{M_{it}}{P_t} - \frac{L_{it}^{1+\nu}}{1+\nu} \right]$$

The budget constraint for period t is (there is no profit income because of the linear technology):

$$P_t C_{it} + M_{it} = W_{it} L_{it} + X_t M_{it-1}$$

where X_t is a common multiplicative monetary shock, equal to M_t/M_{t-1}, and W_{it} is the wage that will be chosen by households of type i. Wage rigidity is obtained by making the assumption, similar to Rotemberg (1982a, 1982b), that there is a quadratic cost of changing the wage W_{it}. This cost is in real terms:

$$\frac{\zeta}{2} Y_t \left(\frac{W_{it}}{W_{it-1}} - 1\right)^2$$

1. Compute the demand L_{it} for labor of type i.
2. Give the intertemporal maximization program of households of type i.
3. Compute the first-order conditions for wages. Take the symmetrical solution, make a log-linear approximation and give the dynamic relation linking successive wages.
4. Solve for the dynamics of wages and employment when the money process is:

$$m_t - m_{t-1} = \varepsilon_t$$

where ε_t is a white noise.

14

Consumption, Investment, Inventories, and Credit

14.1 Introduction

In the preceding chapters we studied intertemporal general equilibrium models of economies subject to stochastic shocks. To have a better understanding of the mechanisms involved, we chose specifications simple enough to obtain analytical solutions for all variables in the model.

In this chapter we first study further aspects of consumption and investment. We also study two important topics that were not treated explicitly in the preceding chapters: inventories and credit. Although some of the issues we deal with can be treated in a general equilibrium framework, to make the exposition simpler we adopt in this chapter a more partial equilibrium approach.

Section 14.2 studies additional features of consumption. We first show why there is "consumption smoothing," in line with Milton Friedman's (1957) insights on "permanent income." We then study whether uncertainty matters for consumption or whether knowledge of mean income is sufficient to determine it. We see that if utility is quadratic, mean expected income is sufficient to determine consumption (this is "certainty equivalence"). If it is not, however, as compared to the quadratic benchmark, precautionary savings may reduce consumption.

Section 14.3 deals with investment. We show how straight application of profit maximization at the partial equilibrium level of the firm may entail unrealistically high investment demand. We then describe a classic model of investment where the presence of installation costs solves this problem.

We finally show how the extension of the methodology to an imperfectly competitive framework allows us to obtain an investment function that resembles the famous "accelerator."

Section 14.4 introduces inventories. One of the primary purposes for holding inventories is to avoid potential consumer rationing. So we first investigate whether firms would want to ration their consumers, and we find that with storable goods this probability of rationing may be quite small. Another rationale for inventories is production smoothing, and we investigate why production can nevertheless be more volatile than demand. We finally show how imperfectly competitive price making interacts with inventory holding and the relation between rationing and competitiveness.

Section 14.5 studies credit. In all previous chapters, credit was implicitly supposed to adapt passively, and we therefore ignored it. We show that actually, due to moral hazard or adverse selection problems, credit may be rationed.

14.2 Consumption

14.2.1 Permanent Income and Consumption Smoothing

Friedman (1957), using the notion of permanent income, showed that individuals should smooth their consumption over time. We will see how this consumption smoothing will occur. The basic idea is that individual incomes can be more variable than aggregate income. This will give to individuals the possibility of smoothing their individual consumptions.

Consider an economy with n agents indexed by $i = 1, \ldots, n$. They live in periods $0, \ldots, T$ and have the same utility functions:

$$U_i = \sum_{t=0}^{T} \beta^t U(c_{it}) \qquad U' > 0 \qquad U'' < 0 \tag{1}$$

where c_{it} is the consumption of agent i in period t. These agents have incomes y_{it}, $t = 0, \ldots T$. Aggregate income in period t is:

$$Y_t = \sum_i y_{it} \tag{2}$$

Call r_t the real interest rate, and Δ_t the real discount factor, with:

$$\Delta_t = \frac{1}{(1+r_1)\ldots(1+r_t)} \qquad \Delta_0 = 1 \tag{3}$$

The intertemporal budget constraint of agent i is:

$$\sum_{t=0}^{T} \Delta_t c_{it} = \sum_{t=1}^{T} \Delta_t y_{it} \qquad (4)$$

The program of agent i is:

$$\text{Maximize } \sum_{t=0}^{T} \beta^t U(c_{it}) \quad \text{s.t.}$$

$$\sum_{t=0}^{T} \Delta_t c_{it} = \sum_{t=1}^{T} \Delta_t y_{it}$$

The Lagrangian is:

$$\sum_{t=0}^{T} \beta^t U(c_{it}) - \lambda_i \left(\sum_{t=0}^{T} \Delta_t c_{it} - \sum_{t=0}^{T} \Delta_t y_{it} \right) \qquad (5)$$

and the first-order conditions:

$$\beta^t U'(c_{it}) = \lambda_i \Delta_t \qquad (6)$$

Inverting (6) and summing over the i's we find:

$$\sum_i U'^{-1}\left(\frac{\lambda_i \Delta_t}{\beta^t}\right) = \sum_i c_{it} = \sum_i y_{it} = Y_t \qquad (7)$$

If total resources Y_t are constant over time, then Δ_t/β^t is constant, and actually equal to 1 since $\Delta_0 = 1$. Inserting this into the first-order condition (6) we find:

$$U'(c_{it}) = \lambda_i \qquad \forall t \qquad (8)$$

This entails that c_{it} is independent of time, so that:

$$c_{it} = c_i = \frac{1}{T} \sum_{t=0}^{T} y_{it} \qquad \forall t \qquad (9)$$

We see that individual consumptions are completely smoothed. If Y_t is not constant in time, smoothing will be less than perfect, as each agent will have to bear some of the aggregate variability, but individual consumptions will be less variable than individual incomes.

14.2.2 Certainty Equivalence

We now study one case where, under stochastic incomes, it is possible to obtain an explicit solution whatever the uncertainty. This case is based on a quadratic utility function and is known as "certainty equivalence" (Simon, 1956, Theil, 1957) for reasons we shall see shortly. The agent has a quadratic utility function:

$$\sum_t \beta^t E \left(C_t - \frac{a}{2} C_t^2 \right) \tag{10}$$

and his budget constraint in period t is:

$$C_t + S_t = Y_t + R S_{t-1} \tag{11}$$

where Y_t is (stochastic) period t income and S_t period t savings. The household maximizes utility (10) subject to the sequence of budget constraints (11). The corresponding Lagrangian is:

$$E \sum_t^\infty \beta^t \left[\left(C_t - \frac{a}{2} C_t^2 \right) + \lambda_t \left(Y_t + R S_{t-1} - C_t - S_t \right) \right] \tag{12}$$

and the first-order conditions with respect to C_t and S_t:

$$\lambda_t = 1 - a C_t \tag{13}$$

$$\lambda_t = \beta R E_t \lambda_{t+1} \tag{14}$$

Combining them, we obtain the dynamic equation in consumption:

$$C_t = \frac{1 - \beta R}{a} + \beta R E_t C_{t+1} \tag{15}$$

Note that if $\beta R = 1$, this simplifies to:

$$C_t = E_t C_{t+1} \tag{16}$$

Consumption follows a random walk (Hall, 1978). Continuing with the case $\beta R = 1$ we can, using (16) and the household's budget constraints, compute consumption as a function of present and future incomes:

$$C_t = (1 - \beta) \sum_{j=0}^\infty \beta^j E_t \left(Y_{t+j} \right) \tag{17}$$

We see that although there is no insurance scheme for incomes, consumption depends only on future expected incomes, and not at all on the possible dispersion of these incomes, hence the name "certainty equivalence."

14.2.3 Prudence

The previous quadratic utility function has the particular property that its third derivative is identically equal to 0. We will now see that as soon as this is not the case, uncertainty will affect savings and consumption. In particular, we observe a phenomenon of "precautionary savings" (Leland, 1968).

One says that a utility function $U(C)$ displays *prudence* if $U'''(C) > 0$ (Kimball, 1990). By analogy with the measures of risk aversion, one can define a coefficient of *absolute prudence* equal to $-U'''(C)/U''(C)$ and a coefficient of *relative prudence* equal to $-CU'''(C)/U''(C)$. We will see how prudence leads to precautionary savings.

14.2.4 Precautionary Savings

To make the point simply, we consider an economy that extends over two periods. The agent considered has a utility function:

$$U(C_1) + \beta U(C_2) \tag{18}$$

The agent has a sure income Y_1 in the first period, a stochastic income Y_2 in the second period. She is faced with a gross real interest rate R. The budget constraints are, calling S the amount of real savings:

$$C_1 + S = Y_1 \tag{19}$$

$$C_2 = Y_2 + RS \tag{20}$$

The agent's program is thus:

$$\text{Maximize } U(Y_1 - S) + \beta EU(Y_2 + RS)$$

The first-order condition is:

$$U'(Y_1 - S) = \beta R E\left[U'(Y_2 + RS)\right] \tag{21}$$

We now assume that the probability distribution of second-period income Y_2 is function of a parameter σ in such a way that an increase in σ

corresponds to a "more random" probability distribution in the sense of Rothschild and Stiglitz (1970).

Let us differentiate equation (21) with respect to S:

$$-\left[U''\left(Y_{1}-S\right)+\beta R^{2}EU''\left(Y_{2}+RS\right)\right]dS = \beta R\left[\frac{\partial EU'\left(Y_{2}+RS\right)}{\partial \sigma}\right]d\sigma \tag{22}$$

If $U''' > 0$, then marginal utility U' is convex, and therefore:

$$\frac{\partial EU'\left(Y_{2}+RS\right)}{\partial \sigma} > 0 \tag{23}$$

Consequently from (22) $\partial S/\partial \sigma > 0$. Keeping average income constant, an increase in second-period uncertainty increases savings. This is the precautionary savings effect.

An Example

Consider a utility function with constant absolute risk aversion:

$$U\left(C_{t}\right) = -\exp\left(-\alpha C_{t}\right) \qquad \alpha > 0 \tag{24}$$

We note that $U'''\left(C_{t}\right) > 0$, so that we should expect to observe precautionary savings. Total discounted utility is:

$$U = -\exp\left(-\alpha C_{1}\right) - \beta \exp\left(-\alpha C_{2}\right) \qquad \alpha > 0 \tag{25}$$

Using (19) and (20) the intertemporal utility is, as a function of savings:

$$U = -\exp\left(-\alpha Y_{1}+\alpha S\right) - \beta E \exp\left(-\alpha Y_{2}-\alpha RS\right) \tag{26}$$

Differentiating with respect to S we find

$$\exp\left[\alpha\left(1+R\right)S\right] = \beta R \exp\left(\alpha Y_{1}\right) E \exp\left(-\alpha Y_{2}\right) \tag{27}$$

Because $\exp\left(-\alpha Y_{2}\right)$ is a convex function of Y_{2}, an increase in the volatility of Y_{2} with constant mean increases $E\exp\left(-\alpha Y_{2}\right)$, and therefore increases savings.

14.3 Investment

14.3.1 A Simple Framework

We will first study a popular model of investment, where the firm who invests not only has to pay for the investment goods but also is subject to installation costs that will end up to smooth investment.[1]

Historically there are two motivations for introducing such an installation cost function. An initial motivation was that some authors found, at the firm level, a potential discontinuity in investment demand that can occur (as we shall see) when there are no such installation costs in the model.

A second motivation is that investment has sometimes been found too volatile in dynamic stochastic general equilibrium models without installation costs. Their introduction allows us to better calibrate this volatility.

Since the potential discontinuity we hinted at will be more conspicuous in continuous time than in discrete time, we adopt a continuous time framework for the study of this problem and revert to discrete time in section 14.3.4.

Our basic model pictures a firm with a production function:

$$Y_t = AF(K_t) \qquad F'(K_t) > 0 \qquad F''(K_t) < 0 \qquad (28)$$

Note that we do not make explicit the dependence of production on labor, as everything will revolve around capital only. The evolution of capital $\dot{K}_t$ is:

$$\dot{K}_t = J_t \qquad (29)$$

where J_t is the *net* investment of the firm:

$$J_t = I_t - \delta K_t \qquad (30)$$

14.3.2 The Model without Installation Cost

With no installation costs, the firm maximizes discounted profits:

$$\int e^{-\rho t} [AF(K_t) - J_t - \delta K_t] \qquad (31)$$

---

1. A classic article on the investment of the firm is Hall and Jorgenson (1967). The model with installation costs has been notably studied by Eisner and Strotz (1963), Lucas (1967), Gould (1968), Treadway (1969), Abel (1982), and Hayashi (1982). This is surveyed in Abel (1990).

under the accumulation equation (29). The current value Hamiltonian (mathematical appendix A.4.2) is:

$$\mathcal{H}_t = AF(K_t) - J_t - \delta K_t + q_t J_t \tag{32}$$

The first-order condition on J_t:

$$\frac{\partial \mathcal{H}_t}{\partial J_t} = q_t - 1 = 0 \tag{33}$$

and on K_t:

$$\dot{q}_t = \rho q_t - \frac{\partial \mathcal{H}_t}{\partial K_t} = \rho q_t - AF'(K_t) + \delta \tag{34}$$

The variables q_t and K_t immediately jump to their steady-state values q^* and K^* characterized by:

$$q^* = 1 \tag{35}$$

$$AF'(K^*) = \delta + \rho \tag{36}$$

We see that there is a potential discontinuity problem. Imagine, for example, that $A = 1 - \tau$, where τ is a tax rate. Suppose there is a sudden fall in τ. Then K^* should make an instantaneous upward jump, which means an unbounded demand for investment.[2] We now modify the problem of the firm so that optimal behavior is consistent with a smoother evolution of capital.

14.3.3 The Model with Installation Cost

The basic model is the same, but we now assume that there is an installation cost function:

$$\mathcal{C}(J_t) \tag{37}$$

where $\mathcal{C}(J_t)$ is the "installation cost" for new equipment, which we assume to be convex (figure 14.1).

---

2. We may note that, for example, we did not encounter this problem in the dynamic general equilibrium studied in chapter 7. In that framework, other variables can vary, so that capital varies smoothly.

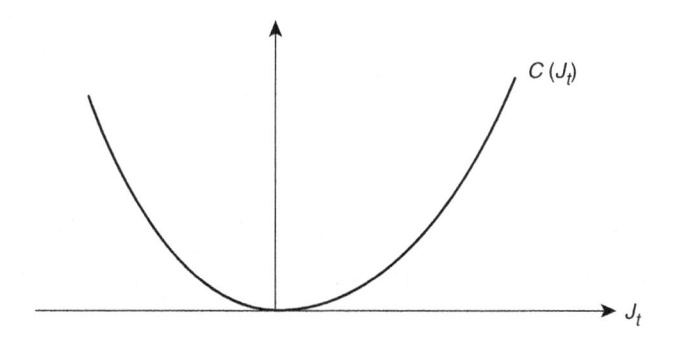

Figure 14.1 The installation cost

Net output in period t is equal to:

$$Y_t - \mathcal{C}(J_t) = AF(K_t) - \mathcal{C}(J_t) \tag{38}$$

The firm maximizes discounted profits:

$$\int_0^\infty e^{-\rho t} \left[AF(K_t) - J_t - \delta K_t - \mathcal{C}(J_t) \right] \tag{39}$$

under the capital accumulation equation (29). The current-value Hamiltonian is:

$$\mathcal{H}_t = AF(K_t) - J_t - \delta K_t - \mathcal{C}(J_t) + q_t J_t \tag{40}$$

The first-order condition on net investment J_t is:

$$\frac{\partial \mathcal{H}_t}{\partial J_t} = q_t - 1 - \mathcal{C}'(J_t) = 0 \tag{41}$$

This yields a net investment function:

$$J_t = \psi(q_t - 1) \qquad \psi = (\mathcal{C}')^{-1} \qquad \psi' > 0 \tag{42}$$

Now the optimality condition on capital yields:

$$\dot{q}_t = \rho q_t - \frac{\partial \mathcal{H}_t}{\partial K_t} = \rho q_t - AF'(K_t) + \delta \tag{43}$$

Combining the foregoing equations, the dynamic system is finally written as:

$$\dot{K}_t = \psi(q_t - 1) \tag{44}$$

$$\dot{q}_t = \rho q_t - AF'(K_t) + \delta \tag{45}$$

The stationary state of this dynamic system is characterized by:

$$q^* = 1 \tag{46}$$

$$J^* = 0 \tag{47}$$

$$AF'(K^*) = \delta + \rho \tag{48}$$

Note that this is the same as in the model without installation costs. We can represent the dynamics (44) and (45) in a (K_t, q_t) graph (figure 14.2).

The locus $\dot{K}_t = 0$ has for equation $q_t = 1$. From (45) the locus $\dot{q}_t = 0$ has for equation:

$$\rho q_t - AF'(K_t) + \delta = 0 \tag{49}$$

which is the downward-sloping line in figure 14.2. We see on this figure that we have saddle path dynamics.

We can consider again the experiment of a change in the parameter A. This is represented in figure 14.3, which shows the dynamics after an increase in A.

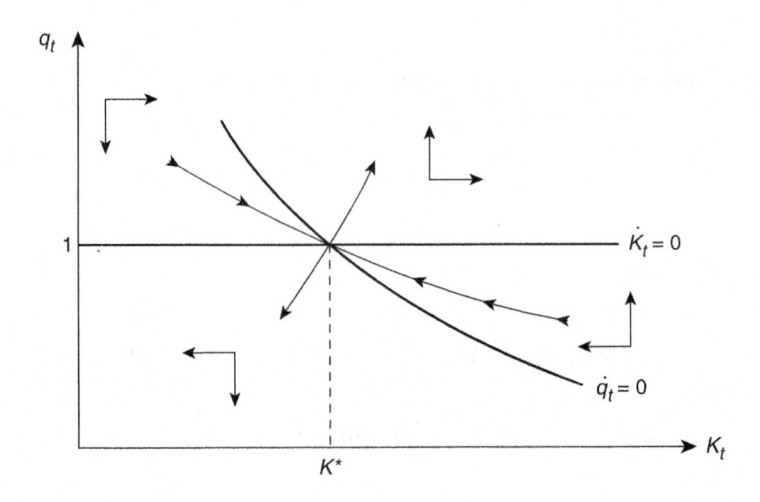

Figure 14.2 The dynamics of K_t and q_t

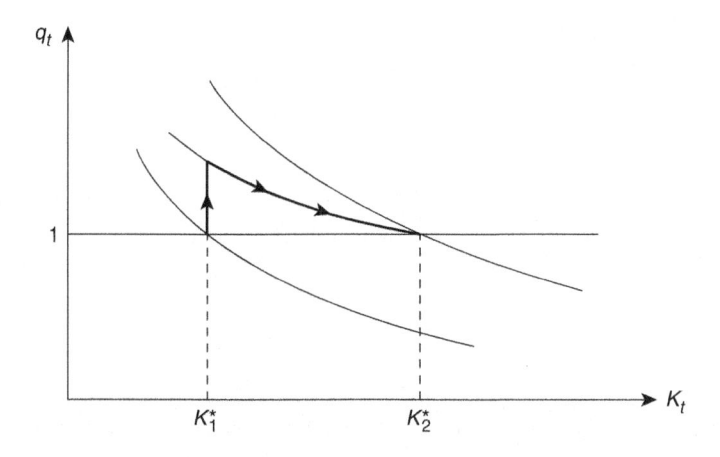

Figure 14.3 Dynamics after an increase in A

When the tax rate is lowered, the long-run equilibrium changes from K_1^* to K_2^*. Because K_t is a predetermined variable, it remains initially at K_1^*. But this time q_t jumps on the stable trajectory corresponding to K_2^*, and investment remains finite. In the long-run, (K_t, q_t) converges toward the long-run equilibrium $(K_2^*, 1)$.

14.3.4 An Imperfect Competition Accelerator

A particularly famous investment function is the so-called accelerator, notably because for a long time it was the central building block in business cycles analysis (Samuelson, 1939). We now show that we can derive an investment function akin to the accelerator in a framework of imperfectly competitive flexible prices.[3]

We revert to discrete time and consider a firm with a production function:

$$Y_t = AK_t \qquad (50)$$

The installation cost incurred by the firm for net investment J_t is:

$$C(J_t) = \frac{aJ_t^2}{2} \qquad (51)$$

---

3. An accelerator-type investment function was derived in a framework of rigid prices by Grossman (1972).

where net investment J_t is again defined by:

$$K_{t+1} = K_t + J_t \tag{52}$$

We assume that the owners of the firms are risk neutral. The managers maximize the expected value of discounted profits:

$$\sum_t \beta^t \left(P_t Y_t - J_t - \delta K_t - \frac{a J_t^2}{2} \right) \tag{53}$$

The firm is in a situation of imperfect competition and chooses the price P_t with a demand curve:

$$D_t = \mathcal{D}_t - d P_t \tag{54}$$

where $\mathcal{D}_t$ is a stochastic demand shock. We assume that the firm satisfies demand, so that:

$$D_t = Y_t = A K_t \tag{55}$$

and combining with (54):

$$P_t = \frac{\mathcal{D}_t - A K_t}{d} \tag{56}$$

Now we insert (56) into (53), so the firm maximizes:

$$E \sum_t \beta^t \left[\frac{\mathcal{D}_t - A K_t}{d} A K_t - J_t - \delta K_t - \frac{a J_t^2}{2} \right] \tag{57}$$

subject to the capital accumulation equation (52). It is shown in appendix 14.1 that the solution for the dynamics of capital is:

$$K_{t+1} = \lambda K_t + \frac{\beta \lambda A}{a d} \sum_{j=1}^{\infty} (\beta \lambda)^{j-1} E_t \mathcal{D}_{t+j} \tag{58}$$

where λ is a root of the characteristic polynomial:

$$\Psi(\lambda) = \beta \lambda^2 - \left(1 + \beta + \frac{2 \beta A^2}{a d} \right) \lambda + 1 = 0 \tag{59}$$

The autoregressive root λ is between 0 and 1 because:

$$\Psi(0) = 1 \tag{60}$$

$$\Psi(1) = -\frac{2\beta A^2}{\alpha a} < 0 \tag{61}$$

Formula (58) belongs to the family of "flexible accelerators" where (1) investment is function of all future expected demand shocks $E_t \mathcal{D}_{t+j}$, $j \geq 1$; and (2) capital has an autoregressive root λ because of the installation costs.

14.4 Inventories

We want to study here a number of issues that are directly related to inventories.[4]

1. Firms typically hold inventories so as not to miss sales when demand is unexpectedly high. On the other hand, carrying inventories has a cost because they depreciate or entail financial costs. We first study why the probability of rationing the consumers is much smaller in markets for storable goods than in markets for nonstorable goods, and therefore why the "traditional" assumption that demand is always served is more likely to be satisfied in that case.

2. Another function of inventories is to smooth production. One would thus expect that the volatility of production is lower than the volatility of sales. But in reality, production is often more volatile than sales, and we will see that this can be explained if demand is autocorrelated (Kahn, 1987).

3. Finally in a model with endogenous prices we will see how price making and inventory holding interact. In particular, we will see that more market power leads to higher inventories and less rationing.

14.4.1 The Common Framework

Let us consider a firm that can produce a storable good at a unit cost c. Denote as P_t the price of the good, Y_t the production, D_t the demand, and I_t the inventory that the firm holds at the beginning of the period.[5] We assume that the firm must decide its production before the demand is

---

4. The issues that we discuss here have been notably studied by Bellman (1957); Arrow, Karlin, and Scarf (1958); Mills (1962); Zabel (1972); Bénassy (1982); Blinder (1986); and Kahn (1987). Overviews of the inventory literature are found in Blinder and Maccini (1991), Kahn (2008), and Ramey and West (1999).

5. In this section I_t will represent inventories, not investment as usual.

known, hence the utility of having inventories. Sales are the minimum of demand and supply, where supply includes both current production and the inventories already available:

$$S_t = \min\left(Y_t + I_t, D_t\right) \qquad (62)$$

Now inventories deteriorate at the rate $1 - \psi$. So the next-period inventories are given by

$$I_{t+1} = \psi\left(Y_t + I_t - S_t\right) \qquad (63)$$

The firm maximizes expected discounted profits:

$$\text{Max } E\left[\sum_{t=0}^{\infty} \beta^t \left(P_t S_t - c Y_t\right)\right] \qquad (64)$$

14.4.2 Customer Rationing: Exogenous Prices

We will be concerned with how much firms ration their customers. In a first step, we assume that the price is exogenously given in all periods and equal to P. Demand is stochastic:

$$D_t = \xi_t \geq 0 \qquad (65)$$

where the ξ_t are positive i.i.d. stochastic variables with a probability density $\phi\left(\xi_t\right)$ and a cumulative density function $\Phi\left(\xi_t\right)$.

We solve the problem using the traditional methods of dynamic programming (mathematical appendix A.5). For that we construct a valuation function for inventories, denoted $V_t\left(I_t\right)$. This is the expected value of discounted profits from time t onward when an optimal production policy is followed, conditional on the initial value of I_t.

To find the recursive equation characterizing $V_t\left(I_t\right)$, we note that the firm can be in one of two regimes: excess supply, where transactions are equal to demand ξ_t, or excess demand, where transactions are equal to supply $Y_t + I_t$. The transition occurs for the threshold value of the stochastic shock ξ_t such that the two are equal, that is:

$$\xi_t = Y_t + I_t \qquad (66)$$

Using this, it is proved in appendix 14.2 that the optimal production strategy of the firm is, when we have an interior solution:

$$Y_t = Q - I_t \qquad (67)$$

That is, the firm produces enough to replenish its "total supply" $Y_t + I_t$ to a level Q. The value of Q itself is given by:

$$\Phi(Q) = \frac{P - c}{P - \beta\psi c} \qquad (68)$$

Now consumers are rationed if $\xi_t > Y_t + I_t = Q$. The probability that customers be rationed is thus:

$$1 - \Phi(Q) = \frac{(1 - \beta\psi)c}{P - \beta\psi c} \qquad (69)$$

We see that patience (a high β) and storability (a high ψ) lead to a lower probability of rationing. This makes the usual assumption that demand is not rationed a reasonable approximation for storable goods.

We also note that the probability of rationing decreases with $P - c$, which is somehow an index of the "profitability" of customers. We come back to the relation between profitability and rationing in section 14.4.4, where prices are endogenized.

14.4.3 Inventories and the Volatility of Production

We want to see whether this model generates production smoothing, and notably whether the variance of production is smaller that the variance of sales. We start with the case considered in the previous section. Combining (62), (65), and (67), we find the level of sales:

$$S_t = \min(Q, \xi_t) \qquad (70)$$

Combining (63), (67), and (70), we find the level of production:

$$Y_t = (1 - \psi)Q + \psi \min(Q, \xi_{t-1}) \qquad (71)$$

Comparing (70) and (71) we see that if, as we assumed, the variables ξ_t are i.i.d., the volatility of production is smaller than the volatility of sales because:

$$\text{Var}(Y_t) = \psi^2 \text{Var}(S_t) \qquad (72)$$

We now show (Kahn, 1987) how demand autocorrelation can create a higher volatility of production. Instead of assuming $D_t = \xi_t$, we assume that demand has an autoregessive component:

$$D_t = \rho D_{t-1} + \xi_t \qquad 0 < \rho < 1 \tag{73}$$

where the ξ_t's are still i.i.d. It is proved in problem 14.4 that the optimal production strategy of the firm is:

$$Y_t = \rho D_{t-1} + Q - I_t \tag{74}$$

We note that this is very similar to (67), except for the addition of the autoregressive term ρD_{t-1}. The threshold value Q is given by the same formula as in equation (68), that is:

$$\Phi(Q) = \frac{P-c}{P-\beta\psi c} \tag{75}$$

Combining (62), (73), and (74), we find that sales are equal to:

$$S_t = \rho D_{t-1} + \min(\xi_t, Q) \tag{76}$$

and combining (63), (74), and (76), we obtain the value of production:

$$Y_t = \rho D_{t-1} + (1-\psi)Q + \psi \min(\xi_{t-1}, Q) \tag{77}$$

We see that because D_{t-1} is correlated with ξ_{t-1} but not with ξ_t, the variance of production may be bigger that that of sales, a feature sometimes observed in reality (Kahn, 1987).

14.4.4 Customer Rationing: Endogenous Price

We continue to study the issue of consumer rationing, but endogenize prices in a framework of imperfect competition where the firm chooses both price and production. The demand function is stochastic with a multiplicative random term:

$$D_t = \xi_t g(P_t) \tag{78}$$

where, as before, the ξ_t are i.i.d. stochastic variables with a probability density $\phi(\xi_t)$ and a cumulative density function $\Phi(\xi_t)$. We prove in appendix 14.2 that the optimal production and price strategies of the firm are given by:

$$Y_t = Q - I_t \tag{79}$$

$$\Phi(q) = \frac{P-c}{P-\beta\psi c} \tag{80}$$

with:

$$q = \frac{Q}{g(P)} \tag{81}$$

We see that q is the threshold value of ξ for which demand and supply are equal. So the probability of rationing is:

$$1 - \Phi(q) = \frac{(1-\beta\psi)c}{P-\beta\psi c} \tag{82}$$

Up to now this looks very much like what we saw in subsection 14.2.2. But this is not anymore the end of the story, since P is now an endogenous variable. And indeed we derive in appendix 14.2 equation (140), which links q and P:

$$\int_0^q \left[g(P) + (P - \beta\psi c)g'(P)\right]\xi\phi(\xi)\,d\xi + \int_q^\infty qg(P)\phi(\xi)\,d\xi = 0 \tag{83}$$

This expression is a bit unintuitive, so to obtain a comprehensible bound on the probability of rationing, we now assume an isoelastic demand curve:

$$g(P) = P^{-1/(1-\eta)} \tag{84}$$

Under this parameterization, equation (83) is rewritten as:

$$\int_0^q (\eta P - \beta\psi c)\xi\phi(\xi)\,d\xi = \int_q^\infty (1-\eta)Pq\phi(\xi)\,d\xi \tag{85}$$

Since $\xi \leq q$ in the interval $[0,q]$, equation (85) then implies that:

$$\int_0^q (\eta P - \beta\psi c)\phi(\xi)\,d\xi \geq \int_q^\infty (1-\eta)P\phi(\xi)\,d\xi \tag{86}$$

This can be rewritten in terms of the probability Φ as:

$$(\eta P - \beta\psi c)\Phi \geq (1-\eta)P(1-\Phi) \tag{87}$$

Combining (80) and (87), we obtain:

$$P \geq \frac{c}{\eta} \qquad (88)$$

The price is thus higher than c/η, the traditional markup formula. After inserting (88) into (80), we finally have:

$$\Phi \geq \frac{1-\eta}{1-\beta\psi\eta} \qquad (89)$$

and the probability $1 - \Phi$ of being rationed is therefore bounded above:

$$1 - \Phi \leq \frac{\eta(1-\beta\psi)}{1-\beta\psi\eta} \qquad (90)$$

We see that this upper bound on $1 - \Phi$, that is, on the probability of being rationed, is an increasing function of η. The intuition is that the more inelastic the demand (a low η), the higher the profits per unit sold, and therefore the lower the desired probability of rationing, because the firm does not want to ration such profitable customers.

14.5 Credit

At the time of the Great Depression, credit had been given a central role in explaining the 1929 crisis. Notably, Irving Fisher (1932, 1933) explained how failure of the credit system had a fundamental role in propagating deflationary shocks.

Later, however, credit more or less disappeared from macroeconomic models. This is mainly because the central macroeconomic model for a few decades, the IS-LM model (Hicks, 1937), had money and not credit as the central monetary explanatory variable.

In more recent times, credit has again become an active subject of study, notably because, as we shall see, theories of imperfect information allow one to explain in a rigorous way why credit markets may not function in a perfectly efficient way and amplify some shocks in a way that cannot be modeled by simply considering money.[6]

---

6. Modern versions started with Jaffee and Russell (1976), Keeton (1979), and Stiglitz and Weiss (1981). See the surveys by Gertler (1988), Jaffee and Stiglitz (1990), and Bernanke and Gertler (1995). The role of credit in fluctuations is notably studied in Bernanke and Gertler (1989), Greenwald and Stiglitz (1993), Kiyotaki and Moore (1997), and Bernanke, Gertler, and Gilchrist (1999).

Consumption, Investment, Inventories, and Credit

A central theme is the possibility of credit rationing. In a nutshell, the argument is the following: in the presence of asymmetric information between lenders and borrowers, the profitability of loans as a function of the interest rate may have the shape shown in figure 14.4.

Beyond the interest rate r^* the profitability goes down because due to information problems, a rise in the interest rate leads to a substantial deterioration of the "quality" of borrowers. If the supply of loans is positively related to their profitability, then the supply of loans will look as the bell-shaped curve in figure 14.5. If the Walrasian equilibrium interest rate is to

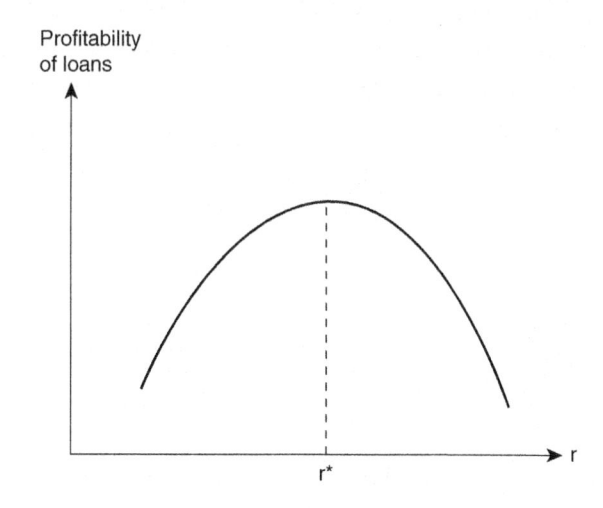

Figure 14.4 The profitability of loans

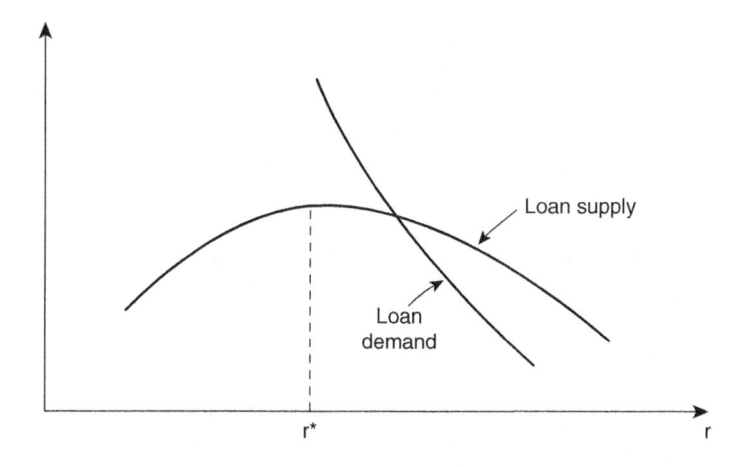

Figure 14.5 A case of credit rationing

the right of r^*, lenders will prefer to lower their interest rate to r^* and ration credit to maximize profitability. There will thus be credit rationing.

Now we describe two very simple models—one based on adverse selection, the other on moral hazard—that will rationalize a curve such as figure 14.4. Before that, we describe a common framework for these two models (our exposition follows Stiglitz and Weiss, 1981).

14.5.1 A Basic Framework

We consider indivisible investments. The bank lends a constant amount B to borrowers at an interest rate r. The gross interest rate is $R = 1 + r$. The gross return on the investment is X, which is a random variable. The ex post distribution of returns between the lender and the borrower follows the lines of the standard debt contract with limited liability.[7] If the investment return is X the borrower receives:

$$\max\,(0, X - RB) \tag{91}$$

and the bank:

$$\min\,(RB, X) \tag{92}$$

We note that the return to the borrower is a convex function of X, which may lead to the choice of investments that are too risky.

Call $\pi(X)$ the density of the probability distribution of the return X. The expected profits of the firm are:

$$\int \max\,(0, X - RB)\,\pi(X)\,dX \tag{93}$$

and those of the bank:

$$\Pi(R) = \int \min\,(RB, X)\,\pi(X)\,dX - B \tag{94}$$

In what follows, we consider a highly simplified distribution of investment projects: (a) project 1 yields X_1 with probability π_1, and 0 with probability

---

7. Townsend (1979) has shown that the standard debt contract can be optimal in case of "costly state verification". See also Gale and Hellwig (1985).

$1-\pi_1$, and (b) project 2 yields X_2 with probability π_2, and 0 with probability $1-\pi_2$. We assume:

$$X_1 < X_2 \qquad \pi_1 > \pi_2 \tag{95}$$

So project 2 is more risky, but more profitable than project 1. No project dominates the other.

14.5.2 An Adverse Selection Story

Assume that there are two types of borrowers, who borrow from the bank and invest in projects 1 or 2. Borrowers of type 1 can only invest in project 1, and are in proportion $\alpha_1 < 1$ in the population. Borrowers of type 2 can only invest in project 2, and are in proportion α_2 in the population, with $\alpha_1 + \alpha_2 = 1$.

The problem comes from the fact that the bank cannot distinguish between the two types of borrowers, so it will have to accept applicants in the same proportion as in the population.

The cut-off interest rates R_1 and R_2 for borrowers of type 1 and 2 are, respectively:

$$R_1 = \frac{X_1}{B} \qquad R_2 = \frac{X_2}{B} \qquad R_1 < R_2 \tag{96}$$

For $R < R_1$ both types apply for a loan, for $R_1 < R < R_2$ only borrowers of type 2 apply, for $R > R_2$ nobody applies. The expected profit of the bank is therefore:

$$\Pi(R) = (\alpha_1 \pi_1 + \alpha_2 \pi_2) RB - B \qquad R < R_1 \tag{97}$$

$$\Pi(R) = \pi_2 RB - B \qquad R_1 < R < R_2 \tag{98}$$

Bank profits will be higher for R_1 than for R_2 if $\Pi(R_1) > \Pi(R_2)$, where $\Pi(R_1)$ is given by equation (97), and $\Pi(R_2)$ by equation (98), that is, if:

$$(\alpha_1 \pi_1 + \alpha_2 \pi_2) X_1 > \pi_2 X_2 \tag{99}$$

or:

$$\frac{X_1}{X_2} > \frac{\pi_2}{\alpha_1 \pi_1 + \alpha_2 \pi_2} \tag{100}$$

This case is represented in figure 14.6.

We see that under condition (100), profitability on loans is not monotonously increasing in the interest rate, but attains a maximum for $R = R_1$, so that we are in a situation similar to that depicted in figure 14.4.

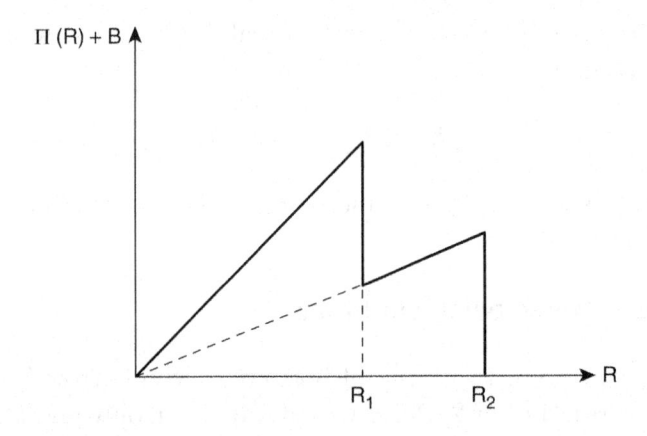

Figure 14.6 An adverse selection story

14.5.3 A Moral Hazard Story

In this case, there is a single type of borrowers. All of them have access to both types of projects and will choose between the two, depending on the interest rate. The representative borrower will choose project 1 if its expected profit is higher than for project 2, that is, if:

$$\pi_1 (X_1 - RB) > \pi_2 (X_2 - RB) \tag{101}$$

This defines a cut-off rate $\hat{R}$, and (101) can be rewritten:

$$R < \hat{R} = \frac{\pi_1 X_1 - \pi_2 X_2}{(\pi_1 - \pi_2) B} \tag{102}$$

Borrowers will choose project 1 if $R < \hat{R}$, project 2 if $R > \hat{R}$. We easily see that:

$$\hat{R} < R_1 = \frac{X_1}{B} \qquad \hat{R} < R_2 = \frac{X_2}{B} \tag{103}$$

Expected bank profit is equal to:

$$\Pi(R) = \pi_1 RB - B \qquad R < \hat{R} \tag{104}$$

$$\Pi(R) = \pi_2 RB - B \qquad R > \hat{R} \tag{105}$$

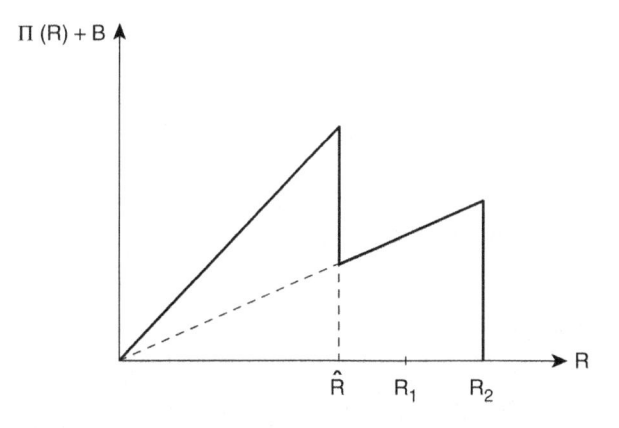

Consumption, Investment, Inventories, and Credit 359

[Figure: graph with axes Π(R)+B vs R, showing two sawtooth peaks at R₁ and R₂, with R̂ marked]

Figure 14.7 A moral hazard story

The profit for $\hat{R}$ (equal to $\pi_1 \hat{R} B - B$) is greater than the profit for R_2 (equal to $\pi_2 R_2 B - B$) if, using (102):

$$\pi_1 \left(\frac{\pi_1 X_1 - \pi_2 X_2}{\pi_1 - \pi_2} \right) > \pi_2 X_2 \tag{106}$$

or:

$$\frac{\pi_1 X_1}{\pi_2 X_2} > \frac{2\pi_1 - \pi_2}{\pi_1} > 1 \tag{107}$$

This case is represented in figure 14.7. Here again, the profitability of loans reaches a maximum for a finite interest rate $\hat{R}$, as in figure 14.4.

Appendix 14.1: An Imperfect Competition Accelerator

We now prove that the dynamics of capital in section 14.3.4 is given by equation (58). Recall that the firm maximizes:

$$E \sum_t \beta^t \left[\frac{\mathcal{D}_t - AK_t}{\alpha} AK_t - J_t - \delta K_t - \frac{aJ_t^2}{2} \right] \tag{108}$$

subject to the capital accumulation equation:

$$K_{t+1} = K_t + J_t \tag{109}$$

The Lagrangian is:

$$E \sum_t \beta^t \left[\frac{D_t - AK_t}{\alpha} AK_t - J_t - \delta K_t - \frac{aJ_t^2}{2} \right]$$

$$+ E \sum_t \beta^t q_t \left(J_t + K_t - K_{t+1} \right) \qquad (110)$$

The first-order conditions in J_t and K_{t+1} are:

$$q_t = 1 + aJ_t = 1 + a\left(K_{t+1} - K_t\right) \qquad (111)$$

$$q_t = \beta E_t q_{t+1} + \frac{\beta A}{\alpha} E_t D_{t+1} - \frac{2\beta A^2}{\alpha} E_t K_{t+1} - \beta \delta \qquad (112)$$

Because K_{t+1} is known in t, we have $E_t K_{t+1} = K_{t+1}$. Combining (111) and (112), and ignoring irrelevant constants, we obtain:

$$\left(\alpha a + \alpha \beta a + 2\beta A^2\right) K_{t+1} - \alpha a K_t - \alpha \beta a E_t K_{t+2} = \beta A E_t D_{t+1} \qquad (113)$$

This can be rewritten with the lag operator $\mathcal{L}$:

$$\left(\alpha a + \alpha \beta a + 2\beta A^2 - \alpha a \mathcal{L} - \alpha \beta a \mathcal{L}^{-1}\right) K_{t+1} = \beta A E_t D_{t+1} \qquad (114)$$

Now we factor the term within the parenthesis in (114) as:

$$\alpha a + \alpha \beta a + 2\beta A^2 - \alpha a \mathcal{L} - \alpha \beta a \mathcal{L}^{-1} = \chi \left(1 - \lambda \mathcal{L}\right)\left(1 - \mu \mathcal{L}^{-1}\right) \qquad (115)$$

Identifying the terms one by one, we find:

$$\mu = \beta \lambda \qquad \chi = \alpha a / \lambda \qquad (116)$$

where the autoregressive root λ is the smallest root of the characteristic polynomial:

$$\Psi(\lambda) = \beta \lambda^2 - \left(1 + \beta + \frac{2\beta A^2}{\alpha a}\right) \lambda + 1 = 0 \qquad (117)$$

which is equation (59). We compute:

$$\Psi(0) = 1 \qquad (118)$$

$$\Psi(1) = -\frac{2\beta A^2}{\alpha a} > 0 \qquad (119)$$

The smallest root is thus between 0 and 1. Using (115), equation (114) is rewritten as:

$$\chi(1 - \lambda\mathcal{L})(1 - \mu\mathcal{L}^{-1}) K_{t+1} = \beta A E_t \mathcal{D}_{t+1} \qquad (120)$$

and the solution for capital is written, combining (116) and (120):

$$K_{t+1} = \frac{\beta\lambda A E_t \mathcal{D}_{t+1}}{\alpha a (1 - \lambda\mathcal{L})(1 - \beta\lambda\mathcal{L}^{-1})} \qquad (121)$$

or:

$$K_{t+1} = \lambda K_t + \frac{\beta\lambda A}{\alpha a} \sum_{j=1}^{\infty} (\beta\lambda)^{j-1} E_t \mathcal{D}_{t+j} \qquad (122)$$

which is equation (58).

Appendix 14.2: Inventories

In this appendix we derive a number of optimal output-price policies in the presence of inventories.

Exogenous Prices

We use the method of dynamic programming (mathematical appendix, section A.5), and construct a valuation function for inventories, denoted $V_t(I_t)$. This is the expected value of discounted profits from time t onward:

$$E\left[\sum_{t=0}^{\infty} \beta^t (PS_t - cY_t)\right] \qquad (123)$$

when an optimal production policy is followed, and conditional on the initial value of I_t.

As we noted, the firm can be in one of two regimes: excess supply, where transactions are equal to demand ξ_t, or excess demand, where transactions are equal to supply $Y_t + I_t$. The transition occurs for the value of the stochastic shock ξ_t such that the two are equal, that is:

$$\xi_t = Y_t + I_t \tag{124}$$

As a consequence, $V_t(I_t)$ is characterized by the following recursive equation:

$$V_t(I_t) = \text{Max}_{Y_t \geq 0} \left\{ \int_0^{Y_t+I_t} \left[P\xi_t + \beta V_{t+1} \left[\psi \left(Y_t + I_t - \xi_t \right) \right] \right] \phi(\xi_t) \, d\xi_t \right.$$
$$\left. + \int_{Y_t+I_t}^{\infty} \left[P(Y_t + I_t) + \beta V_{t+1}(0) \right] \phi(\xi_t) \, d\xi_t - cY_t \right\} \tag{125}$$

Assuming an interior solution in Y_t, which means that I_t is small enough for current production to be positive, we obtain the optimal production strategy by equating to 0 the partial derivative of the right-hand side of (125) with respect to Y_t. This yields the first order condition:

$$\int_0^{Y_t+I_t} \beta \varphi V'_{t+1} \left[\psi \left(Y_t + I_t - \xi_t \right) \right] \phi(\xi_t) \, d\xi_t$$
$$+ \int_{Y_t+I_t}^{\infty} P\phi(\xi_t) \, d\xi_t - c = 0 \tag{126}$$

We note immediately that this equation is actually an equation in $Y_t + I_t$. This means that for I_t smaller than a threshold value Q (which we will characterize shortly), optimal production is given by:

$$Y_t = Q - I_t \tag{127}$$

This implies that $V_t(I_t)$ is linear in the range $0 \leq I_t \leq Q$. Indeed, inserting the optimal strategy (127) into equation (125), we find:

$$V_t(I_t) = \int_0^Q \left[P\xi_t + \beta V_{t+1} \left[\psi(Q - \xi_t) \right] \right] \phi(\xi_t) \, d\xi_t$$
$$+ \int_Q^{\infty} \left[PQ + \beta V_{t+1}(0) \right] \phi(\xi_t) \, d\xi_t - c(Q - I_t) \tag{128}$$

and thus $V'_t(I_t) = c$ for all $0 \leq I_t \leq Q$. We introduce this value into equation (126) and obtain the following equation, which determines the optimal Q:

$$\int_0^Q \beta\psi c\phi(\xi_t)\,d\xi_t + \int_Q^\infty P\phi(\xi_t)\,d\xi_t - c = 0 \tag{129}$$

Equation (129) can be rewritten more simply, using the cumulative density function of demand Φ:

$$\Phi(Q) = \frac{P-c}{P-\beta\psi c} \tag{130}$$

which is equation (68).

Endogenous Prices

We again solve the problem using dynamic programming and construct a valuation function for inventories denoted $V_t(I_t)$. As before, the firm can be in one of two regimes: excess supply, where transactions are equal to demand $\xi_t g(P_t)$, or excess demand, where transactions are equal to supply $Y_t + I_t$. The transition occurs for the value of the stochastic shock ξ_t such that the two are equal:

$$\xi_t g(P_t) = Y_t + I_t \tag{131}$$

Therefore $V(I)$ is characterized by the following recursive equation (we suppress the time indices to make notation more compact):

$$V(I) = \text{Max}\left\{\int_0^{(Y+I)/g(P)} [P\xi g(P) + \beta V(\psi[Y+I-\xi g(P)])]\,\phi(\xi)\,d\xi \right.$$
$$\left. + \int_{(Y+I)/g(P)}^\infty [P(Y+I) + \beta V(0)]\,\phi(\xi)\,d\xi - cY\right\} \tag{132}$$

Assuming an interior solution in P and Y (which means that I is small enough for current production to be positive), we obtain the optimal price-production strategy by equating to 0 the partial derivatives of the right-hand side of (132) with respect to P and Y. This yields the two equations:

$$\int_0^{(Y+I)/g(P)} [g(P) + Pg'(P) - \beta\psi g'(P) V'(\psi[Y+I-\xi g(P)])]\,\xi\phi(\xi)\,d\xi$$
$$+ \int_{(Y+I)/g(P)}^\infty (Y+I)\,\phi(\xi)\,d\xi = 0 \tag{133}$$

$$\int_0^{(Y+I)/g(P)} \beta\varphi V'\left(\psi\left[Y+I-\xi g(P)\right]\right)\phi(\xi)\,d\xi$$

$$+ \int_{(Y+I)/g(P)}^{\infty} P\phi(\xi)\,d\xi - c = 0 \qquad (134)$$

We note immediately that these two equations are equations in $Y+I$ and P. So for I smaller than a threshold value Q (which we characterize next), the optimal price is independent of I while the optimal production is given by:

$$Y = Q - I \qquad (135)$$

Inserting this optimal strategy into equation (132), we find that $V'(I) = c$ for all $I \leq Q$. We introduce this value into equations (133) and (134) and obtain the following two equations, which determine the optimal P and Q:

$$\int_0^{Q/g(P)} \left[g(P) + Pg'(P) - \beta\psi cg'(P)\right]\xi\phi(\xi)\,d\xi + \int_{Q/g(P)}^{\infty} Q\phi(\xi)\,d\xi = 0 \qquad (136)$$

$$\int_0^{Q/g(P)} \beta\psi c\phi(\xi)\,d\xi + \int_{Q/g(P)}^{\infty} P\phi(\xi)\,d\xi - c = 0 \qquad (137)$$

Let us define:

$$q = \frac{Q}{g(P)} \qquad (138)$$

Equation (137) can be rewritten more simply, using the cumulative density function Φ:

$$\Phi(q) = \frac{P-c}{P-\beta\psi c} \qquad (139)$$

and equation (136) becomes:

$$\int_0^q \left[g(P) + Pg'(P) - \beta\psi cg'(P)\right]\xi\phi(\xi)\,d\xi + \int_q^{\infty} qg(P)\phi(\xi)\,d\xi = 0 \qquad (140)$$

Problems

Problem 14.1: Consumption and Financial Investment

We want to show how random returns influence consumption and savings.[8] A household maximizes expected discounted utility:

$$E \sum_t \beta^t U(C_t)$$

At the beginning of each period t the agent has financial assets $\mathcal{A}_t$, which he allocates between consumption C_t and savings $\mathcal{A}_t - C_t$. These savings are invested in a risky investment that will bring in the next period a stochastic gross rate of return R_{t+1}. To simplify, we assume that R_t is i.i.d.

As a consequence, financial assets next period are equal to:

$$\mathcal{A}_{t+1} = R_{t+1}(\mathcal{A}_t - C_t)$$

We use the method of dynamic programming (mathematical appendix A.5) and define:

$$V_t(\mathcal{A}_t) = \text{Max } E_t \sum_s \beta^{s-t} U(C_s)$$

subject to the constraint that initial assets are $\mathcal{A}_t$.

1. Write the dynamic programming equation linking V_t and V_{t+1}. The problem is actually stationary, so $V_t = V_{t+1} = V$. Write the functional equation giving $V(\mathcal{A}_t)$.
2. Assume

$$U(C_t) = \frac{C_t^{1-\theta}}{1-\theta} \qquad \theta > 0$$

and conjecture that V has the form:

$$V(\mathcal{A}_t) = \frac{\zeta \mathcal{A}_t^{1-\theta}}{1-\theta}$$

Show that optimal consumption is characterized by a constant propensity to consume out of assets. Compute this propensity to consume.

---

8. This model was developed by Samuelson (1969), Hakansson (1970), and Merton (1969, 1971).

Problem 14.2: Investment and Installation Costs (1)

A firm has a production function:

$$Y_t = AK_t - \frac{BK_t^2}{2} \qquad A > 0 \qquad B > 0$$

and an installation cost that is a function of *net* investment:

$$C(J_t) = \frac{aJ_t^2}{2}$$

where $J_t = I_t - \delta K_t$. The firm maximizes discounted profits:

$$\sum_t \left(\frac{1}{1+r}\right)^t [Y_t - I_t - C(J_t)]$$

subject to the equation of accumulation of capital:

$$K_{t+1} = I_t + (1-\delta) K_t = J_t + K_t$$

The Lagrangian is:

$$\sum_t^\infty \left(\frac{1}{1+r}\right)^t \left[AK_t - \frac{BK_t^2}{2} - J_t - \delta K_t - \frac{aJ_t^2}{2}\right]$$

$$+ \sum_t \left(\frac{1}{1+r}\right)^t q_t \left(J_t + K_t - K_{t+1}\right)$$

1. Give the first-order conditions for q_t and K_t.
2. Compute the stationary state.
3. Derive a dynamic relation linking successive values of capital.
4. Show that the dynamics of capital has an autoregressive root λ. Give the characteristic polynomial of which λ is a solution and show that $0 < \lambda < 1$.

Problem 14.3: Investment and Installation Costs (2)

A firm has a production function:

$$Y_t = AK_t - \frac{BK_t^2}{2} \qquad A > 0 \qquad B > 0$$

The difference from problem 14.2 is that the installation cost is now a function of *gross* investment I_t:

$$\mathcal{C}(I_t) = \frac{aI_t^2}{2}$$

and the equation of accumulation of capital is:

$$K_{t+1} = I_t + (1-\delta)K_t$$

The firm maximizes discounted profits:

$$\sum_t \left(\frac{1}{1+r}\right)^t [Y_t - I_t - \mathcal{C}(I_t)]$$

subject to the capital accumulation equation.

1. Following the notation of problem 14.2, give the Lagrangian corresponding to this maximization problem, and derive the first-order conditions in K_t and q_t.
2. Compute the steady state.
3. Derive a dynamic relation linking successive values of capital.
4. Show that the dynamics of capital has an autoregressive root λ between 0 and 1.

Problem 14.4: Inventory and Output with Autocorrelated Demand

We consider the same model as in section 14.4.2, but instead of assuming $D_t = \xi_t$, we assume that demand has an autoregressive component:

$$D_t = \rho D_{t-1} + \xi_t \qquad 0 < \rho < 1$$

where the ξ_t's are i.i.d. The rest of the model is the same.

1. Use the same dynamic programming method as in appendix 14.2, and give the equation, similar to (125), giving $V(I_t)$.
2. Assume an interior solution and derive the first order conditions.

3. Show that for low enough I_t, the optimal production is:

$$Y_t = \rho D_{t-1} + Q - I_t$$

where Q is determined by:

$$\Phi(Q) = \frac{P - c}{P - \beta\psi c}$$

15

Unemployment: Basic Models

15.1 Introduction

In previous chapters we used the convenient fiction of a representative household. When there were fluctuations in employment, the global amount of employment was implicitly shared equally among all workers. This is not really a theory of unemployment but of underemployment.

In reality, although a number of employed workers experience fluctuations in the amount of hours they work individually, we observe that a very large part in the fluctuations of total hours is achieved through variations in the number of workers employed, and therefore in the unemployment rate. In this chapter and the next we study a number of traditional explanations of unemployment.

As we will see, there are many alternative explanations for unemployment. Because of this variety of explanations, our exposition proceeds as follows.

First, in this chapter we attempt to present a large number of explanations in a static, one-period framework. This allows us to capture many salient feature of these theories. The dynamic aspects of the theories are studied in chapter 16.

Section 15.2 describes a simple framework within which subsequent theories will be studied. Section 15.3 describes three classic models of trade union behavior: the monopoly trade union, efficient bargains, and the "right to manage" model.

Section 15.4 studies the "insiders-outsiders" theory, where "selfish" insiders negotiate their wages without concern for the outsiders out of the firm. Section 15.5 studies efficiency wage theories where firms voluntarily pay workers wages above those that would allow them to absorb all the unemployed. Section 15.6 studies various versions of the implicit contracts theories, where relatively rigid wages serve as insurance for workers and may correspondingly create unemployment in some states of nature.

15.2 A Simple Framework

We study in this chapter several unemployment theories with fairly different inspirations.[1] To not bury the reader under a multitude of different frameworks and notations, we use throughout a common unified framework, which we describe now.

15.2.1 Workers' Utility and the Reservation Wage

We assume that each worker either works or does not work. She has a utility $U(c) - e$ when she is employed and $U(c)$ when she is unemployed, where c is consumption and e (like effort) is the disutility of working. We assume that workers consume all their wage income so that $c = \omega$, where ω is the real wage. The utility of a worker who actually works is thus:

$$U(\omega) - e \qquad (1)$$

If the worker is unemployed, she receives a real unemployment benefit b, so in that case $c = b$ and her utility is $U(b)$.

Call L the quantity of labor demanded by the firm, and N the number of workers already in the firm. If $L > N$, the firm must hire outside workers. If $L < N$ the N incumbent workers are assumed to be allocated randomly to the jobs, with equal probabilities. In that case, each of the N incumbent workers has ex ante a probability L/N to be employed and $1 - L/N$ to be unemployed. As a consequence her expected utility is:

$$\frac{L}{N}[U(\omega) - e] + \left(1 - \frac{L}{N}\right) U(b) \qquad (2)$$

A worker actually will not want to work if her real wage ω falls below the reservation wage ϖ defined by:

$$U(\varpi) = U(b) + e \qquad (3)$$

---

1. For overviews on the subject, see Cahuc and Zylberberg (1996); Layard, Nickell, and Jackman (1991); and Oswald (1982, 1985).

Taking into account this reservation wage, the utility function (2) is rewritten:

$$\frac{L}{N}\left[U\left(\omega\right) - U\left(\varpi\right)\right] + U\left(b\right) \qquad \omega \geq \varpi \qquad (4)$$

$$U\left(b\right) \qquad \omega \leq \varpi \qquad (5)$$

15.2.2 Benevolent versus Selfish Trade Unions

We interpreted above L/N as the probability for one of the N workers to be employed, so this formula is, strictly speaking, valid only for $L \leq N$. In the case $L > N$, that is, if the firm hires, two polar cases have been considered in the literature.

If incumbent workers care about those newly hired as much as about themselves (we call this the "benevolent" trade union case), then formula (4) continues to be valid for $L > N$. We rewrite it, omitting constants:

$$V\left(\omega, L\right) = L\left[U\left(\omega\right) - U\left(\varpi\right)\right] \qquad (6)$$

One also finds in the literature the assumption that incumbent workers care only about themselves (the "selfish" trade union case), in which case the utility function (6) is replaced by:

$$V\left(\omega, L\right) = \min\left(L, N\right)\left[U\left(\omega\right) - U\left(\varpi\right)\right] \qquad (7)$$

We generally use the simpler benevolent version, except, of course, when selfishness is at the heart of the theory studied, as it will be when we study the insiders-outsiders theory (section 15.4).

15.2.3 The Firm's Objective

The firm has a production function $AF\left(L\right)$ where A is a variable that can be interpreted as a technological shock, as we have already done. The function $F\left(L\right)$ is assumed to be strictly concave in L.

The objective of the firm is to maximize profits $AF\left(L\right) - \omega L$. The first-order condition in L is that the marginal revenue be equal to the real wage ω:

$$AF'\left(L\right) = \omega \qquad (8)$$

Equation (8) can be inverted. This yields a demand for labor $L\left(\omega, A\right)$, which, because F is strictly concave in L, is decreasing in ω.

15.3 Three Classic Trade Union Models

Before going to more specific theories, we describe three classic models of the interaction between trade unions and firms. The trade union is supposed to adopt the utility of the representative worker.

15.3.1 The Monopoly Union

The most standard model, that of the monopoly union (Dunlop, 1944), assumes that the trade union chooses the wage on behalf of the workers, and then the firm chooses the level of employment it will hire at that wage.

The union will take the demand for labor $L(\omega, A)$ as given, and maximizes the utility of the representative worker $V(\omega, L)$ (formula 6), where L is replaced by $L(\omega, A)$:

$$L(\omega, A)\left[U(\omega) - U(\varpi)\right] \tag{9}$$

The condition for maximization in ω is, assuming an interior maximum:

$$L_\omega(\omega, A)\left[U(\omega) - U(\varpi)\right] + L(\omega, A)U'(\omega) = 0 \tag{10}$$

This maximization determines $\omega(A)$ and $L(A)$, which correspond to the tangency of the labor demand curve and a isoutility curve. This is represented in figure 15.1.

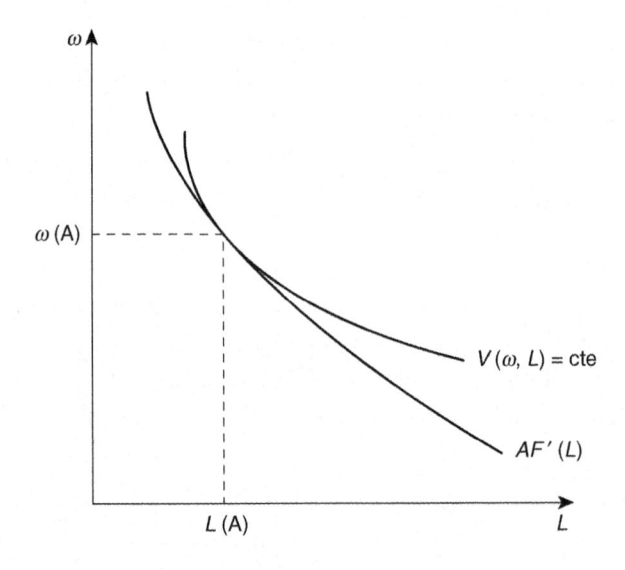

Figure 15.1 The monopoly union

Unemployment: Basic Models

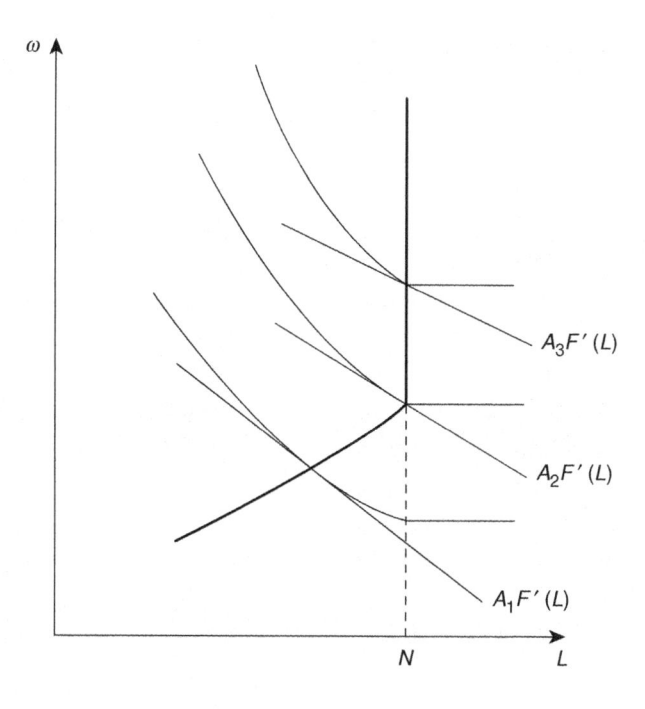

Figure 15.2 Monopoly union: the expansion path

The experiment can be repeated for all possible values of A. The relation between ω and L, as A varies, is called the expansion path (figure 15.2). We may note that if the union is selfish (equation 7), and its membership is N, the expansion path becomes vertical for $L = N$ (this is the case represented in figure 15.2). The trade union will never choose a wage such that employment would become higher than the membership, but rather "appropriate" the benefits of increases in A under the form of increases in the real wage ω.

Also note that in the case of a constant elasticity of the demand for labor, the real wage ω will be constant on the expansion path as long as $L \leq N$. Indeed, call:

$$\epsilon = -\frac{\omega L_\omega(\omega, A)}{L(\omega, A)} \tag{11}$$

Then condition (10) is rewritten:

$$\epsilon[U(\omega) - U(\varpi)] = \omega U'(\omega) \tag{12}$$

which determines a constant ω. As can be expected, the higher ϵ is, the closer ω is to ϖ.

15.3.2 Efficient Bargains

The two-step setup of the monopoly union model makes one suspect that the outcome may not be efficient. To see that, figure 15.3 represents the monopoly union equilibrium, as well as the isoutility curve of the workers, and the isoprofit curve of the firms which goes through the equilibrium point. This confirms that there are combinations of ω and L that make both the firm and the trade union better off. In figure 15.3, these are the combinations in the lentil-shaped area toward which the arrow is pointing.

This led Leontief (1946) and McDonald and Solow (1981) to propose the notion of efficient bargains, that is, Pareto-optimal combinations of ω and L. Graphically the efficient bargains locus is the set of tangency points between isoprofit and isoutility curves (figure 15.4).

We can obtain an analytical characterization of efficient bargains by maximizing a weighted sum of the trade union's utility and the firms' profits:

$$\max L\left[U\left(\omega\right) - U\left(\varpi\right)\right] + \lambda\left[AF\left(L\right) - \omega L\right] \tag{13}$$

where λ is somehow the relative weight of profits. The first-order conditions with respect to L and ω are:

$$U\left(\omega\right) - U\left(\varpi\right) + \lambda\left[AF'\left(L\right) - \omega\right] = 0 \tag{14}$$

$$LU'\left(\omega\right) - \lambda L = 0 \tag{15}$$

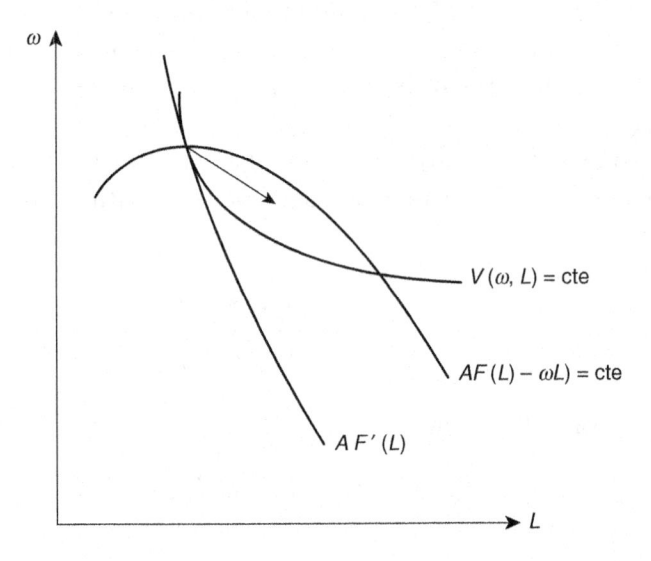

Figure 15.3 The inefficiency of the monopoly union

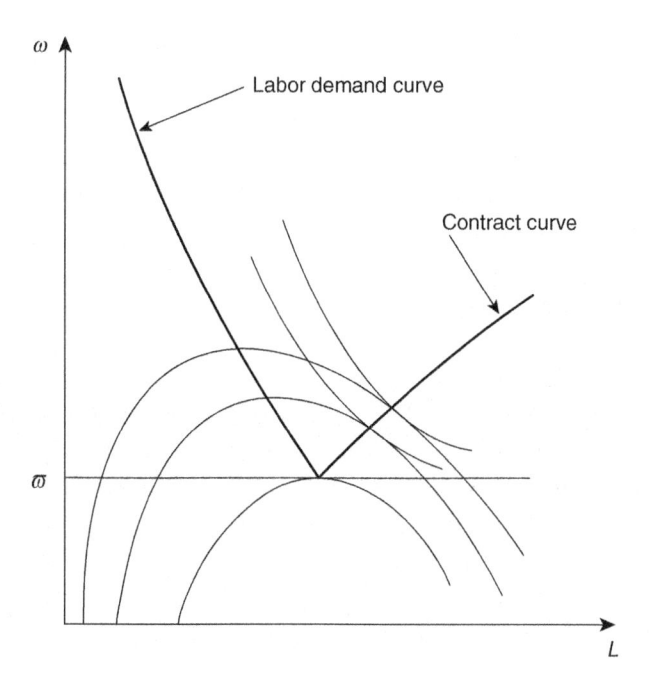

Figure 15.4 Efficient bargains

Eliminating λ, we find the equation of the locus of efficient bargains:

$$U(\omega) - U(\varpi) + U'(\omega)\left[AF'(L) - \omega\right] = 0 \qquad (16)$$

We note first that the curve of efficient bargains intersects the labor demand curve for $\omega = \varpi$. Second, this curve slopes upward, since, differentiating (16) we find:

$$\frac{d\omega}{dL} = \frac{[U'(\omega)]^2 AF''(L)}{U''(\omega)[U(\omega) - U(\varpi)]} > 0 \qquad (17)$$

Along this locus we have, from (16), and if $\omega > \varpi$:

$$AF'(L) < \omega \qquad (18)$$

This means that under such efficient bargains the firm is constrained to employ more workers than it wants at the given real wage. There is thus involuntary exchange in the sense described in chapter 5. As a consequence, and because in reality it is usually not allowed to contract on fixed quantities of labor, one may expect that these efficient contracts might be difficult to implement in the real world. We return to this issue when studying implicit contracts in section 15.6.

We may note that condition (16) defines an infinity of contracts. To determine a single contract, one has to specify a given value of λ (somehow the relative strength of firms in the bargaining), and use both (14) and (15) with this given value of λ.

15.3.3 Right to Manage

The right to manage model (Nickell and Andrews, 1983) shares with the monopoly trade union model the assumption that the quantity of labor is on the demand curve. However, instead of assuming that the wage level is unilaterally determined by the trade union, it is assumed that this wage level is bargained between the firm and the trade union. As before, we assume that the trade union's utility is:

$$V(\omega, L) = L[U(\omega) - U(\varpi)] \qquad (19)$$

The firm's production function is:

$$Y = \frac{AL^{1-\alpha}}{1-\alpha} \qquad 0 < \alpha < 1 \qquad (20)$$

The demand for labor is thus:

$$L(\omega, A) = \left(\frac{\omega}{A}\right)^{-1/\alpha} \qquad (21)$$

and the corresponding real profits:

$$\Pi(\omega, A) = \frac{\alpha A}{1-\alpha}\left(\frac{\omega}{A}\right)^{(\alpha-1)/\alpha} \qquad (22)$$

The result of the negotiation is given by the maximum of the Nash product:[2]

$$(V - \bar{V})^\gamma (\Pi - \bar{\Pi})^{1-\gamma} \qquad 0 \leq \gamma \leq 1 \qquad (23)$$

where γ is an index of negotiation power of the trade union, and $\bar{V}$ and $\bar{\Pi}$ are what the trade union and the firm would respectively obtain in the case

---

2. See Nash (1950); Rubinstein (1982); Hoel (1986); Binmore, Rubinstein, and Wolinski (1986). See mathematical appendix A.6 for a justification of this Nash bargaining solution as the outcome of a bargaining process with alternating offers over time.

negotiations fail. We have:

$$\bar{V} = 0 \qquad \bar{\Pi} = 0 \qquad (24)$$

The Nash product (23) thus becomes:

$$[L(\omega, A)]^\gamma [U(\omega) - U(\varpi)]^\gamma [\Pi(\omega, A)]^{1-\gamma} \qquad (25)$$

Maximization of this expression with respect to ω gives the condition:

$$\frac{U(\omega) - U(\varpi)}{\omega U'(\omega)} = \frac{\alpha\gamma}{1 - \alpha + \alpha\gamma} \qquad (26)$$

As an example, if $U(\omega) = \omega^a$, $a \leq 1$, the above condition yields:

$$\frac{\omega^a - \varpi^a}{a\omega^a} = \frac{\alpha\gamma}{1 - \alpha + \alpha\gamma} \qquad (27)$$

We see that the real wage ω, and therefore the level of unemployment, is an increasing function of γ, the index of bargaining power of the trade union.

15.4 Insiders and Outsiders

15.4.1 The Intuition

When the insiders-outsiders theory appeared,[3] it became popular quickly because it naturally produced both higher unemployment than the traditional model and a more persistent one, too. Before going to a formalization, we briefly summarize the central argument.

Those who negotiate wages in a firm are the insiders, that is, workers already in firms. When they negotiate, they take into account the utility of the insiders, not that of outsiders, that is, the unemployed. If business conditions improve, they will negotiate a wage increase rather than an increase in employment, because this employment increase would not bring them any direct utility.

We now formalize this mechanism within the framework of the "right to manage" wage negotiations already studied.

---

3. See notably Lindbeck and Snower (1986, 1987, 1988), Carruth and Oswald (1987), Gottfries and Horn (1987), and Drazen and Gottfries (1994).

15.4.2 A Simple Formalization

We consider a negotiation between a firm and a trade union. The firm has the production function already seen:

$$Y = \frac{AL^{1-\alpha}}{1-\alpha} \qquad 0 < \alpha < 1 \qquad (28)$$

The trade union is now of the selfish type, and therefore its utility function is:

$$V(\omega, L) = L\left[U(\omega) - U(\varpi)\right] \qquad L \leq N \qquad (29)$$

$$V(\omega, L) = N\left[U(\omega) - U(\varpi)\right] \qquad L \geq N \qquad (30)$$

where N is the number of insiders already in the firm.

15.4.3 Resolution

As in section 15.3.3, we assume that the result of the negotiation is given by the maximum of the Nash product:

$$\left(V - \bar{V}\right)^{\gamma} \left(\Pi - \bar{\Pi}\right)^{1-\gamma} \qquad (31)$$

with:

$$\bar{V} = 0 \qquad \bar{\Pi} = 0 \qquad (32)$$

Let us recall the value of the demand for labor and profits (formulas 21 and 22):

$$L(\omega, A) = \left(\frac{\omega}{A}\right)^{-1/\alpha} \qquad \Pi(\omega, A) = \frac{\alpha A}{1-\alpha}\left(\frac{\omega}{A}\right)^{(\alpha-1)/\alpha} \qquad (33)$$

We can distinguish three cases.

- If $L < N$ the utility of the trade union is (29). Inserting this, and the values of $L(\omega, A)$ and $\Pi(\omega, A)$ in equation (33), into (31), we find that the result of the negotiation corresponds to the maximum of:

$$\left[U(\omega) - U(\varpi)\right]^{\gamma} \left(\frac{\omega}{A}\right)^{(\alpha-1-\alpha\gamma)/\alpha} \qquad (34)$$

We obtain the result already seen (formula 26):

$$\frac{U(\omega) - U(\varpi)}{\omega U'(\omega)} = \frac{\alpha\gamma}{1 - \alpha + \alpha\gamma} \qquad (35)$$

- If $L > N$, the trade union is not concerned by any potential supplementary employment, since all of its constituency is employed anyway. As a result the utility of the trade union is now (30), and the Nash bargaining maximand becomes:

$$[U(\omega) - U(\varpi)]^\gamma \left(\frac{\omega}{A}\right)^{(1-\gamma)(\alpha-1)/\alpha} \qquad (36)$$

The first-order condition is:

$$\frac{U(\omega) - U(\varpi)}{\omega U'(\omega)} = \frac{\alpha\gamma}{(1-\gamma)(1-\alpha)} \qquad (37)$$

- Finally there is a third case, intermediate between the two preceding ones, where the firm neither hires nor fires. In that case wage and employment decisions are particularly simple:

$$L = N \qquad (38)$$

$$\omega = AN^{-\alpha} \qquad (39)$$

where $AN^{-\alpha}$ is the marginal productivity when insiders are all employed.

15.4.4 Interpretation

Equations (35) and (37) actually define two values of the real wage, respectively $\omega_{\min}$ and $\omega_{\max}$. We describe the three cases as a function of the technology shock A:

- If $A/N^\alpha < \omega_{\min}$, the real wage is blocked at $\omega_{\min}$ and the firm fires workers:

$$\omega = \omega_{\min} \qquad L = \left(\frac{A}{\omega_{\min}}\right)^{1/\alpha} < N \qquad (40)$$

- If $A/N^\alpha > \omega_{\max}$, the real wage is blocked at $\omega_{\max}$ and the firm hires:

$$\omega = \omega_{\max} \qquad L = \left(\frac{A}{\omega_{\max}}\right)^{1/\alpha} > N \qquad (41)$$

- Finally if $\omega_{\min} \leq A/N^\alpha \leq \omega_{\max}$, employment remains blocked at the level N and adjustment occurs through wages:

$$L = N \qquad \omega = AN^{-\alpha} \qquad (42)$$

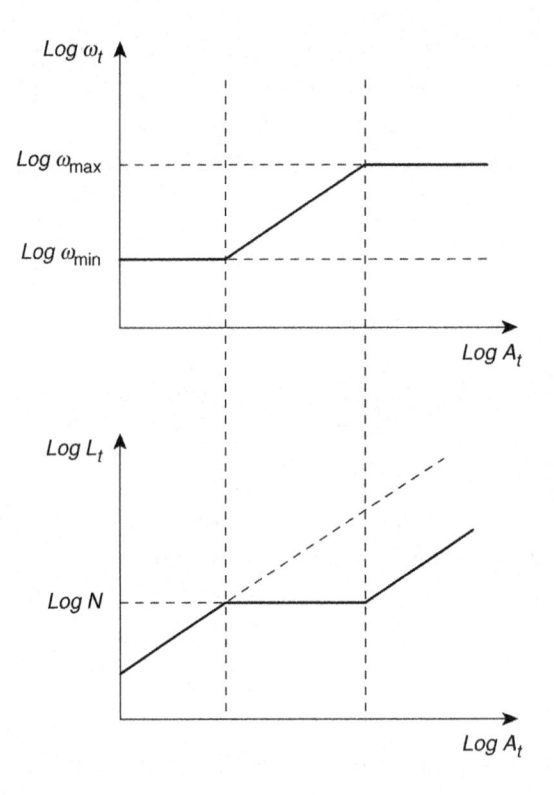

Figure 15.5 The insiders-outsiders model

The three cases are represented in figure 15.5. We may note that if $\gamma = 1$, $\omega_{\max}$ is infinite, so the firm never hires.

We see that the situation is much less favorable to employment than that of the benevolent trade union (which corresponds to formulas 35 and 40). In particular, a positive shock will often translate into wage increases for the insiders rather than an increase in employment. Furthermore, the existence of a range where employment remains constant (equation 42) may lead to a phenomenon of persistence in the level of employment.

15.5 Efficiency Wages

Contrary to some theories above, which are based on some form of market power, efficiency wage theories[4] explain why, even though involuntarily

---

4. For synthetic expositions of various theories of efficiency wages, see Akerlof and Yellen (1986), Katz (1986), Weiss (1991), and Yellen (1984).

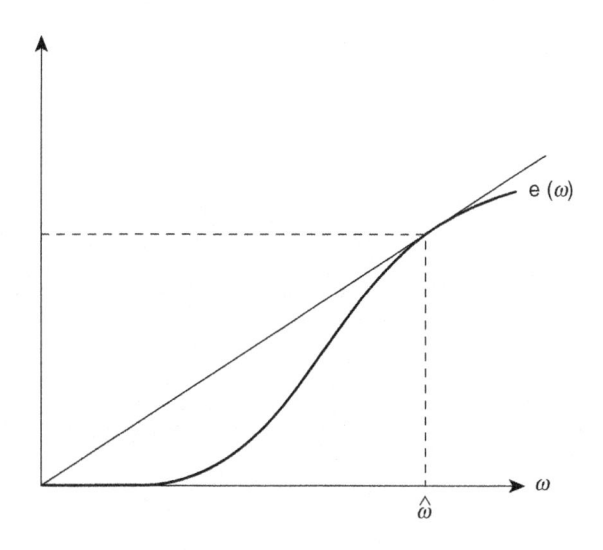

Figure 15.6 Wages and effort

unemployed people would be willing to work at a wage less than the going wage rate, the firms themselves nevertheless do not want to cut wages.

The basic idea is that for various reasons, some of which we describe here, there is a positive relation between wages and workers' productivity, or effort, hence the name "efficiency wages." One often finds in such theories a relation between effort and wages like the one depicted in figure 15.6.

The reasons for positing such a relation were initially based on nutritional arguments (see, for example, Leibenstein, 1957): the real wage determines the quantity of food intake, which is itself a main determinant of productivity. The important feature of the curve is that it is not concave throughout, and this assumption makes sense for the nutritional argument. Indeed, if the food intake is below a minimal vital level, the worker simply cannot work at all, and $e(\omega)$ coincides with the horizontal axis for low values of ω. A nonconcavity necessarily ensues.

15.5.1 The Basic Argument

We describe a first illustrative model due to Solow (1979). It is assumed that effective labor is $e(\omega)L$, where the function $e(\omega)$ looks as the one shown in figure 15.6, and L is the number of workers hired. The firm chooses unilaterally both the real wage ω and the level of employment L. So the program of the firm is:

$$\text{Maximize } F\left[e(\omega)L\right] - \omega L$$

The first-order conditions for ω and L are, assuming an interior maximum:

$$F'\left[e\left(\omega\right)L\right]e'\left(\omega\right) = 1 \qquad (43)$$

$$F'\left[e\left(\omega\right)L\right]e\left(\omega\right) = \omega \qquad (44)$$

These two conditions can be combined to yield:

$$e'\left(\hat{\omega}\right) = \frac{e\left(\hat{\omega}\right)}{\hat{\omega}} \qquad (45)$$

$$F'\left[e\left(\hat{\omega}\right)L\right] = \frac{\hat{\omega}}{e\left(\hat{\omega}\right)} \qquad (46)$$

Condition (45) defines the "efficiency wage" $\hat{\omega}$ at which $\omega/e\left(\omega\right)$ is minimal (figure 15.7). Condition (46) says that the marginal productivity of efficiency labor is equal to marginal cost at the efficiency wage, the traditional condition.

We see that even if there is no minimum wage and workers are willing to take wage cuts, this mechanism will create a downward wage rigidity, because firms themselves do not want to lower wages below $\hat{\omega}$. The type of unemployment that may result is thus involuntary.

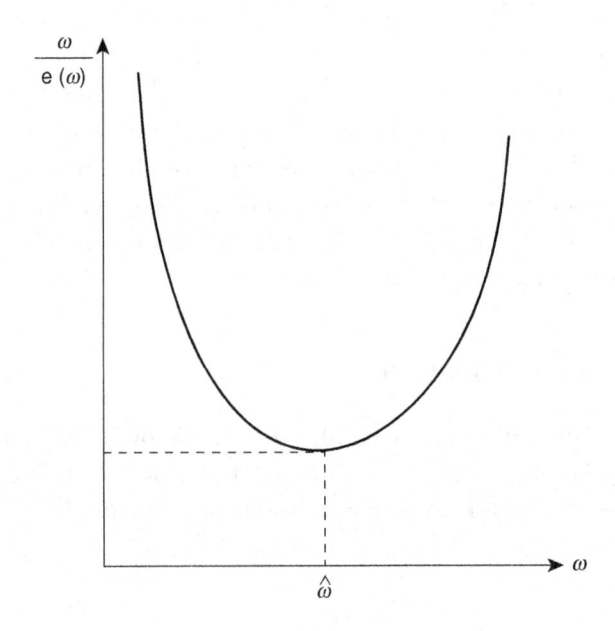

Figure 15.7 The efficiency wage

15.5.2 Efficiency Wages and Imperfect Information

Since the early efficiency wage theories, which were based on nutritional arguments, several other arguments have been proposed. We give two examples, based on imperfect information.

Adverse selection theories. Some productivity characteristics of workers are assumed to be not observable, so the employers cannot directly control the "quality" of the workers. Consequently the quality mix of applicants depends on the wage offered, and the quality mix of those who quit depends on the wage paid to current employees. Thus higher wages can lead to a higher quality of the labor force.

Moral hazard theories. The firm has imperfect information on some actions of workers (for example, their effort) due to monitoring costs. Firms use a high wage as an incentive not to shirk. Of course there must be an effective threat to workers caught shirking, such as firing them, as in the model that we describe next.

15.5.3 The Shirking Model

We describe a well-known model in the second category, the "shirking model" (Shapiro and Stiglitz, 1984). Although the original model is dynamic, we describe a "static" version of the model, which is somewhat simpler and nevertheless captures the essentials of the model. In the next chapter we describe the original dynamic version.

We recall briefly the basic features of the economy. There is a large number of firms producing a homogeneous output with the production function:

$$Y = F(L) \qquad (47)$$

There are N_0 workers who supply one unit of labor each. Each worker is either employed or unemployed. An unemployed worker receives an unemployment benefit b from which she derives a utility $U(b)$.

We assume that existing technology is productive enough to ensure full employment (i.e., $L = N_0$) when markets are competitive, that is:

$$F'(N_0) \geq \varpi \qquad (48)$$

where the reservation wage ϖ has already been defined (equation 3).

The worker who has a job has now two options. She can either make the effort e, in which case her utility is $U(\omega) - e$, or shirk, making no effort, in which case her utility is $U(\omega)$. In this last case she will be detected with probability d and fired.

15.5.4 The No-shirking Condition

If the worker does not shirk, her utility is $U(\omega) - e$. If she shirks, her utility will be $dU(b) + (1-d)U(\omega)$, as she will remain employed with probability $1-d$, and be fired with probability d. She will not shirk only if the first utility is greater than the second, that is, if:

$$U(\omega) - e \geq dU(b) + (1-d)U(\omega) \tag{49}$$

or:

$$U(\omega) - U(\varpi) \geq \frac{(1-d)e}{d} \tag{50}$$

This no-shirking condition defines a minimal real wage the firm must pay the workers to induce them not to shirk. We may note that for $d = 1$, that is, if there is perfect information, the no-shirking wage is equal to the reservation wage ϖ. But as soon as $d < 1$, this wage will be higher than the reservation wage and there may be unemployment (figure 15.8).

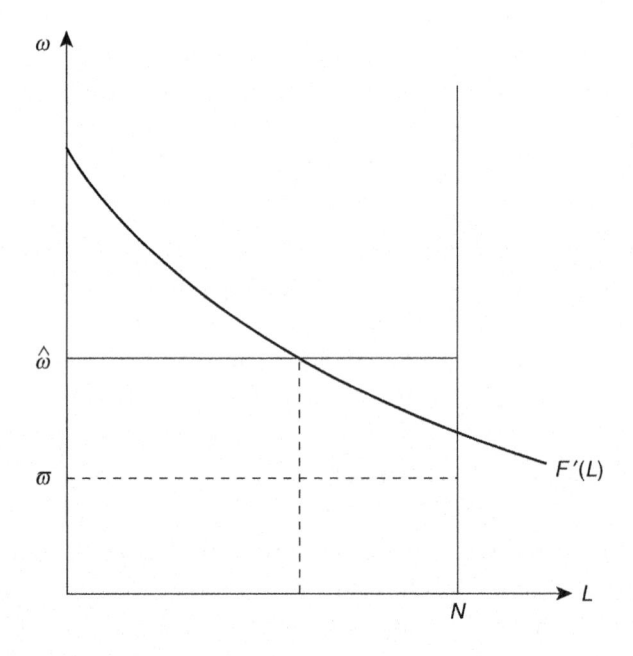

Figure 15.8 The shirking model

15.6 Implicit Contracts

The theory of implicit contracts[5] was designed initially to explain both wage rigidity and underemployment. The basic idea is that firms have better access to financial markets than workers and are less risk averse. As a consequence they can "insure" workers by giving them smoother wages. Indeed, if there was no such scheme, wages would be high in good times and low in bad times. Under implicit contracts the firm gives lower wages in good times, higher in bad ones. This was supposed to result in underemployment in the bad times.

15.6.1 Implicit Contracts: The Traditional Model

The uncertainty in the model is represented by states of nature (see chapter 6) indexed by s. The probability of state s is π_s. Let us call ω_s, ϖ_s, and L_s the real wage, reservation wage, and employment in state s. The revenue of firms in state s is $A_s F(L_s)$. A_s, a stochastic variable, can be interpreted as the value of a technological shock in state s.

The utility of the trade union representing workers is, in the state of nature s:[6]

$$V_s = L_s \left[U(\omega_s) - U(\varpi_s) \right] \tag{51}$$

which generalizes (6) to a stochastic environment. Now the expected utility of the trade union over states of nature is:

$$\sum_s \pi_s V_s = \sum_s \pi_s L_s \left[U(\omega_s) - U(\varpi_s) \right] \tag{52}$$

The firm's profit in state s is:

$$A_s F(L_s) - \omega_s L_s \tag{53}$$

We assume that firms have no risk aversion, so their objective is to maximize expected profits:

$$\sum_s \pi_s \left[A_s F(L_s) - \omega_s L_s \right] \tag{54}$$

---

5. These were initiated in Azariadis (1975), Baily (1974), and Gordon (1974). Synthetic presentations are found in Cooper (1987) and Rosen (1985, 1994).

6. Note that we take here the benevolent version of trade unions' utility, to avoid the discontinuity created by selfishness, and therefore simplify exposition.

The firm and the trade union negotiate on w_s and L_s. We want to obtain a Pareto-optimal situation, so we maximize a weighted sum of the workers' expected utilities and the firms' expected profits, that is, we maximize:

$$\sum_s \pi_s L_s \left[U(w_s) - U(\varpi_s) \right] + \lambda \sum_s \pi_s \left[A_s F(L_s) - w_s L_s \right] \quad (55)$$

where λ represents the weight of firms in the negotiation. The first-order conditions with respect to w_s and L_s are, respectively:

$$U'(w_s) = \lambda \quad (56)$$

$$\left[U(w_s) - U(\varpi_s) \right] + \lambda \left[A_s F'(L_s) - w_s \right] = 0 \quad (57)$$

We see from the first equation that real wages will be the same in all states of nature, so we have indeed produced real wage rigidity. The problem is, as we will see, that this theory does not produce unemployment. The second relation (57) shows, indeed, that:

$$A_s F'(L_s) \leq w_s \quad (58)$$

This means that the level of employment is above that which would be freely decided on by the firm, given the real wage w_s. There is somehow overemployment, although this overemployment is accepted by the firm as part of a comprehensive wage and employment contract.

The situation is actually worse, and we show that employment is even beyond the "equilibrium" level of employment L_{Es} defined by the equality:[7]

$$A_s F'(L_{Es}) = \varpi_s \quad (59)$$

Let us combine equations (56) and (57). We obtain:

$$U(w_s) - U(\varpi_s) = U'(w_s) \left[w_s - A_s F'(L_s) \right] \quad (60)$$

Because of the concavity of the function U:

$$U(w_s) - U(\varpi_s) \geq U'(w_s)(w_s - \varpi_s) \quad (61)$$

Combining (60) and (61) we find:

$$A_s F'(L_s) \leq \varpi_s \quad (62)$$

---

7. The employment level L_{Es} is called "equilibrium" because, if the market is competitive, the real wage will fall to the reservation wage ϖ_s, and L_{Es} is the corresponding labor demand by the firms.

We see that the implicit contract level of employment is above the equilibrium level of employment. A reason for this distortion toward a too-high level of employment is that in this model the workers who actually have a job are "insured" (through the constant real wage), but the unemployed ones are not. The way to insure a maximum number of workers is to (inefficiently) give them extra employment.

So far this theory has succeeded in producing wage rigidity. On the other hand, it somehow produces overemployment instead of the initially expected unemployment. We will now see that introducing the idea of voluntary exchange (chapter 5) into implicit contracts theory helps solve that problem.

15.6.2 Contracts with Voluntary Exchange and Unemployment

A problem with the implicit contracts we have described so far is that, in the real world, one usually does not (or cannot) contract on employment (hence the name "implicit contracts"). The firm would thus have a tendency to renege on the employment part of the contract and return to its labor demand curve. We now study contracts (Bean, 1984; Drèze and Gollier, 1993) that solve that problem by imposing voluntary exchange from the start.

We assume that, to avoid situations of involuntary exchange like (58), the firm cannot be forced to purchase more labor than it wants. As a result, there will be an additional constraint:

$$A_s F'(L_s) \geq \omega_s \qquad (63)$$

So the program will be to maximize:

$$\sum_s \pi_s L_s [U(\omega_s) - U(\varpi_s)] + \lambda \sum_s \pi_s [A_s F(L_s) - \omega_s L_s] \qquad (64)$$

subject to constraint (63) for every state of nature. Call μ_s the multiplier associated with constraint (63). The Lagrangian (55) now becomes:

$$\sum_s \pi_s L_s [U(\omega_s) - U(\varpi_s)] + \lambda \sum_s \pi_s [A_s F(L_s) - \omega_s L_s]$$

$$+ \sum_s \mu_s \pi_s [A_s F'(L_s) - \omega_s] \qquad (65)$$

The first-order conditions with respect to ω_s and L_s are:

$$L_s U'(\omega_s) - \lambda L_s - \mu_s = 0 \qquad (66)$$

$$[U(\omega_s) - U(\varpi_s)] + \lambda [A_s F'(L_s) - \omega_s] + \mu_s A_s F''(L_s) = 0 \qquad (67)$$

We may note that as long as constraint (63) is satisfied, the maximand (64) is always increasing in L_s. This means that the solution will be characterized by:

$$A_s F'(L_s) = \omega_s \tag{68}$$

Then (67) becomes:

$$[U(\omega_s) - U(\varpi_s)] + \mu_s A_s F''(L_s) = 0 \tag{69}$$

Eliminating μ_s between (66) and (69) we get:

$$[U(\omega_s) - U(\varpi_s)] + [U'(\omega_s) - \lambda] A_s L_s F''(L_s) = 0 \tag{70}$$

15.6.3 Unemployment

We now show that the contracts we just defined can produce both wage rigidity and unemployment. We assume an isoelastic production function:

$$F(L_s) = \frac{L_s^{1-\alpha}}{1-\alpha} \qquad 0 \leq \alpha < 1 \tag{71}$$

so that:

$$F'(L_s) = L_s^{-\alpha} \qquad F''(L_s) = -\alpha L_s^{-\alpha-1} \tag{72}$$

Inserting (72) into (68) and (70) and combining the two, we obtain:

$$U(\omega_s) - U(\varpi_s) = \alpha \omega_s [U'(\omega_s) - \lambda] \tag{73}$$

If ϖ_s is constant across states of nature, so will ω_s. A uniform ϖ_s is actually a fairly realistic assumption, because unemployment compensation is usually function of past wages and events, and not of currently negotiated wages or current events.

So this contract, like the traditional implicit contract, produces wage rigidity. We now show that the voluntary exchange contract does produce unemployment.

To get an intuitive comparison between the traditional model of implicit contracts and this model with voluntary exchange, both have been represented in figure 15.9, where the subindex s has been suppressed because everything pertains to the same state of nature.

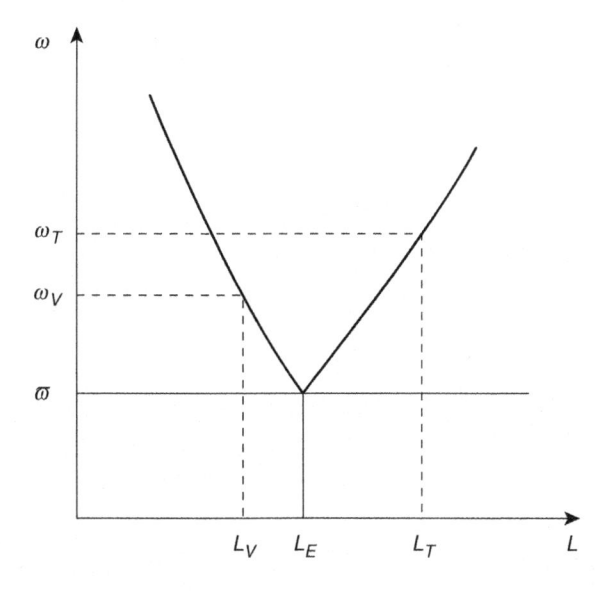

Figure 15.9 Two different implicit contracts

The downward-sloping line is the demand for labor and has for equation:

$$AF'(L) = \omega \tag{74}$$

The upward-sloping line has for equation:

$$U(\omega) - U(\varpi) = U'(\omega)\left[\omega - AF'(L)\right] \tag{75}$$

and is the locus of traditional implicit contracts (equation 60). The two contracts are (ω_T, L_T) and (ω_V, L_V). We see that:

$$L_V < L_E < L_T \tag{76}$$

Whereas the traditional implicit contracts produce overemployment $(L_T > L_E)$, implicit contracts with voluntary exchange produce unemployment $(L_V < L_E)$.

Appendix 15.1: Centralization and Unemployment

A number of authors have observed that there is (on average) less unemployment in countries where (a) wage negotiations are completely centralized, or (b) wage negotiations are, in the contrary, extremely decentralized, for

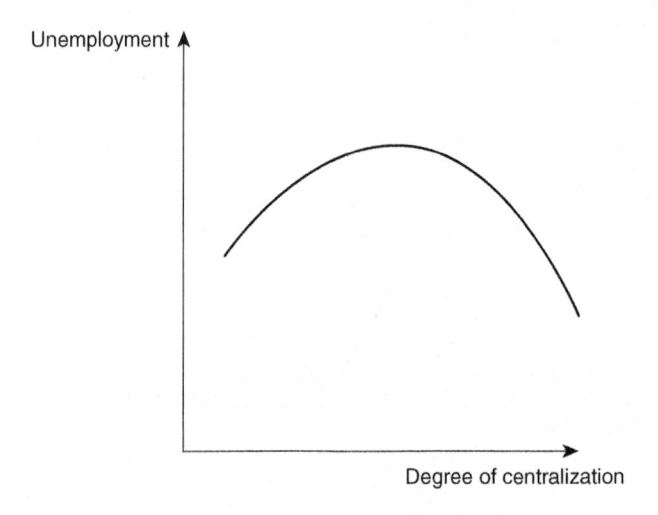

Figure 15.10 Centralization and unemployment

example, at the level of the firm. At the opposite end, unemployment seems to be higher in countries where wage negotiations take place at an intermediate level, such as for example, sectors. In such a case there would be a hump-shaped relationship between the level of unemployment and the degree of centralization in wage negotiations (figure 15.10). This idea was notably worked out by Calmfors and Driffill (1988),[8] and we describe a simple model that displays this property.

The Model

The economy includes two types of agents, households and firm. Households have a utility function:

$$U = LogC - \frac{L}{L_0} \qquad (77)$$

where, as we will see, L_0 will turn out to be the competitive level of employment. There are two types of firms: a first type produces the final consumption good with intermediate goods indexed by $i \in [0,1]$ under the following constant elasticity of substitution (CES) function:

$$Y = \left(\int_0^1 Y_i^\eta di\right)^{1/\eta} \qquad 0 < \eta < 1 \qquad (78)$$

---
8. See also Cahuc and Zylberberg (1991). A survey of the issue is in Calmfors (1993).

Intermediate goods are themselves produced with labor according to the production function:

$$Y_i = AL_i \tag{79}$$

where L_i is the quantity of labor employed in sector i and A a common technological parameter.

All firms behave competitively in the goods markets. Wages are set in an imperfectly competitive manner by trade unions that may operate at a more or less centralized level. This level of centralization will influence the level of employment.

Competitive Equilibrium

As a benchmark for the imperfect competition equilibria that follow, we compute the Walrasian equilibrium of this economy. In that case wages and prices are the same in all sectors:

$$W_i = W \qquad P_i = P \qquad \forall i \tag{80}$$

Households receive only wage income, so consumption C is equal to WL/P, and their utility maximization program is thus:

$$\text{Maximize } Log\left(\frac{WL}{P}\right) - \frac{L}{L_0} \tag{81}$$

where agents choose the quantity of labor L. This yields an employment level $L = L_0$ in all sectors.

Sectoral-level Negotiations

We now assume that wages are decided at the level of each sector. We first determine the demand for goods at the sectoral level. Firms producing the consumption good maximize their profits:

$$\text{Maximize } P\left(\int_0^1 Y_i^\eta di\right)^{1/\eta} - \int_0^1 P_i Y_i di \tag{82}$$

where P_i is the price of intermediate i. This yields the demand for intermediate good i:

$$Y_i = Y\left(\frac{P_i}{P}\right)^{-1/(1-\eta)} \tag{83}$$

where P, the aggregate price index, is linked to the P_i's through the traditional CES price index formula:

$$P = \left(\int_0^1 P_i^{-\eta/(1-\eta)} di\right)^{-(1-\eta)/\eta} \tag{84}$$

Because the firm producing good i is competitive, the price is equal to marginal cost:

$$P_i = \frac{W_i}{A} \tag{85}$$

Combining (79), (83), and (85), we obtain the demand for labor in sector i:

$$L_i = \frac{Y}{A} \left(\frac{W_i}{AP}\right)^{-1/(1-\eta)} \tag{86}$$

The program of the trade union in sector i is thus:

$$\text{Maximize } Log\left(\frac{W_i L_i}{P}\right) - \frac{L_i}{L_0} \quad \text{s.t.}$$

$$L_i = \frac{Y}{A}\left(\frac{W_i}{AP}\right)^{-1/(1-\eta)} \tag{87}$$

whose solution is:

$$L_i = \eta L_0 \tag{88}$$

Firm-level Negotiations

We now assume that each sector consists of firms indexed by k. The sectoral output Y_i results from the aggregation of firms' outputs Y_{ik} through the formula:

$$Y_i = \left(\int_0^1 Y_{ik}^\nu dk\right)^{1/\nu} \tag{89}$$

with:

$$0 < \eta < \nu \leq 1 \tag{90}$$

In (90) we assume that substitutability is greater between firms in the same sector than between firms across different sectors, a quite natural assumption. The demand addressed to firm k is:

$$Y_{ik} = Y_i \left(\frac{P_{ik}}{P_i}\right)^{-1/(1-\nu)} \tag{91}$$

where P_{ik} is the price of firm k in sector i. Using the same method as in the previous section, one finds:

$$L_{ik} = \nu L_0 \tag{92}$$

We see that, because $\nu > \eta$, firm negotiations will bring a level of employment higher than under sectoral negotiations.

Centralized Negotiations

Finally assume that a unique centralized trade union sets the wage W for all workers in the economy. In that case:

$$P_i = \frac{W_i}{A} = \frac{W}{A} \tag{93}$$

and thus, from formula (84):

$$P = \frac{W}{A} \tag{94}$$

The real wage is necessarily equal to A and, knowing that, the centralized trade union thus solves the program:

$$\text{Maximize } Log\,(AL) - \frac{L}{L_0} \tag{95}$$

whose solution is:

$$L = L_0 \tag{96}$$

A Summary

We thus have:
- For centralized negotiations:

$$L = L_0 \tag{97}$$

- For sectoral negotiations:

$$L = \eta L_0 \tag{98}$$

- For firm negotiations:

$$L = \nu L_0 \tag{99}$$

Because $\eta < \nu \leq 1$, we indeed find a hump-shaped curve.

Problems

Problem 15.1: A Tax Scheme to Fight Unemployment

We will describe here a tax scheme to fight unemployment adapted from Jackman and Layard (1986). The basic idea is to tax the wage bill and simultaneously subsidize jobs, the taxes and subsidies balancing each other. The combination, as we shall see, increases employment.

We are in a framework of monopolistic competition. Output is made from the combination of intermediate goods indexed by $i \in [0, 1]$:

$$Y = \left(\int_0^1 Y_i^\eta di \right)^{1/\eta}$$

Firms producing intermediate goods have the same linear production function, which is for firm i:

$$Y_i = L_i$$

Denote ω_i as the real wage in firm i. The wage bill is taxed at the rate t and jobs subsidized at the rate s, so that the real profit of firm i is:

$$p_i Y_i - (1+t)\omega_i L_i + sL_i$$

where p_i is the "real price" of good i. The tax scheme is balanced in the sense that:

$$s \sum_i L_i = t \sum_i \omega_i L_i$$

The average real wage in the economy is ω, and the unemployment rate is u. Unemployed workers receive a real unemployment benefit b. Consequently outside firm i a worker has an expected income equal to:

$$(1-u)\omega + ub$$

We assume that trade unions in firm i set the real wage ω_i so as to maximize "total surplus" that is, so as to maximize:

$$L_i\left[\omega_i - (1-u)\omega - ub\right]$$

1. Compute the demand for labor.
2. Show that a higher t leads to higher employment.

Problem 15.2: A Simple Model of Nominal Wage Rigidity

In the main text of this chapter we assumed that unemployment benefits are expressed in real terms. But in the real world one observes that these benefits are usually not expressed in real terms but are related to the nominal wage of the worker at the time he lost his job. Of course there are some indexing procedures, but they relate to past price evolutions, not to the current price, so that the benefit is not fixed in real terms.

We describe here a simple model, adapted from Dixon (1990), where the fact that unemployment benefits are nominally fixed creates a nominal rigidity.

Output is produced by competitive firms from intermediate goods indexed by $i \in [0, 1]$ via the production function:

$$Y = \left(\int_i Y_i^\eta di\right)^{1/\eta}$$

Production in intermediate sector i is given by:

$$Y_i = L_i$$

The nominal wage W_i in intermediate sector i is determined by a trade union, which maximizes:

$$L_i\left[U\left(\frac{W_i}{P}\right) - U\left(\frac{B}{P}\right)\right]$$

where U is a concave utility function, P the aggregate price level, and B the unemployment benefit, which is expressed here in nominal terms. We take the particular isoelastic utility:

$$U\left(\frac{W}{P}\right) = \frac{1}{1-\theta}\left(\frac{W}{P}\right)^{1-\theta} \qquad \theta \geq 0$$

1. Compute the demand for intermediate labor of type i.
2. Insert this demand for labor into the trade union's utility function. Derive the wage W_i and show that wages display nominal rigidity.

16

A Dynamic View of Unemployment

16.1 Introduction

In the preceding chapter we studied a number of traditional causes for unemployment. To lighten the exposition, we considered only static models. These static models are very useful to understand the various concepts behind each theory of unemployment. On the other hand, a number of theories have developed in which dynamic aspects, such as flows from employment to unemployment and from unemployment to employment, play a prominent role. We present in this chapter a few models that represent such dynamics.

Section 16.2 describes a simple common discrete time dynamic framework, as well as the basic employment flows. Section 16.3 derives a number of dynamic relations that will be common to subsequent models.

Section 16.4 shows how one can go from a static to a dynamic model by extending to a dynamic environment a model already studied in a static framework in the previous chapter, the shirking model (Shapiro and Stiglitz, 1984).

We continue our exploration in section 16.5 by describing a popular model that describes the flows in and out of employment through a matching function.

16.2 A Simple Dynamic Framework

16.2.1 The Economy

We study a discrete time economy. In each period there are N_0 workers, each of which supplies one unit of labor. Workers are either employed or unemployed. An employed worker receives an instantaneous utility equal to $U(\omega) - e$, where ω is the *real* wage and e the level of effort necessary to achieve his work. An unemployed worker has an instantaneous utility $U(b)$, where b is the real level of unemployment benefit. As in the preceding chapter, we define the reservation wage ϖ by:

$$U(\varpi) = U(b) + e \qquad (1)$$

Consumers-workers live forever and discount the future with a discount rate β, $0 < \beta < 1$. On the production side, the economy comprises a large number of firms producing a homogeneous consumption good with an aggregate technology:

$$Y = F(L) \qquad (2)$$

The demand for labor is:

$$L = F'^{-1}(\omega) \qquad (3)$$

where ω is the real wage. We assume that the existing technology allows us to ensure full employment at the reservation wage, that is:

$$F'(N_0) \geq \varpi \qquad (4)$$

16.2.2 Employment Flows

Now we briefly describe the flows in and out of employment and unemployment.[1] We denote by u_t the unemployment rate; by q_t the quits rate, that is, the percentage of employed who lose their job in period t; and by h_t the hiring rate, that is, the percentage of unemployed who find a job in period t.

---

1. Empirical evidence on these flows can be found in Burda and Wyplosz (1994) for Europe, and in Davis and Haltiwanger (1990, 1992, 1999) and Davis, Haltiwanger, and Schuh (1996) for the United States.

In a stationary state there is a simple relation between u_t, q_t, and h_t. Flows into and out of unemployment are equal, so that:

$$(1 - u_t) q_t = u_t h_t \tag{5}$$

or:

$$u_t = \frac{q_t}{h_t + q_t} \tag{6}$$

16.3 A Few Dynamic Relations

16.3.1 Discounted Utilities

Call $\mathcal{V}_t$ the discounted sum of a worker's expected utilities as of time t:

$$\mathcal{V}_t = E\left(\sum_{\tau=t}^{\infty} \beta^{\tau-t} \mathcal{U}_\tau\right) \tag{7}$$

where $\mathcal{U}_\tau$ is the instantaneous utility of a worker in period τ. That worker can either be employed or unemployed. The two possible instantaneous utilities are:

$$\mathcal{U}_\tau = U(\omega_\tau) - e \quad \text{if the worker is employed in } \tau \tag{8}$$

$$\mathcal{U}_\tau = U(b) \quad \text{if the worker is unemployed in } \tau \tag{9}$$

Clearly $\mathcal{V}_t$ will have a different value for employed and unemployed workers. We call, respectively, $\mathcal{V}_t^e$ and $\mathcal{V}_t^u$ the discounted utilities of an employed worker and unemployed worker. These will play an important role in what follows, and we establish a few simple relations between them.

16.3.2 Transitions and Utilities

Consider first an employed worker. In the current period she has an instantaneous utility $U(\omega_t) - e$. She has a probability q_t to quit and become unemployed in $t+1$. So in $t+1$ with probability q_t she will have a utility $\mathcal{V}_{t+1}^u$, and with probability $1 - q_t$ a utility $\mathcal{V}_{t+1}^e$. Consequently we have the following dynamic programming equation giving $\mathcal{V}_t^e$:

$$\mathcal{V}_t^e = U(\omega_t) - e + \beta \left[q_t \mathcal{V}_{t+1}^u + (1 - q_t) \mathcal{V}_{t+1}^e\right] \tag{10}$$

Symmetrically for an unemployed worker who has a probability h_t to be hired:

$$\mathcal{V}_t^u = U(b) + \beta \left[h_t \mathcal{V}_{t+1}^e + (1 - h_t) \mathcal{V}_{t+1}^u \right] \tag{11}$$

16.3.3 Stationary States

We now consider stationary states where:

$$\mathcal{V}_t^e = \mathcal{V}^e \qquad \mathcal{V}_t^u = \mathcal{V}^u \qquad \forall t \tag{12}$$

Relations (10) and (11) become:

$$\mathcal{V}^e = U(\omega) - e + \beta \left[q \mathcal{V}^u + (1 - q) \mathcal{V}^e \right] \tag{13}$$

$$\mathcal{V}^u = U(b) + \beta \left[h \mathcal{V}^e + (1 - h) \mathcal{V}^u \right] \tag{14}$$

Combining (13) and (14) we obtain:

$$\mathcal{V}^e - \mathcal{V}^u = \frac{U(\omega) - e - U(b)}{1 - \beta + \beta(q+h)} = \frac{U(\omega) - U(\varpi)}{1 - \beta + \beta(q+h)} \tag{15}$$

We see that if the real wage is at its competitive value (i.e., $\omega = \varpi$), employed and unemployed workers have the same utility. Second, for a given unemployment rate $u = q/(h+q)$, the difference between discounted utilities is lower if the quit rate q and hiring rate h are high. This is because in such a case workers will go back and forth more frequently between the states of employment and unemployment, which will decrease the difference between the two states.

As we saw (equation 2), h and q are related in a stationary state by:

$$(1-u)q = uh \tag{16}$$

In view of (16), we can rewrite (15) as:

$$\mathcal{V}^e - \mathcal{V}^u = \frac{U(\omega) - e - U(b)}{1 - \beta + \beta q/u} = \frac{U(\omega) - U(\varpi)}{1 - \beta + \beta q/u} \tag{17}$$

16.4 The Shirking Model

We now describe the original dynamic model of Shapiro and Stiglitz (1984). The "static" aspects of the model are those given in section 16.2, and we do not repeat them.

As compared to the model of section 16.3, the central difference is that an employed worker has now two options. She can either make the effort e, in which case her instantaneous utility is $U(\omega) - e$, or shirk, in which case her utility is $U(\omega)$. If she shirks, she will be detected with probability d and fired immediately.

We assume that the quits rate q_t is exogenous and equal to q. The hiring rate h_t and unemployment rate u_t will be determined endogenously.

16.4.1 Dynamic Relations

As before, we call $\mathcal{V}_t$ the discounted sum of a worker's expected utilities:

$$\mathcal{V}_t = E\left(\sum_{\tau=t}^{\infty} \beta^{\tau-t} \mathcal{U}_\tau\right) \tag{18}$$

Because the employed worker can shirk or not, there are now three possible discounted utilities. We accordingly call, respectively, $\mathcal{V}_t^e$, $\mathcal{V}_t^s$, and $\mathcal{V}_t^u$ the discounted utilities of an employed nonshirking worker, employed shirking worker, and unemployed worker.

For the employed nonshirking worker and the unemployed worker, the dynamic relations are very similar to those seen previously (equations 10 and 11). The difference is that a worker who will have a job next period will then have the choice between shirking and not shirking and choose the option that yields the highest utility, so that $\mathcal{V}_{t+1}^e$ should be replaced with $\max(\mathcal{V}_{t+1}^e, \mathcal{V}_{t+1}^s)$. Accordingly the dynamic relations (10) and (11) become:

$$\mathcal{V}_t^e = U(\omega_t) - e + \beta \left[q_t \mathcal{V}_{t+1}^u + (1 - q_t) \max\left(\mathcal{V}_{t+1}^e, \mathcal{V}_{t+1}^s\right)\right] \tag{19}$$

$$\mathcal{V}_t^u = U(b) + \beta \left[(1 - h_t) \mathcal{V}_{t+1}^u + h_t \max\left(\mathcal{V}_{t+1}^e, \mathcal{V}_{t+1}^s\right)\right] \tag{20}$$

Now the expected discounted utility of the shirking worker can be broken into two parts. If she is not detected (with probability $1 - d$), her instantaneous utility is $U(\omega_t)$, and her discounted utility for the next period is the same as that of an employed nonshirking worker (formula 19). If she is detected (with probability d), her instantaneous utility is $U(b)$, and her discounted utility for the next period is the same as that of an unemployed worker (formula 20). Putting these together we obtain

$$\mathcal{V}_t^s = (1-d)\left\{U(\omega_t) + \beta\left[q_t\mathcal{V}_{t+1}^u + (1-q_t)\max\left(\mathcal{V}_{t+1}^e, \mathcal{V}_{t+1}^s\right)\right]\right\}$$
$$+ d\left\{U(b) + \beta\left[(1-h_t)\mathcal{V}_{t+1}^u + h_t\max\left(\mathcal{V}_{t+1}^e, \mathcal{V}_{t+1}^s\right)\right]\right\} \quad (21)$$

16.4.2 Stationary States

We consider again stationary states where:

$$\mathcal{V}_t^e = \mathcal{V}^e \qquad \mathcal{V}_t^s = \mathcal{V}^s \qquad \mathcal{V}_t^u = \mathcal{V}^u \qquad \forall t \quad (22)$$

Relations (19), (20), and (21) become:

$$\mathcal{V}^e = U(\omega) - e + \beta\left[q\mathcal{V}^u + (1-q)\max(\mathcal{V}^e, \mathcal{V}^s)\right] \quad (23)$$

$$\mathcal{V}^u = U(b) + \beta\left[(1-h)\mathcal{V}^u + h\max(\mathcal{V}^e, \mathcal{V}^s)\right] \quad (24)$$

$$\mathcal{V}^s = (1-d)\left\{U(\omega) + \beta\left[q\mathcal{V}^u + (1-q)\max(\mathcal{V}^e, \mathcal{V}^s)\right]\right\}$$
$$+ d\left\{U(b) + \beta\left[(1-h)\mathcal{V}^u + h\max(\mathcal{V}^e, \mathcal{V}^s)\right]\right\} \quad (25)$$

16.4.3 The No Shirking Condition

Combining (23), (24), and (25) we obtain:

$$\mathcal{V}^s = (1-d)\mathcal{V}^e + d\mathcal{V}^u + (1-d)e \quad (26)$$

The firm does not want the workers to shirk, so it will choose a wage high enough that:

$$\mathcal{V}^e \geq \mathcal{V}^s \quad (27)$$

which, together with (26), yields the no shirking condition:

$$\mathcal{V}^e - \mathcal{V}^u \geq \frac{(1-d)e}{d} \quad (28)$$

Note that this condition very much looks like the one we saw in the static framework of the previous chapter (section 15.5), with the single period utility replaced by a discounted intertemporal utility.

This shows that it is necessary to ensure to employed workers a level of utility substantially higher than that of the unemployed, so as to induce them not to shirk. In accordance with intuition, when the probability of detection is lower, this difference in utilities is higher.

Condition (28), with equality, determines a minimum real wage $\hat{w}$ that is such that $\mathcal{V}^e = \mathcal{V}^s$. Using $\mathcal{V}^e = \mathcal{V}^s$, (23) and (24) become:

$$\mathcal{V}^e = U(\omega) - e + \beta [q\mathcal{V}^u + (1-q)\mathcal{V}^e] \tag{29}$$

$$\mathcal{V}^u = U(b) + \beta [(1-h)\mathcal{V}^u + h\mathcal{V}^e] \tag{30}$$

Note that these are the same as (13) and (14). Subtracting one from the other, we obtain a second relation between $\mathcal{V}^e$ and $\mathcal{V}^u$:

$$\mathcal{V}^e - \mathcal{V}^u = \frac{U(\omega) - e - U(b)}{1 - \beta + \beta(q+h)} = \frac{U(\omega) - U(\varpi)}{1 - \beta + \beta(q+h)} \tag{31}$$

and since in a stationary state h and q are related by $(1-u)q = uh$:

$$\mathcal{V}^e - \mathcal{V}^u = \frac{U(\omega) - e - U(b)}{1 - \beta + \beta q/u} = \frac{U(\omega) - U(\varpi)}{1 - \beta + \beta q/u} \tag{32}$$

This relation is actually the same as (17) and is independent of the shirking aspect of the model. We combine equations (28), with equality, and (32):

$$\frac{U(\omega) - U(\varpi)}{1 - \beta + \beta q/u} = \frac{(1-d)e}{d} \tag{33}$$

This yields a relation with negative slope between the no shirking wage $\hat{\omega}$ and the unemployment rate u:

$$U(\hat{\omega}) - U(\varpi) = \frac{(1-d)e}{d}\left(1 - \beta + \frac{\beta q}{u}\right) \tag{34}$$

On the other hand, the demand for labor is given by the equality between the real wage and the marginal productivity of labor:

$$\omega = F'(L) = F'[(1-u)N_0] \tag{35}$$

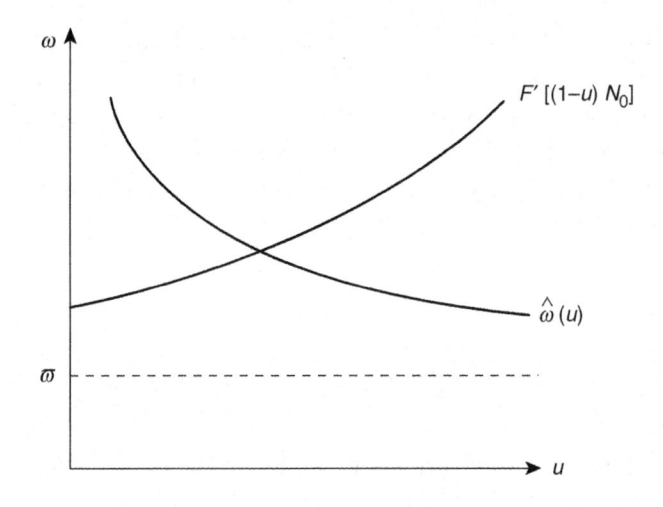

Figure 16.1 The no shirking equilibrium

Equilibrium levels of wages and unemployment are found by solving the system of equations (34) and (35), either algebraically or graphically (figure 16.1).

16.5 Matching in the Labor Market

We will now describe a very popular model of the labor market; the matching function.[2]

16.5.1 The Matching Function

We describe here a discrete time version of the model. In period t a number of unemployed u_t are looking for a job, and vacancies v_t are posted by firms. The matching function shows the flow of successful matches m_t as a function of the unemployment and vacancy rates:

$$m_t = \mathcal{M}(u_t, v_t) \tag{36}$$

---

2. Overviews of the matching and search literature are Diamond (1984); Lippman and McCall (1976); Mortensen (1986); Mortensen and Pissarides (1999a, 1999b); Pissarides (1990); Petrongolo and Pissarides (2001); and Rogerson, Shimer, and Wright (2005). Our exposition borrows particularly from Pissarides (1990).

We assume throughout that the matching function is homogeneous of degree 1 in its arguments:

$$\mathcal{M}(\lambda u_t, \lambda v_t) = \lambda \mathcal{M}(u_t, v_t) \tag{37}$$

We may note that the matching function is a particular rationing scheme, of the type we studied in chapter 5. If the matching process was *frictionless* (in the sense we gave in chapter 5), hirings would be equal to the minimum of unemployed and vacancies:

$$\mathcal{M}(u_t, v_t) = \min(u_t, v_t) \tag{38}$$

In general there are frictions in the matching process. There remains both unmatched vacancies and unemployed workers so that:

$$\mathcal{M}(u_t, v_t) \leq \min(u_t, v_t) \tag{39}$$

We define the degree of labor market tightness:

$$\theta_t = \frac{v_t}{u_t} \tag{40}$$

The probability $f(\theta)$ of a vacancy being filled is given by:

$$\frac{m_t}{v_t} = \frac{\mathcal{M}(u_t, v_t)}{v_t} = \mathcal{M}\left(\frac{1}{\theta_t}, 1\right) = f(\theta_t) \tag{41}$$

Symmetrically the probability for an unemployed worker to become employed is:

$$\frac{m_t}{u_t} = \frac{\mathcal{M}(u_t, v_t)}{v_t} = \theta_t \mathcal{M}\left(\frac{1}{\theta_t}, 1\right) = \theta_t f(\theta_t) \tag{42}$$

We shall assume that m_t/v_t is a decreasing function of θ_t, m_t/u_t an increasing function of θ_t:

$$\frac{\partial (m_t/v_t)}{\partial \theta_t} \leq 0 \qquad \frac{\partial (m_t/u_t)}{\partial \theta_t} \geq 0 \tag{43}$$

so that:

$$f'(\theta_t) \leq 0 \qquad f(\theta_t) + \theta_t f'(\theta_t) \geq 0 \tag{44}$$

16.5.2 The Beveridge Curve

We assume that existing jobs "die" at an exogenous rate q (as "quits"), so that the equation of evolution of the rate of employment is:

$$\ell_{t+1} = (1-q)\ell_t + m_t \qquad (45)$$

with:

$$\ell_t = \frac{L_t}{N_t} \qquad (46)$$

In a steady state, the unemployment rate is constant, so that the flows in and out of unemployment are equal:

$$q(1-u_t) = \theta_t f(\theta_t) u_t \qquad (47)$$

or:

$$u_t = \frac{q}{q + \theta_t f(\theta_t)} \qquad (48)$$

which can also be rewritten:

$$q(1-u_t) = v_t f\left(\frac{v_t}{u_t}\right) \qquad (49)$$

This relation between u_t and v_t is called the Beveridge curve and is represented in figure 16.2.

16.5.3 Firms and Job Creation

We assume that a filled job produces an income $y > 0$ for the firm. When the job is vacant the firm pays a fixed cost $c > 0$ to maintain it and advertise it. Workers arrive at a rate $f(\theta)$ per unit of time.

We call J^o the discounted value of profits for an occupied job, J^v that for a vacant job. The dynamic programming equations applied, respectively, to a vacant job and an occupied job yield:

$$J_t^v = -c + \beta\left\{f(\theta_t) J_{t+1}^o + [1 - f(\theta_t)] J_{t+1}^v\right\} \qquad (50)$$

$$J_t^o = y - \omega + \beta\left\{q J_{t+1}^v + (1-q) J_{t+1}^o\right\} \qquad (51)$$

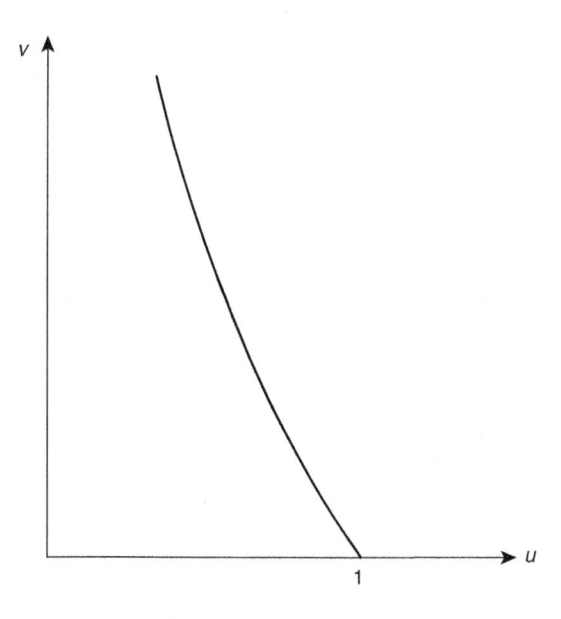

Figure 16.2 The Beveridge curve

where ω is the real wage. In stationary state this yields:

$$J^v = -c + \beta \{f(\theta) J^o + [1 - f(\theta)] J^v\} \tag{52}$$

$$J^o = y - \omega + \beta \{qJ^v + (1-q) J^o\} \tag{53}$$

Because of free entry, in equilibrium:

$$J^v = 0 \tag{54}$$

so that:

$$J^o = \frac{c}{\beta f(\theta)} = \frac{y - \omega}{1 - \beta + \beta q} \tag{55}$$

16.5.4 Workers

Workers receive a real wage ω when employed, and a real unemployment benefit b when unemployed. Call $\mathcal{V}^u$ and $\mathcal{V}^e$ the discounted utilities for unemployed and employed workers, respectively. The dynamic programming equations are for stationary states:

$$\mathcal{V}^u = b + \beta \{\theta f(\theta) \mathcal{V}^e + [1 - \theta f(\theta)] \mathcal{V}^u\} \tag{56}$$

$$\mathcal{V}^e = \omega - e + \beta [q\mathcal{V}^u + (1-q) \mathcal{V}^e] \tag{57}$$

from which we deduce:

$$\mathcal{V}^e - \mathcal{V}^u = \frac{\omega - e - b}{1 - \beta + \beta q + \beta\theta f(\theta)} \tag{58}$$

16.5.5 Wage Setting

It is assumed that the wage in each firm is bargained between firm and workers after they meet, and that it is the solution of the Nash bargaining program (we omit the index of the firm):

$$\text{Maximize } (\mathcal{V}^e - \mathcal{V}^u)^\gamma (J^o - J^v)^{1-\gamma} \tag{59}$$

This leads to the following condition of "surplus sharing":

$$(1-\gamma)(\mathcal{V}^e - \mathcal{V}^u) = \gamma(J^o - J^v) \tag{60}$$

which yields, using (54), (55) and (58):

$$\omega = (1-\gamma)(b+e) + \gamma(y+\theta c) \tag{61}$$

16.5.6 Steady-state Equilibrium

We can gather the equations giving the steady-state equilibrium (equations 48, 55, and 61):

$$u = \frac{q}{q + \theta f(\theta)} \tag{62}$$

$$y - \omega = \frac{(1-\beta+\beta q)c}{\beta f(\theta)} \tag{63}$$

$$\omega = (1-\gamma)(b+e) + \gamma(y+\theta c) \tag{64}$$

The resulting steady state is represented in (u, v) space in figure 16.3.

The downward-sloping curve is the Beveridge curve (equation 62 with $\theta = v/u$). The upward-sloping line is a straight line with slope θ. That value of θ is obtained by combining (63) and (64), which yields the implicit equation:

$$(1-\gamma)(y-b-e) = \gamma\theta c + \frac{(1-\beta+\beta q)c}{\beta f(\theta)} \tag{65}$$

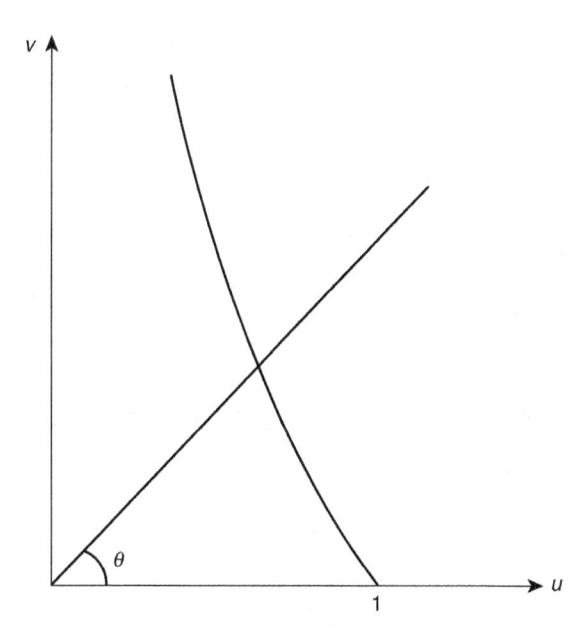

Figure 16.3 The unemployment and vacancies equilibrium

We can use (65) to find the effect of some basic parameters on unemployment and vacancies. For example, differentiating (65) we obtain:

$$\frac{\partial \theta}{\partial \gamma} < 0 \qquad \frac{\partial \theta}{\partial b} < 0 \qquad (66)$$

and combining with the Beveridge curve (62):

$$\frac{\partial u}{\partial \gamma} > 0 \qquad \frac{\partial u}{\partial b} > 0 \qquad (67)$$

$$\frac{\partial v}{\partial \gamma} < 0 \qquad \frac{\partial v}{\partial b} < 0 \qquad (68)$$

16.5.7 Matching and Fluctuations

Up to now, to make the exposition more transparent, we presented the matching model in a deterministic framework. Quite naturally in recent years the matching model was embedded in a DSGE framework with shocks.[3] Whereas such models succeed in reproducing features of the labor market

---

3. See, for example, Merz (1995); Andolfatto (1996); Chéron and Langot (2000); Den Haan, Ramey, and Watson (2000); and Trigari (2009).

like the Beveridge curve, they are less successful on some other aspects. Notably, it appears that in models with productivity shocks the standard matching model fails to reproduce the volatilities of unemployment and vacancies. An interesting debate has developed recently on that issue (see notably Hall, 2005; Shimer, 2005).

One problem seems to be that under the Nash bargaining scheme for wage setting, real wages follow the productivity shocks too closely. A suggestion to overcome that problem has been to introduce some form of wage stickiness.[4] As an example, one possibility would be to assume different degrees of flexibility for the wages of new matches and those of old matches. There are, of course, numerous other possibilities, and the matter seems far from being settled.

Problems

Problem 16.1: Dynamic Wage Negotiations

We combine the "right to manage negotiations" of chapter 15 (section 15.3.3) and the dynamic framework of section 16.3. We assume that wages are negotiated between the firm and a trade union whose utility function is:

$$V_t = L_t \left(\mathcal{V}_t^e - \mathcal{V}_t^u \right)$$

Note the similarity of this utility function with the one used in chapter 15, that is:

$$L_t \left[U(\omega_t) - U(\varpi) \right] = L_t \left[U(\omega_t) - e - U(b) \right]$$

The instantaneous utilities $U(\omega_t) - e$ and $U(b)$ have simply been replaced by the intertemporal discounted ones, $\mathcal{V}_t^e$ and $\mathcal{V}_t^u$.

Firms have the following production function:

$$Y_t = \frac{A L_t^{1-\alpha}}{1-\alpha} \qquad 0 < \alpha < 1$$

The firm and trade union negotiate on the current real wage, taking future events as given. The result of the wage negotiation is given by the maximum

---

4. Note that the debate on wage stickiness and real wages is not really new, since it dates back at least to Dunlop (1938), Keynes (1939), and Tarshis (1939). Two surveys on the empirical side are Abraham and Haltiwanger (1995) and Brandolini (1995).

of the Nash product:

$$\left(V_t - \bar{V}_t\right)^\gamma \left(\Pi_t - \bar{\Pi}_t\right)^{1-\gamma}$$

1. Derive the first-order conditions for the wage negotiation. Give the resulting relation between the real wage and employment.
2. Derive this relation in the particular case where $U(\omega) = Log\omega$
3. Combining this with the aggregate production function, show how the real wage and unemployment rate are determined.

Problem 16.2: A Dynamic Insiders-outsiders Model

We combine the insiders-outsiders model of chapter 15 (section 15.4) with the dynamic framework of sections 16.2 and 16.3. In particular the utility of the trade union is now:

$$V_t = \min\left(L_t, N\right)\left(\mathcal{V}_t^e - \mathcal{V}_t^u\right)$$

Except for this, the model is the same as in problem 16.1

1. Show that the result of the negotiation leads to a relation between the real wage and unemployment.
2. Compute the above relation in the logarithmic case $U(\omega) = Log\omega$. Combining this with the aggregate production function, show how the equilibrium real wage and unemployment rate are determined. Compare with the results of problem 16.1.

Problem 16.3: Matching in the Labor Market: Continuous Time

We consider the dynamic matching model of the labor market (section 16.5), but this time in continuous time. This is actually the original model found notably in Pissarides (1990).

There are u_t unemployed and v_t vacancies at time t. The flow of hirings h_t is given by the matching function:

$$h_t = \mathcal{M}(u_t, v_t)$$

The matching function is homogeneous of degree 1 in its arguments. Denote:

$$f = \frac{h}{v} = \frac{\mathcal{M}(u,v)}{v} = \mathcal{M}\left(\frac{1}{\theta}, 1\right) = f(\theta) \qquad \theta = \frac{v}{u}$$

$$f'(\theta) \leq 0$$

We assume that existing jobs die at an exogenous rate q (as quits), so that the dynamics of unemployment is given by:

$$\dot{u} = q(1-u) - \theta f(\theta) u$$

An occupied job gives a flow of income y. The cost of maintaining a vacancy is c, and the real wage is ω. The real interest rate is r.

1. From the equation giving $\dot{u}$ derive a steady-state relation between u, v, and θ.
2. Denote as J^o and J^v the discounted profits for an occupied job and a vacant job. Give the dynamic programming equations for J^o and J^v.
3. Denote as $\mathcal{V}^e$ and $\mathcal{V}^u$ the discounted utilities of an employed and unemployed household. Give the dynamic programming equations for $\mathcal{V}^e$ and $\mathcal{V}^u$.
4. The wage in each firm is bargained between firm and worker. It is assumed that the resulting wage maximizes the Nash product:

$$(V^e - V^u)^\gamma (J^o - J^v)^{1-\gamma}$$

   Give the resulting wage equation.
5. Using the equilibrium equations previously obtained, characterize the equilibrium of the economy.

17

Policy: The Public Finance Approach

17.1 Introduction

In this and the next two chapters we study issues of optimal government policy. We do not adopt the traditional separation between fiscal and monetary policy, because in a number of issues they are quite inextricably linked. However, we break this study into three relatively homogeneous chapters. Chapter 17 studies the "public finance" approach,"[1] chapter 18 tackles the problem of stabilization, that is, the optimal response of government policy to shocks, external or "internal." Finally, chapter 19 studies the issue of credibility.

Section 17.2 starts with some basic issues in policy design: government objectives, instruments, and information. The next sections present a number of classic results in the theory of optimal financing.

Section 17.3 studies one of the most well-known prescriptions for monetary policy, the Friedman rule, which basically says that since money costs nothing to produce, the nominal interest rate should generally be set to 0.

In section 17.4 we show that when taxes are distortionary, it is better to spread taxation over several periods (tax smoothing). In section 17.5 we go a little deeper into the foundations of the public finance approach and study the issue of Ramsey taxation (Ramsey, 1927). In cases where the fiscal authority can only use distortionary taxation, Ramsey taxation tells us how

---

1. This approach is generally concerned with the optimal financing of public spending and minimizing the distortions associated to it. For general expositions, see Lucas (1986) and Musgrave (2008).

the government should optimally spread taxes across the various goods in the economy.

In section 17.6, we immediately use the lessons of Ramsey taxation and study optimal seigniorage, that is, which part of public spending should be financed by printing money and which part by straight taxation.

17.2 Issues in Policy Design

17.2.1 Government Objectives

In the same way that agents in the private sector maximize a utility function, it is generally assumed that the government maximizes a "social welfare function." In what follows we assume that the government is benevolent, in the sense that this social welfare function is as close as possible to the utility of the private sector. This being said, we must still be aware that this unequivocally determines government's utility only in the very special case where there is a single representative household, like in the Ramsey economy of chapter 7 where the government utility would naturally be (equation 45 in chapter 7):

$$\sum_t \beta^t U(C_t) \tag{1}$$

In general, agents in the economy are heterogeneous, and finding a social welfare function may require a complex political aggregation process, an issue that is tackled in chapter 20.

To give a simple example, we may think of the case where the heterogeneity comes from the demography, for example as in an overlapping generations (OLG) economy where new agents are born over time. In such a case the aggregation process, and therefore optimal policies, will depend on the weight put on each generation. Assume, for example, that the generation born in t has a utility function:

$$U(c_{1t}) + \beta U(c_{2t+1}) \tag{2}$$

In such a case, Samuelson (1967, 1968) proposes the following criterion:

$$\sum_t \phi^t \left[U(c_{1t}) + \beta U(c_{2t+1}) \right] \qquad \phi < 1 \tag{3}$$

where ϕ is some sort of social discount rate. Appendix 17.2 gives a simple application of such a criterion to the choice of optimal financing of government spending.

17.2.2 Instruments

We study both fiscal and monetary policies. Fiscal policy will be characterized by the level of government spending G_t and the real value of taxes T_t. These taxes can be raised in a nondistortionary, lump-sum manner, or by distortionary taxes, for example, through proportional income taxation at the rate τ_t, so that $T_t = \tau_t Y_t$. Appendix 17.1 shows in a very simple example the costs of distortionary taxation as compared to lump sum taxes.

As for monetary policy, two alternative instruments are usually considered, the quantity of money M_t, and the nominal interest rate i_t. We should note that i_t and M_t are not independent instruments, as they are linked by the equilibrium condition on the bonds market (this would correspond to the LM equation in the traditional Keynesian model), so that there is only one degree of freedom.[2]

Finally we note that as may be expected in a general equilibrium approach, it is generally preferable to study optimal monetary and fiscal policies together, notably because they are strongly linked by the intertemporal budget constraint of the government.[3]

17.2.3 Information

Finally a most important issue in governmental policy design is the information available when taking policy decisions. We saw in chapters 2 and 3 how the issue of policy effectiveness, which is essentially based on differences in assumptions on governmental information, had been central in the classical Keynesian battles. In chapter 18 we will show in a rigorous manner that the amount of information available to the government is at the crux of the matter.

17.3 The Friedman Rule

We first do an exercise in optimal policy, corresponding to the famous Friedman rule.[4] This rule says that monetary policy should be conducted so as to achieve a zero nominal interest rate.

---

2. We should note, however, that although there is a link between the two potential instruments, it is not equivalent to use one or the other. For example the Poole (1970) model, described in appendix 2.3, showed us that under imperfect information, the two instruments can give quite different results.

3. This intertemporal government budget constraint actually creates strong links between, and constraints on, monetary and fiscal policies. Following the "unpleasant monetary arithmetic" of Sargent and Wallace (1981), a stimulating exchange has developed on this theme. See notably Darby (1984), Miller and Sargent (1984), Liviatan (1984), Drazen (1984), Aiyagari and Gertler (1985), and Drazen and Helpman (1990).

4. The basic intuition is due to Friedman (1969). Early formalizations can be found in Dornbusch and Frenkel (1973) and Grandmont and Younès (1973).

The basic intuition is most simple and natural: in an optimal policy package, the "price" of money, that is, the nominal interest rate, should be equal to its production cost, that is, zero.

To formalize this intuition we use the cash in advance (CIA) model of chapter 11 (the same exercise could be performed with a money in the utility function specification), but to introduce potential inefficiencies we endogenize output and labor supply.

17.3.1 The Model

Output is produced through a simple production function:

$$Y_t = F(L_t) \tag{4}$$

Households have the following intertemporal utility:

$$\sum_t \beta^t [U(C_t) - \Gamma(L_t)] \qquad \Gamma' > 0 \qquad \Gamma'' > 0 \tag{5}$$

and are subject to the budget constraints:

$$\Omega_{t+1} = (1 + i_t)\Omega_t + W_t L_t t \Pi_t - i_t M_t - P_t C_t \tag{6}$$

where $\Omega_t = M_t + B_t$ and Π_t is firms' profits. Finally they are submitted to CIA constraints:

$$P_t C_t \leq M_t \tag{7}$$

17.3.2 Market Equilibrium

The firm's profit maximization yields:

$$\frac{W_t}{P_t} = F'(L_t) \tag{8}$$

Households maximize their utility function (5) subject to the budget constraints (6) and the CIA constraints (7). The Lagrangian for this problem is:

$$\sum_t \beta^t \left[U(C_t) - \Gamma(L_t) + \nu_t \left(\frac{M_t}{P_t} - C_t \right) \right]$$

$$+ \sum_t \beta^t \lambda_t \left[(1 + i_t)\frac{\Omega_t}{P_t} + \frac{W_t L_t}{P_t} - i_t \frac{M_t}{P_t} - C_t - \frac{\Omega_{t+1}}{P_t} \right] \tag{9}$$

The first-order conditions in C_t, Y_t, and M_t are:

$$U'(C_t) = \lambda_t + \nu_t \tag{10}$$

$$\Gamma'(L_t) = \lambda_t \frac{W_t}{P_t} \tag{11}$$

$$\nu_t = \lambda_t i_t \tag{12}$$

17.3.3 The Optimum

To characterize optimal states, we take as a benchmark the corresponding "real" model without the CIA constraints. We find the optimum by maximizing utility (5) subject to the production function (4):

$$\text{Maximize} \sum_t \beta^t [U(C_t) - \Gamma(L_t)] \quad \text{s.t.}$$

$$C_t = Y_t = F(L_t)$$

The Lagrangian is:

$$\sum_t \beta^t \{U(C_t) - \Gamma(L_t) + \zeta_t [F(L_t) - C_t]\} \tag{13}$$

The first-order conditions are:

$$U'(C_t) = \zeta_t \tag{14}$$

$$\Gamma'(L_t) = \zeta_t F'(L_t) \tag{15}$$

Combining (14) and (15), we find that the optimum is characterized by:

$$\Gamma'(L_t) = U'(C_t) F'(L_t) \tag{16}$$

17.3.4 The Friedman Rule

We now combine the first-order conditions (8), (10), (11), and (12) characterizing the market equilibrium and find:

$$\Gamma'(L_t) = [U'(C_t) - \nu_t] F'(L_t) \tag{17}$$

It is easy to see that the only way to make (16) and (17) consistent with each other is to take $\nu_t = 0$, and therefore from (12):

$$i_t = 0 \qquad (18)$$

This is the Friedman rule.[5]

17.4 Tax Smoothing

The basic idea of tax smoothing is that if the costs of taxation are convex in the tax rates, then taxes financing a certain amount of public spending should be spread over time rather than, say, concentrated in a single period.

17.4.1 The Intuition

We first give the initial intuition and result, due to Barro (1979). Taxes are distortionary. The real cost associated to a real level of taxes T_t is:

$$Y_t f\left(\frac{T_t}{Y_t}\right) \qquad (19)$$

where f is a convex function that summarizes the various distortions associated to tax collection.

The government has an initial debt D_0 and must finance a sequence of public expenses G_t in real terms. Denote Δ_t as the real discount factor at time t, that is:

$$\Delta_t = \frac{1}{(1+r_1)\dots(1+r_t)} \qquad \Delta_0 = 1 \qquad (20)$$

The government budget constraint is:

$$\sum_{t=0}^{\infty} \Delta_t T_t = D_0 + \sum_{t=0}^{\infty} \Delta_t G_t \qquad (21)$$

The government will choose a sequence of taxes T_t so as to minimize total discounted costs associated to taxation, that is:

$$\text{Minimize } \sum_t \Delta_t Y_t f\left(\frac{T_t}{Y_t}\right) \qquad (22)$$

---

5. For further developments on the conditions of validity of the Friedman rule, see notably Abel (1987); Chari, Christiano, and Kehoe (1996); Correia and Teles (1996, 1999); Guidotti and Vegh (1993); Woodford (1990b).

subject to the intertemporal budget constraint (21). The Lagrangian is:

$$\sum_t \Delta_t Y_t f\left(\frac{T_t}{Y_t}\right) + \lambda \left(D_0 + \sum_t \Delta_t G_t - \sum_t \Delta_t T_t\right) \quad (23)$$

and the first-order conditions:

$$f'\left(\frac{T_t}{Y_t}\right) = \lambda \quad \forall t \quad (24)$$

which implies, because f is convex, that T_t/Y_t is constant in time. There is indeed tax smoothing.

17.4.2 A Simple Microfounded Model

We present the tax smoothing insight in a simple model with explicit maximizing by firms and households. Assume there are two periods, 0 and 1. Firms have linear technologies:

$$Y_0 = A_0 L_0 \quad Y_1 = A_1 L_1 \quad (25)$$

Households have the following utility function over these two periods:

$$U = C_0 - \frac{L_0^{1+\nu}}{1+\nu} + \beta\left(C_1 - \frac{L_1^{1+\nu}}{1+\nu}\right) \quad (26)$$

Households receive a real wage ω_t in $t = 0, 1$, and are taxed proportionally at the rate τ_t. Because the utility is linear in consumption, the discount rate β is also the intertemporal price, and consequently the budget constraint is:

$$C_0 + \beta C_1 = \omega_0 (1 - \tau_0) L_0 + \beta \omega_1 (1 - \tau_1) L_1 \quad (27)$$

Maximizing the utility function subject to this budget constraint yields the supplies of labor:

$$L_0 = [\omega_0 (1 - \tau_0)]^{1/\nu} \quad L_1 = [\omega_1 (1 - \tau_1)]^{1/\nu} \quad (28)$$

In view of the technology (25) the real wages are:

$$\omega_0 = A_0 \quad \omega_1 = A_1 \quad (29)$$

Combining (26) and (27) we find that total utility is:

$$U = \omega_0 (1 - \tau_0) L_0 + \beta \omega_1 (1 - \tau_1) L_1 - \frac{L_0^{1+\nu}}{1+\nu} - \beta \frac{L_1^{1+\nu}}{1+\nu} \quad (30)$$

Inserting into (30) the value of labor demand (28) and real wages (29), the expression of total household utility (30) becomes:

$$U = \frac{\nu}{1+\nu} [A_0 (1 - \tau_0)]^{(1+\nu)/\nu} + \beta \frac{\nu}{1+\nu} [A_1 (1 - \tau_1)]^{(1+\nu)/\nu} \quad (31)$$

The government will choose the tax rates τ_0 and τ_1 so as to maximize utility (31) under the constraint that total taxes must finance an exogenously given government spending:

$$\tau_0 A_0 L_0 + \beta \tau_1 A_1 L_1 = G \quad (32)$$

or, inserting the values of L_0 and L_1 (equation 28) into (32):

$$\tau_0 A_0 [A_0 (1 - \tau_0)]^{1/\nu} + \beta \tau_1 A_1 [A_1 (1 - \tau_1)]^{1/\nu} = G \quad (33)$$

The government maximizes utility (31) subject to its budget constraint (33). The Lagrangian is:

$$\frac{\nu}{1+\nu} [A_0 (1 - \tau_0)]^{(1+\nu)/\nu} + \beta \frac{\nu}{1+\nu} [A_1 (1 - \tau_1)]^{(1+\nu)/\nu}$$
$$- \lambda \left\{ \tau_0 A_0 [A_0 (1 - \tau_0)]^{1/\nu} + \beta \tau_1 A_1 [A_1 (1 - \tau_1)]^{1/\nu} \right\} \quad (34)$$

The first-order conditions yield.

$$\frac{\tau_0}{1 - \tau_0} = \frac{\nu (1 + \lambda)}{\lambda} = \frac{\tau_1}{1 - \tau_1} \quad (35)$$

and therefore:

$$\tau_0 = \tau_1 \quad (36)$$

In accordance with Barro's intuition, the tax rates are equalized across periods. Bohn (1990) shows how the argument can be extended to a stochastic environment.

17.5 Optimal Ramsey Taxation

The two previous sections presented two classic examples of the public finance approach to policy. We go a little deeper into the basics of the area and expose one of the pillars of this approach, Ramsey taxation.[7] The problem is: how should a government choose tax rates over various goods when only distortionary taxation is available.[6] We use a particularly simple model, which highlights the basic principles most clearly.

There are a number of goods indexed by $i \in I$. Representative households maximize the utility function:

$$U = \sum_i \frac{C_i^{1-\theta_i}}{1-\theta_i} - L \qquad (37)$$

where the parameter θ_i turns out to be the inverse of the elasticity of the demand for good i.

Denote as $\tau_i \in [0,1]$ the fraction of the value of good i that is taxed by the government. Our problem will be to determine the optimal value of the τ_i's for a given amount of government spending G. The household is subject to the budget constraint:

$$\sum_i p_i C_i = \omega L \qquad (38)$$

where p_i is the selling price of good i and ω the real wage. We further assume a linear technology whereby firms produce one unit of good i with one unit of labor:

$$Y_i = L_i \qquad (39)$$

so that:

$$p_i = \frac{\omega}{1-\tau_i} \qquad (40)$$

and the budget constraint (38) is rewritten:

$$\sum_i \frac{C_i}{1-\tau_i} = L \qquad (41)$$

---

6. The initial insight is found in Ramsey (1927). A general exposition is in Atkinson and Stiglitz (1980). These methods have been applied to numerous fiscal and monetary policy issues. See, for example, Chari, Christiano, and Kehoe (1991) and Chari and Kehoe (1999).

The household maximizes utility (37) subject to the budget constraint (41). This yields:

$$C_i = (1 - \tau_i)^{1/\theta_i} \qquad (42)$$

The budget constraint of the government is:

$$\sum_i \frac{\tau_i C_i}{1 - \tau_i} = G \qquad (43)$$

We assume that the government is benevolent, that is, it has the same utility (37) as the households. The program of the government is:

$$\text{Maximize} \sum_i \frac{C_i^{1-\theta_i}}{1 - \theta_i} - L \qquad \text{s.t.}$$

$$\sum_i \frac{\tau_i C_i}{1 - \tau_i} = G$$

We insert the values of L (formula 41) and C_i (formula 42) into the utility function and budget constraint above. The maximization program becomes:

$$\text{Maximize} \sum_i \frac{\theta_i}{1 - \theta_i} (1 - \tau_i)^{(1-\theta_i)/\theta_i} \qquad \text{s.t.}$$

$$\sum_i \tau_i (1 - \tau_i)^{(1-\theta_i)/\theta_i} = G$$

The Lagrangian is:

$$\sum_i \frac{\theta_i}{1 - \theta_i} (1 - \tau_i)^{(1-\theta_i)/\theta_i} - \lambda \left[\sum_i \tau_i (1 - \tau_i)^{(1-\theta_i)/\theta_i} \right] \qquad (44)$$

The first-order conditions are:

$$\tau_i = \frac{1 + \lambda}{\lambda} \theta_i \qquad (45)$$

We see that the tax rates τ_i are, other things equal, proportional to θ_i, which is the inverse of the elasticity of the demand function for good i (equation 42). Intuitively, the more elastic the demand for a good, the more distortions taxation will create, and thus the government wants to tax where it will create the least distortions.

17.6 Optimal Seigniorage

We immediately apply the foregoing principles to the problem of optimal seigniorage. Seigniorage is the amount of real resources the government can raise by printing money. What is often called the problem of optimal seigniorage is actually the more general problem of how the government should optimally share the financing of a given amount of expenses between seigniorage and proper taxation. Phelps (1973) showed how the methods of public finance could be fruitfully applied in this domain. In this section, we address this problem using a model by Helpman and Sadka (1979).

17.6.1 The Model

We consider an OLG model à la Samuelson (1958). Households have the following utility function:[7]

$$U\left(C_{1t}, C_{2t+1}, L_t\right) = \frac{C_{1t}^{1-\theta_1}}{1-\theta_1} + \beta \frac{C_{2t+1}^{1-\theta_2}}{1-\theta_2} - L_t \qquad \theta_1 \geq 0 \qquad \theta_2 \geq 0 \qquad (46)$$

In the first period of their life, households work L_t and consume C_{1t}. They consume C_{2t+1} in the second period. Households save from the first period to the next under the form of money balances, which yield no interest.

Firms have a simple linear technology:

$$Y_t = L_t \qquad (47)$$

We assume that the government can tax first- and second-period consumptions at different rates, respectively, τ_1 and τ_2. Accordingly the budget constraint of the consumer is written:

$$\frac{P_t C_{1t}}{1-\tau_1} + \frac{P_{t+1} C_{2t+1}}{1-\tau_2} = W_t L_t \qquad (48)$$

We denote the real wage W_t/P_t as ω_t, and the inflation rate as π_t. Equation (48) is rewritten:

$$\frac{C_{1t}}{1-\tau_1} + \frac{(1+\pi_{t+1}) C_{2t}}{1-\tau_2} = \omega_t L_t = Y_t \qquad (49)$$

---

7. Note that we use different elasticities for C_{1t} and C_{2t}, as this will play a central role in the results.

We consider only stationary states in which all real variables and the rate of inflation are constant, which yields the following budget constraint:

$$\frac{C_1}{1-\tau_1} + \frac{(1+\pi)\,C_2}{1-\tau_2} = \omega L = Y \tag{50}$$

17.6.2 The Government's Financing Options

The government must finance an amount G of public spending. Combining (50) and the identity $C_1 + C_2 + G = Y$, we obtain the government's budget constraint:

$$\frac{\tau_1 C_1}{1-\tau_1} + \frac{\tau_2 C_2}{1-\tau_2} + \frac{\pi C_2}{1-\tau_2} = G \tag{51}$$

The two first terms are the traditional taxes. The third term is the inflation tax. This is related to the seigniorage, because at least in steady states inflation and monetary creation are usually linked.

17.6.3 Market Equilibrium

Because of the linear production function, $\omega = 1$. Maximizing the utility function subject to this budget constraint yields the demand functions:

$$C_1 = (1-\tau_1)^{1/\theta_1} \tag{52}$$

$$C_2 = \left(\frac{1-\tau_2}{1+\pi}\right)^{1/\theta_2} \tag{53}$$

We insert these two values into the household's budget constraint to find the supply of labor:

$$L = (1-\tau_1)^{(1-\theta_1)/\theta_1} + \left(\frac{1-\tau_2}{1+\pi}\right)^{(1-\theta_2)/\theta_2} \tag{54}$$

Inserting (52), (53), and (54) into (46), we compute the utility derived from these transactions:

$$U = \frac{\theta_1}{1-\theta_1}(1-\tau_1)^{(1-\theta_1)/\theta_1} + \frac{\theta_2}{1-\theta_2}\left(\frac{1-\tau_2}{1+\pi}\right)^{(1-\theta_2)/\theta_2} \tag{55}$$

Inserting the values of consumptions (52) and (53) into (51), we obtain the following expression for the government's budget constraint:

$$\frac{\tau_1(1-\tau_1)^{1/\theta_1}}{1-\tau_1} + \frac{\tau_2}{1-\tau_2}\left(\frac{1-\tau_2}{1+\pi}\right)^{1/\theta_2} + \frac{\pi}{1-\tau_2}\left(\frac{1-\tau_2}{1+\pi}\right)^{1/\theta_2} = G \tag{56}$$

17.6.4 Optimal Seigniorage and Taxes

The government maximizes (55) subject to (56). The Lagrangian is:

$$\frac{\theta_1}{1-\theta_1}(1-\tau_1)^{(1-\theta_1)/\theta_1} + \frac{\theta_2}{1-\theta_2}\left(\frac{1-\tau_2}{1+\pi}\right)^{(1-\theta_2)/\theta_2}$$
$$-\lambda\left[\tau_1(1-\tau_1)^{(1-\theta_1)/\theta_1} + (\tau_2+\pi)(1+\pi)^{-1/\theta_2}(1-\tau_2)^{(1-\theta_2)/\theta_2}\right] \quad (57)$$

Although there are apparently three free parameters (τ_1, τ_2, and π), there are actually only two independent variables, τ_1 and $(\tau_2+\pi)/(1+\pi)$, and therefore two first-order conditions, which are:

$$\tau_1 = \theta_1 \frac{1+\lambda}{\lambda} \quad (58)$$

$$\frac{\tau_2+\pi}{1+\pi} = \theta_2 \frac{1+\lambda}{\lambda} \quad (59)$$

From these formulas we see a number of things. First, if seigniorage is not used ($\pi = 0$), we find the usual result in optimal taxation that the tax rate should be highest for the goods whose demand is inelastic. More precisely, τ_1 and τ_2 are proportional to θ_1 and θ_2. This is in accordance with the results on Ramsey taxation that we saw in section 17.5.

Now these two goods are not actually different goods, but the same good consumed by people at different stages of life. It is thus difficult to envision that they could be taxed differently. In such a case, inflation will act as a surrogate for differential taxation. To see how this works, we write $\tau_1 = \tau_2 = \tau$, and eliminate λ between (58) and (59). We obtain:

$$\pi = \frac{(\theta_2 - \theta_1)\tau}{\theta_1 - \theta_2 \tau} \quad (60)$$

We see that unless $\theta_2 = \theta_1$, optimal inflation is different from zero.

Appendix 17.1: The Cost of Distortionary Taxation

We use a very simple example to compute the costs generated by distortionary taxation, and we show how they relate to relevant elasticities.

The Model

We take a highly streamlined model. Households have the following utility function:

$$U = C - \frac{L^{1+\nu}}{1+\nu} \tag{61}$$

The production function is:

$$Y = AL \tag{62}$$

Finally the government spends an amount G, so that equilibrium on the goods market requires:

$$Y = C + G \tag{63}$$

The Optimum

As a benchmark, we first compute the optimum in this economy. Combining (62) and (63) we find that consumption is:

$$C = AL - G \tag{64}$$

so that one will maximize:

$$AL - G - \frac{L^{1+\nu}}{1+\nu} \tag{65}$$

whose solution is:

$$L^* = A^{1/\nu} \qquad C^* = A^{(1+\nu)/\nu} - G \tag{66}$$

$$U = U^* = \frac{\nu}{1+\nu} A^{(1+\nu)/\nu} - G \tag{67}$$

Market Equilibrium: Lump-sum Taxes

We assume that government spending G is financed by lump-sum taxes T:

$$T = G \tag{68}$$

In view of the linear production function (62), the real wage is equal to A, so that the household solves the following program:

$$\text{Maximize } C - \frac{L^{1+\nu}}{1+\nu} \quad \text{s.t.}$$

$$C = AL - T$$

This yields, taking into account that $T = G$:

$$L_1 = A^{1/\nu} \qquad C_1 = A^{(1+\nu)/\nu} - G \tag{69}$$

$$U_1 = \frac{\nu}{1+\nu} A^{(1+\nu)/\nu} - G \tag{70}$$

We note immediately that this is the same as in the optimum, so lump-sum taxation creates no distortion.

Market Equilibrium: Distortionary Taxes

We now assume distortionary taxes. The government taxes labor income at the rate τ. The after-tax real wage is thus $A(1-\tau)$ and the household solves:

$$\text{Maximize } C - \frac{L^{1+\nu}}{1+\nu} \quad \text{s.t.}$$

$$C = A(1-\tau)L$$

The solution is:

$$L_2 = [A(1-\tau)]^{1/\nu} \qquad C_2 = [A(1-\tau)]^{(1+\nu)/\nu} \tag{71}$$

$$U_2 = \frac{\nu}{1+\nu} [A(1-\tau)]^{(1+\nu)/\nu} \tag{72}$$

Now the tax rate τ will be determined by the condition that taxes finance public spending, that is, $G = \tau AL$, or:

$$G = \tau A [A(1-\tau)]^{1/\nu} \tag{73}$$

Formula (73) shows that we have a "Laffer curve" situation (figure 17.1), since there is a tax rate $\hat{\tau}$ beyond which tax receipts actually decrease with the tax rate. Maximizing (73) with respect to τ we find that $\hat{\tau}$ is equal to:

$$\hat{\tau} = \frac{\nu}{1+\nu} \tag{74}$$

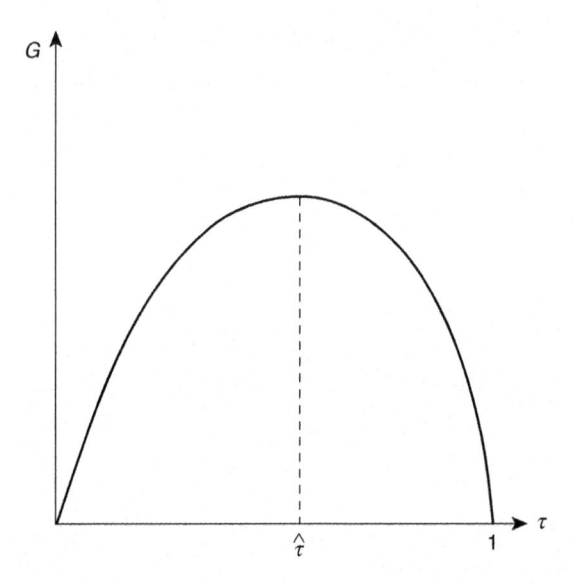

Figure 17.1 A Laffer curve

As should be expected, an elastic labor supply (i.e., a low ν) will lead to fewer taxation possibilities for the government.

Now we compute the difference between the two utilities:

$$U_1 - U_2 = \frac{\nu}{1+\nu} A^{(1+\nu)/\nu} - G - \frac{\nu}{1+\nu} [A(1-\tau)]^{(1+\nu)/\nu} \quad (75)$$

It is actually convenient to use τ as our working variable. In view of equation (73) this becomes:

$$U_1 - U_2 = \frac{\nu}{1+\nu} A^{(1+\nu)/\nu} \left[1 - (1-\tau)^{(1+\nu)/\nu}\right] - \tau A [A(1-\tau)]^{1/\nu} \quad (76)$$

We note that this is equal to 0 for $\tau = 0$. Now we compute:

$$\frac{\partial (U_1 - U_2)}{\partial \tau} = \frac{\tau}{\nu} A^{(1+\nu)/\nu} (1-\tau)^{(1-\nu)/\nu} > 0 \quad (77)$$

So $U_1 - U_2$ is positive and increasing in τ.

A Particular Case

To have a particularly simple and intuitive expression, we further consider the particular case $\nu = 1$, that is, a quadratic utility function:

$$U = C - \frac{L^2}{2} \tag{78}$$

Then the lump-sum case becomes:

$$L_1 = A \qquad C_1 = A^2 - G \tag{79}$$

$$U_1 = \frac{A^2}{2} - G \tag{80}$$

and the distortionary case:

$$L_2 = A(1-\tau) \qquad C_2 = A^2(1-\tau)^2 \tag{81}$$

$$U_2 = \frac{A^2(1-\tau)^2}{2} \tag{82}$$

where G and τ are related by:

$$\tau(1-\tau)A^2 = G \tag{83}$$

Combining (80), (82), and (83) we find that the difference between the two utilities has the particularly simple form:

$$U_1 - U_2 = \frac{A^2\tau^2}{2} \tag{84}$$

Appendix 17.2: Optimal Seigniorage in an OLG Model

We want to study in a model with overlapping generations how the relative weight that the government puts on the various generations influences the optimal seigniorage. We consider an OLG model à la Samuelson (1958). The households born in t have a utility function:

$$U_t = Log C_{1t} + \beta Log C_{2t+1} \tag{85}$$

Following Samuelson (1967, 1968) we assume that the government has the following social utility function:

$$\sum_{t=-1}^{\infty} \phi^t U_t = \sum_{t=-1}^{\infty} \phi^t \left[LogC_{1t} + \beta LogC_{2t+1} \right] \qquad \phi < 1 \qquad (86)$$

where ϕ is a parameter representing the relative weight between two successive generations.

The young household receives a fixed income Y_0 and is taxed lump-sum T_t when young. It can save under the form of money, which it will spend in the second period. The intertemporal budget constraint is:

$$P_t C_{1t} + P_{t+1} C_{2t+1} = P_t (Y_0 - T_t) \qquad (87)$$

Maximizing the utility function (85), subject to the budget constraint (87), yields:

$$C_{1t} = \frac{Y_0 - T_t}{1 + \beta} \qquad (88)$$

The old household has at the outset of period t a quantity of money M_{t-1} which it spends entirely, so that:

$$C_{2t} = \frac{M_{t-1}}{P_t} \qquad (89)$$

The government finances public spending G_t with taxes or monetary creation:

$$M_t - M_{t-1} = P_t (G_t - T_t) \qquad (90)$$

We also have:

$$C_{2t} = Y_0 - C_{1t} - G_t = Y_0 - G_t - \frac{Y_0 - T_t}{1 + \beta} \qquad (91)$$

Maximizing the social welfare function (86) is actually equivalent to maximizing:

$$\sum_{t=0}^{\infty} \phi^t \Upsilon_t \qquad (92)$$

with:

$$\Upsilon_t = LogC_{1t} + \frac{\beta}{\phi} LogC_{2t} \tag{93}$$

We insert (88) and (91) into (93):

$$\Upsilon_t = Log\left(\frac{Y_0 - T_t}{1+\beta}\right) + \frac{\beta}{\phi} Log\left[Y_0 - G_t - \frac{Y_0 - T_t}{1+\beta}\right] \tag{94}$$

Maximizing (94) with respect to T_t we find:

$$\phi(1+\beta)(Y_0 - G_t) = (\beta + \phi)(Y_0 - T_t) \tag{95}$$

Combining (89), (90), (91), and (95) we find:

$$M_t = \phi M_{t-1} \tag{96}$$

Because $\phi < 1$, the optimal seigniorage is actually negative!

Problems

Problem 17.1: The Cost of Distortionary Taxation

Households have a utility function:

$$U = LogC - L$$

The production function is:

$$Y = AL$$

The government carries an exogenous amount of public spending G, and the equation of goods market equilibrium is thus:

$$Y = C + G$$

1. Compute the optimum of this economy. Compute the utility of the household.

2. Compute the market equilibrium assuming that G is financed with lump-sum taxes $T = G$. Compute the associated utility. Compare with the optimum.
3. Compute the market equilibrium assuming that G is financed with distortionary taxes on labor: $G = \tau w L$, where w is the real wage. Compute the associated utility.
4. Compute the cost of distortionary taxation.

Problem 17.2: Optimal Seigniorage with Lump-sum Taxes

We consider an OLG model à la Samuelson (1958). Households live two periods. The household born in period t works an amount L_t in the first period and consumes C_{1t} and C_{2t+1} in the first and second periods, respectively. It has a utility function:

$$U\left(C_{1t}, C_{2t+1}, L_t\right)$$

and budget constraints:

$$P_t C_{1t} + M_t = W_t L_t + \Pi_t - P_t T_t$$

$$P_{t+1} C_{2t+1} = M_t$$

where Π_t are firm's profits and T_t the real value of lump-sum taxes. Assume a production function:

$$Y_t = F(L_t) \qquad F'(L_t) > 0 \qquad F''(L_t) < 0$$

The government spends G_t in real terms. Equilibrium on the goods market requires:

$$C_{1t} + C_{2t} + G_t = Y_t$$

The government can finance its spending G_t by taxes or monetary creation. The government's budget balance yields:

$$P_t G_t = P_t T_t + M_t - M_{t-1}$$

1. Derive the household's and firm's first-order conditions in market equilibrium.
2. Derive the conditions for an intertemporal optimum such that the utility of the representative household is maximized.

3. Compute the optimal values of T_t and $M_t - M_{t-1}$ to finance a given level of spending G_t.

Problem 17.3: Seigniorage and the Cagan Model

We consider the Cagan (1956) model we saw in chapter 3 and show how to compute the rate of inflation that will raise a maximum amount through seigniorage. The demand for money is given by:

$$\frac{M_t^d}{P_t} = \mathcal{M}(\pi_t^e) = A \exp(-\alpha \pi_t^e)$$

The real seigniorage S_t generated by an increase in the quantity of money is:

$$S_t = \frac{\dot{M}_t}{P_t}$$

We call μ_t the rate of increase in the quantity of money:

$$\mu_t = \frac{\dot{M}_t}{M_t}$$

1. Compute the value of real seigniorage as a function of μ_t and π_t^e.
2. Assume a constant rate of growth of money: $\mu_t = \mu$. Compute the value of μ that will raise the maximum amount of seigniorage in steady state.

18

Stabilization Policies

18.1 Introduction

Economies are perpetually subject to destabilizing influences. These can come from exogenous shocks, as in dynamic stochastic general equilibrium (DSGE) models. They can also come from the internal functioning of the economy (the Samuelsonian multiplier-accelerator is the best-known example). Finally, as we will see when studying interest rate rules, destabilization can come from government policy itself.

The stabilization issue is the determination of whether and how government should try to stabilize the economy. It is certainly one of the most debated topics in macroeconomics. Over the years the field has undergone major changes, in both ideas and methods.

In an early stage, beginning with Keynes (1936), Keynesians have strongly advocated activist countercyclical policies. One the other hand, somebody like Milton Friedman battled against such policies most of his life. Although there were a few valid arguments against activism, like model uncertainty or instrument instability (appendixes 18.1 and 18.2), the general opinion until the early 1970s was rather in favor of activism.

A major change occurred with the advent of rational expectations. Notably Lucas (1972, 1976) forcefully advocated the use of structural models as against earlier ad hoc models. Sargent and Wallace (1975, 1976) pointed out the extreme importance of informational assumptions and initiated the "ineffectiveness" debate. We will pay particular attention to these issues in this chapter.

The current trend is to use for policy analysis some rigorously microfounded models, for example in the DSGE tradition that we described in chapters 10, 12, and 13. Although the general methodology is the same for all these models, when we look at the literature we still find a bewilderingly wide array of answers. The reason is clear: even when authors all use a fully rigorous framework like DSGE, they make different assumptions about price and wage rigidities, assets available, the form of monetary or fiscal we will thus not policy, the number of instruments, the information available to agents, and so on. It turns out that the nature of optimal policies can be very sensitive to specific assumptions, and as a result, a synthesis does not appear to be in sight yet; we will thus not attempt to present one. Rather, in the main body of this chapter, we work by way of examples and consider some selected microfounded models, which will show us applications of the general method to a few relevant issues.

In section 18.2 we consider a Walrasian economy faced with stochastic public spending, and we study the problem of choosing optimal financing between taxes and monetary creation to adapt to these stochastic shocks. This model somehow bridges the gap between the public finance approach of the previous chapter and the stochastic stabilization aspects emphasized in this one.

In section 18.3 we reexamine the famous ineffectiveness result of Sargent and Wallace (see chapter 3), according to which government policies are ineffective if the government has no more information than the private sector. We show that more sophisticated policies allow one to actually circumvent the ineffectiveness result. This result is derived from a microfounded model where all agents are explicitly maximizing. It shows very clearly the importance of informational assumptions for the design of stabilization policies.

We move in section 18.4 to another important aspect of government policy design: how to avoid that government fiscal and monetary policies themselves create indeterminacies and therefore instability. This issue is not an abstract, one, as some apparently innocuous policies may lead to indeterminacy and therefore instability. For example, as we already mentioned, Sargent and Wallace (1975) showed that a simple policy of pegging the nominal interest rate would lead to indeterminacy. In section 18.4 we concentrate on monetary interest rate rules. A famous prescription emerges from the literature, the Taylor principle (Taylor, 1993), which says (in its simpler form) that the nominal interest rate should respond more than one for one to inflation. We show that this principle guarantees local determinacy, but unfortunately not global determinacy. We then investigate a few alternative solutions to the problem of determinacy.

18.2 Optimal Monetary and Fiscal Financing

As we indicated, the issue of optimal monetary and fiscal policies has given rise in the latest years to a large and rigorous literature.[1] Rather than undertaking a presumptuous attempt to give a synthetical view of very diverse results, we will demonstrate the methods in the domain, based on rigorous microfounded models, by applying them to some central issues.

The first issue, which we investigate in this section, is that of the optimal monetary-fiscal policy in the presence of stochastic shocks. More precisely, we assume that the value of desired public consumption is a stochastic variable, and we ask what part of it should be financed by money creation (seigniorage) and which part by straight taxation. This will be made in a rigorous DSGE framework, which will both demonstrate the general method and make a link with the public finance approach of the previous chapter.

18.2.1 The Model

We consider a Walrasian overlapping generations model à la Samuelson (1958) with the following utility function:

$$U_t = LogC_{1t} + \beta LogC_{2t+1} - L_t \qquad (1)$$

In the first period of their life, households work L_t, and this labor income is taxed at the rate τ_t. Households save from the first period to the next under the form of money balances that yield no interest. Accordingly their budget constraints for the two periods of their life are:

$$P_t C_{1t} + M_t = (1 - \tau_t) W_t L_t \qquad (2)$$

$$P_{t+1} C_{2t+1} = M_t \qquad (3)$$

Firms have a linear technology:

$$Y_t = L_t \qquad (4)$$

Finally real government spending is G_t, which is an i.i.d. stochastic variable with bounded support.

---

1. A (partial) list includes Adao, Correia, and Teles (2003); Aiyagari, Marcet, Sargent, and Seppälä (2002); Calvo and Guidotti (1993); Chari, Christiano, and Kehoe (1994); Correia, Nicolini, and Teles (2008); Erceg, Henderson, and Levin (2000); Henderson and Kim (1999); Ireland (1996); Khan, King, and Wolman (2003); King and Wolman (1999); McCallum and Nelson (1999); Rotemberg and Woodford (1997, 1999); Schmitt-Grohe and Uribe (2004); Siu (2004); Woodford (2003); and Yun (2005).

18.2.2 Market Equilibrium

In view of the linear production function (4), we have:

$$W_t = P_t \tag{5}$$

The old household arrives in period t with a quantity of money M_{t-1}, so its consumption is:

$$C_{2t} = \frac{M_{t-1}}{P_t} \tag{6}$$

The young household maximizes the expected value of the utility (1) subject to the budget constraints (2) and (3). In view of (6), it will solve the program:

$$\text{Maximize } Log C_{1t} + \beta Log M_t - L_t \quad \text{s.t.}$$

$$P_t C_{1t} + M_t = (1 - \tau_t) W_t L_t$$

Calling λ_t the Lagrange multiplier of the date t budget constraint, the first-order conditions are:

$$\lambda_t P_t C_{1t} = 1 \tag{7}$$

$$\lambda_t M_t = \beta \tag{8}$$

$$\lambda_t (1 - \tau_t) W_t = 1 \tag{9}$$

These yield in particular a consumption function:

$$P_t C_{1t} = \frac{(1 - \tau_t) W_t L_t}{1 + \beta} \tag{10}$$

and a constant amount of labor:

$$L_t = L = 1 + \beta \tag{11}$$

Combining (5) and (10) we find:

$$C_{1t} = \frac{(1 - \tau_t) L}{1 + \beta} \tag{12}$$

and since $Y_t = L$:

$$C_{2t} = Y_t - C_{1t} - G_t = \frac{(\beta + \tau_t) L}{1 + \beta} - G_t \qquad (13)$$

We assume that the government maximizes the expected utility of the representative household:

$$Log C_{1t} + \beta Log C_{2t+1} - L_t \qquad (14)$$

Employment L_t is constant and equal to L, so inserting (12) and (13) into (14) we find that the household's utility is equal to:

$$Log \left[\frac{(1 - \tau_t) L}{1 + \beta} \right] + \beta Log \left[\frac{(\beta + \tau_t) L}{1 + \beta} - G_t \right] - L \qquad (15)$$

Differentiating with respect to τ_t, we find the optimal tax rate:

$$\tau_t = \frac{G_t}{L} = \frac{G_t}{Y} \qquad (16)$$

We see that government spending is 100 percent financed by taxation. Optimal seigniorage is 0.

This result of 100 percent financing by taxes and zero seigniorage might look a bit surprising because, after all, taxes are distortionary. Actually, we can find a useful simple intuition for this result in the model of optimal seigniorage seen in the previous chapter, section 17.5. There we had a more general utility function:

$$\frac{C_{1t}^{1-\theta_1}}{1 - \theta_1} + \beta \frac{C_{2t+1}^{1-\theta_2}}{1 - \theta_2} - L_t \qquad (17)$$

and accordingly we found that the optimal rates of taxation τ and inflation π were related by:

$$\pi = \frac{(\theta_2 - \theta_1) \tau}{\theta_1 - \theta_2 \tau} \qquad (18)$$

Our assumption of logarithmic utility function (equation 1) corresponds to $\theta_1 = \theta_2 = 1$, which yields:

$$\pi = 0 \qquad (19)$$

The government will not use inflationary money creation to finance its spending.

Although it is rigorously demonstrated and intuitively founded, this result should nevertheless not be considered fully general. Indeed, Calvo and Guidotti (1993) build a no less rigorous model with infinitely lived agents. They consider a particular specification where unexpected inflation entails no social cost. As a result, variations in government spending are optimally financed by costless money creation (and subsequent inflation) rather than costly distortionary taxes. This shows that different prescriptions can be obtained from equally rigorous models.

18.3 Government Information and the Policy Effectiveness Debate

18.3.1 The Debate

We will now demonstrate that the problem of information is of fundamental importance in the stabilization issue. For that purpose we study a debate that has been central in shaping ideas about stabilization, that about government information and the effectiveness of government policies.

Until the early 1970s, it was usually admitted, following Keynesian intuitions, that wage or price rigidities provide a valid case for activist counter cyclical demand policies. A devastating critique was made by Sargent and Wallace (1975). They showed that policy effectiveness in most traditional Keynesian models was essentially due to an "informational advantage" implicitly given to the government in such models. More precisely, the government is allowed to react to recent shocks, while the private sector is locked into "old" wage or price contracts, themselves based on old shocks. If the government is not allowed to use more information about shocks than the private sector, then government policies become ineffective (a very simple model developing this argument is presented in appendix 18.3).

This line of attack was particularly damaging, notably as most Keynesian models, even some of those constructed with rational expectations after Sargent and Wallace (1975), were vulnerable to this critique. Moreover the informational advantage critique is truly compelling because, even if a government has more information than the private sector, it could be considered its duty to release any such superior information to private agents, and to intervene only if the result is not sufficient.

In two insightful articles, Turnovsky (1980) and Weiss (1980)[2] showed in traditional models that policy could be effective even when government was

---

2. See also King (1982, 1983) and Andersen (1986a, 1986b).

no more informed than the private sector. Of course this has to be confirmed in a model with maximizing agents, and in this section we describe a model adapted from Bénassy (2001a, 2002a). As we shall see, it fully confirms the Turnovsky-Weiss results.

18.3.2 The Model

We use an overlapping generations (OLG) model à la Samuelson (1958). Households live two periods. Households of generation t work L_t, consume C_{1t} when young, and save a quantity of money M_t, which is the only asset in the economy. They consume C_{2t+1} when old, and maximize the expected value of their utility U_t, with:

$$U_t = \alpha_t Log\, C_{1t} + Log\, C_{2t+1} - (1+\alpha_t) L_t \qquad (20)$$

where $\alpha_t > 0$ is a demand shock. The representative firm in period t has a production function

$$Y_t = A_t L_t \qquad (21)$$

where A_t is a common i.i.d. productivity shock. Government's policy consists in giving to the old households transfers $\mathcal{T}_t$ in nominal terms.

18.3.3 Timing and Information

Because the issue raised by Sargent and Wallace (1975) about the respective informations of the public and private sector is central to the debate, the timing of actions and information is important. In period t events occur in three stages.

1. Government decides its policy variable, the transfer $\mathcal{T}_t$. We assume that $\mathcal{T}_t$ is function only of macroeconomic variables up to $t-1$ included (and therefore *not* of any variable or shock revealed in period t).
2. The price is preset at its expected market-clearing value, without knowing the values of period t shocks A_t and α_t.
3. The shocks α_t and A_t become known to the private sector, and transactions are carried out accordingly.

Because policy decisions in period t are based on information up to $t-1$, the government is no more informed than the private agents.

18.3.4 Walrasian Equilibrium

We compute the Walrasian equilibrium as a benchmark. We begin with old households. They start period t with a quantity of money M_{t-1}, which they carried from the previous period. They receive a transfer $\mathcal{T}_t$, so that they have a total quantity of money available equal to:

$$M_t = M_{t-1} + \mathcal{T}_t \qquad (22)$$

and their consumption is thus given by

$$C_{2t} = \frac{M_t}{P_t} \qquad (23)$$

We now write the maximization program of the young household born in t. When young, it receives wages $W_t L_t$ (profits are 0 because of the linear technology). It will receive $\mathcal{T}_{t+1}$ from the government when old.[3] If it consumes C_{1t} in the first period of its life, it will begin the second period of life with a quantity of money:

$$M_t = W_t L_t - P_t C_{1t} \qquad (24)$$

In view of (23), the expected value of $Log\, C_{2t+1}$ is, up to an unimportant constant, equal to $Log\, (M_t + \mathcal{T}_{t+1})$, so that the household in the first period of its life solves the following program:

Maximize $\alpha_t Log\, C_{1t} + Log\, (M_t + \mathcal{T}_{t+1}) - (1 + \alpha_t) L_t$ s.t.

$$M_t = W_t L_t - P_t C_{1t}$$

The first-order conditions in C_{1t} and L_t are:

$$(1 + \alpha_t) P_t C_{1t} = \alpha_t (W_t L_t + \mathcal{T}_{t+1}) \qquad (25)$$

$$W_t = (1 + \alpha_t)(W_t L_t - P_t C_{1t} + \mathcal{T}_{t+1}) \qquad (26)$$

The equilibrium condition on the goods market is:

$$C_{1t} + C_{2t} = Y_t \qquad (27)$$

---

3. Note that because $\mathcal{T}_{t+1}$ is function of information in period t, it is therefore known with certainty in period t.

Because the goods market clears, we further have:

$$\frac{W_t}{P_t} = A_t \qquad (28)$$

Combining (24), (25), and (26), we find the value of the Walrasian wage:

$$W_t^* = (1 + \alpha_t)(M_t + \mathcal{T}_{t+1}) \qquad (29)$$

18.3.5 Preset Wages

Assume now that at the beginning of period t, wages are preset based on information available then (which does *not* include the values of A_t and α_t), and that at this wage households supply the quantity of labor demanded by firms. We make the assumption, traditional since Gray (1976), that the preset wage is equal to the expected value of the Walrasian wage:[4]

$$W_t = E_{t-1} W_t^* \qquad (30)$$

where the expression of W_t^* is given by formula (29). Combining (29) and (30), the preset wage is equal to:

$$W_t = E_{t-1}(1 + \alpha_t)(M_t + \mathcal{T}_{t+1}) \qquad (31)$$

Under preset wages, equation (26) does not hold anymore, but the other equilibrium equations (23), (24), (25), (27), and (28) still hold. Combining them, we find that the preset wage equilibrium is characterized by the following values for consumptions and employment:

$$C_{1t} = \frac{\alpha_t (M_t + \mathcal{T}_{t+1}) A_t}{W_t} \qquad (32)$$

$$C_{2t} = \frac{M_t A_t}{W_t} \qquad (33)$$

$$L_t = \frac{\alpha_t (M_t + \mathcal{T}_{t+1})}{W_t} + \frac{M_t}{W_t} \qquad (34)$$

---

4. Derivations of similar relations in a framework of imperfect competition can be found, for example, in Bénassy (2002b), Woodford (2003), and many others.

18.3.6 The Optimality of Activist Policies

We now show that under preset wages optimal policies are activist. Indeed, the optimal policy is characterized by:

$$\frac{M_t + \mathcal{T}_{t+1}}{M_t} = \frac{1 + \alpha_a}{1 + \alpha_t} \tag{35}$$

where:

$$\alpha_a = E(\alpha_t) \tag{36}$$

Proof: To prove condition (35), we maximize the utility of the representative household. We simply insert the values of consumptions and labor (formulas 32, 33, and 34) into the utility function (20), which yields:

$$U_t = \alpha_t Log\left[\frac{\alpha_t (M_t + \mathcal{T}_{t+1}) A_t}{W_t}\right] + Log\left(\frac{M_t A_t}{W_t}\right)$$

$$- (1 + \alpha_t)\left[\frac{\alpha_t (M_t + \mathcal{T}_{t+1})}{W_t} + \frac{M_t}{W_t}\right] \tag{37}$$

We maximize (37) subject to the wage equation (31). As it turns out, the wage equation (31) is not binding, so we can maximize (37) without constraint.[5] We start with the future transfers $\mathcal{T}_{t+1}$, which can be chosen freely based on period t information. Maximization in $\mathcal{T}_{t+1}$ yields:

$$M_t + \mathcal{T}_{t+1} = \frac{W_t}{1 + \alpha_t} \tag{38}$$

Inserting this into (37), we find, eliminating irrelevant constants:

$$U_t = Log\left(\frac{M_t A_t}{W_t}\right) - (1 + \alpha_t)\frac{M_t}{W_t} \tag{39}$$

Taking the expectation and maximizing with respect to W_t, we find:

$$W_t = (1 + \alpha_a) M_t \tag{40}$$

Combining (38) and (40), we find formula (35).

---

5. Different (but longer) proofs with similar results are implemented, for example, in Bénassy (2002b).

Properties of the Optimal Policy

We see that the optimal policy (35) is an activist countercyclical one: a negative demand shock today (low α_t) triggers high transfers tomorrow (high $\mathcal{T}_{t+1}$) and conversely for a positive demand shock.

We may also note that government needs not respond to productivity shocks, as price movements satisfactorily take care of them. If price movements are restricted, government will have to react to productivity shocks (problem 18.3).

Finally, we note a quite striking property of this optimal policy. Indeed, combining (29) and (38), we find:

$$W_t = W_t^* \qquad (41)$$

The wage is always equal to its Walrasian value! Although the wage is preset before the shocks are known, the labor market is always cleared under our optimal policy.

18.3.7 An Intuitive Explanation

The fact that a government with no more information than the private sector can nevertheless succeed in stabilizing the economy, despite wages being set in advance without knowledge of the shocks, may be quite surprising. We give a simple intuition behind this striking result. We rewrite the equation for employment (equation 34):

$$L_t = \frac{\alpha_t \left(M_t + \mathcal{T}_{t+1}\right)}{W_t} + \frac{M_t}{W_t} \qquad (42)$$

Suppose that after the wage has been set, a negative demand shock (a low α_t) hits the economy. If the government has no systematic policy, this shock will clearly lead, in view of (42), to a *decrease* in the quantity of labor. This is the traditional effect. Now if the government is known to lead the countercyclical policy (35), then the private sector will know in advance that the future transfers $\mathcal{T}_{t+1}$ will be high, and from the foregoing formula this will, on the contrary, tend to *increase* the quantity of labor. When policy is calibrated to be (35), these two conflicting effects cancel out, and the economy remains at full employment. Of course, the zero unemployment result is due to our particular specifications, but the fact that an adequate activist policy can be beneficial is a robust result.

18.4 Interest Rate Rules and Determinacy

We will study in this section a very important topic in the design of optimal policies—that of whether such policies lead to determinate or indeterminate dynamics.

This subject has become particularly topical since the article of Sargent and Wallace (1975), who showed that a policy of pegging the nominal interest rate would lead to nominal indeterminacy.

Because of that article, the topic of which interest rate rules lead to determinacy has been a particularly lively subject of research in monetary economics. In this section we focus on this important debate and characterize which interest rate rules can lead to determinacy. We first give a few definitions about interest rate rules.

18.4.1 Taylor Rules and the Taylor Principle

The recent debate has actually concentrated around "Taylor rules" (Taylor, 1993), where the nominal interest rate responds to inflation:[6]

$$1 + i_t = \Phi(\Pi_t) \qquad \Phi(\Pi_t) \geq 1 \tag{43}$$

with $\Pi_t = P_t/P_{t-1}$. We also define the elasticity of this function:

$$\phi(\Pi_t) = \frac{\partial Log\Phi(\Pi_t)}{\partial Log\Pi_t} = \frac{\Pi_t \Phi'(\Pi_t)}{\Phi(\Pi_t)} \tag{44}$$

One says that the Taylor principle is satisfied at Π_t if $\phi(\Pi_t) > 1$. The intuitive idea behind this is that under the Taylor principle, an increase in inflation brings an increase in the real interest rate, which is supposed to create a stabilizing effect in the economy (Taylor, 1998).

18.4.2 The Model

To rigorously assess the validity of various statements about policy, we carry the analysis in a microfounded model. We use the simple cash-in-advance (CIA) Ricardian model that we described in chapter 11 (section 11.5).

---

6. In Taylor (1993) the nominal interest rate responds also to the level of activity, but the subsequent debates have mostly emphasized inflation, so we concentrate on it here.

Recall briefly the main characteristics: there is an infinitely lived household with utility function:

$$U_t = \sum_{s=t}^{\infty} \beta^{s-t} Log\, C_s \tag{45}$$

which is subject in each period t to a CIA constraint:

$$P_t C_t \leq M_t \tag{46}$$

This household receives in period t an exogenous endowment Y_t, which grows at the rate ζ:

$$\frac{Y_{t+1}}{Y_t} = \zeta \tag{47}$$

18.4.3 Dynamics

As we saw in chapter 11, a household's intertemporal utility maximization subject to the budget constraints and the CIA constraints yields an Euler-type equation:

$$P_{t+1} C_{t+1} = \beta (1 + i_t) P_t C_t \tag{48}$$

Combining with the equilibrium condition $C_t = Y_t$ we obtain:

$$P_{t+1} Y_{t+1} = \beta (1 + i_t) P_t Y_t \tag{49}$$

and finally inserting the Taylor rule (43):

$$P_{t+1} Y_{t+1} = \beta \Phi(\Pi_t) P_t Y_t \tag{50}$$

Dividing both sides of equation (50) by $\zeta P_t Y_t$, it becomes:

$$\Pi_{t+1} = \frac{\Phi(\Pi_t)}{\xi} \tag{51}$$

with:

$$\xi = \frac{\zeta}{\beta} \tag{52}$$

The parameter ξ is the steady-state gross real interest rate.

18.4.4 Local Determinacy

From (51), steady states Π, if they exist, are characterized by:

$$\Pi = \frac{\Phi(\Pi)}{\xi} \qquad (53)$$

Linearizing (51) around a steady state, we obtain:

$$\Pi_{t+1} - \Pi = \frac{\Phi'(\Pi)}{\xi}(\Pi_t - \Pi) \qquad (54)$$

Because Π_t is a nonpredetermined variable, the condition for local determinacy is that the coefficient of Π_t be greater than 1 (mathematical appendix, section A.11.6), that is:

$$\frac{\Phi'(\Pi)}{\xi} > 1 \qquad (55)$$

which, in view of (53), can be rewritten:

$$\phi(\Pi) = \frac{\Pi \Phi'(\Pi)}{\Phi(\Pi)} > 1 \qquad (56)$$

We see that the Taylor principle is indeed valid as a local determinacy condition.

18.4.5 The Problem of Global Determinacy

We just saw that the Taylor principle yields local determinacy. But it was shown by Benhabib, Schmitt-Grohé, and Uribe (2001) that this property unfortunately does not carry over to global determinacy. The reason appears clearly in figure 18.1.

The steady states are intersections of the curve $\Phi(\Pi_t)/\xi$ with the 45-degree line. The Taylor principle is satisfied if the slope of the curve at the intersection is greater than 1. This is the case at Π_2, which is locally determinate.

The problem is that the Taylor principle cannot be satisfied everywhere. Indeed, because the nominal interest rate must be positive everywhere, that is, $\Phi(\Pi_t) \geq 1$ for all Π_t, there must be at least another intersection, like Π_1, where the slope at the intersection is smaller than 1. Π_1 is indeterminate, and as a consequence we have global indeterminacy. In fact, there is an infinity of admissible trajectories, starting on the left of Π_2, and all converging toward Π_1. The Taylor principle thus fails to deliver global determinacy.

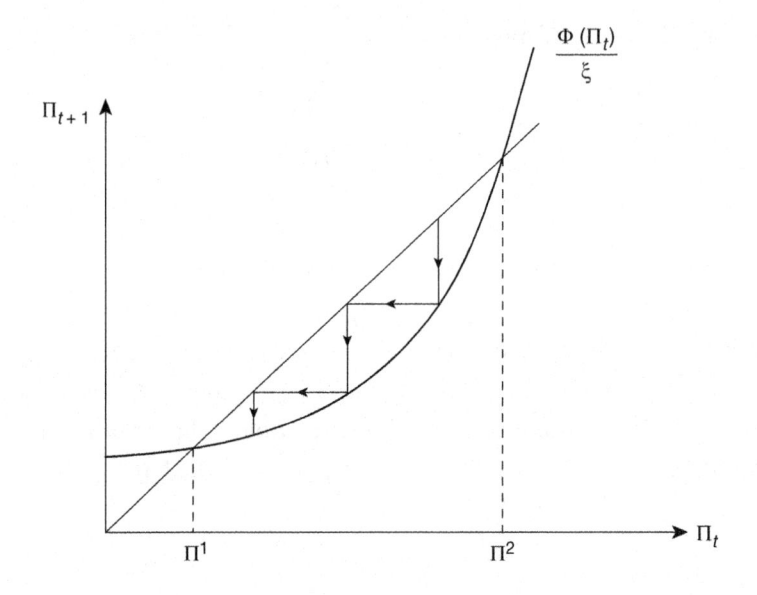

Figure 18.1 Global indeterminacy

18.4.6 Further Developments

At the time being, the issue of monetary rules and determinacy is not settled. We indicate a few recent directions of development.

Inflation Forecast Targeting

Like most contributors to the literature on Taylor rules, we took the interest rate rule to be a function of current inflation (equation 43). But it could be as well a function of past or expected inflation. In fact, some recent developments in the literature have focused on "inflation forecast targeting,"[7] where the authors insist notably on the importance of setting credible inflation forecast targets. The central bank of New Zealand adopted such a strategy in the early 1990s, and a few other central banks followed. Contributions emphasizing the important differences between this and traditional Taylor rules are Bernanke and Mishkin (1997), Bernanke and Woodford (2005), Svensson (1997, 1999b, 2002, 2003), and Svensson and Woodford (2005).

---

7. The most popular name is actually "inflation targeting," but it may invite confusion with traditional Taylor rules, which are, after all, concerned with inflation targeting as well.

Output and the Taylor Rule

Taylor's original contribution had output as well as inflation in the Taylor rule. So in that case the linearized version of the Taylor rule equation is generalized to:

$$i_t - i^* = \phi_\pi (\pi_t - \pi^*) + \phi_y y_t \tag{57}$$

To derive the determinacy conditions, we have to specify a relation between output and inflation. We assume that a new Keynesian Phillips curve relation holds:

$$\pi_t = \beta E_t \pi_{t+1} + \kappa y_t \tag{58}$$

In such a case, Bullard and Mitra (2002) and Woodford (2003) show that the condition for local determinacy becomes:

$$\phi_\pi + \frac{1-\beta}{\kappa} \phi_y > 1 \tag{59}$$

Price Level Targeting

A reason that is often given as a cause of potential indeterminacies, at least in monetary models, is that indeterminacy stems from the lack of a "nominal anchor," that is, a nominal variable that is "backward looking," and to which current prices are linked. A method to create such a nominal anchor is to target not inflation but nominal prices, hence the name "price level targeting." The debate about the pros and cons of price targeting is not settled; the reader will find interesting arguments in McCallum (1981); Dittmar, Gavin, and Kydland (1999a, 1999b); Svensson (1999a); Dittmar and Gavin (2000); and Vestin (2006).

The Pigou Effect

Another way to create a nominal anchor is actually the Pigou effect, or real balance effect, which we studied already in chapter 11. We found that in economies not satisfying Ricardian equivalence (such as OLG type economies) dynamic price equations contain the value of nominal assets. Because these are backward-looking variables, we have a nominal anchor. Appendix 18.5 shows that in such economies we can find sufficient conditions on interest rate rules that ensure *global* determinacy in conjunction with reasonable fiscal policies.

Appendix 18.1: Model Uncertainty and Stabilization

We expose a model due to Brainard (1967), which shows that model uncertainty, in the sense of uncertainty on the coefficients of the model, can lead to an optimal response of governmental instruments that is lower than if the coefficients of the model were deterministic.

The Model

Let output y_t be related to the government policy instrument x_t by the following relation:

$$y_t = a_t x_t + \varepsilon_t \tag{60}$$

where a_t and ε_t are independent[8] i.i.d. stochastic variables with means and variances, respectively, μ_a and σ_a^2 for a_t, 0 and σ_ε^2 for ε_t. The government chooses the value of its instrument x_t so as to minimize:

$$E\left(y_t - \bar{y}\right)^2 \tag{61}$$

We assume that x_t must be determined before the values of a_t and ε_t are known. Because y_t does not depend on any past value, the government will choose a constant x_t.

The Deterministic Case

As a benchmark, let us begin with the case where the model has deterministic parameters, that is, $\sigma_a^2 = 0$ and $a_t = \mu_a$. In that case the government maximizes:

$$E\left(\mu_a x_t + \varepsilon_t - \bar{y}\right)^2 \tag{62}$$

which yields:

$$x_t = x^* = \frac{\bar{y}}{\mu_a} \tag{63}$$

---

8. Brainard (1967) considers the case where a_t and ε_t are correlated, but this is not central to the argument.

The Uncertainty Case

We now go back to the more general case where the parameter a_t is uncertain. Inserting the value of y_t (equation 60) into (61) and eliminating irrelevant constants, we find that the government should minimize:

$$x_t^2 E\left(a_t^2\right) + 2x_t E\left(a_t \varepsilon_t\right) - 2x_t E\left(a_t\right) \bar{y} \tag{64}$$

and since:

$$E\left(a_t^2\right) = \sigma_a^2 + \mu_a^2 \qquad E\left(a_t \varepsilon_t\right) = 0 \qquad E\left(a_t\right) = \mu_a \tag{65}$$

the quantity to be minimized (64) is equal to:

$$x_t^2 \left(\sigma_a^2 + \mu_a^2\right) - 2x_t \mu_a \bar{y} \tag{66}$$

Differentiating with respect to x_t we find the optimal value of the instrument:

$$x_t = x^* = \frac{\mu_a \bar{y}}{\sigma_a^2 + \mu_a^2} \tag{67}$$

In accordance with Brainard's intuition, this is smaller than the value of the instrument when the parameter is deterministic (formula 63).

Appendix 18.2: Instrument Instability

We investigate in this appendix another well-known argument against policy activism—that of instrument instability. Some time ago, Friedman (1961) advocated against policy activism because of long lags and uncertainty. This issue notably was followed by Baumol (1961), Howrey (1967), and Holbrook (1972).

We describe in this section a model due to Holbrook (1972). The idea is that because the effects of policy instruments have long delayed lags, full stabilization could imply explosive dynamics of the policy variables. We shall see that although the point is valid, one can devise stabilization policies that circumvent (at least partly) the problem.

The Model

Let y_t denote output, and x_t a governmental policy instrument. The dynamic evolution of output is given by:

$$y_t = ay_{t-1} + bx_t + cx_{t-1} + \varepsilon_t \tag{68}$$

where ε_t is an i.i.d. stochastic shock with mean zero and variance σ_ε^2. As in the preceding appendix, the policy instrument x_t has to be decided before ε_t is known, so it can depend on past values but not current ones. In such a case, the minimal possible variance of y_t is that of the shock ε_t itself, that is, σ_ε^2.

Instrument Instability

At first sight, it looks like an adequate policy could achieve full stabilization. Indeed, consider the policy:

$$x_t = -\frac{ay_{t-1} + cx_{t-1}}{b} \tag{69}$$

Inserting this into formula (68) we find:

$$y_t = \varepsilon_t \tag{70}$$

Fluctuations are reduced to their absolute minimum ε_t. The problem is that, if $b < c$, the instrument x_t will be explosive (formula 69). We now investigate whether some partial stabilization is nevertheless feasible and desirable in that case.

Partial Stabilization

We do not look for the optimal stabilization policy, but for a simple "partial stabilization" policy that dominates inaction. Let us define the composite variable:

$$z_t = ay_t + cx_t \tag{71}$$

The "full stabilization" policy (69) can be rewritten:

$$x_t = -\frac{z_{t-1}}{b} \tag{72}$$

For the case $c > b$, we now investigate particular partial stabilization policies of the type:

$$x_t = -\frac{\theta z_{t-1}}{b} \qquad 0 \leq \theta \leq 1 \tag{73}$$

The dynamic equation (68) becomes:

$$y_t = (1-\theta) z_{t-1} + \varepsilon_t \tag{74}$$

The dynamics of the composite variable z_t is:

$$z_t = \left[a(1-\theta) - \frac{\theta c}{b}\right] z_{t-1} + a\varepsilon_t \tag{75}$$

The solution can be expressed with the help of the lag operator $\mathcal{L}$:

$$z_t = \frac{a\varepsilon_t}{1 - [a(1-\theta) - \theta c/b]\mathcal{L}} \tag{76}$$

and we deduce y_t:

$$y_t = (1-\theta) z_{t-1} + \varepsilon_t = \varepsilon_t + \frac{a(1-\theta)\varepsilon_{t-1}}{1 - [a(1-\theta) - \theta c/b]\mathcal{L}} \tag{77}$$

Now a first condition not to have instrument instability is that the autoregressive root in the denominator be smaller than 1 in absolute value, that is:

$$-1 < a(1-\theta) - \frac{\theta c}{b} < 1 \tag{78}$$

which yields:

$$\theta < \frac{b(1+a)}{ab+c} = \hat{\theta} \tag{79}$$

We may note that $\hat{\theta} > 1$ when $b > c$, so in this case full stabilization ($\theta = 1$) is feasible, as we have seen.

We now move to the troublesome case $b < c$. Then $\hat{\theta} < 1$. We can compute the variance of y_t, which will be finite if $\theta < \hat{\theta}$:

$$\sigma_y^2 = \sigma_\varepsilon^2 + \frac{a^2(1-\theta)^2 \sigma_\varepsilon^2}{1 - [a(1-\theta) - \theta c/b]^2} \tag{80}$$

The variance σ_y^2 as a function of θ looks as in figure 18.2, which is drawn for the case $b < c$.

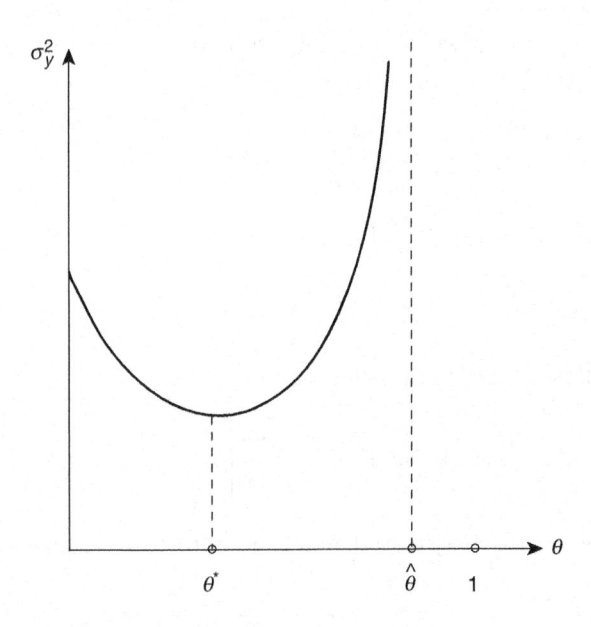

Figure 18.2 Partial stabilization and output variance

The variance σ_y^2, as given by (80), attains a minimum for a value $\theta^* < \hat{\theta}$, with:

$$\theta^* = \frac{b(b + ac)}{c(ab + c)} \qquad (81)$$

So, although this model displays potential instrument instability, it will be better to use a policy like (73) with $\theta = \theta^*$ rather than doing nothing.

Appendix 18.3: The Ineffectiveness Argument: A Simple Model

Because it played a critical role in the debates about policy activism, we want to give here a particularly simple version of the Sargent and Wallace (1975) argument on policy ineffectiveness.

Consider an economy with a linear production function and a fixed supply of labor (everything is expressed in logarithms in this appendix):

$$y_t = \ell_t \qquad (82)$$

$$\ell_t^s = \ell_0 \qquad (83)$$

We have a simple log-linear demand for goods:

$$y_t = m_t - p_t + v_t \tag{84}$$

where v_t is a stochastic demand shock. This solves easily. The price is equal to the wage:

$$p_t = w_t \tag{85}$$

and the demand for labor is thus, combining (82), (84), and (85):

$$\ell_t = m_t - w_t + v_t \tag{86}$$

Equating this labor demand to the fixed labor supply (83) yields the Walrasian wage:

$$w_t^* = m_t + v_t - \ell_0 \tag{87}$$

Now we make the traditional asssumption (Gray, 1976) that the actual wage is preset at the expected value of the Walrasian wage:

$$w_t = E_{t-1} w_t^* = E_{t-1} m_t + E_{t-1} v_t - \ell_0 \tag{88}$$

Combining (86) and (88), we obtain the level of employment:

$$\ell_t - \ell_0 = m_t - E_{t-1} m_t + v_t - E_{t-1} v_t \tag{89}$$

We assume that the government's objective is to stabilize employment (actually the policies we will derive also stabilize inflation). We want to investigate two distinct possibilities, depending on which information the government is allowed to use.

Traditional Keynesian Analysis

In traditional Keynesian analysis, say, of the IS-LM type, it is implicitly assumed that the government can use all information up to and within period t included. In such a case, one optimal policy is of the type:

$$m_t = \mu - v_t \tag{90}$$

Inserting (90) into (89), we find that employment is:

$$\ell_t = \ell_0 \tag{91}$$

We see that government can completely stabilize employment. But clearly here the government has an enormous informational advantage over the private sector. The private sector is locked into wage contracts based on period $t-1$ information, whereas the government can react with full knowledge of period t shocks.

The Ineffectiveness Result

So let us now suppose, as Sargent and Wallace (1975) suggested, that government can only use period $t-1$ information. Then the "innovations" $m_t - E_{t-1}m_t$ and $v_t - E_{t-1}v_t$ in formula (89) are independant. If the government wants to reduce fluctuations in employment, then the best it can do is to have a fully predictable policy such that:

$$m_t = E_{t-1}m_t \tag{92}$$

Under condition (92), employment is given by (equation 89):

$$\ell_t - \ell_0 = v_t - E_{t-1}v_t \tag{93}$$

No matter which policy it uses, government will be unable to suppress a minimal amount of fluctuations, driven by the innovations in the demand shock $v_t - E_{t-1}v_t$. This is the famous ineffectiveness result.

We may note that although it cannot stabilize employment, the government can, in this very simple model, stabilize inflation by selecting, among policies characterized by (92), a policy of the type:

$$m_t = \mu - E_{t-1}v_t \tag{94}$$

We can indeed compute, combining (85), (88), and (94):

$$p_t = \mu - \ell_0 \tag{95}$$

and inflation is always equal to 0.

Appendix 18.4: Fiscal Policy and Determinacy

Most of the debate around Taylor rules concentrated on monetary policy only, as we did in section 18.4. Studying monetary policy in isolation is clearly only a first step, and we now introduce fiscal policy to study determinacy. A new possibility for determinacy will emerge, related to the fiscal theory of the price level (Leeper, 1991; Sims, 1994; Woodford, 1994, 1995), which we already encountered in chapter 11 (section 11.6).

Fiscal Policy

We use the same model as in section 18.4, but we now specify fiscal policy explicitly. The evolution of nominal assets Ω_t is given by the government budget constraint:

$$\Omega_{t+1} = \Omega_t + i_t B_t - P_t T_t \tag{96}$$

where T_t is real taxes. We will express taxes in a way that makes explicit the fiscal deficit:

$$P_t T_t = i_t B_t - D(\Omega_t, P_t Y_t) \tag{97}$$

The function $D(\Omega_t, P_t Y_t)$, the fiscal deficit in nominal terms, is assumed to be homogeneous of degree 1 in its two arguments. The argument $P_t Y_t$ corresponds to an income tax, and the argument Ω_t reflects the fact that the government may want to raise taxes to diminish its financial liabilities Ω_t. Putting together equations (96) and (97), we find:

$$\Omega_{t+1} = \Omega_t + D(\Omega_t, P_t Y_t) \tag{98}$$

We will not use this equation as such, but rather use as working variables inflation Π_t and the predetermined variable $\mathcal{X}_t$ defined as:

$$\mathcal{X}_t = \frac{\Omega_t}{P_{t-1} Y_{t-1}} \tag{99}$$

Combining (98) and (99), and using the homogeneity property of the function D, we find that (98) can be rewritten:

$$\mathcal{X}_{t+1} = F\left(\frac{\mathcal{X}_t}{\zeta \Pi_t}\right) \tag{100}$$

where the "fiscal function" F is defined as:

$$F\left(\frac{\mathcal{X}_t}{\zeta \Pi_t}\right) = \frac{\mathcal{X}_t}{\zeta \Pi_t} + D\left(\frac{\mathcal{X}_t}{\zeta \Pi_t}, 1\right) \tag{101}$$

We assume $F' > 0$ and denote the elasticity of F as f.

Local Determinacy

We now have two dynamic equations, (51) and (100), in Π_t and X_t:

$$\Pi_{t+1} = \frac{\Phi(\Pi_t)}{\xi} \tag{102}$$

$$\mathcal{X}_{t+1} = F\left(\frac{\mathcal{X}_t}{\zeta \Pi_t}\right) \tag{103}$$

Steady states $(\Pi, \mathcal{X})$ of this system (when they exist) are characterized by:

$$\Pi = \frac{\Phi(\Pi)}{\xi} \qquad \mathcal{X} = F\left(\frac{\mathcal{X}}{\zeta \Pi}\right) \tag{104}$$

Linearizing (102) and (103) around a steady state $(\Pi, \mathcal{X})$ we find:

$$\Pi_{t+1} - \Pi = \phi (\Pi_t - \Pi) \tag{105}$$

$$\mathcal{X}_{t+1} - \mathcal{X} = -\frac{\mathcal{X} f}{\Pi}(\Pi_t - \Pi) + f(\mathcal{X}_t - \mathcal{X}) \tag{106}$$

or in matrix form:

$$\begin{bmatrix} \Pi_{t+1} - \Pi \\ \mathcal{X}_{t+1} - \mathcal{X} \end{bmatrix} = \begin{bmatrix} \phi & 0 \\ -\mathcal{X} f/\Pi & f \end{bmatrix} \begin{bmatrix} \Pi_t - \Pi \\ \mathcal{X}_t - \mathcal{X} \end{bmatrix} \tag{107}$$

where ϕ and f are the elasticities of the functions Φ and F. The two eigenvalues of this matrix are ϕ and f. Because there is one predetermined variable, $\mathcal{X}_t$, and one nonpredetermined, Π_t, there will be local determinacy if one of the roots has modulus smaller than 1, the other bigger (see mathematical appendix, section A.11). So we have two possibilities for local determinacy (this duality was uncovered by Leeper, 1991). The first is:

$$\phi > 1 \qquad f < 1 \tag{108}$$

We recognize with $\phi > 1$ the Taylor principle. So this is the traditional condition. But we see that there is a second possibility for local determinacy, specifically:

$$\phi < 1 \qquad f > 1 \tag{109}$$

The condition $\phi < 1$ says that the Taylor principle is not satisfied. But $f > 1$ means that the ratio of government's financial liabilities to nominal income will have divergent dynamics along off-equilibrium paths (equation 106). Such a condition is related to the fiscal theory of the price level (FTPL) that we briefly discusssed in chapter 11. As we indicated then, one would like to avoid such policies, which may have potentially destabilizing effects in real life situations. The next appendix presents monetary policies which allow to obtain global determinacy without such FTPL type policies.

Appendix 18.5: The Pigou Effect and Global Determinacy

We saw in section 18.4 that notably because of the zero lower bound on nominal interest rates, traditional interest rate rules fail to make the dynamic economic system globally determinate. This is, of course, quite bothersome, and we want to show that introducing non-Ricardian features and a Pigou effect in to the picture will allow us to find monetary rules that, together with reasonable fiscal policies, will lead to global determinacy (Bénassy, 2009).

The Model

We use the Weil (1987, 1991) model, which we described in chapter 11, section 11.8, and which we now recall briefly.

As compared with traditional models, such as that of section 18.4, the central difference is that new generations of households are born each period. We denote as $N_t = (1+n)^t$, $n > 0$, the number of households alive in t.

Consider a household born in period j. We denote by c_{jt}, y_{jt}, τ_{jt}, and m_{jt} its consumption, endowment, taxes, and money holdings at time $t \geq j$. This household maximizes the following utility function:

$$U_{jt} = \sum_{s=t}^{\infty} \beta^{s-t} Log\, c_{js} \qquad (110)$$

while being subject to CIA constraints $P_t c_{jt} \leq m_{jt}$. All generations receive the same exogenous income and pay the same taxes:

$$y_{jt} = y_t = \frac{Y_t}{N_t} \qquad \tau_{jt} = \tau_t = \frac{T_t}{N_t} \qquad (111)$$

and real income per head grows at the rate ζ:

$$\frac{y_{t+1}}{y_t} = \zeta \qquad \frac{Y_{t+1}}{Y_t} = (1+n)\zeta \qquad (112)$$

Dynamic Equations

It was shown in chapter 11 (appendix 11.3) that the dynamics of prices in this model are given by:

$$P_{t+1}Y_{t+1} = \beta(1+n)(1+i_t)P_tY_t - (1-\beta)n\Omega_{t+1} \tag{113}$$

As we already emphasized, the last term represents the Pigou effect. The aggregate household's financial wealth at the beginning of period t, Ω_t, evolves according to the government's budget constraint:

$$\Omega_{t+1} = \Omega_t + i_tB_t - P_tT_t \tag{114}$$

Fiscal and Monetary Policy

We now spell precisely monetary and fiscal policies. For monetary policy we assume, as in section 18.4, a Taylor rule:

$$1 + i_t = \Phi(\Pi_t) \tag{115}$$

As for fiscal policy, because we want to concentrate on monetary policy, we assume a particularly simple and reasonable policy, balanced budget:[9]

$$P_tT_t = i_tB_t \tag{116}$$

Accordingly nominal assets will remain constant in time:

$$\Omega_{t+1} = \Omega_t = \Omega \tag{117}$$

The Dynamic System

As in appendix 18.4, we use as working variables inflation Π_t and the predetermined variable:

$$\mathcal{X}_t = \frac{\Omega_t}{P_{t-1}Y_{t-1}} \tag{118}$$

Inserting the Taylor rule (115) into the dynamic equation (113), and dividing both sides of equation (113) by $\zeta(1+n)P_tY_t$, we obtain a first

---

9. One can actually use, at the price of added complexity, more general fiscal policies and still obtain similar results (Bénassy, 2009).

dynamic equation:

$$\Pi_{t+1} = \frac{\Phi(\Pi_t)}{\xi} - \nu \mathcal{X}_{t+1} \qquad (119)$$

where $\xi = \zeta/\beta$ is the gross real interest rate of the traditional model (equation 52) and:

$$\nu = \frac{(1-\beta)n}{(1+n)\zeta} \qquad (120)$$

As for fiscal policy, using the auxiliary variable $\mathcal{X}_t$, (117) becomes:

$$\mathcal{X}_{t+1} = \frac{\mathcal{X}_t}{\zeta(1+n)\Pi_t} \qquad (121)$$

The dynamic system consists of equations (119) and (121).

Global Determinacy

We will show that in this non-Ricardian world, it is possible to find interest rate rules $\Phi(\Pi_t)$ such that global determinacy obtains, in spite of the positive interest rate problem. We indeed demonstrate the following property.

Global determinacy *Let us assume*:

$$\Phi'(\Pi_t) \geq \xi = \frac{\zeta}{\beta} \qquad \forall \Pi_t \qquad (122)$$

Then there is a unique globally determinate equilibrium.

Proof: The result is actually crystal clear if we depict the dynamics in $(\Pi_t, \mathcal{X}_t)$ space (figure 18.3).

From (121) we see that the locus $\mathcal{X}_{t+1} = \mathcal{X}_t$ corresponds to the vertical line of equation:

$$\Pi_t = \frac{\gamma}{\zeta(1+n)} \qquad (123)$$

As for the locus $\Pi_{t+1} = \Pi_t$, from (119) and (121) its equation is:

$$\frac{\Phi(\Pi_t)}{\xi} - \Pi_t = \frac{\nu \mathcal{X}_t}{\zeta(1+n)\Pi_t} \qquad (124)$$

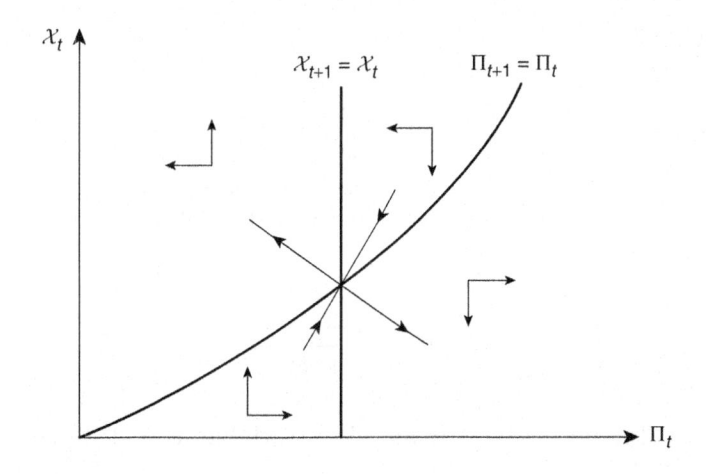

Figure 18.3 Global determinacy

Differentiating (124) logarithmically we find:

$$\frac{\Pi_t \left[\Phi'(\Pi_t) - \xi\right]}{\Phi(\Pi_t) - \xi \Pi_t} \frac{d\Pi_t}{\Pi_t} = \frac{d\mathcal{X}_t}{\mathcal{X}_t} - \frac{d\Pi_t}{\Pi_t} \qquad (125)$$

Now under assumption (122):

$$\Phi(\Pi_t) - \xi \Pi_t = \Phi(0) + \int_0^{\Pi_t} \left[\Phi'(\Pi_s) - \xi\right] d\Pi_s > 0 \qquad (126)$$

Using (122) and (126), equation (125) implies that the curve $\Pi_{t+1} = \Pi_t$ is upward-sloping, as depicted in figure 18.3.

We finally move to the study of global determinacy of the equilibrium. The dynamics of the system is given by:

$$\mathcal{X}_{t+1} > \mathcal{X}_t \quad \text{if} \quad \mathcal{X}_t < \frac{\mathcal{X}_t}{\zeta(1+n)\Pi_t} \qquad (127)$$

$$\Pi_{t+1} > \Pi_t \quad \text{if} \quad \nu F \left[\frac{\mathcal{X}_t}{\zeta(1+n)\Pi_t}\right] < \frac{\Phi(\Pi_t)}{\xi} - \Pi_t \qquad (128)$$

This is represented by the arrows in figure 18.3 where it appears that the unique equilibrium has saddle path dynamics and global determinacy.

A Generalization

We finally consider a simple generalization of our model, which will allow us to substantially weaken the requirements of condition (122). In equation (112) we assumed that all agents have exactly the same income and taxes. We replace (112) with the following assumption:

$$y_{jt} = \psi^{t-j} y_t \qquad \tau_{jt} = \psi^{t-j} \tau_t \qquad \psi \leq 1 \qquad (129)$$

where y_t and τ_t are the income and taxes of an agent born in period t. Equation (129) means that agent's relative resources diminish with age. Under this assumption one can prove (Bénassy, 2009) that for $n > 0$ condition (122) is replaced by:

$$\Phi'(\Pi_t) \geq \frac{\psi \zeta}{\beta} \qquad (130)$$

With a low value of ψ, this is a less constraining requirement on monetary policy. We see that consideration of a non-Ricardian framework not only gives global determinacy but at a "price" that may be potentially low.

Problems

Problem 18.1: Policy Effectiveness: Different Timings

The timing of information is of utmost importance for the issue of the effectiveness of economic policy. To demonstrate it, we study two different versions of an AD-AS system. The AS equation is the same for the two versions:

$$y_t = \xi \left(p_t - E_{t-1} p_t \right) \qquad \text{AS}$$

but there are now two different AD curves:

$$y_t = m_t - p_t + b E_{t-1} \left(p_{t+1} - p_t \right) + \varepsilon_t \qquad \text{AD1}$$

$$y_t = m_t - p_t + b E_t \left(p_{t+1} - p_t \right) + \varepsilon_t \qquad \text{AD2}$$

Where the ε_t's are i.i.d stochastic variables. The AD1 curve is the same as in problem 3.1, and we saw that it leads to policy ineffectiveness.

The only difference between AD1 and AD2 is that the second term is based on period $t - 1$ information in AD1, and on period t information for

AD2. The central difference is in the information available to the private sector to predict inflation.

1. Consider the model with AD2 and investigate monetary policies of the following type:

$$m_t = \phi \varepsilon_{t-1}$$

   conjecture that the solution in p_t is of the form:

$$p_t = \nu \varepsilon_t + \chi \varepsilon_{t-1}$$

   and solve using the method of undetermined coefficients
2. Show that there is a strictly positive value of ϕ that allows us to fully stabilize output, so that policy is effective.

Problem 18.2: The Effectiveness of Government Policy

We extend the simplified model of appendix 18.3 to introduce elements of forward behavior, and we shall see that this introduces the possibility of government policy effectiveness. Instead of the demand curve:

$$y_t = m_t - p_t + v_t$$

We take a demand curve that depends on expected inflation:

$$y_t = m_t - p_t + bE_t\left(p_{t+1} - p_t\right) + v_t$$

The rest of the model is the same. The production function is:

$$y_t = \ell_t$$

and labor supply is constant:

$$\ell_t^s = \ell_0$$

1. Compute the Walrasian wage w_t^*.
2. Assume that the wage is preset at the expected value of the Walrasian wage:

$$w_t = E_{t-1} w_t^*$$

Compute the demand for labor.

3. Show that there is a monetary policy based on previous period information such that employment is completely stabilized.

Problem 18.3: Information and Policy Effectiveness: Preset Prices

In section 18.3 we presented a rigorous DSGE model with preset wages where it is optimal for the government to lead an activist policy. Here we study a model where a similar conclusion is obtained under the assumption of preset prices.

We again use an OLG structure. Households of generation t maximize the expected value of their utility U_t, with:

$$U_t = Log\, C_{1t} + \beta Log\, C_{2t+1} - L_t$$

The representative firm in period t has a production function:

$$Y_t = A_t L_t$$

where A_t is a common stochastic technology shock.

Old households enter period t holding a quantity of money M_{t-1} carried from the previous period. In period t events occur in three steps. First, the government gives a nominal transfer $\mathcal{T}_t$ to the old households. As in section 18.3, $\mathcal{T}_t$ is function only of macroeconomic variables up to $t-1$ included. Second, the price is set by the private sector at its expected market-clearing value, without knowing the values of the period t shock A_t. Finally, the shock A_t becomes known to the private sector, the wage clears the labor market, and transactions are carried out accordingly. Because policy decisions in t are based on information up to $t-1$, the government is never more informed than the private sector.

1. As a benchmark, compute the Walrasian equilibrium.
2. We now assume that the price is preset at the expected value of the Walrasian price:

$$P_t = E_{t-1} P_t^*$$

Compute the preset price equilibrium.
3. Compute the optimal policy and show that the price is always equal to its Walrasian value.

19

Dynamic Consistency and Credibility

19.1 Introduction

When studying optimal government policies extending over several periods, we implicitly assumed that the government would choose an optimal sequence of decisions in the initial period, and then simply implement the corresponding sequence of decisions over time. But in the mid-1970s, notably following the seminal article by Kydland and Prescott (1977), economists became aware of the so-called dynamic consistency problem. In a nutshell, the problem is that a policy decision to be implemented in a future period $t > 0$, which looked optimal from period 0, may not look optimal anymore when time t has come. As a result the government will want to renege on its announced policy. Because the public is supposed to have rational expectations, this means that the initially announced policy was not credible, and as a result the government will not be able to implement its optimal policy.[1]

A typical example, which we will study below, is capital taxation. The government wants to achieve an optimal amount of capital accumulation. Because capital accumulation is sensitive to future capital taxation, the government would like to credibly announce a low future taxation of capital. But once capital is installed, it becomes insensitive to taxation, and taxing it becomes equivalent to lump-sum taxation. So in a later period, when

---

1. This issue has created a substantial body of literature. For surveys, see Chari, Kehoe, and Prescott (1989); Cukierman (1982); Persson and Tabellini (1990, 1999); and Rogoff (1989). A collection of important articles is in Persson and Tabellini (1994).

capital has become a fixed asset, the government will be tempted to tax it heavily. Coming back to the initial period, the private sector will not believe the low tax announcement of the government, and therefore there will be underinvestment.

Section 19.2 presents the simplest example of the problem of time consistency. The simplicity of the condition for a time consistency problem shows that this may be a pervasive feature of any policy problem with a truly dynamic dimension. Section 19.3 gives a simple version of the capital taxation problem that we briefly outlined, and shows that there is indeed an intrinsic dynamic consistency problem.

Section 19.4 develops the most popular application of this theory—that of monetary policy design. It shows that the credibility issue can create an inflationary pressure, and that there is a trade-off between credibility and flexibility. Finally section 19.5 exposes, for the monetary policy case, a number of possible solutions to the credibility problem.

19.2 The Dynamic Consistency Intuition

Consider a situation where the private sector and the government interact in two periods (the timing is fundamental here). In the first period private agents take a decision x; in the second period the government takes a decision g. The private sector has a utility function $U(x,g)$, the government has a utility function $V(x,g)$.

It is assumed that the private sector rationally anticipates the decision g of the government. So it chooses its own decision x by maximizing $U(x,g)$ with given g, which yields:

$$x = X(g) \qquad (1)$$

We now turn to the government. We see that the choice will be quite different depending on whether it can commit on its policy before the private sector moves.

19.2.1 Commitment

We first assume that the government can commit to a policy in both periods. It will thus maximize its utility $V(x,g)$ subject to the reaction function of the private sector (equation 1), that is, it will maximize:

$$V[X(g),g] \qquad (2)$$

The first-order condition in g is:

$$\frac{\partial V}{\partial x}\frac{\partial X}{\partial g} + \frac{\partial V}{\partial g} = 0 \tag{3}$$

19.2.2 No Commitment

But in reality, if the government cannot commit, it will choose the value of g in the second period, at a time where x is *given*. In the second period the government thus maximizes $V(x,g)$ with given x, which yields the first-order condition:

$$\frac{\partial V}{\partial g} = 0 \tag{4}$$

We assume that $\partial V/\partial x \neq 0$, that is, that the government cares about private sector's actions, a natural assumption.

Comparing (3) and (4) we see that there will be a difference between the first-order conditions of the two cases as soon as the private sector's actions today depend on government's actions tomorrow (i.e., if $\partial X/\partial g \neq 0$). This is the dynamic consistency problem.

19.3 Capital Taxation and Dynamic Consistency

We will now develop a simple model of capital taxation and underinvestment.

19.3.1 The Model

We consider a model with two periods, 1 and 2. The household consumes in both periods, respectively, C_1 and C_2. In the first period it receives an exogenous income Y and invests K. Its budget constraints are:

$$C_1 + K = Y \tag{5}$$

$$C_2 = (1-\tau)RK \tag{6}$$

where R is the gross return on capital, τ the tax rate on capital income. These taxes are levied in the second period to finance an amount of government spending G:

$$G = \tau RK \tag{7}$$

The household maximizes the following utility function:

$$U = C_1 + \beta \frac{C_2^{1-\theta} + \zeta G^{1-\theta}}{1-\theta} \qquad 0 < \theta < 1 \tag{8}$$

where ζ is somehow the relative weight of government spending as compared to private consumption in households' utilities.

We assume that the government has the same utility as the private sector:

$$V = C_1 + \beta \frac{C_2^{1-\theta} + \zeta G^{1-\theta}}{1-\theta} \tag{9}$$

so that the problem will not come from a possible discrepancy between the objectives of the government and those of the private sector.

19.3.2 The Demand for Capital

In the first period the representative household maximizes its utility, taking governement spending G as given. So inserting (5) and (6) into (8), the household maximizes:

$$Y - K + \frac{\beta \left[(1-\tau) RK\right]^{1-\theta}}{1-\theta} \tag{10}$$

which yields the demand for capital:

$$K = \beta^{1/\theta} \left[(1-\tau) R\right]^{(1-\theta)/\theta} \tag{11}$$

As should be expected, capital invested depends negatively on the expected tax rate.

19.3.3 The Time Consistent Solution

To find the time consistent solution, we start from the second period. Capital K is given, since it has been decided in the first period. Accordingly second-period consumption and government spending are given by:

$$C_2 = (1-\tau) RK \tag{12}$$

$$G = \tau RK \tag{13}$$

The government chooses τ in the second period so as to maximize second-period utility, that is, so as to maximize:

$$C_2^{1-\theta} + \zeta G^{1-\theta} = (RK)^{1-\theta} \left[(1-\tau)^{1-\theta} + \zeta \tau^{1-\theta}\right] \tag{14}$$

The derivative with respect to τ is proportional to:

$$\zeta\tau^{-\theta} - (1-\tau)^{-\theta} \qquad (15)$$

Equating it to 0 yields:

$$\tau = \frac{\zeta^{1/\theta}}{1+\zeta^{1/\theta}} \qquad (16)$$

This is the time consistent tax rate.[2]

19.3.4 The Commitment Solution

Now imagine that the government can commit to a value of τ from the first period. It will thus maximize the utility function (9), where C_1, C_2, and G are given by equations (5), (6), and (7), and K itself is given by equation (11). The maximand is thus (after simplifications):

$$Y + \frac{\beta^{1/\theta}R^{(1-\theta)/\theta}}{1-\theta}\left[\theta(1-\tau)^{(1-\theta)/\theta} + \zeta\tau^{1-\theta}(1-\tau)^{(1-\theta)^2/\theta}\right] \qquad (17)$$

The derivative of this function with respect to τ is proportional to:

$$\zeta(\theta - \tau) - \theta\tau^\theta(1-\tau)^{1-\theta} \qquad (18)$$

This derivative is negative for $\tau \geq \theta$, and also for $\tau = \zeta^{1/\theta}/(1+\zeta^{1/\theta})$. Moreover, the maximand (17) is concave for $\tau \leq \theta$, so finally the optimal tax rate τ^* is such that:

$$\tau^* < \min\left(\theta, \frac{\zeta^{1/\theta}}{1+\zeta^{1/\theta}}\right) \qquad (19)$$

This optimal tax rate is clearly smaller than the time consistent one (equation 16). So the inability for the government to commit leads to overtaxation and underinvestment.

19.4 Monetary Policy and Credibility

We now move to the study of monetary policy and see how the problem of dynamic consistency can interfere with the design of monetary policy to produce an inflationary bias.[3]

---

2. The time consistent policy is also sometimes called "discretionary."
3. See notably Kydland and Prescott (1977), Calvo (1978), and Barro and Gordon (1983b).

19.4.1 The Basic Model

We consider a game between the private sector and the government. The game occurs in two steps. In a first step, the private sector sets the nominal wage on the basis of expected prices:

$$w_t = p_t^e + \omega \qquad (20)$$

where ω is a target real wage. In the second step, the government chooses the quantity of money m_t. Price and output are determined by two traditional supply-demand equations:

$$y_t = \xi(p_t - w_t) + \varepsilon_t \qquad (21)$$

$$y_t = m_t - p_t \qquad (22)$$

where ε_t is a stochastic shock.

This game, where the private sector first chooses w_t and the government then chooses m_t, can be rewritten as a game where the private sector chooses expected inflation π_t^e in the first step, and the government chooses actual inflation π_t in the second step.

To show that, we first combine (20) and (21). Output is given by the following reduced-form equation:

$$y_t = y^* + \xi(p_t - p_t^e) + \varepsilon_t \qquad (23)$$

with:

$$y^* = -\xi\omega \qquad (24)$$

Because $\pi_t = p_t - p_{t-1}$ and $\pi_t^e = p_t^e - p_{t-1}$, (23) can be rewritten:

$$y_t = y^* + \xi(\pi_t - \pi_t^e) + \varepsilon_t \qquad (25)$$

where π_t^e is the private sector's expected inflation at the time where wages are set (equation 20). The shock ε_t occurs in the second step, and it is observed by the government but not by the private sector.

The government has a utility function:

$$V_t = -\left[(y_t - \bar{y})^2 + \theta\pi_t^2\right] \qquad (26)$$

Note that the level $\bar{y}$ around which the government wants to stabilize output may be higher than y^*, due for example to imperfect competition on the goods or labor markets.

19.4.2 Commitment

We investigate first what will happen if, by some means or another, the government can commit to a given value of inflation π_t. The solution in that case is particularly simple. Indeed, because π_t is known for sure, then $\pi_t^e = \pi_t$, and from equation (25):

$$y_t = y^* + \varepsilon_t \qquad (27)$$

The government has no control over output. The best it can do is then to keep inflation at 0:

$$\pi_t = 0 \qquad (28)$$

Under this policy we compute the expected utility:

$$E(V_t) = -\left[(\bar{y} - y^*)^2 + \sigma^2\right] \qquad (29)$$

where:

$$\sigma^2 = E\left(\varepsilon_t^2\right) \qquad (30)$$

19.4.3 Discretionary Policy

The problem with the foregoing solution is that once the private sector has chosen π_t^e, the government may want to choose a level of inflation different from the one to which it has committed. To see that this will be indeed the case, we place ourselves in the second stage, when π_t^e has already been chosen. The program of the government is thus:

$$\text{Maximize } -\left[(y_t - \bar{y})^2 + \theta \pi_t^2\right] \quad \text{s.t.}$$

$$y_t = y^* + \xi(\pi_t - \pi_t^e) + \varepsilon_t$$

The solution is:

$$\pi_t = \frac{\xi^2 \pi_t^e + \xi(\bar{y} - y^*) - \xi \varepsilon_t}{\theta + \xi^2} \qquad (31)$$

Take the expectation of (31). Because of rational expectations $\pi_t^e = E(\pi_t)$. Because $E(\varepsilon_t) = 0$, this yields:

$$\pi_t^e = \frac{\xi^2 \pi_t^e + \xi(\bar{y} - y^*)}{\theta + \xi^2} \qquad (32)$$

or:

$$\pi_t^e = \frac{\xi(\bar{y} - y^*)}{\theta} = \pi_d \qquad (33)$$

The value π_d is called the discretionary inflation rate. Inserting this value of π_t^e into equation (31) we find the value of inflation:

$$\pi_t = \frac{\xi(\bar{y} - y^*)}{\theta} - \frac{\xi \varepsilon_t}{\theta + \xi^2} \qquad (34)$$

and inserting (33) and (34) into (25) we obtain the level of output:

$$y_t = y^* + \frac{\theta \varepsilon_t}{\theta + \xi^2} \qquad (35)$$

We may first note, eliminating ε_t between (34) and (35), that inflation and output are related by:

$$\theta \pi_t = \xi(\bar{y} - y_t) \qquad (36)$$

Inserting (34) and (35) into the government's utility function (26) we find:

$$E(V_t) = -\left[\frac{\theta + \xi^2}{\theta}(\bar{y} - y^*)^2 + \frac{\theta}{\theta + \xi^2}\sigma^2\right] \qquad (37)$$

19.4.4 Commitment Versus Discretion

We want to compare the levels of welfare respectively attained under commitment V_c and discretion V_d. We make a first comparison assuming away any uncertainty. So we reproduce equations (29) and (37), making $\sigma = 0$:

$$V_c = -(\bar{y} - y^*)^2 \qquad (38)$$

$$V_d = -\frac{\theta + \xi^2}{\theta}(\bar{y} - y^*)^2 \qquad (39)$$

We clearly see that the commitment solution is unambiguously superior to the discretionary one.

Under discretionary policy the government would like to surprise the private sector, creating unexpected inflation to boost output beyond its natural level y^*. Of course, under rational expectations such attempts are self-defeating, and all the government obtains in the end is more inflation, and no more output, hence the lower utility.

19.4.5 Credibility Versus Flexibility

Now we introduce another relevant issue—that of flexibility. In our framework, since the government commits on π_t, this means that π_t cannot react to the value of ε_t in the commitment case, whereas it can in the discretion case. So the government has more "flexibility" in the discretion case.

To see how this affects the comparison between V_c and V_d, we first recall their values under uncertainty (equations 29 and 37):

$$V_c = -\left[(\bar{y} - y^*)^2 + \sigma^2\right] \tag{40}$$

$$V_d = -\left[\frac{\theta + \xi^2}{\theta}(\bar{y} - y^*)^2 + \frac{\theta}{\theta + \xi^2}\sigma^2\right] \tag{41}$$

Subtracting the two we find:

$$V_c - V_d = \frac{\xi^2}{\theta}(\bar{y} - y^*)^2 - \frac{\xi^2 \sigma^2}{\theta + \xi^2} \tag{42}$$

As we just saw, if $\sigma^2 = 0$, the commitment policy is clearly better than the discretionary one, which has an inflationary bias. But if $\sigma^2 > 0$, then the comparison is less clear-cut because the discretionary policy allows the government to respond to unexpected shocks.

19.5 Solutions to the Credibility Problem

We now investigate a few solutions to the dynamic consistency problem that will allow the government to come closer to an optimum solution in the above monetary policy game.

19.5.1 Delegation

We examine a first solution to the time inconsistency problem; delegation (Rogoff, 1985). The idea is that because the problem is an inflationary bias, society will delegate decisions on money creation to an agent who is particularly averse to inflation. For that reason this method is often called the theory of the conservative central banker.

We assume that there are many agents indexed by i in the population. Agent i has a utility function:

$$U_{it} = -\left[(y_t - \bar{y})^2 + \theta_i \pi_t^2\right] \tag{43}$$

We see that different agents may give different weights to inflation, which will appear through different values of the θ_i's. The distribution of the parameter θ_i in the population is given by a cumulative distribution $\Psi(\theta_i)$.

It is now assumed that policy choices are delegated to a central banker, who is a member of the population with a particular value of the parameter θ_b. The problem is: which value of θ_b should be chosen? A naive answer could be that somehow a democratic election process would yield a θ_b equal to the median value of the θ_i's.[4] Rogoff (1985) showed that actually there will be a systematic bias toward more "conservative" central bankers (an agent is called more conservative if he puts more weight on inflation). We now make the argument formal.

We assume that the outcome is the time consistent one, so if the central banker's parameter is θ_b, output and inflation in each period are given by (equations 34 and 35):

$$\pi_t = \frac{\xi(\bar{y} - y^*)}{\theta_b} - \frac{\xi \varepsilon_t}{\theta_b + \xi^2} \tag{44}$$

$$y_t = y^* + \frac{\theta_b \varepsilon_t}{\theta_b + \xi^2} \tag{45}$$

Inserting these into (40), we find that the expected utility of agent i is:

$$E(U_i) = -\left(1 + \theta_i \frac{\xi^2}{\theta_b^2}\right)(y^* - \bar{y})^2 - \frac{\theta_b^2 + \theta_i \xi^2}{(\theta_b + \xi^2)^2}\sigma^2 \tag{46}$$

We first note that if $\sigma^2 = 0$, the utility of agent i is maximized for $\theta_b = \infty$. The central banker will be unanimously chosen at the most conservative end of society. The intuition is clear: everybody wants the lowest possible inflation, and therefore the most possible conservative central banker.

Now if the variance of shocks is not 0, an infinite θ_b will not be optimal. To find the optimal value, let us differentiate (46) with respect to θ_b. The first-order condition is:

$$\frac{(\theta_b - \theta_i)\sigma^2}{(\theta_b + \xi^2)^3} = \frac{\theta_i(y^* - \bar{y})^2}{\theta_b^3} \tag{47}$$

in which we see that we will always have $\theta_b > \theta_i$. This means that the preferred central banker of agent i is always more conservative than agent i himself. If the central banker is elected, he will be the choice of the median voter and therefore always be more conservative than the median voter.

---

4. See chapter 20 for a description of the median voter theory.

19.5.2 Contracts for Central Bankers

The analysis of the previous section showed a dilemma when choosing the value of the parameter θ_b: on one hand, a high value of θ_b leads to a lower inflation, which is a good thing. On the other hand, a value of θ_b higher than θ_i also reduces the coefficient of reaction to shocks ε_t below the value that individual i would consider optimal.

This dilemma comes from the fact that we have restricted the central banker's utility function to belong to the class of the utility functions of the individuals in society. This need not be the case, and one may give, possibly through an explicit contract, a different objective to the central banker (Persson and Tabellini, 1993; Walsh, 1995). Let us continue to assume that agent i has the following objective function:

$$V = -\left[(y_t - \bar{y})^2 + \theta_i \pi_t^2\right] \qquad (48)$$

whereas the central banker's objective function is:

$$V_b = -\left[(y_t - \bar{y})^2 + \theta_b \pi_t^2 + \gamma_b \pi_t\right] \qquad (49)$$

The two first terms in (49) are the central banker's "intrinsic" utility function, characterized by the parameter θ_b. The parameter γ_b reflects the "central banker's contract," whereby he is rewarded whenever realized inflation is low. The problem is to choose values of θ_b and γ_b that will be best for society.

Assume again that the private sector chooses π_t^e first. The program of the central banker is now:

$$\text{Maximize } -\left[(y_t - \bar{y})^2 + \theta_b \pi_t^2 + \gamma_b \pi_t\right] \qquad \text{s.t.}$$

$$y_t = y^* + \xi(\pi_t - \pi_t^e) + \varepsilon_t$$

The solution is:

$$\pi_t = \frac{\xi^2 \pi_t^e + \xi(\bar{y} - y^*) - \xi \varepsilon_t - \gamma_b}{\theta_b + \xi^2} \qquad (50)$$

The time consistent value of π_t^e is given by $\pi_t^e = E(\pi_t)$, which yields:

$$\pi_t^e = \frac{\xi(\bar{y} - y^*) - \gamma_b}{\theta_b} \qquad (51)$$

Inserting this value into equation (50) we find the value of inflation:

$$\pi_t = \frac{\xi(\bar{y} - y^*) - \gamma_b}{\theta_b} - \frac{\xi \varepsilon_t}{\theta_b + \xi^2} \qquad (52)$$

and inserting (51) and (52) into (25) yields the level of output:

$$y_t = y^* + \frac{\theta_b \varepsilon_t}{\theta_b + \xi^2} \qquad (53)$$

We can now evaluate the expected utility of agent i:

$$E(U_i) = -(\bar{y} - y^*)^2 - \theta_i \left[\frac{\xi(\bar{y} - y^*) - \gamma_b}{\theta_b}\right]^2 - \frac{\theta_b^2 + \xi^2 \theta_i}{(\theta_b + \xi^2)^2} \sigma^2 \qquad (54)$$

We first optimize on γ_b. Because γ_b appears only in the second bracket, we immediately find:

$$\gamma_b = \xi(\bar{y} - y^*) > 0 \qquad (55)$$

The optimal γ_b is positive, which means that the central banker's contract will indeed impose a penalty on inflation. We may note that the coefficient γ_b of this penalty does not depend on the individual parameter θ_i so that this value of γ_b will be unanimously chosen. We further note, combining equations (52) and (55), that this value of γ_b yields an average discretionary value of inflation equal to 0.

Given this value of γ_b, there remains only the last term to maximize, which yields:

$$\theta_b = \theta_i \qquad (56)$$

Each agent thus wants a central banker who exactly mimics his own preferences. The bias toward conservative central bankers has disappeared, since the linear term takes care of the discretionary inflation. If the central banker is elected, his θ_b will be equal to the parameter θ_i of the median voter.

Appendix 19.1: Reputation and Credibility

We now study a model due to Barro and Gordon (1983a),[5] which underscores that reputational effects may induce a government to behave in a credible manner.

Instead of having a purely short-run objective, the government maximizes a discounted sum of utilities. Its intertemporal utility in period t is:

$$\mathcal{W} = \sum_t \beta^t V_t \qquad (57)$$

with (as above):

$$V_t = -\left[(y_t - \bar{y})^2 + \theta \pi_t^2\right] \qquad (58)$$

To simplify the exposition we assume that the shock ε_t is always 0, so output is determined by (equation 25):

$$y_t = y^* + \xi (\pi_t - \pi_t^e) \qquad (59)$$

19.5.3 The Reputational Mechanism

At the beginning of each period, the government announces an inflation rate π_t^a. It will decide later the "true" inflation rate π_t. The basic idea behind the reputational mechanism is that if in one period the government has announced an inflation rate and not kept its promise, in the next period the private sector will not believe it, whatever the announcements. In such a case the private sector will expect the discretionary value of inflation π_d:

$$\pi_{t-1} \neq \pi_{t-1}^a \qquad \Rightarrow \qquad \pi_t^e = \pi_d \qquad (60)$$

where we recall that π_d is equal to (equation 33):

$$\pi_d = \frac{\xi (\bar{y} - y^*)}{\theta} \qquad (61)$$

Another case where the private sector will not believe the government is when the government announces a rate of inflation so low that it cannot be

---

5. See also Backus and Driffill (1985a, 1985b) and Barro (1986).

credible. We show shortly that there is a threshold inflation rate $\hat{\pi}$ such that the private sector should not believe an announcement below $\hat{\pi}$, so:

$$\pi_t^a < \hat{\pi} \quad \Rightarrow \quad \pi_t^e = \pi_d \tag{62}$$

If the government has kept its promises in the previous period, and makes an announcement above $\hat{\pi}$, then the agents will believe the government:

$$\pi_{t-1} = \pi_{t-1}^a \text{ and } \pi_t^a > \hat{\pi} \quad \Rightarrow \quad \pi_t^e = \pi_t^a \tag{63}$$

A Credible Inflation Threshold

Now we want to compute the threshold level of inflation $\hat{\pi}$. For that we compare two scenarios: (a) the government announces π in all periods and never cheats, (b) the scenario is the same, but the government cheats in the first period only. These two scenarios will differ only in the first and second periods, so we compute:

$$V_t + \beta V_{t+1} \tag{64}$$

for these two cases. Consider the first scenario (a). Assume that the government has announced $\pi_t^a = \pi$ and that the private sector believes it. Because the governement does not cheat, the utility in both periods will be:

$$V_t = V_{t+1} = -\left[(\bar{y} - y^*)^2 + \theta \pi^2\right] \tag{65}$$

and the discounted utility (64) in scenario (a):

$$-(1+\beta)\left[(\bar{y} - y^*)^2 + \theta \pi^2\right] \tag{66}$$

If the government cheats in the first period (scenario b), it will choose a level of inflation (see equation 31 with $\pi_t^e = \pi$):

$$\pi_t = \frac{\xi}{\theta + \xi^2}(\bar{y} - y^* + \xi \pi) \tag{67}$$

yielding output:

$$y_t - \bar{y} = -\frac{\theta}{\theta + \xi^2}(\bar{y} - y^* + \xi \pi) \tag{68}$$

and a first-period utility:

$$V_t = -\left(\frac{\theta}{\theta + \xi^2}\right)(\bar{y} - y^* + \xi\pi)^2 \tag{69}$$

In the second period of scenario (b), the private sector will not trust the government anymore. So inflation will be at the discretionary level:

$$\pi_{t+1}^e = \pi_d = \frac{\xi(\bar{y} - y^*)}{\theta} \tag{70}$$

and the second-period utility will be (equation 37 with $\sigma = 0$):

$$V_{t+1} = -\frac{\theta + \xi^2}{\theta}(\bar{y} - y^*)^2 \tag{71}$$

So in scenario (b) the discounted utility (64) is:

$$-\left(\frac{\theta}{\theta + \xi^2}\right)(\bar{y} - y^* + \xi\pi)^2 - \beta\frac{\theta + \xi^2}{\theta}(\bar{y} - y^*)^2 \tag{72}$$

The inflation announcement π will be credible if the utility when the government does not cheat (66) is higher than the utility when it cheats (72). Using the relation:

$$\bar{y} - y^* = \frac{\theta\pi_d}{\xi} \tag{73}$$

This yields the condition:

$$(1+\beta)\left[\left(\frac{\theta\pi_d}{\xi}\right)^2 + \theta\pi^2\right] < \left(\frac{\theta}{\theta+\xi^2}\right)\left(\frac{\theta\pi_d}{\xi} + \xi\pi\right)^2 + \beta\frac{\theta+\xi^2}{\theta}\left(\frac{\theta\pi_d}{\xi}\right)^2 \tag{74}$$

or after simplifications:

$$\pi > \hat{\pi} = \frac{\theta - \beta(\theta + \xi^2)}{\theta + \beta(\theta + \xi^2)}\pi_d \tag{75}$$

We first see that if $\beta = 0$, the only announcement that can be sustained by this reputational mechanism is $\hat{\pi} = \pi_d$, as should have been expected.

But as soon as $\beta > 0$, lower inflation rates can be sustained, and this reputational mechanism will help fight the inflationary bias of the discretionary solution.

Problems

Problem 19.1: A Kydland-Prescott Model

Consider a two-period model (Kydland and Prescott, 1977). Private agents take decisions (x_1, x_2), the government (g_1, g_2). The government maximizes a social utility function:

$$U(x_1, x_2, g_1, g_2)$$

Private agents have the following response functions:

$$x_1 = X_1(g_1, g_2)$$
$$x_2 = X_2(x_1, g_1, g_2)$$

It is assumed that private agents have rational expectations and that government knows perfectly the foregoing response functions.

1. Assume that the government can commit in the first period on both g_1 and g_2. Characterize the first-order conditions of the equilibrium.
2. Assume that the governement will choose g_2 in the second period, and can only commit on g_1 in the first period. Characterize the equilibrium.
3. Compare the two equilibria and indicate when they will be the same.

Problem 19.2: Punishment for Lying and Credibility

The model is very similar to that of section 19.4. The difference is that in the first stage of the game the government "announces" a level of inflation π_t^a which it claims to implement in the second stage. If the government "lies," in the sense that the actual inflation rate π_t in the second stage is different from π_t^a, the government will incur a "punishment" $\mu(\pi_t - \pi_t^a)^2$. As a result, the government's utility function is:

$$V_t = -\left[(y_t - \bar{y})^2 + \theta \pi_t^2 + \mu(\pi_t - \pi_t^a)^2\right]$$

where the two first terms have already been seen in chapter 19 (section 19.4), and the third one is the punishment.

Output is determined by:

$$y_t = y^* + \xi \left(\pi_t - \pi_t^e \right)$$

1. We assume that the government cannot commit in advance. Compute the time consistent inflation announcement π_t^a.
2. Compute the equilibrium inflation. How does this inflation rate depend on the "punishment parameter" μ?

Problem 19.3: Time Consistent Inflation with a Phillips Curve

We consider a deterministic model. The government wants to minimize:

$$\sum \beta^t \left[(y_t - \bar{y})^2 + \theta \pi_t^2 \right]$$

subject to a new Keynesian Phillips curve:

$$\pi_t = \beta \pi_{t+1} + \kappa \left(y_t - y^* \right)$$

1. Compute the time consistent rate of inflation.

20

Political Economy

20.1 Introduction

Up to this point, when analyzing economic policy, we always assumed that there was a policy maker with a single and well-defined objective function at any time. This can be actually a good representation if there is, as in the Ramsey model, a single representative agent and the government simply mimics his utility function. But for real-life democracies, this is obviously a huge simplification of reality, as politicians in power are supposed to represent millions of people, each with his or her own preferences.

The problem is, of course, that agents' preferences over different outcomes are usually highly heterogeneous. The problem of political economy is to describe rationally the social decision process when such heterogeneity is present or, in other words, show how to aggregate the heterogeneous preferences of all agents into a single "social utility function" for society. In reality we observe many possible processes. A popular one is democratic voting, by which various politicians propose political platforms, and some form of majority voting determines who is elected.

Political economy is a rapidly expanding and difficult subject, and in this chapter we only scratch the surface of things.[1]

In section 20.2 we start with a result that exemplifies the fundamental difficulties of the field; Arrow's impossibility theorem, which basically says

---

1. For extensive expositions of the field, the reader should consult Alesina (1988), Persson and Tabellini (1990, 1999, 2000), Drazen (2000), and Grossman and Helpman (2001).

that there is no aggregation procedure which always satisfies a number of natural conditions.

Of course, we do not want to stay with a negative result, and section 20.3 describes a highly popular model in which aggregation is possible, the "median voter" model. It has the striking property that the politicians participating in the election propose the same platform, the preferred choice of the median voter, even when they have preferences that differ from it.

Section 20.4 applies the median voter model to a classic subject of political economy, voting on redistribution. Section 20.5 shows how political instability, that is, the possibility of changing majority, can lead to recurrent budget deficits.

The median voter result is not only striking but counterfactual, as politicians in the real world do present different electoral platforms. Section 20.6 returns to the median voter result and shows that introducing a stochastic element can lead politicians to move away from the median outcome and toward their own preferred alternative.

20.2 Arrow's Impossibility Theorem

We consider a society composed of n individuals indexed by $i = 1, \ldots, n$. Define $N = \{1, \ldots, n\}$. These individuals have to make choices between mutually exclusive alternatives in a set Σ. Alternatives in the set Σ will be denoted x, y, $z \ldots$ Each agent i has a preference ordering over the alternatives in Σ. We shall note:

$$x \mathcal{R}_i y \iff i \text{ prefers } x \text{ to } y \text{ or is indifferent between the two} \qquad (1)$$

We will maintain throughout the two following assumptions:

Completeness: For all (x,y), one must have at least $x \mathcal{R}_i y$ or $y \mathcal{R}_i x$.
Transitivity: For all (x,y,z), $x \mathcal{R}_i y$ and $y \mathcal{R}_i z$ imply $x \mathcal{R}_i z$

A *profile* of preference orderings is a description of the preference orderings of all individuals $i = 1, \ldots, n$. A *social welfare function* is a functional which, to each profile of individual preference orderings $\mathcal{R}_i$, associates a social ordering $\mathcal{R}_N$:

$$\mathcal{R}_N = \mathcal{F}(\mathcal{R}_1, \ldots \mathcal{R}_i, \ldots \mathcal{R}_n) \qquad (2)$$

20.2.1 Arrow's Impossibility Theorem

We first indicate four properties that one might naturally wish to be satisfied by the social welfare function. Arrow's theorem will tell us that they cannot be satisfied together.

Condition U (unrestricted domain): The social welfare function is defined for all possible profiles of preference orderings.

Condition P (Pareto principle): If every individual prefers x to y, then x is socially preferred to y:

$$x \mathcal{R}_i y \quad \forall i \quad \Longrightarrow \quad x \mathcal{R}_N y \tag{3}$$

Condition I (independence of irrelevant alternatives): Consider a subset S of Σ, and two profiles $(\mathcal{R}_1, \ldots, \mathcal{R}_n)$ and $(\mathcal{R}'_1, \ldots, \mathcal{R}'_n)$. If these profiles have the same ordering of the alternatives in the subset S for every individual, then they determine the same social ordering on S.

Condition D (nondictatorship): There is no individual whose preferences are the social preferences according to the social welfare function.

We can now give the central result of this literature (Arrow, 1951).

Arrow's impossibility theorem: *If there are at least three alternatives, there is no social welfare function that satisfies properties U, P, I, and D.*

20.2.2 The Condorcet Paradox

Majority voting is a particular social welfare function. Let us define $\mathcal{P}(x, y)$ as the proportion of individuals i who prefer x to y, that is, such that $x \mathcal{R}_i y$. Majority voting is the social ordering $\mathcal{R}_M$ defined by:

$$x \mathcal{R}_M y \quad \Longleftrightarrow \quad \mathcal{P}(x, y) \geq \mathcal{P}(y, x) \tag{4}$$

The Condorcet paradox (Condorcet, 1785) shows that majority voting may not lead to a transitive social ordering. Let us indeed consider a situation with three alternatives, x, y, and z, and three agents, 1, 2, and 3, with the following individual preferences (we assume preferences are strict):

$$x \mathcal{R}_1 y \mathcal{R}_1 z \tag{5}$$

$$y \mathcal{R}_2 z \mathcal{R}_2 x \tag{6}$$

$$z \mathcal{R}_3 x \mathcal{R}_3 y \tag{7}$$

We see that majority voting leads to the following two-by-two rankings:

$$x \mathcal{R}_M y \quad y \mathcal{R}_M z \quad z \mathcal{R}_M x \tag{8}$$

Transitivity is not respected.

20.3 The Median Voter

Because there is no general solution for constructing a social welfare function, people have sought to escape Arrow's impossibility theorem by, for example, restricting the range of preferences of the agents in the economy.

We now describe a well-known particular solution to this problem, that of the median voter.[2] We consider a population of individuals indexed by i. These individuals have to choose collectively a variable x that can take any value along the real line. Each individual i ranks the possible values of x through his individual utility function $U_i(x)$. We assume that $U_i(x)$ has a "bliss point" x_i^*:

$$x_i^* = \mathrm{argmax}\, U_i(x) \tag{9}$$

We further make the traditional assumption that each function U_i has the "single peakedness" property, defined as follows: the function $U(x)$ is single peaked if it has a maximum x^* and:

$$x'' < x' < x^* \quad \Rightarrow \quad U(x') > U(x'') \tag{10}$$

$$x'' > x' > x^* \quad \Rightarrow \quad U(x') > U(x'') \tag{11}$$

Members of the population are ranked by the value of their bliss point x_i^*. We denote by $\Phi(x_i^*)$ the cumulative distribution of x_i^*. In what follows the median voter plays an important role. This median voter, denoted M, is defined by:

$$\Phi(x_M^*) = 1/2 \tag{12}$$

Two politicians, denoted A and B, compete for the votes of the population. Each proposes a particular value of x, denoted respectively as x_A and x_B. Each voter votes for the candidate that gives him the highest utility, that is:

$$U_i(x_A) > U_i(x_B) \quad \Longrightarrow \quad \text{Agent } i \text{ votes for } A \text{ with probability } 1$$

$$U_i(x_A) < U_i(x_B) \quad \Longrightarrow \quad \text{Agent } i \text{ votes for } B \text{ with probability } 1$$

$$U_i(x_A) = U_i(x_B) \quad \Longrightarrow \quad \text{Agent } i \text{ splits his vote with probability } 1/2 \tag{13}$$

---

2. See notably Black (1948) and Downs (1957).

20.3.1 Opportunistic Politicians

We say that politicians are opportunistic if their only goal in choosing their electoral platform is to maximize the probability of being elected. In that case we have the first median voter result:

The median voter (1): *If the two politicians are opportunistic, they both propose the bliss point of the median voter:*

$$x_A = x_B = x_M^* \qquad (14)$$

Proof To prove this, let us first check that $x_A = x_B = x_M^*$ is a Nash equilibrium. Indeed, if either A or B deviates, he will decrease his probability of winning from 1/2 to 0.

Now imagine that one of the two platforms, say x_B, is different from x_M^*. Two cases can occur. (a) $x_A = x_M^*$. In that case, B will change his election probability from 0 to 1/2 by setting $x_B = x_M^*$. (b) $x_A \neq x_M^*$. Then either A or B has a probability of winning inferior to 1 and he can increase it to 1 by moving to x_M^*. The initial position could not be an equilibrium.

As a consequence, $x_A = x_B = x_M^*$ is the only Nash equilibrium.

20.3.2 Partisan Politicians

The above median voter result is not totally surprising, because both politicians only care about being elected and do not have any personal preference about the platform they propose. But we will see that the same result also applies if the two politicians are partisan.

A politician is called *partisan* if he cares not only about his probability of winning the election but also about his own political platform (x_A or x_B). To make the exposition simple, we assume that the preference of, say, politician A, is the following:

$$\Pi_A(x_A)\left[\Lambda + \theta_A V_A(x_A)\right] \qquad V_A'(x_A^*) = 0 \qquad (15)$$

where Π_A is the probability for A to be elected, Λ the utility of just being elected, $V_A(x_A)$ the utility that A derives from the electoral platform x_A, and θ_A the weight that A attributes to his political preferences. Opportunistic politicians correspond to the particular case $\theta_A = 0$.

Now we have a second, and actually more striking, median voter result.

The median voter (2): *If politicians have utilities of the form (15), both politicians propose the bliss point of the median voter:*

$$x_A = x_B = x_M^* \tag{16}$$

Proof Let us first show that $x_A = x_B = x_M^*$ is a Nash equilibrium. Indeed, A and B have a probability of vote of 50 percent. If any of the two deviates, he will fall to 0.

We now assume that one of the two is not at x_M^*, say x_B. Figure 20.1 plots the probability $\Pi_A(x_A)$ for A to be elected as a function of his electoral platform x_A. In figure 20.1 $\varphi(x_B)$ is the value of x_A (besides x_B) such that the median voter is indifferent between x_B and $\varphi(x_B)$, that is:

$$U_M(x_B) = U_M[\varphi(x_B)] \tag{17}$$

There we see that, notably because of the discontinuities, A's best response to x_B will always be in the open interval between x_B and $\varphi(x_B)$:

$$x_A \in\,]x_B, \varphi(x_B)[\tag{18}$$

Another way to express (18) is:

$$U_M(x_A) > U_M(x_B) \tag{19}$$

Now a similar reasoning can be made, exchanging the roles of x_A and x_B, so that:

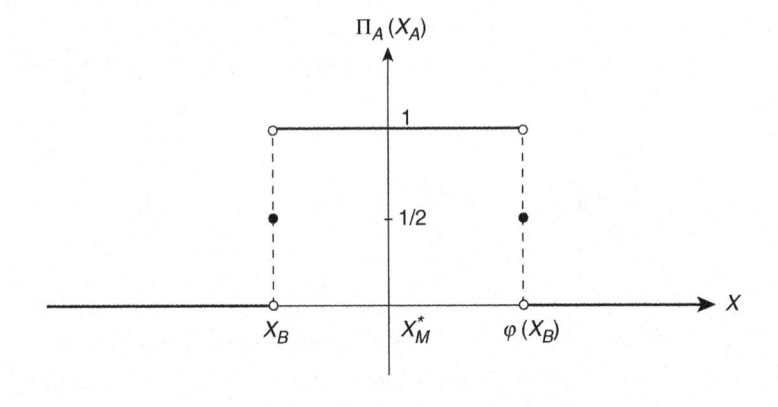

$$U_M(x_B) > U_M(x_A) \tag{20}$$

Figure 20.1 Probability of A's election

But (19) and (20) are inconsistent, so the only Nash equilibrium is $x_A = x_B = x_M^*$.

20.4 Voting and Redistribution

We now give a classic application of the median voter theory, that of voting and redistributive taxation.[3] Society is heterogeneous because different households have different productivities. We denote individual productivity by A. This productivity has a density function $\phi(A)$. All households have the same utility function:

$$U = C - \frac{L^{1+\nu}}{1+\nu} \qquad \nu > 0 \qquad (21)$$

The government taxes incomes at the rate τ and redistributes T in a lump sum, where T, the sum of individual taxes, is given by:

$$T = \tau \int_A AL(A)\phi(A)\,dA \qquad (22)$$

Consumption is thus equal to:

$$C = (1-\tau)AL + T \qquad (23)$$

20.4.1 Equilibrium

Households maximize utility (21) subject to the budget constraint (23). This yields the supply of labor:

$$L = [(1-\tau)A]^{1/\nu} \qquad (24)$$

So the lump-sum subsidy is:

$$T = \tau(1-\tau)^{1/\nu} \int A^{(1+\nu)/\nu}\phi(A)\,dA \qquad (25)$$

Let us call:

$$\gamma = \frac{1+\nu}{\nu} > 1 \qquad (26)$$

$$T = \tau(1-\tau)^{\gamma-1} \int A^\gamma \phi(A)\,dA = \tau(1-\tau)^{\gamma-1} E(A^\gamma) \qquad (27)$$

---

3. Classic references are Romer (1975) and Roberts (1977).

We can compute the utility of each household as a function of its own productivity A:

$$U = C - \frac{L^{1+\nu}}{1+\nu} = (1-\tau)AL + T - \frac{L^{1+\nu}}{1+\nu}$$

$$= \frac{(1-\tau)^\gamma A^\gamma}{\gamma} + \tau(1-\tau)^{\gamma-1} E(A^\gamma) \qquad (28)$$

We compute the derivative of this utility with respect to the tax rate:

$$\frac{\partial U}{\partial \tau} = (1-\tau)^{\gamma-2}\left[(1-\gamma\tau)E(A^\gamma) - (1-\tau)A^\gamma\right] \qquad (29)$$

The value of this derivative for $\tau = 0$ is equal to $E(A^\gamma) - A^\gamma$. If $A^\gamma > E(A^\gamma)$ the agent's preferred tax rate $\tau(A)$ is 0. If $A^\gamma < E(A^\gamma)$ there is an interior maximum for:

$$\tau(A) = \frac{E(A^\gamma) - A^\gamma}{\gamma E(A^\gamma) - A^\gamma} < 1 \qquad (30)$$

which is agent A's preferred tax rate. The tax rate τ^* that will come out of the voting process is simply the preferred tax rate of the median voter.

20.4.2 An Example

We consider the case where $a = Log A$ is a normal variable with mean μ and variance σ^2. In such a case one may compute (see mathematical appendix, section A.7):

$$E(A^\gamma) = \exp\left(\gamma\mu + \frac{\gamma^2\sigma^2}{2}\right) \qquad (31)$$

The productivity of the median voter is $A = e^\mu$, so combining this with (30) and (31), we find that the tax rate τ^* that will come out of a vote is:

$$\tau^* = \frac{\exp(\gamma^2\sigma^2/2) - 1}{\gamma\exp(\gamma^2\sigma^2/2) - 1} \qquad (32)$$

20.5 The Political Economy of Budget Deficits

Many countries nowadays experience sizable budget deficits, and we present in this section a model that is a mix of Persson and Svensson (1989) and Tabellini and Alesina (1990),[4] which shows that political change may lead to budget deficits. In a nutshell, we have a model with two parties that have different "tastes" about either the size of public spending (Persson and Svensson) or its composition (Tabellini and Alesina). For example, in the model we present below one party likes private consumption more than public consumption, the reverse is true for the other party.

Note that these differences in tastes do not imply that any of these parties are intrinsically prone to deficit. In fact, we will see that if either of the two parties was sure to stay in power in the two periods, it would have the same spending pattern in both periods, and deficits would be 0.

Now if there is a positive probability that the political majority will change in the second period, the party currently in power may want to run a deficit and accumulate debt, simply because it wants to have more money to spend when controlling 100 percent of the spending, and less when the other party controls that spending.[5] So the party in power, because it may lose the elections in the next period, wants to "overspend" today on its preferred good, thus creating a deficit.

20.5.1 The Model

We consider a model with two periods, 1 and 2. Private agents have the same income Y in the two periods. We denote by C_1 and C_2, G_1 and G_2, and T_1 and T_2 the values of consumption, government spending, and lump-sum taxes in the two periods. The government runs a deficit in the first period:

$$D = G_1 - T_1 \qquad (33)$$

Because we study optimal fiscal policy in such a framework, we want to use a model where Ricardian equivalence does not hold, for otherwise fiscal policy would not matter. We use the following setup:[6] the economy is a small open economy. Government has access to the world capital market where

---

[4]. See also Alesina and Tabellini (1990).

[5]. We will actually see in appendix 20.1 that this reasoning does not apply to all possible parameters, and this lack of control of spending in the second period may sometimes lead to a surplus.

[6]. This is found in both Persson and Svensson (1989) (in a variation of their main model) and in Tabellini and Alesina (1990). An alternative (Persson and Svensson, 1989) is to assume distortionary taxation.

it can borrow or lend at the world interest rate. To simplify computations, we take this world interest rate equal to be 0. Households, however, do not have access to this world capital market. As a result we have:

$$C_1 = Y - T_1 \qquad C_2 = Y - T_2 \qquad (34)$$

$$G_1 = T_1 + D \qquad G_2 = T_2 - D \qquad (35)$$

In period 1 the party in power has to decide, using D and T_1 as instruments, on the values of C_1 and G_1. Different agents have different utilities about C_1 and G_1, indexed by a coefficient α_i. The utility of agent i for period 1 is:

$$V_i(C_1, G_1) = \alpha_i U(C_1) + (1 - \alpha_i) U(G_1) \qquad 0 \leq \alpha_i \leq 1 \qquad (36)$$

where the function U is increasing and concave. The distribution of the α_i's may change from period 1 to period 2 and therefore lead to a change in government.

20.5.2 A Polarized Society

In this section we consider the particular case where α_i can only take the two extreme values 0 and 1, that is, agents (denoted A and B) care only about one of the two (private or public) goods.[7]

$$V_A(C_1, G_1) = U(C_1) \qquad V_B(C_1, G_1) = U(G_1) \qquad (37)$$

We also assume $U(0) = 0$. We assume that party A is in power in the first period. Available income is $Y + D$, and so party A spends the sum of income and deficit on C_1. Nothing is spent on G_1:

$$C_1 = Y + D \qquad G_1 = 0 \qquad (38)$$

Similarly in period 2 total income available is $Y - D$. If party A stays in power, it will spend all available money on C_2:

$$C_2 = Y - D \qquad G_2 = 0 \qquad (39)$$

Now if party B is in power in period 2, we will have a symmetrical outcome:

$$G_2 = Y - D \qquad C_2 = 0 \qquad (40)$$

---

7. Appendix 20.1 considers a case where each agent cares about both goods, although with a different weight.

20.5.3 Deficit

Assume that with probability π, party B will take over in the next period. We can compute the total expected utility of party A. It is equal to (we assume that the discount rate is equal to 1):

$$\mathcal{W}_A = U(Y+D) + (1-\pi)U(Y-D) \qquad (41)$$

Both terms in the maximand $\mathcal{W}_A$ are concave in D. So the optimum level of deficit is obtained by equating to 0 the derivative with respect to D:

$$\frac{\partial \mathcal{W}_A}{\partial D} = U'(Y+D) - (1-\pi)U'(Y-D) = 0 \qquad (42)$$

Equation (42) is an implicit equation in D. We may note that in the case where $\pi = 0$ (i.e., when the party in power is sure of remaining in office) the deficit will be 0, as we had indicated earlier.

Now as soon as $\pi > 0$, party 1 will run a deficit in the first period. This deficit will be increasing with the probability π of a government change. Indeed, differentiating (42), we find:

$$\frac{\partial D}{\partial \pi} = -\frac{U'(Y-D)}{U''(Y+D) + (1-\pi)U''(Y-D)} > 0 \qquad (43)$$

As an example, in the case where $U(C) = C^{1-\theta}/(1-\theta)$, formula (42) yields:

$$\left(\frac{Y+D}{Y-D}\right)^{1/\theta} = 1 - \pi \qquad (44)$$

or:

$$\frac{D}{Y} = \frac{1 - (1-\pi)^{1/\theta}}{1 + (1-\pi)^{1/\theta}} \qquad (45)$$

20.6 Platform Heterogeneity

We have seen in section 20.3 that whether politicians are partisan or opportunistic, they propose the same platform, that of the median voter. This does not really correspond to reality, where proposed platforms are usually quite different. Therefore, we would like to have a model where different political platforms can coexist in equilibrium.

We now present a model, probabilistic voting, where partisan politicians will end up proposing different platforms.[8] For that purpose we introduce an element of randomness in the voting process. Instead of using rule (13), voter i will vote for candidate A if:

$$U_i(x_A) + \delta > U_i(x_B) \tag{46}$$

where δ is a stochastic variable, which may represent, for example, the relative charisma of candidate A. To simplify the exposition we assume that δ is the same for all agents and uniformly distributed in the interval $[-\Delta, +\Delta]$. The median voter theory described in section 20.3 corresponds to $\Delta = 0$.

The threshold between voting for A or B corresponds to the median voter, whose utility is function is $U_M(x)$. So A will receive a majority of votes for all values of δ such that:

$$\delta > U_M(x_B) - U_M(x_A) \tag{47}$$

so that, with the uniform probability distribution above, the probability of a vote for A is:

$$\Pi_A(x_A) = \frac{\Delta + U_M(x_A) - U_M(x_B)}{2\Delta} \tag{48}$$

Of course this must be between 0 and 1, so that the value of $\Pi_A(x_A)$ is finally:

$$\Pi_A(x_A) = \min\left\{1, \max\left[0, \frac{\Delta + U_M(x_A) - U_M(x_B)}{2\Delta}\right]\right\} \tag{49}$$

The probability $\Pi_A(x_A)$ is represented in figures 20.2 and 20.3, which are drawn under the assumption $x_B < x_M^*$. We note that $\Pi_A(x_A) = 1/2$ when $x_A = x_B$. Furthermore, $\Pi_A(x_A) = 0$ for the two values of x_A (if they exist) such that:

$$U_M(x_A) = U_M(x_B) - \Delta \tag{50}$$

---

8. Probabilistic voting has notably been developed by Hinich (1977), Coughlin and Nitzan (1981), and Ledyard (1981, 1984). For a survey, see Coughlin (1992).

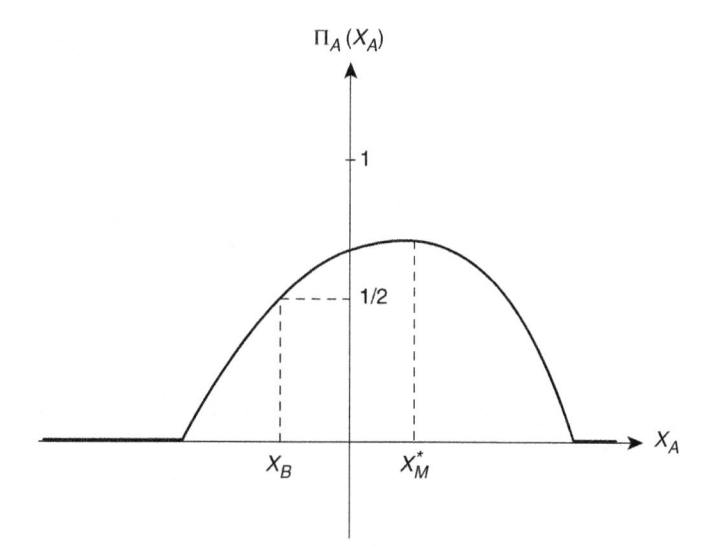

Figure 20.2 Probability of a vote for A

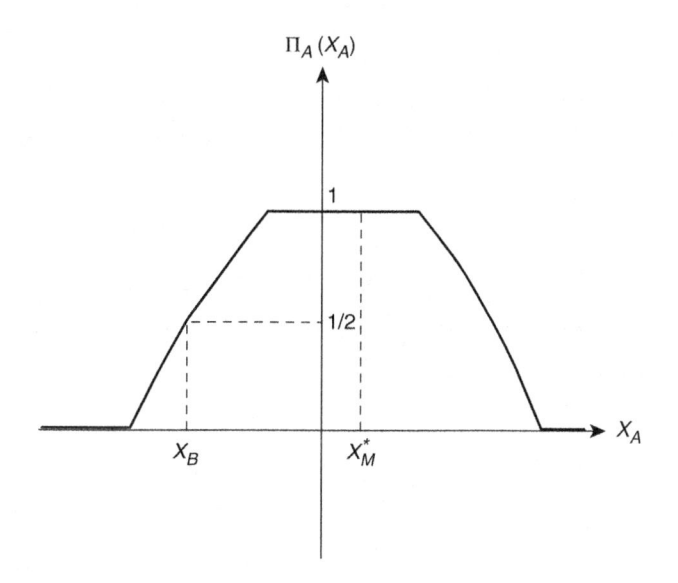

Figure 20.3 Probability of a vote for A

Figure 20.2 has been drawn under the assumption that $\Pi_A(x_A)$, as given in (48), is smaller than 1 for all x_A, which implies:

$$U_M(x_M^*) - U_B(x_B) < \Delta \tag{51}$$

If this condition is not satisfied, then $\Pi_A(x_A)$ has a flat part at the top and looks as it does in figure 20.3. Now we assume that A maximizes the "opportunistic" utility function (15):

$$\Pi_A(x_A)[\Lambda + \theta_A V_A(x_A)] \qquad V_A'(x_A^*) = 0 \qquad V_A(x_A) \geq 0 \qquad (52)$$

which, using (48), is rewritten:

$$[\Delta + U_M(x_A) - U_M(x_B)][\Lambda + \theta_A V_A(x_A)] \qquad (53)$$

The derivative of (53) with respect to x_A is:

$$U_M'(x_A)[\Lambda + \theta_A V_A(x_A)] + [\Delta + U_M(x_A) - U_M(x_B)]\theta_A V_A'(x_A) \qquad (54)$$

Assuming $\theta_A > 0$ and $\Delta > 0$, we see that this derivative is positive for $x_A \leq x_M^*$ and negative for $x_A \geq x_A^*$. There is thus a maximum between x_M^* and x_A^*. Moreover, the derivative at $x_A = x_M^*$ is equal to:

$$[\Delta + U_M(x_M^*) - U_M(x_B)]\theta_A V_A'(x_M^*) \qquad (55)$$

and is thus strictly positive if $\theta_A > 0$, so that the final equilibrium $(\hat{x}_A, \hat{x}_B)$ will be such that:

$$x_B^* < \hat{x}_B < x_M^* < \hat{x}_A < x_A^* \qquad (56)$$

where $\hat{x}_A$ and $\hat{x}_B$ are the equilibrium platforms of candidates A and B. We see that these platforms are a compromise between the politicians' true preferences and those of the median voter.

Appendix 20.1: The Political Economy of Deficits

We now study an extension of the model of section 20.5, where the two parties have utility for both private and public consumption, although in different degrees.

The Model

As in section 20.5 we assume that party A is in power in the first period, but that with probability π party B will take over in the next period. We still assume that agent i's utility over the two goods is:

$$V_i(C_1, G_1) = \alpha_i U(C_1) + (1 - \alpha_i) U(G_1) \qquad 0 \leq \alpha_i \leq 1 \qquad (57)$$

In section 20.5 we had assumed that the α_i's could take only the values 0 and 1. Here we assume that the utilities of partisans of parties A and B are symmetrical and, respectively:

$$V_A(C_1, G_1) = \alpha U(C_1) + (1 - \alpha) U(G_1) \qquad (58)$$

$$V_B(C_1, G_1) = \alpha U(G_1) + (1 - \alpha) U(C_1) \qquad (59)$$

We assume that $\alpha \geq 1/2$, so party A puts more weight on private consumption and party B puts more weight on public consumption.

As an example, we consider below the following utility:

$$U(C) = C^{1-\theta}/(1-\theta) \qquad (60)$$

The Demands for Private and Public Consumptions

Governement spending is equal to $Y + D$ in the first period and $Y - D$ in the second period. If party A is in power in the first period, it will solve:

$$\text{Maximize } V_A(C_1, G_1) = \alpha U(C_1) + (1-\alpha) U(G_1) \qquad \text{s.t.}$$

$$C_1 + G_1 = Y + D$$

We assume that $V_A(C_1, G_1)$ is homothetic, so that the solution is:

$$C_1 = \phi(\alpha)(Y+D) \qquad (61)$$

$$G_1 = [1 - \phi(\alpha)](Y+D) \qquad (62)$$

where the function $\phi(\alpha)$ has the following properties:

$$\phi(1-\alpha) = 1 - \phi(\alpha) \qquad \phi'(\alpha) > 0 \qquad (63)$$

$$\phi(0) = 0 \qquad \phi(1/2) = 1/2 \qquad \phi(1) = 1 \qquad (64)$$

As an example with the utility function (60):

$$\phi(\alpha) = \frac{\alpha^{1/\theta}}{\alpha^{1/\theta} + (1-\alpha)^{1/\theta}} \tag{65}$$

To find what will happen in the second period, we essentially have to replace $Y + D$ by $Y - D$. If party A is in power:

$$C_2 = \phi(\alpha)(Y - D) \tag{66}$$

$$G_2 = [1 - \phi(\alpha)](Y - D) \tag{67}$$

If party B is in power in the second period, the outcome is symmetrical, simply replacing α with $1 - \alpha$:

$$C_2 = \phi(1 - \alpha)(Y - D) \tag{68}$$

$$G_2 = [1 - \phi(1 - \alpha)](Y - D) = \phi(\alpha)(Y - D) \tag{69}$$

Total Utility and the First Order Conditions

We can now compute the expected total utility, as viewed by party A from the first period. It is equal to:

$$\begin{aligned} \mathcal{W}_A = &\alpha U\left[\phi(\alpha)(Y+D)\right] + (1-\alpha) U\left[\phi(1-\alpha)(Y+D)\right] \\ &+ \zeta U\left[\phi(\alpha)(Y-D)\right] + (1-\zeta) U\left[\phi(1-\alpha)(Y-D)\right] \end{aligned} \tag{70}$$

with:

$$\zeta = \alpha + \pi - 2\alpha\pi \tag{71}$$

Terms in the maximand $\mathcal{W}_A$ are concave in D. So the optimum level of deficit is obtained by equating to 0 the derivative with respect to D:

$$\begin{aligned} \frac{\partial \mathcal{W}_A}{\partial D} = &\alpha\phi(\alpha) U'\left[\phi(\alpha)(Y+D)\right] + (1-\alpha)\phi(1-\alpha) U'\left[\phi(1-\alpha)(Y+D)\right] \\ &- \zeta\phi(\alpha) U'\left[\phi(\alpha)(Y-D)\right] - (1-\zeta)\phi(1-\alpha) U'\left[\phi(1-\alpha)(Y-D)\right] = 0 \end{aligned} \tag{72}$$

We first note that if $\pi = 0$, then $\zeta = \alpha$, and equation (72) yields a zero deficit, as we had already found in the model of section 20.5.

When is There a Deficit?

We now consider the case $\pi > 0$. To know the sign of the eventual deficit, we compute the derivative of $\mathcal{W}_A$ with respect to D at the point $D = 0$. This is equal to:

$$\left(\frac{\partial \mathcal{W}_A}{\partial D}\right)_{D=0} = \pi\,(2\alpha - 1)\,\{\phi(\alpha)\,U'[\phi(\alpha)\,Y] - \phi(1-\alpha)\,U'[\phi(1-\alpha)\,Y]\} \tag{73}$$

We see that besides the case $\pi = 0$, there is another case, $\alpha = 1/2$, where the deficit will surely be 0. In that case, the two parties have exactly the same preferences, so that the change of party in power is not a real change.

Now if $\alpha > 1/2$ and $\pi > 0$, the deficit will be positive if:

$$\phi(\alpha)\,U'[\phi(\alpha)\,Y] - \phi(1-\alpha)\,U'[\phi(1-\alpha)\,Y] > 0 \tag{74}$$

A sufficient condition for that is that $xU'(x)$ be increasing in x, or:

$$U'(x) + xU''(x) > 0 \tag{75}$$

which may also be written as:

$$-\frac{xU''(x)}{U'(x)} < 1 \tag{76}$$

In other words the degree of relative risk aversion should be smaller than 1. As an example, with the utility function (60) the deficit is given by the equation:

$$\left(\frac{Y+D}{Y-D}\right)^{1/\theta} = 1 + \pi\,(2\alpha - 1)\,\frac{(1-\alpha)^{(1-\theta)/\theta} - \alpha^{(1-\theta)/\theta}}{\alpha^{1/\theta} + (1-\alpha)^{1/\theta}} \tag{77}$$

The condition for a positive deficit is:

$$\theta < 1 \tag{78}$$

This condition tells us that, a contrario, if $\theta > 1$, this model will predict a budget surplus. This result is actually not so mysterious: indeed with $\theta > 1$, what party A dreads most is have a very low consumption C_2 if party B is elected in the next period. As we already saw (equation 68):

$$C_2 = \phi(1-\alpha)(Y-D) \tag{79}$$

The only thing party A controls in (79) is D, and if it wants to avoid a low C_2 by all means, the only option is a surplus.

Problems

Problem 20.1: Redistribution and Voting Ex Ante

We consider the setting of section 20.4, but we assume here that, instead of voting after productivities are revealed, agents must make a decision on the tax rate *before* they know what their individual productivity will be. So each agent will maximize the expected utility:

$$E(U) = E\left(C - \frac{L^{1+\nu}}{1+\nu}\right)$$

1. Compute the ex ante expected utility of an agent.
2. What will be the tax rate chosen?

Problem 20.2: Ex Ante Voting with Risk Aversion

We continue with the same setting as in problem 20.1, but we introduce some risk aversion. Assume that the utility of each agent is:

$$U = \frac{1}{1-\theta}\left(C - \frac{L^{1+\nu}}{1+\nu}\right)^{1-\theta} \qquad \theta \geq 0$$

To simplify computations we assume that the distribution of productivities is log-normal, that is, $a = Log A$ is a normal variable with mean μ and variance σ^2.

1. Compute the ex ante expected utility of an agent.
2. Show that the optimal tax rate is now strictly positive.

Problem 20.3: Platform Differentiation

The median voter approach described in section 20.3 is very similar to a model of firm competition where firms would choose the optimal location on a line. We saw that this location game led both competitors to choose the median position, that is, minimal differentiation. We now describe a model due to Hotelling (1929) where firms compete in both locations *and* prices, and as a result choose maximal differentiation.

The set of consumers is represented by the segment $[0, 1]$, along which consumers are spread with a uniform density equal to 1. Each consumer buys exactly one unit of a good sold by two firms indexed by $i = A, B$. Firm A is located at the point of abscissa a, firm B at the point of abscissa b, with $0 \leq a \leq b \leq 1$. Firms have a production cost per unit c, and set prices p_a and p_b. A consumer who buys from firm i must pay a transportation cost τd_i^2, where d_i is the distance between him and firm i. Because the goods of the two firms are identical except for location, each consumer buys from the firm that has the lowest total cost $p_i + \tau d_i^2$.

Choices occur in two stages. In a first stage, firms choose their locations a and b. In the second stage, they choose prices p_a and p_b, taking locations a and b as given.

1. Assume we are in the second stage. Compute the demands D_a and D_b that are addressed to firms A and B as a function of locations a and b and prices p_a and p_b.
2. We take locations a and b as given. Compute the Nash equilibrium in prices. Compute the profits of each firm.
3. Consider the first stage. Firms choose their locations a and b, knowing that in the second stage these locations will give rise to the price equilibrium described in question 2. Each firm chooses its location taking the other firm's location as given. Compute the Nash equilibrium in locations. Deduce the full characteristics (locations and prices) of the equilibrium. Comment.

A

Mathematical Appendix

A.1 Matrices

A.1.1 General Properties

A matrix is a collection of numbers arranged in a rectangular table. The typical entry will be denoted a_{ij}, where $i = 1, \ldots m$ is the line index and $j = 1, \ldots n$ is the column index. A typical matrix looks as follows:

$$A = \begin{bmatrix} a_{11} & & a_{1n} \\ & a_{ij} & \\ a_{m1} & & a_{mn} \end{bmatrix} \quad (A.1)$$

Most often we use matrices where a_{ij} is a real number, but it can be a complex number as well.

A number of operations can be performed on matrices. They can be multiplied by scalars:

$$B = \lambda A \quad \Leftrightarrow \quad b_{ij} = \lambda a_{ij} \quad (A.2)$$

If two matrices A and B have the same dimension (m, n) they can be added or subtracted:

$$C = A + B \quad \Leftrightarrow \quad c_{ij} = a_{ij} + b_{ij} \qquad (A.3)$$

$$C = A - B \quad \Leftrightarrow \quad c_{ij} = a_{ij} - b_{ij} \qquad (A.4)$$

The transpose of a matrix is the matrix obtained by exchanging rows and columns:

$$B = A^T \quad \Leftrightarrow \quad b_{ij} = a_{ji} \qquad (A.5)$$

Two matrices A and B (in that order) can be multiplied if the number of columns of A is the same as the number of lines of B. Let us denote by ℓ that common number. The product matrix is defined by:

$$C = AB \quad \Leftrightarrow \quad c_{ij} = \sum_{k=1}^{\ell} a_{ik} b_{kj} \qquad (A.6)$$

A.1.2 Square Matrices

We will particularly work with square matrices such that $m = n$. For such matrices we define the trace T as the sum of entries on the main diagonal:

$$T(A) = \sum_{i=1}^{n} a_{ii} \qquad (A.7)$$

An important special case is the *identity matrix*, denoted I, which is composed of ones along the main diagonal, and zeros everywhere else.

A.1.3 Determinants

The determinant of a matrix is a central element for all the uses that will follow. The determinant of a matrix A will be denoted $|A|$ or $D(A)$. For a matrix of dimension 1 the definition is particularly simple:

$$A = [a_{11}] \quad \Longrightarrow \quad D(A) = |A| = a_{11} \qquad (A.8)$$

To define the determinant of a matrix of dimension $n > 1$, we work recursively. Call A_{ij} the matrix obtained by deleting from A row i and column j:

$$A_{ij} = \begin{bmatrix} a_{1,1} & a_{1,j-1} & a_{1,j+1} & a_{1,n} \\ a_{i-1,1} & a_{i-1,j-1} & a_{i-1,j+1} & a_{i-1,n} \\ a_{i+1,1} & a_{i+1,j-1} & a_{i+1,j+1} & a_{i+1,n} \\ a_{m,1} & a_{m,j-1} & a_{m,j+1} & a_{m,n} \end{bmatrix} \qquad (A.9)$$

Now the cofactor C_{ij} is deduced from A_{ij} through:

$$C_{ij} = (-1)^{i+j} D\left(A_{ij}\right) \qquad (A.10)$$

Finally the determinant $|A|$ is obtained by "cofactor expansion". This expansion can be implemented in two ways: expansion through the ith row:

$$|A| = \sum_{j=1}^{n} a_{ij} C_{ij} \qquad (A.11)$$

or expansion through the jth column:

$$|A| = \sum_{i=1}^{n} a_{ij} C_{ij} \qquad (A.12)$$

It does not matter which row or which column is used. Take as an example the matrix of dimension 2:

$$A = \begin{bmatrix} a_{11} & a_{12} \\ a_{21} & a_{22} \end{bmatrix} \qquad (A.13)$$

Applying the above steps to this matrix we find:

$$D\left(\begin{bmatrix} a_{11} & a_{12} \\ a_{21} & a_{22} \end{bmatrix}\right) = a_{11}a_{22} - a_{12}a_{21} \qquad (A.14)$$

A.1.4 Matrix Inversion

Consider a square matrix A. The matrix inverse of A, which we denote as A^{-1}, is a matrix such that:

$$AA^{-1} = A^{-1}A = I \tag{A.15}$$

where I is the identity matrix. If the determinant $\mid A \mid$ is different from 0, the inverse matrix is unique and computed as follows:

$$A^{-1} = \frac{1}{\mid A \mid} C^T \tag{A.16}$$

The matrix C, or matrix of cofactors, is simply deduced from matrix A by replacing every entry a_{ij} by its cofactor C_{ij}, which was defined in (A.10):

$$C = \begin{bmatrix} C_{11} & & C_{1n} \\ & C_{ij} & \\ C_{n1} & & C_{nn} \end{bmatrix} \tag{A.17}$$

As an example, applying these formulas to the matrix (A.13) we find the inverse:

$$A^{-1} = \frac{1}{a_{11}a_{22} - a_{12}a_{21}} \begin{bmatrix} a_{22} & -a_{21} \\ -a_{12} & a_{11} \end{bmatrix} \tag{A.18}$$

A.1.5 Eigenvalues and Eigenvectors

Consider a square matrix A. An eigenvalue λ and the associated eigenvector x are defined by:

$$Ax = \lambda x \tag{A.19}$$

In other words, the eigenvector x premultiplied by A is equal to a multiple of itself. This can be rewritten:

$$(A - \lambda I)x = 0 \tag{A.20}$$

This equation has a nontrivial solution in x if $\mid A - \lambda I \mid = 0$ (otherwise $x = 0$ is the only solution). Taking again the example of matrix (A.13) this yields:

$$D\left(\begin{bmatrix} a_{11} - \lambda & a_{12} \\ a_{21} & a_{22} - \lambda \end{bmatrix}\right) = 0 \qquad (A.21)$$

or:

$$\Psi(\lambda) = (a_{11} - \lambda)(a_{22} - \lambda) - a_{12}a_{21} = 0 \qquad (A.22)$$

The polynomial $\Psi(\lambda) = \mid A - \lambda I \mid$ is called the *characteristic polynomial*. In the two-dimensional case, it can be rewritten:

$$\Psi(\lambda) = \lambda^2 - T(A)\lambda + D(A) \qquad (A.23)$$

In the general case, the values of the sum and product of the eigenvalues are:

$$\sum_{i=1}^{n} \lambda_i = T(A) \qquad (A.24)$$

$$\prod_{i=1}^{n} \lambda_i = D(A) \qquad (A.25)$$

A.2 Functions

A.2.1 Derivatives

We start with functions of a single argument $f(x)$, where x is a scalar. We define the first and second derivatives:

$$f'(x) = \lim_{\delta \to 0} \frac{f(x + \delta) - f(x)}{\delta} \qquad (A.26)$$

$$f''(x) = \lim_{\delta \to 0} \frac{f'(x + \delta) - f'(x)}{\delta} \qquad (A.27)$$

We can similarly define the derivatives of higher order:

$$f^{(n+1)}(x) = \lim_{\delta \to 0} \frac{f^{(n)}(x + \delta) - f^{(n)}(x)}{\delta} \qquad (A.28)$$

where the common usage is to denote:

$$f'(x) = f^{(1)}(x) \qquad f''(x) = f^{(2)}(x) \qquad (A.29)$$

We now move to functions of more than one argument. We still denote the function as $f(x)$, but now $x = (x_1, \ldots, x_i, \ldots, x_n)$ is a vector. The partial derivative with respect to argument x_i is defined as:

$$\frac{\partial f}{\partial x_i}(x) = \lim_{\delta \to 0} \frac{f(x_1, \ldots, x_i + \delta, \ldots, x_n) - f(x_1, \ldots, x_i, \ldots, x_n)}{\delta} \quad (A.30)$$

We can also define second order partial derivatives:

$$\frac{\partial^2 f}{\partial x_i \partial x_j} = \frac{\partial}{\partial x_i}\left(\frac{\partial f}{\partial x_j}\right) \quad (A.31)$$

Note that the order of derivation does not matter:

$$\frac{\partial}{\partial x_i}\left(\frac{\partial f}{\partial x_j}\right) = \frac{\partial^2 f}{\partial x_i \partial x_j} = \frac{\partial^2 f}{\partial x_j \partial x_i} = \frac{\partial}{\partial x_j}\left(\frac{\partial f}{\partial x_i}\right) \quad (A.32)$$

A.2.2 Taylor Expansions

Consider a function $f(x)$ that is continuously differentiable up to the order N. Then there exists $\gamma \in [0, \delta]$ such that:

$$f(x + \delta) = f(x) + \sum_{n=1}^{N-1} \frac{\delta^n}{n!} f^{(n)}(x) + \frac{\delta^N}{N!} f^{(N)}(x + \gamma) \quad (A.33)$$

where $n! = 1 \times 2 \times \ldots \times n$.

A.2.3 Homogeneous and Homothetic Functions

A function $F(x) = F(x_1, \ldots, x_n)$ is homogeneous of degree k if:

$$F(\lambda x_1, \ldots, \lambda x_n) = \lambda^k F(x_1, \ldots, x_n) \quad \lambda > 0 \quad (A.34)$$

If $F(x_1, \ldots, x_n)$ is homogeneous of degree k, then its partial derivatives $\partial F / \partial x_i$ are homogeneous of degree $k - 1$. Furthermore, the function F and its derivatives satisfy the following identity:

$$\sum_{i=1}^{n} x_i \frac{\partial F}{\partial x_i} = k F(x_1, \ldots, x_n) \quad (A.35)$$

A function $F(x)$ is homothetic if:

$$F(x) = F(y) \Longrightarrow F(\lambda x) = F(\lambda y) \quad (A.36)$$

There is a relation between homothetic and homogeneous functions. Consider a homothetic function such that $F(\lambda x)$ is increasing in λ. Then there exist a homogeneous function g and an increasing function f such that:

$$F(x) = f[g(x)] \tag{A.37}$$

A.2.4 Elasticities and Log-linear Differentiation

The elasticity of a function of a single variable $f(x)$ is equal to:

$$\varepsilon[f(x)] = \frac{dLog f(x)}{dLog x} = \frac{x}{f(x)} \frac{df(x)}{dx} \tag{A.38}$$

The elasticity of a product of functions is the sum of their elasticities:

$$\varepsilon[f(x)g(x)] = \varepsilon[f(x)] + \varepsilon[g(x)] \tag{A.39}$$

The elasticity of a sum of functions is a weighted average of their elasticities:

$$\varepsilon[f(x) + g(x)] = \frac{f(x)}{f(x) + g(x)} \varepsilon[f(x)] + \frac{g(x)}{f(x) + g(x)} \varepsilon[g(x)] \tag{A.40}$$

We consider a function of several variables $f(x) = f(x_1, \ldots, x_n)$. The partial elasticity of f with respect to x_i is equal to:

$$\varepsilon_i[f(x)] = \frac{\partial Log f(x)}{\partial Log x_i} = \frac{x_i}{f(x)} \frac{\partial f(x)}{\partial x_i} \tag{A.41}$$

If a function is homogeneous of degree k, then its partial elasticities sum to k:

$$f(\lambda x_1, \ldots, \lambda x_n) = \lambda^k f(x_1, \ldots, x_n) \implies \sum_{i=1}^{n} \varepsilon_i[f(x)] = k \tag{A.42}$$

A.2.5 Elasticities of Substitution

Consider a function of several variables $f(x) = f(x_1, \ldots, x_n)$. The marginal rate of substitution between x_i and x_j is equal to f'_i / f'_j where:

$$f'_i = \frac{\partial f}{\partial x_i} \qquad f'_j = \frac{\partial f}{\partial x_j} \tag{A.43}$$

Now the elasticity of substitution between x_i and x_j is equal to:

$$\sigma_{ij} = \frac{\partial Log\left(x_i/x_j\right)}{\partial Log\left(f'_i/f'_j\right)} \qquad \text{along the curve } f(x) = c \qquad (A.44)$$

where c is a constant. The constant elasticity of substitution function that we already saw in appendix 1.1 has constant elasticity of substitution:

$$f(x_1,\ldots,x_n) = \left(\sum_{i=1}^{n} a_i x_i^{(\sigma-1)/\sigma}\right)^{\sigma/(\sigma-1)} \qquad (A.45)$$

$$\sigma_{ij} = \sigma \qquad \forall i,j \qquad (A.46)$$

A.2.6 Concavity and Convexity

A subset S of R^n is *convex* if:

$$\forall x \in S \quad \forall y \in S \quad \forall \lambda \in [0,1] \qquad \lambda x + (1-\lambda) y \in S \qquad (A.47)$$

A function $f(x)$ defined on a convex subset S of R^n is *concave* if for every $\lambda \in [0,1]$ and every $x \in S$ and $y \in S$, we have:

$$f[\lambda x + (1-\lambda) y] \geq \lambda f(x) + (1-\lambda) f(y) \qquad (A.48)$$

A function $f(x)$ is *strictly concave* if for $0 < \lambda < 1$ and every $x \in S$ and $y \in S$, we have:

$$f[\lambda x + (1-\lambda) y] > \lambda f(x) + (1-\lambda) f(y) \qquad (A.49)$$

Similarly the function $f(x)$ is *convex* if:

$$f[\lambda x + (1-\lambda) y] \leq \lambda f(x) + (1-\lambda) f(y) \qquad (A.50)$$

and it is strictly convex if:

$$f[\lambda x + (1-\lambda) y] < \lambda f(x) + (1-\lambda) f(y) \qquad (A.51)$$

If f is twice continuously differentiable, we can characterize concavity through second-order derivatives. In particular, if f is function of a single variable, f is concave if:

$$f''(x) \leq 0 \qquad (A.52)$$

If f is a function of two variables, the two following conditions are sufficient:

$$f_{11} \leq 0 \tag{A.53}$$

$$f_{11} f_{22} - (f_{11})^2 \geq 0 \tag{A.54}$$

Note that (A.53) and (A.54) imply $f_{22} \leq 0$, so these two conditions are more symmetrical than they look.

A.3 Static Optimization

A.3.1 First- and Second-order Conditions

Consider a function $F(x) = F(x_1, \ldots, x_n)$ defined over a set $S \subset R^n$. A point x^* is a maximum of the function over S if:

$$F(x^*) \geq F(x) \qquad \forall x \in S \tag{A.55}$$

Traditionally the conditions for a maximum are separated between the first-order conditions (which involve the first-order derivatives) and the second-order conditions (which involve the second-order derivatives). The first-order conditions are:

$$\frac{\partial F}{\partial x_i} = 0 \qquad \forall i = 1, \ldots, n \tag{A.56}$$

In the case where the function F has a single argument, the second-order condition is $F''(x^*) < 0$, so that sufficient conditions for a maximum are:

$$F'(x^*) = 0 \qquad F''(x^*) < 0 \tag{A.57}$$

A.3.2 Maximization Under Equality Constraints

Consider the following problem:

$$\text{Maximize } F(x) = F(x_1, \ldots, x_n) \quad \text{s.t.}$$
$$g_i(x) = g_i(x_1, \ldots, x_n) = 0 \qquad i = 1, \ldots, m$$

We define the *Lagrangian* as:

$$\mathcal{L}(x, \lambda) = F(x) + \sum_{i=1}^{m} \lambda_i g_i(x) \qquad (A.58)$$

The parameter λ_i is called the *Lagrange multiplier* associated to the ith constraint. The first-order necessary conditions for a maximum are:

$$\frac{\partial \mathcal{L}}{\partial x_i} = 0 \quad \forall i = 1, \ldots, n \qquad \frac{\partial \mathcal{L}}{\partial \lambda_i} = 0 \quad \forall i = 1, \ldots, m \qquad (A.59)$$

If $\mathcal{L}(x, \lambda)$ is concave in x, then the solution to these equations is indeed a maximum.

A.3.3 An Envelope Theorem

We now assume that both the maximand and the constraints are functions of a vector of parameters a, so that the maximization program is:

$$\text{Maximize } F(x, a) \quad \text{s.t.}$$
$$g_i(x, a) = 0 \quad i = 1, \ldots, m$$

The Lagrangian is now defined as:

$$\mathcal{L}(x, \lambda, a) = F(x, a) + \sum_{i=1}^{m} \lambda_i g_i(x, a) \qquad (A.60)$$

Define the value function as:

$$V(a) = \max_x \{F(x, a) \mid g_i(x, a) = 0 \quad i = 1, \ldots, m\} \qquad (A.61)$$

Then the *envelope theorem* says:

$$\frac{\partial V(a)}{\partial a_i} = \frac{\partial \mathcal{L}(x, \lambda, a)}{\partial a_i} \quad \forall i \qquad (A.62)$$

where the value of x in (A.62) is a solution of the maximization program. As an example of application of this theorem, we give a very simple interpretation of the Lagrange multiplier when $F(x,a) = F(x)$ and the constraint $g_i(x,a) = 0$ takes the particular form:

$$g_i(x) = a_i \tag{A.63}$$

Then direct application of the envelope theorem shows that:

$$\lambda_i = \frac{\partial V(a)}{\partial a_i} \tag{A.64}$$

The Lagrange multiplier is equal to the marginal contribution of a unit of a_i to the overall value function.

A.3.4 Maximization Under Inequality Constraints

Consider the following problem:

$$\text{Maximize } F(x,a) \quad \text{s.t.}$$

$$g_i(x,a) \geq 0 \quad i = 1, \ldots, m$$

where F and the g_i's are concave in x. We define the *Lagrangian* as:

$$\pounds(x, \lambda, a) = F(x,a) + \sum_{i=1}^{m} \lambda_i g_i(x,a) \tag{A.65}$$

where λ_i is again the Lagrange multiplier associated to the ith constraint. Sufficient conditions for a maximum are:

$$\frac{\partial \pounds(x^*, \lambda, a)}{\partial x_i} = 0 \quad i = 1, \ldots, m \tag{A.66}$$

$$\lambda_i \geq 0 \quad \lambda_i = 0 \text{ if } g_i(x^*, a) > 0 \quad i = 1, \ldots, m \tag{A.67}$$

The value function is now defined as:

$$V(a) = \max \{F(x,a) \mid g_i(x,a) \geq 0 \quad i = 1, \ldots, m\} \tag{A.68}$$

and the envelope theorem now says:

$$\frac{\partial V(a)}{\partial a_i} = \frac{\partial \pounds(x, \lambda, a)}{\partial a_i} \quad \forall i \tag{A.69}$$

A.4 Dynamic Optimization

Consider the following dynamic maximization problem:

$$\text{Maximize} \int_0^T F(x_t, u_t, t)\, dt \quad \text{s.t.}$$

$$\dot{x}_t = g(x_t, u_t, t)$$

where x_t is called the state variable, u_t the control variable, $\dot{x}_t = dx_t/dt$, and the initial value x_0 is historically given. We define the *Hamiltonian* $\mathcal{H}_t$ as:

$$\mathcal{H}_t(x_t, u_t, \lambda_t, t) = F(x_t, u_t, t) + \lambda_t g(x_t, u_t, t) \quad (A.70)$$

where λ_t is a multiplier similar to the Lagrange multiplier. Necessary conditions for a maximum are:

$$\frac{\partial \mathcal{H}_t}{\partial u_t} = 0 \quad (A.71)$$

$$\dot{x}_t = \frac{\partial \mathcal{H}_t}{\partial \lambda_t} \quad (A.72)$$

$$\dot{\lambda}_t = -\frac{\partial \mathcal{H}_t}{\partial x_t} \quad (A.73)$$

There can be other conditions depending on the constraints on the endpoints. (a) If x_T is free, then $\lambda_T = 0$. (b) If $x_T \geq \bar{x}_T$, then $\lambda_T \geq 0$. (c) If x_T is given, then λ_T is free.

A.4.1 Some Sufficient Conditions

If the Hamiltonian function $\mathcal{H}_t(x_t, u_t, \lambda_t, t)$ is concave in (x_t, u_t), then the conditions (A.71) to (A.73) are sufficient for a maximum (Mangasarian, 1966).

If the Hamiltonian is not concave in (x_t, u_t), there is a weaker sufficient condition (Arrow and Kurz, 1970): let us denote as $u^*(x_t, \lambda_t, t)$ the value of the control variable that maximizes $\mathcal{H}_t(x_t, u_t, \lambda_t, t)$ for given (x_t, λ_t, t), and define the *maximized Hamiltonian* $\mathcal{H}_t^*$ as

$$\mathcal{H}_t^*(x_t, \lambda_t, t) = \mathcal{H}_t[x_t, u^*(x_t, \lambda_t, t), \lambda_t, t] \quad (A.74)$$

Then a sufficient condition for the above conditions to yield a maximum is that the maximized Hamiltonian be concave in x_t.

A.4.2 The Current Value Hamiltonian

In many applications the function F contains a discount factor and is written as:

$$F(x_t, u_t, t) = e^{-\rho t} f(x_t, u_t, t) \tag{A.75}$$

so that the maximization problem is:

$$\text{Maximize} \int_0^T e^{-\rho t} f(x_t, u_t, t)\, dt \quad \text{s.t.}$$

$$\dot{x}_t = g(x_t, u_t, t)$$

We now use a new Hamiltonian multiplier variable $\mu_t = \lambda_t e^{\rho t}$ and define the current value Hamiltonian $\mathcal{H}_t^c$ as:

$$\mathcal{H}_t^c = f(x_t, u_t, t) + \mu_t g(x_t, u_t, t) \tag{A.76}$$

Then necessary conditions for optimality are:

$$\frac{\partial \mathcal{H}_t^c}{\partial u_t} = 0 \tag{A.77}$$

$$\dot{x}_t = \frac{\partial \mathcal{H}_t^c}{\partial \mu_t} \tag{A.78}$$

$$\dot{\mu}_t = \rho \mu_t - \frac{\partial \mathcal{H}_t^c}{\partial x_t} \tag{A.79}$$

A.4.3 Transversality Conditions

For infinite horizon optimization problems, such as those we encountered in the Ramsey model in chapter 7, a first set of optimality conditions usually consists of first-order conditions, for example, the Euler equations of the consumer. We encountered a second type of condition, the *transversality condition*. We give here, by way of example, a simple intuitive description of what this transversality condition means.[1]

To make the exposition particularly simple, we use the same framework as that of the Ramsey model with fixed incomes and in discrete time that we studied in chapter 4. We consider an infinitely lived agent who in period t

---

1. More advanced treatments are found, among others, in Chiang (1992), Dixit (1990), Intriligator (1971), and Michel (1982, 1990).

receives an exogenous income Y_t and consumes C_t. She has an intertemporal utility:

$$\sum_{t=0}^{\infty} \beta^t U(C_t) \qquad (A.80)$$

and is subject to the budget constraints:

$$D_{t+1} = R_{t+1}(D_t + Y_t - C_t) \qquad (A.81)$$

where D_t is the amount of government debt (the only asset) the agent holds at the beginning of period t. She thus solves the following optimization problem:

$$\text{Maximize} \quad \sum_{t=0}^{\infty} \beta^t U(C_t) \quad \text{s.t.}$$

$$D_{t+1} = R_{t+1}(D_t + Y_t - C_t)$$

The Lagrangian for this program is:

$$\sum_{t=0}^{\infty} \beta^t \left[U(C_t) + \lambda_t \left(D_t + Y_t - C_t - \frac{D_{t+1}}{R_{t+1}} \right) \right] \qquad (A.82)$$

The first-order conditions for C_t and D_t are, respectively:

$$U'(C_t) = \lambda_t \qquad (A.83)$$

$$\lambda_t = \beta R_{t+1} \lambda_{t+1} \qquad (A.84)$$

Combining (A.83) and (A.84) we obtain the traditional *Euler equation*:

$$U'(C_t) = \beta R_{t+1} U'(C_{t+1}) \qquad (A.85)$$

Now define the discount factors:

$$\Delta_t = \frac{1}{R_1 \ldots R_t} \qquad \Delta_0 = 1 \qquad (A.86)$$

So we have:

$$\Delta_t = R_{t+1} \Delta_{t+1} \qquad (A.87)$$

The budget equation (A.81) is rewritten:

$$\Delta_{t+1} D_{t+1} = \Delta_t (D_t + Y_t - C_t) \tag{A.88}$$

Sum equations (A.88) from time 0 to time T. We obtain:

$$\Delta_{T+1} D_{T+1} + \sum_{t=0}^{T} \Delta_t C_t = D_0 + \sum_{t=0}^{T} \Delta_t Y_t \tag{A.89}$$

Now the *transversality condition* says that the limit, as time goes to infinity, of the discounted value of asset holdings must go to 0, that is:

$$\text{Lim}_{t \to \infty} \Delta_t D_t = 0 \tag{A.90}$$

Indeed, if this limit was positive, there would be "purchasing power left at infinity." The agent could transfer this purchasing power to any early date and consume more at this date. This means that the initial situation would not be optimal. Conversely if this limit was negative, this would mean that the state would permanently finance this agent's consumptions, which we rule out.

A.5 Dynamic Programming

The technique of dynamic programming (Bellman, 1957), is a specific optimization technique used to solve maximization problems of the following type:[2]

$$\text{Maximize} \sum_{t=1}^{T} \beta^t U_t (x_t, u_t) \quad \text{s.t.}$$

$$x_{t+1} = g_t (x_t, u_t)$$

The variable u_t is the control variable, which is chosen by the maximizing agent. The variable x_t is the state variable, which embeds all information necessary at date t. Both u_t and x_t can be vectors as well as scalars.

Note that we have described a deterministic, finite horizon problem. This is the first we study, followed by deterministic infinite horizon and a stochastic problem.

---

2. Although discounting is not necessary for the finite horizon case, we introduce it from the start for the homogeneity of the exposition.

A.5.1 Deterministic Finite Horizon

The method of dynamic programming is based on a *value function*, denoted as V_t, which represents the maximal utility that can be expected as of period t included, for a given initial value x_t:

$$V_t(x_t) = \text{Max} \sum_{s=t}^{T} \beta^{s-t} U_s(x_s, u_s) \quad \text{s.t.}$$

$$x_{s+1} = g_s(x_s, u_s) \qquad s \geq t$$

This program is solved recursively, starting with the last period:

$$V_T(x_T) = \text{Max}_{u_T} U_T(x_T, u_T) \tag{A.91}$$

Now the value function in $T-1$ is obtained by:

$$V_{T-1}(x_{T-1}) = \text{Max}_{u_{T-1}} \{U_{T-1}(x_{T-1}, u_{T-1}) + \beta V_T[g_T(x_{T-1}, u_{T-1})]\} \tag{A.92}$$

and similarly for all previous periods:

$$V_t(x_t) = \text{Max}_{u_t} \{U_t(x_t, u_t) + \beta V_{t+1}[g_{t+1}(x_t, u_t)]\} \tag{A.93}$$

A.5.2 Deterministic Infinite Horizon

This time we solve the problem:

$$\text{Maximize} \sum_{t=1}^{\infty} \beta^t U_t(x_t, u_t) \quad \text{s.t.}$$

$$x_{t+1} = g_t(x_t, u_t)$$

The difference is that because the horizon is infinite, there is no such thing as starting from the last period. One usually studies stationary problems such that the functions U and g are time independent. In that case, the value function will also be time independent and satisfy the functional equation:

$$V(x) = \text{Max}_u \{U(x, u) + \beta V[g(x, u)]\} \tag{A.94}$$

A.5.3 A Stochastic Problem

We now assume that the law of transition is also function of a stochastic variable ε_t (this will be defined precisely in sections A.7 and A.8, which the reader may want to read before this section):

$$x_{t+1} = g_t\left(x_t, u_t, \varepsilon_{t+1}\right) \tag{A.95}$$

where the probability distribution of the variable ε_{t+1} depends on x_t and u_t. The dynamic equation giving the value function in the finite horizon case becomes:

$$V_t\left(x_t\right) = \text{Max}_{u_t} \left\{ U_t\left(x_t, u_t\right) + \beta E_t V_{t+1} \left[g_{t+1}\left(x_t, u_t, \varepsilon_{t+1}\right)\right] \right\} \tag{A.96}$$

which replaces (A.93), and the functional equation for the infinite horizon case:

$$V\left(x\right) = \text{Max}_u \left\{ U\left(x, u\right) + \beta E V \left[g\left(x, u, \varepsilon\right)\right] \right\} \tag{A.97}$$

which replaces (A.94).

A.6 Noncooperative Games

We are in a noncooperative game situation when economic agents interact, each choosing independently an action, which will be called his strategy. Assume there are n agents indexed by $i = 1, \ldots, n$. Agent i has a strategy s_i. The utility function of agent i is function of all strategies:

$$U_i\left(s_1, \ldots, s_n\right) = U_i\left(s_i, s_{-i}\right) \tag{A.98}$$

where s_{-i} is the set of all strategies, except that of agent i:

$$s_{-i} = \{s_j \mid j \neq i\} \tag{A.99}$$

A.6.1 Nash Equilibrium

A pure strategy Nash equilibrium (Nash, 1953) is a set of strategies s_i^*, $i = 1, \ldots n$, such that:

$$U_i\left(s_i^*, s_{-i}^*\right) \geq U_i\left(s_i, s_{-i}^*\right) \qquad \forall s_i \tag{A.100}$$

We can express this in terms of the best response function $\psi(s_{-i})$:

$$\psi_i(s_{-i}) = \arg\max_{s_i} U_i(s_i, s_{-i}) \qquad (A.101)$$

A Nash equilibrium is a set of s_i^* such that each strategy is a best response to the other ones:

$$s_i^* \in \psi_i(s_{-i}^*) \qquad (A.102)$$

If the utility functions are differentiable, the Nash equilibrium satisfies the following necessary conditions:

$$\frac{\partial U_i}{\partial s_i} = 0 \qquad \forall i = 1, \ldots, n \qquad (A.103)$$

A.6.2 A Two-period Game

We consider a two-period, two-player game and see that depending on the timing of the play the solutions obtained can be quite different.

The players are denoted X and Y. Their strategies in periods 1 and 2 are, respectively, (x_1, x_2) for X and (y_1, y_2) for Y, and their utility functions:

$$U_X(x_1, y_1, x_2, y_2) \qquad (A.104)$$
$$U_Y(x_1, y_1, x_2, y_2) \qquad (A.105)$$

A.6.3 Nash Equilibrium with Commitment

We first assume that each player decides in the first period her strategies for both the first and the second period. In other words, she can commit to a second-period strategy. We say there is commitment. The optimality conditions for players X and Y are, respectively:

$$\frac{\partial U_X}{\partial x_1} = 0 \qquad \frac{\partial U_X}{\partial x_2} = 0 \qquad (A.106)$$

$$\frac{\partial U_Y}{\partial y_1} = 0 \qquad \frac{\partial U_Y}{\partial y_2} = 0 \qquad (A.107)$$

A.6.4 Subgame Perfect Nash Equilibrium

In reality games are usually played sequentially. Even if players announce their second-period strategies in the first period, they are not bound by this announcement. In particular x_2 and y_2 are effectively decided on in the second period, when x_1 and y_1 have already been played and cannot be changed. As a result we obtain what is called a *subgame perfect*, or *time consistent* equilibrium (Selten, 1975; Kydland and Prescott, 1977).

To characterize this equilibrium, we place ourselves in the second period. At this stage x_1 and y_1 are given. We have a Nash equilibrium in x_2 and y_2 characterized by:

$$\frac{\partial U_X}{\partial x_2} = 0 \qquad \frac{\partial U_Y}{\partial y_2} = 0 \qquad (A.108)$$

In particular conditions (A.108) yield the best response functions:

$$x_2 = X_2(x_1, y_1, y_2) \qquad (A.109)$$

$$y_2 = Y_2(x_1, y_1, x_2) \qquad (A.110)$$

Going back to the first period, each player knows that the values that will be played in the second period are given by equations (A.109) and (A.110), so that players X and Y maximize, respectively:

$$U_X[x_1, y_1, X_2(x_1, y_1, y_2), Y_2(x_1, y_1, x_2)] \qquad (A.111)$$

$$U_Y[x_1, y_1, X_2(x_1, y_1, y_2), Y_2(x_1, y_1, x_2)] \qquad (A.112)$$

Player X maximizes with respect to x_1, player Y with respect to y_1. The first-order conditions are, respectively, for players X and Y:

$$\frac{\partial U_X}{\partial x_1} + \frac{\partial U_X}{\partial x_2}\frac{\partial X_2}{\partial x_1} + \frac{\partial U_X}{\partial y_2}\frac{\partial Y_2}{\partial x_1} = 0 \qquad (A.113)$$

$$\frac{\partial U_Y}{\partial y_1} + \frac{\partial U_Y}{\partial x_2}\frac{\partial X_2}{\partial y_1} + \frac{\partial U_Y}{\partial y_2}\frac{\partial Y_2}{\partial y_1} = 0 \qquad (A.114)$$

We may first note that if $\partial X_2/\partial y_1 = 0$ and $\partial Y_2/\partial x_1 = 0$, then the solutions of the system (A.106, A.107) and of system (A.108, A.113, A.114) are the same. But as soon as the second-period optimal strategies of a player depend on the other player's first-period strategy, the two outcomes will be different.

A.6.5 Bargaining: The Strategic Approach

We now describe the strategic approach to bargaining.[3] Assume that agents X and Y bargain over the partition of a cake of size 1. Denote X's share of the cake by x, and Y's share by $y = 1 - x$. Their respective undiscounted utility functions are for period t:

$$U_X(x) \quad \text{and} \quad U_Y(y) \tag{A.115}$$

The traditional Nash cooperative solution (Nash, 1950) says that x is solution of:

$$x = \text{Argmax } \{\gamma_X Log[U_X(x)] + \gamma_Y Log[U_Y(1-x)]\} \tag{A.116}$$

where γ_X and γ_Y represent X's and Y's weights in the negotiation.

Now we show that such a solution can actually be obtained as the outcome of a bargaining process in time where the two agents make alternating offers to each other (Rubinstein, 1982).

More precisely, in even periods X proposes to Y a partition x of the cake, with $y = 1 - x$. If Y accepts, this partition is implemented. If Y refuses, she will make in the next odd period a proposition for a partition, and so on. If an agreement is reached in period t, the two players receive respectively the following discounted utilities:

$$\delta_X^t U_X(x) \quad \text{and} \quad \delta_Y^t U_Y(1-x) \tag{A.117}$$

where δ_X and δ_Y are, respectively, X's and Y's discount rates. We will now show that the dynamic game just described yields a solution that is very similar to that in formula (A.116).

Linear Utilities

We begin with the case of linear utility functions (Rubinstein, 1982):

$$U_X(x) = x \quad U_Y(y) = y \tag{A.118}$$

We find the solution by determining the maximal and minimal share of the pie that X can obtain. Let us start with the maximum, denoted x_M (table A.1).

---

3. See Nash (1950); Rubinstein (1982); Binmore, Rubinstein, and Wolinski, (1986); and Hoel (1986).

If X can obtain at most x_M in period 2, because of discounting she will be ready to accept $\delta_X x_M$ in period 1, which gives Y at least $1 - \delta_X x_M$. Now if Y must get at least $1 - \delta_X x_M$ in period 1, because of discounting she must be given at least $\delta_Y (1 - \delta_X x_M)$ in period 0, which leaves X with at most $1 - \delta_Y (1 - \delta_X x_M)$ in period 0.

Time	Offer made by	X obtains at most	Y obtains at least
0	X	$1 - \delta_Y (1 - \delta_X x_M)$	
1	Y		$1 - \delta_X x_M$
2	X	x_M	

Table A.1 Bounds on alternating offers

We note that player X is in the same situation in period 0 and in period 2, so the outcomes for X must be the same, which yields:

$$x_M = 1 - \delta_Y (1 - \delta_X x_M) \tag{A.119}$$

so that:

$$x_M = \frac{1 - \delta_Y}{1 - \delta_X \delta_Y} \tag{A.120}$$

This was for the maximum attainable x_M. The same reasoning applies to the minimum x_m, and we find the same number. So the shares of the two players are uniquely defined and equal to:

$$x = x_M = x_m = \frac{1 - \delta_Y}{1 - \delta_X \delta_Y} \tag{A.121}$$

$$1 - x = \frac{\delta_Y (1 - \delta_X)}{1 - \delta_X \delta_Y} \tag{A.122}$$

We note that because of the discrete time, the solution is asymmetrical. Playing first confers an advantage to X. Note, indeed, that if $\delta_X = \delta_Y = \delta$, we have:

$$x = \frac{1}{1 + \delta} > \frac{1}{2} \tag{A.123}$$

Now we can make the problem symmetrical by assuming that the time span between offers tends to 0. For that we take, calling Δ this time span:

$$\delta_X = e^{-\rho_X \Delta} \qquad \delta_Y = e^{-\rho_Y \Delta} \tag{A.124}$$

Then we find in the limit, when $\Delta \longrightarrow 0$:

$$x = \frac{\rho_Y}{\rho_X + \rho_Y} \qquad 1 - x = \frac{\rho_X}{\rho_X + \rho_Y} \tag{A.125}$$

This is now symmetrical and similar to the generalized Nash solution, with:

$$\gamma_X = \frac{1}{\rho_X} \qquad \gamma_Y = \frac{1}{\rho_Y} \tag{A.126}$$

We see that the implicit bargaining power of the two agents is inversely related to their impatience.

Concave Utilities

We now consider the more general case (Hoel, 1986) where the utilities $U_X(x)$ and $U_Y(y)$ are concave and such that $U_i(0) = 0$. Then consider the two numbers x and y defined by:

$$U_X(y) = \delta_X U_X(x) \tag{A.127}$$

$$U_Y(1 - x) = \delta_Y U_Y(1 - y) \tag{A.128}$$

A reasoning similar to what we made for linear utilities shows that the outcome is $(x, 1 - x)$. Indeed let us assume that x is the minimum that X can expect in period 2. Then in period 1, Y must at least propose a value y such that:

$$U_X(y) = \delta_X U_X(x) \tag{A.129}$$

Now in period 0, X must propose to Y a value $1 - x$ that will give her the same utility as $1 - y$ in period 1, that is:

$$U_Y(1 - x) = \delta_Y U_Y(1 - y) \tag{A.130}$$

Because U_X and U_Y are concave, the values x and y given by (A.127) and (A.128) are unique. To make the problem symmetrical, we take again:

$$\delta_X = e^{-\rho_X \Delta} \qquad \delta_Y = e^{-\rho_Y \Delta} \tag{A.131}$$

and go to the limit $\Delta \to 0$. The system (A.127), (A.128) yields:

$$\lim_{\Delta \to 0} x = \text{Argmax} \left\{ \frac{\text{Log}\left[U_X(x)\right]}{\rho_X} + \frac{\text{Log}\left[U_Y(1-x)\right]}{\rho_Y} \right\} \quad \text{(A.132)}$$

which has the first-order condition:

$$\frac{1}{\rho_X} \frac{U_X'(x)}{U_X(x)} = \frac{1}{\rho_Y} \frac{U_Y'(1-x)}{U_Y(1-x)} \quad \text{(A.133)}$$

As an example, if:

$$U_X(x) = x^{\kappa_X} \qquad U_Y(x) = x^{\kappa_Y} \quad \text{(A.134)}$$

then:

$$x = \frac{\kappa_X \rho_Y}{\kappa_X \rho_Y + \kappa_Y \rho_X} = \frac{\kappa_X/\rho_X}{(\kappa_X/\rho_X) + (\kappa_Y/\rho_Y)} \quad \text{(A.135)}$$

A.7 Stochastic Variables

A.7.1 Probabilities

We consider an experiment whose outcome is not known in advance and can take values in a set Ω. Ω, called the sample space, is the set of all possible outcomes. A subset $A \subset \Omega$ is called an event. If the subset A is a point in Ω, it is called an elementary event.

For example, if the experiment consists in tossing a coin, there are two elementary events, heads and tails, and $\Omega = \{\text{heads, tails}\}$.

A probability function is a real valued function $P(A)$ defined for every subset $A \subset \Omega$ and satisfying the following axioms:

- $0 \leq P(A) \leq 1$
- $P(\Omega) = 1$
- If $A \cap B = \emptyset$ then $P(A \cup B) = P(A) + P(B)$

Consider two events, A and B. Events A and B are stochastically independent if:

$$P(A \cap B) = P(A) P(B) \quad \text{(A.136)}$$

The probability that A occurs, given that B has occurred, that is, the conditional probability $P(A \mid B)$, is defined by:

$$P(A \mid B) = \frac{P(A \cap B)}{P(B)} \quad \text{if } P(B) > 0 \tag{A.137}$$

A.7.2 One-dimensional Random Variables

We start with a random variable X, which can take values $x \in R$, where R is the real line. If the potential values form a discrete set, we denote as $f(x)$ the probability that X takes the value x. The function $f(x)$ has the property that:

$$\sum_{x \in R} f(x) = 1 \tag{A.138}$$

The probability of an event A is:

$$P(X \in A) = \sum_{x \in A} f(x) \tag{A.139}$$

Similarly, if the random variable is continuous, the probability that X is in the interval $[x, x + dx]$ is $f(x)\, dx$ with:

$$\int_R f(x)\, dx = 1 \tag{A.140}$$

The function $f(x)$ is called the *probability density function*. The probability of an event A is:

$$P(X \in A) = \int_A f(x)\, dx \tag{A.141}$$

One defines also the *cumulative distribution function* $F(z)$:

$$F(z) = \text{Prob } (X \leq z) \tag{A.142}$$

It is easily derived from the probability density function. In the discrete case:

$$F(z) = \sum_{x \leq z} f(x) \tag{A.143}$$

and in the continuous case:

$$F(z) = \int_{x \leq z} f(x)\, dx \tag{A.144}$$

A.7.3 Moments of Random Variables

The mean, or expected value, of the random variable X is given by:

$$\mu = E(X) = \sum_x x f(x) \qquad (A.145)$$

for the discrete case, and:

$$\mu = E(X) = \int_{-\infty}^{+\infty} x f(x)\, dx \qquad (A.146)$$

for the continuous case. More generally, the expectation of a function of the random variable $h(X)$ is:

$$E[h(X)] = \sum_x h(x) f(x) \qquad (A.147)$$

for the discrete case, and:

$$E[h(X)] = \int_{-\infty}^{+\infty} h(x) f(x)\, dx \qquad (A.148)$$

for the continuous case.

If the function h is convex, we have Jensen's inequality:

$$h[E(X)] \leq E[h(X)] \qquad (A.149)$$

Some of the expectations defined in (A.147) and (A.148) are often used in economics. Notably one defines the central moment of order k as:

$$\mu_k = E(X - \mu)^k \qquad (A.150)$$

A particularly used moment is the central moment of order 2, called the *variance*:

$$\text{Var}(X) = E(X - \mu)^2 \qquad (A.151)$$

One also defines the *standard deviation* as the square root of the variance:

$$\sigma(X) = [\text{Var}(X)]^{1/2} \qquad (A.152)$$

A.7.4 Two-dimensional Random Variables

We consider two random variables X and Y. They have a joint density function $f(x,y)$. The expectation of a function h is defined in the discrete case as:

$$E[h(X,Y)] = \sum_{x,y} h(x,y) f(x,y) \qquad (A.153)$$

and in the continuous case as:

$$E[h(X,Y)] = \int_{-\infty}^{+\infty} \int_{-\infty}^{+\infty} h(x,y) f(x,y) \, dx dy \qquad (A.154)$$

An important second-order moment is the *covariance* between the two variables:

$$\text{Cov}(X,Y) = E\{[X - E(X)][Y - E(Y)]\} \qquad (A.155)$$

If $\text{Cov}(X,Y) = 0$, then X and Y are said to be uncorrelated. One defines the coefficient of correlation between X and Y:

$$\text{Corr}(X,Y) = \frac{\text{Cov}(X,Y)}{\sigma(X)\sigma(Y)} \qquad (A.156)$$

One easily checks that:

$$-1 \leq \text{Corr}(X,Y) \leq 1 \qquad (A.157)$$

We have the following useful relations between the second order moments:

$$\text{Var}(X+Y) = \text{Var}(X) + \text{Var}(Y) + 2\,\text{Cov}(X,Y) \qquad (A.158)$$

$$\text{Var}(X-Y) = \text{Var}(X) + \text{Var}(Y) - 2\,\text{Cov}(X,Y) \qquad (A.159)$$

A.7.5 Some Classic Distributions

We briefly describe a few classic distributions for which we give the density function, mean, variance, and, when possible, the moments of order k.

The Normal Distribution

The normal distribution is defined for $x \in [-\infty, +\infty]$ and has the density function:

$$f(x) = \frac{1}{\sigma\sqrt{2\pi}} \exp\left[-\frac{(x-\mu)^2}{2\sigma^2}\right] \qquad (A.160)$$

The mean and variance are:

$$E(X) = \mu \qquad (A.161)$$

$$\text{Var}(X) = \sigma^2 \qquad (A.162)$$

The Log-normal Distribution

The log-normal distribution is defined for $x \in [0, +\infty]$ and the variable $Log\,x$ is normal, so x has the density function:

$$f(x) = \frac{1}{\sigma\sqrt{2\pi}} \exp\left[-\frac{(Log\,x - \mu)^2}{2\sigma^2}\right] \qquad (A.163)$$

The mean, variance, and moment of order k are:

$$E(X) = \exp\left(\mu + \frac{\sigma^2}{2}\right) \qquad (A.164)$$

$$\text{Var}(X) = \exp(2\mu)\left[\exp(2\sigma^2) - \exp(\sigma^2)\right] \qquad (A.165)$$

$$E\left(X^k\right) = \exp\left(k\mu + \frac{k^2\sigma^2}{2}\right) \qquad (A.166)$$

The Uniform Distribution

The uniform distribution is defined for $x \in [A, B]$ and has the density function:

$$f(x) = \begin{cases} 1/(B-A) & A \leq x \leq B \\ 0 & \text{otherwise} \end{cases} \qquad (A.167)$$

The mean and variance are:

$$E(X) = \frac{A+B}{2} \qquad \text{Var}(X) = \frac{(B-A)^2}{12} \qquad (A.168)$$

Mathematical Appendix

The Exponential Distribution

The exponential distribution has the density function:

$$f(x) = \begin{cases} \lambda \exp(-\lambda x) & x \geq 0 \\ 0 & x < 0 \end{cases} \quad (A.169)$$

and its mean and variance are:

$$E(X) = \frac{1}{\lambda} \qquad \text{Var}(X) = \frac{1}{\lambda^2} \quad (A.170)$$

A.7.6 Multivariate Normal Laws and Conditional Probabilities

Assume that X and Y are jointly normal with means μ_X and μ_Y, variances σ_X^2 and σ_Y^2 and covariance σ_{XY}. Then the stochastic variable Y conditional on X is a normal variable with the following mean and variance:

$$E(Y \mid X) = \mu_Y + \frac{\sigma_{XY}}{\sigma_Y^2}(X - \mu_X) \quad (A.171)$$

$$\sigma^2(Y \mid X) = \sigma_Y^2 \left(1 - \frac{\sigma_{XY}^2}{\sigma_X^2 \sigma_Y^2}\right) \quad (A.172)$$

A.8 Time Series and Stochastic Processes

Call Z the set of integers and consider a set of random variables X_t indexed by $t \in Z$. The infinite vector $X = \{X_t, t \in Z\}$ is called a discrete time series.

A.8.1 Stationary Processes

A process is second-order stationary (we henceforth call it *stationary* for brevity) if:

$$EX_t^2 < \infty \qquad \forall t \in Z \quad (A.173)$$

$$EX_t = EX_s \qquad \forall t \in Z, \ \forall s \in Z \quad (A.174)$$

$$\text{cov}(X_t, X_{t+h}) = \gamma(h) \qquad \forall t \in Z, \ \forall h \in Z \quad (A.175)$$

For a stationary process we define the autocorrelation function as:

$$\rho(h) = \frac{\gamma(h)}{\gamma(0)} \quad (A.176)$$

A.8.2 White Noises

A white noise of dimension 1 is a process $(\varepsilon_t, t \in Z)$ where the ε_t's are centered and uncorrelated:

$$E(\varepsilon_t) = 0 \qquad E(\varepsilon_t \varepsilon_s) = 0 \quad t \neq s \qquad (A.177)$$

We can also define a white noise of dimension n, where this time the ε_t's are vectors of the same dimension, and with the same matrix of variance-covariance Ω. They are also centered and uncorrelated in time:

$$E(\varepsilon_t) = 0 \qquad E(\varepsilon_t \varepsilon_s^T) = 0 \quad t \neq s \qquad (A.178)$$

A.8.3 Expectations

Quite often in this book we use the expectation at some time t of a variable at a later date, say $t+j$. To make that precise, we first define the information set at date $t \in Z$ as the set of all informations available at date t, which we denote as $\mathcal{I}_t$. As an example of what $\mathcal{I}_t$ contains, if the agent observes a particular variable X_t, a usual assumption is that $\mathcal{I}_t$ contains the current and past values of X_t:

$$\{X_t, X_{t-1}, \ldots\} \in \mathcal{I}_t \qquad (A.179)$$

Now the expectation at t of X_{t+j}, which we denote $E_t(X_{t+j})$ is simply defined as the mathematical expectation of X_{t+j}, conditional on the information contained in $\mathcal{I}_t$.

To give a simple example of such an expectation, we consider the following process:

$$X_t = X_{t-1} + \varepsilon_t \qquad (A.180)$$

where ε_t is a white noise. Such a process is called a *random walk*. We can write X_{t+j} as:

$$X_{t+j} = X_t + \varepsilon_{t+1} + \ldots + \varepsilon_{t+j} \qquad (A.181)$$

Because the expected values, as of period t, of all the white noises $\varepsilon_{t+1}, \ldots, \varepsilon_{t+j}$ are equal to 0, we find:

$$E_t X_{t+j} = X_t \qquad (A.182)$$

Now a useful property of these expectations is the *law of iterated expectations*:[4]

$$E_t \left(E_{t+i} X_{t+j} \right) = E_t \left(X_{t+j} \right) \qquad 0 \leq i \leq j \qquad (A.183)$$

A.8.4 Lag Operators

We call *lag operator* $\mathcal{L}$ the operator such that:

$$\mathcal{L} \left(X_t \right) = X_{t-1} \qquad (A.184)$$

$$\mathcal{L}^j \left(X_t \right) = X_{t-j} \qquad (A.185)$$

This operator is linear and invertible. Its inverse $\mathcal{L}^{-1}$ is defined by:

$$\mathcal{L}^{-j} \left(X_t \right) = E_t X_{t+j} \qquad (A.186)$$

Note that there are two "times" involved: the time t at which the expectation is taken, and the time $t+j$ at which the variable occurs. When shifting time forward, we shift only the time at which the variable occurs, not the time at which the expectation is taken.

A very useful property of these lag operators is that we can make computations with them as if they were algebraic numbers, provided all expectations are taken as of the same period. We see an application of this shortly when computing solutions to a rational expectations dynamic equation.

A.8.5 Lag Polynomials

One can define polynomial series in the operator $\mathcal{L}$. Consider a time series $X = (X_t, t \in Z)$ and a sequence $(a_i, i \in Z)$ such that:

$$\sum_{i=-\infty}^{+\infty} | a_i | < +\infty \qquad (A.187)$$

Then the process defined by:

$$Y_t = \sum_{i=-\infty}^{+\infty} a_i X_{t-i} \qquad (A.188)$$

---

4. This is actually valid if $\mathcal{I}_t \subset \mathcal{I}_{t+i} \subset \mathcal{I}_{t+j}$, that is, if the information set expands over time.

is stationary. We note:

$$A(\mathcal{L}) = \sum_{i=-\infty}^{+\infty} a_i \mathcal{L}^i \qquad (A.189)$$

The process Y_t can be rewritten as:

$$Y_t = A(\mathcal{L}) X_t \qquad (A.190)$$

A.8.6 Simple Inversion Formulas

In several occasions in this book we have to find the inverses of simple operators like $1 - \lambda\mathcal{L}$ or $1 - \mu\mathcal{L}^{-1}$, where the absolute values of λ and μ are smaller than 1. As we indicated, we can treat the lag operator like an algebraic number, so the inverse of $1 - \lambda\mathcal{L}$ is:

$$\sum_{i=0}^{+\infty} \lambda^i \mathcal{L}^i \qquad (A.191)$$

and that of $1 - \mu\mathcal{L}^{-1}$:

$$\sum_{i=0}^{+\infty} \mu^i \mathcal{L}^{-i} \qquad (A.192)$$

A.8.7 ARMA Processes

We say that the process X_t is *autoregressive* of order p, or $AR(p)$ if it can be written as:

$$A(\mathcal{L}) X_t = \varepsilon_t \qquad (A.193)$$

where ε_t is a white noise and $A(\mathcal{L})$ is a polynomial of order p:

$$A(\mathcal{L}) = a_0 + a_1 \mathcal{L} + \ldots + a_p \mathcal{L}^p \qquad (A.194)$$

We say that the process X_t is a *moving average* of order q, or $MA(q)$ if it can be written as:

$$X_t = B(\mathcal{L}) \varepsilon_t \qquad (A.195)$$

Mathematical Appendix

where ε_t is a white noise and $B(\mathcal{L})$ is a polynomial of order q:

$$B(\mathcal{L}) = b_0 + b_1 \mathcal{L} + \ldots + b_q \mathcal{L}^q \qquad (A.196)$$

Finally, the process X_t is an *autoregressive moving average* of order (p, q), or ARMA (p, q) if it can be written as:

$$A(\mathcal{L}) X_t = B(\mathcal{L}) \varepsilon_t \qquad (A.197)$$

where the polynomials $A(\mathcal{L})$ and $B(\mathcal{L})$ have been defined in equations (A.194) and (A.196).

A.8.8 Martingales

A process $\mathcal{M} = (\mathcal{M}_t, t \in Z)$ is a *martingale* if:

$$E(\mathcal{M}_t \mid \mathcal{I}_t) = \mathcal{M}_t \qquad \forall t \qquad (A.198)$$

$$E(\mathcal{M}_t \mid \mathcal{I}_{t-1}) = \mathcal{M}_{t-1} \qquad \forall t \qquad (A.199)$$

For example, the random walk defined in equation (A.180) is a martingale.

A.9 Solutions to a Rational Expectations Dynamic Equation

We already studied (in chapter 3) the solutions to a simple dynamic equation involving the current and expected values of the endogenous variable. We now study a dynamic equation involving the lagged value as well. We want to solve the dynamic equation:

$$\mathcal{A} x_t - \mathcal{B} x_{t-1} - \mathcal{C} E_t x_{t+1} = \mathcal{D} z_t \qquad (A.200)$$

where x_t is the endogenous variable, z_t an exogenous random variable, and:

$$\mathcal{A} > 0 \quad \mathcal{B} > 0 \quad \mathcal{C} > 0 \quad \mathcal{A} > \mathcal{B} + \mathcal{C} \qquad (A.201)$$

We present the two most used techniques for solving such equations, that of lag operators, and that of undetermined coefficients.

A.9.1 Lag Operators

Using the lag operator defined in section A.8.4, we rewrite equation (A.210) as:

$$\left(\mathcal{A} - \mathcal{B}\mathcal{L} - \mathcal{C}\mathcal{L}^{-1}\right) x_t = \mathcal{D} z_t \tag{A.202}$$

We want to factorize the parentheses in (A.202) as:

$$\left(\mathcal{A} - \mathcal{B}\mathcal{L} - \mathcal{C}\mathcal{L}^{-1}\right) = \chi \left(1 - \lambda \mathcal{L}\right)\left(1 - \mu \mathcal{L}^{-1}\right) \tag{A.203}$$

Identifying the terms one by one we find:

$$\lambda \chi = \mathcal{B} \qquad \mu \chi = \mathcal{C} \tag{A.204}$$

$$\chi \left(1 + \lambda \mu\right) = \mathcal{A} \tag{A.205}$$

We thus have from (A.204):

$$\mu = \frac{\lambda \mathcal{C}}{\mathcal{B}} \qquad \chi = \frac{\mathcal{B}}{\lambda} \tag{A.206}$$

and, inserting (A.206) into (A.205), we find that the autoregressive root λ is solution of the characteristic polynomial:

$$\Psi\left(\lambda\right) = \mathcal{C}\lambda^2 - \mathcal{A}\lambda + \mathcal{B} = 0 \tag{A.207}$$

We have:

$$\Psi\left(0\right) = \mathcal{B} > 0 \tag{A.208}$$

$$\Psi\left(1\right) = \mathcal{B} + \mathcal{C} - \mathcal{A} < 0 \tag{A.209}$$

There is thus one root λ between 0 and 1. We must also verify that the other root μ in (A.203) is smaller than 1, which boils down to $\lambda < \mathcal{B}/\mathcal{C}$. This is indeed the case, because:

$$\Psi\left(\frac{\mathcal{B}}{\mathcal{C}}\right) = \frac{\mathcal{B}}{\mathcal{C}}\left(\mathcal{B} + \mathcal{C} - \mathcal{A}\right) < 0 \tag{A.210}$$

The solution is therefore, from (A.202), (A.203), and (A.204):

$$x_t = \frac{\mathcal{D} z_t}{\chi \left(1 - \lambda \mathcal{L}\right)\left(1 - \mu \mathcal{L}^{-1}\right)} = \frac{\lambda \mathcal{D} z_t}{\mathcal{B} \left(1 - \lambda \mathcal{L}\right)\left(1 - \mu \mathcal{L}^{-1}\right)} \tag{A.211}$$

which can be rewritten:

$$x_t = \lambda x_{t-1} + \frac{\lambda \mathcal{D}}{\mathcal{B}} \sum_{j=0}^{\infty} \mu^j E_t(z_{t+j}) \quad (A.212)$$

with μ defined in (A.206).

A.9.2 The Method of Undetermined Coefficients

The method of undetermined coefficients consists in conjecturing a solution with unknown coefficients and determining the value of these coefficients using the constraints imposed by rational expectations. Here we conjecture a solution of the form:

$$x_t = \lambda x_{t-1} + \sum_{j=0}^{\infty} \kappa_j E_t z_{t+j} \quad (A.213)$$

From that we deduce:

$$E_t x_{t+1} = \lambda x_t + \sum_{j=0}^{\infty} \kappa_j E_t z_{t+1+j} = \lambda x_t + \sum_{j=1}^{\infty} \kappa_{j-1} E_t z_{t+j}$$

$$= \lambda^2 x_{t-1} + \lambda \sum_{j=0}^{\infty} \kappa_j E_t z_{t+j} + \sum_{j=1}^{\infty} \kappa_{j-1} E_t z_{t+j} \quad (A.214)$$

Inserting (A.213) and (A.214) into the initial formula (A.200), we obtain:

$$\mathcal{A}\left(\lambda x_{t-1} + \sum_{j=0}^{\infty} \kappa_j E_t z_{t+j}\right) - \mathcal{B} x_{t-1}$$

$$-\mathcal{C}\left(\lambda^2 x_{t-1} + \lambda \sum_{j=0}^{\infty} \kappa_j E_t z_{t+j} + \sum_{j=1}^{\infty} \kappa_{j-1} E_t z_{t+j}\right) = \mathcal{D} z_t \quad (A.215)$$

Identifying to 0 the term in x_{t-1} we find the characteristic equation giving λ:

$$\Psi(\lambda) = \mathcal{C}\lambda^2 - \mathcal{A}\lambda - \mathcal{B} = 0 \quad (A.216)$$

Note that this is the same as (A.207). So there is one root λ such that:

$$0 < \lambda < 1 \quad (A.217)$$

Now identifying to 0 the term in z_t in (A.215) yields:

$$\kappa_0 = \frac{\mathcal{D}}{\mathcal{A} - \lambda\mathcal{C}} \qquad (A.218)$$

and using (A.216):

$$\kappa_0 = \frac{\lambda\mathcal{D}}{\mathcal{B}} \qquad (A.219)$$

Finally identifying to 0 the term in $E_t z_{t+j}$ gives:

$$\kappa_j = \frac{\mathcal{C}}{\mathcal{A} - \lambda\mathcal{C}} \kappa_{j-1} = \eta \kappa_{j-1} \qquad (A.220)$$

We may note, again using (A.216), that $\eta = \mu$, where $\mu < 1$ was defined in (A.206). Finally we find:

$$x_t = \lambda x_{t-1} + \frac{\lambda\mathcal{D}}{\mathcal{B}} \sum_{j=0}^{\infty} \mu^j E_t \left(z_{t+j}\right) \qquad (A.221)$$

This is the same expression as (A.212).

A.10 Dynamic Systems

A.10.1 Generalities

Consider a n-dimensional vector x_t. A discrete time dynamic system is characterized by a function F that depicts how this vector evolves over time:

$$x_{t+1} = F(x_t) \qquad (A.222)$$

A steady state x^*, or equilibrium, of this dynamic system is a fixed point of the above mapping:

$$x^* = F(x^*) \qquad (A.223)$$

Consider the eigenvalues of the linearization of F around x^*. The equilibrium is called:

1. A *sink* if all eigenvalues are of modulus smaller than 1.
2. A *source* if all eigenvalues are of modulus greater than 1.

Mathematical Appendix

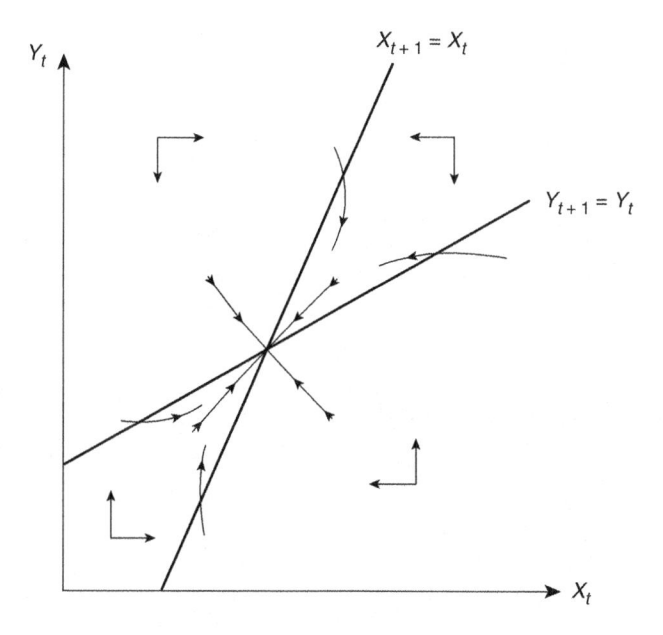

Figure A1 A sink

3. A *saddle* in the other cases.

The three cases are represented in figures A.1, A.2, and A.3 for a two-dimensional system.

A.10.2 A Two-dimensional Linear System

Consider the following linear discrete time dynamic system:

$$\begin{bmatrix} y_{t+1} \\ z_{t+1} \end{bmatrix} = A \begin{bmatrix} y_t \\ z_t \end{bmatrix} \tag{A.224}$$

where the matrix A is defined as:

$$A = \begin{bmatrix} a & b \\ c & d \end{bmatrix} \tag{A.225}$$

and where the variables y_t and z_t have been redefined as deviations from their stationary values y^* and z^*, so that there is no constant term.

We are looking for λ's and associated values of y_t and z_t such that:

$$\begin{bmatrix} y_{t+1} \\ z_{t+1} \end{bmatrix} = A \begin{bmatrix} y_t \\ z_t \end{bmatrix} = \lambda \begin{bmatrix} y_t \\ z_t \end{bmatrix} \tag{A.226}$$

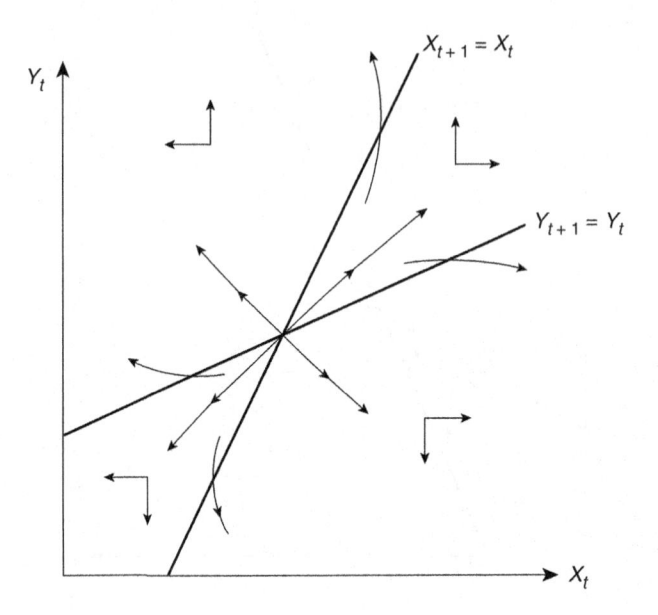

Figure A2 A source

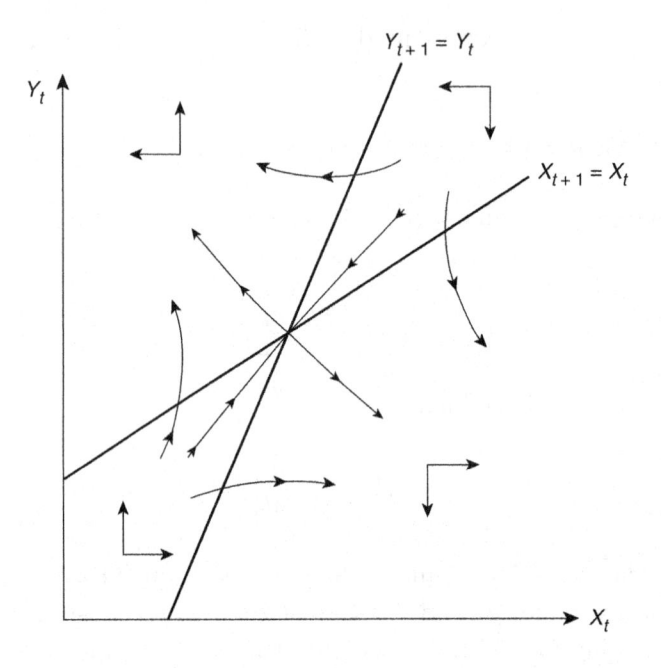

Figure A3 A saddle

where λ is a scalar. We know from section A.1 that λ's must be such that the determinant of the matrix $A - \lambda I$ is equal to 0, that is:

$$\begin{vmatrix} a - \lambda & b \\ c & d - \lambda \end{vmatrix} = 0 \qquad (A.227)$$

so λ is given by the following equation:

$$\Psi(\lambda) = \lambda^2 - (a+d)\lambda + ad - bc = 0 \qquad (A.228)$$

$\Psi(\lambda)$ is the *characteristic polynomial*, and its roots are called the eigenvalues. We recognize that $ad - bc$ is the determinant D of the matrix A. The term $a + d$ is called the trace and noted T. The characteristic polynomial is rewritten:

$$\Psi(\lambda) = \lambda^2 - \lambda T + D = 0 \qquad (A.229)$$

This characteristic polynomial is represented in figure A.4. We now indicate for which combinations of T and D one obtains a sink, a saddle, or a source.

Let us start with the case of a sink. For that case to obtain, the two roots λ_1 and λ_2 must be smaller than 1 in absolute value. Looking at figure A.4, we see that there are three conditions:

$$(a) \qquad \Psi(1) > 0 \qquad (A.230)$$

$$(b) \qquad \Psi(-1) > 0 \qquad (A.231)$$

$$(c) \qquad \lambda_1 \lambda_2 < 1 \qquad (A.232)$$

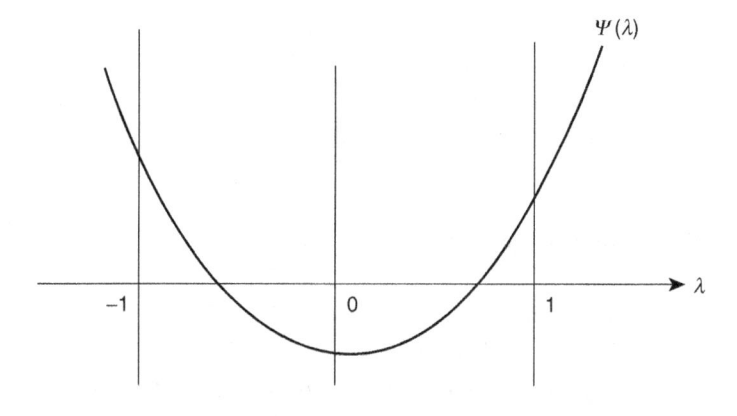

Figure A4 The characteristic polynomial

In terms of T and D this yields, respectively:

$$\text{(a)} \quad 1 - T + D > 0 \tag{A.233}$$

$$\text{(b)} \quad 1 + T + D > 0 \tag{A.234}$$

$$\text{(c)} \quad D < 1 \tag{A.235}$$

Using similar graphs, one sees that for a saddle there are two possible combinations:

$$1 - T + D > 0 \quad \text{and} \quad 1 + T + D < 0 \tag{A.236}$$

or:

$$1 - T + D < 0 \quad \text{and} \quad 1 + T + D > 0 \tag{A.237}$$

Finally, for a source there are also two possible combinations:

$$1 - T + D > 0 \quad \text{and} \quad 1 + T + D > 0 \quad \text{and} \quad D > 1 \tag{A.238}$$

or:

$$1 - T + D < 0 \quad \text{and} \quad 1 + T + D < 0 \quad \text{and} \quad D < -1 \tag{A.239}$$

All the foregoing combinations are represented in figure A.5.

Finally we must separate the cases where the roots are real from those where they are complex. The roots are real if the discriminant of equation (A.229) is positive, that is, if:

$$4D < T^2 \tag{A.240}$$

which is also represented in figure A.5. Above the parabola $D = T^2/4$, the roots are real; below the parabola, the roots are complex.

A.11 Determinacy

An important problem in macrodynamics is that of determinacy, that is, the uniqueness or multiplicity of admissible dynamic trajectories.

At this stage there is no really satisfactory theory to say what happens when a system is indeterminate. There seems to be an agreement, however, that such a situation may be associated with some instability in economic

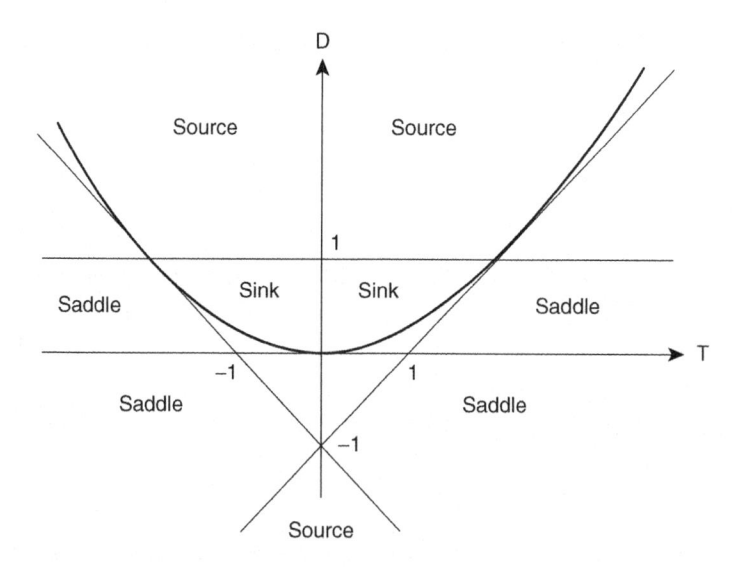

Figure A5 Roots and dynamics

variables (because one may possibly jump from one trajectory to the other), and one usually looks for policies that will make the system determinate. We want to indicate a few simple conditions for a dynamic system to have a determinate solution.

A.11.1 Global and Local Determinacy

There are actually, implicitly or explicitly, two different determinacy criteria in the literature: global and local determinacy.

There is *global determinacy* if there is only one admissible trajectory. That criterion is easy to enunciate but sometimes difficult to prove. So many people use a "local" criterion. One says that a dynamic system displays *local determinacy* around an equilibrium if there is only one admissible trajectory in a neighborhood of that equilibrium. That criterion will be easier to handle because, as we shall see, it can be assessed by looking only at the eigenvalues of the dynamic system.

A.11.2 Predetermined and Nonpredetermined Variables

Another fundamental distinction for the determinacy issue is that between predetermined and nonpredetermined variables. Predetermined variables are, as their name says, fully determined at time t, for example, because they are functions of past variables. As an example, a typical predetermined variable is fixed capital, because the traditional equation of evolution of capital is:

$$K_t = (1 - \delta) K_{t-1} + I_{t-1} \tag{A.241}$$

A nonpredetermined variable, on the contrary, can take any value at time t. In particular it can "jump" to any value. For example, prices are usually thought of as nonpredetermined variables, at least in a Walrasian environment.

A.11.3 The Dynamic System

Let us call Y_t the n-dimensional vector of predetermined variables, Z_t the m-dimensional vector of nonpredetermined variables. The dynamic system is written:

$$\begin{bmatrix} Y_{t+1} \\ Z_{t+1} \end{bmatrix} = A \begin{bmatrix} Y_t \\ Z_t \end{bmatrix} + \Omega_t \tag{A.242}$$

where A is a square matrix of dimension $(m + n)$ and Ω_t is a vector of exogenous variables. The "initial conditions" consist in the value of the predetermined variables at time 0, Y_0.

We first study two particular cases, and then give a more general condition, all for local determinacy.

A.11.4 Determinacy: Predetermined Variables

We start with the case where there is only one predetermined variable.

$$Y_{t+1} = aY_t + b \tag{A.243}$$

We see on figure A.6 that if $a < 1$ there is one admissible trajectory[5] starting from some given Y_0, whereas if $a > 1$ trajectories are divergent and there is no admissible trajectory.

---

5. In this literature the usual definition of an admissible trajectory is a nonexplosive or nondivergent trajectory.

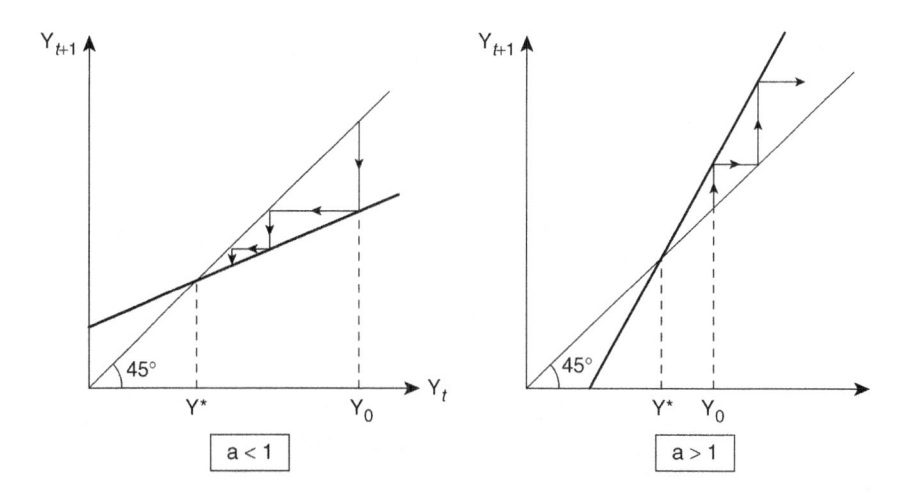

Figure A6 Determinacy: a predetermined variable

A.11.5 Determinacy: Nonpredetermined Variables

We now consider the case of a single nonpredetermined variable:

$$Z_{t+1} = aZ_t + b \qquad (A.244)$$

Although the trajectories (figure A.7) look fairly similar to those in figure A.6, the interpretation is almost opposite, because in the case of non predetermined variables there are no such things as initial conditions.

In the case where $a < 1$, there is an infinity of admissible trajectories, which all converge toward the long-run equilibrium Z^*. There is thus indeterminacy. In the contrary if $a > 1$, all trajectories such that $Z_0 \neq Z^*$ are divergent. Only the stationary trajectory such that $Z_t = Z^*$ for all t is admissible. The dynamic system is thus determinate.

A.11.6 A General Condition for Local Determinacy

Extending the foregoing intuitions to a system with n predetermined variables and m nonpredetermined variables, we have the following result (Blanchard and Kahn, 1980).

Local determinacy: *If the number of eigenvalues of A outside the unit circle is equal to the number of nonpredetermined variables, there exists a unique locally determinate solution.*

In this book we have most often encountered two particular cases: (a) there is only one nonpredetermined variable, in which case the (only)

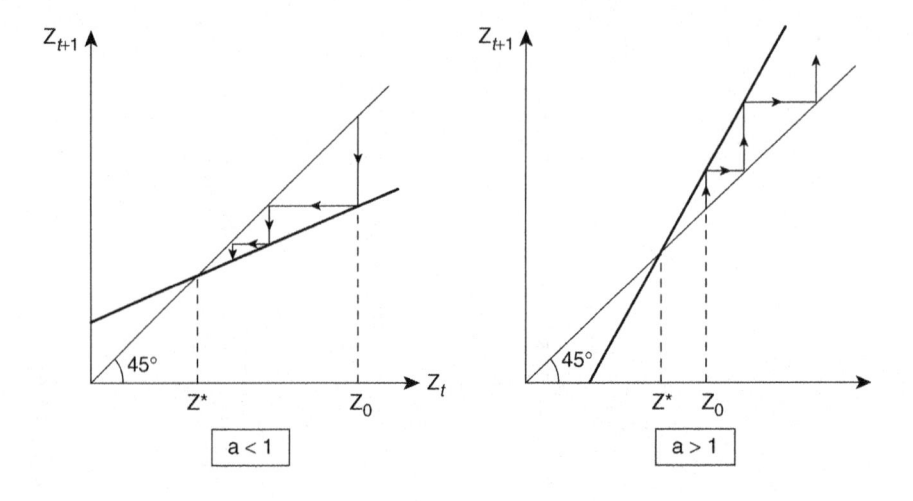

Figure A7 Determinacy: a nonpredetermined variable

eigenvalue must be greater than 1 for determinacy; and (b) there is one predetermined variable and one nonpredetermined variable, in which case one eigenvalue must be greater than 1 (in absolute value) the other one smaller than 1.

A.12 Some Useful Calculations

We derive a few formulas that have been used without proof in chapters 12 and 13.

A.12.1 A Computation for Chapter 12

We want to compute:

$$E\left(\Theta Log\Theta\right) \tag{A.245}$$

where $\theta = Log\Theta$ is a normal variable with mean μ_θ and variance σ_θ^2 such that:

$$E\left(\Theta\right) = 1 \tag{A.246}$$

Condition (A.246) implies:

$$\mu_\theta + \frac{\sigma_\theta^2}{2} = 0 \tag{A.247}$$

Take θ as the working variable. The expression in (A.245) is equal to:

$$\int_{-\infty}^{+\infty} \theta e^{\theta} \exp\left[-\frac{(\theta - \mu_\theta)^2}{2\sigma_\theta^2}\right] d\theta \tag{A.248}$$

Let us denote:

$$z = \theta - \mu_\theta \tag{A.249}$$

The expression in (A.248) becomes:

$$\exp\mu_\theta \int_{-\infty}^{+\infty} z \exp\left(z - \frac{z^2}{2\sigma_\theta^2}\right) dz + \mu_\theta \exp\mu_\theta \int_{-\infty}^{+\infty} \exp\left(z - \frac{z^2}{2\sigma_\theta^2}\right) dz \tag{A.250}$$

Now:

$$\exp\left(z - \frac{z^2}{2\sigma_\theta^2}\right) = \exp\left(\frac{\sigma_\theta^2}{2}\right) \exp\left[-\frac{(z - \sigma_\theta^2)^2}{2\sigma_\theta^2}\right] \tag{A.251}$$

Insert (A.251) into (A.250). The expression (A.250) becomes:

$$\exp\left(\mu_\theta + \frac{\sigma_\theta^2}{2}\right) \int_{-\infty}^{+\infty} z \exp\left[-\frac{(z - \sigma_\theta^2)^2}{2\sigma_\theta^2}\right] dz$$

$$+ \mu_\theta \exp\left(\mu_\theta + \frac{\sigma_\theta^2}{2}\right) \int_{-\infty}^{+\infty} \exp\left[-\frac{(z - \sigma_\theta^2)^2}{2\sigma_\theta^2}\right] dz \tag{A.252}$$

Formula (A.252) simplifies to:

$$(\mu_\theta + \sigma_\theta^2) \exp\left(\mu_\theta + \frac{\sigma_\theta^2}{2}\right) \tag{A.253}$$

so that, in view of (A.247):

$$E(\Theta Log\Theta) = \frac{\sigma_\theta^2}{2} \tag{A.254}$$

A.12.2 A Computation for Chapter 13

We want to establish the formulas:

$$\sum_{j=0}^{\infty} j\lambda^j = \frac{\lambda}{(1-\lambda)^2} \qquad (A.255)$$

$$\sum_{j=t}^{\infty} j\lambda^j = \frac{t\lambda^t}{1-\lambda} + \frac{\lambda^{t+1}}{(1-\lambda)^2} \qquad (A.256)$$

We first compute:

$$\Upsilon_t = \sum_{j=0}^{t} j\lambda^j \qquad (A.257)$$

We make the change of variable $j = 1 + i$:

$$\Upsilon_t = \sum_{i=0}^{t-1} (1+i)\lambda^{1+i} = \lambda \left[\sum_{i=0}^{t-1} (1+i)\lambda^i \right]$$

$$= \lambda \left(\sum_{i=0}^{t-1} \lambda^i \right) + \lambda \left(\sum_{i=0}^{t-1} i\lambda^i \right) = \lambda \frac{1-\lambda^t}{1-\lambda} + \lambda \left(\Upsilon_t - t\lambda^t \right) \qquad (A.258)$$

So:

$$\Upsilon_t = \frac{\lambda(1-\lambda^t)}{(1-\lambda)^2} - \frac{t\lambda^{t+1}}{1-\lambda} \qquad (A.259)$$

Taking the limit $t = \infty$ in (A.259) we find:

$$\Upsilon = \sum_{j=0}^{\infty} j\lambda^j = \frac{\lambda}{(1-\lambda)^2} \qquad (A.260)$$

which is formula (A.255). Finally we combine (A.257) and (A.260) to obtain:

$$\sum_{j=t}^{\infty} j\lambda^j = \Upsilon - \Upsilon_{t-1} = \frac{t\lambda^t}{1-\lambda} + \frac{\lambda^{t+1}}{(1-\lambda)^2} \qquad (A.261)$$

which is formula (A.256).

A.13 References

Although the above mathematical appendix should give sufficient mathematical material to read the book, some readers may want to pursue some particular directions further. The following is a (nonexhaustive) list of more advanced sources: Bellman (1957); Broze, Gourieroux, and Szafarz (1985, 1990); Chiang (1984, 1992); Chiang and Wainwright (2005); De la Fuente (2000); Dixit (1990); Gourieroux and Monfort (1995, 1996); Hirsch and Smale (1974); Intriligator (1971); Léonard and van Long (1992); Seierstad and Sydsaeter (1987); Stachurski (2009); and Sydsaeter, Strom, and Berck (2000).

Bibliography

Abel, Andrew B. (1982), "Dynamic effects of permanent and temporary tax policies in a q model of investment," *Journal of Monetary Economics*, vol. 9, 353–373.

Abel, Andrew B. (1987), "Optimal monetary growth," *Journal of Monetary Economics*, vol. 19, 437–450.

Abel, Andrew B. (1990), "Consumption and investment," in B. M. Friedman and F. H. Hahn (eds.), *Handbook of Monetary Economics*, Amsterdam: North Holland.

Abel, Andrew B. (2008), "Ricardian equivalence theorem," in S. N. Durlauf and L. E. Blume (eds.), *The New Palgrave Dictionary of Economics*, 2nd edition. London: Palgrave Macmillan.

Abraham, Katherine G., and John C. Haltiwanger (1995), "Real wages and the business cycle," *Journal of Economic Literature*, vol. 33, 1215–1264.

Adao, Bernardino, Isabel Correia, and Pedro Teles (2003), "Gaps and triangles," *Review of Economic Studies*, vol. 70, 699–713.

Aghion, Philippe, Christopher Harris, Peter Howitt, and John Vickers (2001), "Competition, imitation and growth with step-by-step innovation," *Review of Economic Studies*, vol. 68, 467–492.

Aghion, Philippe, and Peter W. Howitt (1992), "A model of growth through creative destruction," *Econometrica*, vol. 60, 323–351.

Aghion, Philippe, and Peter W. Howitt (1998), *Endogenous Growth Theory*. Cambridge, Mass.: MIT Press.

Aiyagari, S. Rao, and Mark Gertler (1985) "The backing of government bonds and monetarism," *Journal of Monetary Economics*, vol. 16, 19–44.

Aiyagari, S. Rao, Albert Marcet, Thomas Sargent, and Juha Seppälä (2002), "Optimal taxation without state-contingent debt," *Journal of Political Economy*, vol. 10, 1220–1254.

Akerlof, George A., and Janet L. Yellen (1985a), "A near-rational model of the business cycle with wage and price inertia," *Quarterly Journal of Economics*, vol. 100, supplement, 823–838.

Akerlof, George A., and Janet L. Yellen (1985b), "Can small deviations from rationality make significant differences to economic equilibria?," *American Economic Review*, vol. 75, 708–721.

Akerlof, George A., and Janet L. Yellen (1986), *Efficiency Wage Models of the Labor Market*. Cambridge: Cambridge University Press.

Alesina, Alberto (1988), "Macroeconomics and politics," *NBER Macroeconomics Annual*, vol. 3, 13–52.

Alesina, Alberto, and Guido Tabellini (1990), "A positive theory of fiscal deficits and government debt," *Review of Economic Studies*, vol. 57, 403–414.

Allais, Maurice (1947), *Economie et Intérêt*. Paris: Imprimerie Nationale.

Andersen, Torben M. (1985a), "Price and output responsiveness to nominal changes under differential information," *European Economic Review*, vol. 29, 63–87.

Andersen, Torben M. (1985b), "Price dynamics under imperfect information," *Journal of Economic Dynamics and Control*, vol. 9, 339–361.

Andersen, Torben M. (1986a), "Differential information and the role for an active stabilization policy," *Economica*, vol. 53, 321–338.

Andersen, Torben M. (1986b), "Pre-set prices, differential information and monetary policy," *Oxford Economic Papers*, vol. 38, 456–480.

Andersen, Torben M. (1994), *Price Rigidity: Causes and Macroeconomic Implications*. Oxford: Oxford University Press.

Andolfatto, David (1996), "Business cycles and labor market search," *American Economic Review*, vol. 86, 112–132.

Arrow, Kenneth J. (1951), *Social Choice and Individual Values*. New York: Wiley; Second edition, 1963.

Arrow, Kenneth J. (1953), "Le rôle des valeurs boursières pour la répartition la meilleure des risques," *Cahiers du Séminaire d'Econométrie*. Paris: CNRS, 41–48.

Arrow, Kenneth J. (1959), "Toward a theory of price adjustment," in M. Abramowitz (ed.), *The Allocation of Economic Resources*. Stanford, Calif.: Stanford University Press, 41–51.

Arrow, Kenneth J. (1963), "The role of securities in the optimal allocation of risk-bearing," *Review of Economic Studies*, vol. 31, 91–96.

Arrow, Kenneth J. (1971), *Essays in the Theory of Risk Bearing*. Chicago: Markham.

Arrow, Kenneth J., Hollis B. Chenery, Bagicha S. Minhas, and Robert M. Solow (1961), "Capital-labor substitution and economic efficiency," *Review of Economics and Statistics*, vol. 43, 225–250.

Arrow, Kenneth J., and Gérard Debreu (1954), "Existence of an equilibrium for a competitive economy," *Econometrica*, vol. 22, 265–290.

Arrow, Kenneth J., and Frank H. Hahn (1971), *General Competitive Analysis*. San Francisco: Holden-Day.

Arrow, Kenneth J., Samuel Karlin, and Herbert Scarf (1958), *Studies in the Mathematical Theory of Inventory and Production*. Stanford, Calif.: Stanford University Press.

Arrow, Kenneth J., and Mordecai Kurz (1970), *Public Investment, the Rate of Return and Optimal Fiscal Policy*. Baltimore: Johns Hopkins University Press.

Ascari, Guido (2000), "Optimising agents, staggered wages and persistence in the real effects of money shocks," *Economic Journal*, vol. 110, 664–686.

Ascari, Guido, and Neil Rankin (2002), "Staggered wages and output dynamics under disinflation," *Journal of Economic Dynamics and Control*, vol. 26, 653–680.

Atkinson, Anthony, and Joseph Stiglitz (1980), *Lectures in Public Economics*. New York: McGraw-Hill.

Azariadis, Costas (1975), "Implicit contracts and underemployment equilibria," *Journal of Political Economy*, vol. 83, 1183–1202.

Azariadis, Costas (1981a), "Self-fulfilling prophecies," *Journal of Economic Theory*, vol. 25, 380–396.

Azariadis, Costas (1981b), "A reexamination of natural rate theory," *American Economic Review*, vol. 71, 946–960.

Azariadis, Costas, and Roger Guesnerie (1986), "Sunspots and cycles," *Review of Economic Studies*, vol. 53, 725–737.

Backus, David, and John Driffill (1985a), "Inflation and reputation," *American Economic Review*, vol. 75, 530–538.

Backus, David, and John Driffill (1985b), "Rational expectations and policy credibility following a change in regime," *Review of Economic Studies*, vol. 52, 211–221.

Baily, Martin N. (1974), "Wages and employment under uncertain demand," *Review of Economic Studies*, vol. 41, 37–50.

Ball, Laurence (1994a), "Credible disinflation with staggered price-setting," *American Economic Review*, vol. 84, 282–289.

Ball, Laurence (1994b), "What determines the sacrifice ratio?," in N. G. Mankiw (ed.), *Monetary Policy*. Chicago: University of Chicago Press.

Ball, Laurence (1995), "Disinflation with imperfect credibility," *Journal of Monetary Economics*, vol. 35, 5–23.

Ball, Laurence, and David Romer (1990), "Real rigidities and the nonneutrality of money," *Review of Economic Studies*, vol. 57, 183–203.

Barro, Robert J. (1972), "A theory of monopolistic price adjustment," *Review of Economic Studies*, vol. 34, 17–26.

Barro, Robert J. (1974), "Are government bonds net wealth?," *Journal of Political Economy*, vol. 82, 1095–1117.

Barro, Robert J. (1979), "On the determination of public debt," *Journal of Political Economy*, vol. 87, 940–971.

Barro, Robert J. (1986), "Reputation in a model of monetary policy with incomplete information," *Journal of Monetary Economics*, vol. 17, 1–20.

Barro, Robert J. (1989), "The Ricardian approach to budget deficits," *Journal of Economic Perspectives*, vol. 3, 37–54.

Barro, Robert J. (1991), "Economic growth in a cross section of countries," *Quarterly Journal of Economics*, vol. 106, 407–443.

Barro, Robert J., and David B. Gordon (1983a), "Rules, discretion and reputation in a model of monetary policy," *Journal of Monetary Economics*, vol. 12, 101–121.

Barro, Robert J., and David B. Gordon (1983b), "A positive theory of monetary policy in a natural rate model," *Journal of Political Economy*, vol. 91, 589–610.

Barro, Robert J., and Herschel I. Grossman (1971), "A general disequilibrium model of income and employment," *American Economic Review*, vol. 61, 82–93.

Barro, Robert J., and Herschel I. Grossman (1976), *Money, Employment and Inflation*. Cambridge: Cambridge University Press.

Barro, Robert, and Xavier Sala-i-Martin (1991), "Convergence across states and regions," *Brookings Papers on Economic Activity*, no. 1, 107–182.

Barro, Robert, and Xavier Sala-i-Martin (1992), "Convergence," *Journal of Political Economy*, vol. 100, 223–251.

Barro, Robert and Xavier Sala-i-Martin (1995), *Economic Growth*. New York: McGraw-Hill.

Barro, Robert, and Xavier Sala-i-Martin (2004), *Economic Growth*, 2nd edition. Cambridge, Mass.: MIT Press.

Baumol, William J. (1952), "The transactions demand for cash: an inventory theoretic approach," *Quarterly Journal of Economics*, vol. 66, 545–556.

Baumol, William J. (1961), "Pitfalls in contracyclical policies: some tools and results," *American Economic Review*, vol. 43, 21–26.

Baumol, William J. (1986), "Productivity growth, convergence and welfare: What the long-run data show," *American Economic Review*, vol. 76, 1072–1085.

Baumol, William J., and Edward N. Wolff (1988), "Productivity growth, convergence and welfare," *American Economic Review*, vol. 78, 1155–1159.

Bean, Charles (1984), "Optimal wage bargains," *Economica*, vol. 51, 141–149.

Bellman, Richard (1957), *Dynamic Programming*. Princeton, N.J.: Princeton University Press.

Bénassy, Jean-Pascal (1975), "Neo-Keynesian disequilibrium theory in a monetary economy," *Review of Economic Studies*, vol. 42, 503–523.

Bénassy, Jean-Pascal (1976), "The disequilibrium approach to monopolistic price setting and general monopolistic equilibrium," *Review of Economic Studies*, vol. 43, 69–81.

Bénassy, Jean-Pascal (1977), "A neo Keynesian model of price and quantity determination in disequilibrium," in G. Schwödiauer (ed.), *Equilibrium and Disequilibrium in Economic Theory*. Boston: Reidel.

Bénassy, Jean-Pascal (1982), *The Economics of Market Disequilibrium*. New York: Academic Press.

Bénassy, Jean-Pascal (1984), "A non-Walrasian model of the business cycle," *Journal of Economic Behavior and Organisation*, vol. 5, 77–89.

Bénassy, Jean-Pascal (1987), "Imperfect competition, unemployment and policy," *European Economic Review*, vol. 31, 417–426.

Bénassy, Jean-Pascal (1988), "The objective demand curve in general equilibrium with price makers," *Economic Journal*, vol. 98, supplement, 37–49.

Bénassy, Jean-Pascal (1990), "Non-Walrasian equilibria, money and macroeconomics," in B. Friedman and F. H. Hahn (eds.), *Handbook of Monetary Economics*. Amsterdam: North Holland.

Bénassy, Jean-Pascal (1995), "Money and wage contracts in an optimizing model of the business cycle," *Journal of Monetary Economics*, vol. 35, 303–315.

Bénassy, Jean-Pascal (1996), "Analytical solutions to an RBC model with imperfect competition, increasing returns and underemployment," *Recherches Economiques de Louvain*, vol. 62, 287–297.

Bénassy, Jean-Pascal (1998), "Is there always too little research in endogenous growth with expanding product variety?," *European Economic Review*, vol. 42, 61–69.

Bénassy, Jean-Pascal (1999), "Analytical solutions to a structural signal extraction model: Lucas 1972 revisited," *Journal of Monetary Economics*, vol. 44, 509–521.

Bénassy, Jean-Pascal (2001a), "On the optimality of activist policies with a less informed government," *Journal of Monetary Economics*, vol. 47, 45–59.

Bénassy, Jean-Pascal (2001b), "The Phillips curve and optimal policy in a structural signal extraction model," *Review of Economic Dynamics*, vol. 4, 58–74.

Bénassy, Jean-Pascal (2002a), "Optimal monetary and fiscal policies under wage and price rigidities," *Macroeconomic Dynamics*, vol. 6, 429–441.

Bénassy, Jean-Pascal (2002b), *The Macroeconomics of Imperfect Competition and Nonclearing Markets: A Dynamic General Equilibrium Approach*. Cambridge, Mass.: MIT Press.

Bénassy, Jean-Pascal (2002c), "Rigidités nominales dans les modèles d'équilibre général intertemporel stochastique," *L'Actualité économique*, vol. 78, 423–457.

Bénassy, Jean-Pascal (2003a), "Staggered contracts and persistence: microeconomic foundations and macroeconomic dynamics," *Louvain Economic Review*, vol. 69, 125–144.

Bénassy, Jean-Pascal (2003b), "Output and inflation dynamics under price and wage staggering: Analytical results," *Annales d'Economie et de Statistique*, no. 69, 1–30.

Bénassy, Jean-Pascal (2007), *Money, Interest and Policy: Dynamic General Equilibrium in a Non Ricardian World*. Cambridge, Mass.: MIT Press.

Bénassy, Jean-Pascal (2009), "Interest rate rules and global determinacy: an alternative to the Taylor principle," *International Journal of Economic Theory*, vol. 5, 359–374.

Benhabib, Jess, ed. (1992), *Cycles and Chaos in Economic Equilibrium*. Princeton, N.J.: Princeton University Press.

Benhabib, Jess (2008), "Chaotic dynamics in economics," in S. N. Durlauf and L. E. Blume (eds.), *The New Palgrave Dictionary of Economics*, 2nd edition. London: Palgrave Macmillan.

Benhabib, Jess, and Richard H. Day (1982), "A characterization of erratic dynamics in the overlapping generations model," *Journal of Economic Dynamics and Control*, vol. 4, 37–55.

Benhabib, Jess, and Roger E. A. Farmer (1994), "Indeterminacy and increasing returns," *Journal of Economic Theory*, vol. 63, 19–41.

Benhabib, Jess, and Roger E. A. Farmer (1996), "Indeterminacy and sector-specific externalities," *Journal of Monetary Economics*, vol. 37, 421–443.

Benhabib, Jess, and Roger E. A. Farmer (1999), "Indeterminacy and sunspots in macroeconomics," in J. B. Taylor and M. Woodford (eds.), *Handbook of Macroeconomics*, volume 1. Amsterdam: North Holland.

Benhabib, Jess, and Kazuo Nishimura (1979), "The Hopf bifurcation and the existence and stability of closed orbits in multisector models of optimal economic growth," *Journal of Economic Theory*, vol. 21, 421–444.

Benhabib, Jess, Stephanie Schmitt-Grohé, and Martin Uribe (2001), "The perils of Taylor rules," *Journal of Economic Theory*, vol. 96, 40–69.

Benhabib, Jess, and Yi Wen (2004), "Indeterminacy, aggregate demand, and the real business cycle," *Journal of Monetary Economics*, vol. 51, 503–530.

Bernanke, Ben S., and Mark Gertler (1989), "Agency costs, net worth, and business fluctuations," *American Economic Review*, vol. 79, 14–31.

Bernanke, Ben S., and Mark Gertler (1995), "Inside the black box: the credit channel to monetary policy transmission," *Journal of Economic Perspectives*, vol. 9, 27–48.

Bernanke, Ben S., Mark Gertler, and Simon Gilchrist (1999), "The financial accelerator in a quantitative business cycle framework," in J. B. Taylor and M. Woodford (eds.), *Handbook of Macroeconomics*. Amsterdam: North Holland.

Bernanke, Ben S., and Frederic S. Mishkin (1997), "Inflation targeting: A new framework for monetary policy?," *Journal of Economic Perspectives*, vol. 11, 97–116.

Bernanke, Ben S., and Michael Woodford (2005), *The Inflation Targeting Debate*. Chicago: University of Chicago Press.

Bernheim, B. Douglas (1987), "Ricardian equivalence: An evaluation of theory and evidence," *NBER Macroeconomics Annual*, vol. 2, 263–304.

Bils, Mark, and Peter J. Klenow (2004), "Some evidence on the importance of sticky prices," *Journal of Political Economy*, vol. 112, 947–985.

Binmore, Ken, Ariel Rubinstein, and Asher Wolinsky (1986), "The Nash bargaining solution in economic modelling," *Rand Journal of Economics*, vol. 17, 176–188.

Black, Duncan (1948), "On the rationale of group decision making," *Journal of Political Economy*, vol. 56, 23–34.

Blanchard, Olivier J. (1979), "Backward and forward solutions for economies with rational expectations," *American Economic Review*, vol. 69, 114–118.

Blanchard, Olivier J. (1985), "Debts, deficits and finite horizons," *Journal of Political Economy*, vol. 93, 223–247.

Blanchard, Olivier J., and Charles M. Kahn (1980), "The solution of linear difference models under rational expectations," *Econometrica*, vol. 48, 1305–1311.

Blanchard, Olivier, and Nobuhiro Kiyotaki (1987), "Monopolistic competition and the effects of aggregate demand," *American Economic Review*, vol. 77, 647–666.

Blinder, Alan S. (1986), "Can the production smoothing model be saved?," *Quarterly Journal of Economics*, vol. 101, 431–454.

Blinder, Alan S., and Louis J. Maccini (1991), "Taking stock: a critical assessment of recent research on inventories," *Journal of Economic Perspectives*, vol. 5, 73–96.

Bohn, Henning (1990), "Tax smoothing with financial instruments," *American Economic Review*, vol. 80, 1217–1230.

Boldrin, Michele, and Michael Woodford (1990), "Equilibrium models displaying endogenous fluctuations and chaos: A survey," *Journal of Monetary Economics*, vol. 25, 189–222.

Bourguignon, François, and Christian Morrisson (2002), "Inequality among world citizens: 1820–1992," *American Economic Review*, vol. 92, 727–744.

Brainard, William (1967), "Uncertainty and the effectiveness of policy," *American Economic Review*, vol. 57, 411–425.

Brandolini, A. (1995), "In search of a stylized fact: Do real wages exhibit a consistent pattern of cyclical variability?," *Journal of Economic Surveys*, vol. 9, 103–163.

Branson, William H., and Julio J. Rotemberg (1980), "International adjustment with wage rigidity," *European Economic Review*, vol. 13, 309–332.

Breeden, Douglas T. (1979), "An intertemporal asset pricing model with stochastic consumption and investment opportunities," *Journal of Financial Economics*, vol. 7, 265–296.

Brock, William A. (1974), "Money and growth: The case of long-run perfect foresight," *International Economic Review*, vol. 15, 750–777.

Brock, William A. (1975), "A simple perfect foresight monetary model," *Journal of Monetary Economics*, vol. 1, 133–150.

Broze, Laurence, Christian Gourieroux, and Ariane Szafarz (1985), "Solutions of dynamic rational expectations models," *Econometric Theory*, vol. 1, 341–368.

Broze, Laurence, Christian Gourieroux, and Ariane Szafarz (1990), *Reduced Forms of Rational Expectations Models*. Chur: Harwood Academic Publishers.

Brunnermeier, Markus K. (2008), "Bubbles," in S. N. Durlauf and L. E. Blume (eds.), *The New Palgrave Dictionary of Economics*, 2nd edition. London: Palgrave Macmillan.

Buchanan, James M. (1976), "Barro on the Ricardian equivalence theorem," *Journal of Political Economy*, vol. 84, 337–342.

Buiter, Willem H. (1988), "Death, birth, productivity growth and debt neutrality," *The Economic Journal*, vol. 98, 279–293.

Buiter, Willem H., and Ian Jewitt (1981), "Staggered wage setting with real wage relativities: Variations on a theme of Taylor," *Manchester School*, 211–228.

Buiter, Willem, and Marcus Miller (1985), "Costs and benefits of an anti-inflationary policy: Questions and issues," in V. E. Argy and J. W. Nevile (eds.), *Inflation and Unemployment: Theory, Experience and Policy Making*. London: George Allen and Unwin.

Bullard, James, and Kaushik Mitra (2002), "Learning about monetary policy rules," *Journal of Monetary Economics*, vol. 49, 1105–1129.

Burda, Michael, and Charles Wyplosz (1994), "Gross worker and job flows in Europe," *European Economic Review*, vol. 38, 1287–1315.

Cagan, Philip (1956), "The monetary dynamics of hyperinflation," in M. Friedman (ed.), *Studies in the Quantity Theory of Money*. Chicago: University of Chicago Press.

Cahuc, Pierre, and André Zylberberg (1991), "Niveaux de négociations salariales et performances macroéconomiques," *Annales d'économie et de Statistique*, no. 23, 1–12.

Cahuc, Pierre, and André Zylberberg (1996), *Labor Economics*. Cambridge, Mass.: The MIT Press.

Calmfors, Lars (1993), "Centralisation of wage bargaining and macroeconomic performance—a survey," *OECD Economic Studies*, no. 21, 161–191.

Calmfors, Lars, and John Driffill (1988), "Bargaining structure, corporatism and macroeconomic performance," *Economic Policy*, no. 6, 13–61.

Calvo, Guillermo (1978), "On the time consistency of optimal policy in a monetary economy," *Econometrica*, vol. 46, 1411–1428.

Calvo, Guillermo (1983), "Staggered prices in a utility-maximizing framework," *Journal of Monetary Economics*, vol. 12, 383–398.

Calvo, Guillermo, and Pablo E. Guidotti (1993), "On the flexibility of monetary policy: the case of the optimal inflation tax," *Review of Econmic Studies*, vol. 60, 667–687.

Camerer, Colin (1989), "Bubbles and fads in assets prices," *Journal of Economic Surveys*, vol. 3, 3–41.

Campbell, John Y. (1994), "Inspecting the mechanism: an analytical approach to the stochastic growth model," *Journal of Monetary Economics*, vol. 33, 463–506.

Campbell, John Y. (1999), "Asset prices, consumption, and the business cycle," in J. B. Taylor and M. Woodford (eds.), *Handbook of Macroeconomics*, volume 1C. Amsterdam: North Holland.

Caplin, Andrew, and Daniel F. Spulber (1987), "Menu costs and the neutrality of money," *Quarterly Journal of Economics*, vol. 102, 703–725.

Carlstrom, Charles T., and Timothy S. Fuerst (2001), "Timing and real indeterminacy in monetary models," *Journal of Monetary Economics*, vol. 47, 285–298.

Carlton, Dennis (1986), "The rigidity of prices," *American Economic Review*, vol. 76, 637–658.

Carruth, Alan, and Andrew J. Oswald (1987), "On union preferences and labour market models: Insiders and outsiders," *The Economic Journal*, vol. 97, 431–445.

Cass, David (1965), "Optimum growth in an aggregative model of capital accumulation," *Review of Economic Studies*, vol. 32, 233–240.

Cass, David, and Karl Shell (1983), "Do sunspots matter?," *Journal of Political Economy*, vol. 91, 193–227.

Cecchetti, Steven G. (1986), "The frequency of price adjustment: A study of the newsstand prices of magazines," *Journal of Econometrics*, vol. 31, 255–274.

Chang, W. W., and D. J. Smyth (1971), "The existence and persistence of cycles in a nonlinear model: Kaldor's 1940 model reexamined," *Review of Economic Studies*, vol. 38, 37–44.

Chari, Varadarajan V., Lawrence J. Christiano, and Patrick Kehoe, (1991), "Optimal fiscal and monetary policy: Some recent results," *Journal of Money, Credit and Banking*, vol. 23, 519–539.

Chari, Varadarajan V., Lawrence J. Christiano, and Patrick J. Kehoe (1994), "Optimal fiscal policy in a business cycle model," *Journal of Political Economy*, vol. 102, 617–652.

Chari, Varadarajan V., Lawrence J. Christiano, and Patrick J. Kehoe (1996), "Optimality of the Friedman rule an economies with distorting taxes," *Journal of Monetary Economics*, vol. 37, 203–223.

Chari, Varadarajan V., and Patrick Kehoe (1999), "Optimal fiscal and monetary policy," in J. B. Taylor and M. Woodford (eds.), *Handbook of Macroeconomics*, volume 1A. Amsterdam: North Holland.

Chari, Varadarajan V., Patrick J. Kehoe, and Edward C. Prescott (1989), "Time consistency and policy," in R. J. Barro (ed.), *Modern Business Cycle Theory*. Cambridge, Mass.: Harvard University Press.

Chéron, Arnaud, and François Langot (2000), "Phillips and Beveridge curves revisited," *Economics Letters*, vol. 69, 371–376.

Chiang, Alpha C. (1984), *Fundamental Methods of Mathematical Economics*. 3rd edition. New York: McGraw-Hill.

Chiang, Alpha C. (1992), *Elements of Dynamic Optimization*. New York: McGraw-Hill.

Chiang, Alpha C., and Kevin Wainwright (2005), *Fundamental Methods of Mathematical Economics*. New York: McGraw-Hill.

Chiappori, Pierre-André, and Roger Guesnerie (1991), "Sunspot equilibria in sequential markets models," in W. Hildenbrand and H. Sonnenschein (eds.), *Handbook of Mathematical Economics*, volume 4. Amsterdam: North Holland.

Cho, Jang-Ok (1993), "Money and the business cycle with one-period nominal contracts," *Canadian Journal of Economics*, vol. 26, 638–659.

Cho, Jang-Ok, and Thomas F. Cooley (1995), "Business cycles with nominal contracts," *Economic Theory*, vol. 6, 13–34.

Cho, Jang-Ok, Thomas F. Cooley, and Louis Phaneuf (1997), "The welfare cost of nominal wage contracting," *Review of Economic Studies*, vol. 64, 465–484.

Christiano, Lawrence J., and Martin Eichenbaum (1992), "Liquidity effects and the monetary transmission mechanism," *American Economic Review*, vol. 82, 346–353.

Christiano, Lawrence J., Martin Eichenbaum, and Charles Evans (1999), "Monetary policy shocks: What have we learned and to what end?," in J. B. Taylor and M. Woodford (eds.), *Handbook of Macroeconomics*, volume 1A. Amsterdam: North Holland.

Christiano, Lawrence J., Martin Eichenbaum, and Charles Evans (2005), "Nominal rigidities and the dynamic effects of a shock to monetary policy," *Journal of Political Economy*, vol. 113, 1–45.

Clower, Robert W. (1965), "The Keynesian counterrevolution: a theoretical appraisal," in F. H. Hahn and F. P. R. Brechling (eds.), *The Theory of Interest Rates*. London: Macmillan.

Clower, Robert W. (1967), "A reconsideration of the microfoundations of monetary theory," *Western Economic Journal*, vol. 6, 1–9.

Cogley, Timothy, and James M. Nason (1993), "Impulse dynamics and propagation mechanisms in a real business cycle model," *Economics Letters*, vol. 43, 77–81.

Cogley, Timothy, and James M. Nason (1995), "Output dynamics in real-business-cycle models," *American Economic Review*, vol. 85, 492–511.

Collard, Fabrice, and Harris Dellas (2005), "Poole in the new-Keynesian model," *European Economic Review*, vol. 49, 887–907.

Condorcet, Marquis de (1785), *Essai sur l'Application de l'Analyse à la Probabilité des Décisions Rendues à la Pluralité des Voix*. Paris.

Cooley, Thomas F. (ed.) (1995), *Frontiers of Business Cycle Research*. Princeton, N.J.: Princeton University Press.

Cooley, Thomas F., and Gary D. Hansen (1989), "The inflation tax in a real business cycle model," *American Economic Review*, vol. 79, 733–748.

Cooley, Thomas F., and Lee E. Ohanian (1991), "The cyclical behavior of prices," *Journal of Monetary Economics*, vol. 28, 25–60.

Cooper, Russell W. (1987), *Wage and Employment Patterns in Labor Contracts: Microfoundations and Macroeconomic Implications*. Chur: Harwood Academic Publishers.

Correia, Isabel, Juan Pablo Nicolini, and Pedro Teles (2008) "Optimal fiscal and monetary policy: equivalence results," *Journal of Political Economy*, vol. 116, 141–170.

Correia, Isabel, and Pedro Teles (1996) "Is the Friedman rule optimal when money is an intermediate good?," *Journal of Monetary Economics*, vol. 38, 223–244.

Correia, Isabel, and Pedro Teles (1999) "The optimal inflation tax," *Review of Economic Dynamics*, vol. 2, 325–346.

Coughlin, P. (1992), *Probabilistic Voting Theory*. Cambridge: Cambridge University Press.

Coughlin, P., and S. Nitzan (1981) "Electoral outcomes with probabilistic voting and Nash social welfare maxima," *Journal of Public Economics*, vol. 15, 113–121.

Cukierman, Alex (1992), *Central Bank Strategy, Credibility and Independence*. Cambridge, Mass.: MIT Press.

Dana, Rose-Anne, and Pierre Malgrange (1984), "The dynamics of a discrete version of a growth cycle model," in J. P. Ancot (ed.), *Analysing the Structure of Econometric Models*. Amsterdam: M. Nijhoff.

Danthine, Jean-Pierre, and John B. Donaldson (1990), "Efficiency wages and the business cycle puzzle," *European Economic Review*, vol. 34, 1275–1301.

Danthine, Jean-Pierre, and John B. Donaldson (1991), "Risk sharing, the minimum wage and the business cycle," in W. Barnett et al. (eds.), *Equilibrium Theory and Applications: A Conference in Honor of Jacques Drèze*. Cambridge: Cambridge University Press.

Danthine, Jean-Pierre, and John B. Donaldson (1992), "Risk sharing in the business cycle," *European Economic Review*, vol. 36, 468–475.

Darby, Michael (1984), "Some pleasant monetarist arithmetic," *Federal Reserve Bank of Minneapolis Quarterly Review*, spring 1984.

Davis, Steven J., and John Haltiwanger (1990), "Gross job creation and destruction: Microeconomic evidence and macroeconomic applications," *NBER Macroeconomics Annual*, 123–168.

Davis, Steven J., and John Haltiwanger (1992), "Gross job creation, gross job destruction and employment reallocation," *Quarterly Journal of Economics*, vol. 107, 123–168.

Davis, Steven J., and John Haltiwanger (1999), "Gross job flows," in O. Ashenfelter and D. Card (eds.), *Handbook of Labor Economics*, volume 3. Amsterdam: North Holland.

Davis, Steven J., John Haltiwanger, and Scott Schuh (1996), *Job Creation and Destruction*. Cambridge, Mass.: MIT Press.

Debreu, Gérard (1959), *Theory of Value*. New York: Wiley.

De la Croix, David, and Philippe Michel (2002), *A Theory of Economic Growth. Dynamics and Policy in Overlapping Generations*. Cambridge: Cambridge University Press.

De la Fuente, Angel (1997), "The empirics of growth and convergence: a selective review," *Journal of Economic Dynamics and Control*, vol. 21, 23–73.

De la Fuente, Angel (2000), *Mathematical Methods and Models for Economists*. Cambridge: Cambridge University Press.

De Long, J. Bradford (1988), "Productivity growth, convergence and welfare: Comment," *American Economic Review*, vol. 78, 1138–1154.

Den Haan, Wouter J., Garey Ramey, and Joel Watson (2000), "Job destruction and propagation of shocks," *American Economic Review*, vol. 90, 482–498.

Devereux, Michael B., Allen C. Head, and Beverly J. Lapham (1993), "Monopolistic competition, technology shocks and aggregate fluctuations," *Economics Letters*, vol. 41, 57–61.

Devereux, Michael B., and James Yetman (2003), "Predetermined prices and the persistent effects of money on output," *Journal of Money, Credit and Banking*, vol. 35, 729–741.

Diamond, Peter A. (1965), "National debt in a neoclassical growth model," *American Economic Review*, vol. 55, 1126–1150.

Diamond, Peter A. (1984), *A Search-Equilibrium Approach to the Micro Foundations of Macroeconomics*. Cambridge, Mass.: MIT Press.

Dinopoulos, Elias, and Peter Thompson (1998), "Schumpeterian growth without scale effects," *Journal of Economic Growth*, vol. 3, 313–335.

Dittmar, Robert, and William T. Gavin (2000), "What do new-Keynesian Phillips curves imply for price-level targeting?," *Federal Reserve Bank of Saint Louis Review*, March–April, 21–30.

Dittmar, Robert, William T. Gavin, and Finn E. Kydland (1999a), "The inflation-output variability tradeoff and price-level targets," *Federal Reserve Bank of Saint Louis Review*, January–February, 23–31.

Dittmar, Robert, William T. Gavin, and Finn E. Kydland (1999b), "Price-level uncertainty and inflation targeting," *Federal Reserve Bank of Saint Louis Review*, July–August, 23–33.

Dixit, Avinash K. (1990), *Optimization in Economic Theory*, 2nd edition. Oxford: Oxford University Press.

Dixit, Avinash K., and Joseph E. Stiglitz (1977), "Monopolistic competition and optimum product diversity," *American Economic Review*, vol. 67, 297–308.

Dixon, Huw (1987), "A simple model of imperfect competition with Walrasian features," *Oxford Economic Papers*, vol. 39, 134–160.

Dixon, Huw (1990), "Imperfect competition, unemployment benefit and the non-neutrality of money: An example," *Oxford Economic Papers*, vol. 42, 402–413.

Dixon, Huw, and Neil Rankin (1994), "Imperfect competition and macroeconomics, a survey," *Oxford Economic Papers*, vol. 46, 171–199.

Domar, Evsey D. (1946), "Capital expansion, rate of growth, and employment," *Econometrica*, vol. 14, 137–147.

Dornbusch, Rudiger, and Jacob A. Frenkel (1973), "Inflation and growth: Alternative approaches," *Journal of Money, Credit and Banking*, vol. 5, 141–156.

Downs, A. (1957), *An Economic Theory of Democracy*. New York: Harper and Row.

Dowrick, Steve, and Duc-Tho Nguyen (1989), "OECD comparative economic growth 1950–1985: Catch-up and convergence," *American Economic Review*, vol. 79, 1010–1030.

Drazen, Allan (1984), "Tight money and inflation: Further results," *Journal of Monetary Economics*, vol. 15, 113–120.

Drazen, Allan (2000), *Political Economy in Macroeconomics*. Princeton, N.J.: Princeton University Press.

Drazen, Allan, and Nils Gottfries (1994), "Seniority rules and the persistence of unemployment," *Oxford Economic Papers*, vol. 46, 228–244.

Drazen, Allan, and Elhanan Helpman (1990), "Inflationary consequences of anticipated macroeconomic policies," *Review of Economic Studies*, vol. 57, 147–166.

Drèze, Jacques H. (1975), "Existence of an exchange equilibrium under price rigidities," *International Economic Review*, vol. 16, 301–320.

Drèze, Jacques H. (1991), *Underemployment Equilibria*. Cambridge: Cambridge University Press.

Drèze, Jacques H., and Christian Gollier (1993), "Risk sharing on the labour market and second-best wage rigidities," *European Economic Review*, vol. 37, 1457–1482.

Dunlop, John T. (1938), "The movement in real and money wage rates," *Economic Journal*, vol. 48, 413–434.

Dunlop, John T. (1944), *Wage Determination under Trade Unions*. New York: Macmillan.

Durlauf, Steven N., Paul A. Johnson, and Jonathan Temple (2005), "Growth econometrics," in P. Aghion and S. N. Durlauf (eds.), *Handbook of Economic Growth*, volume 1A. Amsterdam: North Holland.

Durlauf, Steven N., and Danny Quah (1999), "The new empirics of economic growth," in J. B. Taylor and M. Woodford (eds.), *Handbook of Macroeconomics*, volume 1A. Amsterdam: North Holland.

Eicher, Theo S., and Stephen J. Turnovsky (1999), "Non-scale models of economic growth," *Economic Journal*, vol. 109, 394–415.

Eisner, Robert, and Robert H. Strotz (1963), "Determinants of business investment," in Commission on Money and Credit (ed.), *Impacts of Monetary Policy*. Englewood Cliffs, N.J.: Prentice Hall.

Epstein, Larry G., and Stanley Zin (1989), "Substitution, risk aversion and the temporal behavior of consumption and asset returns I: A theoretical framework," *Econometrica*, vol. 57, 937–969.

Erceg, Christopher J., Dale W. Henderson, and Andrew T. Levin (2000), "Optimal monetary policy with staggered wage and price contracts," *Journal of Monetary Economics*, vol. 46, 281–313.

Erceg, Christopher J., and Andrew T. Levin (2003), "Imperfect credibility and inflation persistence," *Journal of Monetary Economics*, vol. 50, 915–944.

Ethier, Wilfred J. (1982), "National and international returns to scale in the modern theory of international trade," *American Economic Review*, vol. 72, 389–405.

Evans, George W. (1985), "Expectational stability and the multiple equilibria problem in rational expectations models," *Quarterly Journal of Economics*, vol. 100, 1217–1233.

Evans, George W., and Seppo Honkapohja (1999), "Learning dynamics," in J. B. Taylor and M. Woodford (eds.), *Handbook of Macroeconomics*, volume 1. Amsterdam: North Holland.

Evans, George W., and Seppo Honkapohja (2001), *Learning and Expectations in Macroeconomics*. Princeton, N.J.: Princeton University Press.

Evans, George W., and Seppo Honkapohja (2008), "Learning in Macroeconomics," in S. N. Durlauf and L. E. Blume (eds.), *The New Palgrave Dictionary of Economics*, 2nd edition. London: Palgrave Macmillan.

Farmer, Roger E. A. (1990), "RINCE preferences," *Quarterly Journal of Economics*, vol. 105, 43–60.

Farmer, Roger E. A. (1993), *The Macroeconomics of Self-Fulfilling Prophecies*. Cambridge, Mass.: MIT Press. Second edition, 1999.

Farmer, Roger E. A., and Jang-Ting Guo (1994), "Real business cycles and the animal spirits hypothesis," *Journal of Economic Theory*, vol. 63, 42–72.

Feldstein, Martin S. (1974), "Social security, induced retirement, and induced capital accumulation," *Journal of Political Economy*, vol. 82, 905–926.

Feldstein, Martin S. (1976), "Social security and saving: The extended life cycle theory," *American Economic Review*, vol. 66, papers and proceedings, 77–86.

Feldstein, Martin S., and Jeffrey Liebman (2002), "Social security," in A. Auerbach and M. Feldstein (eds.), *Handbook of Public Economics*, volume 4. Amsterdam: North Holland.

Fischer, Stanley (1977a), "Long-term contracts, rational expectations, and the optimal money supply rule," *Journal of Political Economy*, vol. 85, 191–205.

Fischer, Stanley (1977b), "Wage indexation and macroeconomic stability," *Carnegie Rochester Conference Series on Public Policy*, vol. 5, 107–147.

Fisher, Irving (1932), *Booms and Depressions*. New York: Adelphi.

Fisher, Irving (1933), "The debt-deflation theory of great depressions," *Econometrica*, vol. 1, 337–357.

Frankel, M. (1962), "The production function in allocation and growth: A synthesis," *American Economic Review*, vol. 52, 995–1022.

Friedman, Milton (1957), *A Theory of the Consumption Function*. Princeton, N.J.: Princeton University Press.

Friedman, Milton (1961), "The lag in effect of monetary policy," *Journal of Political Economy*, vol. 69, 447–466.

Friedman, Milton (1968), "The role of monetary policy," *American Economic Review*, vol. 58, 1–17.

Friedman, Milton (1969), "The optimum quantity of money," in M. Friedman (ed.), *The Optimum Quantity of Money and Other Essays*. London: Macmillan.

Fuerst, Timothy S. (1992), "Liquidity, loanable funds and real activity," *Journal of Monetary Economics*, vol. 29, 3–24.

Fuhrer, Jeff, and George Moore (1995), "Inflation persistence," *Quarterly Journal of Economics*, vol. 110, 127–159.

Gabisch, Günter, and Hans-Walter Lorenz (1987), *Business Cycle Theory*. Berlin: Springer-Verlag. Second edition, 1989.

Gabszewicz, Jean-Jaskold, and Jean-Philippe Vial (1972), "Oligopoly 'à la Cournot' in a general equilibrium analysis," *Journal of Economic Theory*, vol. 42, 381–400.

Gale, David (1973), "Pure exchange equilibrium of dynamic economic models," *Journal of Economic Theory*, vol. 6, 12–36.

Gale, Douglas, and Martin Hellwig (1985), "Incentive-compatible debt contracts: The one-period problem," *Review of Economic Studies*, vol. 52, 647–663.

Galor, Oded, and Harl E. Ryder (1989), "Existence, uniqueness and stability of equilibria in an overlapping-generations model with productive capital," *Journal of Economic Theory*, vol. 19, 360–375.

Gertler, Mark (1988), "Financial structure and aggregate economic activity: An overview," *Journal of Money, Credit and Banking*, vol. 20, 559–588.

Goldman, Steven M. (1972), "Hyperinflation and the rate of growth in the money supply," *Journal of Economic Theory*, vol. 5, 250–257.

Goodwin, Richard M. (1951), "The non-linear accelerator and the persistence of business cycles," *Econometrica*, vol. 19, 1–17.

Goodwin, Richard M. (1982), *Essays in Economic Dynamics*. New York: Macmillan.

Gordon, Donald F. (1974), "A neo-classical theory of Keynesian unemployment," *Economic Inquiry*, vol. 12, 431–459.

Gottfries, Nils, and Henrik Horn (1987), "Wage formation and the persistence of unemployment," *Economic Journal*, vol. 97, 877–884.

Gould, John P. (1968), "Adjustment costs in the theory of investment of the firm," *Review of Economic Studies*, vol. 35, 47–55.

Gourieroux, Christian, and Alain Monfort (1995), *Statistics and Econometric Models*. Cambridge: Cambridge University Press.

Gourieroux, Christian, and Alain Monfort (1996), *Time Series and Dynamic Models*. Cambridge: Cambridge University Press.

Grandmont, Jean-Michel (1985), "On endogenous competitive business cycles," *Econometrica*, vol. 53, 995–1045.

Grandmont, Jean-Michel, and Yves Younès (1973), "On the efficiency of a monetary equilibrium," *Review of Economic Studies*, vol. 40, 149–165.

Gray, Jo-Anna (1976), "Wage indexation: A macroeconomic approach," *Journal of Monetary Economics*, vol. 2, 221–235.

Gray, Jo-Anna (1978), "On indexation and contract length," *Journal of Political Economy*, vol. 86, 1–18.

Greenwald, Bruce, and Joseph Stiglitz (1993), "Financial markets imperfections and business cycles," *Quarterly Journal of Economics*, vol. 108, 77–114.

Grossman, Gene M., and Elhanan Helpman (1991a), "Quality ladders in the theory of growth," *Review of Economic Studies*, vol. 58, 43–61.

Grossman, Gene M., and Elhanan Helpman (1991b), *Innovation and Growth in the Global Economy*. Cambridge, Mass.: MIT Press.

Grossman, Gene M., and Elhanan Helpman (2001), *Special Interest Politics*. Cambridge, Mass.: MIT Press.

Grossman, Herschel I. (1972), "A choice-theoretic model of an income investment accelerator," *American Economic Review*, vol. 62, 630–641.

Guesnerie, Roger, and Michael Woodford (1992), "Endogenous fluctuations," in J. J. Laffont (ed.), *Advances in Economic Theory*. Cambridge: Cambridge University Press.

Guidotti, Pablo E., and Carlos A. Vegh (1993), "The optimal inflation tax when money reduces transactions costs," *Journal of Monetary Economics*, vol. 31, 189–205.

Guvenen, Fatih, and Hanno Lustig (2008a), "Consumption based asset pricing models (theory)," in S. N. Durlauf and L. E. Blume (eds.), *The New Palgrave Dictionary of Economics*, 2nd edition. London: Palgrave Macmillan.

Guvenen, Fatih, and Hanno Lustig (2008b), "Consumption based asset pricing models (empirical performance)," in S. N. Durlauf and L. E. Blume (eds.), *The New Palgrave Dictionary of Economics*, 2nd edition. London: Palgrave Macmillan.

Haavelmo, Trygve (1945), "Multiplier effects of a balanced budget," *Econometrica*, vol. 13, 311–318.

Hahm, Sangmoon (1987), "Information acquisition in an incomplete information model of business cycle," *Journal of Monetary Economics*, vol. 20, 123–140.

Hairault, Jean-Olivier, and Franck Portier (1993), "Money, new-Keynesian macroeconomics and the business cycle," *European Economic Review*, vol. 37, 1533–1568.

Hakansson, Nils H. (1970), "Optimal investment and consumption strategies under risk for a class of utility functions," *Econometrica*, vol. 38, 587–607.

Hall, Robert E. (1978), "Stochastic implications of the life cycle permanent income hypothesis: Theory and evidence," *Journal of Political Economy*, vol. 86, 971–987.

Hall, Robert E. (2005), "Employment fluctuations with equilibrium wage stickiness," *American Economic Review*, vol. 95, 50–65.

Hall, Robert E., and Dale Jorgenson (1967), "Tax policy and investment behavior," *American Economic Review*, vol. 57, 391–414.

Hansen, Gary D. (1985), "Indivisible labor and the business cycle," *Journal of Monetary Economics*, vol. 16, 309–327.

Harrod, Roy F. (1939), "An essay in dynamic theory," *Economic Journal*, vol. 49, 14–33.

Hart, Oliver D. (1982), "A model of imperfect competition with Keynesian features," *Quarterly Journal of Economics*, vol. 97, 109–138.

Hayashi, Fumio (1982), "Tobin's marginal q and average q: A neoclassical interpretation," *Econometrica*, vol. 50, 213–224.

Helpman, Elhanan (1981), "An exploration in the theory of exchange-rate regimes," *Journal of Political Economy*, vol. 89, 865–890.

Helpman, Elhanan (2004), *The Mystery of Economic Growth*. Cambridge, Mass.: Harvard University Press.

Helpman, Elhanan, and Efraim Sadka (1979), "Optimal financing of the government's budget: Taxes, bonds or money?," *American Economic Review*, vol. 69, 152–160.

Henderson, Dale, and Jinill Kim (1999), "Exact utilities under alternative monetary rules in a simple macro model with optimizing agents," *International Tax and Public Finance*, vol. 6, 507–535.

Hercowitz, Zvi, and Michael Sampson (1991), "Output, growth, the real wage, and employment fluctuations," *American Economic Review*, vol. 81, 1215–1237.

Heston, Alan, Robert Summers, and Bettina Aten (2009), "PennWorld Table, version 6.3," Center for International Comparison of Productivities, Incomes and Prices at the University of Pennsylvania, Philadelphia.

Hicks, John R. (1937), "Mr. Keynes and the 'Classics': A suggested interpretation," *Econometrica*, vol. 5, 147–59.

Hicks, John R. (1950), *A Contribution to the Theory of the Trade Cycle*. Oxford: Oxford University Press.

Hinich, Melvin J. (1977), "Equilibrium in spatial voting: The median voter result is an artifact," *Journal of Economic Theory*, vol. 18, 208–219.

Hirsch, Morris W., and Steven Smale (1974), *Differential Equations, Dynamical Systems and Linear Algebra*. New York: Academic Press.

Hirshleifer, Jack (1971), "The private and social value of information and the reward to inventive activity," *American Economic Review*, vol. 61, 561–574.

Hoel, Michael (1986), "Perfect equilibia in sequential bargaining games with non-linear utility functions," *Scandinavian Journal of Economics*, vol. 88, 383–400.

Holbrook, Robert S. (1972), "Optimal economic policy and the problem of instrument instability," *American Economic Review*, vol. 62, 57–65.

Hornstein, Andreas (1993), "Monopolistic competition, increasing returns to scale and the importance of productivity shocks," *Journal of Monetary Economics*, vol. 31, 299–316.

Hotelling, Harold (1929), "Stability in competition," *Economic Journal*, vol. 39, 41–57.

Howitt, Peter W. (1999), "Steady endogenous growth with population and R & D inputs growing," *Journal of Political Economy*, vol. 107, 715–730.

Howitt, Peter W. (2008), "Endogenous growth theory," in S. N. Durlauf and L. E. Blume (eds.), *The New Palgrave Dictionary of Economics*, 2nd edition. London: Palgrave Macmillan.

Howrey, E. Philip (1967), "Stabilization policy in linear stochastic systems," *Review of Economics and statistics*, vol. 49, 404–411.

Huffman, Gregory W. (1993), "An alternative neo-classical growth model with closed-form decisions rules," *Economics Letters*, vol. 42, 59–63.

Hunt, E. K., and Howard J. Sherman (1972), *Economics: An Introduction to Traditional and Radical Views*. New York: Harper and Row.

Inada, Kenichi (1964), "Some structural characteristics of turnpike theorems," *Review of Economic Studies*, vol 31, 43–58.

Intriligator, Michael D. (1971), *Mathematical Optimization and Economic Theory*. Englewood Cliffs, N.J.: Prentice Hall.

Iraola, Miguel A., and Manuel S. Santos (2008), "Speculative bubbles," in S. N. Durlauf and L. E. Blume (eds.), *The New Palgrave Dictionary of Economics*, 2nd edition. London: Palgrave Macmillan.

Ireland, Peter N. (1996), "The role of countercyclical monetary policy," *Journal of Political Economy*, vol. 104, 704–723.

Jackman, Richard, and Richard Layard (1986), "A wage-tax, worker subsidy policy for reducing the 'natural' rate of unemployment," in W. Beckerman (ed.), *Wage Ridity and Unemployment*. London: Gerald Duckworth.

Jacobsen, Hans-Jörgen, and Christian Schultz (1990), "A general equilibrium macro model with wage bargaining," *Scandinavian Journal of Economics*, vol. 92, 379–398.

Jaffee, Dwight, and Thomas Russell (1976), "Imperfect information, uncertainty and credit rationing," *Quarterly Journal of Economics*, vol. 90, 651–666.

Jaffee, Dwight, and Joseph Stiglitz (1990), "Credit rationing," in B. Friedman and F. H. Hahn (eds.), *Handbook of Monetary Economics*. Amsterdam: North Holland.

Jeanne, Olivier (1998), "Generating real persistent effects of monetary shocks: How much nominal rigidity do we really need?," *European Economic Review*, vol. 42, 1009–1032.

Jones, Charles I. (1995), "R&D-based models of economic growth," *Journal of Political Economy*, vol. 103, 758–784.

Jones, Charles I. (1997a), "Convergence revisited," *Journal of Economic Growth* vol. 2, 131–153.

Jones, Charles I. (1997b), "On the evolution of the world income distribution," *Journal of Economic Perspectives*, vol. 11, no. 3, 19–36.

Jones, Charles I. (1999), "Growth: With or without scale effects?," *American Economic Review*, vol. 89, papers and proceedings, 139–144.

Jones, Robert A. (1976), "The origin and development of media of exchange," *Journal of Political Economy*, vol. 84, 757–775.

Kahn, James A. (1987), "Inventories and the volatility of production," *American Economic Review*, vol. 77, 667–679.

Kahn, James A. (2008), "Inventory investment," in S. N. Durlauf and L. E. Blume (eds.), *The New Palgrave Dictionary of Economics*, 2nd edition. London: Palgrave Macmillan.

Kaldor, Nicholas (1940), "A model of the trade cycle," *Economic Journal*, vol. 50, 78–92.

Kashyap, Anil K. (1995), "Sticky prices: New evidence from retail catalogs," *Quarterly Journal of Economics*, vol. 110, 245–274.

Katz, Lawrence F. (1986), "Efficiency wage theories: A partial evaluation," *NBER Macroeconomics Annual*, vol. 1, 235–276.

Keeton, William (1979), *Equilibrium Credit Rationing*. New York: Garland.

Keynes, John Maynard (1936), *The General Theory of Employment, Interest and Money*. New York: Harcourt Brace.

Keynes, John Maynard (1937), "Alternative theories of the rate of interest," *Economic Journal*, vol. 47, 241–252.

Keynes, John Maynard (1939), "Relative movements of real wages and output," *Economic Journal*, vol. 49, 34–51.

Khan, Aubhik, Robert G. King, and Alexander L. Wolman (2003), "Optimal monetary policy," *Review of Economic Studies*, vol. 70, 825–860.

Killingsworth, M. R., and James J. Heckman (1986), "Female labor supply: A survey," in O. Ashenfelter and R. Layard (eds.), *Handbook of Labor Economics*, volume 1. Amsterdam: North Holland.

Kimball, Miles S. (1990), "Precautionary savings in the small and in the large," *Econometrica*, vol. 58, 53–73.

King, Robert G. (1982), "Monetary policy and the information content of prices," *Journal of Political Economy*, vol. 90, 247–279.

King, Robert G. (1983), "Interest rates, aggregate information, and monetary policy," *Journal of Monetary Economics*, vol. 12, 199–234.

King, Robert G., and Charles I. Plosser (1984), "Money, credit and prices in a real business cycle," *American Economic Review*, vol. 74, 363–380.

King, Robert G., Charles I. Plosser, and Sergio T. Rebelo (1988a), "Production, growth and business cycles, I: The basic neoclassical model," *Journal of Monetary Economics*, vol. 21, 195–232.

King, Robert G., Charles I. Plosser, and Sergio T. Rebelo (1988b), "Production, growth and business cycles, II: New directions," *Journal of Monetary Economics*, vol. 21, 309–341.

King, Robert G., and Sergio T. Rebelo (1999), "Resuscitating real business cycles," in J. B. Taylor and M. Woodford (eds.), *Handbook of Macroeconomics*, volume 1B. Amsterdam: North Holland.

King, Robert G., and Alexander L. Wolman (1999), "What should the monetary authority do when prices are sticky," in J. B. Taylor (ed.) *Monetary Policy Rules*. Chicago: University of Chicago Press.

Kiyotaki, Nobuhiro, and John Moore (1997), "Credit cycles," *Journal of Political Economy*, vol. 105, 211–248.

Kocherlakota, Narayana R. (1996), "The equity premium: It's still a puzzle," *Journal of Economic Literature*, vol. 34, 42–71.

Koopmans, Tjalling C. (1965), "On the concept of optimal economic growth," in *The Economic Approach to Development Planning*. Amsterdam: North Holland.

Kreps, David, and Evan L. Porteus (1978), "Temporal resolution of uncertainty and dynamic choice theory," *Econometrica*, vol. 46, 185–200.

Kydland, Finn E., editor (1995), *Business Cycle Theory*. Aldershot, UK: Edward Elgar.

Kydland, Finn E., and Edward Prescott (1977), "Rules rather than discretion: The inconsistency of optimal plans," *Journal of Political Economy*, vol. 87, 473–492.

Kydland, Finn E., and Edward Prescott, (1982), "Time to build and aggregate fluctuations," *Econometrica*, vol. 50, 1345–1370.

Lau, Sau-Him Paul (2002), "Further inspection of the stochastic growth model by an analytical approach," *Macroeconomic Dynamics*, vol. 6, 748–757.

Layard, Richard, Stephen Nickell, and Richard Jackman (1991), *Unemployment: Macroeconomic Performance and the Labour Market*. Oxford: Oxford University Press.

Ledyard, J. O. (1981), "The paradox of voting and candidate competition: A general equilibrium analysis," in A. L. Roth and J. Kagel (eds.), *The Handbook of Experimental Economics*. Princeton, N.J.: Princeton University Press.

Ledyard, J. O. (1984), "The pure theory of large two-candidate elections," *Public Choice*, vol. 44, 7–41.

Leeper, Eric M. (1991), "Equilibria under 'active' and 'passive' monetary and fiscal policies," *Journal of Monetary Economics*, vol. 27, 129–147.

Leibenstein, Harvey (1957), *Economic Backwardness and Economic Growth: Studies in the Theory of Economic Development*. New York: Wiley.

Leijonhufvud, Axel (1968), *On Keynesian Economics and the Economics of Keynes*. Oxford: Oxford University Press.

Leland, Hayne E. (1968) "Saving and uncertainty: The precautionary demand for saving," *Quarterly Journal of Economics*, vol 82, 465–473.

Léonard, Daniel, and Ngo van Long (1992), *Optimal Control Theory and Static Optimization in Economics*. Cambridge: Cambridge University Press.

Leontief, Wassily (1946), "The pure theory of the guaranteed annual wage contract," *Journal of Political Economy*, vol. 54, 76–79.

Lindbeck, Assar, and Dennis J. Snower (1986), "Wage setting, unemployment and insider-outsider relations," *American Economic Review*, vol. 76, 235–239.

Lindbeck, Assar, and Dennis J. Snower (1987), "Union activity, unemployment persistence and wage-employment ratchets," *European Economic Review*, vol. 31, 157–167.

Lindbeck, Assar, and Dennis J. Snower (1988), *The Insider-Outsider Theory of Employment and Unemployment*. Cambridge, Mass.: MIT Press.

Lippman, Steven A., and John J. McCall (1976), "The economics of job search: A survey," *Economic Inquiry*, vol. 14, 347–368.

Liviatan, Nissan (1984), "Tight money and inflation," *Journal of Monetary Economics*, vol. 13, 5–15.

Long, John B., and Charles I. Plosser (1983), "Real business cycles," *Journal of Political Economy*, vol. 91, 39–69.

Lucas, Robert E. Jr. (1967), "Adjustment costs and the theory of supply," *Journal of Political Economy*, vol. 75, 321–334.

Lucas, Robert E. Jr. (1972), "Expectations and the neutrality of money," *Journal of Economic Theory*, vol. 4, 103–124.

Lucas, Robert E. Jr. (1973), "Some international evidence on output-inflation trade-offs," *American Economic Review*, vol. 63, 326–334.

Lucas, Robert E. Jr. (1976), "Econometric policy evaluation: A critique," in K. Brunner and A. H. Meltzer (eds.), *The Phillips Curve and Labor Markets*, vol. 1 of *Carnegie-Rochester Conference Series on Public Policy*, Amsterdam: North Holland.

Lucas, Robert E. Jr. (1978), "Asset prices in an exchange economy," *Econometrica*, vol. 46, 1429–1445.

Lucas, Robert E. Jr. (1982), "Interest rates and currency prices in a two-country world," *Journal of Monetary Economics*, vol. 10, 335–359.

Lucas, Robert E. Jr. (1986), "Principles of fiscal and monetary policy," *Journal of Monetary Economics*, vol. 17, 117–134.

Lucas, Robert E. Jr. (1987), *Models of Business Cycles*. Oxford: Basil Blackwell.

Lucas, Robert E. Jr. (1988), "On the mechanics of economic development," *Journal of Monetary Economics*, vol. 22, 3–42.

Lucas, Robert E. Jr. (1990), "Liquidity and interest rates," *Journal of Economic Theory*, vol. 50, 237–264.

Lucas, Robert E. Jr., and Leonard A. Rapping (1969), "Real wages, employment and inflation," *Journal of Political Economy*, vol. 77, 721–754.

Lucas, Robert E. Jr., and Thomas J. Sargent, editors (1981), *Rational Expectations and Econometric Practice*. London: George Allen and Unwin.

Maddison, Angus (1982), *Phases of Capitalist Development*. Oxford: Oxford University Press.

Maddison, Angus (1989), *The World Economy in the Twentieth Century*. Paris: OECD.

Maddison, Angus (1991), *Dynamic Forces in Capitalist Development*. Oxford: Oxford University Press.

Maddison, Angus (1995), *Monitoring the World Economy, 1820–1992*. Paris: OECD.

Maddison, Angus (2001), *The World Economy: A Millennial Perspective* Paris: OECD.

Mangasarian, O. L. (1966), "Sufficient conditions for the optimal control of nonlinear systems," *SIAM Journal of Control*, vol. 4, 139–152.

Mankiw, N. Gregory (1985), "Small menu costs and large business cycles: A macroeconomic model of monopoly," *Quarterly Journal of Economics*, vol. 100, 529–539.

Mankiw, N. Gregory, and Ricardo Reis (2002), "Sticky information versus sticky prices: A proposal to replace the new-Keynesian Phillips curve," *Quarterly Journal of Economics*, vol. 117, 1295–1328.

Mankiw, N. Gregory, David Romer, and David N. Weil (1992), "A contribution to the empirics of economic growth," *Quarterly Journal of Economics*, vol. 107, 407–437.

McCallum, Bennett T. (1981), "Price level determinacy with an interest rate policy rule and rational expectations," *Journal of Monetary Economics*, vol. 8, 319–329.

McCallum, Bennett T. (1984), "A linearized version of Lucas's neutrality model," *Canadian Journal of Economics*, vol. 17, 138–145.

McCallum, Bennett T. (1986), "Some issues concerning interest rate pegging, price level determinacy and the real bills doctrine," *Journal of Monetary Economics*, vol. 17, 135–160.

McCallum, Bennett T. (1989a), "Real business cycle models," in R. J. Barro (ed.), *Modern Business Cycle Theory*. Cambridge, Mass.: Harvard University Press.

McCallum, Bennett T. (1989b), *Monetary Economics: Theory and Policy*. New York: Macmillan.

McCallum, Bennett T. (1994), "A semi-classical model of price level adjustment," *Carnegie Rochester Conference Series on Public Policy*, vol. 41, 251–284.

McCallum, Bennett T., and Marvin Goodfriend (1987), "Demand for money: Theoretical studies," in J. Eatwell, M. Milgate, and P. Newman (eds.), *The New Palgrave Dictionary of Economics*. London: Macmillan.

McCallum, Bennett T., and Edward Nelson (1999), "Performance of operational policy rules in an estimated semiclassical structural model," in J. B. Taylor (ed.), *Monetary Policy Rules*. Chicago: University of Chicago Press.

McDonald, Ian M., and Robert M. Solow (1981), "Wage bargaining and unemployment," *American Economic Review*, vol. 71, 896–908.

Mehra, Rajnish, and Edward C. Prescott (1985), "The equity premium: A puzzle," *Journal of Monetary Economics*, vol. 15, 145–161.

Merton, Robert C. (1969), "Lifetime portfolio selection under uncertainty: The continuous time case," *Review of Economics and Statistics*, vol. 51, 247–257.

Merton, Robert C. (1971), "Optimum consumption and portfolio rules in a continuous time model," *Journal of Economic Theory*, vol. 3, 373–413.

Merz, Monika (1995), "Search in the labor market and the real business cycle," *Journal of Monetary Economics*, vol. 36, 269–300.

Michel, Philippe (1982), "On the transversality condition in infinite horizon optimal problems," *Econometrica*, vol. 50, 975–985.

Michel, Philippe (1990), "Some clarifications on the transversality condition," *Econometrica*, vol. 58, 705–723.

Miller, Preston J., editor (1994), *The Rational Expectations Revolution: Readings from the Front Line*. Cambridge, Mass.: MIT Press.

Miller, Preston J., and Thomas Sargent (1984), "A reply to Darby," *Federal Reserve Bank of Minneapolis Quarterly Review*, spring 1984.

Mills, Edwin S. (1962), *Price, Output and Inventory Policy*. New York: Wiley.

Mortensen, Dale T. (1986), "Job search and labor market analysis," in O. Ashenfelter and R. Layard (eds.), *Handbook of Labor Economics*, volume 2. Amsterdam: North Holland.

Mortensen, Dale T., and Christopher A. Pissarides (1999a), "New developments in models of search in the labor market," in O. Ashenfelter and D. Card (eds.), *Handbook of Labor Economics*, volume 3B. Amsterdam: North Holland.

Mortensen, Dale T., and Christopher A. Pissarides (1999b), "Job reallocation, employment fluctuations and unemployment," in J. B. Taylor and M. Woodford (eds.) *Handbook of Macroeconomics*, volume 1B. Amsterdam: North Holland.

Musgrave, Richard A. (2008), "Public finance," in S. N. Durlauf and L. E. Blume (eds.), *The New Palgrave Dictionary of Economics*, 2nd edition. London: Palgrave Macmillan.

Muth, John F. (1960), "Optimal properties of exponentially weighted forecasts," *Journal of the American Statistical Association*, vol. 55, 290–306.

Muth, John F. (1961), "Rational expectations and the theory of price movements," *Econometrica*, vol. 29, 315–335.

Nash, John F.(1950), "The bargaining problem," *Econometrica*, vol. 18, 155–162.

Nash, John F. (1953), "Two-person cooperative games," *Econometrica*, vol. 21, 128–140.

Negishi, Takashi (1961), "Monopolistic competition and general equilibrium," *Review of Economic Studies*, vol. 28, 199–228.

Negishi, Takashi (1977), "Existence of an under-employment equilibrium," in G. Schwödiauer (ed.), *Equilibrium and Disequilibrium in Economic Theory*. Boston: Reidel.

Negishi, Takashi (1979), *Microeconomic Foundations of Keynesian Macroeconomics*. Amsterdam: North Holland.

Nickell, Stephen J., and Martyn J. Andrews (1983), "Unions, real wages and employment in Britain 1951–79," *Oxford Economic Papers*, vol. 35, 507–530.

Niehans, Jürg (1969), "Money in a static theory of optimal payments arrangements," *Journal of Money, Credit and Banking*, vol. 1, 706–726.

Niehans, Jürg (1978), *The Theory of Money*. Baltimore: Johns Hopkins University Press.

Nishimura, Kiyohiko G. (1986), "Rational expectations and price rigidity in a monopolistically competitive market," *Review of Economic Studies*, vol. 53, 283–92.

Nishimura, Kiyohiko G. (1992), *Imperfect Competition, Differential Information and Microfoundations of Macroeconomics*. Oxford: Oxford University Press.

O'Driscoll, Gerald P. Jr. (1977), "The Ricardian nonequivalence theorem," *Journal of Political Economy*, vol. 85, 207–210.

Ostroy, Joseph (1973), "The informational efficiency of monetary exchange," *American Economic Review*, vol. 63, 597–610.

Ostroy, Joseph, and Ross Starr (1974), "Money and the decentralization of exchange," *Econometrica*, vol. 42, 1093–1114.

Oswald, Andrew J. (1982), "The microeconomic theory of the trade-union," *Economic Journal*, vol. 92, 576–595.

Oswald, Andrew J. (1985), "The economic theory of trade unions: An introductory survey," *Scandinavian Journal of Economics*, vol. 87, 160–193.

Parkin, Michael (1986), "The output-inflation trade-off when prices are costly to change," *Journal of Political Economy*, vol. 94, 200–224.

Patinkin, Don (1956), *Money, Interest and Prices*. New York: Harper and Row. Second edition, 1965.

Pencavel, John (1986), "Labor supply of men: A survey," in O. Ashenfelter and R. Layard (eds.), *Handbook of Labor Economics*, volume 1. Amsterdam: North Holland.

Persson, Torsten, and Lars E. O. Svensson (1989), "Why a stubborn conservative would run a deficit: Policy with time-inconsistent preferences," *Quarterly Journal of Economics*, vol. 104, 325–345.

Persson, Torsten, and Guido Tabellini (1990), *Macroeconomic Policy, Credibility and Politics*. Chur: Harwood Academic Publishers.

Persson, Torsten, and Guido Tabellini (1993), "Designing institutions for monetary stability," *Carnegie Rochester Conferences Series on Public Policy*, vol. 39, 53–84.

Persson, Torsten, and Guido Tabellini, editors (1994), *Monetary and Fiscal Policy. Volume 1: Credibility*. Cambridge, Mass.: MIT Press.

Persson, Torsten, and Guido Tabellini (1999), "Political economics and macroeconomic policy," in J. B. Taylor and M. Woodford (eds.), *Handbook of Macroeconomics*, volume 1A. Amsterdam: North Holland.

Persson, Torsten, and Guido Tabellini (2000), *Political Economics. Explaining Economic Policy*. Cambridge, Mass.: MIT Press.

Petrongolo, Barbara, and Christopher A. Pissarides (2001), "Looking into the black box: A survey of the matching function," *Journal of Economic Literature*, vol. 39, 390–431.

Phelps, Edmund S. (1961), "The golden rule of accumulation: A fable for growthmen," *American Economic Review*, vol. 51, 638–643.

Phelps, Edmund S. (1966), *Golden Rules of Economic Growth*. New York: Norton.

Phelps, Edmund S. (1967), "Phillips curves, expectations of inflation and optimal unemployment over time," *Economica*, vol. 34, 254–281.

Phelps, Edmund S. (1968), "Money-wage dynamics and labor market equilibrium," *Journal of Political Economy*, vol. 76, 678–711.

Phelps, Edmund S. (1973), "Inflation in the theory of public finance," *Swedish Journal of Economics*, vol. 75, 67–82.

Phelps, Edmund S. (1978), "Disinflation without recession: Adaptive guideposts and monetary policy," *Weltwirtschaftliches Archiv*, vol. 114, 783–809.

Phelps, Edmund S., and John B. Taylor (1977), "Stabilizing powers of monetary policy under rational expectations," *Journal of Political Economy*, vol. 85, 163–190.

Phillips, A. W. (1958), "The relationship between unemployment and the rate of change of money wages in the United Kingdom, 1861–1957," *Economica*, vol. 25, 283–299.

Pigou, Arthur C. (1943), "The classical stationary state," *Economic Journal*, vol. 53, 343–351.

Pissarides, Christopher A. (1990), *Equilibrium Unemployment Theory*. Cambridge, Mass.: MIT Press. Second edition, 2000.

Plosser, Charles I. (1989), "Understanding business cycles," *Journal of Economic Perspectives*, vol. 3, 51–77.

Poole, William (1970), "Optimal choice of monetary instruments in a simple stochastic macro model," *Quarterly Journal of Economics*, vol. 84, 197–216.

Portes, Richard (1981), "Macroeconomic equilibrium and disequilibrium in centrally planned economies," *Economic Inquiry*, vol. 19, 559–758.

Pratt, John W. (1964), "Risk aversion in the small and in the large," *Econometrica*, vol. 32, 122–136.

Pritchett, Lant (1997), "Divergence, big time," *Journal of Economic Perspectives*, vol. 11, 3–17.

Quah, Danny T. (1996a), "Empirics for economic growth and convergence," *European Economic Review*, vol. 40, 1353–1375.

Quah, Danny T. (1996b), "Twin peaks: Growth and convergence in models of distribution dynamics," *Economic Journal*, vol. 106, 1045–1055.

Ramey, Valerie A., and Kenneth D. West (1999), "Inventories," in J. B. Taylor and M. Woodford (eds.), *Handbook of Macroeconomics*, volume 1B. Amsterdam: North Holland.

Ramsey, Frank P. (1927), "A contribution to the theory of taxation," *Economic Journal*, vol. 37, 47–61.

Ramsey, Frank P. (1928), "A mathematical theory of saving," *Economic Journal*, vol. 38, 543–559.

Rebelo, Sergio (1991), "Long-run policy analysis and long-run growth," *Journal of Political Economy*, vol. 99, 500–521.

Rebelo, Sergio (2005), "Real business cycles models: Past, present and future," *Scandinavian Journal of Economics*, vol. 107, 217–238.

Roberts, John M. (1995), "New Keynesian economics and the Phillips curve," *Journal of Money, Credit and Banking*, vol. 27, 975–984.

Roberts, Kevin (1977), "Voting over income tax schedules," *Journal of Public Economics*, vol. 8, 329–340.

Rogerson, Richard (1988), "Indivisible labor, lotteries and equilibrium," *Journal of Monetary Economics*, vol. 21, 3–16.

Rogerson, Richard, Robert Shimer, and Randall Wright (2005), "Search-theoretic models of the labor market: A survey," *Journal of Economic Literature*, vol. 43, 959–988.

Rogoff, Kenneth (1985), "The optimal degree of commitment to an intermediate monetary target," *Quarterly Journal of Economics*, vol. 100, 1169–1189.

Rogoff, Kenneth (1989), "Reputation, coordination and monetary policy," in R. J. Barro (ed.), *Modern Business Cycle Theory*. Cambridge, Mass.: Harvard University Press.

Romer, Paul M. (1986), "Increasing returns and long-run growth," *Journal of Political Economy*, vol. 94, 1002–1037.

Romer, Paul M. (1987), "Growth based on increasing returns due to specialization," *American Economic Review*, vol. 77, papers and proceedings, 56–62.

Romer, Paul M. (1990), "Endogenous technical change," *Journal of Political Economy*, vol. 98, supplement, 71–102.

Romer, Paul M. (1994), "The origins of endogenous growth," *Journal of Economic Perspectives*, vol. 8, 3–22.

Romer, T. (1975), "Individual welfare, majority voting and the properties of a linear income tax," *Journal of Public Economics*, vol. 7, 163–168.

Rose, Hugh (1967), "On the non-linear theory of the employment cycle," *Review of Economic Studies*, vol. 34, 153–173.

Rosen, Sherwin (1985), "Implicit contracts: A survey," *Journal of Economic Literature*, vol. 23, 1144–1175.

Rosen, Sherwin (1994), *Implicit Contract Theory*. Aldershot: Edward Elgar.

Rotemberg, Julio J. (1982a), "Monopolistic price adjustment and agregate output," *Review of Economic Studies*, vol. 44, 517–531.

Rotemberg, Julio J. (1982b), "Sticky prices in the United States," *Journal of Political Economy*, vol. 90, 1187–1211.

Rotemberg, Julio J. (1983), "Aggregate consequences of fixed costs of price adjustments," *American Economic Review*, vol. 73, 433–436.

Rotemberg, Julio J. (1987), "The new-Keynesian microfoundations," *NBER Macroeconomics Annual*, vol. 2, 69–104.

Rotemberg, Julio J., and Michael Woodford (1992), "Oligopolistic pricing and the effects of aggregate demand on economic activity," *Journal of Political Economy*, vol. 100, 1153–1207.

Rotemberg, Julio J., and Michael Woodford (1995), "Dynamic general equilibrium models with imperfectly competitive product markets," in T. F. Cooley (ed.), *Frontiers of Business Cycle Research*. Princeton, N.J.: Princeton University Press.

Rotemberg, Julio J., and Michael Woodford (1997), "An optimization based econometric framework for the evaluation of monetary policy," *NBER Macroeconomics Annual*, vol. 12, 297–346.

Rotemberg, Julio J., and Michael Woodford (1999), "Interest rate rules in an estimated sticky price model," in J. B. Taylor (ed.), *Monetary Policy Rules*. Chicago: University of Chicago Press.

Rothschild, Michael, and Joseph E. Stiglitz (1970), "Increasing risk: I. A definition," *Journal of Economic Theory*, vol. 2, 225–243.

Rubinstein, Ariel (1982), "Perfect equilibrium in a bargaining model," *Econometrica*, vol. 50, 97–109.

Sala-i-Martin, Xavier X. (1996), "The classical approach to convergence analysis," *Economic Journal*, vol. 106, 1019–1036.

Samuelson, Paul A. (1939), "Interaction between the multiplier analysis and the principle of acceleration," *Review of Economics and Statistics*, vol. 21, 75–78.

Samuelson, Paul A. (1958), "An exact consumption-loan model of interest with or without the social contrivance of money," *Journal of Political Economy*, vol. 66, 467–482.

Samuelson, Paul A. (1967), "A turnpike refutation of the golden rule in a welfare-maximizing many-year plan," in K. Shell (ed.), *Essays on the Theory of Optimal Economic Growth*. Cambridge, Mass.: MIT Press.

Samuelson, Paul A. (1968), "The two-part golden rule deduced as the asymptotic turnpike of catenary motions," *Western Economic Journal*, vol. 6, 85–89.

Samuelson, Paul A. (1969), "Lifetime portfolio selection by dynamic stochastic programming," *Review of Economics and Statistics*, vol. 51, 239–246.

Samuelson, Paul A. (1975), "Optimum social security in a life-cycle growth model," *International Economic Review*, vol. 16, 539–544.

Samuelson, Paul A., and Robert M. Solow (1960), "Analytical aspects of anti-inflation policy," *American Economic Review*, vol. 50, 177–194.

Sargent, Thomas J., and Neil Wallace (1973), "The stability of models of money and growth with perfect foresight," *Econometrica*, vol. 41, 1043–1048.

Sargent, Thomas J., and Neil Wallace (1975), "Rational expectations, the optimal monetary instrument and the optimal money supply rule," *Journal of Political Economy*, vol. 83, 241–254.

Sargent, Thomas J., and Neil Wallace (1976), "Rational expectations and the theory of monetary policy," *Journal of Monetary Economics*, vol. 2, 169–183.

Sargent, Thomas J., and Neil Wallace (1981), "Some unpleasant monetarist arithmetic," *Federal Reserve Bank of Minneapolis Quarterly Review*, fall, 1–17.

Sarkovskii, A. (1964), "Coexistence of cycles of a continuous map of the line into itself," *Ukrainskyi Matematychnyi Zhurnal*, vol. 16, 61–71.

Schinasi, Garry (1982), "Fluctuations in a dynamic intermediate-run IS-LM model: Applications of the Poincaré-Bendixson theorem," *Journal of Economic Theory*, vol. 28, 369–375.

Schmitt-Grohe, Stephanie, and Martin Uribe (2004), "Optimal fiscal and monetary policy under sticky prices," *Journal of Economic Theory*, vol. 114, 198–230.

Segerstrom, Paul S. (1998), "Endogenous growth without scale effects," *American Economic Review*, vol. 88, 1290–1310.

Segerstrom, Paul S., T.C. A. Anant, and Elias Dinopoulos (1990), "A Schumpeterian model of the product life cycle," *American Economic Review*, vol. 80, 1077–1091.

Seierstad, Atle, and Knut Sydsaeter (1987), *Optimal Control Theory with Economic Applications*. Amsterdam: North Holland.

Selten, Reinhard (1975), "Reexamination of the perfectness concept for equilibrium points in extensive games," *International Journal of Game Theory*, vol. 4, 25–55.

Shapiro, Carl, and Joseph E. Stiglitz (1984), "Equilibrium unemployment as a worker discipline device," *American Economic Review*, vol. 74, 433–444.

Shell, Karl (1977), "Monnaie et allocation intertemporelle," *Séminaire d'économétrie*. Paris: CNRS.

Shell, Karl (2008), "Sunspot equilibrium," in S. N. Durlauf and L. E. Blume (eds.), *The New Palgrave Dictionary of Economics*, 2nd edition. London: Palgrave Macmillan.

Sheshinski, Eytan, and Yoram Weiss (1977), "Inflation and costs of price adjustment," *Review of Economic Studies*, vol. 44, 287–303.

Shimer, Robert (2005), "The cyclical behavior of equilibrium unemployment and vacancies," *American Economic Review*, vol. 95, 25–49.

Sidrauski, Miguel (1967), "Rational choice and patterns of growth in a monetary economy," *American Economic Review*, vol. 57, supplement, 534–544.

Siegel, Jeremy J., and Richard Thaler (1997), "Anomalies: The equity premium puzzle," *Journal of Economic Perspectives*, vol. 11, 191–200.

Silvestre, Joaquim (1982), "Fixprice analysis in exchange economies," *Journal of Economic Theory*, vol. 26, 28–58.

Silvestre, Joaquim (1983), "Fixprice analysis in productive economies," *Journal of Economic Theory*, vol. 30, 401–409.

Silvestre, Joaquim (1993), "The market-power foundations of macroeconomic policy," *Journal of Economic Literature*, vol. 31, 105–141.

Silvestre, Joaquim (1995), "Market power in macroeconomic models: New developments," *Annales d'Economie et de Statistique*, no. 37–38, 319–356.

Simon, Herbert A. (1956), "Dynamic programming under uncertainty with a quadratic criterion function," *Econometrica*, vol. 24, 74–81.

Sims, Christopher A. (1994), "A simple model for the determination of the price level and the interaction of monetary and fiscal policy," *Economic Theory*, vol. 4, 381–399.

Singer, D. (1978), "Stable orbits and bifurcations of maps of the interval," *SIAM Journal of Applied Mathematics*, vol. 35, 260–267.

Singleton, Kenneth J. (1990), "Specification and estimation of intertemporal asset pricing models," in B. M. Friedman and F. H. Hahn (eds.), *Handbook of Monetary Economics*. Amsterdam: North Holland.

Siu, Henry E. (2004), "Optimal fiscal and monetary policy with sticky prices," *Journal of Monetary Economics*, vol. 51, 575–607.

Smets, Frank, and Raf Wouters (2003), "An estimated dynamic stochastic general equilibrium model of the euro area," *Journal of the European Economic Association*, vol. 1, 1123–1175.

Smith, R. Todd (1992), "The cyclical behavior of prices," *Journal of Money, Credit and Banking*, vol. 24, 413–430.

Smulders, Sjak, and Theo van de Klundert (1995), "Imperfect competition, concentration and growth with firm-specific R&D," *European Economic Review*, vol. 39, 139–160.

Sneessens, Henri R. (1987), "Investment and the inflation-unemployment tradeoff in a macroeconomic rationing model with monopolistic competition," *European Economic Review*, vol. 31, 781–808.

Snower, Dennis (1983), "Imperfect competition, unemployment and crowding out," *Oxford Economic Papers*, vol. 35, 569–584.

Solow, Robert M. (1956), "A contribution to the theory of economic growth," *Quarterly Journal of Economics*, vol. 70, 65–94.

Solow, Robert M. (1957), "Technical change and the aggregate production function," *Review of Economics and Statistics*, vol. 39, 312–320.

Solow, Robert M. (1960), "Investment and technical progress," in K. J. Arrow, S. Karlin and P. Suppes (eds.), *Mathematical Methods in the Social Sciences*. Stanford: Stanford University Press.

Solow, Robert M. (1979), "Another possible source of wage stickiness," *Journal of Macroeconomics*, vol. 1, 79–82.

Solow, Robert M., and Joseph Stiglitz (1968), "Output, employment and wages in the short run," *Quarterly Journal of Economics*, vol. 82, 537–560.

Stachurski, John (2009), *Economic Dynamics: Theory and Computation*. Cambridge, Mass.: MIT Press.

Stiglitz, Joseph E., and Andrew Weiss (1981), "Credit rationing in markets with imperfect information," *American Economic Review*, vol. 71, 393–410.

Summers, Robert, and Alan Heston (1991), "The Penn world table (mark 5): An expanded set of international comparisons, 1950–1988," *Quarterly Journal of Economics*, vol. 106, 327–368.

Svensson, Lars E. O. (1985), "Money and asset prices in a cash-in-advance economy," *Journal of Political Economy*, vol. 93, 919–944.

Svensson, Lars E. O. (1986), "Sticky goods prices, flexible asset prices, monopolistic competition and monetary policy," *Review of Economic Studies*, vol. 53, 385–405.

Svensson, Lars E. O. (1997), "Inflation forecast targeting: implementing and monitoring inflation targets," *European Economic Review*, vol. 41, 1111–1146.

Svensson, Lars E. O. (1999a), "Price-level targeting versus inflation targeting: A free lunch?," *Journal of Money, Credit and Banking*, vol. 31, no. 3, 277–295.

Svensson, Lars E. O. (1999b), "Inflation targeting as a monetary policy rule," *Journal of Monetary Economics*, vol. 43, 607–654.

Svensson, Lars E. O. (2002), "Inflation targeting: Should it be modeled as an instrument rule or a targeting rule?," *European Economic Review*, vol. 46, 771–780.

Svensson, Lars E. O. (2003), "What is wrong with Taylor rules? Using judgment in monetary policy through targeting rules," *Journal of Economic Literature*, vol. 41, 426–477.

Svensson, Lars E. O., and Michael Woodford (2005), "Implementing optimal policy through inflation-forecast targeting," in B. S. Bernanke and M. Woodford (eds.), *The Inflation-Targeting Debate*. Chicago: University of Chicago Press.

Swan, Trevor W. (1956), "Economic growth and capital accumulation," *Economic Record*, vol. 32, 334–361.

Sydsaeter, Knut, Arne Strom, and Peter Berck (2000), *Economists' Mathematical Manual*, 3rd edition. Berlin: Springer-Verlag.

Tabellini, Guido, and Alberto Alesina (1990), "Voting on the budget deficit," *American Economic Review*, vol. 80, 37–49.

Tarshis, Lorie (1939), "Changes in real and money wage rates," *Economic Journal*, vol. 49, 150–154.

Taylor, John B. (1979), "Staggered wage setting in a macro model," *American Economic Review*, vol. 69, 108–113.

Taylor, John B. (1980), "Aggregate dynamics and staggered contracts," *Journal of Political Economy*, vol. 88, 1–23.

Taylor, John B. (1983), "Union wage settlements during a disinflation," *American Economic Review*, vol. 73, 981–993.

Taylor, John B. (1993), "Discretion versus policy rules in practice," *Carnegie-Rochester Conference Series on Public Policy*, vol. 39, 195–214.

Taylor, John B. (1998), "Monetary policy and the long boom," *Federal Reserve Bank of Saint-Louis Review*, vol. 80, no. 6, 3–11.

Taylor, John B. (1999), "Staggered price and wage setting in macroeconomics," in J. B. Taylor and M. Woodford (eds.), *Handbook of Macroeconomics*, volume 1B. Amsterdam: North Holland.

Temple, Jonathan (1999), "The new growth evidence," *Journal of Economic Literature*, vol. 37, 112–156.

Theil, Henri (1957), "A note on certainty equivalence in dynamic planning," *Econometrica*, vol. 25, 346–349.

Tirole, Jean (1985), "Asset bubbles and overlapping generations," *Econometrica*, vol. 53, 1071–1100.

Tobin, James (1956), "The interest-elasticity of transactions demand for cash," *Review of Economics and Statistics*, vol. 38, 241–247.

Townsend, Robert (1979), "Optimal contracts and competitive markets with costly state verification," *Journal of Economic Theory*, vol. 21, 265–293.

Treadway, A. B. (1969), "On rational entrepreneurial behavior and the demand for investment," *Review of Economic Studies*, vol. 36, 227–239.

Trigari, Antonella (2009), "Equilibrium unemployment, job flows, and inflation dynamics," *Journal of Money, Credit and Banking*, vol. 41, 1–33.

Turnovsky, Stephen J. (1980), "The choice of monetary instrument under alternative forms of price expectations," *Manchester School*, vol. 48, 39–62.

Uzawa, Hirofumi (1965), "Optimum technical change in an aggregative model of economic growth," *International Economic Review*, vol. 6, 12–31.

Van de Klundert, Theo, and Sjak Smulders (1997), "Growth, competition and welfare," *Scandinavian Journal of Economics*, vol. 99, 99–118.

Veendorp, E. C. H. (1970), "General equilibrium theory for a barter economy," *Western Economic Journal*, vol. 8, 1–23.

Vestin, David (2006), "Price-level versus inflation targeting," *Journal of Monetary Economics*, vol. 53, 1361–1376.

Von Neumann, John, and Oskar Morgenstern (1944), *Theory of Games and Economic Behavior*. Princeton, N.J.: Princeton University Press

Wallace, Neil (1992), "Lucas's signal extraction model: A finite state exposition with aggregate real shocks," *Journal of Monetary Economics*, vol. 30, 433–447.

Walras, Léon (1874), *Eléments d'économie politique pure*. Lausanne: Corbaz. London: Allen and Unwin. Definitive edition translated by William Jaffe: *Elements of pure economics* (1954).

Walsh, Carl E. (1995), "Optimal contracts for central bankers," *American Economic Review*, vol. 85, 150–167.

Walsh, Carl E. (1998), *Monetary Theory and Policy*. Cambridge, Mass.: MIT Press. Second edition, 2003.

Weil, Philippe (1987), "Permanent budget deficits and inflation," *Journal of Monetary Economics*, vol. 20, 393–410.

Weil, Philippe (1989a), "Overlapping families of infinitely-lived agents," *Journal of Public Economics*, vol. 38, 183–198.

Weil, Philippe (1989b), "The equity premium puzzle and the risk-free rate puzzle," *Journal of Monetary Economics*, vol. 24, 401–421.

Weil, Philippe (1990), "Nonexpected utility in macroeconomics," *Quarterly Journal of Economics*, vol. 105, 29–42.

Weil, Philippe (1991), "Is money net wealth?," *International Economic Review*, vol. 32, 37–53.

Weil, Philippe (1992), "Equilibrium asset prices with undiversifiable labor income risk," *Journal of Economic Dynamics and Control*, vol. 16, 969–990.

Weiss, Andrew (1991), *Efficiency Wages: Models of Unemployment, Layoffs and Wage Dispersion*. Oxford: Oxford University Press.

Weiss, Laurence (1980), "The role for active monetary policy in a rational expectations model," *Journal of Political Economy*, vol. 88, 221–233.

Weitzman, Martin L. (1985), "The simple macroeconomics of profit sharing," *American Economic Review*, vol. 75, 937–952.

Woodford, Michael (1990a), "Learning to believe in sunspots," *Econometrica*, vol. 58, 277–307.

Woodford, Michael (1990b), "The optimum quantity of money," in B. F. Friedman and F. H. Hahn (eds.), *Handbook of Monetary Economics*. Amsterdam: North Holland.

Woodford, Michael (1994), "Monetary policy and price level determinacy in a cash-in-advance economy," *Economic Theory*, vol. 4, 345–380.

Woodford, Michael (1995), "Price level determinacy without control of a monetary aggregate," *Carnegie-Rochester Conference Series on Public Policy*, vol. 43, 1–46.

Woodford, Michael (2003), *Interest and Prices: Foundations of a Theory of Monetary Policy*. Princeton, N.J.: Princeton University Press.

Yaari, Menahem E. (1965), "Uncertain lifetime, life insurance, and the theory of the consumer," *Review of Economic Studies*, vol. 32, 137–150.

Yellen, Janet L. (1984), "Efficiency wage models of unemployment," *American Economic Review*, vol. 74, 200–205.

Young, Alwyn (1998), "Growth without scale effects," *Journal of Political Economy*, vol. 106, 41–63.

Yun, Tack (1996), "Nominal price rigidity, money supply endogeneity and business cycles," *Journal of Monetary Economics*, vol. 37, 345–370.

Yun, Tack (2005), "Optimal monetary policy with relative price distortions," *American Economic Review*, vol. 95, 89–109.

Zabel, Edward (1972), "Multiperiod monopoly under uncertainty," *Journal of Economic Theory*, vol. 5, 524–536.

Index

Absolute convergence, 13
Accelerator with imperfect
    competition, 347–349, 359–361
Activist policies, optimality of, 443–444
Adaptive expectations, 32, 51
    and signal extraction, 60–62
AD-AS model, 27–28
AK model, 181–183
ARMA processes, 532–533
Arrow securities, 125–126
Arrow's impossibility theorem, 484–485
Arrow-Debreu equilibrium, 122–125, 139–142
Asset pricing, 127–129, 215–217
Autoregressive process, 532
Autoregressive root, 534

Balanced budget multiplier, 26
Balanced growth, 12
Bargaining, dynamic, 521–524
Barter exchange, 259–260
Baumol-Tobin money demand, 38–39
Beveridge curve, 406
Blanchard-Kahn condition, 543–544
Bubble solutions, 55–56

Budget deficits and political economy, 491–493, 496–500
Business cycles
    competitive, 205–234
    with imperfect competition, 275–277
    with imperfect information, 277–284, 285–287
    with nominal rigidities, 291–336

Cagan model, 50–54
    with adaptive expectations, 51–52
    with rational expectations, 52–54
Calvo contracts, 303–304
    and disinflation, 323–326
Calvo-Fischer contracts, 305–306
    and disinflation, 327–328
Capital augmenting technical progress, 21
Capital taxation and dynamic consistency, 468–470
Cash in advance and money, 245–247
Central bankers and inflation
    contracts, 476–477
    delegation, 474–475
    reputation, 478–480

Centralization and unemployment, 389–394
Certainty equivalence, 340–341
Characteristic polynomial, 534
Classical unemployment, 102
Cobb-Douglas production function, 5–6, 10
Cobweb dynamics, 47–48
Competitive business cycles, 205–234
Complete markets, 121–125
   and asset pricing, 127–128
Concavity, 509–510
Conditional convergence, 4, 14–16
Conditional probabilities, 529
Condorcet paradox, 485
Constant elasticity of substitution (CES) production function, 18–20
Consumption, 338–342
Consumption capital asset pricing model, 215–217
Consumption function, 25
Convergence, 4, 12–16
   absolute, 13
   conditional, 14–16
Convergence clubs, 4
Convexity, 509–510
Correlation, 527
Correlations, 273–275
   in real business cycles, 210–211
   with nominal rigidities, 298–300
   with nonclearing markets, 108–111
Covariance, 527
Credibility, 466–482
   solutions to the problem of, 474–477, 478–480
Credit, 354–359
   and adverse selection, 357–358
   and moral hazard, 358–359
Credit rationing, 355–359
Cycles and money, 270–290

Debt in Diamond model, 174–177
Depreciation and propagation, 211–212
Derivatives, 506–507
Determinacy, 540–544
   and fiscal policy, 456–459
   global, 541
   global, and Pigou effect, 459–463
   and interest rate rules, 445–450
   local, 541
   and nonpredetermined variables 543–544
   and predetermined variables, 542–543
Determinants, 503–504
Diamond model, 162–177
   with debt, 174–177
Disinflation, 33–34, 322–329
   and Calvo contracts, 323–326
   and Calvo-Fischer contracts, 327–328
Distortionary taxation
   cost of, 425–429
   and Ramsey model, 156–158
Double coincidence of wants, 237
Dynamic consistency, 466–482
   basic intuition, 467–468
   and capital taxation, 468–470
Dynamic programming, 516–518
Dynamic stochastic general equilibrium (DSGE) models, 207–217
   with market clearing, 207–217
   with imperfect competition, 275–277
   with imperfect information, 277–287
   with nominal rigidities, 308–316
Dynamic systems, 536–540

Effective demands and supplies, 92–93
Efficiency wages, 380–384
Efficient bargains, 374–376
Eigenvalues, 505–506
Eigenvectors, 505–506
Elasticities, 508
Elasticity of substitution, 508–509
Embodied technical progress, 20–21
Employment flows, 398–399
Employment fluctuations, 213–215, 224–227
Employment function, 93
Employment lotteries, 224–227
Endogenous cycles, 220–224

Endogenous growth, 4, 180–204
  and technical progress, 183–184
Endogenous productivity increases, 190–193, 198–201
Envelope theorem, 511–512
Euler equation, 68, 148
Excludable goods, 183
Exogenous growth, 4, 145
Exogenous technical progress, Ramsey model, 155
Expectations, 530–531
  adaptive, 32
  rational, 45–64
Expected utility, 119–120
Exponential distribution, 529

Factors of production, 4
Financial assets, 118–144
First order conditions, 510
Fiscal policy, 415
Fiscal theory of the price level, 250–251, 255
Fischer model, 294–295
Fixprice macroeconomic model, 100–105
Frictionless markets, 89
Friedman rule, 415–418
Functions, 506–510
Fundamental solution, 55

Games, non cooperative, 518–524
Global determinacy, 541
  and Pigou effect, 459–463
Golden rule, 4, 9–10, 167–168
Golden rule capital, 9
Government information and policy effectiveness, 439–444
Government objectives, 414–415
Government policy under imperfect competition, 105–108
Government spending, optimal financing of, 436–439
Government spending, Ramsey model, 154–155
Gray model, 293–294

Great Divergence, 3
Growth
  endogenous, 4, 180–204
  exogenous, 4

Hamiltonian, 513
  current value, 514
  maximized, 513
Homogeneous functions, 507–508
Homothetic functions, 507–508
Human capital, 4, 16–18

Imperfect competition and cycles, 275–277
Imperfect competition in macroeconomic models, 105–108
Imperfect information
  and optimal policy, 41–43
  and cycles, 275–277
Implicit contracts, 385–389
Impulse response functions, 306–308, 320–322
Inada conditions, 5, 18
Incomplete markets, 125–127, 135–138
Incomplete markets and asset pricing, 129
Indeterminacy, 56–57, 218–219, 241–242, 249
Indeterminacy, nominal, 249
Indexation, 39–40
Inefficient dynamic equilibrium, 10
Inflation targeting, 448
Insiders-outsiders, 377–380
Instrument instability, 451–454
Interest rate pegging, 249, 254–255, 258–259
Interest rate rules
  and determinacy, 445–450
  and global determinacy, 447–448, 459–463
  and local determinacy, 447
Intertemporal budget constraint, 67
Intertemporal elasticity of substitution, 149

Intertemporal equilibria, 65–84
Intertemporal substitution and fluctuations, 213–215
Inventories, 349–354, 361–364
   and imperfect competition, 352–354
   and rationing, 350–351
   and volatility, 351–352
Investment, 343–349
IS-LM model, 26–27
Iterated expectations, 531

Keynesian cross, 25–26
Keynesian unemployment, 100–102

Laffer curve, 427–428
Lag operators, 531, 534–535
Lag polynomials, 531–532
Lagrange multiplier, 511
Learning and rational expectations, 57–60
Leontief production function, 18
Liquidity effect, 254
Liquidity puzzle, 248
Local determinacy, 541
   in monetary overlapping generations models, 77
Loglinear differentiation, 508
Lognormal distribution, 528
Lucas's signal extraction model, 277–284

Macroeconomic models with imperfect competition, 105–108
Martingales, 533
Matching and fluctuations, 409–410
Matching function, 404–405
Matching in labor market, 404–410
Matrices, 502–506
Mean of a random variable, 526
Median voter, 486–489
   and redistribution, 489–490
Medium of exchange, 239, 259–260
Menu costs, 316–318
Monetary exchange 260–262
Monetary paradoxes, 247–251

Monetary policy, 415
   and commitment, 472
   and credibility, 470–474
   discretionary policy, 472–473
Monetary shocks and rigidities, 110
Money, 235–269
Money and cycles, 270–290
Money demand, 27
   Baumol-Tobin model, 38–39
Money and overlapping generations, 76–78, 240–242
Money in the utility function, 242–245
Monopoly union, 372–373
Multiplier, 26
Muth model, 47–49

Nash equilibrium, 518–519
   subgame perfect, 520
Natural rate of unemployment, 29, 314–315
New Keynesian Phillips curve, 304–305, 312
Nominal indeterminacy, 249
Nominal price stickiness and imperfect information, 277–284
Nominal rigidities
   Calvo model, 303–304
   Calvo-Fischer model, 305–306
   Fischer model, 294–295
   and fluctuations, 291–336
   Gray model, 293–294
   and impulse response functions, 306–308
   and menu costs, 316–318
   and real rigidities, 318–319
   Rotemberg model, 301–302
   Taylor model, 295–297
Non cooperative games, 518–524
Non Ricardian monetary model, 251–255
Nonclearing markets and imperfect competition, 85–117
Nonexpected utility, 132–135
Nonpredetermined variables, 541–542
Normal distribution, 528

Optimal savings rate, 10
Optimization
   dynamic, 513–516
   with inequality constraints, 512
   static, 510–512
Overaccumulation, 168–169
Overlapping generations model, 70–76, 161–179
Overlapping generations and money, 76–78, 240–242

Paradoxes in monetary models, 247–251
Pensions, 169–174
   fully funded, 170–171
   pay as you go, 171–174
Permanent income, 338–339
Phillips curve, 29–31, 284
   and inflationary expectations, 31–34
   new -Keynesian, 304–305, 312
   with wages, 315–316
Physical capital, 4
Pigou effect, 255, 257–258, 265–267
   and global determinacy, 449–450, 459–463
   and taxes, 266–267
Policy
   Friedman rule, 415–418
   optimal seigniorage, 423–425, 429–431
   and public finance, 413–433
   Ramsey taxation, 421–422
   and stabilization, 434–465
   tax smoothing, 418–420
Policy, commitment vs no commitment, 467–468
Policy effectiveness, 34–38, 439–444
   and rational expectations, 49–50
Policy ineffectiveness, 454–456
Policy instruments, 415
Political economy, 483–501
Political economy and budget deficits, 491–493, 496–500
Political heterogeneity, 493–496

Politicians
   opportunistic, 487
   partisan, 487–489
Poole model, 41–43
Precautionary savings, 341–342
Predetermined variables, 541–542
Price level targeting, 449
Price making, 94–97
Probabilities, 524–525
Production function
   Cobb-Douglas, 5
   constant elasticity of substitution (CES), 6, 18–20
   Leontief, 18
Propagation in cycles, 211–212
Prudence, 341
Public finance and policy, 413–433

Quantity signals, 90–92
Queueing system, 111–112

Ramsey model, 66–70, 145–160
   in discrete time, 155–156
Ramsey-OLG model, 78–81
Ramsey OLG monetary model, 255–259
Ramsey taxation, 421–422
Random variables, 525–527
   moments of, 526
   one dimensional, 525
   two dimensional, 527
Random walk, 530
Rational expectations, 45–64
   bubble solutions, 55–56
   definition, 46
   dynamic solutions, 54–57
   fundamental solution, 55
   indeterminacy, 56–57
   learning, 57–60
   and policy effectiveness, 49–50
   solution of dynamic equations, 533–536
   sunspots, 56–57
Rationing schemes, 89–91, 111–112
Real balance effect, 255

Real rigidities
   and nominal rigidities, 318–319
   and persistence, 313–314
Real business cycles, 206, 207–217
Redistribution and median voter, 489–490
Reservation wage, 370–371
Returns to diversity, 185, 190
Ricardian equivalence, 69–70, 152–153
   and overlapping generations model, 75–76
Right to manage, 376–377
Risk aversion, 119–121
Risk aversion and substitutability, 132–135
Risk free rate, 129–130, 134–135
Risk free rate puzzle, 135–138
Risk premium, 131
   absolute, 120
   relative, 121
Rival goods, 183
Romer model, 184–190
Rotemberg model, 301–302, 308–316
Rule of the minimum, 90

Saddle, 536–538
Saddle path, 150–151
Savings rate, 6
Scale effects, 194–195
Second order conditions, 510
Securities, 125–126
Seigniorage, optimal, 423–425, 429–431
Shirking model, 383–384
   dynamic version of, 401–404
Shocks and correlations with nonclearing markets, 108–111
Short side rule, 89–90
Signal extraction, 60–62, 277–284
Sink, 536–538
Social welfare function, 484–485
Solow residual, 11
Solow-Swan model, 4–6
   dynamics, 7
   speed of convergence, 8

Source, 536–538
Stabilization policies, 434–465
   and instrument instability, 451–454
   and model uncertainty, 450–451
Standard deviation, 526
States of nature, 119
States of the world, 119
Stationary processes, 529
Stochastic processes, 529–533
Stochastic productivity increases, 198–201
Stochastic variables, 524–529
Subgame perfect Nash equilibrium, 520
Substitutability, 132–135
Sunspots, 56–57, 217–220
Suppressed inflation, 103

Targeting
   inflation, 448
   price level, 449
Tax smoothing, 418–420
Taylor expansions, 507
Taylor model, 295–297
Taylor principle, 445
Taylor rules, 445
Technical progress, 4, 11–12
   capital augmenting, 11, 21
   embodied, 20–21
   and endogenous growth, 183–184
   labor augmenting, 11
Technology shocks with rigidities, 110
Time series, 529–533
Trade-unions 371, 372–377
   benevolent, 371
   efficient bargains, 374–376
   monopoly union, 372–373
   right to manage, 376–377
   selfish, 371
Transactions, 88
Transactions in nonclearing markets, 88–90
Transactions schemes, 89
Transitional dynamics, 195–198
Transversality condition, 148–149, 514–516

Uncertainty, 118–144
Undetermined coefficients, 535–536
Unemployment, 369–396, 397–412
  and centralization, 389–394
  a dynamic view, 397–412
  efficiency wages, 380–384
  implicit contracts, 385–389
  insiders-outsiders, 377–380
  and matching, 404–410
  natural rate of, 29
  and shirking model, 383–384, 401–404
Uniform distribution, 528

Variance of a random variable, 526
Voluntary exchange, 89

Walrasian dynamics and correlations, 273–275
Walrasian theory, 86–87
Weil model, 263–267
White noise, 530

CPSIA information can be obtained at www.ICGtesting.com
Printed in the USA
LVOW03*1106040815

448590LV00010B/22/P